THE KING
IN HIS BEAUTY

THE KING

IN HIS BEAUTY

A Biblical Theology of
the Old and New Testaments

THOMAS R. SCHREINER

B

Baker Academic

a division of Baker Publishing Group
Grand Rapids, Michigan

Published by Baker Academic
a division of Baker Publishing Group
P.O. Box 6287, Grand Rapids, MI 49516-6287
www.bakeracademic.com

Printed in the United States of America

Library of Congress Cataloging-in-Publication Data
Schreiner, Thomas R.
    The King in his beauty : a Biblical theology of the Old and New Testaments / Thomas R. Schreiner.
        pages cm
    Includes bibliographical references and indexes.
    ISBN 978-0-8010-3939-3 (cloth)
    1. Bible—Theology. 2. Bible—Criticism, interpretation, etc. I. Title.
BS543.S386 2013
230′.041—dc23   2012050805

21   22   23   24   25   12   11   10   9   8   7

To Diane,
my beloved wife and coheir in the kingdom

CONTENTS

PREFACE

It has been a great joy to write this book, though I am keenly aware of its limitations. I can scarcely express my debt to other scholars who confirmed, sharpened, and corrected my thinking. I am also aware that I have barely scratched the surface in terms of secondary sources. I tried to read enough to get a sense of what biblical scholarship was saying about the theology of the various books examined. But I was not concerned about being comprehensive; I mainly cite sources that proved to be of help in understanding the theology of the Bible. My hope is that this book will be understandable for college students, laypersons, seminary students, and pastors. It is not intended to be a technical work for scholars. Obviously, in a work of this scope virtually all readers will disagree with me somewhere on something, but I hope I will stimulate all to reflect on the majesty and beauty of the biblical message.

A word should be said about how I wrote this book. I wrote the first draft inductively without consulting other sources, based on my own work in the biblical text. Subsequently I read widely, incorporating many insights from others. Except for one or two short sections, I wrote the NT portion without consulting my previous writing on Pauline and NT theology. Obviously, there are many points of contact with what I wrote before, since my views have not changed substantially about NT theology.

I am grateful especially to Southern Baptist Theological Seminary for granting me a sabbatical and to President R. Albert Mohler Jr. and Vice President and Dean Russell Moore for supporting my scholarship. Thanks are also due to Jim Kinney from Baker Academic for his encouragement and support for this project and to Brian Bolger for his fine editing work that improved the final product. I am particularly thankful for Joshua Greever, my PhD student and Garrett Fellow, who ran to the library again and again to check out books and to copy articles for me, and for his help in the dreary task of compiling my bibliography from my footnotes. Joshua also read the book carefully, making a number of suggestions for improvement. Joshua has been an immense help, and his willingness and eagerness to assist me have been a great encouragement.

I am dedicating this book to my beloved wife, Diane, who has recently survived a near fatal bicycle accident. She has been like Tabitha in her love and service to me and to many others, and like Tabitha she has been, as it were, raised from the dead (Acts 9:36–41). I can't express adequately what a gift Diane has been to me.

Prologue

By now it is common consensus that no one theme adequately captures the message of the Scriptures.[1] It is not my intention to dispute that hypothesis here, for almost any center chosen tends to domesticate one theme or another.[2] I maintain that there are a number of different ways to put together the story line and theology of the Scriptures that are legitimate. We should not insist, therefore, that one theme captures the whole. Indeed, the word "center" is ambiguous. Are we talking about the central theme of the story or the ultimate reason for the story?[3] Here my focus is on one of the major themes in the narrative. I have argued elsewhere that the ultimate reason and purpose for the story is the glory of God, and hence in this book I will not focus on the reason for the story.[4] Here the intent is to focus on the story line as it unfolds. The theme pursued must be flexible enough to comprehend several different interlocking themes in Scripture so that it summarizes the fundamental message of the Bible. I intend to argue in this book that the "kingdom of God," if that term is defined with sufficient flexibility, fits well as a central theme of the

1. Writing a biblical theology of the whole Bible is a daunting task. It is not the purpose of this book to give a final word, for that is impossible. I am convinced that a biblical theology of the whole Bible can be written from a number of different and complementary perspectives. I have been preceded and helped by a number of scholars who have written a biblical theology of the whole Bible. See Childs, *Biblical Theology*; Fuller, *Unity of the Bible*; Scobie, *Ways of Our God*; VanGemeren, *Progress of Redemption*; Hamilton, *God's Glory in Salvation*; Beale, *Biblical Theology*; Gentry and Wellum, *Kingdom through Covenant*.

2. In this work I quote a number of different writers from various perspectives. I usually quote these sources when they say something insightful, but it does not follow, of course, that the author quoted necessarily agrees with me in terms of the larger picture that I am presenting. Indeed, any given author may differ from me dramatically.

3. Vern Poythress ("Kinds of Biblical Theology") rightly argues that a variety of perspectives can be adopted in doing biblical theology.

4. See Schreiner, *Paul*; idem, *New Testament Theology*.

entire Bible.[5] Let me hasten to say that such a thesis does not rely upon a word study approach, for it is quite obvious that the kingdom of God cannot be a central theme if we count up how many times the words "king," "kingdom," or "rule" and "reign" appear, for in many books of the Bible they do not appear at all.[6] Instead, the contention here is that the phrase "kingdom of God" thematically captures, from a biblical theology standpoint, the message of Scripture. Now I would immediately add that God brings in the kingdom for the glory and praise of his name. Scripture unfolds *the story* of the kingdom, and God's glory is *the reason* for the story.[7] In this book I focus on one of the central themes of the story.

Perhaps it will help if I sketch in what I mean by "the kingdom of God." First of all, it designates the rule of God. In one sense, God is always the King of kings and the Lord of lords, reigning over everything that happens. But in another sense, God's rule has been flouted since the fall of humankind, and the Scriptures tell the story of the kingdom regained. The objection to seeing the kingdom as central is that it does not seem to fit with the Writings of the Hebrew Bible—for example, the book of Proverbs. I will argue in due course that Proverbs (and the other books from the Writings in the OT) fits with such a notion, even though the term "kingdom" is virtually absent in Proverbs. I will demonstrate that the Wisdom literature features the supremacy of God in everyday life, showing that he rules over the particulars of our existence. We will see that Proverbs, Job, and Ecclesiastes teach that the fear of Yahweh is the beginning of wisdom. To fear the Lord is to live under his lordship. The focus on God as King is evident in the regular refrain found in Scripture, particularly the OT, where God is identified as the Lord. As Lord, he is the sovereign one, the creator of all, the one who deserves praise and obedience. In other words, saying that the theme of Scripture is God's kingship is verified and confirmed by the constant refrain that God is the Lord.[8]

Focusing on God as King in the abstract apart from human beings does not do justice to the breadth found in the Scriptures.[9] For the central message of Scripture also includes human beings—the crown of creation—who are created in God's image.[10] Since God is King and Lord, it is his purpose and

5. I agree with G. K. Beale (*Biblical Theology*, 168–84) that there is a coherent story line in the Scriptures.
6. On this matter, see Goldingay, *Israel's Faith*, 59–60.
7. I tried to unpack this foundational reason in two earlier books: Schreiner, *Paul*; idem, *New Testament Theology*. See also Hamilton, *God's Glory in Salvation*.
8. For the centrality of lordship in the Scriptures, see Frame, *Doctrine of God*.
9. See Goldingay, *Israel's Faith*, 59–83.
10. Others have rightly argued that one of the major themes in Scripture relates to God's people. See Scobie, *Ways of Our God*, 469–651; Martens, "People of God."

design that he be glorified in all things and by all people. Some have complained that such a God is narcissistic, but that objection misses the point. For God as King glorifies himself by giving himself to his human beings in love. God is honored as King when human beings receive and depend upon his love and experience his salvation. God's glory and God's love must not be placed into two separate compartments. Rather, God is glorified as Lord in his love for human beings.[11] The sovereignty of God and his kingship take place in history, in the story recounted in the Scriptures, revealed supremely in the ministry and person of Jesus Christ.

A close relationship exists between God's kingdom and his covenant.[12] Indeed, the divine covenants are the means by which God's rule is established.[13] God's lordship becomes a reality as he dwells with his people, as they experience his gracious presence.[14] This fits with Desmond Alexander's remark that "the theme of God's presence on the earth is especially significant for understanding the biblical meta-story."[15] God's love for human beings is manifested in his covenants with human beings, for in the covenant God promises that he will accomplish salvation for his people and be their God.

The lordship of God, however, cannot be confined to God's love, for the Scriptures call attention to another dimension of the story. God expresses his kingship also in punishing his enemies, in judging those who resist the overtures of his love.[16] Some of God's subjects rebel against his kingly rule and his sovereign love. Their recalcitrance and rebellion will not ultimately succeed. The story line of the Scriptures indicates that evil will be destroyed and pacified. The subjects who refuse to bow the knee will be judged, and God's rule over all and glory will be manifested in judgment as well.

We must beware of another abstraction in understanding God's lordship. God's kingdom certainly consists of his rule over angels and human beings, but the emphasis on rule must not blind us to the truth that there is also a realm. History does not take place in an ethereal sphere. God created the entire

11. See the careful articulation of both divine sovereignty and God's relatedness to the world in Childs, *Biblical Theology*, 356–58.

12. A covenant signifies a relationship in which there are obligations made under oath. For the definition of the term, see Gentry and Wellum, *Kingdom through Covenant*, 132–33.

13. Meredith Kline says that "covenants function as administrative instruments of God's kingly rule" (*Kingdom Prologue*, 3). So also Gentry and Wellum, *Kingdom through Covenant*; Dumbrell, *Covenant and Creation*, 42. For a survey of covenant in the Scriptures along with his own proposal, see Hahn, *Kinship by Covenant*.

14. Rightly Martens, "People of God," 230. See also Terrien, *Elusive Presence*.

15. Alexander, *Eden to the New Jerusalem*, 14–15.

16. See Hamilton, *God's Glory in Salvation*, 37–65. He defends the notion that God's glory is expressed "in salvation through judgment."

universe, and the lordship of God and his relationship with human beings take place on earth. Place matters in this story. God is King over the world and over the universe, but history raises questions about his lordship over this world. The incursion of evil represents a rebel kingdom that threatens God's sovereignty and seeks to undo his love. This world, with all its beauty, is vitiated by sin. The drama of God as King and human beings as his subjects is worked out in history and in a certain place. The story of Scripture is not only the relationship between God and human beings; it also relates to the universe. What is the destiny of the world that God has made? The Scriptures promise that there will be a new heaven and a new earth—a new creation where the glory of God will illumine the cosmos. So, the kingdom of God has a threefold dimension, focusing on God as King, on human beings as the subjects of the King, and the universe as the place where his kingship is worked out.

A final comment should be made about the approach of this book. It is not my purpose to interact with critical reconstructions of Israel's history or literature. The same could be said regarding the NT history. Careful interaction with such reconstructions is a significant part of the scholarly endeavor, but no book can accomplish everything.[17] It is also a historical fact that particular books were recognized and accepted as canonical, though I maintain also that the church was providentially led by God to recognize which writings belonged to authoritative Scripture.[18] Hence, my goal in this book is to unpack the canonical writings in their final form.[19] We are still faced with an important decision with regard to the OT. Should the canon be explored in terms of its Hebrew order or the Christian order?[20] Some regard this issue to

17. I concur with most conservative evangelicals in believing that the accounts in the Scriptures are historical, whether we are speaking of Genesis or the Gospels. My view will surface in this book, but it is not my intention to defend it. The goal of this book is to set forth the theology of the Bible in its final, canonical form.

18. See Kruger, *Canon Revisited*, for an important work on this topic.

19. The canonical approach is well known through the groundbreaking work of Brevard Childs. For a similar approach, see Rendtorff, *Canonical Hebrew Bible*. For a very different reading, see Brueggemann, *Theology of the Old Testament*. Brueggemann adopts a postmodern approach in which a Christian reading is not privileged. Clearly, the present book moves in a very different direction. Even though Brueggemann trumpets postmodernism, there are a number of positivistic, dogmatic, and modernist statements in his book, though his work also contains many helpful insights. I am not denying that the postmodern turn rightly uncovered many problems in the modernist agenda. I would suggest that the way forward is to presuppose the truth of the Christian worldview and the authority and the complete truthfulness of the Scriptures. For a full exposition of this view, see Frame, *Knowledge of God*; idem, *Word of God*. My work is similar to Brueggemann's in that I am not seeking here to investigate the historical truth of the OT, though I do believe that the OT is historically reliable.

20. The trend is to examine the OT in its Hebrew order. For a robust defense, see Seitz, *Fellowship of the Prophets*. See also Hamilton, *God's Glory in Salvation*, 59–63; Gentry and

be of major importance, but its significance is exaggerated.[21] In my judgment, the central themes of OT theology are not affected dramatically whether one follows the Hebrew order or the order used in English translations. I am assuming here that the ordinary reader of English who is not even aware of the Hebrew order is at no disadvantage in trying to understand the theology of the OT. Therefore, in this book I follow the English order.

I should also note that my approach to various books differs. Some books are examined chronologically, others thematically, and in the Psalms the canonical ordering of the books is explored. I am not suggesting in any particular case that the approach adopted here is the *right* approach. I would simply maintain that it is one fruitful way to examine the message of the Scriptures.

Wellum, *Kingdom through Covenant*, 95n308. The fact that the Writings are not in the same order in every list indicates that the order is not as crucial as some claim.

21. Childs says, "In my opinion, there are far too many unverified assumptions with such an argument to rest much weight on it. A far more fruitful avenue of investigation would be to explore the effect of a canonical ordering on the reading of the book and the differing theologies involved in the canonical arrangements of the Hebrew and Greek Bibles" (*Old Testament as Scripture*, 564).

ABBREVIATIONS

General

chap(s).	chapter(s)
cf.	compare
e.g.	for example
esp.	especially
ibid.	in the same source
idem	by the same author
i.e.	that is
par(s).	parallel(s)
p(p.)	page(s)
rev.	revised
v(v).	verse(s)

Divisions of the Canon

NT	New Testament
OT	Old Testament

Ancient Versions

LXX	Septuagint
MT	Masoretic Text

Modern Versions

HCSB	Holman Christian Standard Bible
KJV	King James Version
NIV	New International Version
NRSV	New Revised Standard Version

Hebrew Bible / Old Testament

Gen.	Genesis
Exod.	Exodus
Lev.	Leviticus
Num.	Numbers
Deut.	Deuteronomy
Josh.	Joshua
Judg.	Judges
Ruth	Ruth
1–2 Sam.	1–2 Samuel
1–2 Kings	1–2 Kings
1–2 Chron.	1–2 Chronicles
Ezra	Ezra
Neh.	Nehemiah
Esther	Esther
Job	Job
Ps./Pss.	Psalms
Prov.	Proverbs
Eccles.	Ecclesiastes
Song	Song of Songs
Isa.	Isaiah
Jer.	Jeremiah
Lam.	Lamentations

Ezek.	Ezekiel
Dan.	Daniel
Hosea	Hosea
Joel	Joel
Amos	Amos
Obad.	Obadiah
Jon.	Jonah
Mic.	Micah
Nah.	Nahum
Hab.	Habakkuk
Zeph.	Zephaniah
Hag.	Haggai
Zech.	Zechariah
Mal.	Malachi

New Testament

Matt.	Matthew
Mark	Mark
Luke	Luke
John	John
Acts	Acts
Rom.	Romans
1–2 Cor.	1–2 Corinthians
Gal.	Galatians
Eph.	Ephesians
Phil.	Philippians
Col.	Colossians
1–2 Thess.	1–2 Thessalonians
1–2 Tim.	1–2 Timothy
Titus	Titus
Philem.	Philemon
Heb.	Hebrews
James	James
1–2 Pet.	1–2 Peter
1–3 John	1–3 John
Jude	Jude
Rev.	Revelation

Apocrypha and Septuagint

1–4 Macc.	1–4 Maccabees
Sir.	Sirach
Wis.	Wisdom of Solomon

Old Testament Pseudepigrapha

Pss. Sol.	Psalms of Solomon

Mishnah and Talmud

m.	Mishnah
'Abot	'Abot
Sukkah	Sukkah

Secondary Sources

AB	Anchor Bible
AUMSR	Andrews University Monographs: Studies in Religion
BibJudS	Biblical and Judaic Studies
BibOr	Biblica et orientalia
BibSem	Biblical Seminar
BST	The Bible Speaks Today
BTB	Biblical Theology Bulletin
BTNT	Biblical Theology of the New Testament
BZAW	Beihefte zur Zeitschrift für die alttestamentliche Wissenschaft
CBQ	Catholic Biblical Quarterly
CC	Continental Commentaries
CEP	Contemporary Evangelical Perspectives
ConBNT	Coniectanea biblica: New Testament Series
ExpTim	Expository Times
FBBS	Facet Books: Biblical Series
FFNT	Foundation and Facets: New Testament
GDNES	Gorgias Dissertations: Near East Series
GTJ	Grace Theological Journal
HBSt	Herders biblische Studien
HS	Hebrew Studies
HSM	Harvard Semitic Monographs

IBC	Interpretation: A Bible Commentary for Teaching and Preaching
Int	*Interpretation*
ITC	International Theological Commentary
JBL	*Journal of Biblical Literature*
JETS	*Journal of the Evangelical Theological Society*
JPSTC	JPS Torah Commentary
JPTSup	Journal of Pentecostal Theology: Supplement Series
JRH	*Journal of Religious History*
JSNTSup	Journal for the Study of the New Testament: Supplement Series
JSOT	*Journal for the Study of the Old Testament*
JSOTSup	Journal for the Study of the Old Testament: Supplement Series
LS	*Louvain Studies*
NAC	New American Commentary
NICNT	New International Commentary on the New Testament
NICOT	New International Commentary on the Old Testament
NIVAC	NIV Application Commentary
NovT	*Novum Testamentum*
NovTSup	Novum Testamentum Supplements
NSBT	New Studies in Biblical Theology
NTS	*New Testament Studies*
NTT	New Testament Theology
NVBS	New Voices in Biblical Studies
OBT	Overtures to Biblical Theology
OTL	Old Testament Library
PBM	Paternoster Biblical Monographs
RB	*Revue biblique*
SBJT	*Southern Baptist Journal of Theology*
SBLAB	Society of Biblical Literature Academia Biblica
SBLDS	Society of Biblical Literature Dissertation Series
SBLSymS	Society of Biblical Literature Symposium Series
SBT	Studies in Biblical Theology
SJT	*Scottish Journal of Theology*
SNTSMS	Society for New Testament Studies Monograph Series
SNTW	Studies of the New Testament and Its World
TJ	*Trinity Journal*
TOTC	Tyndale Old Testament Commentaries
TynBul	*Tyndale Bulletin*
VT	*Vetus Testamentum*
VTSup	Supplements to Vetus Testamentum
WBC	Word Biblical Commentary
WTJ	*Westminster Theological Journal*
WUNT	Wissenschaftliche Untersuchungen zum Neuen Testament
ZECNT	Zondervan Exegetical Commentary: New Testament

Part 1

CREATION TO THE EDGE OF CANAAN

1

GENESIS

Creation

The story commences where the book of Genesis begins, with the creation of the heavens and the earth (1:1).[1] There is no reflection on what God was doing before creation, nor does the writer recount the creation of angels. Speculative issues have no interest for the writer of Genesis.[2] The first creation account (1:1–2:3) heralds the majesty and power of God, for by his word he creates and orders the world in six days. Umberto Cassuto sums up the message of God's creation of the world:

> Not many gods but One God; not theogony, for a god has no family tree; nor wars nor strife nor the clash of wills, but only One Will, which rules over everything, without the slightest let or hindrance; not a deity associated with nature and identified with it wholly or in part, but a God who stands absolutely above nature, and outside of it, and nature and all its constituent elements, even the sun and all other entities, be they never so exalted, are only His creatures, made according to His will.[3]

The simplicity and the depth of God's creative power are evident because all things come into existence by his word.[4] As Ps. 33:6 says, "By the word of the

1. In defense of this reading of Gen. 1:1, see Cassuto, *From Adam to Noah*, 20; Wenham, *Genesis 1–15*, 11–15. See also von Rad, *Genesis*, 48–49. Von Rad says, "It is amazing to see how sharply little Israel demarcated herself from an apparently overpowering environment of cosmological and theogonic myths" (p. 49).
2. God clearly created the world thoughtfully and with wisdom (Prov. 8:22–31). See Goldingay, *Israel's Gospel*, 43–49.
3. Cassuto, *From Adam to Noah*, 8.
4. Von Rad says, "Gen. 1 presents the results of concentrated theological and cosmological reflection in a language which is concise and always utterly direct in expression" (*Israel's Historical Traditions*, 141). See also his comments on p. 142.

LORD the heavens were made, and by the breath of his mouth all their host."[5] God's creation of the entire universe communicates his sovereignty and lordship, for the creator of all is also the Lord of all. The account of creation in Genesis also differs from the creation accounts in surrounding ancient Near Eastern cultures, since the one God is the creator of all things.[6] In creating the world Yahweh shows his sovereignty over all other powers and gods (Pss. 74:12–14; 89:5–13).[7] The implication of creation, as Paul House affirms, is that "God has no rivals. God has jurisdiction over all created persons and things."[8] As Jeremiah says, "The gods who did not make the heavens and the earth shall perish from the earth and from under the heavens" (Jer. 10:11). Psalm 96:5 echoes the same theme: "For all the gods of the peoples are worthless idols, but the LORD made the heavens."

The creator of all is also the King of all, and his lordship is extended over a place—a realm. As Gerhard von Rad says, "If the world was called into being by the free will of God, then it is his very own possession, and he is its Lord."[9] He is the King of the created cosmos. Therefore, the creation of the universe demonstrates that God is the Lord of the whole world, and that his lordship will not be limited to Israel.[10] Since God is the creator, it follows that "the creation exists for the praise and glory of its creator God."[11] "The earth is full of God's glory [Ps. 24:1] because what fills the earth constitutes his glory."[12] In other words, we see the glory of God when we delight in, reflect upon, and enjoy the world he has created.[13] God's creative power supports the notion that "Genesis describes God's work in regal terms, even without using the word 'king.'"[14] God's wisdom, power, and goodness in creating the world demonstrate his sovereignty over all things (see Ps. 145).

In reading the creation account, how should we interpret the "let us" in Gen. 1:26? Some have argued that it is a *pluralis majestatis* ("plural of majesty"), or that it includes angels or the heavenly assembly.[15] It is doubtful that

5. On the power of God's word, see Goldingay, *Israel's Gospel*, 49–52.

6. House, *Old Testament Theology*, 60. For a full discussion of this matter, see Waltke, *Old Testament Theology*, 197–203. See also Collins, *Genesis 1–4*. Contrary to Brueggemann (*Theology of the Old Testament*, 158–59), God's creation is *ex nihilo*.

7. See Goldingay, *Israel's Gospel*, 64–75.

8. House, *Old Testament Theology*.

9. Von Rad, *Israel's Historical Traditions*, 143.

10. See Childs, *Old Testament as Scripture*, 155.

11. C. Wright, *Old Testament Ethics*, 114.

12. Ibid., 115.

13. "But the creation not only declares the glory of God (Ps. 19:1); creation's fullness is also an essential part of that glory" (ibid., 116).

14. Ibid., 121.

15. For the options, see Waltke, *Old Testament Theology*, 212–15. In support of the idea that the heavenly assembly is in view, see Gentry, "Kingdom through Covenant."

the author thought specifically of the Trinity in using this expression, or that the earliest Israelite readers read the text in such a way, for the Trinity is only clearly revealed in the NT. Recent developments in hermeneutics, however, have rightly corrected an overemphasis on authorial intent.[16] Interpreters of sacred Scripture must also consider the canonical shape of the Scriptures as a whole, which is to say that we must also take into account the divine author of Scripture.[17] Nor does appeal to a divine author open the door to arbitrariness or subjectivity, for the meaning of the divine author is communicated through the words and canon of Scripture. It is not the product of human creativity but is textually located and circumscribed.

A canonical approach supports a trinitarian reading, which is suggested by the actual words of the text and confirmed by the entire canon.[18] The Spirit's role in creation is signified by his "hovering over the face of the waters" (Gen. 1:2).[19] Psalm 33:6, cited above, probably alludes to the work of the Spirit, for the word "breath" is the word used for "Spirit" (*rûaḥ*), and hence here the writer attributes the creation of the world to the Spirit.[20] In light of the NT revelation on the divinity of the Spirit, it is warranted to see the Spirit as creator. The Son's role as creator is even clearer from a canonical perspective. John's Gospel commences, "In the beginning" (John 1:1), an unmistakable allusion to Gen. 1:1. Another allusion to Genesis immediately surfaces, for John 1:3 speaks of the role of the "Word" in the beginning, claiming that "all things were made" by the one who is the "Word." Hence, the "Word" that spoke creation into existence (Gen. 1:3, 6, 9, 11, 14, 20, 24, 26) is identified as the Son of God—Jesus the Christ (John 1:14). Hence, from a canonical perspective, the "let us" in Gen. 1:26 should be understood as a reference to the Trinity.[21]

The other feature of the creation in Gen. 1:1–2:3 that must be considered is the creation of man and woman in the image of God (1:26–27). Clearly, this is the climax of creation, and the previous days anticipate the creation of human beings on the sixth day.[22] What is particularly striking is that "man" (*'ādām*) is created as male and female in the image of God (1:27). Theologians

16. See, e.g., Hays, *Echoes of Scripture*.

17. See Poythress, *God-Centered Biblical Interpretation*.

18. Hermeneutically, I am suggesting that the meaning of the text must also be investigated canonically. In other words, neither Moses nor the original readers could grasp fully the meaning of what is said here.

19. Against von Rad, *Genesis*, 49; Goldingay, *Israel's Gospel*, 82.

20. Again, I am defending this reading in light of the whole canon of Scripture.

21. See House, *Old Testament Theology*, 61–62.

22. But C. Wright (*Old Testament Ethics*, 126–27) rightly cautions that this is misunderstood if human beings think of themselves, rather than God, as the center of creation, noting also that there is a sense in which the Sabbath rest is the climax of God's creative work.

have long reflected on the meaning and significance of the creation of human beings in God's image. If we pay attention to the text, the focus is on human beings as the vice-regents of creation. We read the mandate for human beings in 1:28: "Be fruitful and multiply and fill the earth and subdue it and have dominion over the fish of the sea and over the birds of the heavens and over every living thing that moves on the earth." Human beings are made in God's image in that they are to rule the world for God. The regal nature of the image is confirmed by the use of images in the ancient Near East where "a ruler's image was set up in distant parts of his kingdom to indicate that his authority reached there."[23]

Certainly, other elements of the divine image are implied by the mandate to rule.[24] But the biblical text calls attention to human beings as those having the responsibility and privilege of subduing the world for God. As Stephen Dempster says, "The male and female as king and queen of creation are to exercise rule over their dominion, the extent of which is the entire earth."[25] Peter Gentry rightly argues in a detailed study that the image of God is not functional here; rather, it is ontological, for human beings are in the image of God because they are servant kings and sons of God, and as a result of being made in God's image they rule the world for God.[26] The importance of human beings being created in God's image can scarcely be exaggerated. Indeed, the central three themes of this book appear right here. God is the sovereign creator who extends his kingship over the world. But he extends his rule through human beings, for as God's image-bearers they must govern the world for God's glory and honor. As von Rad remarks, "God set man in the world as the sign of his own sovereign authority, in order that man should uphold and enforce his—God's—claims as lord."[27] And their rule is not abstract, for God's reign is to be implemented in the world of space and time, over the good creation that God has made. Dempster rightly ties together the themes of Gen. 1: "Another way of describing this emphasis on human dominion and dynasty would be the simple expression 'the kingdom of God.'"[28] Indeed, there are indications that human beings functioned as priest-kings.[29] Adam

23. Alexander, *Eden to the New Jerusalem*, 78. See also Mathews, "Genesis," 142; Dumbrell, *Covenant and Creation*, 34.

24. See Gentry and Wellum, *Kingdom through Covenant*, 613–16.

25. Dempster, *Dominion and Dynasty*, 59. C. Wright says, "Human dominion over the rest of creation is to be an exercise of kingship that reflects God's own kingship" (*Old Testament Ethics*, 121). So also Levenson, *Persistence of Evil*, 112–17.

26. Gentry, "Kingdom through Covenant," 22–33.

27. Von Rad, *Israel's Historical Traditions*, 146; cf. von Rad, *Genesis*, 59–60.

28. Dempster, *Dominion and Dynasty*, 62.

29. See Beale, *Church's Mission*, 66–70.

is commanded to "work and keep" the land (2:15). These two verbs are often used of priests and their work in the tabernacle/temple (Num. 3:7–8; 8:25–26; 18:5–6; 1 Chron. 23:32; Ezek. 44:14). Adam was to begin by ruling the garden for God and presumably to extend God's reign over the whole earth.[30]

The seventh day of creation (Gen. 2:1–3) stands apart because on it God does not create but instead rests, since he has completed his creative work.[31] God's rest plays a significant role thematically in the story line of the Bible. God's rest indicates that "he was now reigning over the creation for the good of his people."[32] According to Joshua, Israel enjoys rest from its enemies when it possesses the land promised to it (Josh. 23:1). Israel's Sabbath observance also replicates the rest of the Lord on the seventh day (Deut. 5:12–15). The theme of rest points to the refreshment and joy found in God's presence, for the seventh day never ends.[33] The Sabbath rest of God, according to Hebrews, finds its fulfillment in the new creation, where believers will enjoy a heavenly and eternal rest during the eschaton (Heb. 4:1–11). Meredith Kline observes that the final rest will take place after the Lord's victory over his satanic enemies (Rev. 19–20).[34] Then human beings will enjoy fellowship with God and see the King in his beauty.

The second creation account (Gen. 2:4–25) supplements the first by zeroing in on the creation of the man and the woman and their unique responsibility. God's special covenant love for human beings is emphasized by the use of the term "Yahweh," whereas the first creation account, in recounting the creation of the cosmos, regularly used the word "God" ('ĕlōhîm). The Lord's care for human beings is relayed by the terms used for his creation of both the man and the woman. The Lord "formed" the man from the dust and "breathed" life into him (2:7). Furthermore, he fashioned the woman from the rib of the man (2:21–22). According to Gen. 1, man and woman, as those who image God, are to display his image as they rule the world for God.

In Gen. 2 this rule begins in the garden that the Lord planted. The garden is, as Dempster says, "the throne-room . . . of the kingdom."[35] The man and the woman are to "work it and keep it" (2:15). The garden, as others have observed, anticipates the tabernacle (Exod. 25–31), and hence it "was the place where human beings could enjoy the fellowship and presence of God."[36]

30. Ibid., 82–83.
31. The Lord rests because he has finished (Goldingay, *Israel's Gospel*, 127).
32. Hafemann, "Covenant Relationship," 40. See also Kline, *Kingdom Prologue*, 23.
33. Dumbrell, *Faith of Israel*, 40.
34. Kline, *Kingdom Prologue*, 23.
35. Dempster, *Dominion and Dynasty*, 62.
36. Sailhamer, *Pentateuch as Narrative*, 98. Cf. Ezek. 28:13.

"Paradise was a sanctuary, a temple-garden."[37] Desmond Alexander notes a number of parallels between the tabernacle/temple and the garden:[38] (1) the Lord walks in both (Gen. 3:8; Lev. 26:12); (2) both Eden and the tabernacle are guarded by cherubim, and they are accessed from the east; (3) the lampstand may symbolize the tree of life (Gen. 2:9; 3:22; Exod. 25:31–35);[39] (4) the verbs used in Gen. 2:15 are also used of the work of the Levites in the sanctuary (Num. 3:7–8; 18:5–6); (5) a river comes from Eden and also flows from Ezekiel's temple (Gen. 2:10; Ezek. 47:1–12); (6) stones found in Eden are also in the tabernacle (Gen. 2:11–12; Exod. 25:7, 11, 17, 31); (7) both are on a mountain, which is sacred land in the ancient Near East. The temple imagery indicates that "God intends that the world become his dwelling place."[40]

The man and the woman, however, do not exercise their rule autonomously. They are ever subject to the will of God.[41] The Lord showers his goodness upon them by placing them in an idyllic garden with verdant trees from which they are nourished. At the same time, the man and the woman would reveal their submission to God's lordship by refusing to eat from "the tree of the knowledge of good and evil" (Gen. 2:17). Indeed, partaking of that tree will bring death. The "tree of life" (Gen. 2:9; 3:22, 24) anticipates the final joy of human beings who know the Lord (Rev. 22:2, 14, 19). The call to obedience forecasts the Mosaic covenant, where God's people are summoned to keep his commandments, thereby showing their devotion to him.[42] God's covenant is integrally related to his rule over his people, for God's covenant with his people always involves a relationship.[43] Furthermore, one of the refrains of

---

37. Kline, *Kingdom Prologue*, 31. He goes on to say, "The garden of Eden was a microcosmic, earthly version of the cosmic temple, and the site of a visible, local projection of the heavenly temple" (p. 32).

38. Alexander, *Paradise to the Promised Land*, 21–23; idem, *Eden to the New Jerusalem*, 21–23. See also Beale, *Church's Mission*, 66–80; Dumbrell, *Faith of Israel*, 19–20; Waltke, *Genesis*, 57–75; Gentry and Wellum, *Kingdom through Covenant*, 211–16; Levenson, *Sinai and Zion*, 129. Levenson says that "the Temple was conceived as a microcosm, a miniature world," and "the world . . . as a macro-temple" is "the palace of God in which all are obedient to his commands" (*Persistence of Evil*, 86).

39. Jenson, *Graded Holiness*, 112.

40. Alexander, *Eden to the New Jerusalem*, 26.

41. "On the one hand, the sovereign King delegates to humanity the authority to rule under him. On the other hand, God's issuing of a commandment assumes man has the moral capacity to choose freely whether to obey or disobey God" (Waltke, *Old Testament Theology*, 259).

42. Scholars have long debated whether God's relationship with Adam and Eve was covenantal. It seems to me that the arguments defending a covenantal idea are stronger. See Gentry, "Kingdom through Covenant," 19–22; Gentry and Wellum, *Kingdom through Covenant*, 177–221; Dumbrell, *Covenant and Creation*, 15–26. For the contrary view, see Williamson, *Sealed with an Oath*, 52–58, 69–76.

43. It is commonly recognized that the relationship in the covenant is familial. See Hahn, *Kinship by Covenant*, 59–67.

Scripture is covenantal, where God pledges, "I will be your God and you will be my people," showing that God's covenant and rule are personal.[44]

The Fall and the Flood

The fall of Adam and Eve into sin signifies their rejection of God's lordship over their lives (Gen. 3).[45] The author of Genesis betrays no interest in where the serpent came from, nor does he inform the reader about how the serpent became evil.[46] Still, there is no idea that the serpent is equal in power to God, nor that something that God created (see Gen. 1) was actually evil.[47] Clearly, the serpent is most unusual because he talks with Eve, and talking is not normal for animals![48] The serpent is strikingly different from the other animals, for it is quite clear from 2:19–20 that Adam's naming of the animals symbolized his dominion over them. Kline notes that such naming represents wisdom,[49] so that already in the creation account we have a link between wisdom themes and lordship. The other animals are not "crafty" (3:1) and are unable to converse with Adam and Eve. Presumably, Adam and Eve were to evict the serpent from the garden by obeying the Lord.[50] They were "to keep or guard the garden so that it would remain holy."[51] Instead, they capitulated to the serpent's blandishments and transgressed the Lord's command by eating from the tree of the knowledge of good and evil.[52]

By failing to obey God's command, they manifested their stubborn independence and their desire to be godlike (3:5). As von Rad remarks, "The unthinkable and terrible is described as simply and unsensationally as possible."[53]

44. See Martens, "People of God," 225.

45. Eating of the tree of the knowledge of good and evil means that Adam and Eve were arrogating to themselves a godlike status. So von Rad, *Israel's Historical Traditions*, 155; Waltke, *Old Testament Theology*, 257–58; Dumbrell, *Covenant and Creation*, 37–38.

46. See Waltke, *Old Testament Theology*, 261.

47. Rightly House, *Old Testament Theology*, 64.

48. Dempster (*Dominion and Dynasty*, 67) rightly criticizes the idea that people in those days believed in talking snakes. So also Alexander, *Eden to the New Jerusalem*, 103.

49. Kline, *Kingdom Prologue*, 48. He comments, "Man's culture was to provide a human replica of the divine kingship manifested in the Glory-Archetype" (p. 49).

50. Kline, *Kingdom Prologue*, 54–55, 77; Beale, *Church's Mission*, 87; Hamilton, *God's Glory in Salvation*, 75. Kline (*Kingdom Prologue*, 75) observes that the judgment of the serpent in the garden anticipated the responsibility of human beings to judge angels (1 Cor. 6:2–3) in the future.

51. Alexander, *Eden to the New Jerusalem*, 26.

52. Beale (*Biblical Theology*, 35) says that distinguishing good from evil is the judicial function of kings (2 Sam. 14:17; 19:35; 1 Kings 3:9; Isa. 7:15–16). See Clark, "Yahwist's Use of 'Good and Evil.'"

53. Von Rad, *Genesis*, 90.

The precious fellowship that they enjoyed with God was shattered. As Kline says, Eve "idolized herself as well as Satan, for she arrogated to herself the divine prerogative of final judgment in discerning between good and evil and in defining the meaning of reality in general. Her new theology was evidenced in her assumption of a critical stance over against the word of God."[54] Nor did their rejection of God's lordship only touch upon their relationship with God. The created world, with all its beauty, was also, as the apostle Paul later noted, "subjected to futility" (Rom. 8:20). The ground that was fertile and yielded fruitful trees now sprouted "thorns and thistles" (Gen. 3:18). The exercise of dominion over the world was now marred by sin so that frustration, pain, and boredom were part and parcel of work. Similarly, the joy of bearing children was now tarnished by the pain that accompanies childbirth (3:16). Adam and Eve were evicted from the garden and now lived east of Eden (3:22–24).

Human beings were to rule the world for God, but now both they and the world were blighted by sin. Nevertheless, a ray of hope shines through the narrative. The Lord promises a future victory over the serpent through the offspring of the woman (3:15).[55] The victory will not be easy, however, for it will come through intense conflict with the offspring of the serpent. In the story line of the Bible Jesus the Christ is the offspring predicted here (see Gal. 3:16), who will triumph over Satan through his death and resurrection. The Lord bestowed his grace upon Adam and Eve by clothing them with the skins of animals (Gen. 3:21). The clothing may indicate the "royal authority" of Adam and Eve.[56] Such clothing anticipates the slaughter of animals for sacrifices, and it is warranted canonically to see the climactic fulfillment in Christ's sacrifice for his people. Adam apparently grasped the significance of the promise in 3:15, for he expressed hope for the future through the children of Eve, who "is the mother of all living" (3:20).[57] The story line of the Scriptures details how the curses pronounced here will be reversed through the blessings promised to Abraham.[58] Indeed, as Kenneth Mathews points out, the verbal and noun form of "blessing" appears eighty-eight times in

54. Kline, *Kingdom Prologue*, 78.
55. Against von Rad (*Genesis*, 93), there is a messianic dimension to the prophecy here. Rightly Hamilton, "Skull Crushing Seed"; Alexander, *Eden to the New Jerusalem*, 106.
56. So Beale, *Biblical Theology*, 228.
57. Rendtorff observes that the "biblical primordial history shows its readers . . . the greatness and beauty of creation and its derailment and endangering by humans. But it also reassures them that God wants to retain and maintain his creation despite human sinfulness" (*Canonical Hebrew Bible*, 20).
58. Rightly Mathews, "Genesis," 143; Hamilton, "Seed of the Woman"; against Sailhamer, *Pentateuch as Narrative*, 301.

Genesis, showing that is a major theme.[59] A new Eden, a new creation, will come through Jesus Christ.[60]

Adam and Eve did not comprehend the horrific evil that they had unleashed into the world. It is possible that Eve believed that Cain was the promised child who would triumph over the serpent and his children (4:1). Cain did not turn out to be the promised deliverer. On the contrary, it became clear that he sided with the serpent. The battle between the children of the serpent and the children of the woman had begun. Abel's sacrifice was pleasing to God, while Cain's was rejected (4:2–7). We learn from Hebrews that the fundamental reason why Abel's sacrifice was pleasing to God was that it was offered in faith (Heb. 11:4), which suggests that Abel sought the Lord for the forgiveness of his sins. Cain is not criticized for failing to bring animal sacrifices, for he brought to the Lord the fruits of his labor. Perhaps there is a suggestion in Genesis that Cain kept for himself the best produce (Gen. 4:3–4). In any case, Hebrews informs us that Cain did not bring his offering in faith. Hence, his offering was not motivated by trust in God. We see from the beginning that mechanical obedience is not pleasing to the Lord, that he demands obedience that flows from a heart of faith (see Rom. 1:5; 16:26). Cain demonstrated that he belonged to the children of the serpent (1 John 3:12; cf. John 8:44; Rev. 12:15–17) by slaying Abel, the offspring of the woman.[61] It is thereby apparent that victory over the serpent will not come easily, that the victory of the woman's offspring will be gained only through intense conflict. The kingdom of God will reign over all, but its triumph will be realized at great cost. At the same time, the Lord reveals his patience and grace in response to Cain's sin, for he does not destroy him but instead shows him mercy.

Culture, craftsmanship, and improved ranching were introduced through Cain's line (Gen. 4:20–22), and yet at the same time the moral character of Cain's descendants declined, and this is evident particularly in the case of Lamech (4:19, 23–24). Human culture, artistry, and technological skill are gifts of God, but they may be used to advance evil rather than good.[62] The riches and beauty of human culture may be dazzling so that the evil perpetrated is hidden from perception. The offspring of the woman continue through Seth (4:25–26), but the trajectory dips rapidly downward. The daughters of men begin to intermarry with the sons of God, and the latter

59. Mathews, "Genesis," 141.
60. This suggests that the land promise, including the promise given to Abraham, will embrace the entire creation (see Williamson, "Promise and Fulfillment," 27).
61. See Alexander, *Eden to the New Jerusalem*, 107–8.
62. See Kline, *Kingdom Prologue*, 113.

most probably are demons (6:1–4), though the identity of the sons of God remains controversial.[63]

The influence of the serpent was now becoming rampant on the earth so that the earth was filled with corruption (6:5, 11). As David Clines notes, "There is an ever-growing 'avalanche' of sin, a 'continually widening chasm between man and God.' There is a movement from disobedience to murder, to reckless killing, to titanic lust, to total corruption and violence, to the full disruption of humanity."[64] Clines goes on to say, "God responds to the extension of human sin with increasingly severe punishment: from expulsion from the garden to expulsion from the tillable earth, to the limitation of human life, to the near annihilation of mankind, to the 'dissolution of mankind's unity.'" But Clines also rightly sees that God's grace is featured. "God not only punishes Adam and Eve, but also withholds the threatened penalty of death; he not only drives out Cain, but also puts his mark of protection upon him; not only sends the Flood, but saves the human race alive in preserving Noah and his family."[65] Von Rad memorably makes the same point about the flood: "It shows God as the one who judges sin, and it stands at the beginning of the Bible as the eternally valid word about God's deadly anger over sin. Thus it protects every succeeding word of grace from any kind of innocuousness (Verharmlosung); it undergirds the understanding of God's will for salvation as a pure miracle."[66]

The offspring of the woman after the flood is restricted to Noah and his family. The promise that God's kingdom would triumph seemed distant and improbable. The account of the flood generation underscores the depth and horror of human sin. Human beings are not stained with a light imperfection (8:21; cf. 6:5); the evil that besets the human race is at the core of human-ity and is not easily erased. The story of the flood generation reveals that human beings, left to themselves, turn toward violence and evil. Any student of twentieth-century history acquainted with the atrocities inflicted by Hitler, Stalin, Mao, and Pol Pot should not find it difficult to understand the evil that bedevils the human race.

The judgment and destruction of all of humankind through the flood also demonstrates that the children of the serpent will not ultimately win. God's kingdom is realized not only through salvation but also through judgment.[67]

---

63. For a discussion of this matter, see Mathews, *Genesis 1:1–11:26*, 323–32.

64. Clines, *Theme of the Pentateuch*, 70. Clines in the afterword clarifies that he would have written the book somewhat differently and more tentatively in 1996 than he first conceived of it in 1976.

65. Ibid.

66. Von Rad, *Genesis*, 129.

67. This is the theme of the important work by Hamilton, *God's Glory in Salvation*.

The head of the serpent will be crushed, and God is glorified in the vanquishing of his foes. In addition, the story of Noah illustrates the truth that God saves and rescues those who trust and obey him, even if they are a small remnant (see 1 Pet. 3:20; 2 Pet. 2:5). The wonder and the grace of salvation stand out when set against the backdrop of God's wrath unleashed upon the world. The land is both cleansed and judged by the flood.[68] God's wrath, as Abraham Heschel points out, "is not a blind, explosive force, operating without reference to the behavior of man, but rather voluntary and purposeful, motivated by concern for right and wrong."[69] Heschel rightly observes that indifference to evil is itself a great evil.[70]

The offspring of the woman, Noah and his family, triumphed over the offspring of the serpent. God made a covenant with Noah and all humankind (Gen. 9:8–17),[71] pledging that the world would not be destroyed by water again.[72] The preservation of the world means that the saving promises for the world will be realized before the end comes. God's creation of human beings will not end up being a failed experiment where the world ends up being destroyed. The "bow" that God sets in the sky is the sign of the covenant, standing here for a weapon of war that God will not unleash on human beings.[73] Nevertheless, the root problem with human beings has not been solved, but God will show mercy as Peter Gentry and Stephen Wellum rightly see, "The condition of humanity after the cataclysmic judgement remains the same after the flood as it was before; so the judgement has not altered or changed the condition of the human heart. The implication is that God would be completely justified in wiping out every generation of humanity by means of a great judgement. There is only one reason why he does not: because of his own grace and mercy towards us. The earth is maintained and preserved in spite of the human situation. Thus the covenant made with Noah creates a firm stage of history where God can work out his plan for rescuing his fallen world."[74]

68. Alexander (*Eden to the New Jerusalem*, 28–29) underestimates the judgment, but he does see the role for cleansing.

69. Heschel, *The Prophets*, 282. Heschel goes on to say that God's anger "is a secondary emotion, never the ruling passion, disclosing only a part of God's way with man" (pp. 282–83).

70. Ibid., 284. Heschel remarks, "The Lord is long-suffering, compassionate, loving, and faithful, but He is also demanding, insistent, terrible, and dangerous" (p. 285).

71. Gentry and Wellum comment, "The statements in verses 8–17 are highly repetitive and monotonous to western ears. This repetition is like a cathedral bell pealing and ringing out again and again, reverberating into the future, that God is committing himself to all his living creatures while the earth lasts. There can be no mistaking of the parties specified in the covenant" (*Kingdom through Covenant*, 168).

72. Incidentally, covenants can be either egalitarian or hierarchical, so we must be careful of saying that the term is used univocally. So Goldingay, *Israel's Faith*, 183–84.

73. Gentry and Wellum, *Kingdom through Covenant*, 170.

74. Ibid., 169.

The author of Genesis consciously draws parallels between the new start with Noah and the initial creation of Adam and Eve, indicating that a fresh era has commenced, that we have something like a new creation after the flood.[75] We find the following parallels:[76] (1) creation out of water and chaos (1:2; 7:11–12, 17–24); (2) birds, animals, and creeping things are brought in to swarm upon the earth (1:20–21, 24–25; 8:17–19); (3) God establishes days and seasons (1:14–18; 8:22); (4) animals are commanded to be fruitful and multiply (1:22; 8:17); (5) repetition of the mandate to be fruitful and multiply (1:28; 9:1, 7); (6) dominion over the world is reestablished (1:28; 9:2); (7) God provides food for humans (1:29–30; 9:3); (8) human beings are still in the image of God (1:26–27; 9:6). All of these features signal that the plan to rescue the human race from sin and the serpent has not ended. Of course, the parallels between the days of Adam and of Noah do not stand at every point, for Noah's world was still stained by sin, whereas the original creation was free from the curse.

Babel and Abraham

The salvation of Noah and the new start with his family are not a return to paradise. Sin is still pervasive (6:5; 8:21). Noah, like Adam in the garden, also sinned in a garden by getting drunk from the fruit of the vine (9:21). And just as Adam and Eve were ashamed of their nakedness after their sin (3:7), so Noah was shamed by his nakedness (9:21–23). Ham's dishonoring of his father (9:22–25) demonstrates that the children of the serpent were not extinguished by the flood but rather were alive and well upon planet earth.[77] But God in his mercy promises not to wipe out the human race by a flood, marking this promise by the covenant sign of the rainbow (9:8–17).[78] God puts aside his bow of war for the preservation of the human race.[79] Human government was also instituted to deter evil (9:6) so that the human society does not descend into anarchy.[80] This is not to say, however, that the fundamental problem with human

75. Dumbrell (*Covenant and Creation*, 15–26) argues that the Noahic covenant represents the reaffirmation of an existing covenant made with Adam and is not the inauguration of a new covenant. See also Hahn, *Kinship by Covenant*, 95. For a confirmation of Dumbrell's view that responds to criticisms and puts it on a firmer foundation, see Gentry and Wellum, *Kingdom through Covenant*, 155–61.

76. See G. Smith, "Genesis 1–11," 310–11. See also Gentry and Wellum, *Kingdom through Covenant*, 161–65.

77. See Kline, *Kingdom Prologue*, 161–62.

78. See Williamson, *Sealed with an Oath*, 64–65, 67–69.

79. So von Rad, *Genesis*, 134; Dumbrell, *Covenant and Creation*, 29–30. Hahn (*Kinship by Covenant*, 50–59) rightly emphasizes that covenant is closely linked with oaths.

80. See Kline, *Kingdom Prologue*, 160.

beings had been solved. Indeed, the power of evil increased exponentially, so that by the time of Babel human arrogance had crested again (11:1–9). The building of what probably was a ziggurat represented the apex of anthropocentrism instead of theocentrism. They built "to make a name for ourselves" (11:4) instead of living to make a name for God.[81] Perhaps human beings also sinned by congregating in one place instead of dispersing throughout the earth. The Lord reigns over all, and he judged human beings by introducing linguistic diversity and dispersing them throughout the world.[82]

The new start that commenced with Noah was looking more and more like the old world. The entirety of the human race was the offspring of the serpent. The tentacles of evil had all of humankind in its grasp, so that none were able to resist its allure. "Babel expressed a naïve and total confidence in what human achievement could effect. . . . It was the beginning of the utopian humanistic dream to which mankind has always aspired."[83] Nevertheless, the final chapter had not been written, and the promise that God's kingdom would triumph through the offspring of the woman was not withdrawn.[84] Von Rad observes that in the early accounts in Genesis each word of judgment was followed by a promise of grace, but such a gracious word is not expressed after Babel, raising the question of whether "God's relationship to the nations is now finally broken; is God's gracious forbearance now exhausted; has God rejected the nations in wrath forever?"[85] The calling of Abraham answers those questions. Mark Strom says, "Abraham would receive the very things for which the people at Babel had grasped: he would have a great name; he would father a great nation; and he would become a source of blessing throughout all the earth. In other words, the Lord would maintain his purposes for creation and humanity through Abraham and those who followed him."[86]

God had promised, after all, that he would "put enmity" between the offspring of the woman and the offspring of the serpent (3:15). When all seemed lost, the Lord called Abraham to the land of promise. "No matter how drastic

81. On the significance of God's name, see Goldingay, *Israel's Faith*, 106–8.
82. Quoting Procksch, von Rad says about Yahweh coming down to see what was happening at Babel, "Yahweh must draw near, not because he is nearsighted, but because he dwells at such tremendous height and their work is tiny. God's movement must therefore be understood as remarkable satire on man's doing" (*Genesis*, 149).
83. Dumbrell, *Covenant and Creation*, 63.
84. See Clines, *Theme of the Pentateuch*, 84–86. Clines (p. 74) also argues that the Table of Nations (Gen. 10) is placed before the incident at Babel (11:1–9) to preclude the idea that judgment is the final word.
85. Von Rad, *Genesis*, 153.
86. Strom, *Symphony of Scripture*, 26. For a full discussion of Yahweh's relationship to the nations, see Goldingay, *Israel's Faith*, 732–833.

human sin becomes, destroying what God has made good and bringing the world to the brink of uncreation, God's grace never fails to deliver humankind from the consequences of their sin."[87] Abraham's obedience, however, cannot be ascribed to his own virtue or wisdom. Abraham himself was from a family of idolaters (Josh. 24:2) and hence was classed among the "ungodly" (see Rom. 4:5).[88] The Lord "took" Abraham from Ur and led him to Canaan (Josh. 24:3).[89] Abraham was one man against the world, but he was a man of the world who had been summoned out of the world by the grace of God. Abraham's leaving Ur for the land of promise also functions as an anticipation of the exodus of Israel from Egypt, where Israel by the mercy of God left Egypt and settled in Canaan.

The focus upon God's grace does not cancel out the reality of Abraham's obedience.[90] Instead, it functions as the foundation upon which his obedience rested. Abraham obeyed the divine summons by leaving his country, relatives, and family without knowing the place of his destination (12:1). Alexander rightly says, "First, the fulfillment of the divine promises is conditional upon Abraham's obedience."[91] Abraham here functions as a new Adam, obeying the Lord in contrast to Adam. And yet, according to Hebrews, such obedience flowed from Abraham's faith: "By faith Abraham obeyed when he was called to go out to a place that he was to receive as an inheritance. And he went out, not knowing where he was going" (Heb. 11:8). So Alexander is mistaken when he says that Abraham merited the promises.[92] The discontinuity between Adam and Abraham must also be emphasized, for Adam before his transgression did not stand in need of forgiveness of sins. Even though Abraham obeyed the Lord in contrast to Adam, he still needed God's forgiveness, for he was not entirely free from sin. He lied twice about Sarah (Gen. 12:11–20; 20:1–18) and resorted to Hagar for children instead of trusting God's promise (16:1–16). Significantly, the writer of Genesis does not identify Abraham's obedience as his righteousness, even though Abraham's obedience is mentioned first (12:4). When the narrator reflects

---

87. Clines, *Theme of the Pentateuch*, 83.

88. Rightly Hafemann, "Covenant Relationship," 43.

89. In Josh. 24:3 "take" (*lāqaḥ*) signals election (Goldingay, *Israel's Gospel*, 196). The election of Abraham is clear in the biblical story (see also Gen. 18:19; Neh. 9:7; Isa. 41:8; 51:2). See Rendtorff, *Canonical Hebrew Bible*, 21; Dumbrell, *Covenant and Creation*, 57–58.

90. Waltke ("Phenomenon of Conditionality") rightly says that the covenant is both irrevocable and conditional. God certainly will fulfill his covenant, but it will not be fulfilled by a disobedient generation.

91. Alexander, *Paradise to the Promised Land*, 50.

92. Ibid., 55. Von Rad rightly observes that Abraham's obedience was rooted in faith (*Genesis*, 161).

upon why Abraham was right with God, he attributes it to his faith, not his obedience (15:6).[93] Paul follows the lead of Genesis in insisting that Abraham was right with God by faith instead of by virtue of his works (Rom. 4:1–25; Gal. 3:1–9). The centrality of God's grace is again featured as the answer to human corruption.[94]

The promises made to Abraham were the means by which God would undo the devastation wrought by Adam and would bring in his kingdom. The Lord promised Abraham land, children, and blessing (Gen. 12:1–3).[95] The blessing and dominion given to Adam are now given to Abraham.[96] The promise that God would make "a great nation" from Abraham signifies the promise of the kingdom.[97] The command given to Adam to be fruitful and multiply (1:28) is now a promise given to Abraham and his offspring (17:2, 5, 6; 22:17; 26:4, 24; 28:3; 35:11; 47:27; 48:4).[98] Contrary to many English translations, Abraham is *commanded* to be a blessing in 12:2 so that, like Adam, he was enjoined to bring blessing to the world.[99]

The land was Canaan, the offspring Isaac, and the blessing was universal so that it encompassed all the peoples of the world (12:3). The serpent, then, would be defeated by the children of Abraham, and so it is now clear in the story that the children of the woman (3:15) would come from the family of Abraham. The promise that the Lord would make Abraham's name great has kingly associations (12:2; cf. 11:4; 2 Sam. 7:9), pointing to the promise that kings would come from Abraham (17:6, 16; cf. 35:11).[100] Blessing for the world would come from a royal figure. The land of Canaan, in a sense, represented a new Eden where the Lord would rule over his people.[101] The land was Canaan, but there were intimations that it comprehended the whole world. Abraham's "offspring" would "possess the gate of [their] enemies" (22:17). Just as the blessing through Abraham would be universal, so the land would include the

93. Contrary to Goldingay (*Israel's Gospel*, 266), who thinks Abraham is counted as righteous in Gen. 15:6.

94. This is not the first time Abraham believed, but it was a confirmation and reaffirmation of faith that he already possessed (see Dumbrell, *Covenant and Creation*, 56).

95. Clines (*Theme of the Pentateuch*) argues that the promise to the patriarchs is the theme of the Pentateuch.

96. N. T. Wright, *Climax of the Covenant*, 21–26; Beale, *Biblical Theology*, 48.

97. Gentry and Wellum, *Kingdom through Covenant*, 243–45.

98. Ibid., 226–28.

99. See ibid., 230–34. As Gentry and Wellum point out, the two commands are supported by three promises, showing that the commands will be fulfilled through divine grace and enabling. Goldingay (*Israel's Gospel*, 201–2) interprets the imperative in Gen. 12:2 as a promise, but Williamson (*Sealed with an Oath*, 79) and Terrien (*Elusive Presence*, 74–75) see it as a command.

100. So Gentry and Wellum, *Kingdom through Covenant*, 236.

101. On the theme of the land, see C. Wright, *Old Testament Ethics*, 76–99.

entire world (Rom. 4:13; Heb. 11:13–16; Rev. 21:1–22:5).[102] It would begin with Canaan, which would be the Lord's outpost in a world gone dramatically wrong.

Though the Lord began with one man, the blessing promised was intended for all peoples everywhere. The promise that the world would be renewed through the children of one man emblazons the truth that salvation is of the Lord and is due entirely to his grace. Human beings naturally side with the serpent, but the Lord will triumph over evil and reclaim the world for his glory and for the good of human beings. The centrality of grace is underlined through the covenant enacted with Abraham, showing that the kingdom would be realized through covenant.[103] The promises of land, seed, and universal blessing were covenant promises.

Was the covenant with Abraham conditional or unconditional? In one sense it was conditional, for it depended upon Abraham's obedience. The logic of Gen. 26:4–5 is clear: "I will multiply your offspring as the stars of heaven and will give to your offspring all these lands. And in your offspring all the nations of the earth shall be blessed, because Abraham obeyed my voice and kept my charge, my commandments, my statutes, and my laws." The text specifically says here that the blessings were granted to Abraham "because" he obeyed the Lord's directives.[104] In a more profound sense, however, the covenant was unconditional.[105] The decisive text here is Gen. 15. The Lord promised Abraham that his children would be as uncountable as the stars. In the latter part of Gen. 15 we find a covenant ceremony where the Lord pledged to Abraham that he would possess the land of Canaan. Abraham brought animals and cut them in half. Sleep and darkness descended upon Abraham. Typically, the covenant partners walked through the divided animals together, symbolizing the truth that they would be cut off if they violated the provisions of the covenant. "To walk between the carcasses is to submit oneself to the fate of the slaughtered animals as a penalty for covenant breaking."[106]

Jeremiah 34, reflecting on the same covenantal custom, pronounced a judgment on those who transgressed the stipulations of the covenant: "I will make them like the calf that they cut in two and passed between its parts" (Jer. 34:18). But in the Abrahamic covenant the Lord alone "passed between these pieces" as "a smoking fire pot and a flaming torch" (Gen. 15:17). The Lord alone passing

102. So Williamson, "Promise and Fulfillment," 18–20; Gentry and Wellum, *Kingdom through Covenant*, 708–9, 711.

103. See Gentry and Wellum, *Kingdom through Covenant*.

104. Contrary to Kline (*Kingdom Prologue*, 198–99), Abraham's obedience should not be seen here as a treasury of merits for others.

105. Gentry and Wellum (*Kingdom through Covenant*, 608–11) rightly argue that it is incorrect to say that some covenants are conditional while others are unconditional.

106. Waltke, *Old Testament Theology*, 319.

between the pieces symbolizes that the fulfillment of the covenant depends upon him alone.[107] The parallel in Jer. 34:18 indicates that "God is invoking the curse on himself, if he fails to fulfill the promise."[108] Ultimately, the covenant will be fulfilled. God himself pledges that it will be so. The unconditionality of the covenant does not remove the need for human obedience. Any person who fails to obey will not enjoy the covenant blessings, and hence the demand for obedience remains in all its starkness. Nevertheless, the grace of God, not the obedience of human beings, remains central, for God will see to it that the covenantal demands are fulfilled by his grace.

It is significant, then, that the covenant of circumcision in Gen. 17, with its requirement of circumcision, is subsequent to the covenant ratified in Gen. 15 (cf. Rom. 4:9–12).[109] The priority of faith and divine grace is thereby underscored. This is not to say that the covenant in Gen. 17 is bereft of grace. After Abraham and Sarah wrongly tried to fulfill the promise through Hagar (chap. 16), chapter 17 begins with the Lord saying, "I am God Almighty" (17:1), signifying that the covenant would be fulfilled through the power of God.[110] The covenant sign of circumcision, where Abram's name was changed to "Abraham" ("father of many nations"),[111] functions as a concrete reminder to Abraham that his children were the result of the grace of God, not Abraham's own sexual virility. Furthermore, the rite signified that all of Israel was consecrated to God.[112]

We have seen that God's kingdom will be realized through the offspring of the woman (3:15), and Gen. 12 clarifies that the offspring will be from Abraham's family. Genesis 12–50 focuses on the promise of offspring. The promise of receiving the land was not fulfilled in Abraham's day. Indeed, Stephen emphasizes that Abraham did not own even a foot of the land (Acts 7:5), which fits well with the narrative in Genesis. The only land that Abraham received was a place to bury Sarah (Gen. 23).[113] Abraham, Isaac, and Jacob

107. So also Williamson, *Sealed with an Oath*, 86. For a fuller discussion of the covenant here, see Gentry and Wellum, *Kingdom through Covenant*, 251–56.

108. Wenham, *Genesis 1–15*, 332.

109. But against Williamson (*Sealed with an Oath*, 89–90), it should not be interpreted as a separate and distinct covenant from that pledged in Gen. 15. Rightly Gentry and Wellum, *Kingdom through Covenant*, 263–70, 275–80.

110. My thanks to Joshua Greever for this insight.

111. For the sake of simplicity I use "Abraham" even before his name was changed.

112. So Gentry and Wellum, *Kingdom through Covenant*, 272–75 (citing the work of John Meade).

113. The patriarchs were resident aliens in Canaan and did not see the fulfillment of the land promise. A burial place for the dead does not signify a fulfillment of the land promises but rather functions as an indication that the promise will be fulfilled in the future (see Williamson, "Promise and Fulfillment," 29–30).

were nomads in the land, living as shepherds with their flocks. Hebrews 11:9 captures the story of Genesis in saying that the patriarchs lived as foreigners in tents in the land that God promised them. In addition, the promise of universal blessing, though it was reiterated to Abraham several times (Gen. 18:18; 22:18; 26:4), was not fulfilled during Abraham's life.

The drama of the story, then, focuses on the promise of offspring, but the promise that Abraham will have children becomes a reality only through conflict (3:15). Indeed, the promise of children was threatened when Sarah was included in the harems of Pharaoh (12:10–20) and Abimelech (20:1–18). Abraham could not have children if his wife no longer belonged to him![114] The narrative does not focus upon Abraham's cowardice and fear in lying about his wife, though certainly he failed to do what God commanded in these instances.[115] Instead, it emphasizes God's dramatic intervention for Abraham's sake, showing that nothing will prevent the Lord from fulfilling his promise.[116] God brought a plague upon Pharaoh's house until Pharaoh realized that he had Abraham's wife and returned her to Abraham (12:17–20). Similarly, God threatened in a dream to kill Abimelech because he had taken Sarah (20:3), and as a result Abimelech returned her to Abraham. Nothing can thwart God's fulfillment of his promises—neither Abraham's failures of faith nor the opposition of unbelieving kings.

Another threat to the promise was the impotence and barrenness of Abraham and Sarah. Abraham worried that his servant Eliezer would be the heir, but God astonished him with the promise that his children would be as many as the stars (15:1–5). Sarah and Abraham, however, devised another plan to fulfill the promise, and Hagar (Sarah's servant) was given to Abraham so that she could bear a child for him and Sarah (chap. 16). The plan worked, and Ishmael was born. But Ishmael was a child derived from the flesh (human ingenuity and ability) rather than the Spirit (see Gal. 4:23, 28–29). God's promise, however, was that the son of the promise would be born to Abraham *and Sarah* (Gen. 17:15–22), thereby underscoring that only God could fulfill the promise, that nothing is "too hard for the LORD" (18:14). The kingdom is the Lord's, and it will be introduced into the world only through his work.

114. Rightly Rendtorff, *Canonical Hebrew Bible*, 25.
115. As Gentry and Wellum point out, Abraham builds altars in honor of God only in Canaan: "There is no altar during his sojourns in Egypt or in Gerar; only half-truths, lies, and troubles" (*Kingdom through Covenant*, 235).
116. "One must always discern the chief thing in God's actions. Here the narrative is one-sidedly concentrated on that, and we have difficulty in following it because the moral problem of Abraham's guilt worries us" (von Rad, *Genesis*, 169).

Paul reflects on this narrative, concluding that Isaac rather than Ishmael was the child of the promise (Rom. 9:6–9). This coheres with the story in Genesis, for the covenantal promise that Abraham would have children was limited to Isaac (Gen. 17:19, 21). Isaac is characterized as "the only son" of Abraham (22:2, 12, 16). Hence, the line of promise was restricted to Isaac and his children. A strange twist in the story emerges in Gen. 22, for God commanded Abraham to sacrifice his son Isaac.[117] The command is astonishing, for it is only through Isaac that the offspring of the woman who would slay the serpent would come. Why would God instruct Abraham to put to death the one through whom the promises would be realized? Several explanations are offered in the account. First, the Lord tested Abraham, thereby confirming the blessing promised to him,[118] for he was willing to obey the most radical directive imaginable (22:16–18). The Lord underscores repeatedly that the child enjoyed by Abraham and Sarah was nothing short of a miracle. Second, Abraham's obedience must not be sundered from his faith. Abraham was convinced, even though God commanded that he sacrifice Isaac, that Isaac would return with him from the sacrifice. Abraham said to the young men as he and Isaac left them to offer the sacrifice, "I and the boy will go over there and worship and come again to you" (22:5). In a narrative such as this, carefully constructed and dramatically effective, the inclusion of such words cannot be waved off as insignificant. Abraham truly believed that Isaac would return with him. The test is the call "to obey when God seems to contradict himself."[119]

The author of Hebrews read the narrative similarly, concluding that Abraham believed that the Lord would raise Isaac from the dead if he was sacrificed (Heb. 11:17–19). Such an interpretation is confirmed by another theme that is woven into the story. When Isaac questioned where the sacrifice would come from, Abraham told him, "God will provide for himself the lamb for a burnt offering, my son" (Gen. 22:8). The words of Abraham were prophetic, for when Abraham was about to sacrifice Isaac, he was instructed to desist and a ram was offered in his place, which confirmed Abraham's belief that "the LORD will provide" (22:14). The sacrifice of the ram in place of Isaac anticipates the final fulfillment of the promise of the offspring, where the true offspring of Abraham, Jesus Christ, fulfills what Isaac only forecasts typologically (Gal. 3:16). The atonement provided by the Lord becomes a reality in the sacrifice of Jesus Christ, who is the beloved Son of God (Rom. 8:32).

117. As Hahn (*Kinship by Covenant*, 134) points out, in Gen. 15; 17; 22 the sacrifices demanded from Abraham escalate—animals, circumcision, Isaac—though the blessings promised escalate as well.
118. The oath formula indicates a covenant is in view (ibid., 109–11).
119. Rendtorff, *Canonical Hebrew Bible*, 29.

The Promise for New Generations

The Genesis narrative continues to focus on the promise of children, though the entirety of the covenant made with Abraham is confirmed to Isaac: offspring, land, and universal blessing (26:3–4). The offspring of the woman (Isaac) was now one man against the world, and the question is whether godly children would survive in a world where the offspring of the serpent desired to annihilate them. The first challenge for Isaac was to find a wife who worshiped the Lord, for if Isaac married a woman who turned his heart and the heart of his children away from the Lord, the promise of future salvation through Abraham's children would be nullified. Hence, Gen. 24 recounts the narrative of how Abraham's servant found a wife (Rebekah) from Abraham's relatives instead of from the Canaanites. Thereby the purity of the line of promise was preserved. Nevertheless, the integrity of the family was compromised when Isaac, like Abraham, lied about whether Rebekah was his wife so that she was taken into Abimelech's harem (26:7). The Lord showed favor to Isaac just as he did to Abraham, for when Abimelech realized that Rebekah was married to Isaac, God threatened anyone who would violate their union with death (26:8–11). The promise was also endangered because Rebekah, like Sarah, was barren. But the Lord, in response to Isaac's prayer, granted Rebekah children (25:21). The promised offspring survived only by the intervention of God, underlining the truth that the Lord graciously fulfills what he has pledged.

Nor was the fulfillment of the promise dependent merely on Isaac and Rebekah producing children. For the children of Isaac and Rebekah were not necessarily the offspring of the woman merely because they were their physical children. Esau and Jacob were the twin children of Isaac and Rebekah, and one would expect that the promise would be transmitted through the older son (Esau). The Lord prophesied, however, that the older son would serve the younger (25:23). Paul, in commenting on the choice of Jacob, highlights God's election (Rom. 9:11–13). The choice of Jacob could not be ascribed to Jacob's virtue or moral heroism; rather, it finds its roots in the grace and election of God. Jacob's deception and manipulation verify his moral impoverishment, confirming Paul's reading. Since all people are children of the serpent by nature, the promise of victory over the serpent will become a reality only by virtue of God's mercy. Esau's casual disregard for his birthright demonstrated that he was not a son of the promise (Gen. 25:29–34), for it is almost inconceivable that he would give it up for the sake of one lunch (Heb. 12:16). The mystery of God's sovereignty in choosing Jacob is relayed in the story of the blessing, for Rebekah and Jacob shamefully conspired together so that Jacob, rather than Esau, would receive the blessing from Isaac (27:1–40).

Despite (not because of!) their machinations, the Lord granted the blessing to Jacob rather than Esau.

Immediately, God's promise was in peril, for Esau was enraged and vowed to kill Jacob (27:41). But as the people of God flee from Satan into the wilderness (Rev. 12:14), so Jacob fled from Esau and traveled to his relatives in Haran (Gen. 27:42–46). Jacob's life was preserved, and unlike Esau, he did not intermarry with Hittite women who worshiped false gods (27:46). Esau's murderous intentions became the means by which Jacob would marry women who were devoted to the Lord, so that the parents of the children to come were devoted to Yahweh. As Jacob traveled to Haran to escape from Esau, the Lord met him at Bethel and confirmed to him the promise of Abraham: land, offspring, and universal blessing (28:13–15).[120] As Rolf Rendtorff says, "When Jacob has experienced the most devastating bankruptcy, when all seems lost and blessing seems to have turned to a curse, God adds his blessing to him."[121] There is no need to linger over the details of Jacob's marriages to Leah and to Rachel. The promise was no longer limited to just one son; all twelve of Jacob's sons were recipients of the promise. Hence, the promise of many offspring began to be fulfilled as Jacob's children multiplied.

Threats to the preservation of Jacob's children continued. Jacob left Laban without notice because the tension and the strife between them were constant. When Laban discovered that Jacob had left and overtook Jacob, he intended to inflict harm upon Jacob and his family (chap. 31). God warned Laban, however, to refrain from injuring Jacob, implying that if Laban did so, he would be severely punished (31:24, 29). Jacob's fears were not ended, however, for immediately after he left Laban, reports arrived that Esau was riding to meet him with four hundred men (32:6–7). Naturally, Jacob was afraid, for the last thing he had heard from Esau was that his brother wanted to kill him, and hence he prayed earnestly to the Lord for deliverance (32:11). Jacob's wrestling with God and prevailing is a significant moment in his life, for his name is changed to "Israel" (32:24–30). As Dempster says, this means that he "will be God's conquering warrior in the earth."[122] Such a name change verifies that victory over the serpent will come through the one who is named "Israel." And Jacob's prayer for protection was answered, for Esau did not come for war but to renew their friendship (chap. 33).

Another threat to the promise loomed on the horizon. Shechem the son of Hamor from the Shechemites was smitten with Dinah and raped her, prevailing

120. Alexander (*Eden to the New Jerusalem*, 31–32) points out that Mount Moriah and Bethel are anticipations of the temple where Yahweh dwells.

121. Rendtorff, *Canonical Hebrew Bible*, 30.

122. Dempster, *Dominion and Dynasty*, 87.

upon his father to work out an arrangement by which he could marry her (34:1–4). Why is this rather strange story included? If the Israelites intermarried with the Shechemites, the children of Jacob would lose their purity because of uniting with people who worshiped other gods. Hence, the children of the serpent would triumph over and overwhelm the children of the woman. Ironically, the means by which Israel was protected from intermarriage involved subterfuge and murder, for Jacob's sons persuaded all the Shechemite males to submit to circumcision before they would agree to intermarry (chap. 34). After the surgery Simeon and Levi dishonorably murdered the Shechemites while they were sore (34:25–26), and the remaining brothers gleefully looted their possessions (34:27–29). Simeon and Levi were punished for their cruelty, and as a result they were scattered among the twelve tribes and were not given a specific portion of land as an inheritance (49:5–7). Even though the narrator did not comment immediately in Gen. 34 on the actions of Simeon and Levi, it is clear that he saw these deeds as evil. Nonetheless, the Lord's purposes were realized through their malfeasance, for the Israelites were prevented from intermarrying with the Shechemites.

Another danger surfaced, however, because of the evil perpetrated by Simeon and Levi. Now the family of Jacob (and the realization of the promise of the kingdom) faced the danger of attack from the Canaanites and Perizzites, who would retaliate for Israel's slaughter (34:30). The only explanation for Israel's preservation was divine intervention, for "a terror from God fell upon the cities that were around them, so that they did not pursue the sons of Jacob" (35:5). The Lord then appeared to Jacob and confirmed the promise of Abraham to him again, pledging offspring, land, and blessings for all peoples (35:9–13). The stories of the preservation of Jacob and his children drive home one of the main themes of the narrative: the preservation of Jacob's offspring is not due to human ingenuity or even human virtue. Only God's covenant promise can explain why this small family escaped disaster after disaster and was preserved intact.

Judah and Joseph

The story of Joseph dominates Gen. 37–50, though the account of Judah bearing children through Tamar is inset into the narrative (chap. 38). Why is this rather sordid story about Judah and Tamar included in the narrative? If we consider the entire narrative of Genesis, we find a significant clue in 49:8–10:[123]

123. See Mathews, "Genesis," 144.

"Judah, your brothers shall praise you; your hand shall be on the neck of your enemies; your father's sons shall bow down before you. Judah is a lion's cub; from the prey, my son, you have gone up. He stooped down; he crouched as a lion and as a lioness; who dares rouse him? The scepter shall not depart from Judah, nor the ruler's staff from between his feet, until tribute comes to him; and to him shall be the obedience of the peoples." The writer clarifies here that from Judah will come the ruler who will defeat the Lord's enemies. The promise that the offspring of the woman will triumph over the serpent will be obtained through the family of Judah. The blessing promised to Abraham through all nations will be realized finally through Judah's family.[124]

How does the story of Gen. 38 relate to this promise of future rule? Brevard Childs says, "Judah demonstrated an unfaithfulness which threatened to destroy the promise of a posterity, which was only restored by the faithfulness of a Canaanite wife."[125] Hence, the birth of Perez and Zerah is significant because the promises made to Abraham will finally be fulfilled through Judah's descendants. John Sailhamer also makes a crucial observation. Jacob's words in Gen. 49 relate to the "days to come" (49:1), forecasting a coming ruler from Judah.[126] The same phrase (translated as "in the latter days") occurs in Num. 24:14, where Balaam predicts Israel's triumph over Moab. Indeed, the parallels do not stop there. The language about a lion is picked up from Gen. 49: "He crouched, he lay down like a lion and like a lioness; who will rouse him up?" (Num. 24:9).[127] A coming ruler who will triumph over Moab is also foretold: "I see him, but not now; I behold him, but not near: a star shall come out of Jacob, and a scepter shall rise out of Israel; it shall crush the forehead of Moab and break down all the sons of Sheth" (Num. 24:17).[128] The kingdom of God will become a reality through a ruler from the tribe of Judah.

We turn to the Joseph narrative, which encompasses Gen. 37–50. The purpose here is to see the overarching purpose of the account. It is apparent throughout Genesis that the offspring of Abraham were not necessarily characterized by virtue. The moral weaknesses of Jacob and his sons are quite evident. The treachery of Joseph's brothers reached its apex when they sold him into Egypt and lied to their father about his death. In the midst of Joseph's sufferings, the theme that the Lord was with him is underscored, whether he was in Potiphar's house or in the prison (39:2–3, 23). Since God gave him the ability to

---

124. Sailhamer (*Pentateuch as Narrative*, 140) notes the emphasis on "blessing" in Gen. 49:28.

125. Childs, *Old Testament as Scripture*, 157.

126. Sailhamer, *Old Testament Theology*, 211.

127. See Beale, *Biblical Theology*, 99.

128. See Sailhamer, *Old Testament Theology*, 211–12. Sailhamer (p. 247) sees at the end of the Pentateuch (Deut. 33) prominence for Judah as well.

interpret dreams, he became the second in command in Egypt, conserving and distributing food during the seven years of abundance and the seven years of famine. Joseph's story is full of human interest, but what is its role in terms of the purpose of Genesis? Joseph himself declared the purpose in the dramatic scene where he disclosed his identity to his brothers: "And now do not be distressed or angry with yourselves because you sold me here, for God sent me before you to preserve life. For the famine has been in the land these two years, and there are yet five years in which there will be neither plowing nor harvest. And God sent me before you to preserve for you a remnant on earth, and to keep alive for you many survivors. So it was not you who sent me here, but God. He has made me a father to Pharaoh, and lord of all his house and ruler over all the land of Egypt" (45:5–8). Joseph did not minimize the evil his brothers inflicted upon him (50:20), but he saw the larger purposes of God in the events that transpired. The Lord sovereignly regulated circumstances so that Joseph would be a ruler in Egypt, and thus Jacob's family was sustained in Egypt during the famine so that a remnant would continue to exist (45:11).

The offspring of the woman would not be annihilated by the children of the serpent. In fact, the children of the serpent (the Egyptians) play a vital role in Israel's survival. Ultimately, the Lord even rules over Satan and mysteriously uses him to accomplish his will (cf. Job 1–2). At the same time, the promise of offspring was being fulfilled, for now there were seventy persons in Jacob's family (Gen. 46:6–27). The children were not yet as numerous as the stars, but they were on their way to the realization of what God had promised. Nor did the Israelites intermarry with the Egyptians, so as to pollute the holy seed. They had an occupation as shepherds that the Egyptians detested, and so they were able to live separately in Goshen (46:33–47:6).

Israel's population was growing, and they were safe in Egypt, but they were in the wrong place. They were destined for the land of Canaan. It was there that the kingdom would be established, but the land was not to be theirs yet. God's justice must be preserved, and evicting the Canaanites from their land was not yet fitting.[129] The Canaanites would not be removed from the land for four generations, since their "iniquity" was "not yet complete" (15:16). Canaan eventually would belong to Israel. Hence, Jacob insisted that Joseph bury him in Canaan rather than Egypt (47:29–31; 50:5–13). Like Abraham, the only portion of Canaan that Jacob possessed was a tomb, but the Lord's promise was not revoked (48:3–4).

---

129. It is interesting to note that the narrator believes that the slaughter of the Shechemites was evil, but the same conclusion is not drawn regarding the Canaanites in the land. In the latter case, their evil was great enough to warrant their complete annihilation. In that respect, they were like the generation of the flood, which deserved utter destruction.

Genesis concludes with Joseph's death in Egypt, before which he reminded Israel of the promise that they would inherit the land promised to the patriarchs, and instructed them to bring him to Canaan in the future (50:24–26). So Genesis ends with Israel in the wrong place. The kingdom is the Lord's, but Egypt was not where they were supposed to be. The offspring of Abraham were scarcely as many as the stars. They did not live in the land of Canaan, and worldwide blessing was not even close. Still, the family of the patriarchs survived and was even beginning to thrive. The Lord had preserved them even though they were small and weak, even while they were sojourners in the land promised to them (Ps. 105:11–15). He had showered his grace on Abraham, Isaac, and Jacob by making a covenant with them and showing them grace again and again. The preservation of the offspring clearly was the Lord's work, for Abraham's family survived despite barrenness, sin, stupidity, squabbles, and famine. Genesis teaches that the kingdom will come, for ultimately it depends upon the Lord. It will be realized through his promise rather than human virtue.

2

EXODUS

The Great Escape

The promise of the coming of the kingdom would be secured through the covenant made with Abraham, a covenant that promised children, land, and worldwide blessing. We saw at the end of Genesis that these promises had scarcely advanced at all. Clearly, the patriarchs lived in faith that the Lord would fulfill his promises in the future. Israel was not in Canaan but in Egypt, and obviously the whole world had not been renewed through Abraham's family. Indeed, as Genesis concludes, the entire family is limited to about seventy people. Nevertheless, the promise that the family of Abraham, Isaac, and Jacob would be like the stars of heaven (Gen. 15:5) began to be fulfilled in Exodus (cf. Gen. 46:3; Deut. 26:5).[1] We read in Exod. 1:7, "But the people of Israel were fruitful and increased greatly; they multiplied and grew exceedingly strong, so that the land was filled with them."[2] The offspring of the serpent, however, continued, like Cain with Abel, to try to stamp out the children of Abraham. Pharaoh was filled with fear at Israel's burgeoning population, and therefore, as a child of the serpent, he tried to wipe them out (1:8–22). Nothing, however, could ultimately frustrate the Lord's sovereign plan.[3] "Insignificant" midwives defied Pharaoh's orders and preserved Israel

---

1. The many children born "is like a new beginning of creation" (Rendtorff, *Canonical Hebrew Bible*, 34). Goldingay (*Israel's Gospel*, 290) wrongly downplays the fulfillment here.

2. As Enns ("Exodus," 147) points out, creation language is used here.

3. Sailhamer points out the irony in the Exodus narrative: "The more the king tries to thwart God's blessing the more that blessing increases. . . . God is at work in these events to bring about his plan, and no one, not even the great power of the gentile nations, can stand in his way" (*Pentateuch as Narrative*, 242).

(1:15–21). Indeed, the sovereignty of God manifested itself in a "quieter" and ironic way. The eventual deliverer of Israel and destroyer of Egypt was rescued by Pharaoh's own daughter, raised in Pharaoh's palace (2:1–10), and educated in Egyptian wisdom (Acts 7:22). When Pharaoh realized that Moses was his adversary, he tried to put him to death (Exod. 2:15), but Moses fled into exile, which pointed forward to Jesus' exile (back into Egypt!) to escape from another king (Herod the Great) from Satan's line (Matt. 2:13–15).[4]

Israel suffered miserably under Egyptian rule and cried out for deliverance. The Lord remembered his covenant promise, showing his unfailing love for his people (Exod. 2:23–25). Moses was the man appointed to lead Israel out of Egypt, though the narrative stresses Moses' feeling that he was utterly incapable of being the deliverer (chaps. 3–4). Moses knew that he was a sinner and that he was nothing in himself, which is why he is commended for his humility (Num. 12:3). The story does not elevate Moses to greatness by emphasizing his courage. He does not represent a brave "general" who is ready to rescue God's people. Instead, he pleads and begs to be relieved of his duty, for he is deeply conscious of his inadequacy. Moses' greatness stems not from his own inner strength but rather from his recognition that without God he could do nothing. Only God could save Israel from their enemies. Moses is merely a "servant" in the Lord's house (Exod. 14:31; Num. 12:7; cf. Heb. 3:5).

God revealed himself to Moses as "I AM" (Exod. 3:14), and the meaning and translation of the Hebrew have precipitated much discussion. We can safely land, though, on what the text emphasizes. The Lord ("Yahweh") appeared to Moses as the God who keeps his covenant with his people. He will fulfill his covenantal promise by rescuing Israel from Egypt and by bringing them into the land of promise (3:7–10, 16–17).[5] Hence, "I AM" emphasizes that the Lord is the God of the covenant, that he is fulfilling his promises as "the God of Abraham, the God of Isaac, and the God of Jacob" (3:15). The Lord is the living God and always keeps his promises, and the realization of the promises is not in question, since he is the Lord over all. Yahweh will be remembered and praised forever for being the covenant-keeping God. The kingdom surely will come, for the Lord always fulfills his promises.

The emphasis on covenant also helps to explain the strange passage in 4:24–26, where the Lord threatens to kill Moses. Apparently, Moses, presumably at the behest of Zipporah, refused to circumcise his son. The Lord

4. Pharaoh is "an anti-God/anti-creation figure" (Enns, "Exodus," 147).
5. For discussion, see Waltke, *Old Testament Theology*, 364–67; Martens, *God's Design*, 22–23; Dumbrell, *Covenant and Creation*, 82–84. Childs (*Book of Exodus*, 76) emphasizes that God will reveal himself by his future work on Israel's behalf. See his discussion of the verse, including the history of interpretation (pp. 82–83, 85–87).

threatened to slay Moses because he had refused to keep the covenant stipulation that God had ordained. Those who were not circumcised would be "cut off" from the covenant (Gen. 17:9–14). Moses could scarcely be the agent of covenantal deliverance when he himself did not apply the covenantal sign to his own sons! Covenantal blessing only comes to those who obey the Lord, as the Lord reminded Moses and Zipporah on that unusual night.

How the Lord delivered Israel from Egypt was imprinted on their memory, and it became the stuff of liturgy and festivals (Passover and Unleavened Bread). The nation was now large as the Lord promised, but they had no land of their own and were enslaved to a people much more powerful and sophisticated than they. Israel reflected both in story and in song (e.g., Exod. 15:1–18; Ps. 105:23–45) on the astonishing deliverance that they received through the hand of Moses. If Abraham was the father of the nation, the exodus from Egypt under Moses represented Israel's Independence Day. They were freed from oppression and misery in a most astonishing and unexpected way. They walked away free from one of the great superpowers of ancient history and never forgot it. When we get to the prophets, we will see that when the nation languished, the prophets promised them a new exodus. The Lord would deliver them again as he had in the past. The exodus, then, became the paradigm, a type, of the Lord's redeeming love. The story of the exodus, then, was not merely history. It also signified God's purpose for Israel for the future. As von Rad says, "In the deliverance from Egypt Israel saw the guarantee for all the future, the absolute surety for Jahweh's will to save."[6] The exodus can be conceived of as the new creation of Israel, pointing toward the new creation in the future.[7]

The Exodus narrative details how the Lord saved his people from the Egyptian behemoth, delivering them by sending ten plagues upon Egypt and Pharaoh.[8] The story of the plagues is recounted in some detail (chaps. 7–10), and the narrative builds to a climax. Pharaoh is deeply conflicted in the story. He cannot abide the thought of losing free slave labor, and yet the misery of the plagues is unbearable. Pharaoh cannot help thinking that the plagues will cease. Surely, they are "freak accidents," and not the work of the God of Israel. Hence, Pharaoh repeatedly promises to let Israel go if only he and Egypt can get relief from the plagues, convinced all along that the plagues will end. Surely, the narrative of the plagues represents storytelling at its best, for the tension in the account builds to a climax as plague after plague strikes Egypt, and Pharaoh continues to harden his heart and stubbornly declines to

6. Von Rad, *Israel's Historical Traditions*, 176.

7. Dumbrell, *Covenant and Creation*, 101.

8. Alexander observes that more often the "plagues" are described as "signs" and "wonders" (*Paradise to the Promised Land*, 67).

let Israel leave Egypt. Pharaoh's inability to see the obvious is underlined by his servants who say to him, "How long shall this man be a snare to us? Let the men go, that they may serve the LORD their God. Do you not yet understand that Egypt is ruined?" (10:7). It is evident that Yahweh was fulfilling his covenant promises to Israel and exercising his sovereignty and rule over Pharaoh and Egypt.

Nor is Pharaoh's intransigence presented one-dimensionally. On one level, Pharaoh resisted the Lord by hardening his heart (7:14, 22; 8:32; 9:34), and yet it was also the case that the Lord hardened Pharaoh's heart (4:21; 7:3, 13; 8:15, 19; 9:7, 12, 35; 10:1, 20, 27; 11:10; 14:4, 8; cf. 14:17).[9] Pharaoh's obstinacy was not the only reality; the Lord reigned and ruled over his decisions without infringing upon the authenticity of his choices.[10] The psalmist reflects on the same reality but widens its scope to include all of Egypt, saying that the Lord "turned [the Egyptians'] hearts to hate his people, to deal craftily with his servants" (Ps. 105:25). This verse is misunderstood if the Lord's sovereign work in the heart of the Egyptians is interpreted as removing moral responsibility from the Egyptians, for moral blame is still assigned to the Egyptians for their hatred. The biblical writers do not finally and fully resolve the tension between divine sovereignty and human freedom. They affirm the authenticity of human decisions, and yet they see God's sovereign hand behind all that occurs (Prov. 16:33; 21:1).[11]

Why were there ten plagues? Clearly the Lord, as creator and ruler of the cosmos, could have liberated Israel from Egypt immediately. The infliction of plague after plague, however, impressed upon the Israelites (and the Egyptians!) that Yahweh was Lord, and that the liberation of Israel was not a freakish accident. It was the outworking of the Lord's plan. Pharaoh began the whole conversation by asking, "Who is the LORD?" (Exod. 5:2). By the end of the plagues, he knew the answer to that question.[12] Hence, Israel knew from their deliverance that they were loved by the Lord. Indeed, the narrative articulates why ten plagues were visited upon Pharaoh: "For by now I could have put out my hand and struck you and your people with pestilence, and you would have been cut off from the earth. But for this purpose I have raised you up, to show you my power, so that my name may be proclaimed in all the

9. Some of these texts may indicate Pharaoh's hardening his own heart, but in any case we have texts that say that Pharaoh hardened his own heart and others that say that the Lord hardened Pharaoh's heart. For helpful explanations of what is happening here, see Beale, "Hardening of Pharaoh's Heart"; Piper, *Justification of God*, 159–71.

10. The text does not explain how this is so, but it clearly states both that God is sovereign over Pharaoh's choices and that Pharaoh hardened his own heart.

11. "Everything happens by God's determination" (Goldingay, *Israel's Faith*, 78).

12. See Sailhamer, *Pentateuch as Narrative*, 249–50.

earth" (9:15–16). The Lord could have crushed Pharaoh as easily as one steps on an ant, but he preserved him in order to show his own sovereign power and greatness. The salvation of Israel and the judgment of Egypt became the theater for God's glory—the place where his character and his name were displayed to the world. The refrain that punctuates the narrative is that God inflicted punishment on Egypt so that they would know that "I am the LORD" (7:5, 17; 8:22; 10:2; 12:12; 14:4, 18) or, as Moses tells Pharaoh at one point, "so that you may know that there is no one like the LORD our God" (8:10). Pharaoh should "fear the LORD God" (9:30). The lordship and the kingship of God are revealed in the liberation of Israel. We see here one of the main themes of the book. Israel's redemption and Egypt's judgment reveal the incomparability of Yahweh, so that all people know that there is no one like the Lord, and that he is to be feared both as a loving savior and as a mighty judge and a sovereign king. The Lord is a mighty and incomparable warrior against whom no enemy can triumph.[13]

It should also be emphasized that the Lord was fulfilling his covenant to the patriarchs in liberating Israel from Egypt. Exodus 6:6–8 emphasizes the Lord's faithfulness to his covenant promises: "I am the LORD, and I will bring you out from under the burdens of the Egyptians, and I will deliver you from slavery to them, and I will redeem you with an outstretched arm and with great acts of judgment. I will take you to be my people, and I will be your God, and you shall know that I am the LORD your God, who has brought you out from under the burdens of the Egyptians. I will bring you into the land that I swore to give to Abraham, to Isaac, and to Jacob. I will give it to you for a possession. I am the LORD." In being redeemed and freed from Egypt, Israel realized that Yahweh was fulfilling the promise that he had given to the patriarchs. Yahweh was Israel's God, and hence he saved them and delivered them in accord with his promises. The fulfillment of the covenant explains the difficult text where God says that he did not make himself known as "the LORD" (*yhwh*) to the patriarchs but is now providing such a revelation to Moses and his generation (6:3). At first glance, this appears to be an outright contradiction because "Yahweh" is used with reference to the patriarchs. The purpose of the statement, however, is not to deny that God revealed himself to patriarchs as Yahweh. What is distinctive is that the realization and the fulfillment of the covenant promises were only now taking place.[14] The exodus generation was coming to know Yahweh as the covenant-keeping God.

13. See Longman and Reid, *God Is a Warrior*; Rendtorff, *Canonical Hebrew Bible*, 45; Waltke, *Old Testament Theology*, 393–94; Brueggemann, *Theology of the Old Testament*, 139–44.
14. Rightly Waltke, *Old Testament Theology*, 367–69. For a discussion of the history of interpretation and modern critical views, see Childs, *Book of Exodus*, 112–14. Childs says, "Now

Two themes interlock here. On the one hand, the Lord fulfilled his covenant by delivering Israel from slavery in Egypt.[15] Israel's liberation represented their redemption and testified to the Lord's love for his people.[16] Israel's salvation was inseparable from Egypt's judgment, for just as the Israelites passed through the waters of the sea unscathed, the Egyptians were destroyed (14:13, 30). By defeating Pharaoh, the Lord got "glory over Pharaoh and all his host, his chariots and his horsemen" (14:17). The song of triumph interprets poetically the victory that the Lord gained over Egypt. What should be observed first is that the song is one of praise. The God-centeredness of biblical revelation surfaces here. When the Lord delivers his people, they praise and exalt him. One striking theme that emerges here is that the Lord's judgment and salvation demonstrate that he is the King: "The LORD will reign forever and ever" (15:18). But he reigns over his people so that he could dwell with them and show them his love. Israel is "planted" on God's mountain (15:17), where Yahweh's "sanctuary" is. What we see here anticipates what we will see in more detail in the book of Psalms. The sovereignty and the kingship of the Lord are wedded inextricably to praise, for the Lord of the universe should be praised and exalted for his goodness and his redeeming love and for his judgment of the wicked. And the psalms emphasize that the Lord is especially praised in the temple, in his sanctuary as the King of the universe. The NT sees the exodus as a foreshadowing and type of the redemption accomplished by Jesus Christ (e.g., Col. 1:12–14), where God's people are freed from their sins by Christ's atoning work. Ultimately, the whole of creation will be his temple (Rev. 21–22), where he reigns over his people and dwells with them.

The victory that the Lord won was celebrated yearly in Israel in the festivals of Passover and Unleavened Bread (Exod. 12–13). Parents were to tell the story of what happened to their children so that Israel would never forget that Yahweh brought them out of Egypt "with a strong hand" (13:9). If Israel forgot, they would cease to be thankful, and if thankfulness vanished, so would faith and obedience. The Passover was particularly significant. The Lord could have rescued Israel simply by destroying all the firstborn in Egypt. The Passover events, however, reminded Israel that they deserved judgment as well. The Lord would "pass over" the firstborn in Israel only if blood was applied to

God reveals himself to Moses as Yahweh who remembers his covenant, and who moves to bring his promise to completion" (p. 115). He continues, "Now God reveals himself through his name as the God who fulfills his promise and redeems Israel from Egypt" (p. 115).

15. Waltke summarizes what Yahweh did this way. Israel "was delivered to live as a free people in their own land" (*Old Testament Theology*, 391).

16. If we read the Scriptures canonically (including the NT witness), the exodus functions primarily as a type of spiritual redemption, not economic or political or social liberation. Against C. Wright (*Old Testament Ethics*, 156), who makes all of these parallel.

the lintel and the doorposts of the house. The Lord impressed upon Israel that they were not inherently better than the Egyptians. They were rescued from the wrath of the Lord only if they responded in faith to his instructions by putting the blood of lambs on their houses. It is easy for us to read the story abstractly, but it is quite violent, for lambs were slain and their blood was applied to houses. Certainly the Passover represents "redemption" and "liberation" for Israel. It probably signifies substitution as well, for the blood of the lamb is spilled instead of the blood of the firstborn. According to the NT, Passover points ahead to the sacrifice of Christ, whereby he gave his life for the deliverance of his people (1 Cor. 5:7). The Lord's Supper almost certainly is a Passover meal (Matt. 26:26–29; Mark 14:22–25; Luke 22:15–20),[17] and the blood of Jesus represents the new covenant where the blood of "the lamb of God" (John 1:29) has been shed for his people.

Unleavened bread was also eaten in memory of the great exodus event (Exod. 12:15–20, 34, 39; 13:3, 6–7), for the Israelites were pressed for time and thus the bread could not be leavened before they left Egypt. Remembrance in Israel was not limited to mentally recalling what happened in the past; true remembrance meant participation in the story of the past. Israel's deliverance in the past represented the liberation of all generations. Observing the feasts of Passover and Unleavened Bread helped Israel relive Yahweh's salvation of his people. Paul suggests that the removal of leaven should not have been a mechanical exercise (1 Cor. 5:7–8). It symbolizes the removal of evil from the lives of God's people. Those who are delivered in God's redeeming love should live in a way that expresses their joy at being rescued from evil. Paul argues that since believers enjoy deliverance through Christ's Passover sacrifice, they are now free from evil (1 Cor. 5:7) and should live in accord with the freedom that they already enjoy.

The Mosaic Covenant

The next major event in redemptive history is the inauguration of the Mosaic covenant on Mount Sinai. Yahweh delivered his people from Egypt on the basis of his covenant with the patriarchs: Abraham, Isaac, and Jacob (Exod. 2:23–25; 6:2–9). At this juncture he establishes a covenant at Sinai with Israel. Some scholars have argued that there is a parallel with suzerain-vassal treaties of the second millennium BC in which a king makes a pact with his vassals.[18] These treaties often had six elements: (1) the preamble, where the sovereign

17. See Köstenberger, "Last Supper."
18. See Mendenhall, *Law and Covenant*; Kline, *Treaty of the Great King*; Hillers, *Treaty-Curses*.

is introduced; (2) the historical prologue, which summarizes the relationship of the parties in question; (3) the stipulations of the covenant; (4) the deposition of the covenant in the sanctuary for periodic reading; (5) witnesses to the covenant; and (6) the curses and blessings of the covenant. Although some scholars, for both historical and exegetical reasons, doubt whether there is truly a parallel,[19] it seems that there are solid grounds for thinking that the parallel holds.[20] The historical parallel suggests that Israel's covenant with Yahweh fits with the historical-cultural world in which they lived. Whatever one makes of the suzerain-vassal notion, it is clear from Exodus (and Deuteronomy) that virtually all the elements of the treaty are present conceptually. Yahweh's covenant with Israel involved both God's promises to his people and the obligation of the people to obey.[21] Israel was to live under the authority of its great King.

It is imperative to point out that the Lord's deliverance of the people from Egypt (preamble and historical prologue) precedes the giving of covenant stipulations.[22] Yahweh reminds Israel at Sinai "how I bore you on eagles' wings and brought you to myself" (19:4). Similarly, before the giving of the Ten Commandments God says, "I am the LORD your God who brought you out of the land of Egypt, out of the house of slavery" (20:2). It is immediately evident that the Sinai covenant should not be identified as a legalistic one.[23] The Lord delivers his people by his grace, and they are to respond to his redemptive work on their behalf with obedience.[24] It was not the Israelites' moral virtue that caused the Lord to save them from Egyptian bondage; he delivered them because of his mercy and love, which were undeserved and unmerited.

The events at Sinai also reminded Israel of the Lord's mysterious holiness. He comes to the people "in a thick cloud" (19:9, 16). When the Lord descends, a terrible storm erupts on the mountain with thunder and lightning and smoke and something akin to an earthquake (19:16–19; 20:18–21). The thick cloud and darkness indicate that the glory of the Lord is hidden from the people, and the storm reveals the holiness and fierce wrath of the Lord. Hence, the people tremble (19:16; 20:18). If they do not follow the Lord's instructions about washing, consecration, and purity, and if they transgress, then the wrath of the Lord will break out against them. The

19. For a summary of these objections, see Williamson, *Sealed with an Oath*, 26–28. See also McCarthy, *Old Testament Covenant*, 10–34; Weinfeld, *Deuteronomy*, 59–157.
20. So J. A. Thompson, "Suzerain-Vassal Concept"; Lucas, "Covenant, Treaty, and Prophecy."
21. So Goldingay, *Israel's Faith*, 186–87.
22. See Von Rad, *Israel's Historical Traditions*, 194.
23. See Gentry and Wellum, *Kingdom through Covenant*, 312.
24. Rightly Childs, *Old Testament as Scripture*, 174; C. Wright, *Old Testament Ethics*, 28–29; Dumbrell, *Covenant and Creation*, 91.

covenant that Israel is making is not with a deity whom they can manipulate or domesticate to serve their own ends. He is the sovereign Lord of the whole earth, judging the sin of those who turn against him, and thus Israel should fear him (20:18, 20). At the same time, he is the loving Lord, who has just rescued his people from Egyptian oppression. Israel comes trembling to their holy and loving Lord.

The Sinai covenant is conditional. John Goldingay says, "It is not exactly that Yhwh's commitment to Israel is conditional on Israel's commitment. Rather, it demands it."[25] Israel must keep the stipulations of the covenant, or else it will be broken. After the Lord emphasizes his deliverance of Israel, he declares to them the conditions and privileges of the covenant: "If you will indeed obey my voice and keep my covenant, you shall be my treasured possession among all peoples, for all the earth is mine; and you shall be to me a kingdom of priests and a holy nation" (19:5–6). Like Adam, Israel serves as priest-king.[26] The promise of a nation given to Abraham is also picked up here.[27] The entire nation of Israel will be a kingdom of priests that will have access to God and mediate his blessings to others.

Israel's priestly blessing to the nations is disputed. It could be that Yahweh summons Israel in a missional sense.[28] It is more likely that Israel would mediate blessings to the nations if it was consecrated to the Lord and kept his law.[29] Israel was not instructed (unlike the NT) to bring the message of the love of God to other nations. Other nations would be attracted to Yahweh when they saw the blessings that belonged to Israel as the chosen and consecrated people of the Lord. William Dumbrell says that "Israel's primary role in this connection consisted in attracting the world to her form of government (i.e., the kingdom of God) by her embodied holiness."[30] They will be a theocracy—God's special and distinct people on the earth—if they keep the provisions of the covenant. In the story line of the OT, however, Israel fails in its role as priest-king, just as Adam did in the garden. The people are corrupted by evil and suffer exile

25. Goldingay, *Israel's Faith*, 188. He goes on to say that the covenant with Israel is not a "contract." Israel must submit to Yahweh, but the "must" means that there are conditions.
26. Alexander, *Eden to the New Jerusalem*, 84.
27. Dumbrell, *End of the Beginning*, 129.
28. So Waltke, *Old Testament Theology*, 407; Brueggemann, *Theology of the Old Testament*, 431; Beale, *Church's Mission*, 117–21.
29. C. Wright (*Old Testament Ethics*, 6, 74) says that Israel was to be a "model" for the nations.
30. Dumbrell, *Faith of Israel*, 38. See also the helpful discussion in Dumbrell, *Covenant and Creation*, 85–90. He says that Israel's role as a "*separated* divine possession is being underscored. . . . Just as a priest is separated from an ancient society in order to serve it and serves it by his distinctiveness, so Israel serves her world by maintaining her distance and difference from it" (*Covenant and Creation*, 90).

for their sin. Ultimately, Israel's role as priest-king is fulfilled in Jesus Christ. He is the true Adam, the true Israel, God's faithful priest and true king. As the Melchizedekian priest, according to Hebrews, he brings human beings into fellowship with God through his atoning sacrifice. He restores the relationship Adam had in the garden, but it is even better than this, for believers are guaranteed a place in the heavenly city, where sin cannot touch them. At the same time Hebrews teaches that Jesus, as a result of his sacrifice, is seated as king at the right hand of God. On the basis of his shed blood he intercedes as a priest for his people.[31]

The roles of priest and king are not restricted to Jesus Christ. These roles are also given by the Christ to his people, to those who are united with him by faith. Peter emphasizes in the NT that the church of Jesus Christ, composed of both Jews and Gentiles, now fulfills the role that belonged to Israel in the OT (1 Pet. 2:9). Just as Israel was his special possession, now the church of Jesus Christ is the Lord's special possession (Eph. 1:14; 1 Pet. 2:9), his kingdom of priests and a holy nation. A crucial difference must be noted, however, for the church is not a theocracy. Its members do not belong to a particular political entity. Believers in Jesus Christ come from countries and realms all over the world. They are a kingdom of priests and a holy nation as the church of Jesus Christ. The different roles of Israel and the church are illustrated by the temple, for the temple was in one place (Jerusalem). But Jesus is the true temple in the NT, and the church of Jesus Christ is his temple, and thus God's presence in the NT resides wherever his people are, not being specially confined to one place or one nation.[32]

The stipulations of the Sinai covenant are declared in the Ten Commandments (20:2–17). Here the charter regulations of the covenant are set forth in broad strokes, detailing what it means for Israel to be loyal to their covenant Lord and King. The most striking feature in the commandments is the supremacy of God: "The most important thing is the duty of exclusive acknowledgement and worship of the one and only God."[33] No other "gods" should be worshiped or set before the Lord (20:3). Worshiping the image of any other creature or thing on the earth will provoke the jealous wrath of God (20:4–6), showing that the Lord must be first in Israel's affections and actions. "We may see in the prohibition of images an assertion of the unfettered character of Yahweh, who will not be captured, contained, assigned, or

31. Joshua Greever interacted with me helpfully on this section, and I am thankful for his suggestions, some of which I have incorporated.

32. My thanks to Joshua Greever for his thoughts on this matter.

33. Rendtorff, *Canonical Hebrew Bible*, 501. See also Brueggemann, *Theology of the Old Testament*, 183 (though against Brueggemann, the command assumes monotheism).

managed by anyone or anything, for any purpose."[34] Similarly, the Lord's name must not be trifled with (20:7). He is the ever holy one, and his name must be honored and venerated. "The holy could much more aptly be designated the great stranger in the human world, that is, a datum of experience which can never really be co-ordinated into the world in which man is at home, and over against which he initially feels fear rather than trust—it is, in fact, the 'wholly other.'"[35] Dishonoring or trivializing his name will have severe consequences.[36]

The only commandment that addresses the desires of the heart is the tenth, where the Lord prohibits coveting (20:17). The first and tenth commandments address the same issue. Whatever one covets or desires in one's heart represents what one worships. Nothing and no one should capture one's affections above the Lord. As von Rad says, "The intolerant claim for exclusive worship is something unique in the history of religion."[37] The Lord must be first in one's passions and affections. Once we see that the first and tenth commandments address the same issue, it is clear that all the commandments fall under the same banner. Those who steal fail to trust the Lord for his provision and live as if they do not have a sovereign Lord who will supply all their needs. Those who do not honor their parents as an authority signify that they are rejecting the authority of the Lord over them, for God's will is communicated through parents. Those who murder view themselves as sovereign over life instead of entrusting both their lives and the lives of others to the will of God. So too, those who commit adultery are not satisfied to live with the wife or husband God has given them. They become their own "lords" and find their joy outside of the will of God. Those who violate God's commands proclaim, like Adam, that they are independent and wise enough to determine what should be done. The Ten Commandments, then, reveal one's relationship with God, but they also set forth what it means to love other human beings, what it means to live in human society. It is the charter for a right relationship with God and a right relationship with others. We live with one another in peace when we honor our parents, do not murder others, or steal their possessions, or lie to one another, or take another's spouse. Those who honor God also honor other human beings and respect their dignity as creatures made in God's image.

The Ten Commandments represent in strikingly declarative statements the will of God for Israel. Israel's obedience is not legalistic. Instead, Israel's obedience demonstrates that it is centered on God and worships him as the center

---

34. Brueggemann, *Theology of the Old Testament*, 184–85.
35. Von Rad, *Israel's Historical Traditions*, 205.
36. On God's holiness, see Brueggemann, *Theology of the Old Testament*, 288–93.
37. Von Rad, *Israel's Historical Traditions*, 208.

of its life.[38] Sailhamer wrongly argues that in the Pentateuch life according to the law is contrasted with the way of faith.[39] We find in Exod. 21–23 detailed commands that relate to specific situations.[40] The broad declarations of the Ten Commandments must be applied to the specifics of everyday life. The authority of the Lord comprehends all of life, and in everything that Israel does it must seek to please him,[41] just as Christians are to do everything for God's glory (1 Cor. 10:31). The Lord's sovereignty over Israel is not an abstract concept. He speaks to the will of Israel, summoning its people to follow him.

Israel responded to the demands of Yahweh as the covenant Lord by pledging to do all that he had commanded (19:8; 24:3). The older dispensational view that Israel sinned by agreeing to keep the covenant stipulations misses the point of the text dramatically. Israel was expected, indeed commanded, to agree to the conditions of the covenant. This is not an equal pact. The great sovereign stipulated his commands for his vassals. The covenant was established with a covenant meal, with offerings and sacrifices, and with blood that was sprinkled on the altar and the people, being affirmed with the words "Behold the blood of the covenant that the LORD has made with you in accordance with all these words" (24:8). The establishing of the covenant with blood, as Heb. 9:15–22 explains, signifies that "without the shedding of blood there is no forgiveness of sins" (9:22). Israel, because of its sin, was unworthy to enter into covenant with the Lord. It needed forgiveness of sins, which the Lord granted in his covenant mercy.[42]

After the covenant was established, a stunning event occurred. Moses, Aaron, Nadab, Abihu, and the seventy elders enjoyed a covenantal meal in God's presence (24:9–11). We are told that "they saw the God of Israel" (v. 9) and "beheld God" (v. 11). The goal of the covenant is captured in the experience of seeing God. The greatest delight (indeed the goal of all of redemptive history) is to "see his face" (Rev. 22:4). It seems that the experience of seeing God enjoyed by Moses and his companions is an anticipation of what Revelation describes,

38. C. Wright, *Old Testament Ethics*, 45.

39. Sailhamer, *Meaning of the Pentateuch*, 39–42, 153–56. I reject Sailhamer's contention that the additional laws were given because of Israel's sin in making the golden calf so that the Sinai covenant was fundamentally changed as more laws were added. Hence, he sees the priesthood and tabernacle as instituted because Israel became afraid and failed to draw near to God by refusing to go up to Mount Sinai as directed (Exod. 19). He also mistakenly claims that the covenant of Deut. 29–30 is different from the Sinai covenant. See his discussion on pp. 42, 351–54, 362–65, 374–415, 537–62. For trenchant criticisms of Sailhamer's reading, see Dempster, "Magnum Opus"; Hamilton, "Sailhamer's *The Meaning of the Pentateuch*."

40. For an unpacking of the specifics of OT law in more general terms, see the excellent survey in C. Wright, *Old Testament Ethics*, 281–326.

41. See also Brueggemann, *Theology of the Old Testament*, 186.

42. For another interpretation, see Gentry and Wellum, *Kingdom through Covenant*, 349–54.

and yet they probably did not see God's face, for the Lord says later in Exodus, "You cannot see my face, for man shall not see me and live" (33:20). The reference to God's feet in 24:10 suggests that Moses and his friends saw God in some sense, but did not see his face.[43] Still, there is a sense of mystery and ineffability in the account that cannot be captured in descriptions of the event.

The Tabernacle

Exodus devotes considerable space to the tabernacle, giving instructions for its construction (25:1–31:18) and then describing how it was built (35:1–40:38).[44] The fundamental purpose of the tabernacle actually picks up from the unusual event described in 24:9–11, where Moses and his friends saw God. The tabernacle was the place where the Lord dwelt with his people. The word "tabernacle," which Exodus uses fifty-five times, emphasizes that the Lord dwells with his people. Another phrase that describes the Lord's presence with Israel is "tent of meeting." Thirty-three times in Exod. 27–40 this term is used to designate the tabernacle. The Lord places his tabernacle in the midst of Israel so he can meet with and enjoy fellowship with his people. The Lord "will meet with" Israel at the mercy seat (25:22; 30:6), and he "will meet with" them at "the tent of meeting" (29:42–43; 30:36). The fundamental purpose of the tabernacle was to devise a means by which Israel could maintain its fellowship with God (29:45).[45] Why are the instructions about the tabernacle repeated twice, though with some variations? Philip Jenson's answer seems correct: "It reinforces the significance and importance of the action and the reality of the divine dimension being approached. . . . The formal repetitions of the Priestly texts reflect the central significance of the new cultic order set up at Sinai, focused on the Tabernacle."[46]

The construction of the tabernacle must follow the pattern prescribed by God (25:9; 26:30). It seems that the tabernacle and temple, following the example of other ancient Near Eastern cultures, corresponded with the heavenly world.[47] Hebrews 8:5 picks up on this requirement, arguing that there is a typological significance in the tabernacle.[48] It always pointed to something

43. Rightly Rendtorff, *Canonical Hebrew Bible*, 58.
44. See the discussion in Jenson, *Graded Holiness*, 89–114.
45. Rendtorff (*Canonical Hebrew Bible*, 65) points out that the fundamental purpose of the covenant was God's presence with Israel. See also Alexander, *Eden to the New Jerusalem*, 35–36.
46. Jenson, *Graded Holiness*, 100.
47. So Niehaus, *Ancient Near Eastern Themes*, 91–93, 111–13.
48. For the notion that the tabernacle represents the meeting place of God with human beings, the cosmic mountain, see Dumbrell, *Covenant and Creation*, 102–3.

greater than itself. I noted previously the parallels between Eden and the tabernacle and will not mention all of them again here. But some are especially important and bear restating. Both Eden and the tabernacle are attended by cherubim and are entered from the east. The lampstand may symbolize the tree of life (Gen. 2:9; 3:22; Exod. 25:31–35). The verbs used in Gen. 2:15 are also used of the work of the Levites in the sanctuary (Num. 3:7–8; 18:5–6). Stones found in Eden are also in the tabernacle (Gen. 2:11–12; Exod. 25:7, 11, 17, 31). Just as the Lord dwelt with Adam and Eve in Eden, so he meets with his people and resides in the tabernacle. The tabernacle and the temple are also a place where the Lord rests (1 Chron. 28:2; 2 Chron. 6:41; Ps. 132:7–8, 13–14; Isa. 66:1; cf. Gen. 2:1–3).[49]

Dumbrell notes that in Exodus the Sabbath command closes (31:12–17) the first instruction of building the tabernacle and then opens the next account of its building (35:1–3). He remarks, "The tabernacling presence of God in Israel was intended to ensure for her the enjoyment of the very great covenant blessing, namely, that of 'rest' in the promised land."[50] G. K. Beale notes that the temple was built by Solomon only after Yahweh gave him "rest on every side" (1 Kings 5:4).[51] Hence, Yahweh's sitting in the tabernacle/temple represents his triumph over his enemies and his reign over all (Exod. 15:17).[52]

Interestingly, Vern Poythress argues that the tabernacle is patterned after the heavens and the earth.[53] The outer court may stand for the earthly world, where human beings live. Perhaps the holy place stands for the skies, the heavens seen by human beings. And the holy of holies represents the invisible realms of the cosmos, where God and the angels dwell.[54] Hence, the tabernacle may represent a microcosm, just as it recalls Eden.[55] The Lord will ultimately fill the world with the beauty of his presence. As Habakkuk says, "For the earth will be filled with the knowledge of the glory of the LORD as the waters cover the sea" (Hab. 2:14; cf. Isa. 11:9). The tabernacle anticipates the day when the whole earth will be God's temple.[56] This vision is fulfilled in Rev. 21–22, where there is no need for a temple because God and the Lamb are the temple in the new Jerusalem (21:22). In both the creation account and

49. Beale, *Church's Mission*, 60–63.
50. Dumbrell, *Covenant and Creation*, 104. He goes on to say, "Both tabernacle and sabbath thus witness to God's rule over creation."
51. Beale, *Church's Mission*, 63.
52. Ibid.
53. Poythress, *Shadow of Christ*.
54. So Beale, *Church's Mission*, 32–33 (see pp. 34–38).
55. See Alexander, *Eden to the New Jerusalem*, 37–42 (with cautions about being too dogmatic about seeing this connection).
56. For the centrality of the temple theme, see Beale, *Church's Mission*.

in the building of the tabernacle a word of blessing followed the completion of the work (Gen. 2:1–3; Exod. 39:43). It also seems that both the creation and the tabernacle were completed in seven stages (Gen. 1; Exod. 25:1; 30:11, 17, 22, 34; 31:1, 12).[57]

Yahweh specially met Israel at the mercy seat, which was guarded by the cherubim whose wings overstretched the seat (Exod. 25:17–22; 37:6–8). In the same way, the cherubim guarded God's holiness in Eden so that sinners could not enter the garden (Gen. 3:24). Exodus describes how the mercy seat was in the innermost section of the tabernacle, in the section identified as the holy of holies (26:33–34) or the most holy place. The tabernacle was divided into compartments. There was a courtyard, an outer sanctum, and an inner sanctum. In the courtyard was the altar of burnt offering, where sacrifices were offered to the Lord (27:1–8; 38:1–7). Here sacrifices were offered so that sins could be forgiven and thanks could be rendered to the Lord. The altar was made of bronze instead of gold. Sacrifices had to be offered first because human beings are unholy and cannot enter the presence of the Lord without atonement.

Indeed, the whole structure of the tabernacle emphasizes that God's presence cannot and must not be entered casually. The Lord is inaccessible because of human sin and uncleanness. One must enter several compartments in order to arrive in his presence. Furthermore, the ordination of priests (chaps. 28–29) drives home this point further. The outer and inner sanctums of the tabernacle are not open to everyone. They are reserved only for the priests, which indicates the terrifying and beautiful holiness of the Lord. The procedures and specifications that the Lord prescribes must be followed in order to meet with him. The tabernacle (and the temple built later) "guards the perfection of the divine presence. The laws that regulate the liturgy there are expressly designed to thwart the irruption of profane experience into the zone of the sacred."[58] One must offer sacrifices in the courtyard, and then only priests can enter the outer sanctum, in which is the bread of the presence, the lampstand, and the altar of incense. And only the high priest once a year is permitted to enter the inner sanctum, where the ark of the covenant resides with the mercy seat and the cherubim (see Lev. 16). It is striking that gold is reserved for the inner and outer sanctums, whereas bronze is in the courtyard, signifying the special presence of God in the former places. The issued precautions and the series of compartments underscore the truth that God is separated from human

57. Sailhamer, *Pentateuch as Narrative*, 298–99; Beale, *Church's Mission*, 61; Enns, "Exodus," 149.
58. Levenson, *Sinai and Zion*, 127.

beings, primarily because of the sin of human beings. The OT stresses the seriousness of sin constantly, for human beings are prone to explain it away and to think of it as relatively trivial. As Childs says, sin "is not a deviation from some abstract moral standard, but is an offence directed against Yahweh himself."[59] Hence, the tabernacle was constructed so that those who enjoyed fellowship with Yahweh would not die.[60]

Exodus 32–34

Yahweh's presence at the mercy seat with the overshadowing of the cherubim also represents his reign over Israel.[61] He reigns from his throne in heaven and also from his throne at the mercy seat. We read that the Lord "is enthroned on the cherubim" (1 Sam. 4:4; 2 Sam. 6:2; cf. 1 Chron. 13:6), and the psalms also say that the Lord is "enthroned upon the cherubim" (Pss. 80:1; 99:1). In particular, it seems fair to conclude, since forgiveness was obtained at the mercy seat, that the Lord's reign over Israel was gracious and saving. Exodus 32–34, however, immediately reveals a fundamental problem with Israel and the Sinai covenant. The covenant was established with Israel by grace, but the covenant was also conditional. While Moses was up on the mountain, the Israelites turned away from the Lord and fashioned a golden calf (32:1–8). Scholars dispute whether they worshiped other gods or worshiped Yahweh in the image of the calf. In either case, they violated the stipulations of the Sinai covenant. What is particularly astonishing is that Israel turned to blatant idolatry almost immediately after the covenant was ratified (32:8).

Israel's behavior reveals a fundamental truth about the Sinai covenant. Even though the covenant is gracious, since the Lord liberated Israel in his mercy, the hearts of the Israelites were not transformed through the covenant. The grace of the Lord in the Sinai covenant did not extend, generally speaking, to the renewal of Israel's heart so that they actually obeyed the Lord. One of the fundamental problems with the Sinai covenant is thus revealed (see Rom. 7:1–25; 2 Cor. 3:4–18; Gal. 3:15–25). In one sense the covenant is gracious, but in another sense it is conditional and dependent upon human obedience.[62] Hence, an internal defect in the Mosaic covenant appears (see Heb. 7:11–19), though the flaw is located in the human heart. Israel is "stiff-necked" (Exod.

---

59. Childs, *Biblical Theology*, 574.
60. Jenson, *Graded Holiness*, 111–12.
61. Jenson (ibid., 112–13) is among many who argue that one of the themes of the tabernacle is God's presence.
62. See Meyer, *End of the Law*.

32:9; 33:3, 5; 34:9) and, apparently, unregenerate.[63] Thus, one of the recurrent themes of the biblical story line appears: the pervasiveness and deeply rooted evil in the human heart, and the inability of the law to root out sin.

It is true the covenant with Abraham also had conditional elements, but the Lord promised that ultimately the covenant with Abraham would be fulfilled. At the end of the day, the fulfillment of the Abrahamic covenant was dependent on the Lord, for he passed through the cut-up animals in the covenant ceremony alone (Gen. 15), signifying that he would fulfill the covenant. The covenant with Abraham would be enjoyed only by an obedient generation, but God would see to it that there would be an obedient generation. In other words, in the covenant with Abraham the Lord guaranteed that he would fulfill the promises of offspring, land, and blessing. When it comes to the Mosaic covenant, there was no such promise that the covenant would be perpetuated. That is, there was no promise that the Mosaic covenant would last forever. Such a reading fits with Paul's claim that the Mosaic covenant was intended to be an interim covenant, designed to last until the coming of the Messiah (Gal. 3:15–25). Indeed, Paul makes it clear that the Abrahamic covenant is one of promise and thus would certainly be fulfilled. The covenant with Moses, however, depended on human performance, and therefore it could be broken by human disobedience.

Israel's worship of the golden calf constituted a breaking of the covenant,[64] and therefore the Lord threatened to destroy them and make a great nation of Moses and his descendants (Exod. 32:10).[65] As Childs says, Israel's sin here should not be construed "as an accidental misdeed, but as a representative reaction, constitutive to human resistance to divine imperatives."[66] This signature event, immediately after the covenant was enacted, forecast Israel's inability to do Yahweh's will.[67] Moses' intercession staved off God's anger, reminding the Lord not of the Sinai covenant but rather of the covenant promises to the patriarchs (32:11–13). Moses then descended from the mountain and flung the tablets of the covenant from his hand, breaking them (32:15–19). The shatter-

63. There was a remnant that was regenerate, but they were the exception, not the rule.
64. The threatened destruction echoes the wiping out of the world by the flood, but here the Lord threatens to wipe out Israel. Moses stands as a kind of new Noah who intercedes for Israel (so Rendtorff, *Canonical Hebrew Bible*, 61–62).
65. Dempster (*Dominion and Dynasty*, 113) points out a fascinating feature of the narrative in the Pentateuch. Israel was judged more strictly for disobedience after the terms of the Sinai covenant were stated. For instance, violation of the Sabbath before the covenant merited rebuke (Exod. 16:27–30), but after Sinai death was meted out to the one who transgressed Sabbath regulations (Num. 15:32–36).
66. Childs, *Old Testament as Scripture*, 175.
67. Dumbrell, *Faith of Israel*, 40.

ing of the tablets did not represent a selfish fit of anger on Moses' part. The broken tablets represent the breaking of the covenant between Yahweh and Israel. The Lord did not annihilate Israel, which it deserved for its blatant rejection of the covenant stipulations immediately after the covenant was ratified. Moses again interceded for Israel, asking if he could atone for their covenant betrayal, but Moses himself needed atonement as a flawed human being, and hence he could not atone for the sins of the people (32:30–32). Atonement will await one who is greater than Moses.

Yahweh relented from destroying Israel utterly, but he would not dwell in Israel's midst because of its recalcitrant heart (33:1–6). The tent that was placed outside of Israel's camp further illustrates Israel's corruption (33:7–11). The Lord would not reside in a tent in Israel's camp, for Israel's wickedness required judgment. Thus, only Moses and Joshua and those who sought the Lord were able to meet the Lord in the tent, where the nearness of his presence and the joy of his fellowship were present. Indeed, the Lord spoke "to Moses face to face, as a man speaks to his friend" (33:11), and the communion with the Lord was so precious that Joshua "would not depart from the tent" (33:11). The majority of Israel, however, were unable to draw near to the tent and to enjoy the Lord's gracious presence because of their sin.

Moses was not finished interceding for Israel in Exod. 32–34. The prospect of traveling to Canaan without the presence of the Lord was intolerable. Israel's strength and distinctiveness came not from within, but only from God himself. Hence, Moses pleaded with Yahweh to forgive his people so that Israel could enjoy God's gracious presence as they inherited the promises (33:12–17). Moses prayed boldly, asking the Lord "show me your ways" (33:13) and "show me your glory" (33:18). The beauty of seeing and knowing the Lord, which is the final goal of biblical revelation, was graciously revealed to Moses. God's glory consists in the revelation of his goodness and the proclamation of his name (33:19). His glory is also declared in his withholding his mercy from some and disclosing it to others (33:19), for no one deserves God's mercy. His judgment is a revelation of his character as well, for the wonder of God is manifested in his justice as well as his mercy. The glory that Moses sees is mediated. He cannot get a "straight-shot" look at the Lord and live, and so he is hidden "in a cleft of the rock" and covered (33:20–23).

The Lord approached Moses and revealed his name to him, which signifies God's character (34:5). What is disclosed in the revelation of God's name and the disclosure of his glory? Here we find one of the most famous texts in the OT:[68] "The Lord passed before him and proclaimed, 'The Lord, the

---

68. See Brueggemann, *Theology of the Old Testament*, 215–18.

LORD, a God merciful and gracious, slow to anger, and abounding in steadfast love and faithfulness, keeping steadfast love for thousands, forgiving iniquity and transgression and sin, but who will by no means clear the guilty, visiting the iniquity of the fathers on the children and the children's children, to the third and the fourth generation'" (34:6–7). The Lord reveals that he is a God of mercy and grace who delights in showing saving love and in forgiving sinners. At the same time, he is also a God of justice who punishes those who rebel against his lordship. Still, the accent is on his love and grace, for he is gracious to "thousands," while repaying sin "to the third and fourth generation." The importance of this self-revelation of God is evident, for this verse is recalled again and again by OT writers (Num. 14:18; Neh. 9:17; Pss. 86:15; 103:8; 145:8; Joel 2:13; Jon. 4:2; Nah. 1:3). Clearly, God's grace is supremely revealed in Jesus Christ, who is the true tabernacle of the Lord (John 1:14), who is "full of grace and truth."

Moses' prayer for the revelation of the Lord's glory is intertwined with a plea for a renewal of the covenant. The Lord answers in the affirmative, and thus Moses cuts two new tablets to represent the covenant renewal (Exod. 34:1–4). Since the covenant is renewed, the Lord promises to dwell with Israel, forgiving them for their covenantal betrayal. The placement of the chapters on the construction of the tabernacle after Moses' intercession indicates that his prayer was answered. The Lord graciously dwells with Israel, even if access to the Lord is still limited to the sanctuary of the tabernacle. When the tabernacle was set up, the Lord's glory descended upon it in a cloud (40:34–38). The cloud, which represented the glory and mystery of God's presence, led Israel on its journeys in the wilderness, showing that Moses' prayer for the divine presence was answered.

Conclusion

As Exodus concludes, the promise that Israel would become a mighty and large nation was answered. The covenant promises were becoming a reality. God's kingdom was coming on earth as it was in heaven. Furthermore, Yahweh redeemed his people by delivering them from Egyptian slavery. The gracious work of the Lord was celebrated in story and song and festival, especially in the feast of Passover. As the sovereign Lord, God entered into covenant with his people, reminding them of his gracious mercy and giving them covenantal stipulations. Furthermore, he laid out the plan for a tabernacle, in which he was to dwell among the people of Israel. Israel shockingly violated the covenant by making and worshiping the golden calf almost immediately after the covenant was ratified. Upon Moses' intercession, the Lord forgave his people and deigned to go with them. The book concludes with the Lord's glorious and protective presence in the tabernacle. Israel was on the way to the land of promise, anticipating the fulfillment of another one of the promises of the covenant with Abraham.

3

LEVITICUS

Introduction

Exodus concludes with Yahweh's presence among the people of Israel. Despite Israel's recalcitrance and proneness toward abandoning the Lord, he dwells among his people via the tabernacle. Leviticus stops the narrative and considers how the Lord can continue to live in the midst of Israel, a sinful people.[1] Or another way of putting it is that Leviticus describes how Israel lives in the Lord's presence.[2] Dumbrell says, "Leviticus is a political document describing Israel as theocracy, an entity ruled by God."[3] This fits with the notion that God's kingship and lordship are central to the story line of the Scriptures. Leviticus is particularly concerned with holiness and purity, explicating how the holy one of Israel may continue to dwell with Israel.[4] Leviticus refers sixty times to what is done "before the LORD," showing that the Lord's presence is central in the book.[5] The Lord's design for Israel is summed up in the truth that he delivered Israel from Egypt so "that I might be their God" (26:45).[6] Another way of expressing the same truth is found in 26:12: "And I will walk among you and will be your God, and you shall be my people." As John Hartley says,

---

1. Clines says that Leviticus "spell[s] out in detail the means by which the relationship now established is to be maintained" (*Theme of the Pentateuch*, 54).
2. Wenham, *Leviticus*, 16–18.
3. Dumbrell, *Faith of Israel*, 48.
4. For helpful studies on holiness, see Gammie, *Holiness in Israel*; Jenson, *Graded Holiness*. See also the illuminating discussion of purity regulations in Goldingay, *Israel's Life*, 607–22.
5. The phrase appears in Leviticus more than any other OT book (cf. Numbers 38x, Deuteronomy 27x, Exodus 22x).
6. So Clines, *Theme of the Pentateuch*, 56.

"There is a trace of the happiness and wonder of Yahweh's presence as well as a deep fear aroused by the nearness of God."[7]

The importance of fellowship with the Lord is communicated by the phrase "tent of meeting," which occurs forty-one times in Leviticus. Interestingly, the term "tabernacle" is used only three times. The "tent of meeting" emphasizes that the Lord dwells with his people, that their greatest joy comes from fellowship with him. But the Lord is the holy one, and thus the purity of the people must be maintained through sacrifices, by their following purity regulations, and by doing the will of the Lord. The holiness of the Lord shows that the book is profoundly God-centered. God is fearsome in his holiness, and his holiness is intense and dangerous to sinful humans. Hence, the people are warned not to "profane my holy name" (20:3; 22:32). The danger of profaning the Lord's name is portrayed in the account of the man who blasphemed God's name, for he is put to death for such a heinous act (24:10–16). As Hartley says, "It is little wonder that the vision of the holy God is both awe-inspiring and frighteningly terrible (9:23–24). Humans either retreat in dread or bow in contrite worship."[8]

Sacrifices

The first seven chapters of Leviticus describe the sacrifices required in Israel. Five different kinds of sacrifices are specified: burnt offerings (1:1–17; 6:8–13), grain offerings (2:1–16; 6:14–23), peace or fellowship offerings (3:1–17; 7:11–36), sin/purification offerings (4:1–5:13; 6:24–30), and guilt/reparation offerings (5:14–6:7; 7:1–10). If we consider the sacrifices as a whole, their fundamental purpose is to atone for sins before God so that fellowship may be maintained with him. Some of the sacrifices focus on atonement, while others signify the joy and fellowship between the Lord and human beings. Still, we must guard against separating these two features of the sacrifices too sharply from each other, since they are intertwined.

Remarkably, Leviticus does not unpack in detail the reason for sacrifices, though some clues are provided. A fundamental text, which explains the significance of shedding the blood of animals, is 17:11. "For the life of the flesh is in the blood, and I have given it for you on the altar to make atonement for your souls, for it is the blood that makes atonement by the life."[9] The pouring

7. Hartley, *Leviticus*, lxiii.
8. Hartley, *Leviticus*, lvi–lvii.
9. For a thorough study of this text, see Rodriguez, "Substitution in the Hebrew Cultus," 233–57. Milgrom (*Leviticus 1–16*, 1082–83) admits that the verb *kipper* refers to ransom from

out of one's blood indicates that one has died, that life has been surrendered. The shedding of the animal's blood (i.e., the giving up of its life), secures atonement, which means that the sins of the offender have been forgiven by virtue of the life sacrificed in its place. The sacrifices, then, have a representative and substitutionary function. The blood of the animal is spilled in place of the blood of the offender.[10] The verb for "to atone" is *kipper* in Hebrew and *hilaskomai* in Greek. Careful study demonstrates that the latter verb has to do with the appeasement or the satisfaction of God's wrath.[11] Some earlier scholars defended the idea that blood atones because it designates the offering of life to God, so that blood signifies the release of life instead of the giving up of one's life in death. Against this idea, the spilling of blood signifies death, since it is evident that animals and humans die when their blood is poured out. The shedding of blood spells the death of the victim, and therefore atonement comes through the death of that which was sacrificed. It is not difficult to see that the animal's blood is shed in place of the death of human beings. Gordon Wenham also sees the "principle of substitution" here, for "animal life takes the place of human life."[12]

The fundamental reason for the sacrifices was atonement, so that sinners could be forgiven by the holy one. Wenham remarks, "They all presuppose that the animal victim is a substitute for the worshipper, makes atonement for him, and thereby restores him to favour with God."[13] The laying on of hands plays an important role in understanding the purpose of the sacrifices (Exod. 29:10, 15, 19; Lev. 4:15; 8:14, 18, 22; 16:21). The laying of hands on animals most likely indicates that the animal functions as a substitute for a person.[14]

---

anger in some texts but denies that any notion of ransom from God's wrath is present in cultic texts. His attempt to segregate cultic from noncultic texts is unsuccessful (rightly Kiuchi, *Purification Offering*, 39–66, 87–101; Gammie, *Holiness in Israel*, 37–41; Groves, "Atonement in Isaiah 53," 65–68). The substitutionary character of the verb *kipper* is defended well by Nicole, "Atonement in the Pentateuch," 47–50. See also Peterson, "Atonement in the Old Testament," 10–12; Kiuchi, *Purification Offering*, 101–9. Against Milgrom, see also Childs, *Biblical Theology*, 506.

10. See Wenham, *Leviticus*, 245. Against Martens, *God's Design*, 63–64.

11. See esp. Morris, *Apostolic Preaching*, 112–28; Nicole, "Atonement in the Pentateuch," 39–40, 46. The sacrifice by Noah after the flood communicates the idea that the sacrifice averted God's wrath (Gen. 8:20–21). So Wenham, "Old Testament Sacrifice," 80–81.

12. Wenham, "Old Testament Sacrifice," 82; see also Nicole, "Atonement in the Pentateuch," 35–50, esp. 36–40.

13. Wenham, "Old Testament Sacrifice," 84. See also the discussion on burnt offerings and peace offerings in Rodriguez, "Substitution in the Hebrew Cultus," 225–32.

14. See Kiuchi, *Purification Offering*, 112–19. Fiddes (*Past Event and Present Salvation*, 73) thinks that propitiation cannot be in view because sin cannot be transferred to a pure animal, as that animal would no longer be pure. Rodriguez ("Substitution in the Hebrew Cultus," 217–19), however, argues from Lev. 10:16–18 that the animal was still considered to be holy and at the same time bore the sin of the people.

The sins of human beings are transferred, so to speak, to the animal.[15] The sacrifice of the animals was no abstraction. The animal was violently killed so that blood and gore poured out. The death of the animals shows that the penalty for sin is death. It seems likely that the "pleasing aroma" of the sacrifices designates the notion that sacrifices satisfy God's wrath, that they appease his anger (e.g., Gen. 8:21; Exod. 29:28; Lev. 1:9; 2:2; 3:5; 4:31; 17:6).[16]

If the laying on of hands symbolizes the transfer of sin from the person to the animal, then it seems to follow that the death of the animal is substitutionary.[17] The laying on of one hand occurs when the sacrifice is for a single individual (Lev. 1:4; 3:2, 8, 13; 4:4, 24, 29, 33), and the laying on of two hands occurs when the sacrifice is for the community or more than one individual (e.g., Exod. 29:10, 15; Lev. 4:15; 8:14, 18; 16:21).[18] Wenham comments, "What he [the worshiper] does to the animal, he does symbolically to himself. The death of the animal portrays the death of himself"; he goes on to say, "The animal is a substitute for the worshipper. Its death makes atonement for the worshipper. Its immolation on the altar quietens God's anger at human sin."[19] Human beings were required to approach God in the way specified. If they deviated from what he commanded, they would experience his wrath. The story in Leviticus of Nadab and Abihu illustrates this truth. They offered "unauthorized fire before the LORD" (10:1), and a fire descended from the Lord and annihilated them (10:2). As Hartley says, "The glory would devour anyone who approached the holy unclean or unworthily."[20] The God-centeredness of the narrative is striking. Nadab and Abihu were consumed because their actions blemished God's holiness and did not glorify the Lord (10:3). The flaming fire that consumed Nadab and Abihu represents the anger of the Lord that was not mollified, since his instructions were flouted in the tabernacle.

15. Against Milgrom (*Leviticus 1–16*, 151–52), who says that laying on of a single hand designates ownership instead of transference. Levine (*Leviticus*, 6) rejects the transfer of sin notion. Nicole ("Atonement in the Pentateuch," 44–45) is more persuasive in suggesting that substitution is in view. Kiuchi (*Purification Offering*, 112–19) maintains that only substitution is intended. The objection that substitution cannot be in view because some of the sacrifices were meal offerings is not compelling (Fiddes, *Past Event and Present Salvation*, 73). Rodriguez ("Substitution in the Hebrew Cultus," 146–47) observes that even though expiation is not the central purpose of meal offerings, the notion of expiation cannot be excluded (Lev. 5:11–13; 1 Sam. 3:14). Nicole ("Atonement in the Pentateuch," 45) notes that the grain offering was "an exception among exceptions" and hence cannot become the lodestar by which sacrifices are interpreted.

16. See Hartley, *Leviticus*, lxviii; Wenham, "Old Testament Sacrifice," 84. Martens (*God's Design*, 59–60) rightly sees both propitiation and expiation in view here. Contrary to Goldingay, *Israel's Life*, 145–46.

17. In defense of substitution in the OT, see also G. Williams, "Punishment of Sin," 68–81.

18. So Paul R. Williamson, "Because He Loved Your Forefathers."

19. Wenham, "Old Testament Sacrifice," 77, 82.

20. Hartley, *Leviticus*, lxiii–lxiv.

Most remarkably, access to the inner sanctum, the holy of holies, where God's presence was specially manifested, was permitted only once a year, on the Day of Atonement (Lev. 16).[21] Clearly, such a limitation signified that human beings could not enter into the Lord's presence casually. He is the wholly other one, and hence access to his presence is severely limited (cf. Heb. 9:6–8). Indeed, only one person once a year could deign to enter into his presence. Anyone who entered the inner sanctum (the holy of holies) was liable to face the same death experienced by Nadab and Abihu, since God's presence in the cloud was over the mercy seat, and therefore the Lord instructed Aaron about what he must do "so that he may not die" (Lev. 16:2; cf. 16:3). Furthermore, on the Day of Atonement the high priest must be careful to follow the rituals exactly as prescribed. Human creativity and ingenuity are excluded. Humble obedience to the Lord's directives is required of the high priest. No one can obtain access to the Lord without approaching him in the way prescribed.

On the Day of Atonement sacrifices were required both of the high priest and of the people (16:5–6, 11, 15). The cleansing of the holy place, the tent of meeting, and the altar were not merely purificatory, if by that one means that it was a ritual ceremony unrelated to human sin. They had to be cleansed with blood "because of the uncleannesses of the people of Israel and because of their transgressions, all their sins" (16:16). The place of God's indwelling was defiled by the sinfulness of Israel. It follows, then, that the sacrifices were offered to obtain forgiveness. Two goats were brought forward. The goat that was slaughtered was offered as a sin/purification offering, and its blood was sprinkled on the mercy seat (God's very presence) to secure forgiveness for Israel's iniquities (16:15). It seems quite clear that the goat offered as a sin/purification offering was slain in place of Israel, so that it took upon itself the punishment that Israel deserved.

The substitutionary character of the sacrifices is underlined in the whole ritual. The second goat, Azazel, which was released into the wilderness, is in some ways rather mysterious. Nonetheless, Azazel probably pictures vividly the same truth that we saw with the goat offered as a sin/purification offering. We should note the wording in 16:21–22: "And Aaron shall lay both his hands on the head of the live goat, and confess over it all the iniquities of the people of Israel, and all their transgressions, all their sins. And he shall put them on the head of the goat and send it away into the wilderness by the hand of a man who is in readiness. The goat shall bear all their iniquities on itself to a remote area, and he shall let the goat go free in the wilderness." These verses

---

21. For a good discussion on limited access to the realm of the holy, see Jenson, *Graded Holiness*, 107–8.

demonstrate clearly that the laying on of hands signifies substitution. When Aaron laid his hands on the goat, he confessed the sins of Israel, and the sins are conveyed to the head of the goat, the very place where Aaron lays both his hands.[22] Verse 22 confirms that substitution is in view, for the goat bears the sins of the Israelites into the wilderness.[23] The live goat functions as the substitute that bears the penalty (eviction to the wilderness) for Israel's sins. It is also probably the case that the goat was sent into the wilderness to die.[24] In any case, Geerhardus Vos rightly argues that in order to grasp the truth being conveyed, we must take both of the goats together, for there was "in reality one sacrificial object; the distribution of suffering death and of dismissal into a remote place simply serving the purpose of clearer expression, in visible form, of removal of sin after expiation had been made, something which the ordinary sacrificial animal could not well express, since it died in the process of expiation."[25] The inclusion of Azazel, then, illustrates further the punishment warranted by sin. Both death and departure from God's presence are the penalty for human sin. The sacrifices on the Day of Atonement, therefore, highlight both the holiness and grace of God. The Lord is holy, for no one can stand in his presence without forgiveness of sins, but he is also gracious, for he provides the means of atonement because of his love for his people. As 17:11 emphasizes, the Lord has given ("I have given it") sacrifices to secure atonement. Just as the Lord was gracious to Adam and Eve after their sin and clothed them (Gen. 3:21), so too the sacrifices that mollify his anger are from him and are the fruit of his love.

At this juncture, we will look briefly at the sacrifices that Israel regularly offered. In the burnt offering the animal is entirely consumed by fire. One of the purposes of the offering was to obtain forgiveness for sins committed. "He shall lay his hand on the head of the burnt offering, and it shall be accepted for him to make atonement for him" (Lev. 1:4). As noted earlier, the laying on of hands signifies the transference of sins from human beings to the animal. The atoning and substitutionary character of the sacrifice is evident, for the sacrifice wins atonement and acceptance for the one offering it.[26] The atoning

22. So Wenham, "Old Testament Sacrifice," 79.

23. Milgrom (*Leviticus 1–16*, 1021) objects that Azazel was not sacrificed or punished for others. It is true that the Azazel rite is not an example of sacrificial substitution, but Rodriguez ("Substitution in the Hebrew Cultus," 219–20) rightly argues that the role of laying on of hands in the rite signals that substitution is in view.

24. In support of the view that Azazel was sent away to die, see Martens, *God's Design*, 54; Peterson, "Atonement in the Old Testament," 15; G. Williams, "Punishment of Sin," 79.

25. Vos, *Biblical Theology*, 163. I owe this citation to Nicole, "Atonement in the Pentateuch," 26–27.

26. See House, *Old Testament Theology*, 129.

character of the burnt offering seems to be present also in Job, where Job's three friends offer burnt offerings and thereby avoid being dealt with "according to your folly" (Job 42:8). Conversely, in Jer. 14:12 the people will not be accepted and will be judged by the Lord, even though they offer burnt offerings, which suggests that ordinarily burnt offerings play a role in the forgiveness of sins. We see the same idea in 1 Chron. 6:49: "But Aaron and his sons made offerings on the altar of burnt offering and on the altar of incense for all the work of the Most Holy Place, and to make atonement for Israel, according to all that Moses the servant of God had commanded." Burnt offerings were not only for atonement; they were offered also to signify thanksgiving to God and consecration to him. The psalmist offers burnt offerings to the Lord in accord with what he has vowed, as he is filled with joy because the Lord has delivered him from his enemies (Ps. 66:13–15). The atoning function of the burnt offering is not absent, but the accent is on the gratefulness with which the sacrifice is offered. Similarly, Ezra and his friends offered burnt offerings in praise to the Lord when the Lord protected them on their trip from Babylon to Jerusalem (Ezra 8:35; cf. 2 Sam. 6:17–18; 2 Chron. 29:32). Such praise to God also was expressed with burnt offerings when the Philistines returned the ark to Israel (1 Sam. 6:14). So too, the parents of Samson offered sacrifices to honor the Lord when he revealed to them directions for Samson's future (Judg. 13:16, 23).

The grain offering (Lev. 2:1–16) fundamentally expresses thanksgiving and praise to God, and if it was offered with the right attitude, it was pleasing to the Lord (Exod. 29:41; Lev. 23:18; Isa. 66:3; Jer. 14:12). Manoah and his wife offer grain offerings in thanksgiving in response to the revelation about the birth of Samson and his future greatness (Judg. 13:19, 23). Even in the case of the grain offering, however, it cannot be separated entirely from the atoning function of sacrifices, since it is regularly offered in conjunction with the other sacrifices. The focus in peace offerings (Lev. 3:1–17) is not on atonement. The worshiper's aim was to enjoy fellowship with the Lord and to renew a relationship with him. God instituted sacrifices so that human beings could enjoy the wonder and loveliness of his presence. Sacrifices were not merely a mechanical means by which sins were erased before the holy one of Israel.[27] Goldingay says that such offerings may designate "self-giving to God" or express "gratitude" or "fulfill a vow."[28]

Sin/purification and guilt/reparation offerings remind us that the fundamental reason why fellowship is disrupted between God and human beings

27. Rightly Martens, *God's Design*, 60–61.
28. Goldingay, *Israel's Life*, 142–43.

is sin. Hence, the sin/purification offering (4:1–5:13; 6:24–30) and the guilt/reparation offering (5:14–6:7; 7:1–10) play a major role in the sacrificial cultus.[29] It is difficult to nail down the distinction between the sin/purification offering and the guilt/reparation offering. There is some evidence to support the idea that the guilt/reparation offering relates to more serious sins. In any case, both offerings focus on human sin that requires atonement.[30] Some scholars think that it is better to identify the sin offering as the purification offering and the guilt offering as the reparation offering, arguing that personal sin is not invariably in view, since a sin/purification offering is presented in cases of childbearing (Lev. 12:6, 8), leprosy (Lev. 14:19, 22, 31), bodily discharges (Lev. 15:15, 30), and pollution from a corpse (Num. 6:11).[31] Such texts preclude a simplistic understanding of the sin/purification offering.[32] Clearly, such offerings are not always due to personal sin. And yet it is likely that even in the cases that are cultic, where personal sin is not the focus, the defilement incurred is a pointer to the sin of human beings. So it seems fitting to say that the fundamental purpose of the sin/purification and guilt/reparation offerings is to obtain forgiveness. A verse from Proverbs sums up the purpose of the guilt/reparation offering: "Fools mock at the guilt/reparation offering, but the upright enjoy acceptance" (Prov. 14:9). The word "acceptance" indicates the function of the guilt/reparation offering. The one who offers a guilt/reparation offering will receive forgiveness of sins and be restored to a right relationship with the Lord.

The prophets declaim against superstitious or mechanical offering of sacrifices (e.g., Isa. 1:11–13; Jer. 6:20; 7:21–23; Hosea 6:6; Amos 4:4–5; 5:22–24; Mic. 6:6). Formerly, many scholars maintained that the prophets rejected sacrifices altogether, but it is generally recognized now that they did not repudiate sacrifices and offerings per se but criticized a mechanical, external, superficial, and magical view of sacrifices, as if sacrifices could atone even if they were offered with a wrong attitude (cf. Prov. 15:8; 21:3, 7). The notion that faith is "spiritual" without a material dimension is foreign to the faith

29. Contrary to Goldingay (Israel's Life, 143), who thinks sin can be forgiven merely by repentance.

30. Wenham says about the sin/purification offering, "Sin not only angers God and deprives him of his due, it also makes his sanctuary unclean. A holy God cannot dwell amid uncleanness. The purification offering purifies the place of worship, so that God may be present among his people" (Leviticus, 89).

31. So Jenson, Graded Holiness, 156.

32. Many of the offerings relate to life and death. For example, those with skin diseases look "as if" they are "falling apart," as if they are "dying" (see Goldingay, Israel's Life, 634). But death only comes from sin, and hence even these sacrifices cannot be separated entirely from sin.

of Israel.[33] The Lord himself provided the sacrifices so that Israel could enjoy forgiveness of sins and fellowship with him.

If we consider sacrifices canonically, they point to the sacrifice of Christ. Hebrews emphasizes that old covenant sacrifices are inferior since they did not truly cleanse the worshiper in conscience and did not bring complete and permanent forgiveness of sins (7:1–10:18).[34] Bold access to the holy place (God's very presence) is no longer limited to the Day of Atonement, where God's presence is accessed only once a year. Now, believers boldly enter God's presence every day through the blood of Jesus Christ (9:6–8; 10:19–22). According to Romans, the sin offering is fulfilled in Jesus Christ (8:3), so that "there is no condemnation" for those who belong to him (8:1). His sacrifice has brought justification and redemption through his blood (3:24–26). Glad fellowship with God has been restored forever through the once-for-all sacrifice of Jesus Christ.

Cleanness

The theme of Leviticus is the holiness of the Lord. Human beings cannot approach him without sacrifice, since they are defiled by sin. A corresponding theme is the necessity of cleanness to enter the Lord's presence. Hence, instructions are given regarding the priesthood (chaps. 8–10), and other regulations are prescribed that relate to food, skin diseases, and bodily discharges (chaps. 11–15). Also given are instructions for the ordination of priests (chaps. 8–10).[35] The ordination account underscores the unworthiness of Aaron and his sons to serve as priests. They are not inherently qualified to minister before the Lord. Therefore, they must be cleansed with water and must wear holy garments to serve in the priesthood (8:6–9, 13).

Priests can serve only if they are ritually pure. When serving in the sanctuary, they cannot wear ordinary garments, for only that which is set apart can be worn in the Lord's presence. Furthermore, high priests must be anointed with oil, which sets them apart for holy use (8:12). Perhaps most important, Aaron and his sons had to offer a bull for a sin/purification offering and rams for a burnt offering (8:14–29). These offerings were designed to "make atonement" for Aaron and his sons (8:34). They could not serve as priests based on

33. See von Rad, *Israel's Historical Traditions*, 260.

34. Dumbrell (*Faith of Israel*, 42–43) fails to see this clearly in saying that OT sacrifices atoned for sin. The very point of Hebrews is that the repetition of the sacrifices symbolizes the truth that animal sacrifices did not finally secure forgiveness. In terms of the story line of Scripture, they pointed to the sacrifice of Christ as the final and definitive sacrifice.

35. See the helpful discussion in Jenson, *Graded Holiness*, 116–30.

their own dignity and worthiness, for they had violated the Lord's precepts. Therefore, before ordination they had to be cleansed of their sins through sacrifice. Placing blood on the right ears, right thumbs, and right toes of the priests (8:23–24) symbolizes that the priests were cleansed and consecrated to the Lord. It could be argued that purification rather than sin is the fundamental issue, since the altar also needed to be purified with blood (8:15). The parallel text in 16:16, however, suggests that the altar needs purification because of human sin: "Thus he shall make atonement for the Holy Place, because of the uncleannesses of the people of Israel and because of their transgressions, all their sins. And so he shall do for the tent of meeting, which dwells with them in the midst of their uncleannesses." It follows, then, that a wedge should not be driven between purification and sin. The offerings by Aaron and his sons purified the tabernacle and its furniture, but they also cleansed Aaron and his sons from sin so they could serve as the Lord's priests.

Chapter 9 of Leviticus relays the service in the tabernacle after the Lord gave instructions on sacrifices (chaps. 1–7) and the priests were duly ordained. The text underscores that all the offerings (sin/purification offering, guilt/reparation offering, burnt offering, grain offering, and peace offering) were brought to obtain forgiveness of sins. "Draw near to the altar and offer your sin offering and your burnt offering and make atonement for yourself and for the people, and bring the offering of the people and make atonement for them, as the LORD has commanded" (9:7). Such sacrifices were offered so "that the glory of the LORD may appear to you" (9:6). Sacrifices were brought so that Israel could enjoy the beauty and joy of the Lord's presence without being annihilated by his intense holiness. The Lord, in his love, provided forgiveness so that his people would have fellowship with him. The chapter emphasizes that Aaron and his sons did exactly what the Lord commanded. One enters the Lord's presence only as he prescribes. The chapter concludes with the Lord's glory manifesting itself to the people (9:23). Indeed, fire fell from heaven and consumed the offerings on the altar, showing the flaming holiness of the Lord but also his gracious presence with his people (9:24).

The contrast with chapter 10 could not be more striking. Nadab and Abihu violated the directives the Lord set forth by offering "unauthorized fire," and, in a quid pro quo, fire descended from the Lord and obliterated them (10:1–2). Clearly, the Lord's wrath was displayed because they did not approach him properly (10:6–7). The particular responsibility of priests is emphasized: "You are to distinguish between the holy and the common, and between the unclean and the clean, and you are to teach the people of Israel all the statutes that the LORD has spoken to them by Moses" (10:10–11). Nadab and Abihu, as priests, violated egregiously these instructions. They presented the common as if it were holy, the unclean as if clean. No priest could serve the Lord who did not glorify the Lord by upholding his holiness (10:3). Chapter 10 emphasizes that priests were to distinguish between what is holy and clean and what is not (10:10–11), and in the case of Nadab and Abihu the failure to follow the Lord's instructions is highlighted.

The importance of distinguishing between the clean and unclean (chaps. 11–15) is sandwiched by the death of Nadab and Abihu (chap. 10) and the Day of Atonement (chap. 16), showing that these instructions must not be taken lightly.[36] Necessary distinctions are explicated relative to dietary matters (chap. 11), cleanness after childbirth (chap. 12), skin diseases (chaps. 13–14), and bodily discharges (chap. 15).

Readers throughout history have attempted to discern the reason for purity regulations, whether they are related to food, skin diseases, or bodily discharges.[37] It has been quite common to say that the laws were given for dietary reasons. Such an explanation is never given, however, in the biblical text, though it is clear that some of the laws in Leviticus would have a health benefit. From a canonical standpoint, there is a significant problem with such an interpretation. It is clear in the NT that the food laws are no longer applicable to the church of Jesus Christ (Mark 7:19; Acts 10:1–11:18; Rom. 14:14, 20; 1 Cor. 8:4–8; Col. 2:16–23). It is hard to see why Jesus and the apostles would permit believers to eat food that was disallowed in the OT if such food was banned in the OT for health reasons. Others maintain that the laws were given because the foods or practices banned were used in paganism. However, bulls were often used in pagan sacrifice just as they were in Israel, and so this solution fails to convince.

Mary Douglas thinks that the food laws focus on that which is whole, complete, and perfect, and food that does not conform to its class is unclean.[38] This rationale may represent one of the reasons for uncleanness. The explanation, however, is quite general and vague and lacks specific support, for it is difficult to perceive, from the Israelite standpoint, what constituted wholeness and completeness in every instance.[39] In some cases her explanations border on being tautologous and hence do not illumine the text clearly. To say that

36. Sprinkle, "Laws of Clean and Unclean," 641.

37. For a summary of scholarship and a helpful explanation of the rationale here, see Sprinkle, "Laws of Clean and Unclean"; see also Jenson, *Graded Holiness*, 75–83; House, *Old Testament Theology*, 136. My own discussion here is dependent upon Sprinkle, though he would not necessarily endorse all my conclusions. For a fuller discussion on the theories of clean and unclean foods, see Houston, *Purity and Monotheism*, 68–123.

38. Douglas, *Purity and Danger*, 51–57. See also Wenham, *Leviticus*, 20–21, 23–25. For a summary and analysis of Douglas's views, see Houston, *Purity and Monotheism*, 93–114.

39. See Houston, *Purity and Monotheism*, 74.

prohibited food is imperfect because it is unclean does not in itself provide an explanation as to why food is imperfect or unclean. Another view emphasizes that the regulations separated sexuality from the realm of the holy. Joe Sprinkle rightly notes that such a theory does not mean that sex is evil; rather, the point is that sex is earthly rather than heavenly.[40] But this theory pertains only to laws that relate to sexuality, so it is hardly comprehensive. Others suggest that the purity laws discourage violence and the consumption of meat.[41] The dietary laws, then, promote the value of life. This theory, though it may have some elements of truth, is not entirely convincing. The animals forbidden are not designated as "holy to the Lord." Instead, they are classified as unclean and abominable, which is a strange way of inculcating reverence for life. Furthermore, there is no indication that the quantity of meat to be eaten was limited.[42]

Sprinkle suggests the most satisfying explanation for the regulations regarding cleanness.[43] Israel's laws separated them from the Gentiles to prevent Israel from being contaminated by the idolatry and evil practiced by the Gentiles.[44] The food laws made it difficult for Jews to enjoy table fellowship with Gentiles, and if peoples do not share at table together, they are less likely to influence one another. The NT clearly teaches that during the old covenant it was God's intention for Jews to be separated from Gentiles. The era of such separation has now ended in Jesus Christ, for the laws relating to cleanness are no longer binding (see Acts 10:1–11:18). The separation between Jews and Gentiles has ended with the coming of Jesus Christ (Eph. 2:11–22; 3:2–13). Now Jews and Gentiles in Christ are equally members of the people of God (Gal. 3:28). In the old covenant, however, the law separated Jews from Gentiles so that the Jews would not imbibe the idolatry and pagan practices that were endemic among Gentiles.

Sprinkle also suggests that the laws in some instances can be divided into three categories.[45] There was clean food that could be offered in sacrifice, clean food that could be eaten but not sacrificed, and unclean food that could not be eaten. Priests were marked out as especially holy because of their cultic work, ordinary Israelites were clean as God's people, and Gentiles were unclean. So too, the tabernacle was particularly holy because the Lord dwelt in it. The land of Israel was also holy because the Lord gave it to his people, but the land of the Gentiles was profane. Interestingly, this matches the tabernacle

---

40. Sprinkle, "Laws of Clean and Unclean," 650.
41. Milgrom, *Leviticus*, 103–9. See also Goldingay, *Israel's Life*, 624–28.
42. For these two criticisms, see Houston, *Purity and Monotheism*, 77–78.
43. See Sprinkle, "Laws of Clean and Unclean," 651–53.
44. So also Hartley, *Leviticus*, 144.
45. Sprinkle, "Laws of Clean and Unclean," 651.

itself, where the holiest space was the holy of holies, the outer sanctum was less holy, and the courtyard was less holy still.

Most significantly, the laws given emphasize the holiness of the Lord. It probably is the case that there was no inherent rationale for some of the laws given to Israel. As Childs emphasizes, the laws were stipulated to point to Yahweh's lordship over his people.[46] Israel lives in subjection to the holy one of Israel. An explanation for the food laws is provided in Lev. 11:44–45: "For I am the LORD your God. Consecrate yourselves therefore, and be holy, for I am holy. You shall not defile yourselves with any swarming thing that crawls on the ground. For I am the LORD who brought you up out of the land of Egypt to be your God. You shall therefore be holy, for I am holy." The Israelites are to obey the instructions of the Lord and dedicate their lives to him so that they are a separate and distinct people to the Lord.

By following his rules and precepts, the people of Israel show that they uniquely belong to the Lord, and they call attention to the Lord's holiness. He is the wholly other one. Even though the laws relating to cleanness are no longer required for NT believers, 1 Pet. 1:15–16 picks up the admonition to be holy as the Lord is holy. Believers are to live a life of moral rectitude, showing that they are those who have been redeemed by the Lord. Even if the specific regulations about cleanness do not apply to believers, the call to live consecrated lives applies to the people of God. Believers are to live in a way that distinguishes them from the pagan world.

Leviticus emphasizes that the tabernacle where the Lord dwells is not to be defiled with human uncleanness of any kind. Hence, anyone who has leprosy must live outside the camp (13:45–46). Similarly, after relaying the instructions regarding the bodily discharges, chapter 15 concludes by saying, "Thus you shall keep the people of Israel separate from their uncleanness, lest they die in their uncleanness by defiling my tabernacle that is in their midst" (15:31). The tabernacle must not be contaminated by those who are menstruating or who have had an emission of semen or other bodily discharges.

Laws relative to cleanness do not necessarily pertain to sin.[47] Someone who has a skin disease or engages in sexual relations has not necessarily sinned, nor is it sinful to menstruate or to sow one's field with two kinds of seed or wear garments with two different kinds of cloth (19:19). Sprinkle rightly argues that an analogy is drawn between such uncleanness and sin. The ceremonial uncleanness of the people metaphorically and analogically points to their sinfulness. Those who suffer from skin diseases are required to offer sacrifices,

---

46. Childs, *Old Testament as Scripture*, 186.
47. Sprinkle, "Laws of Clean and Unclean," 653.

including the sin/purification and the guilt/reparation offering, for atonement so that they can be cleansed and enter the sanctuary (14:10–20). The reference to the sin/purification offering and the guilt/reparation offering do not necessarily prove that a person who has a skin disease has sinned. The offerings can be described, as noted above, as the purification and reparation offering, respectively. And yet it seems correct to draw an analogy between such uncleanness (which is not strictly sin) and the sinfulness of Israel. Israel's physical uncleanness testifies to its mortality and lack of wholeness and perfection and is thus an emblem of its sin. We are not surprised to discover, therefore, that later writers pick up the language of uncleanness and defilement to describe wickedness (e.g., Ps. 51:7; Isa. 6:5; Ezek. 14:11).[48]

The NT maintains that the Mosaic covenant is no longer in force (e.g., 2 Cor. 3:7–18; Gal. 3:15–4:7; Heb. 7:11–19).[49] Hence, believers are no longer subject to purity regulations (see Rom. 14:14, 20). The separation between Jews and Gentiles that was part and parcel of OT revelation has passed away in Christ (Eph. 2:11–22). All believers in Christ are members of the people of God, and the stipulations of the law are no longer binding upon them. The temple no longer represents the place of God's presence where atonement is offered. Jesus is the new temple (John 2:19–20; 4:20–24), and believers are the temple of the Holy Spirit (1 Cor. 3:16; 2 Cor. 6:16). Therefore, the purity regulations that relate to the temple no longer apply to those who are members of the new covenant. The NT applies the language of cleanness and uncleanness to believers metaphorically, so that sin is still designated as uncleanness (e.g., Rom. 6:19; 2 Cor. 12:21; Eph. 5:3; 1 Thess. 4:7), and believers are to cleanse themselves from evil (2 Cor. 7:1). Jesus' sacrifice on the cross cleanses believers from the impurity of sin (1 John 1:7). The Lord calls believers to be pure in heart (Matt. 5:8; cf. 2 Tim. 2:22) and to have a clean conscience (1 Tim. 1:5; 3:9; 2 Tim. 1:3), and such purity is manifested in the love of believers for one another (1 Pet. 1:22).

Laws

In one sense all of Leviticus is filled with laws. The instructions regarding sacrifices, the priesthood, and cleanness consist of laws. But here we will consider the instructions found in chapters 18–27. It is not my intention to examine these laws in detail, nor is there space here to attempt to explain the structure of this section, since it is extremely difficult to discern the rationale

48. See Hartley, Leviticus, 146.
49. See esp. ibid., 147, which I drew upon for this paragraph.

for the order of the commands. Rather, my purpose here is to offer some general observations so that the overall message of Leviticus relative to the law can be determined.

It is fair to say that the laws in Leviticus relate directly to the theme of holiness. Even though 19:2 is not intended to summarize the laws contained in chapters 18–27, the words "be holy, for I the LORD your God am holy" aptly capture the message of these chapters. Israel's holiness is reflected in the way it lives, and if Israel is holy, it lives under Yahweh's reign and rule. Understanding the laws in terms of holiness helps us understand specific instructions given to Israel. For instance, peace offerings must not be eaten after two days, for then the food is profaned and no longer is deemed holy (19:5–8). Those who offer their children to Molech "make my sanctuary unclean and . . . profane my holy name" (20:3). The call to obedience should not be understood as an impersonal ethic or as a list of duties. Those who rebel against the Lord's instructions fail to honor God and defile his sanctuary. Sorcery is despicable (20:6), for it constitutes a blatant rejection of God's lordship and flouts God's holiness (20:7). The call to obedience is deeply personal: "You shall be holy to me, for I the LORD am holy and have separated you from the peoples, that you should be mine" (20:26). Israel's life is to be patterned after the Lord, who distinguished them from all nations and called Israel to himself. A holy life reflects the character of the God who rescued them from Egyptian bondage. Those who fail to honor the blind, the deaf, and the elderly reveal that they do not fear the Lord (19:14, 32).

Indeed, any injury to others stems from a failure to fear and honor God (25:17), showing that the ethical life is profoundly God-centered. Similarly, treating a fellow Israelite who is poor "ruthlessly" evinces a lack of fear of God (25:43). Priests have special responsibilities because they particularly represent the Lord's holiness (21:6–8; 22:1–16). They must not marry a prostitute, a divorced woman, or a woman who is defiled (21:7) and must be careful to maintain ritual purity (21:1–6). Nor can those who have blemishes or defects serve as priests (21:18–21). High priests have yet a higher standard because they are even closer to the holy. A high priest may not leave the sanctuary even for the death of his father or mother (21:10–12) and must marry a virgin (21:13–15). The days and feasts that Israel is mandated to observe are "holy convocations" (23:2). The holiness of such festivals and days is emphasized (23:3, 4, 7, 8, 20, 21, 24, 27, 35, 36, 37). The days are set apart especially to the Lord, and hence they are designated as "to the Lord" (23:3, 6, 8, 34, 41). These days and festivals are a gift to Israel, for they are free from work and are occasions for celebration and rest (23:39, 41). In the same way, the years of Jubilee are set aside as a special rest and release for

Israel (chap. 25). Holiness is emphasized even when the word is not used. For instance, the sexual conduct of the Israelites must be distinguished from the behavior of the Egyptians and Canaanites (18:3, 27–28). Surely, we have the concept of Israel being a distinct and holy people even if the word "holy" is not used.

Israel's obedience, as already noted, is related to their covenant relationship with the Lord. As Christopher Wright says, "The ethical teaching of the Old Testament is first and foremost God-centered."[50] Again and again in Leviticus the Lord demands obedience because "I am the LORD" (18:5, 6, 21; 19:12, 14, 16, 18, 28, 30, 32, 37; 21:12; 22:2, 3, 8, 30, 31, 33; 26:2) or "I am the LORD your God" (18:2, 4, 30; 19:3, 4, 10, 25, 31, 34, 36; 20:7; 23:22, 43; 24:22; 25:17, 38, 55; 26:1). The Lord demands obedience because Israel belongs to him, because he is Israel's master and covenant Lord. The call to obey, however, is rooted in the grace of the Lord, in his delivering Israel from Egypt. The people of Israel are regularly reminded that they are to keep God's commands because they have been redeemed from Egyptian slavery (19:36; 22:33; 23:43; 25:38, 42, 55; 26:13). The summons to obedience is presented not as an oppressive duty but rather as a grateful response to the Lord's saving love. The Lord who saved them declares how they should live under his lordship. It is not as if the Lord motivates Israel only by reminding them of his past grace; he also emphasizes that he sanctifies them.[51] The basis for a command is often that the Lord sanctifies Israel, so that we read, "Keep my statutes and do them; I am the LORD who sanctifies you" (20:8). In the same way, "They shall therefore keep my charge, lest they bear sin for it and die thereby when they profane it: I am the LORD who sanctifies them" (22:9). Some of the major themes found in the regulations of Leviticus come together in 22:32–33: "And you shall not profane my holy name, that I may be sanctified among the people of Israel. I am the LORD who sanctifies you, who brought you out of the land of Egypt to be your God: I am the LORD." Israel's responsibility is to live in such a way that they do not profane and debase God's name. They are to do everything for the glory of the Lord. By living in holiness, they will sanctify God's name, displaying his holiness to the world. Israel is motivated to obey because Yahweh is their covenant Lord and liberated them from Egypt. At the same time, if they obey, the Lord gets the credit, since he is the Lord "who sanctifies" them. As Childs says, "God is the sanctifier, but Israel must strive for holiness."[52] Even in Israel's obedience the Lord receives glory, for he provides them with

---

50. C. Wright, *Old Testament Ethics*, 46.
51. See Wenham, *Leviticus*, 22.
52. Childs, *Biblical Theology*, 423.

the ability to obey.[53] That the Lord sanctifies Israel is a refrain that occurs in other texts as well (21:8, 15, 23; 22:16).

On the one hand, the Lord provides Israel the ability to obey; on the other hand, Israel is summoned to obey and threatened if they refuse. Apparently, Moses believed that both of these themes belonged to the full-orbed reality that Israel needed to know. Chapter 26 is a decisive chapter in Leviticus, for Israel is promised blessings if they obey and curses if they rebel. The blessings and curses of the covenant are announced to Israel. If Israel obeys, the people will live in the land that the Lord promised Abraham and will enjoy the Lord's covenantal presence. The supreme blessing of the covenant is expressed in 26:11–12: "I will make my dwelling among you, and my soul shall not abhor you. And I will walk among you and will be your God, and you shall be my people." If Israel obeys, the Lord will dwell in their midst and will walk with them day by day as he walked with Adam and Eve in the garden. He will satisfy every need, since they will be his people and he will be their God.

Hartley emphasizes that the laws of Leviticus focus on the themes of justice and love.[54] For instance, the "eye for eye, tooth for tooth" principle (24:19–20) is the fundamental principle of justice in the courts. "When compared to, say, the Middle Assyrian laws, the law of Moses was remarkably just. Often in other ancient Near Eastern cultures the punishment was much harsher than the crime committed. This demonstrates Yahweh's commitment to justice and righteousness."[55] The punishment inflicted by judges must be proportional to the crime.[56] One must not resort to cruelty and exact a stricter penalty than is warranted, nor should one fall prey to favoritism and wink an eye at a malfeasance because of partiality (19:15). Those who murder others with malice aforethought should be put to death as an expression of justice (24:21). Employees must be paid fairly and promptly (19:13). Just weights and measures are required, for justice, contrary to the view of some OT scholars, also involves conformity to a norm.[57]

The law also calls for love because love and justice are not contrary to each other but rather complement each other. Therefore, one is called upon to love one's neighbor as oneself (19:18). Vengeance, grudges, and hatred are

---

53. We see here the tension between divine sovereignty and human responsibility. For the obedience of any was due to the grace of God. Apparently, however, this grace was limited to a remnant, for most did not obey (see Deut. 29:4).

54. Hartley, *Leviticus*, lxii.

55. This comment is from Joshua Greever.

56. Rightly C. Wright, *Old Testament Ethics*, 335n8; Dumbrell, *Faith of Israel*, 47; Wenham, *Leviticus*, 312. The words here should not be interpreted as if such punishments were always carried out literally (see Goldingay, *Israel's Life*, 445).

57. Rightly Seifrid, "Righteousness Language," 415–22.

forbidden (19:17–18). Love reaches to the heart and transforms the way one treats enemies. Love treats the elderly with dignity and respect (19:32), and the resident alien is to be loved and not rejected as a foreigner (19:33–34). Gleanings in the field must not be hoarded; they are to be left for the poor so that their material needs are cared for (19:9–10).

The holiness of Israel is expressed in its sexual ethic. Sexual relations with one's sister, brother, father, mother, daughter, son, uncle, aunt, and other close relatives are forbidden (18:6–17; 20:11–12, 17, 19–21). Adultery is contrary to the holiness of the Lord, warranting the death penalty (20:10). Homosexuality is proscribed and characterized as an abomination (20:13), and bestiality is a crime deserving death (20:15–16).

Israel will experience covenant blessings if it obeys the Lord and carries out his commands (26:1–13). More space is given to the covenant curses that will follow if Israel disobeys the Lord (26:14–39). The focus on the curses suggests that Israel will rebel and experience the Lord's opposition in the coming years. And yet judgment is not the last word. The Lord, in his grace, will not abandon Israel. If Israel confesses its sin and humbles itself before the Lord, and its heart is circumcised through a miracle of grace, then the Lord will remember his covenant with Abraham, Isaac, and Jacob (26:40–42). He will show them mercy on the basis of the covenant made with Abraham. "Yet for all that, when they are in the land of their enemies, I will not spurn them, neither will I abhor them so as to destroy them utterly and break my covenant with them, for I am the Lord their God. But I will for their sake remember the covenant with their forefathers, whom I brought out of the land of Egypt in the sight of the nations, that I might be their God: I am the Lord" (26:44–45). The Lord promises to be faithful to his covenant with Abraham and to bring about a new exodus. Ultimately, the land belongs not to the people but to the Lord (chap. 25).[58] The Lord will be king over his people. They will dwell in the land, and he will dwell among them.

Conclusion

Leviticus reveals what it means to live under the lordship of the holy one, the one who is wholly other from us. Yahweh cannot dwell in the midst of his people without atonement. Human beings are stained by sin, needing to be cleansed to remain in God's presence. We find in Leviticus that Yahweh himself provides the means of forgiveness through sacrifices. Salvation is of the Lord,

58. C. Wright, *Old Testament Ethics*, 95–96.

and he is the one who saves his people. If the theology of sacrifice in Leviticus is interpreted canonically, forgiveness of sins is realized not through animal sacrifices but instead through Jesus Christ as the crucified and risen Lord.

Leviticus also emphasizes that one must be clean and pure in order to abide in God's presence. The priests and people are given many regulations to remind them that belonging to God and dwelling in his presence are inestimable privileges, that the holy one may be approached only by one who is clean. Israel itself must be holy to approach the holy one. Lastly, living under Yahweh's lordship means that Israel must live a holy life. The Lord is the one who sanctifies them, but Israel must also pursue actively a holy life. The people must separate themselves from all that is evil and devote themselves to what is good. Yahweh provides forgiveness for his people so that they may live in a way that pleases him, so that they may lead pure lives that testify that they are truly the people of the Lord.

According to the NT, the holy one is Jesus Christ. Believers are holy and blameless because they belong to him. They have been sanctified in Jesus Christ (e.g., 1 Cor. 1:30; 6:11). Believers have also received the Holy Spirit, who empowers them as the new and true Israel to live holy lives, to live in a way that is pleasing to God. The holy conduct of believers (1 Pet. 1:15–16) marks them as God's people, showing that they are truly in the circle of the redeemed.

4

NUMBERS

We have seen that the Lord promises Abraham land, offspring, and universal blessing. The book of Exodus opens with Israel multiplying rapidly. The Lord was fulfilling his covenant promise for his people. Nevertheless, they were not yet in the land of promise, and thus the Lord freed them from Egypt and entered into a covenant with them, instructing them how they were to live under his covenant lordship. Israel sinned in a dramatic way by making a golden calf (Exod. 32–34). They broke the covenant almost immediately after it was enacted. Moses interceded with the Lord, and he forgave them. As a result the Lord resided in their midst via the tabernacle. The book of Leviticus does not advance the narrative, but it emphasizes that the Lord is ever the holy one. The Lord could not continue to dwell in the midst of Israel if they did not offer sacrifices for the forgiveness of their sins. Furthermore, Leviticus specifies that access to the Lord is allowed only on his terms. Only those appointed as priests had access to the tabernacle, and the inner sanctum was accessible only once a year and only by the high priest. A number of instructions regarding purity were given as a reminder that Israel needed to be cleansed in order to enter the Lord's presence. Israel was not inherently pure enough to live in the Lord's presence. Finally, the Lord communicates through a number of laws what it means to be a holy people to the Lord, so that Israel understood what it meant to live under his dominion and lordship.

Preparation: Purity and Obedience to Enter the Land

The book of Numbers picks up the narrative from Exodus, though the story is interwoven with laws relating to cultic matters. If we consider the story in

Numbers as a whole, we see that the book begins with a generation that should have entered the land of promise but failed to do so because of disobedience and unbelief. The book concludes, though, with the census of a new generation poised to inherit the land. The end of the story takes us back to the beginning, reminding the reader what the former generation should have done. Thematically, then, the promise of the land plays a central role in the account.[1] Numbers commences with a census, and the number of those able to fight was more than six hundred thousand (1:46). Clearly, the Lord had fulfilled his promise of countless offspring made to Abraham. Furthermore, the counting of the fighting force demonstrates that Israel was ready to possess the land.

The strength of Israel, however, did not ultimately come from its army. Israel's uniqueness and power came from the presence of the Lord in its midst. The word "tabernacle" is used thirty-two times in Numbers (second only to Exodus, with fifty-five, and far more than in any other book in the OT), denoting the Lord's dwelling with his people. The phrase "tent of meeting" occurs fifty-four times, more than any other book in the OT (cf. thirty-three in Exodus, forty-one in Leviticus). Clearly, Numbers focuses on the Lord's special presence with his people. As Childs says, "The effect is that the entire emphasis falls on characterizing the nature of being separated to God in preparation for becoming a pilgrim people on the move."[2] Hence, the army had to arrange its camp just as the Lord directed, for the tabernacle where Yahweh dwells must be separated from all that is unholy. Judah occupies a special place in the camp (2:3–4), forecasting the truth that a king would come from it.[3] The Levites were specially appointed to care for the tabernacle and its furnishings, and they were to set up their camp around the tabernacle and to guard it (1:47–54).[4] By following the Lord's instructions, they would ensure that the Lord's wrath would not fall upon Israel. The theme of holiness, therefore, continues from Leviticus. This was no ordinary camp or army, for the Lord dwelt in the midst of Israel. His presence was what made Israel distinct, and if Israel followed the Lord's instructions, they would know the joy and glory of his presence.

The arrangements of the camp were dictated specifically so that each tribe knew its place (2:1–34). The holiness of the camp explains why particularly detailed instructions were given to Aaron and his sons and to the Levites (chaps. 3–4), for the priests were nearest to the Lord, and the fearsome holiness of the Lord made it imperative that the priests do exactly what the Lord demanded.

1. So Clines, *Theme of the Pentateuch*, 57.
2. Childs, *Old Testament as Scripture*, 197.
3. Sailhamer, *Pentateuch as Narrative*, 371.
4. For the special role of the Levites, see Jenson, *Graded Holiness*, 130–35.

Therefore, they were reminded about the destruction of Nadab and Abihu (3:4), and the importance of "guarding" their charge is underscored repeatedly (3:7–10, 25, 31, 32, 36, 38).[5] Those who were closer to the sanctuary were to be especially careful, guarding the divine presence, since any outsider who entered the Lord's presence was to be slain (3:38). A gradation of responsibilities existed, and those who transcended their boundaries were in danger of death. When the tent was moved, only the sons of Aaron could cover the holy articles (4:1–20). The Kohathites were charged with carrying the articles, but they could not uncover the holy things and touch them "lest they die" (4:15). If the Kohathites looked at the holy articles even for a moment, God would strike them dead (4:20). The Gershonites were not as close to the holy articles as the Kohathites, and they had the responsibility of carrying the curtains and hangings in the tabernacle (4:24–28), while the Merarites were even more distant, being charged with carrying the frames, bars, and other accessories in the tabernacle (4:29–33). The Lord would not go up with Israel to the land of promise (in answer to Moses' prayer [Exod. 33:7–34:12]) if Israel did not treat him as holy and awesome by following his specific instructions.

Chapters 5–6 follow the detailed instructions for Israel's camp by emphasizing the need for purity. Lepers must dwell outside the camp (5:1–4). Being unclean, they would bring defilement into the camp (see Lev. 13–14). Those who sin were to make full restitution (5:5–8), and if a husband suspected his wife of jealousy, she had to undergo the water rite to determine whether she had been faithful (5:11–31).[6] Instructions were also given for the Nazirite vow by which a man devoted himself to the Lord (6:1–21). The regulations were given so that Israel could live in the Lord's presence and under his lordship. Thus, the priestly blessing that concludes the chapter represented God's intention for his people (6:24–26). The Lord desired to bless and guard his people so that they would enjoy the radiance and joy and peace of his gracious love.

The emphasis on purity and obedience continues in chapters 7–10, showing again the paramount importance of holiness in the camp. Every tribe gave generously for the dedication of the altar (chap. 7), showing that every tribe had been blessed by the Lord economically, and that every tribe was joyfully contributing for offerings in the tent of meeting, where the Lord met with his people.[7] The Levites were set aside and ordained for their duties (chap. 8).

5. There probably is an allusion here to Adam, who did not guard the garden rightly and failed to evict the unholy serpent that entered the garden.
6. Though the instructions seem strange, they protected wives from "arbitrary violence or from divorce on the basis of mere suspicion" (Goldingay, *Israel's Life*, 376).
7. My thanks to my friend Tom Rogstad for his reflections on the role of Numbers 7 in the narrative.

Before they could serve they had to be cleansed (8:6–7), and atonement had to be offered on their behalf (8:8–12). They could serve only after being purified and after atonement had been offered, showing again the holiness of the Lord (8:15). Similarly, the observance of the Passover was restricted to those who were clean (9:1–14), and its placement here is significant. Israel celebrated Passover before entering the land of promise, for they could enter the land only as a pure and obedient people. The cloud, the fire, the tabernacle, and the tent of meeting all underscore the Lord's glorious presence with his people in 9:15–22. What is particularly emphasized, however, is Israel's need to follow the Lord's guidance. Israel set off from the camp only when the cloud lifted, and they were entirely dependent on the Lord's command. If the cloud remained many days, Israel remained stationed in the camp; if it lifted after a few days, they set out. The last two verses drive home the point: "Whether it was two days, or a month, or a longer time, that the cloud continued over the tabernacle, abiding there, the people of Israel remained in camp and did not set out, but when it lifted they set out. At the command of the LORD they camped, and at the command of the LORD they set out. They kept the charge of the LORD, at the command of the LORD by Moses" (9:22–23). This text foreshadows, by way of contrast, Israel's forthcoming disobedience. Israel would retain its blessing only if they followed the Lord, and hence a dark cloud surfaces on the horizon.

Chapter 10 opens with instructions regarding the trumpets. The trumpets summoned Israel to assemble, to set out from the camp, to celebrate festivals, and to battle (10:1–10). Israel, then, set off for the land the Lord had promised, following carefully the instructions for the camp that the Lord had given them (10:11–28). The Israelite camp and march were under the Lord's protection, guidance, and rule, for the ark of the covenant and the cloud preceded and protected them on their journeys (10:33–34).[8] The ark is closely associated with Yahweh's kingship and rule. It is the footstool for his feet (cf. 1 Chron. 28:2; Ps. 132:7; Isa. 60:13; 66:1), so that "the ark of the covenant extends the heavenly throne to earth."[9] Israel's army could not boast of superior military ability, nor were they a well-crafted fighting force. Their success depended entirely on the Lord's presence and favor. Inheriting the land depended upon the Lord routing their enemies (10:35), and they would find true rest in the land only if the Lord's presence remained among them (10:33, 36).[10]

8. So Ollenburger, *Zion*, 37; Beale, *Church's Mission*, 113.
9. Alexander, *Eden to the New Jerusalem*, 33.
10. Clines (*Theme of the Pentateuch*, 57–59) notes that the first ten chapters of Numbers emphasize the movement of Israel into the land.

The Disobedient Generation

The Lord had delivered his people from Egypt, entered into covenant with them, dwelt in their midst via the tabernacle, and gave them instructions to maintain his presence among them. Israel would prosper only if they remained pure and followed divine instructions. One of the major themes of Numbers is Israel's remarkable failure to believe in the Lord's promises and to obey what he commanded. Chapters 11–12 forecast and anticipate Israel's rebellion, demonstrating the depth of evil present in the people liberated from Egypt. Camp was scarcely broken when they complained about their circumstances, sparking the anger of the Lord (11:1–3). Furthermore, they grumbled about eating manna every day, longing for meat (11:4–10, 18–20, 31–35). Clearly, they were rebelling against God's lordship, dishonoring him by wishing to return to Egypt instead of traveling to Canaan. In essence, they were rejecting Yahweh as their God, saying that their lives would have been better had he not intervened on their behalf. This was tantamount to saying that the Lord was evil, and hence the Lord responded in anger and sent a plague among them, showing his holiness in his judgment of those who failed to trust him.

A contrasting inset in chapter 11 is quite illuminating. Moses felt overwhelmed by the grumbling of the people, despairing of his ability to bear with the people alone (11:10–15). The fundamental flaw with Israel is revealed by this incident: the people lacked the Holy Spirit. The Lord answered Moses' prayer by giving the Spirit to the seventy elders so that they could bear the burden of the people with Moses (11:16–17, 24–25). Joshua was concerned that Eldad and Medad remained in the camp and prophesied (11:26–29). But Moses was truly a man of the Spirit, for he was not defiled by a selfish will. He was meek and humble (12:3), so he did not grow envious over others who were inspired to prophesy by the Spirit. Instead, he longed for all of Israel to have the Spirit and function as prophets (11:29). Miriam and Aaron, however, were consumed with a selfish will and fell prey to jealousy, complaining about Moses' foreign wife and objecting that the Lord did not speak only through Moses (12:1–2). They failed to recognize that the Lord uniquely spoke through Moses, and in rejecting Moses' special stature as a leader, they were resisting what the Lord had ordained, and thereby they defied the sovereign Lord (12:4–15). Therefore, the Lord's anger flared up against Miriam and Aaron, and the former was struck with a skin disease for a week, suggesting that she played the primary role in the attack against Moses.

The rebellion of Israel, which was intimated in chapters 11–12, manifests itself fully in chapters 13–14. Despite Israel's false steps in chapters 11–12, they continued to journey to Canaan (11:35; 12:16). Spies were sent out to reconnoiter the land, and they found it to be lush and fruitful, just as the Lord promised (13:23–24, 26–27). However, fear paralyzed them, for they were persuaded that they could not dislodge the current inhabitants, given their military strength and stature (13:28–29, 31–34). They convinced the people that the proposed conquest was a futile endeavor, and the people wept (14:1). Indeed, the congregation turned against Moses and Aaron, complaining that life would have been better in Egypt, and that the Lord had liberated them only to slay them with the sword of their enemies (14:2–3). They lamented that their wives and children would face death and started a campaign to reverse the exodus and return to Egypt (14:3–4).

Their disobedience was akin to what was previewed in chapter 11. The people were persuaded that the Lord was not a gracious God; rather, like Eve in the garden (Gen. 3:1–6), they believed that God had evil intentions for their lives. Joshua and Caleb remonstrated with the people, reminding them of the Lord's goodness, for the land was delightful and fruitful, and the Lord had promised them victory over their foes by virtue of his presence with his people (14:6–9). The people refused to glorify God by believing his promises, even after having been liberated from Egypt! Instead, they threatened to stone Joshua and Caleb (14:10). The glory of the Lord appeared to the people, though it was not his saving but rather his judging presence (14:10). The congregation's sin was no light matter; by failing to believe in the Lord despite all that he had done for them, they were despising the Lord himself (14:11).

As in Exodus, the Lord threatens to destroy the people and make a great nation of Moses and his descendants (14:12). But again, as in Exodus, Moses intercedes for the people, reminding the Lord that his own reputation would be besmirched if he destroyed Israel (14:13–20). The Lord's name and presence were inextricably intertwined with Israel's fate, so if he annihilated them, the Lord's power and presence among his people would be questioned by surrounding nations, for if Israel ceased to exist it would call into question Yahweh's power. Moses reminded the Lord of his great name and character, for he is a God who "is slow to anger and abounding in steadfast love, forgiving iniquity and transgression, but he will by no means clear the guilty, visiting the iniquity of the fathers on the children, to the third and the fourth generation" (14:18). Israel's betrayal warranted their judgment and annihilation, but the Lord, in response to Moses' intercession and as a revelation of his saving love, spared them.

The forgiveness granted by the Lord did not mean that there would be no judgment at all. He spared Israel from utter and complete destruction, but those who despised him and tested him over and over, despite seeing his power and saving love when they were freed from Egypt, would not inherit the promised land (14:21–23). The centrality of the Lord's name is apparent, for the Lord swears, "But truly, as I live, and as all the earth shall be filled with the glory of the LORD" (14:21). The Lord's glory was manifested in both salvation and judgment. His name was glorified in showing mercy by sparing the people, and it was glorified also in judgment. Indeed, the Lord's intention was that his glory would spread throughout the earth so that it would not be confined to Israel. The Lord's judgment paradoxically fulfilled what the disobedient generation in Israel asked for. They wanted to die in the wilderness (14:2), and their wish was being granted (14:29, 32). Ironically, they claimed to be worried about their children, but their children would be the ones to inherit the land (14:3, 31), though their enjoyment of the land would be delayed because of the unfaithfulness of their parents.

Israel lurched into irrationality, for after the Lord assured those of the age twenty and older that they would die in the wilderness, they vainly and recklessly tried to enter the promised land and were cut down relentlessly, just as the Lord said (14:40–45), for they were deprived of the Lord's saving presence. The reason for Israel's failure is captured in 14:43–44: "'Because you have turned back from following the LORD, the LORD will not be with you.' But they presumed to go up to the heights of the hill country, although neither the ark of the covenant of the LORD nor Moses departed out of the camp." Israel could not conquer without the presence of the Lord.

The disobedient generation's faithlessness and disobedience were paradigmatic. They anticipate the remainder of the OT, where Israel regularly failed to keep Yahweh's commands.[11] Both Paul (1 Cor. 10:1–12) and the writer of Hebrews (3:7–4:13) remind their readers of the generation that failed to inherit the promise, stressing that their readers must persevere in faith and obedience until the end in order to be saved. Verbal adherence to the Christian faith and participation in sacramental realities do not guarantee enjoying the final inheritance. Only those who continue to trust in divine promise and who obey the Lord's instructions will be saved on the last day.

Numbers shows that the rebellion and ungratefulness that resided in Israel were not exhausted by their refusal to enter the land of Canaan. The Levite Korah and the Reubenites Dathan and Abiram protested the singular authority of Moses and Aaron, complaining that everyone was equally holy (16:1–3). The Levites participating in the rebellion espoused a radical egalitarianism by maintaining that they were worthy of the priesthood as well (16:10). Fundamentally, their protest, which mirrored the problem with the wilderness generation, was a rejection of God's lordship (16:11). Korah and his friends

11. See Rendtorff, *Canonical Hebrew Bible*, 73.

assembled their partisans against Moses and Aaron, and "the glory of the LORD appeared" to all (16:19), threatening destruction of the entire congregation except for Moses and Aaron (16:21). The majority of Israel was spared only by separating themselves from Korah and his friends. The glory of the Lord manifested itself in judgment, as the earth swallowed up Korah, Dathan, Abiram, and their families (16:30–33). Similarly, the glory of the Lord blazed forth in judgment, consuming the 250 men who were offering incense (16:35). The ferocity of the judgment revealed that the sin of those destroyed here was intentional (cf. 15:30–31), deserving the same fate as the Sabbath breaker (15:32–36). These men were guilty of despising the Lord himself (16:30). The fierce anger of the Lord indicates again the awesome holiness of the Lord; no one is qualified to come before him apart from the way he has directed (16:40).

The amazing blindness of the "lost" generation is evident in the way they responded to the death of Korah and his compatriots. Instead of being provoked to reexamine their lives and to grief and repentance, they blamed Moses and Aaron for the death of those who perished, which is strikingly irrational because Korah and his friends died in an earthquake and in something like a lightning strike from heaven (16:31–35, 41). Once again the glory of the Lord appeared to the congregation, threatening to destroy the congregation entirely (16:42–45). A plague that killed more than fourteen thousand Israelites broke out, and the Lord's wrath was stanched only by atonement, with the result that the nation was not wiped out (16:46–49).

If we stop to consider the progress of the story thus far, we note that the holiness of the Lord and the evil of Israel made it difficult for Israel to enter into the land. Israel's complaints about Aaron's priestly role could not go on, and so the Lord caused Aaron's rod to bud and flower in order to demonstrate that only Aaron and his sons could serve as priests (chap. 17). The "disobedient generation" lurched from one thought and action to another, realizing that they deserved to perish. They could not draw near to the Lord's tabernacle because of their depravity, and so they despaired of life, exclaiming that they were all destined to perish (17:12–13).

Chapter 18 responds to the concern expressed at the end of chapter 17. Israel could not live in the Lord's presence unless they followed the Lord's instructions. The priests and Levites must guard the sanctuary by doing what the Lord mandated. If the Levites (Korah and his friends!) arrogantly took upon themselves priestly duties, they would perish (18:3; cf. 17:10). If they wanted to avoid the holy wrath of the Lord from breaking out, they must follow the instructions the Lord gave, for only those whom the Lord had chosen could serve in the tabernacle (18:4–5). The holiness of the Lord must be guarded, for "any outsider who comes near shall be put to death" (18:7). Chapter 17 concludes with Israel wondering how they can avoid dying, and chapter 18 emphasizes that only the priests and Levites should serve in the tabernacle, just as the Lord directed, so that Israel would not die (18:22).

The instructions regarding the heifer (chap. 19) address the same issue.[12] The ashes of the heifer are for the water of impurity by which Israel can be cleansed from defilement contracted from corpses and other sources that pollute the people.[13] Refusing to be cleansed was no minor matter, for those who were tainted and unclean would be cut off from the assembly because they had defiled the Lord's sanctuary (19:20). Israel's need for cleansing, Yahweh's holiness, and his provision for atonement are again highlighted.

The failure of the wilderness generation surfaces again in chapter 20. The fate of the lost generation is symbolized in the deaths of Miriam and Aaron. Israel's years in the wilderness have not been characterized by increased faith or greater obedience. Indeed, the heart of Israel has not changed one whit. When water supplies ran low, the people voiced the wish that they had died with others who were punished by the Lord! They romanticized Egypt as an ideal home and thus regretted the Lord's saving them from Egyptian bondage (20:5). The pattern woven through Numbers surfaces again. The glory of the Lord appears ready to judge and destroy the nation for their blatant disobedience. Numbers makes it exceedingly clear that God's glory is manifested not merely in salvation but also in his judgment of his people.[14] Nor was Moses himself exempt from the Lord's judgment, for he too failed to display the Lord's holiness, since he struck the rock in anger instead of speaking to it as instructed (20:7–12). No one, the text emphasizes, can trifle with the holiness of the Lord. Moses himself would not enter the land, for no one enjoys special privileges. All must honor the holiness of the Lord or face his judgment.

A New Generation: The Promises Are Not Revoked

Israel was promised that they would inherit the land, but Numbers also highlights the awesome and fearsome holiness of the Lord. Israel, despite all of the Lord's goodness to them, failed to believe and hence faced judgment. Nevertheless, Israel's disobedience did not mean that the Lord would cancel his promises. The wilderness generation was judged for their lack of faith and consequent disobedience, but this was not the last word. Their children, whom

12. See Sailhamer, *Pentateuch as Narrative*, 394.
13. Chapters 18–19 emphasize that Yahweh provides atonement for his people (so Childs, *Old Testament as Scripture*, 198).
14. This is the theme of Hamilton's *God's Glory in Salvation*.

they said would perish (14:3), finally possessed the land (14:31). Similarly, after the disobedient generation was barred from the land (chap. 14), it seemed as if the end had come for Israel. The following chapter (chap. 15), which specifies required offerings, at first glance seems to be irrelevant and disconnected from the narrative. Actually, the chapter is vitally connected to the narrative, for the sacrifices required are to be offered "when you come into the land you are to inhabit, which I am giving you" (15:2). The promise of the land was not revoked, despite Israel's disobedience. They most certainly would enter the land and eat its bread (15:18–19). Forgiveness was still available for those who transgressed.[15]

The last section of Numbers (chaps. 21–36) reveals that a corner has been turned. A new day in which Israel would enter the land was coming. Hence, Israel conquered Arad (21:1–3), Sihon (21:21–30), and Og (21:31–35) and was on the move to Canaan in fulfillment of the promise (21:10–20). However, this is not to say that the fundamental problem with Israel was removed. They complained again about being liberated from Egypt, and so the Lord sent serpents to slay the people (21:5–6). But there is a new feature in the story. Israel confessed its sin on its own initiative, asking Moses to function as an intercessor (21:7). The pathway to forgiveness was counterintuitive. A bronze serpent was fashioned and placed upon a pole, and those who looked upon that serpent, trusting in the Lord's promise of forgiveness, were healed (21:8–9). In the NT, of course, John picks up this narrative and applies it to Jesus' work upon the cross, promising that those who believe in the crucified and risen Lord will enjoy eternal life (John 3:14–15).

The Balaam oracles dominate the next section of Numbers (chaps. 22–24). The issue of whether Israel is blessed or cursed permeates the chapters. Words related to blessing occur eleven times in these chapters, whereas the language of curse is found sixteen times. These chapters, then, address the promise originally made to Abraham, for the Lord pledged that those who cursed Abraham would be cursed and those who blessed him would be blessed (Gen. 12:3). The Moabites were destined for a curse because they longed to curse Israel. Balaam, contrary to the wishes of Balak the ruler of Moab and contrary to his own inclinations (Num. 23:7–8), pronounced a blessing upon Israel again and again. The promises given to Abraham will become a reality for Israel. The placement of these chapters is quite striking, for the preceding narrative portrays Israel as disbelieving, quarrelsome, and longing to return to Egypt. Nevertheless, the Lord's promises have not been withdrawn from this recalcitrant and refractory people.

15. So Childs, *Old Testament as Scripture*, 198.

The sovereignty of the Lord is featured in the account. Balaam clearly desired to please Balak the king of Moab and to curse Israel, thereby ensuring a hefty financial reward for himself. But he was constrained by the Lord to speak only what the Lord commanded. Balaam prided himself on his ability to discern the future, probably via examination of animal entrails and perhaps by interpreting the flying of birds. Ironically and humorously, his donkey knew better than he did what the Lord was doing and had to instruct Balaam about what was going on (22:22–34). Therefore, it was impressed upon Balaam that he had to speak the Lord's word (22:35). Balaam impressed immediately upon Balak the decisive issue: "Behold, I have come to you! Have I now any power of my own to speak anything? The word that God puts in my mouth, that must I speak" (22:38). Balaam will speak what God shows him (23:3), and God put the words in his mouth (23:5). When Balak was angry because Balaam blessed Israel instead of cursing them, he reminded Balak that he was compelled to speak God's word (23:12). And the Lord continued to place his words, on every occasion in which Balaam prophesied, in his mouth (23:16). Balaam was compelled by what the Lord said (23:26; 24:13). The Spirit of the Lord took hold of Balaam and spoke through him (24:2). Hence, no curse or spell could counteract the blessing intended for Israel (23:23). Indeed, the blessing that the Lord promised to Israel was irrevocable (23:19), and thus the words of Balaam cannot be attributed to a passing fancy or to the caprice of the moment.

Some of the particular features of the blessing promised to Israel should be noted. The promise of offspring to Abraham was confirmed, for the children of Israel would be as uncountable as dust and innumerable (23:10). Indeed, Israel will conquer all its enemies with the strength of a wild ox and a lion (23:22–24; 24:8–9). What made Israel distinctive was the Lord's presence with them, and the second oracle points to a kingly rule in Israel: "the shout of a king is among them" (23:21). Indeed, "his king shall be higher than Agag, and his kingdom shall be exalted" (24:7). The rule of a king is expanded upon in Balaam's final oracle (24:17–24). Israel's rule over the nations will commence in the distant future, hinting that the possession of the land in the near future will not lead to immediate triumph for Israel. A scepter and a star will arise from Israel to rule over Israel's enemies. The assertion that the star "will crush the forehead of Moab" (24:17) probably functions as an allusion to Gen. 3:15, reminding readers that the offspring of the woman will crush the head of the serpent.[16] We are reminded again (cf. Gen. 49:8–12) that

16. So also Dempster, *Dominion and Dynasty*, 116–17.

the blessing of Abraham will become a reality through a king,[17] which finds its fulfillment in Jesus the Christ. Finally, this king will introduce a paradise comparable to Eden: "Like palm groves that stretch afar, like gardens beside a river, like aloes that the LORD has planted, like cedar trees beside the waters" (Num. 24:6). The land will be as fruitful and as beautiful as a garden.[18] The major themes of this work come together here. The people of the Lord will be returned to something like a land of paradise under the rule of their king. They will triumph over their enemies, and God's lordship over all will be realized.

Balaam spoke of a future day. The story in Numbers departs from Balaam's oracle, returning to the matters at hand. The reality on the ground was dramatically and tragically different (25:1–9). The story is reminiscent of Moses on the mountain with the covenantal tablets, while the people of Israel below worshiped the golden calf (see Exod. 32–34). Israel's destiny was blessing, according to Balaam, but that should not be interpreted to say that all of Israel would enjoy that blessing. Many in Israel celebrated a cultic meal in honor of the fertility god Baal and worshiped him. Perhaps the leaders were particularly responsible for the defection, for they were hanged for their infidelity (25:4), and twenty-four thousand died of plague because of the wrath of the Lord (25:9). Phinehas the priest intervened by slaying an Israelite man and a Midianite woman who were engaging in sexual relations near the tabernacle (25:7–18). How could the Lord continue to abide with Israel, since he was holy and they were radically sinful? The need for atonement, which receives its climax in the sacrifice of Jesus Christ, surfaces in this text. Phinehas's actions prepare us for chapter 26. A new census was taken, demonstrating that the Lord had not abandoned Israel, for atonement had been secured despite their sin. Hence, a new generation was prepared to go to war and to win the land (26:2). The number of people was roughly the same as the first census, but the former generation had died out, and a new generation had arrived. The inheritance promised to Abraham had not been revoked.

The promise of a future inheritance was underlined and clarified, and no tribe would lose its inheritance even if a clan did not have sons (27:1–11; 36:1–12). Moses commissioned Joshua, as a man of the Spirit, as the new leader and shepherd of the people who would lead them into the promised inheritance (27:15–23), though much later a new Joshua would arise who would give a better rest (Heb. 4:8–9). The repetition of the offerings also indicates that Israel would enter the land and give thanks to the Lord with offerings

17. See Sailhamer, *Pentateuch as Narrative*, 408–9.
18. See Dempster, *Dominion and Dynasty*, 115–16; Hamilton, *God's Glory in Salvation*, 81–82.

(Num. 28–29). Eleven times we are told that the offerings would be "a pleasing aroma," indicating that the Lord would take pleasure in Israel's offerings and perhaps also that they would avert his wrath from Israel (cf. Gen. 8:21) so that he could continue to dwell among them. The slaughter of Midian (chap. 31), which had ensnared Israel in idolatry (chap. 25), functioned as a warm-up and model for Israel's destruction of its enemies in Canaan.

Numbers closes with other matters that prepare Israel for the conquest of Canaan. Reuben, Gad, and the half-tribe of Manasseh settle in the Transjordan, and the text particularly emphasizes their commitment to help Israel in the conquest of Canaan. Chapter 33 details the stages of Israel's encampments and journeys during the wilderness years, demonstrating that Israel has not yet reached its final destination, that it was on the way to its inheritance. Indeed, the chapter concludes with the instruction that Israel must displace the inhabitants of the land and destroy their idols (33:50–56). Otherwise, the Israelites would fall prey to the worship of false gods and would live in the land without the Lord being their true king, and therefore he would destroy them for not submitting to his lordship. In preparation for Israel entering the land, the Lord delineated the borders of the land and established cities of refuge for those who killed someone accidentally (chaps. 34–35).

Conclusion

Numbers begins with Israel as the camp of the Lord, poised to enter the land of promise, the second element of the promise of Abraham. Israel is the holy people of Yahweh, who dwells in the middle of the camp, and hence they must camp and set out just as he instructs. Yahweh is the holy one of Israel, and he will not remain with Israel if they become defiled. Only an obedient people who live under his lordship will enter the land. Numbers recounts Israel's failure to trust in and obey God's instructions, and hence the wilderness generation instead of entering Canaan was destroyed. Still, Yahweh did not withdraw the promise. The prophecies of Balaam indicate that the blessings of Abraham would become a reality for Israel. Paradise eventually would be regained, and a king from Judah would rule over Israel and destroy Yahweh's enemies. The NT indicates that this king is Jesus the Christ, who triumphed over Satan on the cross. But that was for a day far removed from the time in which Israel lived. Now the children of the wilderness generation were ready to enter the land. A new census was commissioned, indicating that a new army of the Lord over which he ruled would inherit the land.

5

DEUTERONOMY

Introduction and the Land

The theology of Deuteronomy is multifaceted, and it is clearly one of the most important books in the OT. It is quite different from the first four books of the Pentateuch, and hence we must examine its contribution to the narrative. If we were to sum up the book briefly, Deuteronomy calls upon Israel to obey Yahweh in order to enter and stay in the land. Only those who submit to Yahweh's lordship will experience his blessing. It is imperative to see, however, that the call to obedience is predicated upon the grace of God. Grace precedes demand, and in this sense the book anticipates the pattern of salvation found in the NT.

Deuteronomy is not primarily a narrative that rehearses Israel's history. The book concentrates on Israel's responsibility to obey the Lord as they are poised to enter the land of promise. Nevertheless, Deuteronomy cannot be understood apart from the narrative framework that informs the book. The Israelites, situated beyond the Jordan and facing the land promised to their ancestors, are on the cusp of entering the land (1:1–2). The prospect of entering the land informs the entire book.[1] Indeed, "the geographical motif is omnipresent."[2] The promise made to the patriarchs plays a fundamental role: "See, I have set the land before you. Go in and take possession of the land that the LORD swore to your fathers, to Abraham, to Isaac, and to Jacob, to give to them and to their offspring after them" (1:8). One of the central promises

---

1. So Millar, *Now Choose Life*, 67–98; Vogt, *Deuteronomic Theology*, 151; Dumbrell, *Faith of Israel*, 63–64.
2. Dempster, *Dominion and Dynasty*, 118.

in the covenant with Abraham is about to be fulfilled.[3] Israel not only has multiplied in terms of its population (1:10), it also is about to receive the land promise given to Abraham.[4] As Gordon McConville points out, gift precedes demand in Deuteronomy, for repeatedly in the book the verb "give" (*nātan*) is used with the giving of the land of promise to Israel.[5] Strikingly, Deuteronomy emphasizes that Yahweh made his covenant with the generation that was alive and about to enter the land (5:2–3). They are the generation that will inherit the promise of the land, but they must obey the Lord to obtain the promises given, which the preceding generation failed to do. Therefore, Deuteronomy may be seen as a renewal of the covenant for future generations.[6]

The book begins by reflecting on the failure of the preceding generation to obey the Lord and therefore their failure to receive the blessing of enjoying the land (1:19–33). Now a new generation has arisen that is challenged to obey the Lord and to inherit the land pledged to Israel. The Lord has not given Israel the land of Edom, Moab, or Ammon (2:1–23), but the Lord has given them the territory of Sihon and Og (2:26–3:17). Again and again in Deuteronomy the commands given to Israel are set in a framework where life in the land is tied to moral exhortations.[7] A couple of examples should suffice: "And now, O Israel, listen to the statutes and the rules that I am teaching you, and do them, that you may live, and go in and take possession of the land that the Lord, the God of your fathers, is giving you" (4:1; cf. 4:40); "See, I have taught you statutes and rules, as the Lord my God commanded me, that you should do them in the land that you are entering to take possession of it" (4:5; cf. 4:14). Often a new set of instructions is given with the prospect of entering the land in view: "Now this is the commandment, the statutes and the rules that the Lord your God commanded me to teach you, that you may do them in the land to which you are going over, to possess it" (6:1; cf. 8:1). Or the prospect of entering the land is noted: "when the Lord your God brings you into the land that you are entering to take possession of it" (7:1; cf. 19:1). Most scholars agree that chapter 12 commences

3. Craigie (*Deuteronomy*, 36–45) argues that the covenant is central in Deuteronomy. Many think that the treaty form of covenant that was presented under Exodus also applies to Deuteronomy. For hesitation, see Millar, *Now Choose Life*, 42–43.
4. "The land is also the locus of Israel's relationship with Yahweh" (Millar, *Now Choose Life*, 56).
5. McConville, *Law and Theology in Deuteronomy*, 11–13. McConville rightly emphasizes that the gift of the land also calls for Israel's response to God's grace. See also Martens, *God's Design*, 108–12.
6. So Waltke, *Old Testament Theology*, 497–503. House's title for his chapter on Deuteronomy is "The God Who Renews the Covenant" (*Old Testament Theology*, 169).
7. As Millar (*Now Choose Life*, 56–62) observes, the land is a gift from Yahweh, and yet Israel must obey to enter it and stay in it.

a new section of the book, and it begins, "These are the statutes and rules that you shall be careful to do in the land that the LORD, the God of your fathers, has given you to possess, all the days that you live on the earth" (12:1).

The land that Israel is about to possess is a gift from Yahweh, fulfilling the promise that the Lord swore to the fathers (6:23), in which Israel will enjoy rest (3:20; 12:9–10; 25:19). The land is described in lavish terms, calling attention to the goodness of the Lord and reminding readers of the garden of Eden (11:10–12).[8] "For the LORD your God is bringing you into a good land, a land of brooks of water, of fountains and springs, flowing out in the valleys and hills, a land of wheat and barley, of vines and fig trees and pomegranates, a land of olive trees and honey, a land in which you will eat bread without scarcity, in which you will lack nothing, a land whose stones are iron, and out of whose hills you can dig copper. And you shall eat and be full, and you shall bless the LORD your God for the good land he has given you" (8:7–10). The Israelites must never think that wealth and blessing are due to their hard work, for these are gifts from the Lord (8:17–18). Israel's righteousness and godliness are not the reason they will inherit the land; indeed, Israel is identified as stubborn and recalcitrant (9:5–6). The incident of the golden calf functions as the signature and emblem of Israel's rebellion against Yahweh, for the words of the covenant were scarcely inscribed before Israel violated the stipulations of the covenant (9:8–10:5). Israel was spared only by the intercession of Moses, who reminded the Lord of the promises made to Abraham, Isaac, and Jacob.

The Grace of God

The grace of God is a prominent theme in Deuteronomy. Israel is his "treasured possession, out of all the peoples who are on the face of the earth" (7:6). The grace bestowed on Israel is encapsulated in the confessional statement in 26:5–9. Israel sojourned in the wilderness, but the Lord multiplied and prospered the nation. In Egypt Israel was mistreated and persecuted, but the Lord delivered them from Egyptian bondage and brought them into a fruitful land. Why has the Lord specially loved and chosen Israel? Later in Israel's history some of the rabbis attributed it to Israel's willingness to obey the law. The Lord, said the rabbis, reputedly offered the law to Gentile nations as well, but they refused to live under it.[9] The rabbinic narrative attributes to Israel the virtue

8. Dumbrell, *Faith of Israel*, 64–66.
9. See Sifre Deuteronomy 343 (to 33:2); Mekilta Bahodesh 1 (to 19:2b); Mekilta Pisha 5 (to 12:6); Mekilta Beshallah 6 (to 14:31); Sifre Deuteronomy 170 (to 18:9). I owe these references to Sanders, *Paul and Palestinian Judaism*, 88–89.

of recognizing the goodness of the law and the wisdom of living under its instructions. Deuteronomy proposes an answer that is diametrically opposed to this rabbinic interpretation. Why did the Lord choose Israel? Not because they were the only ones to accept Yahweh's offer. It is a matter of grace from start to finish, for Israel was stubborn. The Lord set his love on Israel because he loved Israel and because of the promise given to the patriarchs (7:7–8). Israel had nothing to offer to the Lord, nor was it chosen because of its virtue. As Childs says, Israel's election derives "from the mysterious and inexplicable love of God."[10] The election of Israel is hidden in "the secret things" that "belong to the LORD our God" (29:29).[11] The reason why Yahweh chose Israel eludes and surpasses human understanding. He chose Israel because he wanted to show them his love, even though they were not inclined to follow him. Clearly, Israel did not deserve to be God's special possession, but he chose to dispense his grace on them.

Israel should enter the land with confidence and joy, for they know that the Lord is on their side. The wilderness generation did not trust in the Lord's promise to fight for them, and hence they refused to obey him (1:30). The same warrior God who triumphed over Egypt will give them victory over their enemies. The Lord's care for Israel is not only tough but also tender. He cared for Israel as his beloved son, for "in the wilderness . . . you have seen how the LORD your God carried you, as a man carries his son, all the way that you went until you came to this place" (1:31). The Lord who delivered them so wondrously from Egyptian bondage will not renege on his promises and suddenly abandon his people (4:20, 37; 5:6). He will complete what he started. He would not deliver them from the Egyptians and fail to bring them into the land of promise (6:21–23). Fear could paralyze Israel so that they refused to venture forth and obey the Lord and enter the land. So Yahweh reminds them what he did to the Egyptians, of his signs and wonders by which he liberated them from the superpower of their day (7:17–19; 11:3–4; 29:2–3). Since Yahweh defeated the Egyptians, Israel should not fear the tribal groups in the land of Canaan. The same warrior God who freed them from Egypt would fight for Israel in Canaan as well (3:22; 4:34), and therefore Israel should be full of confidence.

Israel is not summoned to obedience in order to gain God's favor. Repeatedly, they are called upon to remember who Yahweh is, what he has done,

---

10. Childs, *Biblical Theology*, 426. He goes on to say, "For the author Israel's election is not a theoretical concern. . . . Israel can claim no superiority, but its existence is grounded totally in the undeserved and inexplicable sovereign will of God." See the discussion in Goldingay, *Israel's Faith*, 192–209.

11. So also Craigie, *Deuteronomy*, 37.

and not to forget all his benefits. They must recall what the Lord did to the Egyptians (5:15; 7:18; 15:15; 16:3, 12; 24:18, 22) and how he preserved them in the frightening wilderness (8:2). Israel is prone to forget the Lord's mercy and to desist from trusting him (4:9, 23). Israel may begin to take for granted that the Lord delivered them from Egypt and turn away from the Lord (6:12; 8:14). Their hearts may grow cold and distant because they have not cultivated the memory of what the Lord has done for them. We think here of the importance of remembering the Lord's Supper in the NT, for the Lord's Supper celebrates the great act of redemption in the NT, the new exodus by which God delivered his people through the death and resurrection of Jesus Christ. Like Israel, Christians are encouraged to remember God's saving work so that they will not depart from the Lord.

Israel's trust in and obedience to the Lord are based on his incomparability and his love. He is Israel's rock who sustained them in the wilderness (32:4, 30–31). He is the just and faithful God who always keeps his promises (32:4). He is Israel's father and creator (32:6) and has intervened on Israel's behalf. Israel should feel the Lord's love for them. When Israel was in the desert and faced with its "howling waste," the Lord "encircled him" and "cared for him," even "as the apple of his eye" (32:10). The Lord watched over Israel like a mother eagle that "flutters over its young, spreading out its wings, catching them, bearing them on its pinions" (32:11). "Also, God calls them 'Jeshurun' in Deut. 32:15 and 33:5, and both times the LXX translates it with ἠγαπημένος. 'Jeshurun' seems to have been a title indicating the special love God had for Israel."[12]

Israel should obey not only because the Lord is good and loving but also because he is the sovereign and only God. There is no other god besides the Lord (4:35, 39). Idols are helpless and hopeless (4:28; 28:36; 29:17). The other so-called gods are not gods at all (32:17, 21). The Lord's universal sovereignty over all things is expressed clearly: "See now that I, even I, am he, and there is no god beside me; I kill and I make alive; I wound and I heal; and there is none that can deliver out of my hand" (32:39). The uniqueness of Yahweh is set forth, for he is the living God. Life and death are in his hands, so all of life is controlled by him, including sickness and health.[13] As Peter Craigie remarks, "God is the Lord of history *and* of the world of nature. He controls other nations and the course of nature, whether it be health, the fruitfulness of the land, or any other part of the created order."[14]

---

12. A note from Joshua Greever.
13. On the uniqueness of Yahweh, see Clements, *Old Testament Theology*, 72–78.
14. Craigie, *Deuteronomy*, 44.

The Lord's rule over history is confirmed repeatedly in Deuteronomy. Israel should not contend with Edom, "for I will not give you any of their land" (2:5). Nor did the Lord give Israel the land of Moab or the land of Ammon (2:9, 19). Conversely, Yahweh hardened and made obstinate Sihon to give Israel possession of his land (2:30–31). As Gary Millar says, "Throughout the narrative of the opening chapters Yahweh is presented as the one who disposes territory and determines the outcomes of battles."[15] Dread and fear of Israel will come upon the peoples from the Lord (2:25). The Lord will expel nations stronger than Israel to give them the land as an inheritance (4:38). If Israel fears that they cannot conquer nations stronger than they, Yahweh reminds them of the signs and wonders performed in Egypt by which Israel was freed (7:18–19).

Indeed, everything in history conspires to work out God's plan. He will send hornets to drive out the nations inhabiting the land (7:20). The Lord will slowly remove the nations in the land (7:22). Yahweh's sovereignty shows that he is "a great and awesome God" (7:21). The Lord promised to give the nations over to Israel "and throw them into great confusion until they are destroyed" (7:23). The lordship of Yahweh is not an abstract teaching, for it brought great comfort and encouragement to Israel, for they were promised that the Lord would "give kings into your hand" so that they would destroy them (7:24). Israel should be full of confidence, for "no one shall be able to stand against you until you have destroyed them" (7:24). When Israel fights enemies after possessing the land, they need not dread them or be fearful, "for the LORD your God is he who goes with you to fight for you against your enemies, to give you the victory" (20:4). The Lord will deliver such nations into Israel's hand (20:13).

Israel's Obedience

The Lord's rule over history and his grace is tied to one of the major themes of Deuteronomy: the necessity of obedience. It is imperative to see that the obedience called for in the book is not legalistic or external. We can say that the obedience is covenantal, for the Lord calls for obedience in response to his covenant mercy, by which he delivered Israel from slavery in Egypt.[16] Mc-Conville characterizes obedience in Deuteronomy this way: "The sequence then is this: God blesses, Israel obeys, God continues to bless."[17] Israel is blessed if it obeys, but it obeys because it has been blessed. The grace of

15. Millar, *Now Choose Life*, 43.
16. See McConville, *Grace in the End*, 132–34.
17. McConville, *Law and Theology in Deuteronomy*, 17.

Yahweh was manifested in redeeming Israel from Egypt, in liberating them from bondage (7:8; 9:26; 13:5; 15:15; 21:8; 24:18). Egypt is mentioned fifty times in the book. Of course, not every reference to Egypt refers to the exodus, but the majority by far refer to God saving his people from Egyptian bondage. The call to obedience in Deuteronomy, therefore, must be placed in its gracious and covenantal framework. Yahweh has shown himself faithful to his covenant and has delivered his people. In grateful response, Israel is summoned to obey.

Obedience in Deuteronomy is expressed with a variety of verbs, since one verb cannot capture the nature of the obedience demanded.[18] As House says, "Israel must display total allegiance to God."[19] Repeatedly Moses commands Israel to keep (šāmar) the Lord's commands (e.g., 4:2, 6, 40; 5:1, 12, 29, 32; 6:2, 3, 17, 25; 7:11, 12; 8:1, 2). The commandments are not simply to be contemplated and meditated upon. They must be put into action; they must be "done" ('aśâ) (e.g., 1:18; 4:1, 5, 6, 13, 14; 5:1, 27, 31, 32; 6:1, 3, 18, 24, 25; 7:11; 8:1; 11:22, 32; 12:1, 32; 13:19; 15:5; 16:12; 27:10, 26; 28:1, 58; 29:8; 30:12, 13, 14), for they speak to the issues of life in the market and in the family and in the courts, signifying one's complete and utter devotion to the lordship of Yahweh. Peter Vogt rightly remarks that the call to obey Yahweh in Deuteronomy signals the Lord's supremacy.[20] The kingship of Yahweh is expressed in his demand that his people obey him.[21] Vogt says, "The supremacy of Yahweh is also evident in the fact that it is Yahweh who commands."[22] Millar makes the same point, saying that the theology of the book enshrines "the belief that Yahweh is now Israel's absolute ruler who must be obeyed in every detail of life, and that he has given Israel a land in which to enjoy relationship with him together."[23] The call to do what the Lord commands must not be construed as legalistic or external. Israel's obedience shows whether they are truly devoted to Yahweh.

The fundamental issue, then, is whether Israel really knows Yahweh as its Lord. True obedience to Yahweh is expressed not merely in outward obedience but in love.[24] Millar comments, "Above all, the nation must choose to

18. See Millar, Now Choose Life, 47–51.
19. House, Old Testament Theology, 175.
20. Vogt, Deuteronomic Theology, esp. 5–6, 129–30, 134, 151–59, 202, 219–20, 224, 229–31.
21. Craigie (Deuteronomy, 65) argues that the Lord's kingship and his being a warrior are two central themes in Deuteronomy. See also McConville, Grace in the End, 124.
22. Vogt, Deuteronomic Theology, 227.
23. Millar, Now Choose Life, 181.
24. It is often argued that chapters 6–11 provide an exposition of the meaning of the first commandment. See Olson, Deuteronomy, 62–65; Walton, "Deuteronomy," 214–15. Millar (Now Choose Life, 81) also thinks that the dominant theme is love for Yahweh.

love God, and to demonstrate this love by obedience."[25] Not surprisingly, the message of Deuteronomy is expressed in 6:5: "You shall love the LORD your God with all your heart and with all your soul and with all your might." What it means to obey the Lord is to love him with all of one's strength (11:13; 13:3; 30:6).[26] True love can never be separated from the keeping of his commands (7:9; 11:1).[27] Love is not merely a pious feeling; it is an affection that results in concrete obedience to the Lord. Loving the Lord cannot be separated from fearing him, walking in his paths, and serving him (10:12). The various verbs used to depict devotion to the Lord mutually interpret one another in one sense, and in another sense they expand and fill out what it means to live under Yahweh's lordship. Love and fear are not ultimately polar concepts in Deuteronomy. Those who love the Lord fear him (4:10).[28] Those who fear the Lord will never depart from keeping his commands (5:29; 6:2, 24; 13:4; 17:19; 31:12). The honor that the Lord deserves is captured by 6:13: "It is the LORD your God you shall fear. Him you shall serve and by his name you shall swear." Fearing the Lord means, among other things, that one does not swear by any other god.

Another verb that conveys Israel's covenant loyalty is "serve" (*'ābad*). In some contexts "serve" is placed with "worship" (*hištaḥăwâ*), showing that Israel is to be exclusively devoted to Yahweh (4:19; 8:19; 11:16; 17:3; 29:26; 30:17; see also 4:28; 7:4, 16; 12:30; 13:2, 6, 13; 28:14, 36, 64; 29:18), that it must not worship any other gods. The covenantal dimension of the term is also apparent when "serve" is used with the verb "swear" (6:13; 10:20), for Israel's allegiance belongs to Yahweh alone. Indeed, those who serve other gods show that they "despise" the Lord and have broken "my covenant" (31:20). Serving the Lord is also linked with fearing the Lord, walking in his ways, and loving him with all of one's being (10:12). Indeed, the Lord calls upon his people to serve him "with joyfulness and gladness of heart, because of the abundance of all things" (28:47). Israel must serve the Lord with glad-hearted obedience, since he has lavished his kindness upon them.

Another covenantal term that describes Israel's obedience is "hold fast" or "cling to" (*dābaq*). Israel must "hold fast to" the Lord (10:20), which means that it must fear him, love him and walk in his ways (11:22), and listen to his

25. Millar, *Now Choose Life*, 46.

26. For further reflection on this command, see Gentry and Wellum, *Kingdom through Covenant*, 365–69.

27. As Craigie says, "Love was not simply a principle or abstract ethical concept; it was given clear expression in the commandments" (*Deuteronomy*, 42). Vogt (*Deuteronomic Theology*, 156) rightly points to the covenantal dimensions of love.

28. On the fear of the Lord in Deuteronomy, see Waltke, *Old Testament Theology*, 483.

voice (13:5; 30:20). This is the same term used to describe Adam's devotion to his wife: he must "hold fast to" her (Gen. 2:24). Similarly, the same verb is used to describe Ruth's devotion to Naomi, for she "clung to her" (Ruth 1:14). Often, the life that is prescribed for Israel is described as walking (*hālak*) in the ways God has commanded (5:33; 10:12; 26:17; 28:9). Or Israel's obedience or disobedience is characterized as listening (*šāmaʿ*) or failing to listen to the Lord (1:43; 4:1, 30; 8:20; 9:23; 11:13, 27, 28; 12:28; 13:4, 18; 15:5; 18:15, 19; 26:14, 17; 27:10; 28:1, 2, 13, 15, 45, 62; 30:2, 8, 10, 20). Truly listening to the Lord and hearing him results in obeying him, and hence many English versions translate the Hebrew verb for "listen" as "obey."

What is the function of such a diversity of expressions for obeying the Lord? They communicate the comprehensiveness and richness of what it means to obey the Lord. Following the Lord is captured by terms such as "doing," "keeping," and "hearing." Obedience to the Lord must be concrete and practically worked out in everyday life. But obedience is not exhausted by such terms, for there is the danger of thinking that obedience is mere external conformity to the Lord's will. True obedience involves affection—loving the Lord and clinging to him, finding him to be the praise and joy of one's life. Still, such love and loyalty are never abstracted from walking in his ways. Israel indicates that it lives under Yahweh's lordship by doing his will and obeying him.

Interestingly, we find the same diversity when it comes to terms that describe what Israel is to obey.[29] Israel is to obey "statutes" (*ḥuqqîm*). The word "statutes" is used twenty-one times in Deuteronomy, emphasizing that God has prescribed what Israel must do. The word "rules" (*mišpāṭîm*) is used thirty-seven times, focusing on what is right and just. The most important term is "commandments" (*miṣwōt*), which occurs forty-six times, and its verbal form eighty-eight times, emphasizing the Lord's authority, sovereignty, and kingship. Yahweh possesses all authority as the King of the universe to command the people to follow his instructions. What the Lord enjoins may also be described in terms of God's "way" or "ways" (*derek*) (5:33; 8:6; 9:16; 10:12; 11:22, 28; 13:5; 19:9; 26:17; 28:9; 30:6). He knows the paths that will lead to life and joy for his people. Three times we find the word "testimonies" (*ʿēdōt*) (4:45; 6:17, 20), signifying covenant stipulations. The various terms for God's commands emphasize the comprehensiveness of the Lord's sovereignty. He rules over all of Israel's life, and they are to submit to his lordship as his covenant subjects. Of course, one of the most important words to describe what Israel must do is "law" (*tôrâ*). This word occurs twenty-two times. Scholars often say that

29. Not every use of these terms refers to obedience to the law, but in most instances they refer to what the law enjoins.

Torah refers to instruction in a broad sense, but in Deuteronomy the instruction is tied to what God commands and enjoins. The word "law" primarily refers to what the Lord demands from Israel as its covenant Lord.

Yahweh's Supremacy

The commands and statutes in Deuteronomy point to Yahweh's supremacy and kingship over Israel, showing that Israel is to live under Yahweh's kingship in the land by obeying his instructions just as Adam was supposed to live under God's lordship in the garden.[30] It is striking how often idolatry is proscribed in the book, for idolatry substitutes something or someone else for the worship of the one true God. Moses impresses upon Israel that they saw no form when Yahweh appeared to them at Horeb, and hence they must not make any form to represent the Lord (4:15–18), nor should they worship anything else in all of creation (4:19, 23, 25). Vogt says, "Making images is inappropriate because it is contrary to Yahweh's will regarding the way his presence is to be manifested and also because it is too restrictive. Yahweh is God of *all* of heaven above and earth beneath. Therefore, his presence cannot be localized in an idol."[31] Worship must be done the way Yahweh prescribes (12:4). Moses fears that the people will follow the gods of the nations around them and abandon their covenant with the Lord (6:14; 29:18).

The command to love the Lord with all one's being (6:5) is just another way of saying that the Lord must be first in one's life. Clearly, the first three commands of the Ten Commandments focus on God's supremacy (5:7–11). We saw earlier the emphasis on "fearing" God, and such fear reveals that Yahweh is central in one's affections. Yahweh is to be the praise and joy of Israel's heart (10:21). The same truth is evident in the call to "hold fast to" Yahweh. Intermarriage with other nations in the land is strictly forbidden, and their cultic objects are placed under the ban (*ḥērem*) and must be completely and utterly destroyed (7:2–5; 12:2–3). Israel is "holy to the LORD your God" (7:6) and is "his treasured possession," and therefore the peoples in the lands must be killed, or else they will turn Israel away from the Lord. The call to utterly destroy the peoples in Canaan is a shock to modern sensibilities, but despite the attempt of some scholars to say otherwise, it is quite clear that Israel believed that these were instructions from Yahweh himself. The failure to carry out such instructions would imperil the fundamental tenet of Israel's faith: Yahweh's lordship. Israel must cleanse the land from evil, for Canaan

---

30. Dumbrell, *Covenant and Creation*, 126.
31. Vogt, *Deuteronomic Theology*, 133.

is to be a new Eden, a new garden of the Lord, free from evil.[32] The concern is that Israel will forget the Lord and turn to other gods (8:19). Remarkably, Israel turned to idolatry through the worship of the golden calf shortly after entering into covenant with the Lord (9:16). As Millar says, "The golden calf incident sounds a warning that even a place of revelation has the potential to become a place of apostasy."[33] Hence, Israel must resist temptation and worship Yahweh alone.

Yahweh Alone

One of the most prominent, and oft discussed, features of Deuteronomy is the insistence that Israel should worship Yahweh in the place that he chooses (12:5, 11, 14, 18, 21, 26; 14:23, 24, 25; 15:20; 16:2, 6, 7, 11, 15, 16; 17:8, 10; 18:6; 23:16; 31:11). The requirement to worship and offer sacrifices at the place that Yahweh chooses has played a significant role in attempts to reconstruct the history of Israel. But our purpose here is to attend to the function of the requirement in Deuteronomy. It is notable that the place where worship must take place is not named.[34] The point of the instructions is that Israel must worship Yahweh in the way and in the place he commands.[35] Worship must not be left to Israel's creativity or its own devices.[36] Worship is regulated by the word of God with regard to sacrifices, festivals, tithes, offerings, and the reading of the law.

Such worship is not merely a duty. Where Israel offers sacrifices, they will "eat before the Lord your God, and you shall rejoice" (12:7; cf. 12:12, 18). When Israel brings tithes to the place that Yahweh chooses (14:23–25), they are called upon to rejoice. They are to care for the Levite (14:27), but what is

32. On Canaan as a new Eden, see Dumbrell, *Covenant and Creation*, 120.

33. Millar, *Now Choose Life*, 86.

34. "The aim is *not* to identify the place, but to urge Israel to conform her worship to the divine command" (ibid., 110).

35. Wenham ("Central Sanctuary") says that Deuteronomy specifies a central sanctuary but does not exclude other sanctuaries. Alternatively, others maintain that there is a sole and central sanctuary but the location of the sole sanctuary changes over time (see McConville and Millar, *Time and Place in Deuteronomy*, 117–23; Niehaus, "Central Sanctuary"). Still another possibility is that a central sanctuary is to be established only after Israel has conquered and settled in the land (see Pitkänen, *Central Sanctuary*, 97–100). Dumbrell (*Faith of Israel*, 65) sees one sanctuary, which was mobile.

36. Vogt says that "the emphasis is on the contrast between the false worship of Canaanite religion and the proper worship of Yahweh," and "the primary emphasis is *not* on the number of sanctuaries but on the fact that Yahweh is to choose the location of legitimate places of sacrifice and that this stands in strong contrast to the practices depicted as Canaanite" (*Deuteronomic Theology*, 176, 179). See Miller, *Deuteronomy*, 131–32; Millar, *Now Choose Life*, 103.

particularly striking is the emphasis on joy. The Lord says, "Spend the money for whatever you desire—oxen or sheep or wine or strong drink, whatever your appetite craves. And you shall eat there before the LORD your God and rejoice, you and your household" (14:26). Israel's worship of the Lord was not some abstract experience of God; they were to worship him with joy and enjoy the good things of life that he had given them. They were to enjoy fellowship with God. Thus, Vogt rightly says, "Deuteronomy also portrays Yahweh as a God who is present with his people."[37] This same call to joy is reiterated in the feast of Weeks (16:14). The language used is again quite striking: "For seven days you shall keep the feast to the LORD your God at the place that the LORD will choose, because the LORD your God will bless you in all your produce and in all the work of your hands, so that you will be altogether joyful" (16:15). Absolutely joyful! Israel should be invigorated when they worship the Lord at the place that he chooses. Such delight is not self-oriented religion where "everyone does whatever is right in his own eyes" (12:8); rather, it is delight in the Lord and his gifts.

Israel must be on guard against those who claim to speak the word of the Lord as prophets (13:1–18), who encourage Israel to follow after other gods. They must not heed such prophets even if they do signs and wonders (13:1–2). Those who counsel such rebellion against Yahweh must be slain (13:5) because Israel will be destroyed if they follow such advice. Compassion and pity must not be extended even to family members who advocate worship of other gods; they too must be put to death (13:6–11). Such severe measures will prevent the infection of idolatry from spreading in Israel, which will lead to its certain destruction (13:11). Hence, if a certain city begins to promote idolatry, it must face utter annihilation (ḥērem).

Motive Clauses

In Deuteronomy Moses does not only call Israel to obey its covenant Lord and King, he also gives reasons or motives why they should obey. For instance, often obedience is linked to the well-being of Israel. Israel is summoned to obey so that "it may go well with you" (4:40; 5:16, 33; 6:3, 18; 12:25, 28; 22:7). In most of these texts the well-being of Israel is linked with staying in or possessing the land, the inheritance promised to Israel. On the one hand, the reception of the land is a gift (3:18), for Yahweh chose Israel to be his people because of his grace. At the same time, the covenant made with Israel at Sinai has conditional

---

37. Vogt, *Deuteronomic Theology*, 228.

elements. Israel will enter the land only if they trust and obey the Lord (11:8). And they will stay in the land only if they fulfill the conditions of the covenant. If Israel turns away from Yahweh, he will eject them from the land, destroy them, and send them into exile (4:25–27; 8:20). Moses pleads with Israel to walk in the Lord's ways so that they will live in the land Yahweh has given to them (5:33; 11:9). The Lord promises to bless Israel with children, fruitfulness in agriculture, and good health if they are obedient (7:13–15; 11:14–15, 21). In addition, they will triumph over their enemies (7:16) and expel them from the land (9:3). Israel must choose between the blessing and the curse, depending upon whether they obey or not (11:26–28). Curses and blessings dominate the latter part of the book. Curses are called down upon those who violate covenantal stipulations (27:15–26). The sins listed in chapter 27 are those that could be committed in secret, but Yahweh sees and will punish those who violate his statutes.[38] On the other hand, Israel is promised amazing blessings if they obey the Lord (28:1–14). They will triumph over their enemies, enjoy the fruit of the land, and rest in God's care. Conversely, the curses that threaten Israel receive much more attention (28:15–68).

We can see here the parallel between Israel and Adam. Adam was enjoined to obey to receive life and blessing, and so was Israel. Adam, of course, had never sinned before, whereas Israel had already defiled itself with sin. And yet both Adam and Israel shared the same calling. They were to obey the Lord and experience his blessing and life.

Specific Commands

I have already shown that the commands in Deuteronomy are fundamentally God-centered. Israel must not forget the Lord. It must serve him, fear him, love him, listen to him, cleave to him, keep and do his commands, and walk in his ways. Israel must not tolerate idolatry. Millar rightly says, "The biblical laws are theocentric in essence and expression, and as such are necessarily of a different genre from most comparative material."[39] The commandments that Israel is enjoined to keep in chapters 1–11 are unpacked in chapters 12–26.[40] As Vogt says, "The entirety of life in the land is to be lived before Yahweh and, therefore, is religiously significant and is considered as falling to some degree in the realm of worship."[41]

38. See Dempster, *Dominion and Dynasty*, 119.
39. Millar, *Now Choose Life*, 105.
40. See Vogt, *Deuteronomic Theology*, 198.
41. Ibid., 200.

Yahweh is ever the holy one of Israel, and so he specifies who may enter his assembly (23:1–8). Indeed, the Lord dwells in Israel's camp, and therefore the camp must be kept holy, and all that is unclean must be kept outside the camp (23:9–14). Some of the laws, of course, match commands found in Exodus or Leviticus. In some instances details are changed, presumably because Deuteronomy anticipates a new situation in which Israel contemplates entering the land. Israel's holiness and consecration to the Lord are made manifest in its abstention from foods prohibited by Yahweh (14:2–21; cf. 22:8–12). Israel should show its devotion to and submission to the Lord in observing the feasts of Passover, Weeks, and Booths as the Lord commands (16:1–17). The Levites are to be cared for via tithes (18:1–8).

Justice and compassion are central concerns in Deuteronomy.[42] "Justice, and only justice, you shall follow, that you may live and inherit the land that the LORD your God is giving you" (16:20). Thus, judges and other officials must be just and equitable in rendering judgment when cases come before them (16:18–19; 17:8–13). Punishment must fit the crime and be proportional (19:21; cf. 25:1–3); judges should be impartial so that they do not let off easily someone they favor or punish too harshly someone they dislike. Each person should be punished for his or her own sin (24:16). The truth of charges must be established on the basis of witnesses (clear evidence), and false witnesses are to be strictly punished (19:15–20). Incorrigible children who have acted outrageously are to be put to death (21:18–21). Correct and accurate weights and measures must be used (25:13–15). A parapet should be placed on the roof to prevent people from falling off and injuring or even killing themselves (22:8). Cities are set aside so that those who killed another accidentally are not deprived of their lives (19:1–13). One who kidnaps a fellow Israelite and sells him must be put to death (24:7).

When a war is conducted against those who reside outside the land (20:1–20), Yahweh reminds Israel that victory is his prerogative, and thus they should not fear. Apparently, annihilation (ḥērem) was practiced in the land to prevent Israel from falling into idolatry.[43] But cities and countries outside of the land were to be offered peace if they came into conflict with Israel; and if Israel's enemies sued for peace, they were to be conscripted for labor instead of being destroyed. If enemies far from the land insisted on going to war with Israel, only adult males were to be put to death; women, children, and animals were to be spared. The Lord desired to restrain the rapacity and the rage that so

42. Vogt (ibid., 209–16) emphasizes that righteousness is the responsibility of the entire community, not only judges.
43. See Millar, *Now Choose Life*, 133.

often accompany war, warning Israel that they should not destroy all the trees in the land: "Are the trees in the field human, that they should be besieged by you?" (20:19). A similar ecological concern is manifested in 22:6–7, where it is said that a person may take a nest with baby birds, but the mother should not be snatched away as well. Presumably, there is a concern for the continued existence of various kinds of birds in the land, and both laws mentioned here also ensure that the food supply is not exhausted.[44]

The king is not above the Lord, and there is special concern that the king may turn the nation away from the Lord (17:14–20). Hence, a foreigner must not be appointed who is not devoted to Yahweh. Kings must beware of accumulating horses, gold, or wives for themselves, lest they put their trust in such things rather than the Lord. The purpose of the regulations is to circumscribe and limit the power of the king.[45] It is quite striking that the king is to be devoted to the law that is written in a book.[46] The king's whims and preferences must not be the standard for Israel. Yahweh, not the king, must be supreme in Israel, and hence the king should fear the Lord and keep his commands and beware of turning the nation from Yahweh. Moses also predicts that a prophet will arise that is like him in the future (18:15–20). Yahweh will put his words in the mouth of that prophet, and his standing as a prophet of the Lord will be verified by his prophecies coming true. So authoritative is this prophet that anyone who refuses to listen to his words will face Yahweh's judgment. Israel as a nation is governed by the word of Yahweh. No king or prophet or priest determines autonomously what the nation should do. All must submit to the word of Yahweh.

Israel must attend to the poor and generously and graciously meet their needs (15:1–11). One must not refuse to help when a fellow Israelite's ox or sheep are wandering by protesting that one is too busy and occupied with one's own work (22:1–4). Love requires that time be taken away from one's own concerns to assist others. Hebrew slaves should not be a permanent fixture but instead granted freedom after six years (15:12–18), unless they desire to be part of the household forever. When slaves are set free, they must be provided for generously. A penurious and grudging spirit must not be tolerated. We must constantly remind ourselves that Israel's life under the law reflects the supremacy of and submission to Yahweh. Interest must not be charged on loans (23:19–20; cf. 24:6, 10–13), for otherwise the poor will be unable to extricate themselves from their poverty and will be subject to the will of

44. See McConville, *Law and Theology in Deuteronomy*, 17.
45. So Vogt, *Deuteronomic Theology*, 216–18.
46. See again Vogt (ibid., 218), who notes the echo of 8:11–14.

the creditor forever. Hired workers must be paid their wages on time and be treated fairly (24:14–15), and gleanings should be left for the poor (24:20–22). In particular, sojourners, widows, and orphans must be treated justly (24:18; cf. 26:11–13). It is permissible to pluck and eat fruit and grain while walking through a neighbor's field, but not to start harvesting the crop (23:24–25).

Justice and compassion must be shown to wives. If a husband divorces his wife, under no circumstances must he take her again for his wife after she has been married to another man (24:1–4).[47] For instance, a wife taken from a foreign country must be given time to grieve and be treated equitably once she is part of the household (21:10–14). If a man has two wives, he cannot and must not deprive the inheritance from the firstborn son even if he is the child of the wife loved less by her husband (21:15–17). A husband who falsely charges that his wife was not a virgin upon marriage will be whipped publicly and fined, and he may never divorce his wife (22:13–19). Conversely, if a wife is found not to have been a virgin, she must be stoned to death; or if a man and a woman commit adultery, or if a man has sex with a woman who is engaged, both must be slain (22:20–24). The concern for justice is evident in the case of an engaged girl who is forced into sexual intercourse outside the city. In that instance only the man will be put to death, since the woman cried for help but could not be heard (22:25–27). If a man has sex with a woman who is not engaged, he must marry her and never divorce her, since in Israel others would be loath to marry a woman who was no longer a virgin (22:28–29).

The Future

Deuteronomy is a forward-looking book. Israel is enjoined to obey the commands of the Lord so that it will possess and stay in the land. If Israel does not obey the Lord, it will be expelled from the land and go into exile (4:24–28). What is striking is that the failure is described as inevitable. Moses forecasts that Israel will transgress the covenant and be thrust from the land. Exile, however, is not the last word (4:29). Moses looks forward to a day when Israel will repent and seek the Lord ardently, and the Lord will renew his covenant with his people (4:30–31).

One of the prominent themes of Deuteronomy is that blessing and curse are before Israel (11:22–32). If they obey, they will inherit the land and experience its blessings, but if they transgress the law, they will know the curses of the covenant and be ejected from the land. As Israel contemplates entering the

---

47. This legislation protects a wife from the arbitrary decisions of the first husband (Goldingay, *Israel's Life*, 376).

land, Moses impresses upon them again the importance of keeping the law (26:17–18). When Israel crossed the Jordan, they were to plaster stones and write on them the words of the law so that they would remember the importance of doing what the law commands (27:1–10). Some tribes were to stand on Mount Gerizim to bless Israel, and others on Mount Ebal to curse them (27:11–13). The curses of the covenant are immediately emphasized, and as noted, sins that could be done in secret are the focus of the curses (27:15–25). Israel is summoned to do all that the law says (27:26; 28:1, 15, 58; 29:29; 30:8; 31:12; 32:45). Israel must circumcise its heart (10:16) and fear and love and cling to Yahweh by doing what he commands.

If Israel obeys the Lord, they will experience incomparable blessings (28:1–14). Whether in town or in a field, they will know the Lord's favor. Their land will overflow with riches and produce so that the people will exult with joy. No enemy will conquer them, and they will see that the blessing of the Lord rests on Israel.

Remarkably, while the blessings occupy fourteen verses, the curses are rehearsed for more than fifty verses (28:15–68). The reader is thereby signaled that the curses will come, for Israel will not keep the law. The curses, of course, were also given to motivate Israel to obey and to avoid the terrors that will come. Yahweh promised that if Israel transgresses the law, they will suffer poverty, confusion, frustration, pestilence, famine, disease, defeat before their enemies, insanity, rape, removal of sons and daughters from parents, the eating of their children, and finally exile from the land. All these things will occur if Israel does not obey its covenant Lord. They would experience the curses of the covenant because they "did not serve the LORD your God with joyfulness and gladness of heart" (28:47). The horror of disobedience recounted so vividly in chapter 28 leaves the reader dazed at the prospect that awaits Israel if they fail to do what the Lord commanded. Furthermore, as was already noted, it is clear that Israel certainly will transgress the covenant and experience the terrors recounted here. "Israel seems bound to fail."[48]

In the land of Moab the Lord reminds Israel of the covenant made at Horeb and renews it (29:1–2). As Millar says, "This generation is not to think of the covenant at Horeb as a mere memory, but as *a memory which is actualized in the present at Moab*."[49] The covenant does not apply only to the present generation; it applies to Israel in the future, and they must recall the Lord's

48. Millar, *Now Choose Life*, 171.

49. Ibid., 82. Millar goes on to say, "Moab is the fulcrum of the history of Israel in the view of Deuteronomy" (p. 83) (see also p. 85). Against Hahn (*Kinship by Covenant*, 68–70), who sees the covenant in Deut. 29 as distinct from the Sinai covenant. The word "cut" (*kārat*) typically designates a new covenant. Contextually, however, it seems illegitimate to see an entirely new

gracious work in freeing them from Egyptian bondage, in preserving them in the wilderness, and in giving them the land of others (29:3–16). Awful curses are threatened for those who would depart from the Lord; the curses of the covenant will descend upon them with a vengeance (29:17–28).[50] So terrible will be the devastation that people will think of Sodom and Gomorrah. Such ravaging judgments can be avoided if Israel will obey the law, and yet Moses clearly says that the Lord has not given Israel the ability to keep the law (29:4). Such inability does not translate into lack of culpability. Clearly, they should keep the law, even though their hearts are uncircumcised (10:16). Moses prophesies, therefore, that all the curses pronounced will come upon Israel (30:1).[51]

And yet exile and judgment and curse will not persist forever. When Israel is in exile, they should remember what the Lord prophesied and return to the Lord "with all your soul" (30:2). Then the Lord will restore his people and bring them back from exile, and the blessing in the future will far exceed anything that Israel has experienced thus far (30:3–5). The Lord himself will remedy Israel's fundamental defect, for he will circumcise Israel's heart "so that you will love the LORD your God with all your heart and with all your soul, that you may live" (30:6).[52] Israel's new heart will be an eschatological work of the Lord. Then Israel will obey the Lord and experience his great blessings, and its enemies will know God's curse (30:7–10). Here we see an anticipation of the new covenant fleshed out by Jeremiah (Jer. 31:31–34) and Ezekiel (Ezek. 11:18–19; 36:26–27),[53] which has become a reality in Jesus Christ (Luke 22:20; 1 Cor. 11:25; 2 Cor. 3:4–6; Heb. 8:7–13; 10:15–18). When the new covenant was realized, the prophet like Moses (Jesus Christ) announced God's final word to his people (Deut. 18:15–22; Acts 3:22–23; Heb. 1:2).

Somewhat surprisingly, after proclaiming that the exile was inevitable, Moses then emphasizes that the commandment is not too hard for Israel. It is not in heaven or beyond the sea but is near them so they can obey it (30:11–14). Thereby Moses summons Israel to a decision. They must obey to enjoy life instead of disobeying, which results in death (30:15–20). The call to decision fits with all of Deuteronomy, and if we look ahead, we know that the generation under Joshua obeyed and experienced the blessing, but Israel under the judges

---

covenant, so perhaps the word "cut" is used to indicate a supplementation or renewal of what was given at Horeb.

50. "If Israel is to avoid the journey of reversal, then they must abide by the conditions set out at the new Horeb; they must keep this 'new covenant'" (Millar, *Now Choose Life*, 92).

51. Hahn, *Kinship by Covenant*, 77–78. In this sense Dempster is right in saying that there is "a strong undercurrent of doom . . . in Deuteronomy" (*Dominion and Dynasty*, 120).

52. For the fundamental role of this verse, see also McConville, *Grace in the End*, 136–37; Goldingay, *Israel's Faith*, 379–80.

53. See Millar, *Now Choose Life*, 93; Clements, *Old Testament Theology*, 102–3.

was a different story. How can Moses say that the commandment is not too difficult or far away after being so emphatic about Israel's inability to obey and after stressing that they will go into exile? It is difficult to be sure. Perhaps the narrative flow of the book is important here.[54] God will circumcise the hearts of the generation after the exile so that they will obey Yahweh and experience his blessing.[55] It seems that Paul interpreted Deut. 30:11–14 eschatologically (Rom. 10:5–13), for he sees here a reference not to obedience to the law, but to faith in Jesus Christ. When the new exodus occurs (redemption in Christ Jesus!), then God's people will perceive that it is not fundamentally their work that saves (for they are disobedient). They will understand that God has called them to look outside of themselves to Jesus Christ as the risen and exalted Lord. He is the one who has come down from heaven and been raised from the abyss, so that those who believe in him enjoy life.

The closing chapters of Deuteronomy portray the promise and tragedy of Israel. Yahweh promises that he will go before his people so that they will inherit the land and calls them to be courageous, for he is present with them (31:1–6). Joshua is appointed as the new leader of Israel (31:7–8, 14, 23). Israel will live or die by its obedience to the law, and they are instructed to read it every seven years at the feast of Booths (31:9–13, 24–26). Even though Israel was about to enter the land since they were obedient to the Lord, the tone turns dark and depressing. The Lord predicts that Israel will forsake the covenant and abandon the Lord and turn toward other gods (31:16–30). Yahweh will inflict great evil upon them for their refusal to be faithful to him, and Moses is instructed to write down the song (chap. 32) as a witness against Israel. God is faithful, upright, and just (32:3–4), but Israel is "crooked and twisted"; they are not the Lord's true children (32:5). The Lord's tender care for his people is rehearsed (32:7–14). He set his favor upon Israel and protected them, delivering them from Egypt and watching over them in the wilderness. He gave them a rich and bounteous land. But Israel will respond to such bounty by turning against the Lord, by worshiping and serving other gods (32:15–18). In turn, the Lord will unleash his vengeance and jealousy on Israel (32:19–35). He will send forth disasters upon his people, for they are not different from Sodom and Gomorrah and are children of the serpent instead of being the offspring of the woman (32:32–33; cf. Gen. 3:15).

And yet the song in Deut. 32 ends with hope. When Israel sees that it has no ability to do God's will and sinks into exile, the Lord will show compassion on his people and vindicate them (32:36). He will turn and crush Israel's

---

54. See McConville, *Grace in the End*, 137–38.
55. So Millar, *Now Choose Life*, 176.

adversaries (32:37–42) and will have mercy on Israel once again (32:43). Chapter 33 recounts the blessing of Moses for each tribe, anticipating final redemption and vindication.[56] Israel serves an incomparable God who rides in triumph in the heavens (33:26). Israel will tread (cf. Gen. 3:15) upon the backs of their enemies and live in safety and security in the end (33:27–29). But this is the latter end of Israel. First, they will show their inability to do God's will and will suffer the dire consequences. As Craigie says, "Since Israel's defection was largely a result of the arrogance of believing in their own strength, that arrogance and belief in human strength had to be totally demolished before the people were in a position to realize their need of God's strength."[57] The rebellion and stubbornness of the human heart will be illustrated in Israel's history. The desperate need for the grace of God to be poured out will be evident. Only when Israel realizes that it has no power can the day of triumph arrive. Even Moses cannot bring Israel deliverance. He too is a sinner who does not deserve to enter the land (chap. 34).[58] Millar remarks, "The exclusion of Moses from the land is a dark theme which runs through the whole book . . . , serving to adumbrate the consequences of disobedience for the people in the most powerful way."[59] No one is qualified to enter the land or stay in the land because of his or her virtue.

The book ends with the recognition that no prophet like Moses has arisen in Israel (34:10–12). No signs and wonders like those done by Moses were replicated. Israel needs another prophet to arise (18:15–20)—a prophet superior to Moses, a prophet who can circumcise Israel's heart (10:16; 30:6) so that they will truly love and fear and cling to and obey the Lord.[60] As Sailhamer points out, it is clear in both Joshua (Josh. 23:15–16; 24:31) and Judges (Judg. 2:10–15) that a prophet like Moses did not arise in the days immediately following Moses.[61] Indeed, we can say that such a prophet did not arise during the OT era.[62] Only with the coming of Jesus of Nazareth and the dawning of the kingdom did such a prophet arise, and Yahweh fulfilled his promise that he would circumcise the heart of his people.[63]

---

56. So also Dempster, *Dominion and Dynasty*, 121.

57. Craigie, *Deuteronomy*, 387.

58. Dempster goes too far in saying that Moses "is cursed so that Israel can be blessed" (*Dominion and Dynasty*, 122). The point is that despite all of Moses' virtues, someone better than Moses is needed.

59. Millar, *Now Choose Life*, 97. See also Olson, *Deuteronomy*, 17, passim (though Olson's way of expressing it strays at some points from the intention of Deuteronomy).

60. See Sailhamer, *Pentateuch as Narrative*, 456; idem, *The Meaning of the Pentateuch*, 17–19.

61. Sailhamer, *Pentateuch as Narrative*, 479.

62. Sailhamer (*Old Testament Theology*, 249) argues that Deut. 34 also excludes Elijah as a candidate.

63. It is significant that this final word about no prophet arising after Moses is found in chapter 34, which was written after the death of Moses.

Conclusion

In Deuteronomy Israel is poised to enter the land. Moses exhorts Israel to submit to Yahweh's lordship, to obey his commands. Only if Israel obeys its covenant Lord will it possess the land and continue to abide in it. Such obedience is not legalistic but instead represents a grateful response to Yahweh's love and grace. Deuteronomy specifies in some detail what submission to Yahweh looks like in the concrete details of life. The book does not restrict itself to the immediate future. Moses looks into the future, prophesying that Israel will sin and go into exile. They will fail to adhere to covenant stipulations. And yet that is not the end. A new day will come, and a new heart will be given to Israel. Like Adam, they will be expelled from the land, but Yahweh will not repudiate his people. He will circumcise their hearts and restore them to the land, and they will enjoy his presence again. They will see the King in his beauty. A new prophet would arise who would speak the word of the Lord to Israel. This prophet under whom God will bring in his kingdom is none other than Jesus of Nazareth.

INTERLUDE

A Synopsis of
CREATION TO THE EDGE OF CANAAN

Sailhamer says, "One of the central issues in the message of the Pentateuch is the coming king and his eternal kingdom."[1] God created Adam and Eve, placing them in the garden as his vice-regents to extend his rule to the garden and presumably to extend his rule over the remainder of the earth. They failed to trust in and obey the Lord, so that instead of blessing the world, they introduced the curse. Still, God promised that through the offspring of the woman the serpent would be defeated (Gen. 3:15). Such a victory would be no easy prospect, for the battle between the offspring of the serpent and the offspring of the woman was intense. Indeed, evil was so powerful and dominant that the whole world fell under its sway, except for Noah. The Lord demonstrated his sovereignty over all by judging the world through the flood. The offspring of the serpent would never finally triumph over the Lord. God promises in the covenant enacted with Noah that the world would be preserved until God brings in the promised salvation.

The judgment at the flood did not eradicate human sin, and the building of the tower at Babel showed that human beings still lived for their own glory rather than God's. The depth of human sin indicates that the triumph of the offspring of the woman is no minor matter. It will take nothing less than a miracle, for human beings are naturally in alliance with the serpent. The promise of victory over the serpent begins afresh with one man, Abraham. God called him from Ur of the Chaldees, pledging to him land, children, and blessing that would reach the whole world. The same promise is confirmed

1. Sailhamer, *Meaning of the Pentateuch*, 37.

to Isaac and Jacob. What is quite striking is how slowly the promise was fulfilled. The whole of Genesis is occupied with the issue of offspring. How slow and difficult it was for Abraham to have even one son! The Lord wants to drive home the truth that his kingdom will come only by his grace and his strength, not by virtue of human strength. By the end of Genesis, Israel consists of about seventy people—hardly as numerous as the stars in the sky and the sand on the seashore!

By the time of the exodus, Israel had multiplied rapidly, so the promise of many children was becoming a reality. One element of the promise was finally coming true, but hundreds of years had passed, and Israel was enslaved in Egypt. Nonetheless, the promise of land was now on the verge of being fulfilled, for the Lord liberated his people from Egypt through Moses and brought them to the brink of the land of Canaan. Yahweh triumphed over the offspring of the serpent (Pharaoh) and delivered his people. Yahweh established a covenant with Israel; they would remain his people and in the land if they obeyed the covenant stipulations. The covenant was gracious, for Yahweh first delivered his people by his grace, and Israel was called upon to respond in grateful obedience to Yahweh's redemption.

The narrative slows down considerably, for the question of how the Lord can dwell with his people is raised. Yahweh will dwell in the tabernacle in the midst of Israel. But Yahweh's presence in Israel immediately becomes a problem. Right after the covenant was inaugurated, Israel worshiped the golden calf and broke the covenant. How could Yahweh dwell in the midst of such a stubborn and recalcitrant people? Yahweh's presence with his people must not be treated casually or taken for granted. Moses intercedes for Israel, and the people are forgiven, and Yahweh, as the holy one, gives specific directions as to how he can tabernacle in the midst of a sinful people. Israel's sins would need to be forgiven to maintain fellowship with God, and so sacrifices were instituted so they could receive forgiveness, and priests were ordained to minister in the tabernacle. Israel would be destroyed like the flood generation if they did not follow the Lord's instructions or if they tried to enter his presence on their own initiative.

Yahweh dwelt among the people of Israel, but the second element of the promise to Abraham, entrance into the land, was not yet fulfilled. We see a troubling foreshadowing of what is to come in Exodus, for Israel grumbled and complained instead of trusting the Lord. Israel's disobedience climaxes in failing to obey the Lord's direction to take the land of Canaan in Numbers. They feared that the peoples in Canaan were stronger than they, and therefore they refused to follow the Lord's instructions. Israel showed that it was like Adam and in Adam by its disobedience.

Israel was on the cusp of receiving the second element of the promise of Abraham—the promise of the land—when it transgressed the Lord's will. Deuteronomy represents a renewal of the covenant with Israel, as the nation is again given the opportunity to trust the Lord and to enter the land. Deuteronomy sketches in what it means to trust the Lord, for Moses admonishes Israel to be faithful to their covenant Lord: to love him, hold fast to him, fear him, and keep his commands. God promised the land to Israel, but the land was reserved for a people who were obedient and trusting. In a sense, the land was like the garden for Adam and Eve.[2] It was the place where the Lord would reign over Israel, with the promise that blessing would spread over the whole world.

Still, as the story unfolds, one thing becomes clearer and clearer. The promise would become a reality slowly. Hundreds of years had passed since the promise was made to Abraham, and Israel still was not in the land. Why were things progressing so slowly? One of the purposes of the narrative is to reveal the depth of Israel's evil. Turning a world gone wrong into paradise was no easy prospect, for the human race, including Israel, was opposed to Yahweh's lordship. They needed a new Adam, a king and final prophet who would fulfill the promise made to Abraham. There are intimations in the Pentateuch that a future king would come, one from the tribe of Judah, and he would crush the forehead of Moab, fulfilling Gen. 3:15. The blessing for the whole world would only come through him.

2. See Dempster, *Dominion and Dynasty*, 127.

Part 2

THE STORY
OF POSSESSION, EXILE,
AND RETURN

6

JOSHUA

Land

As we come to the book of Joshua, the story makes a striking advance. Now the second element of the promise to Abraham is about to be fulfilled.[1] In Deuteronomy Israel is on the verge of entering the land, while in Joshua they enter it and possess it.[2] The land is not paradise, but it is an anticipation of paradise regained, an outpost of Yahweh's lordship over his people. The importance of land in Joshua can scarcely be overestimated. Scholars have argued that the book can be structured in terms of verbs that relate to the land: (1) chapters 1–5, where Israel must "pass over" (*'ābar*) to enter the land; (2) chapters 6–11, where Israel "takes" (*lāqaḥ*) the land; (3) chapters 12–22, where Israel "divides" and "apportions" (*ḥālaq*) the land; (4) chapters 23–24, where Israel "serves" (*'ābad*) the Lord in the land.[3] The word "land" (*'ereṣ*) occurs 102 times, the word "inheritance" (*naḥălâ*) fifty times, and the word translated "boundary" or "territory" or "border" (*gĕbûl*) eighty-four times, and the word for "cast lots" or for "allotment" (*gôrāl*) twenty-six times. Truly the book of Joshua is consumed with the place where Yahweh rules over his people. Several chapters are devoted to specifying how the land was divided up among the twelve tribes (15:1–19:51; 21:1–42). Selecting the cities of refuge likewise demonstrates that Israel is now in the land (20:1–9). Indeed, the geographical allotment for each

1. Childs (*Old Testament as Scripture*, 244) says the purpose of the book is to show that God's promise regarding the land was fulfilled.
2. "The land is a central goal toward which the action and thought in the Pentateuch moves" (Howard, *Joshua*, 56).
3. See Dempster, *Dominion and Dynasty*, 126.

tribe is recorded in loving detail.[4] The description of how the land was divided is so particular that we can no longer certify the precise borders. The specificity of the promise is clear from the outset of the book: "From the wilderness and this Lebanon as far as the great river, the river Euphrates, all the land of the Hittites to the Great Sea toward the going down of the sun shall be your territory" (1:4). The boundaries of the land are sketched in for Israel. What is clear is that the land is no abstraction. The word often translated as "possess" or "drive out" (*yāraš*) signifies the concreteness of the promise. Israel takes up residence in the land and is called upon to drive out the Canaanites.

Joshua features,[5] then, the fulfillment of Yahweh's promises.[6] The book underscores the theme noted above. Yahweh fulfills his promises. What he swore to the fathers becomes a reality under Joshua's leadership (21:43–45). The author makes sure that we get the point. "Not one word of all the good promises that the LORD had made to the house of Israel had failed; all came to pass" (21:45). The same truth is reiterated in arresting language near the conclusion of the book (23:14–15). These latter words are bounded by the imminence of Joshua's death. Israel enjoys rest in the land just as Yahweh promised, but will Israel be faithful? Several times in the book the fulfillment of the promise is described in terms of the rest (*nûaḥ*) that Yahweh promised to give to Israel (1:13, 15; 21:44; 22:4; 23:1). The word "rest" suggests that life in the land is delightful and refreshing, the place where Israel can enjoy Yahweh's gracious presence and his reign over them, just as Yahweh's rest on the Sabbath foreshadows the rest that human beings will inherit in the new creation forever (Gen. 2:1–3; Heb. 3:12–4:13; Rev. 21–22). The presence and the rule of the Lord with his people are indicated by the ark, which goes before Israel and dwells in its midst (chaps. 3; 4; 6). Ultimately, the presence of the Lord is represented in the setting up of the sanctuary in Shiloh (18:1).[7]

Yahweh's Sovereignty and Grace

Why and how did Israel receive the land? We have already seen that in granting the land to Israel the Lord fulfilled the promises made to Israel's ancestors: Abraham, Isaac, and Jacob. He would never revoke the covenant enacted with them. The reasons for receiving the land, however, cannot be limited to

4. Dempster says that it seems like "geographical overkill" (*Dominion and Dynasty*, 128).
5. I will often use "Joshua" to designate the book. Context will make it clear when the book is intended or when the person Joshua is in mind.
6. On Joshua as a type of Christ, see Hess, "Joshua," 168–71.
7. See Dempster, *Dominion and Dynasty*, 127.

only one theme, for there is a richness and depth in the presentation found in Joshua. We can also say that Israel received the land because of Yahweh's sovereignty and grace. The land was not obtained because of Israel's virtue or strength. It was a gift of Yahweh given to a people who did not deserve such a stunning gift, showing the Lord's covenant love for Israel.

How can Israel venture to possess Canaan when it is inhabited by nations stronger than they? It is because Yahweh promised them the territory (1:4). And he pledges that Israel will defeat their enemies: "No man shall be able to stand before you all the days of your life. . . . I will not leave you or forsake you" (1:5). Yahweh has promised to "give" (*nātan*) the land to Israel (e.g., 1:2, 3, 6, 11, 13, 15; 2:9, 14; 24).[8] Yahweh encourages Israel by underscoring that his promises will most certainly be fulfilled. For instance, when the spies meet the prostitute Rahab, she astounds them with her words, which the narrator places at a crucial juncture in the story: "I know that the LORD has given you the land, and that the fear of you has fallen upon us, and that all the inhabitants of the land melt away before you. For we have heard how the LORD dried up the water of the Red Sea before you when you came out of Egypt, and what you did to the two kings of the Amorites who were beyond the Jordan, to Sihon and Og, whom you devoted to destruction. And as soon as we heard it, our hearts melted, and there was no spirit left in any man because of you, for the LORD your God, he is God in the heavens above and on the earth beneath" (2:9–11). These words are not included only for the sake of the spies; they are intended for all Israel and also for subsequent readers of the book. Rahab knows that Yahweh has given the land as a gift to Israel. Indeed, Rahab is not alone. Everyone in the land is terrified of Israel. They know what Yahweh did in liberating Israel from Egypt, and therefore they are convinced that they will suffer defeat. We hear later in the story a similar confession on the lips of the Gibeonites (9:9–10, 24), which explains why they pretended to come from afar and made a treaty with Israel. The peoples in Canaan acknowledge that Yahweh is sovereign over all, that he reigns over both heaven and earth (cf. Exod. 20:4; Deut. 4:39; 5:8). The God of Israel is the living and true God, and he will drive the peoples who are currently in the land out of it and grant it to Israel (3:10).

Israel's battles testify to the Lord's sovereignty. He is the divine warrior and king who ensures that they will triumph over their enemies.[9] "Without question it was the intention of the narrator to attribute the causation of victory to

8. Howard rightly says, "God is the one who gives the land; even when humans are the agents of the verb's action; they act on God's behalf" (*Joshua*, 78). See his entire discussion (pp. 77–81).
9. For this theme, see von Rad, *Holy War*; Miller, *Divine Warrior*; Martens, *God's Design*, 47–52.

Yahweh alone, yet in no way did that exclude belligerent activity on the part of Israel."[10] The battle of Jericho, the first battle, is rehearsed in some detail in Joshua because it is paradigmatic (chap. 6). The battle plan is quite plainly absurd. Marching around a city every day with trumpets and horns is no way to win a battle. How can Israel triumph by marching around the city seven times on the seventh day and shouting and blowing on trumpets and horns? The answer is that this is no ordinary battle. This is a holy war ordained by the Lord. He has given the victory to Joshua and Israel (6:2, 16). The bizarre strategy confirmed that Israel could not attribute victory to its own military prowess. Their victory was a gift of grace—an astounding work of the Lord.

The lordship of Yahweh over all is reaffirmed in the battle of the south. When some of the peoples heard that Gibeon had made a treaty with Israel, they were enraged and determined to inflict vengeance upon Gibeon (chap. 10). Israel must come to Gibeon's aid because they are now in covenant with them. But how will Israel triumph over so many kings at once? It was one thing to defeat individual cities such as Jericho and Ai. It is quite another to defeat a league of cities all conspiring to destroy Israel. Yahweh reminded Joshua that he is a divine warrior, and therefore they did not need to fear (10:8). The Lord gave Israel's enemies into the hand of Joshua (10:19). Therefore, "the LORD threw them into a panic before Israel" (10:10), and he "threw down" hail on them from heaven (10:11), even stopping the sun and the moon for a whole day so that Israel could defeat its enemies (10:12–14). Obviously, the battle was utterly unique. Never before or since have the sun and moon been stopped. The narrator summarizes why Israel conquered: "the LORD fought for Israel" (10:14). Repeated elements in a story are of special significance, and so it is striking that we are told three more times that Israel conquered cities because the Lord gave them into their hands (10:19, 30, 32). When the author summarizes the defeat of the southern cities, he returns to the refrain that the Lord "fought for Israel" (10:42). He is the divine warrior and king; no one can conquer him. Israel placed their feet on the necks of their enemies, and they were hung on trees (10:24–27). Dempster rightly says, "There are echoes of the woman's crushing the serpent's head and of the placing of the curse upon the seed of the serpent. . . . The hanging of the bodies on trees graphically shows the cursed fate of these kings."[11]

The battle for the northern cities is painted in similar colors (chap. 11). The coalition of kings seems daunting and impossible for Israel (11:5). We are told that "they came out with all their troops, a great horde, in number

10. Von Rad, *Holy War*, 49.
11. Dempster, *Dominion and Dynasty*, 127.

like the sand on the seashore, with very many horses and chariots" (11:4). But Joshua is instructed not to fear, for the Lord "will give over all of them, slain to Israel" (11:6; cf. 11:8). The war was protracted (11:18), indicating that the stylized versions found here gloss over most of the details of the conflict. What is important is why Israel won the victory. We read in 11:20, "For it was the LORD's doing to harden their hearts that they should come against Israel in battle, in order that they should be devoted to destruction and should receive no mercy but be destroyed, just as the LORD commanded Moses." Israel's enemies believed that they attacked Israel strategically and astutely, but in reality they waged war against Israel because Yahweh hardened their hearts. The opponents of Israel thought that they were saving themselves by warring against Israel, but in fact they were destroying themselves, showing that Yahweh as king is sovereign even over the desires of Israel's enemies. He had, so to speak, lured them to war. A caution is in order. The author is scarcely suggesting that the desires and actions of Israel's adversaries were morally blameless because Yahweh had turned their hearts to fight. Actually, the author shows no concern about explaining how the Lord could control the desires of Israel's enemies and how the actions and motives of their opponents could be evil. He simply assumes that both are true. Yahweh is the sovereign King, who rules to such an extent that he reigns over the desires of Israel's adversaries. At the same time, Israel's opponents were morally responsible for the evil they perpetrated.

The grace and sovereignty of Yahweh are captured in Joshua's last speech, where the covenant between Yahweh and Israel is renewed in Shechem (chap. 24). Joshua reminds Israel of their sordid past; like the Canaanites, "they served other gods" on the other side of the Euphrates (24:2). In other words, Abraham was among the ungodly who worshiped idols (cf. Rom. 4:5), and it was Yahweh who rescued him by choosing him and leading him to Canaan (24:3). We have a summary review of the Lord's goodness, for he gave Isaac to Abraham, fulfilling the promise of multiplying his offspring (24:3–4). When Israel was enslaved in Egypt, they were liberated by the power of God (24:5). Even after Israel had escaped from Egypt, danger had not escaped them (24:6–7). Egypt pursued Israel with its vastly superior military force, and any hope of escape was futile. But Yahweh did not let Israel perish. Darkness obscured Israel from the Egyptians, and when they pursued Israel in the sea, they were drowned (24:6–7). The Lord preserved Israel in the wilderness and enabled them to triumph over the Amorites on the east side of the Jordan; Yahweh "gave them into your hand" so that Israel could possess the land (24:8). Balak summoned Balaam to curse Israel, but Yahweh ruled even over the words of a prophet who despised Israel, so the curse was turned into a blessing (24:9–10).

And when Israel crossed the Jordan, the Lord gave all of Israel's enemies into their hands as well (24:11). Israel is told that it was not "by your sword or by your bow" that they conquered nations (24:12). Human resourcefulness and skill and strength could not explain Israel's victory. So lavish was the goodness of the Lord that he gave them a land that was already cultivated (24:13). They enjoyed vineyards and olive orchards that they did not plant, and in many instances they moved into cities that were already built.

David Howard rightly says that God is "the major character" in the book.[12] "He was the giver of the land in fulfillment of his promises, the one to whom allegiance and obedience were owed, who was a holy and jealous God . . . who fought for his people and gave them rest."[13]

Israel's Call to Obey

The book of Joshua is thoroughly covenantal. Yahweh promises to be Israel's protector and king and to win for them great victories as their warrior. Israel in turn is called upon to be faithful and obedient to its covenant Lord.[14] The obedience of Israel is not abstract. The narrator places Joshua at center stage as the man who will lead Israel into the land of promise. We have seen in previous books that Joshua would replace Moses (Num. 27:15–23; Deut. 1:38; 3:28; 31:3, 7–8, 23; 34:9). In the book of Joshua, Israel is summoned to obey Joshua just as it obeyed Moses (1:16–18), for anyone who rebels against the words of Joshua has rejected Yahweh's lordship. Therefore, Yahweh exalted Joshua at the parting of the Jordan so that Israel knew that he was with Joshua just as he was with Moses (3:7; 4:14). Joshua's prominence in the book goes without saying, for his name is mentioned 168 times. He commands the people, strikes down enemies, speaks the word of the Lord, and allots the land. The Lord is with Joshua just as he was with Moses (1:5).[15] As Howard points out, Joshua has a kingly role and anticipates the future kingship in Israel.[16] Nevertheless, Joshua, like Moses, is not the ultimate leader of Israel.

A fascinating and mysterious story is relayed before the first battle in Jericho (5:13–15). Joshua looked up and saw a man with a sword before him. As the leader of Israel, Joshua demanded to know if he was on the side of Israel or its enemies. The man identified himself as "the commander of the army of the

12. Howard, *Joshua*, 56.
13. Ibid.
14. See Childs, *Old Testament as Scripture*, 245–46.
15. However, Joshua is not said to be a prophet like Moses, nor does he reach Moses' stature (Deut. 34:10–12). See Howard, *Joshua*, 55.
16. Ibid., 55–56.

LORD" (5:14). Joshua "fell . . . and worshiped," asking for instructions (5:14). Like Moses, Joshua is told to remove his sandals because he was standing on holy ground.[17] "It is Yhwh in person as commander who now gives Joshua instructions about what is to happen."[18] Joshua is stripped of the illusion that he has the strength or ability to triumph over the enemy. Even as general of the army he was in a subordinate position subject to the instructions of the commander of the Lord's army. He is unholy standing in the presence of the holy one. Joshua's leadership over Israel is rooted in his worship of Yahweh, and victory depends upon this mysterious commander of the army, not in his own competence. Joshua was called upon to be strong, courageous, and careful to keep the Torah (1:6–9), but he needed the grace and forgiveness of Yahweh, just like the rest of Israel.

When Israel was initially defeated at Ai, Joshua implied that Yahweh was to blame, that he had abandoned his promises (7:6–9). Joshua, however, was blind to the real situation, not realizing that Israel had violated the ban on goods in Jericho (7:10–12). Moreover, Israel made a covenant with Gibeon, promising them that they would be allies instead of enemies (chap. 9). The covenant seemed fitting because the Gibeonites gave every evidence of being a people far from Israel. Israel and Joshua failed to perceive that Gibeon was deceiving them, and the blame is attributed to their not asking "counsel from the LORD" (9:14). The narrator clarifies in these two accounts that Joshua's own wisdom and prowess were not responsible for victory. Yahweh exalted him, but his strength did not lie in himself. It was only as one who acknowledged and obeyed the Lord that he enjoyed victory.

What was true of Joshua—he was called to humble obedience—was true also of Israel. At the outset of the book Israel is summoned to rise up and to enter the land with the promise that Yahweh has given them the land (1:2–3). They are to be strong, courageous, and obedient to everything Joshua demands (1:16–18). Israel's trust and obedience are rooted in the saving acts of the Lord. The ark of the Lord precedes Israel into the Jordan (3:11), and the Lord dried up the Jordan just as he did the Red Sea so that Israel crossed over on dry land (3:12–17). The passing through the Jordan confirmed that the God of the exodus continued to dwell with Israel. His mighty works were not at an end, showing that Israel's entrance into the land was a miracle. Hence, Israel's obedience was in response to the Lord's saving love; it was covenant obedience. Stones were taken out of the Jordan as a memorial of what the

17. For the parallels to Moses at the burning bush, see Hamilton, *God's Glory in Salvation*, 148–49.
18. Goldingay, *Israel's Gospel*, 493.

Lord did for Israel so that the children of coming generations might also trust in the Lord and obey him (chap. 4). Both the current and future generations of Israel should know "that the hand of the LORD is mighty, that you may fear the LORD your God forever" (4:24).

The people of the covenant cannot and must not enter the land before they have the sign of the covenant, and therefore Israel was circumcised at Gilgal before possessing the land (5:1–9). The reproach of Egypt was removed at Gilgal because Israel was about to possess the land and to experience rest in its own land. The land pledged to Abraham was about to become theirs, but the blessing of the land belonged only to an obedient people, to a covenant people who took upon themselves the sign of the covenant (cf. Gen. 17:9–14; Exod. 4:24–26; Lev. 12:3). Significantly, Israel celebrated Passover as well, for they were on the verge of entering the land, so it was fitting that Israel celebrated liberation from Egypt because they were freed to possess their own land.

I have already noted the strange plan of battle at Jericho in Joshua (chap. 6), though Israel still played a role, for they were called upon to obey the bizarre instructions. Israel could have rejected the Lord's battle plan as completely impractical and could have complained that it was doomed to failure. Once the walls collapsed, Yahweh had further instructions for Israel. Everything in the city was under the ban (ḥērem) (6:17–19). Everything was to be destroyed, including every human being (6:21, 24). Only Rahab the prostitute and her family were to be spared, along with the silver and gold that were to be kept for the Lord's treasury. It is clear that the command to wipe out the inhabitants came from Yahweh. Apparently, the evil of the Canaanites was so pervasive that it warranted their complete annihilation (cf. Gen. 15:13–16).[19] Perhaps this is the best place to reflect on Rahab as an exception (Josh. 2), for the story indicates that those outside of Israel could also be included in his saving purposes. Indeed, what is astonishing is that Rahab was a prostitute, which demonstrates that forgiveness was available for anyone who was repentant and turned to Yahweh for salvation. Rahab's protection of the spies indicated that she had cast her lot with Israel and with the God of Israel, that she had put her trust in Yahweh (cf. Heb. 11:31; James 2:25).

There was a fly in the ointment, however. Unbeknownst to Joshua and the rest of Israel, the injunction that everything be devoted to Yahweh for destruction or put into the treasury was violated (7:1). Achan had taken some of the devoted things. The alien world of the Bible surfaces here. One might think that the Lord would be pleased, since everyone in Israel obeyed except

19. The Genesis text indicates Yahweh patiently waited four hundred years for the inhabitants of the land to repent. When they did not do so, he acted in judgment.

for one person. Instead, we read that "the anger of the LORD burned against the people of Israel" (7:1). Even though Israel as a whole was ignorant of Achan's sin, thirty-six were slain in battle because of Achan's treachery (7:5). Israel's life was not one of solitary individualism. When Yahweh confronted Joshua, he declared, "Israel has sinned; they have transgressed my covenant" (7:11). The thing under the ban is in Israel's midst and thus Israel itself has "become devoted for destruction" (7:12). Israel will lose the gracious presence of the Lord unless they act. The penalty was remarkably severe, and was inflicted on Achan's entire family (7:14–26). The presence of such an egregious sin in Israel reveals the holiness of the Lord, showing that his commands must not be trifled with. Israel would experience the same fate as the inhabitants of Jericho if they violated the provisions of the covenant. Caleb, however, stands out as the polar opposite of Achan. Caleb could truthfully say, "I wholly followed the LORD my God" (14:8), and he drove out Israel's enemies (15:14).

The lives of Achan and Caleb represent the two ways that Israel could go. Would they choose the blessing or the curse? Despite the remarkable victories recorded in Joshua, there are indications that Israel did not obey to the extent it should, casting a pall over their future prospects. The narrator notes several instances where Israel did not drive out the inhabitants wholly, where the inhabitants of the land continued to dwell with Israel (13:13; 15:63; 16:10; 17:12–13; 19:47). When Israel possessed the land, they followed Yahweh's instructions about building an altar on Mount Ebal, and they read the law (8:30–35), both the blessings and the curses, on Mount Gerizim and Mount Ebal (cf. Deut. 11:29; 27:1–26). Israel's covenantal responsibilities were rehearsed.[20] As the book closes, Joshua reminds Israel that it must be faithful to the covenant. The tribes east of the Jordan are exhorted in Deuteronomic covenantal terms:[21] "Only be very careful to observe the commandment and the law that Moses the servant of the LORD commanded you, to love the LORD your God, and to walk in all his ways and to keep his commandments and to cling to him and to serve him with all your heart and with all your soul" (22:5). Devotion to the covenant is expressed in both affections and actions, in loving the Lord and doing what he says. Israel must "be very strong" and keep what is written in the law of Moses (23:6–8). They are commanded to "cling to the LORD your God" (23:8), love him (23:11), and resist assimilating with the pagan nations (23:7, 12). Transgressing the covenant and worshiping

20. There are two covenant renewals in the book of Joshua, at Mount Ebal (8:30–35) and at Shechem (chap. 24). See Howard, *Joshua*, 59.

21. It is a commonplace in scholarship that Joshua is part of Deuteronomistic history. Theologically, this certainly is the case, but my concern here does not pertain to historical reconstruction.

other gods will have devastating consequences; Yahweh will respond in anger and destroy Israel (23:16).

The covenant renewal at Shechem closes the book (chap. 24). As already noted, the chapter begins by rehearsing the Lord's saving work on behalf of Israel (24:1–13; cf. 24:17–18), his grace that precedes demand. In light of this, Israel must fear Yahweh and renounce worshiping other gods (24:14). Joshua sternly summons Israel to serve the Lord, to be faithful covenant partners (24:15–16). As we saw in Deuteronomy, there is an intimation of what is to come—a hint that the Mosaic covenant is defective because of the hearts of Israel. Joshua proclaims that Israel is not able to serve the Lord, with the result that the jealous wrath of God will burn against them (24:19–20). Still, Joshua's generation insists that they will serve the Lord (24:21). The people make a covenant to serve the Lord (24:22–27), knowing that their words of promise will indict them if they turn away from the Lord. Indeed, Joshua wrote down their covenant promises and set up a stone as a witness to this. The book concludes on an ambiguous note (24:31–33). On the one hand, God had fulfilled his promises! Israel was in the land, and Joseph's bones, just as he requested, were buried in Canaan (cf. Gen. 50). The generation of Joshua continued to serve the Lord. On the other hand, the book ends with the death of Eleazar suggesting that a new day was coming—a day when Israel would not be faithful to the Lord.[22] Perhaps Howard is correct in suggesting that the close of the book intimates that Israel was lacking a godly leader to replace Joshua, that they needed a king to rule them.[23] If so, the book of Judges nicely follows the story in Joshua, and Joshua points ahead canonically to the Messiah proclaimed in the NT.

Conclusion

Joshua represents a major advance in the story line of the Scriptures because the second dimension of the promise to Abraham is fulfilled: Israel possesses the land of Canaan. The narrative emphasizes that Israel dispossessed the nations in the land through the power of Yahweh. Israel could not boast of its military strategy or prowess. It was the Lord's might and sovereignty that accomplished the victory. Israel, like Adam, now lived in a land under the Lord's care, but they entered the land only because they were obedient to their covenantal King, and they would remain in the land only if they continued to trust and obey him. Hence, Joshua summoned the people to serve the Lord, to be faithful to their covenant with Yahweh. If they strayed from the Lord, they would face his judgment.

22. See Dempster, *Dominion and Dynasty*, 128–30.
23. Howard, *Joshua*, 63.

7

JUDGES

Introduction

A new generation dawns with the book of Judges. On the heels of the book of Joshua, we wonder if Israel will be faithful to the covenant that was reaffirmed at the conclusion of Joshua, for it is clear that Israel will prosper only if they obey their covenant Lord and King. Two-thirds of the promise made with Abraham had been fulfilled: Israel enjoyed a large population, and they inhabited the land of Canaan. But would they bless the whole world? Would the universal blessing promised to Abraham become a reality through them? The book of Judges dashes any hopes that worldwide blessing would come anytime soon through Israel.

Israel Needs a King

Careful consideration of the book of Judges shows that the idea that Israel needs a king is pervasive.[1] Gregory Wong sees the theme of the book as "progressive deterioration,"[2] rightly arguing that the fundamental problem with

---

1. Against Block, *Judges, Ruth*, 59; rightly Armerding, "Judges," 175; Alexander, *Servant King*, 47. Dumbrell rightly argues that what happens in Judges relates to the whole of Israel. "It is also customarily suggested that the Book of Judges describes merely local incidents involving isolated tribes. However, no OT book uses the term 'Israel' or the phrase 'all Israel' more frequently in relation to its length. From beginning to end, we are concerned with what will happen representatively to 'all Israel.' Since each local event in a small territory like Palestine inevitably influences the whole, each event assumes an 'all-Israelite' dimension in the writer's mind" (*Faith of Israel*, 78).
2. Wong, *Book of Judges*, 249.

Israel was not political but spiritual.[3] Barry Webb says, "Israel is depicted as spiraling downwards into worse and worse apostasy."[4] Dumbrell observes, "Everything in these bizarre accounts commends God's direct leadership of God's people as the sole guarantee that Israel will have a future."[5] It is more likely, however, that the author thinks that Yahweh's rule over the people will be *mediated* through a human king, seeing a fulfillment of the prophecies found in Gen. 49:8–12 and Num. 24:17. Yahweh's rule will be realized through the offspring of the woman (cf. Gen. 3:15). Such a view fits canonically, for the promise of a human king is picked up in the books that immediately follow Judges. The book of Ruth promises a future king from Boaz's line, and 1–2 Samuel features the fulfillment of that promise. Indeed, 2 Sam. 7 pledges that David's dynasty will never end, that it will last forever.[6] In light of the canon, then, Judges too looks forward to the coming of the Christ.

The book of Joshua testifies to the faithfulness of the Lord, for he grants to Israel the land that he promised. In reading Joshua, we might think that Israel is on the verge of being the agent by which blessing and joy come to the world. And indeed, Judges begins on an optimistic note. Israel is sensitive to the Lord's direction and inquires of him as to who should fight against the Canaanites (1:1). Judah is to take the lead, which perhaps is a hint that Israel's king will come from Judah (1:2). Victories are granted to Judah and Simeon because the sovereign Lord, who rules over all peoples, gives their enemies into their hands (1:2, 4).[7] Triumph belongs not only to Judah but also to Benjamin and Joseph (1:1–26) as the children of the Lord.[8] Certainly, the Lord who was with Joshua continues to dwell in Israel, and where his presence abides, there is victory.

The optimism with which Judges opens collapses with a resounding thud. "No leader after Joshua has arisen. The unity of the nation has been fractured."[9] Suddenly the tone of chapter 1 changes, and a new refrain dominates the

---

3. Ibid., 252. Israel refused to acknowledge Yahweh's authority, and the problem with Israel was attributed to its leaders (see ibid., 253).

4. B. Webb, *Book of Judges*, 112.

5. Dumbrell, *Faith of Israel*, 80. See also Dumbrell, "'No King in Israel'"; Wong, *Book of Judges*, 212–23.

6. Contrary to my thesis, Webb (*Book of Judges*, 202–3, 210, 265n50) does not see the issue of the monarchy playing a central role in Judges.

7. Waltke (*Old Testament Theology*, 594), however, notes that Israel in part adopted Canaanite ways even in its initial victories.

8. Even in this section all is not well. As Wong notes of 1:21, the "failure of Benjamin sets an ominous tone for the whole section" (*Book of Judges*, 29). See also B. Webb, *Book of Judges*, 91.

9. Childs, *Old Testament as Scripture*, 259.

remainder of the chapter (1:27–36). Whether it involved the Israelite tribes of Manasseh, Ephraim, Zebulun, Asher, Naphtali, Dan, or Joseph, the Canaanite peoples were not expelled from the land. They lived in and among Israel. In some instances, Israel subjected the peoples to forced labor, but the Lord clearly enjoined Israel to wipe out the Canaanites entirely lest Israel be snared by the gods of the nations and forsake the Lord. We are not told in chapter 1 that Israel was led astray by idols, but the chapter produces a sense of foreboding. If Israel lives *among* the Canaanites, it likely will not be long before Israel begins to live *like* the Canaanites.

Israel was in the land, but what would their life in the land be like? They are, in a sense, given the same mandate as Adam. Just as Adam was to rule the garden for God's glory, so Israel was to rule the land of promise for his glory. Adam was to remove the serpent from the garden, and Israel was to remove the Canaanites (the children of the serpent) from the land of promise. In many ways, Judges forecasts the remainder of the OT, for Israel, though it starts well, veers away from the Lord. The story of Judges is mixed and ambiguous; there are some bright spots on the horizon. The trend, however, slopes downward instead of upward. The gloomy clouds obscure the rays of the sun.

The substance of Judges is conveyed by chapter 2. The angel of Yahweh speaks to Israel, reminding them of the Lord's covenant love, for he redeemed Israel from Egypt and pledged to be faithful to the covenant (2:1). Israel in turn was required to be faithful to covenant stipulations and to destroy the cultic places of worship in the land (2:2). Since Israel failed to heed the Lord's words, the gods whom they have chosen will become a snare to them (2:3). Israel wept and sacrificed to the Lord (2:4–5), but their weeping and devotion were short-lived. The narrator revisits the days of Joshua: Israel served Yahweh during his lifetime and the lifetime of other leaders during Joshua's era (2:6–7). Those who saw the works of the Lord trusted and obeyed him. But a new generation arose "who did not know the LORD or the work that he had done for Israel" (2:10). Apparently, the Deuteronomic ideal of teaching children to love, fear, and hold fast to the Lord had failed (see Deut. 4:4; 10:20; 11:22; 13:5; 30:20). Israel was in the land but not in the Lord. Since Israel departed from the Lord, they served the Baals and Ashtaroth (2:11–13). A refrain in the book of Judges is that Israel "did what is evil in the eyes of the LORD" (2:11; 3:7, 12; 4:1; 6:1; 10:6; 13:1), which reflects the fundamental problem with Israel, that "everyone did what was right in his own eyes" (17:6; 21:25).[10] Yahweh responded with anger and handed Israel over to their enemies (2:14–15). As Dempster says, "The Israelites experience 'Egyptian' oppression all over again, only this time

10. See B. Webb, *Book of Judges*, 200.

on their own soil."[11] When Israel departed from the covenant, they experienced the curses of the covenant (see Lev. 26; Deut. 26–28).

And yet the Lord did not abandon Israel entirely. He sent judges to save them when they cried out to him in their affliction (2:16, 18). These judges were spiritual and military leaders who delivered Israel in their distress, but they were not kings (17:6; 18:1; 19:1; 21:25). They were not a permanent solution to Israel's problems. And Israel's flaws were profound. They "whored after other gods and bowed down to them" (2:17). They did not heed the instructions of the judges or live in accordance with the commands of the Lord. Israel vacillated (2:19). For a time, they would follow the Lord when a new judge arose, but after the death of the judge they would abandon the Lord and serve and follow other gods. Israel proved itself to be stubborn and recalcitrant by regularly transgressing covenantal obligations (2:20). It was because of Israel's disobedience and apostasy that they could not displace the nations in Canaan (2:21). The Lord allowed nations to remain in Israel to see if Israel would follow his commands (2:22–23; 3:1–5). The true nature of Israel was immediately revealed. They intermarried among the Canaanites and worshiped their gods (3:6–7).

The Judges or Saviors of Israel

When Israel sinned and cried out to the Lord, he raised up "judges" (*šōpĕṭîm*) for his people. Daniel Block argues that the judges are fundamentally saviors and deliverers.[12] Hence, their fundamental role should be described as soteriological rather than legal or judicial. The cycles of disobedience and judgment in the book show both the mercy and the righteousness of the Lord. Yahweh is the holy one of Israel—the awesome King. Israel regularly violated the covenant stipulations (6:8–10), and as a result, in accord with the blessings and curses described in Deuteronomy, they were punished by the Lord. Repeatedly Israel falls under the dominion of foreign peoples because of their sin. What is remarkable, however, is the mercy of Yahweh. Israel's continued unfaithfulness and disobedience warranted irrevocable judgment, and yet the Lord delivers Israel, when they repent and cry out for mercy, again and again. Such deliverances demonstrate that judgment is Yahweh's strange work, that he longs because of his love to bless his people. They also forecast what Paul teaches in Rom. 9–11: God's final word for his people will be a merciful one.

11. Dempster, *Dominion and Dynasty*, 131.
12. Block, *Judges, Ruth*, 23. However, Deborah primarily has a judicial role instead of a saving role (4:4–5). See Wong, *Book of Judges*, 244–45; B. Webb, *Book of Judges*, 134.

Despite Israel's sin, it will not be wiped out entirely; the Israelites, in spite of their sins, remain the people of the King.

The judges or deliverers the Lord sent to rescue his people from oppressors reveal his saving mercy. These victories are "a fulfillment of the promise as the seed of the woman establishes dominion by defeating oppression."[13] What can we say about these saviors?[14] The narrator often calls attention to how unusual they were, indicating that they are unexpected saviors. Deliverance came from Ehud, a man who was left-handed (chap. 3; esp. 3:15, 28), and he slays the king in a most startling way.[15] Perhaps even more astonishing, Deborah, a woman, was a judge of Israel who played a role in its triumph over its enemies (chaps. 4–5). Her sidekick, Barak, lacked the courage to lead Israel on his own, entreating Deborah to go with him to the battle, and another woman, Jael, displays more initiative and courage than Barak when she ingeniously assassinates the enemy commander Sisera.[16] As Webb says, Yahweh was "realizing his providential designs by means which completely overturn human expectations."[17] Israel triumphed over Sisera and Jabin. Yahweh as the great King and sovereign Lord delivered his people from bondage just as he did at Sinai (5:4–5, 11). According to the song in chapter 5, the "human element in the victory is so completely eclipsed by the intervention of heavenly forces that Barak and his forces are not even mentioned in the description of the battle!"[18] The focus of the story is on the "'victorious deeds' of Yahweh himself," and the story is designed to bring praise to Yahweh.[19] Yahweh is utterly unique and "wonderful" (13:18).[20]

When Israel was under the thumb of Midian, Yahweh raised up Gideon as a judge and deliverer (chaps. 6–8). Gideon was a most unlikely leader. He recognized that he was from the weakest clan in Manasseh, and that he was the least honored among his father's children (6:15). The key to victory was that the Lord had sent him and promised to be with him, just as he sent Moses and was with him (6:14, 17). Gideon's faith was faltering and weak, and so he needed sign after sign to verify that Yahweh had truly sent him (6:17–23, 36–40; 7:9–14). He was too fearful to tear down Baal's altar during the day, and so he did it during the night, when he would be unobserved (6:25–27).

---

13. Dempster, *Dominion and Dynasty*, 132.

14. Dumbrell (*Faith of Israel*, 77) points out that the Spirit in Judges is associated with "divine rule."

15. Against Wong (*Book of Judges*, 118–23), there is no suggestion here that Ehud sinned.

16. See Waltke, *Old Testament Theology*, 600.

17. B. Webb, *Book of Judges*, 138.

18. Ibid., 142.

19. Ibid., 144.

20. See ibid., 166–67.

Indeed, like Ehud, Gideon's strength came from Yahweh's Spirit (3:10; 6:34). The Lord underscores that the victory is his, for Gideon's army of twenty-two thousand is whittled down to three hundred in order to show that military prowess could not account for Israel's victory (7:1–8). Gideon wins because Yahweh gave Midian into his hand (7:9, 14–15). The battle plan reminds the reader of the battle of Jericho.[21] Israel blew on trumpets and smashed the jars in their hands, and the Midianite army imploded (7:19–22).

As the story goes on in Judges, it becomes apparent, despite the victories won by the judges, that they are weak and fallible.[22] We saw that Barak was weak and fearful, and Gideon shared the same weaknesses. The faults of the judges whom Yahweh raised up to deliver Israel indicate that Israel needed a king—a man after God's own heart. Indeed, Israel asked Gideon to serve as their king because he saved them from their enemies (8:22). Gideon declined, saying that neither he nor his son (a clear critique of Abimelech [see below]) should serve as king, but rather "the LORD will rule over you" (8:23). Gideon's fallibility immediately emerged, for he made a golden ephod that Israel worshiped instead of the Lord (8:24–27),[23] demonstrating that Gideon was unworthy to be king, and that Israel was failing to subject itself to the lordship of Yahweh.[24]

Actually, Gideon, in spite of his faults as Israel's judge, restrained Israel's defection from Yahweh. After his death the people turned to Baal worship, forgetting about Yahweh's saving deliverance through Gideon (8:33–34). After his death things only got worse (chap. 9). Abimelech (whose name means "my father is king") took on what Gideon refused to do. He appointed himself as king. He was a worthless king and had worthless followers (9:4), for he arrogated leadership to himself by slaying Gideon's seventy sons. Jotham, in his fable of the trees, characterized the rule of Abimelech (9:7–15). His rule was not fruitful and pleasing like the rule of an olive tree, fig tree, or grapevine. Instead, his rule was as worthless and annoying as having a bramble rule over the rest of the trees. The pact between Shechem and Abimelech was mutually advantageous at the outset, but it was an evil collaboration, and in it were the seeds of their mutual destruction. Their downfall was the result

21. See von Rad, *Israel's Historical Traditions*, 328–29.
22. Block argues that the theme of Judges is "the Canaanization of Israelite society during the period of the settlement" (*Judges, Ruth*, 58 [italics removed]). Although I do not see this as the theme of the book, it surely is emphasized, and Block rightly points it out. On the weaknesses and sins of the judges, see also Wong, *Book of Judges*, 156–85.
23. House (*Old Testament Theology*, 219) remarks that the golden ephod reminds us of the golden calf.
24. B. Webb argues that the ephod was intended to be an object of inquiry of the Lord, that it was "an act of piety that goes wrong" (*Book of Judges*, 153).

of the Lord's will (9:20), for he sent an "evil spirit" between Abimelech and the Shechemites (9:23–24). The narrator closes the story by underscoring that God repaid both Abimelech and the Shechemites for the evil that they did, showing that Jotham's fable was no idle word (9:53–54).

Predictably, Israel turned again to false gods and was handed over to the Philistines and Ammonites (10:6–9). Israel was supposed to be the offspring of the woman, but they were virtually indistinguishable from the offspring of the serpent. Israel, by forsaking the Lord, abandoned the covenant, but when they were oppressed, they entreated Yahweh for mercy (10:10–16). The Lord said that he would save them no more, for they were faithless time and again; instead, they should summon the gods whom they worshiped to deliver them (10:13–14). Israel, however, put itself in Yahweh's hands; they ceased serving false gods and "served the Lord" (10:16). The mercy of the Lord is evident, for "he became impatient over the misery of Israel" (10:16) and raised up Jephthah to deliver them (chaps. 11–12). Israel realized it needed a leader (10:18), but once again a most improbable prospect emerged, for Jephthah was the son of a prostitute and rejected by his family (11:1–3). Nevertheless, Israel entreated Jephthah to serve as their leader, for they needed someone with military skills to conquer their enemies (11:6–11). Jephthah reminded the Ammonites of Israel's deliverance from Egypt and their victories east of the Jordan (11:13–26), showing that Yahweh had given Israel the land. Jephthah did not conquer in his own strength but rather triumphed through the Spirit (11:29). At the same time, Jephthah was deeply flawed, and his devotion to Yahweh was mixed with Canaanite religion, so much so that he offered, according to the most likely reading, his own daughter in sacrifice.

Perhaps the most unusual judge of all was Samson (chaps. 13–16). He was blessed with supernatural strength given to him by Yahweh.[25] There is no idea here of a natural power intrinsic to Samson. The narrator emphasizes that the Spirit of the Lord "rushed upon" Samson (14:6, 19; 15:14; cf. 13:25). The narrator calls attention to the Spirit empowering Samson much more emphatically than he does in the case of the other judges. The mighty and unusual deeds, therefore, were God's work in him and functioned as a punishment of the Philistines for their mistreatment of Israel. The Lord was even working in Samson's choice of a wife, for it became the occasion by which the Philistines were harmed (14:1–4). The special role of Samson is underscored, for even before his birth he was called to be a Nazirite, showing his complete devotion to Yahweh by abstaining from alcohol, grapes, raisins, and unclean foods and

25. For echoes of previous stories in Judges in the account of Samson's life, see B. Webb, *Book of Judges*, 164–65.

by refusing to cut his hair (13:4–7, 14–15). The special requirements for Samson as a Nazirite are recounted three times in chapter 13, underlining the truth that he was a unique child dedicated entirely to Yahweh. Samson's uniqueness is communicated also in his being born to a woman who is barren (13:3). Such a birth reminds readers of the births of Isaac and Jacob and Esau, forecasting that the Lord would be with Samson in an extraordinary way. Moreover, the angel of Yahweh appeared to Samson's mother and father, featuring again the significance of Samson's life.

Samson indeed was unusually gifted, but also he was plagued with problems. He was attracted to foreign women instead of those from the covenant people of the Lord. The Lord uses his power to inflict punishment upon the Philistines, but the reality portrayed is complex, for Samson's own desires are defiled by his selfish will, and some of his responses are vindictive and petty (chaps. 14–15). Samson's weaknesses are on display in his encounter with Delilah (16:4–21). As a Nazirite, he should be committed to the Lord, but his heart is seduced by a woman who loves other gods. As Webb says, "He wants to be 'like any other man.'"[26] He betrays to her that the source of his strength is not in himself, and he is literally shorn of his strength. Dempster rightly notes that Samson "represents his own people, who had a supernatural origin, were set apart from among the nations with a distinctive vocation, broke their vows and were enamoured of foreign idols, until finally they lost their identity and spiritual power and became the blind slaves of their oppressors in exile."[27] As Wong points out, Samson falls for foreign women like Israel falls for foreign gods.[28]

But even though Samson, like Israel, was unfaithful to Yahweh, his infidelity was not the last word. The grace of God is communicated in the words "But the hair of his head began to grow again" (16:22). This is "one of those pregnant sentences that is the mark of genius."[29] The Philistines gave praise to their god for triumphing over Samson (16:23–24). But Yahweh was not finished with Samson, and Samson was not finished with the Philistines (16:25–30). Samson brought down the pillars of the house and died along with three thousand Philistines.[30] For the narrator, this was not the work merely of selfish vengeance; it was a work of Yahweh in inflicting retribution upon

---

26. Ibid., 169.

27. Dempster, *Dominion and Dynasty*, 132. See also Childs, *Old Testament as Scripture*, 261; Dumbrell, *Faith of Israel*, 79; B. Webb, *Book of Judges*, 179.

28. Wong, *Book of Judges*, 232.

29. B. Webb, *Book of Judges*, 168, quoting Crenshaw.

30. Webb (ibid., 172) points out that Israel does not call out to the Lord in the Samson cycle, but Samson calls out to the Lord here.

the Philistines, for the account plainly teaches that Yahweh gave Samson the strength to shatter the Philistines. Samson's end also gives hope that Israel will find a new day after exile.[31]

If we assess the judges of Israel as a whole, including the NT witness, we see that they are heralded as those who exercised faith (Heb. 11:32). Such an assessment is not contrary to the OT, for the accounts in Judges focus on the courage and military exploits of those such as Gideon, Jephthah, and Samson. Even though the failings and frailties of the judges also receive attention in Judges, the NT shines the light upon the faith of the judges. Such a perspective corrects a possible misperception of the OT witness. The weaknesses of the judges may lead us to think they are fundamentally failures, but the NT actually confirms the main story that we read in Judges itself. The judges trusted in God and acted on that trust and thereby delivered Israel from its enemies. In other words, the judges should be remembered primarily as people of faith, not as those who disobeyed the Lord. And yet the flaws of the judges also play a canonical role. Clearly, the judges are not the final saviors of Israel. The book of Judges itself underscores that there was no king in Israel, and Israel's fundamental problem was not solved by the judges. Webb, reflecting on Samson's life, says, "The climax combines, paradoxically, achievement and failure, blindness and recognition, resentment and acceptance."[32] Therefore, the book looks forward to a future day when a king would arise. Surely, David is in view here, but David shares the same faults to some extent as the judges, and so ultimately the book points to the arrival of one greater than David—Jesus the Christ. He is the savior of Israel and the world, and he is the true king whom Israel needs.

The End of the Matter

The narrator of Judges dramatically depicts Israel's need for a righteous king in the concluding chapters of the book (chaps. 17–21).[33] That Israel lacked a king is repeatedly noted in these chapters (17:6; 18:1; 19:1; 21:25), and it appears at key junctures in the narrative and functions as a resounding conclusion to the book. The two stories that conclude the book depict the shocking extent of evil in Israel, showing again why leadership is needed. The story in chapters 17–18 illustrates the presence of deviancy in Israel. A young man, Micah, stole from his mother eleven hundred pieces of silver. He confessed his sin and returned

31. So Dumbrell, *Faith of Israel*, 79; against House, *Old Testament Theology*, 220.
32. B. Webb, *Book of Judges*, 172.
33. See Satterthwaite, "'No King in Israel.'"

the money, but the good that he did was turned to evil ends, for the money was used to make idols. A Levite came along and was installed as a priest in Micah's house, but it was a priesthood devoted to the worship of idols.[34] Wong rightly points out that the actions described here echo Gideon's idolatry in the crafting of the ephod.[35] Gideon, like Micah, started out by doing something good by declining the kingship (8:22–23), but, inexplicably, he followed up on this by making an ephod that ensnared Israel in idolatry (8:24–28).

One evil led to another, and the tribe of Dan was seeking out a place of residence and came to Laish. The people in Laish were secure and at peace, but they were brutally and viciously destroyed by the Danites so that the tribe of Dan could possess the city as their home. As Wong argues, the Danites should have offered Laish peace in accord with Deut. 20:10–15.[36] The sheer thuggery of the Danites is evident in their treatment of Micah and the Levite priest. They inquired of the priest in their exploratory mission in which they spied out conditions in Laish. When they returned again to Ephraim, they seized Micah's household idols and convinced the Levite to travel with them so that he could serve as the priest for an entire tribe instead of a single home. When Micah pursued Dan and protested, they threatened his safety and security if he acted further. Micah certainly was no angel, but the behavior of the Danites shows that Israel's spiritual condition was at its nadir. Indeed, the news is even more depressing, for the Levite described was the great-grandson of none other than Moses himself (18:30).

The narrator climaxes the book with another story about a Levite and his concubine. His concubine fled from him, and he pursued her in Bethlehem. On his way back to Ephraim, he spent the night in Gibeah of Benjamin instead of Jerusalem because the latter was still under pagan control. The master's comment "We will not turn aside into the city of foreigners, who do not belong to the people of Israel" (19:12) turns out to be highly ironic, given what happened to him at Gibeah. Remarkably, Gibeah has become like Sodom (cf. Gen. 19). Like Sodom, in Gibeah there is only one person who showed hospitality, inviting the travelers to lodge with him, demonstrating the selfish will that reigned in the town (19:15–20). The narrator underlines this truth by saying, "No one took them into the house to spend the night" (19:15), and repeats this fact in 19:18. Shockingly, like those in Sodom, the men of Gibeah wanted to have sexual relations with the man from the hill country of Ephraim (19:22). The master remonstrated with the men (19:23–24), just

34. The sins of the Levite are well detailed by Wong, *Book of Judges*, 89–91.
35. Ibid., 83–89.
36. Ibid., 39.

as Lot did with the men of Sodom (see Gen. 19:7–8). In the end, the man's own behavior was "appallingly callous."[37] The men of Gibeah seized his concubine, raped her, and abused her all night until she died. When confronted with the evil in Gibeah, Benjamin fell prey to tribal loyalty rather than justice and went to war in defense of Gibeah (chap. 20). The horror of what occurred is memorialized in 19:30: "And all who saw it said, 'Such a thing has never happened or been seen from the day that the people of Israel came up out of the land of Egypt until this day.'" Repeated assaults finally led to the defeat of Benjamin, but the entire account called into question whether Israel was truly the people of the Lord. Indeed, Benjamin as a tribe was almost wiped out, signifying what would happen to Israel as a whole if they defected from Yahweh.[38] Devices were found to prevent Benjamin from dissolving entirely, preserving the integrity of the tribe (chap. 21).

Conclusion

Judges comes to an end. But where is Israel? It is in the land and has a healthy population. Two-thirds of the promise of Abraham had become a reality. But things are not right. Israel was devoted to the Lord for short periods of time when things got desperate, but when life was comfortable, they fell into idolatry and lived no differently from the Canaanites. Clearly, the judges were not a permanent solution for Israel's problem. Instead of being a blessing to the world, Israel seemed to be cursed along with the world. Israel clearly needed a new direction. They needed a king. They needed to be devoted to Yahweh in the land that he gave to them. They needed to live under Yahweh's rule in order to be a blessing to the world. They were not truly enjoying rest in the land that they had received from Yahweh's gracious hand.[39] Canonically, the need for a king is fulfilled in the reign of David, but it finds its final fulfillment in the reign of Jesus Christ.

37. Ibid., 104. Wong (ibid., 103–11) argues that the account in chapter 19 alludes to the story of Samson in chapter 15.

38. Against Wong (ibid., 38), there is no suggestion that the actions taken against Benjamin or Jabesh-gilead were "inappropriate."

39. Rightly House, *Old Testament Theology*, 217.

8

RUTH

Introduction

Fruitful OT theologies have been written using the canonical order found in the MT. If we follow the Hebrew order, Ruth belongs with the Writings and follows Proverbs. Surely this is instructive, for Ruth represents the virtuous woman of Prov. 31.[1] But if we follow the LXX and the order in English Bibles, Ruth is tucked between Judges and 1–2 Samuel. The theological significance of Ruth's placement between Judges and 1–2 Samuel is also instructive. It is a mistake to make too much of the canonical order of either the MT or the LXX. Childs, commenting on this issue relative to Ruth, remarks, "In my opinion, there are far too many unverified assumptions with such an argument to rest much weight on it. A far more fruitful avenue of investigation would be to explore the effect of a canonical ordering on the reading of the book and the differing theologies involved in the canonical arrangements of the Hebrew and Greek Bibles."[2] In other words, both approaches are legitimate, and we should avoid the dogmatism of insisting that there is only one legitimate canonical order in considering the theology of the book of Ruth.

Judges focuses on Israel's need for a king, a ruler who will guide the nation in accord with God's will. Ruth closes with a genealogy that culminates with the man who will serve as Israel's king, David.[3] The books of 1–2 Samuel pick up from Ruth by rehearsing the story of how David became king and served as king. Ruth fits nicely, then, as a bridge book between Judges and 1–2 Samuel.

---

1. Sailhamer, *Old Testament Theology*, 213–14.
2. Childs, *Old Testament as Scripture*, 564. See also B. Webb, *Five Festal Garments*, 52–53.
3. Dempster (*Dominion and Dynasty*, 193–94) rightly emphasizes the significance of the genealogy in Ruth.

The sovereign rule of Yahweh is manifested through the rule of King David. But we are getting ahead of the story, and first we must consider the particular contribution of the book of Ruth.

Suffering

The events of the book of Ruth occurred during the days of the judges (1:1). The link with the book of Judges is immediately established. We know from Judges that the people of Israel adopted a self-referential morality because there was no king (Judg. 17:6; 18:1; 19:1; 21:25). Even the godly in Israel suffered because the nation as a whole was unrighteous, serving other gods instead of clinging to Yahweh. The famine in Israel (Ruth 1:1) was an indication that the people were experiencing the Deuteronomic curses of the covenant (Deut. 28:48; 32:24).[4] The narrator does not imply that Elimelech and Naomi suffered because they had sinned personally.[5] Nor is there any intertextual evidence that clearly supports the notion that they transgressed by leaving Israel and living in Moab (1:2). For example, the woman whose son Elijah had raised from the dead left the land during a famine, but she is not criticized for doing so (2 Kings 8:1–6). In fact, Elisha told her to leave, and she was rewarded when she returned. In any case, Naomi suffered remarkably. Not only was she removed from her homeland but also both her husband and her two sons died in Moab (1:2–5). Both the Moabite women, Ruth and Orpah, suffered as well, since they lost their husbands, though the narrator concentrates on the distress of Naomi.

Naomi recognized the Lord's sovereignty and rule in her affliction.[6] She does not charge Yahweh with sin, but she does affirm his superintendence over all that struck her.[7] She acknowledged that the Lord's hand was stretched out against her (1:13). She engaged in a play on words, as the name "Naomi" means "pleasant," and the word "Mara" means "bitter." She confessed, "Do not call me Naomi; call me Mara, for the Almighty has dealt very bitterly with me" (1:20). The same theme is reiterated in 1:21: "I went away full, and the LORD has brought me back empty. Why call me Naomi, when the LORD

4. So also Block, *Judges, Ruth*, 608.
5. Against Block, *Judges, Ruth*, 609n75; Waltke, *Old Testament Theology*, 863. B. Webb (*Five Festal Garments*, 41–42) may be right, however, that the frequent use of the word "return" (*šûb*) indicates Naomi's repentance.
6. For the emphasis on divine sovereignty in the book, see R. Hubbard, *Book of Ruth*, 68–71; Block, *Judges, Ruth*, 607–10; Gow, "Ruth," 176.
7. Against Webb (*Five Festal Garments*, 43), who sees self-pity and complaint against Yahweh here.

has testified against me and the Almighty has brought calamity upon me?" Naomi's theology here is quite sophisticated, anticipating the book of Job. She does not maintain that her sufferings are the result of her sin, nor does she argue that what happened to her was outside the Lord's control. Yahweh brought calamity upon her. His hand was stretched against her. He made her bitter. And yet Naomi was not suggesting that the Lord was defiled by any evil in what he did to her; the Lord was just and good despite the evils that Naomi experienced from his hand. The Lord remained the King even in the midst of difficult times.

Naomi did not minimize the evils that she experienced; she did not give a saccharine response that was contrary to the depth of human experience. She lamented and grieved over the pain that had come her way. Naomi's grief and pain, however, were not an isolated case. Israel was suffering as well because it was not living under Yahweh's rule.[8] The conclusion of the book of Ruth clarifies that Naomi's story should be set against the backdrop of Israel's need for a king. Naomi's suffering and the suffering of Israel were not the last word. Yahweh would be faithful to his covenant; he would raise up a king over them who would rule righteously and justly. One of the fundamental themes of Ruth, then, is the kingship of the Lord. Robert Hubbard says, "It is a story about the firm, guiding 'hands' of divine providence at work in the world."[9] Even in seemingly mundane and ordinary events Yahweh was working out his plan.[10] Indeed, "while the writer in no way limits the freedom of the people whose lives he describes, he obviously nevertheless rejoices in tracing out the delicate manner in which God works all their actions into his plan."[11] As Ronald Hals points out, Yahweh's purposes and plans are hidden but become evident as time elapses.[12]

Faith

Yahweh had brought suffering into Naomi's life, but her fortunes were about to change. The change of fortune is signaled by the Lord visiting his people and granting them food (1:6). As Hubbard says it is "a harbinger" of divine

8. The analogy does not work at every point if I am right in saying that Naomi's sufferings were not due to personal sin.

9. R. Hubbard, *Book of Ruth*, 63. See also Hals, *Book of Ruth*, 6–9.

10. Waltke, *Old Testament Theology*, 862.

11. Hals, *Book of Ruth*, 18. "The narrator's total hiding of God's hand is rather his forceful affirmation of the Lord's complete sovereignty" (p. 19). The Lord is "seen as acting not intermittently but continuously" (p. 19).

12. Ibid., 16–17.

"intervention."[13] The same God who brought fertility to the field also granted fertility to Ruth so that she bore a son (4:13).[14] The God who brings calamity also promises to bring great blessing. Naomi was about to be blessed by a most unusual source. "Though she [Naomi] does not know it, however, Yahweh has already extended mercy in her bereavement through Ruth's commitment to her."[15] She instructed both her daughters-in-law to return to Moab because there were no future prospects for husbands in Israel (1:6–15). Orpah returned to Moab and to her gods (1:15), but Ruth stunned Naomi by insisting that she would return with her to Israel. Clearly, Ruth had put her faith in Yahweh, the God of Israel. This was illustrated by her "clinging" to Naomi (1:14). The word "cling" (dābaq) is a covenantal term, denoting the responsibility to cling to one's wife (Gen. 2:24) and, even more profoundly, the covenantal obligation to cling to Yahweh (Deut. 10:20; 11:22; 13:5; 30:20). Ruth's devotion to Naomi demonstrated her covenantal attachment to Yahweh, the God of Israel. Ruth's faith in Yahweh is even more clear in the famous words in 1:16–17: "Do not urge me to leave you or to return from following you. For where you go I will go, and where you lodge I will lodge. Your people shall be my people, and your God my God. Where you die I will die, and there will I be buried. May the LORD do so to me and more also if anything but death parts me from you." The word "leave" ('āzab) likewise is covenantal (see Deut. 28:20; 29:24; 31:16; cf. Gen. 2:24). Ruth was not only devoted to Naomi, she was forsaking her people and ethnic background (Moab) and her gods, and attaching herself to Israel and declaring her devotion to Yahweh, the God of Israel. Such a shift of allegiance demonstrated the faith of Ruth.

Reward

The story of Ruth, like the account of Rahab (Josh. 2), anticipates one of the major themes of the covenant of Abraham. The blessing promised to Abraham is not reserved for Israel alone; it belongs to the whole world and includes all people groups. Even though Ruth was, as she says, "a foreigner" (2:10), she was now a citizen of Israel. Boaz captures this truth in his response to Ruth: "All that you have done for your mother-in-law since the death of your husband has been fully told to me, and how you left your father and mother and your native land and came to a people that you did not know before. The LORD repay you for what you have done, and a full reward be given you by the

13. R. Hubbard, Book of Ruth, 65.
14. See R. Hubbard, Book of Ruth, 69; Block, Judges, Ruth, 607.
15. House, Old Testament Theology, 457.

LORD, the God of Israel, under whose wings you have come to take refuge!"
(2:11–12). Ruth's covenant devotion to Yahweh is reiterated again with the verb
"left" (*'āzab*). Ruth, like Abraham (Gen. 12:1–3), left behind her family and
country to join the people of God. Apparently, the exclusion of Moab from
the people of God (Deut. 23:3) admits of exceptions or does not apply to a
Moabitess who married an Israelite.[16] Ruth's obedience warrants repayment
and reward. Such repayment and reward, however, should not be construed
as contradicting the fundamental importance of faith in Ruth's life. Ruth did
not earn or merit reward. Because she trusted in Yahweh, she took refuge
under his wings. In other words, Ruth was repaid for looking to Yahweh as her
fortress and protector and rock. All those who trust in Yahweh are rewarded
for looking to him as their God and King.

Boaz's words became a reality in a way he never anticipated, for Ruth
would be rewarded by marrying Boaz and bearing a child to him. But it was
Yahweh who was working behind the scenes to reward Ruth for her faith. Ruth
just "happened" (2:3) to glean in the part of the field belonging to Boaz. The
sovereign plan of the Lord, though hidden from human beings, is operating.[17]
The benefits of this seemingly chance occurrence were immediately evident.
Boaz protected Ruth from sexual assaults by young men, provided her with
food and nourishment while gleaning, and ensured that she was granted more
food than she could hope for (2:8–9, 13–18, 21–23). God in his grace was re-
warding Ruth for her trust in and obedience to Yahweh. Ruth's trust functions
as a paradigm for all Israel and indeed for the whole world.

Naomi realized that Boaz was a kinsman redeemer (2:20). Words having
to do with redemption occur more than twenty times in Ruth and therefore
provide a significant theme in the book. According to the Israelite custom of
levirate marriage, if a man died without a son, his brother should marry his
brother's wife and have children by her (Deut. 25:5–6). The first son of such
a couple would continue the name of the dead brother. Similarly, a redeemer
would purchase property that a brother sold so that the inheritance could remain in the family (Lev. 25:25). Naomi discerned that Boaz would function as a
redeemer for her family by marrying Ruth, giving Ruth specific instructions to
further such an aim (3:1–6). Ruth's laying down at Boaz's feet unbeknownst to
him while he was sleeping is quite unexpected (3:7–8). There is no hint here of
some kind of illicit sexual activity, since both Ruth and Boaz are commended
as people who are virtuous. The redeemer theme points back to Yahweh's work
in freeing his people at the exodus and forward to what he would do on their

16. See Gow, "Ruth," 177.
17. So R. Hubbard, *Book of Ruth*, 70.

behalf in the future. Given the royal ending of Ruth, it probably anticipates the redemption for Israel that will be secured through David and his offspring.[18] The narrator emphasizes throughout the book the godliness of Boaz and Ruth. What occurred during their night encounter was out of the ordinary, but it was not immoral.[19] Boaz could scarcely characterize Ruth as a "worthy woman" if she had just seduced him in the middle of the night (3:11). Ruth's design is evident in the words of 3:9: "I am Ruth, your servant. Spread your wings over your servant, for you are a redeemer." Just as Ruth sought refuge under Yahweh's wings (2:12), now she asks for the reward of being placed under the protective wings of Boaz.[20] Boaz worked out the details in the gate where business was done so that he could serve as the redeemer to preserve the name of Mahlon and take Ruth for his wife (4:1–10).

One of the striking features of the book of Ruth is that all its characters are commendable; all of them live by and under the grace (*ḥesed*) of the Lord.[21] Naomi graciously releases her daughters-in-law and does not expect them to return with her to Israel (1:8–13). She longs for them to find rest and joy in their homeland. Similarly, Ruth shows her devotion to her mother-in-law by refusing to leave her and by returning with her to Israel (1:15–18). She cares for Naomi by sacrificing her own comfort and gleaning in the fields (2:2–3). Boaz is a model of a man who fears Yahweh. He invokes Yahweh's blessing on his workers, and they wish the same for him (2:4). It appears that the relationship between employer and employees is just and righteous in accord with the will of Yahweh. Boaz cares for and protects Ruth when she is gleaning so that she is spared from abuse and also provides food for her and Naomi (2:8–9). He sees the hand of the Lord in Ruth's life (2:12), and she is deeply grateful for his kindness (2:13).

Indeed, Boaz lavished concern upon Ruth, ensuring that her gleaning was fruitful (2:14–17; cf. 3:15–16). At the same time, Boaz asks for the blessing of Yahweh upon Ruth for her kindness (*ḥesed*) in desiring Boaz, an older man, to be her husband and redeemer (3:10). In the same way, Boaz showed his kindness to Ruth in wanting to serve as her redeemer (3:13). As Childs says, the characters in the book "emerge as models of the faithful life of Israel."[22] Naomi detected the kindness of the Lord in Boaz's treatment of Ruth and

---

18. See Alexander, *Servant King*, 53.
19. Rightly B. Webb, *Five Festal Garments*, 47.
20. See R. Hubbard, *Book of Ruth*, 71.
21. On the importance of this theme, see R. Hubbard, *Book of Ruth*, 65–66, 72–74; Waltke, *Old Testament Theology*, 850–69; Gow, "Ruth," 177; Block, *Judges, Ruth*, 611–15; B. Webb, *Five Festal Garments*, 37–57.
22. Childs, *Old Testament as Scripture*, 567.

Naomi, asking the Lord to bless Boaz for his goodness (2:20). Naomi showed the same kindness to Ruth as well, for she instructed her so that she "could seek rest for you, that it may be well with you" (3:1). Finally, the people rejoice with Naomi at the Lord's blessing in her life through the marriage of Boaz and Ruth and the birth of Obed (4:11–16).

Clearly, Ruth was rewarded for her faith and faithfulness by her marriage to Boaz. And Naomi was rewarded as well.[23] Earlier she lamented that the Lord had made her empty, that his hand was stretched out against her, and that he had made her bitter. But she was only partially right. She did not come back completely empty, for Ruth came with her. Ruth was the means by which the one who was empty was made full, and by which the one who was bitter experienced great joy. Yahweh deserved great praise, for he had not abandoned Naomi (see also 3:17), for there was a son born to Boaz and Ruth, and hence Naomi was preserved and renowned in Israel (4:14–16).

Indeed, the prayer of the people for Ruth and Boaz was answered in a most remarkable way. As Hubbard says, "The genealogy . . . underscores the great reward granted Ruth for her loyalty; she is the honored ancestress of a great Israelite leader. It also subtly recalled the steady, imperceptible hand of God's providence which had guided the story."[24] Thereby Israel was reminded that the Lord would fulfill his promises, even if how he would do so was imperceptible. The people prayed that the Lord would make Ruth "like Rachel and Leah, who together built up the house of Israel," and for Boaz, "May you act worthily in Ephrathah and be renowned in Bethlehem, and may your house be like the house of Perez, whom Tamar bore to Judah, because of the offspring that the LORD will give you by this young woman" (4:11–12). Little could they anticipate how renowned the son would be: he was the ancestor of David the king, as the genealogy at the conclusion of the book spells out (4:17–22). The line of Ruth and Boaz was the line from which the promised offspring would come (cf. Gen. 3:15). He would crush the serpent and his offspring, and he would bring many Gentiles like Ruth under his wings. The promise given to Rachel and Leah and to Tamar and Judah was becoming a reality. History, with fits and starts, with moves backward and forward, was going somewhere. The Lord would reign over the earth, and he would do it through a king, and that king would trace his ancestry to Ruth and Boaz. Hubbard rightly notes, "God's care for Naomi's family turned out to be a piece of his care for all Israel."[25] And in light of the canon, it is part of the piece of his care for the whole world.

23. See R. Hubbard, *Book of Ruth*, 63–64.
24. Ibid., 22.
25. Ibid., 65.

Conclusion

We see in this delightful story Yahweh's care for those who trust in him. The characters in Ruth show by their kindness what life looks like when one lives under Yahweh's rule. We also see Yahweh's grace and sovereignty in the story, for he is working out his purposes, even though hidden from human beings. Those purposes include blessing for the whole world through David and the greater son of David to come. Surprisingly, Ruth forms a link in the chain that would bring David into the world, solving the problem of Judges, where Israel lacked a king. And a future son of David would bring many more Ruths, many more Gentiles into the fold of God's people, and fulfill the promise of universal blessing made to Abraham.

9

1–2 SAMUEL

Introduction

The books that English Bibles identify as 1–2 Samuel are truly one book and should be studied as a whole. The placement of 1–2 Samuel after Judges and Ruth is significant. Judges emphasizes Israel's waywardness, noting that there was no king in Israel (17:6; 18:1; 19:1; 21:25). The book of Ruth relays the story of how Ruth married Boaz, explaining how she and Boaz were ancestors of the one who eventually became king: David. The books of 1–2 Samuel recount the story of how David became king, featuring the covenant promise that the kingdom would never be withdrawn from David's heirs. One of the central themes of the OT emerges in these books. The sovereign rule of Yahweh is exercised through the anointed king of Israel. Yahweh rules over Israel through a mediator, and that mediator is from David's family line. When we include the entire canon, it becomes clear that Yahweh's rule over the whole world, which includes Gentiles, is exercised through the king, who is none other than Jesus the Christ. The story of the king and his kingdom in 1–2 Samuel is conveniently broken up by studying the three main characters of the book: Samuel, Saul, and David.

It seems also that the central themes of 1–2 Samuel are captured by the songs and final words of David. The songs are the hymn of Hannah at the beginning of the book (1 Sam. 2:1–10) and the psalm of David at the conclusion (2 Sam. 22:1–51).[1] The final words are designated as "the last words of David"

1. Childs says, "The thanksgiving hymn [2 Sam. 22] picks up many of the same themes of the song of Hannah, and thus reinforces the same theocentric emphasis now seen in retrospect" (*Old Testament as Scripture*, 274). For the centrality of the songs, see Rendtorff, *Canonical Hebrew Bible*, 103; Dempster, *Dominion and Dynasty*, 134–36; Satterthwaite, "Samuel," 179.

(2 Sam. 23:1),[2] suggesting that these words (2 Sam. 23:2–7) take on unusual importance (particularly because these are not literally his last words in the book, as David says other words in 2 Sam. 24) in interpreting 1–2 Samuel as a whole. The songs and final words of David appear at the beginning (1 Sam. 2:1–10) and at the end (2 Sam. 22:1–23:7), so they function as an inclusio that brackets the entire work. Childs says that "the psalm of ch. 22 offers a theological commentary on the entire history of David."[3] Hence, these songs and final words function as an interpretive key for reading 1–2 Samuel.

We begin with Hannah's song in 1 Sam. 2:1–10. Childs says that it "offers an interpretative key for this history which is, above all, to be understood from a theocentric perspective."[4] The content of the song is rather remarkable, for Hannah does not sing about what we might expect at the birth of a son. Hannah's barrenness in chapter 1 reflects the state of Israel and anticipates the fulfillment of Yahweh's promise, for victory would come through a child born of a woman (Gen. 3:15). Furthermore, Hannah's conflict with Peninnah mirrors the struggle between the righteous and the wicked in Israel, between the remnant that obeyed the Lord and the strong majority that persecuted and mistreated the righteous. We see a prelude here of Saul's mistreatment of David. Peter Leithart rightly says, "Elkanah's family was a microcosm of Israel, divided between the rich and apparently fruitful nobles and the poor and needy who made their home in dust and ashes."[5]

In Hannah's song we are swept into a world where the Lord vindicates and protects the righteous and annihilates the wicked. The story moves from Hannah's personal world to the cosmic scene, where Yahweh's reign over the entire earth is featured. Clearly, the narrator is telling us that the former must be interpreted in light of the latter. The seemingly small events in history must be read against the canvas of the Lord's rule and reign over all of history. And how should history be interpreted? It must be read upside down (1 Sam. 2:1–10). Those who are strong and rich and wicked will not finally triumph. It is the poor who trust in Yahweh who will finally be vindicated. The humble who trust in the Lord will be fed, while the arrogant, who trust in themselves, will go hungry. Obviously, Hannah is not declaring in this psalm that what she sings about has already become a reality. Ultimately and finally, "the wicked shall be cut off in darkness" (2:9). The Lord will thunder against his adversaries and rout them (2:10). Nor are these promises limited to Israel, for "the LORD will judge the ends of the earth" (2:10). Obviously, Hannah forecasts

2. See Dempster, *Dominion and Dynasty*, 144–45.
3. Childs, *Old Testament as Scripture*, 274.
4. Ibid., 273. So also Dumbrell, *Faith of Israel*, 82; House, *Old Testament Theology*, 229.
5. Leithart, *A Son to Me*, 38.

the future when she exclaims that the Lord "will give strength to his king and exalt the power of his anointed" (2:10), for there was no king yet on the scene.

What we have in Hannah's song is the whole of 1–2 Samuel in compact form. Just as Yahweh vindicated Hannah by giving her children (2:5), so he will vindicate poor and weak Israel. The story in chapter 1, like Ruth's story, is a story for all of Israel, and indeed for the whole world. The judgment and destruction of Eli's sons (Hophni and Phinehas) and the exaltation of Samuel illustrate Hannah's theme. Yahweh judges the wicked, who despise him, but exalts the little boy who trusts in him. Indeed, the story of Saul and David recounts the same theme. Saul begins as a humble king who trusts the Lord, but he is subverted along the way and turns to the dark side. The entire book of 1–2 Samuel is about how the Lord exalts David as king through many dangers, toils, and snares and casts down Saul.[6] Yahweh will rule the nation through a king who trusts in him.

What conclusion should be drawn from Yahweh's preservation of the faithful and destruction of the godless? Readers must see that Yahweh is sovereign over all things. He cannot be outwitted or defeated. He will strengthen the poor and needy who trust in him and will sap the strength of those who resist him. As Hannah proclaims, "The LORD kills and brings to life; he brings down to Sheol and raises up" (2:6).[7] Life and death are in his hands, and thus his people should trust him. Yahweh, as the incomparable one, will see to it that righteousness is done. "There is none holy like the LORD; there is none besides you; there is no rock like our God" (2:2). Hannah has experienced the Lord's exaltation in her own life. The Lord "closed her womb" (1:5), but he "remembered her" (1:19) and gave her the child that she fervently and humbly asked of the Lord. Therefore, Hannah and all the poor and weak who trust in the Lord will finally rejoice and exult in the Lord (2:1). The victory and reign of the Lord will bring great joy, for he will accomplish salvation for his people (2:1), just as he did for Hannah and Samuel and David.

The second text that is fundamental for interpreting 1–2 Samuel is 2 Sam. 22, which is David's song of deliverance from Saul and his other enemies (22:1). The striking element of this psalm is how closely it matches Hannah's song. David does not advertise himself as the giant-killer who slew Goliath. Instead he focuses on his weakness and Yahweh's strength. The Lord is his rock, refuge, savior, fortress, and deliverer (22:3). Using striking imagery, David portrays the Lord's intervention on his behalf: "smoke went up from his nostrils" (22:9); "he

---

6. Alexander (*Servant King*, 68) emphasizes that David is exalted because of his humility, his trust in God, and his obedience.

7. For the implications of this statement relative to resurrection, see Levenson, *Restoration of Israel*, 173.

bowed the heavens and came down" (22:10); "he rode on a cherub and flew" (22:11); "coals of fire flamed forth" (22:13). The language of Hannah's song is picked up: "the LORD thundered from heaven" (22:14) should be compared with Hannah's words about what Yahweh will do to his enemies, "against them he will thunder in heaven" (1 Sam. 2:10). The Lord rescued David when there was no hope (22:17–19). Why did the Lord intervene on David's behalf? Because he "kept the ways of the LORD" (22:22). David was "blameless" and free from guilt (22:24). David says that Yahweh rewarded him "according to my righteousness, according to my cleanness in his sight" (22:25). The point of David's story is that the Lord saves the humble (22:28), which fits with Hannah's theme. Yahweh saves those who make him their refuge and put their faith in him (22:31). David's victories, then, are due to God's favor and the empowerment that he received from the Lord (22:34–46).

The judgment over the Lord's enemies, predicted in Hannah's song, has become a reality through Yahweh's king, David. The Lord extends his salvation and judgment through his anointed one. The offspring of the serpent are conquered through the Davidic king. So David, just like Hannah, voices praise to God for being his rock of salvation (22:47, 50). The psalm does not relate just to David; it also points forward to his offspring, for David is promised that his offspring will reign forever (2 Sam. 7). And the whole of 1–2 Samuel clarifies that a better king than David is needed. Yes, David obeyed Yahweh and, as we will see, trusted in the Lord rather than taking revenge on Saul. But he sinned remarkably by committing adultery with Bathsheba and murdering Uriah (2 Sam. 11). A better king is needed—a king who can be rewarded for his righteousness that lasts his whole life long. That king, according to the canonical witness, is Jesus the Christ, the son of David.

The last words of David also play a key role in the book (23:1–7). The narrator in most emphatic terms stresses that the Lord spoke through David (23:1–3). His words are an "oracle"; the Spirit speaks through him; "the God of Israel" utters his words through him. The sweet psalmist of Israel did not utter merely a human word; these are the words of the man whom Yahweh raised up and anointed to be king. And what are the words of the anointed one? He calls attention to the ideal king. The king with whom Yahweh is pleased is radically God-centered. He rules "in the fear of God" (23:3) and dispenses justice in the land. Hannah in her song looked forward to such a king, and by the end of 1–2 Samuel we recognize that Saul failed utterly in this regard, while David mainly succeeded. Israel needs a king who dawns like the light of the sun and blesses the people through gentle rains (23:4). David identifies himself and his house as such a kingdom (23:5), acknowledging that the covenant made with him will stand in perpetuity, whereas the wicked will be destroyed forever (23:6–7). Again, there is an incongruity between the justice of the king and the stains on David's rule. Canonically, we look for a king who is perfectly just, one who will fulfill the covenant with Abraham and bring blessing to the entire world.

Samuel

We can examine 1–2 Samuel nicely by concentrating on three characters: Samuel, Saul, and David. This is not to say that the chapters of the book can be discretely divided up among these characters. There is overlap, such that the career of Saul intrudes significantly into the life of Samuel, and, of course, Saul and David overlap and interact with each other significantly. If we begin with Samuel, it is immediately apparent that he functions as the polar opposite of the sons of Eli (Hophni and Phinehas). Samuel represents the godly and the poor who trust in Yahweh in Hannah's song, whereas Hophni and Phinehas stand for the arrogant, rich, and wicked whom Yahweh will thrust down.[8] Eli, the father of Hophni and Phinehas, is a tragic character. He is characterized, like those in the book of Judges, as the judge of Israel for forty years (1 Sam. 4:18). It is difficult to know if his judging involved saving Israel, as was typical in the book of Judges, or if it focused upon ruling in a more administrative sense. Apparently, Hophni and Phinehas were to serve as his successors, but their blatant evil led to their death before they could succeed Eli. Samuel, however, judged Israel for his entire life (7:15–17), making a circuit of several cities. It appears that Samuel's work as a judge was both judicial and soteriological, for it involved both settled leadership and victories over the Philistines.

Hophni and Phinehas represent the same problem observed in Judges. They did what was right in their own eyes (Judg. 17:6; 21:25). The narrator alternates between Hophni and Phinehas and Samuel, between the wicked and the godly. Hophni and Phinehas are characterized as "worthless men . . . [who] did not know the LORD" (1 Sam. 2:12). They were brutish, grabbing meat for themselves before it was fully cooked (2:13–14), transgressing the Torah by taking meat before the fat was burned (2:15–16). The narrator summarizes their problem: "Thus the sin of the young men was very great in the sight of the LORD, for the men treated the offering of the LORD with contempt" (2:17). Indeed, they had sex with the women serving at the tent of meeting (2:22). Eli's words in the narrative are of great importance, for he is the high priest

---

8. Rightly Leithart, *A Son to Me*, 43.

and judge in Israel. So his words against his sons are full of significance when he warns them that there is no mediation for them if they sin against Yahweh (2:25). The narrator remarks that they did not pay heed to their father's remonstrations, "for it was the will of the LORD to put them to death" (2:25). A prophet ratifies the doleful news, rebuking Eli for being soft on his sons and honoring them more than he honored the Lord (2:27–36). His blindness probably signifies a spiritual blindness as well (3:2), and his "heaviness" (*kābēd*) (4:18) anticipates the glory (*kābôd*) of God departing from him.[9] Yahweh will remove the priesthood from Eli's descendants and slay Hophni and Phinehas on the same day. The judgment threatened is confirmed to Samuel (3:11–14). The Lord "will raise up for myself a faithful priest, who shall do according to what is in my heart and in my mind. And I will build him a sure house, and he shall go in and out before my anointed forever" (2:35).

We have seen that human beings are required to honor Yahweh as king, and Hophni and Phinehas refused to do so, glorifying themselves instead of glorifying the Lord. Samuel, however, gave himself entirely to the Lord. Even when he was a child, Samuel's godliness was evident. "Now the young man Samuel continued to grow both in stature and in favor with the LORD and also with man" (2:26), anticipating Jesus of Nazareth, a child who pleased the Lord more than Samuel did (Luke 2:52). As a young child (1 Sam. 3), Samuel began to hear and declare the words of the Lord as a prophet, even though prophetic words were not common in his day. Perhaps Eli's dimness of sight was parabolic (3:2) of the spiritual state of his family and of all Israel. Samuel's prophetic status was conversely established throughout all of Israel: "And Samuel grew, and the LORD was with him and let none of his words fall to the ground. And all Israel from Dan to Beersheba knew that Samuel was established as a prophet of the LORD" (3:19–20).

The judgment threatened came crashing down on Israel (chap. 4). Israel under the leadership of Hophni and Phinehas superstitiously relied upon the ark to bring them victory. They were likely trying to reproduce the victory at Jericho by bringing the ark into the camp and shouting.[10] But they were routed by the Philistines, and Hophni and Phinehas, in accord with prophecy (2:34), died on the same day. Leithart insightfully remarks that the battle was more like Ai than Jericho, for the "Achans" were "carrying the ark."[11] Furthermore, upon hearing the news, Eli fell back, broke his neck, and died (4:18). The old leadership was swept aside instantaneously. The horror of the news propelled

---

9. So Dumbrell, *Faith of Israel*, 81; Leithart, *A Son to Me*, 48–49.
10. So Leithart, *A Son to Me*, 55.
11. Ibid.

Phinehas's wife into labor, and she died in the process of giving birth, declaring "Ichabod," which is explained twice in terms of the glory departing from Israel (4:21–22). God's glorious presence (the ark) does not and cannot reside with those who despise his name. But the so-called defeat of Israel and Yahweh was a prelude to victory. Before the Lord raises up the nation, he casts down the wicked within it.[12]

The ark of Yahweh was taken by the Philistines, suggesting that Yahweh was subservient and inferior to Philistine gods. But Yahweh is Lord and King. Israel was defeated because they tried to manipulate him, but for Philistines, victory was more than they bargained for. To signify the victory of their gods, the Philistines placed the ark of Yahweh in the temple next to the god Dagon. The utter uselessness of Dagon is humorously portrayed. He fell "face downward on the ground before the ark of the Lord" (5:3), and so he needed help in being put back in his place. It scarcely helped. The next day he fell again, and his head and hands were severed from his trunk (5:4). As Leithart says, the Lord was "forcing Dagon to bow before his throne," and Dagon "apparently was joining with Israel in prostrating himself before the throne of the God of gods."[13] Furthermore, tumors, possibly bubonic plague, broke out wherever the ark of the Lord was taken in Philistia (5:6–12). Clearly, Yahweh was Lord over the Philistines and their gods and must be honored as a great king, for he will always crush the head of the serpent (Gen. 3:15).[14]

The Philistines wondered, however, if everything that happened was mere coincidence. They needed some empirical evidence to verify that Yahweh had really judged them, and so they yoked milk cows to a new cart that had never been yoked before (6:7) and watched to see if they took the ark back to Israel. If so, it would confirm that Yahweh truly judged them. Remarkably, the cows traveled straight to Beth-shemesh, working together for several miles even though they were never yoked previously. Israel rejoiced at the return of the ark, but they were reminded again of the lordship, holiness, and majesty of Yahweh. Those who looked into the ark were struck dead (6:19), and so Israel rightly exclaimed, "Who is able to stand before the Lord, this holy God?" (6:20). Again we see an allusion to Hannah's song. Those who trust and fear the Lord are rescued, but those who transgress him will face his wrath.

Israel must repent and renew the covenant to stand before the Lord (chap. 7). Samuel, as their judge, leads them in the ceremony. The narrator uses Deuteronomic language. Israel is told that they must return "to the Lord with all your

12. Ibid., 57.
13. Ibid.
14. See ibid., 58.

heart," renounce foreign gods, and serve the Lord only, and then they will be delivered from the Philistines (7:3). Israel did so and gathered at Mizpah to renew the covenant (7:4–6), confessing their sins. The Philistines used the opportunity to attack Israel, and Israel cried out in fear (7:7–8). Samuel offered sacrifice and interceded for Israel. Yahweh answered Samuel's prayer and "thundered" against the Philistines, throwing them into confusion so that they were routed before Israel, and Israel took many cites back from the Philistines (7:10–14). The word "thundered" (7:10) echoes Hannah's song and fulfills it (2:10), for Yahweh thundered against his enemies. Yahweh is the holy and sovereign one of Israel. If they are faithful to him, he will be faithful to them. But if they depart from him, they will face the same fate as Hophni and Phinehas.

Chapters 8–12 represent a new stage in Samuel's career and a transition to Saul as the king of Israel. Samuel attempted to keep the institution of judges going in Israel, but his sons were corrupt (like Eli's sons!), and so the people rejected their leadership (8:1–3). What Israel wanted was a king (8:5). The request seems reasonable enough, for there were prophecies that Israel would have a king (Gen. 49:10; Num. 24:17) as well as other indications that a king was coming (Deut. 17:14–20) and needed (Judg. 17:6; 18:1; 19:1; 21:25). One would be mistaken to see an antimonarchial strain in 1–2 Samuel, for Hannah's song indicates that Yahweh will rule the nation through a king (1 Sam. 2:10), and the entire book culminates with David's reign, which will be perpetuated forever in the Davidic covenant (2 Sam. 7).[15] Nonetheless, both Samuel and the Lord were grieved that Israel desired a king (1 Sam. 8:6–7), for in doing so Israel was rejecting Yahweh's kingship over Israel. Deuteronomic language is again used. Israel was "forsaking" Yahweh and "serving other gods" (8:8). Forsaking the Lord never leads to better circumstances, for the king whom they choose will "take" and "take" and "take" (8:11, 13, 14, 16). Then the people will cry out to the Lord for relief from the king whom they themselves chose (8:18)! Clearly, both the Lord and Samuel reluctantly concede that Israel should have a king (8:9, 22; 10:19). It seems that the Lord ultimately wants Israel to have a king, so why the reluctance? The best answer seems to be that the problem with Israel was its motives: it desired a king not in order to serve and cling to the Lord but rather to be like all the other nations and to find security in their battles (8:5, 22).[16] Thereby they were rejecting Yahweh's reign over them.

The appointment of Saul as the first king initially looked very promising according to the charming account found in chapter 9.[17] At first glance, Saul's

15. Rightly Satterthwaite, "Samuel," 179–80.
16. Rightly Satterthwaite, "Samuel," 179.
17. That Saul is from "Gibeah" (Judg. 19–20) may signal the problems coming in the future (Dempster, *Dominion and Dynasty*, 138).

good looks and towering height appear to be just what is needed (9:2). But the word for Saul's height (*gābōah*) echoes Hannah's song, where boastful arrogance (*gĕbōhâ*) is criticized (2:3). Indeed, the narrator later informs us that the Lord pays attention not to outward appearance but instead to the heart, and that no attention should be paid to "the height [*gĕbōah*] of [one's] stature" (16:7).[18] The bizarre circumstances by which Saul and Samuel encounter each other demonstrate that he was the king whom Yahweh appointed to reign over Israel (cf. 9:15–16; 10:1). Saul was also humble, recognizing (after the circumstances of Judg. 19–21) that his tribe was the "least" in Israel, and that his clan was the "humblest" (9:21). Indeed, when Saul was appointed, he was so humble (there is no evidence here that it was false humility) that he was hiding among the baggage (10:21–22). Indeed, Saul was strengthened by the Lord to serve as king, for the Spirit "rushed upon" him, clothing him with power and giving him another heart (10:6, 9–10). Those who knew Saul were astonished that he prophesied (10:11–12), but one man wisely commented, "Who is their father?" (10:12), meaning that there is no genealogical connection for those who prophesy. Prophecy has no human father; it is a sovereign work of God. One cannot rationally trace the channels by which prophecy flows. Even though the Lord did not approve of Israel's desire for a king, those who resisted Saul are described as evil, while those who supported him were "men of valor whose hearts God had touched" (10:26–27).

The choice of Saul as king seems to be vindicated when the town of Jabesh-gilead was threatened by the Ammonites (chap. 11). The "Spirit of God rushed upon Saul" (11:6), and he rescued Jabesh-gilead from disaster and death. Saul showed himself to be magnanimous, forgiving those who opposed his kingship at an hour when he could have inflicted vengeance upon them (11:12–13). Saul's great victory led to the last great act of Samuel's judgeship with the ratification of Saul's kingship and the reminder of Israel's covenantal obligations in chapter 12. Hence, chapter 12 functions as a "covenant renewal event."[19] Samuel had warned the people of the danger of appointing a king and emphasized his moral integrity as Israel's judge (12:1–5). He had not enriched himself at Israel's hands. He also reminded the people of Yahweh's saving acts on behalf of Israel from the days of the exodus up to the present time (12:6–11). Israel had asked for a king to deliver them from the Ammonites (12:12), and Yahweh granted them their request (12:12–13). Israel's fundamental need, however, was not the rule of a king. The question for Israel was the same as it always was. If they served and obeyed Yahweh, both the nation and the king would

18. See ibid., 139.
19. Hahn, *Kinship by Covenant*, 87.

prosper (12:14–15). But if they rebelled, both the people and the king would be destroyed. The renewal of the covenant indicates that the monarchy, the kingship of Israel, is now constitutive of Israel's relationship with Yahweh.[20]

Yahweh, by causing thunder during the wheat harvest, provided concrete evidence that Israel indulged in evil in seeking a king (cf. 2:10). The wheat harvest took place in May–June, which was the dry season. The thunderstorm would destroy some of the heads of grain in the wheat harvest, testifying to God's judgment before the people. The ratification of Saul's kingship was not sentimental. Samuel did not assume that all would be well with the defeat of the Ammonites. The evil that motivated Israel in demanding a king had not vanished. And yet Samuel's response was complex. He did not give up on Israel even though they had pursued an evil course of action. Instead, he exhorts them, "Do not be afraid; you have done all this evil. Yet do not turn aside from following the LORD, but serve the LORD with all your heart. And do not turn aside after empty things that cannot profit or deliver, for they are empty" (12:20–21). Hope still existed for Israel, for if they followed Yahweh, they would still find blessing. Indeed, ultimately, the nation would be blessed, "For the LORD will not forsake his people, for his great name's sake, because it has pleased the LORD to make you a people for himself" (12:22). The apostle Paul picks up this promise in Rom. 11, seeing a future salvation for Israel (Rom. 11:2).

Samuel says that Israel's future is secure because their destiny is tied to Yahweh's name and will. Despite their sin, Yahweh has chosen Israel to be his people and will not finally forsake them, for to do so would be to blemish his own name. Since Israel's destiny is tied to Yahweh's name, he will never abandon them. But this ultimate promise for Israel can never become a pretext for disobedience. Israel must "fear the LORD and serve him faithfully with all your heart" (12:24). If they turn against Yahweh and practice wickedness, both the nation and the king "shall be swept away" (12:25). At the end of the day, the Lord will not forsake Israel and will fulfill his saving promises to his people. Nevertheless, no generation of Israel can presume upon that promise. Finally, there will be an obedient king, but a disobedient king and a rebellious generation of Israelites will experience judgment, not salvation.

Saul can be compared to Adam and to Israel after the Sinai covenant was ratified. In a sense, we can think of Saul as a new Adam and a new Israel, representing a new beginning for the nation. We have already seen that the beginning under Saul was auspicious. He was humble, gracious, and obedient. We will see, however, in chapters 13–15 that he went the same way as Adam

20. Ibid., 87–88.

and Israel in the incident of the golden calf, showing that merely having a king was not the solution to Israel's problems. Saul, in other words, did not heed the words of Samuel uttered at the renewal of the kingship in chapter 12. He did not serve and fear Yahweh, but instead he practiced wickedness, and so his dynasty was "swept away" (12:25).

Saul

I noted earlier that the stories of Samuel and Saul overlap, but Samuel drops into the background and Saul to the forefront in chapter 13. The story begins with an initial victory over the Philistines, though the triumph is attributed to Jonathan rather than Saul (1 Sam. 13:3). Saul's wickedness, however, comes to the fore in the midst of the battle. Samuel instructed Saul to wait for him to arrive before offering the burnt and peace offerings (13:8–14). Samuel failed to come at the promised time, and so Saul went ahead and offered the sacrifices. Right after the sacrifices were offered, Samuel arrived and rebuked Saul for failing to obey instructions. Here is a crucial moment for Saul. If we anticipate the narrative, we note that David repented when rebuked. But Saul made excuses, blaming Samuel for not arriving on time and appealing to what seemed reasonable: his troops were leaving, and the Philistines were preparing for battle. Saul clothed his actions in religious fervor: "I said, '. . . I have not sought the favor of the LORD.' So I forced myself, and offered the burnt offering" (13:12). Instead of admitting that he was motivated by fear and disobeyed, Saul acted as if what he did was actually holy. It was this kind of upside-down perverseness that led Samuel to say that Saul's dynasty would not continue (13:13–14). Saul showed that he was not "a man after [the Lord's] own heart" (13:14). Saul "was becoming as blind as Eli."[21]

Saul's foolishness as a leader is on display in chapter 14, standing in remarkable contrast to the courage and wisdom of his son Jonathan. Jonathan bravely attacked the Philistines, recognizing that "nothing can hinder the LORD from saving by many or by few" (14:6), and that the Lord had delivered the Philistines into their hands (14:12; cf. 14:15), leading to a great victory (14:23). Meanwhile, Saul was dithering in the camp, inquiring of God when he should have been attacking (14:15–19). Nor was he a wise leader, for he hindered Israel from eating in the middle of a battle, when they especially needed energy (14:24). Jonathan, upon hearing of his father's prohibition, recognized that the victory would have been greater if Saul had not deprived

21. Leithart, *A Son to Me*, 86.

Israel of food (14:29–30). Indeed, Saul's prohibition so weakened his troops that they violated the Torah by eating meat with the blood because they were famished (14:32–33). And then Saul was even willing to put his son Jonathan to death for infringing a command that he did not hear, and he was only restrained from doing so by his troops, who showed thereby that they were wiser than their leader (14:39–45).

Saul's victories were significant (14:47–48), but there was a worm at the core of the apple, and this becomes remarkably apparent in chapter 15. The Lord commanded Saul to wipe out the Amalekites root and branch, placing them under a total ban (*ḥērem*) (15:1–6). Saul defeated them, but he failed to carry out all that the Lord demanded: "Saul and the people spared Agag and the best of the sheep and of the oxen and of the fattened calves and the lambs, and all that was good, and would not utterly destroy them. All that was despised and worthless they devoted to destruction" (15:9). The Lord revealed to Samuel what Saul had done, indicating that he regretted appointing Saul as king (15:11, 35). Samuel traveled to meet Saul and to confront him with his evil. Meanwhile, Saul had erected a monument to himself (15:12). Saul, full of bravado, met Samuel, claiming that he had done what the Lord instructed (15:13). But Samuel would have none of it, asking why then did he hear "this bleating of sheep . . . and the lowing of the oxen" (15:14). Saul excused his disobedience, as he did in chapter 13, with spiritual reasoning. They "spared the best of the sheep and of the oxen to sacrifice to the LORD your God" (15:15). Samuel stopped Saul short, reminding him that the Lord chose him when he was nothing to be king over Israel and had sent him on a mission to destroy Amalek entirely (15:17–19). Saul continued to rationalize, insisting that he did obey, and that what was spared would be given to the Lord as a sacrifice (15:21–22). What Saul did not recognize or admit was that he acted with presumption by violating the Lord's command (15:22–23). Just as he "rejected the word of the LORD," so too the Lord rejected him "from being king" (15:23; cf. 15:26, 28). Finally, Saul acknowledged his sin, and the true reason for his disobedience came to light: he feared people rather than fearing the Lord (15:24). But there was no turning back now. Yahweh removed the kingdom from Saul and granted it to another who would obey the Lord (15:28–29). Israel wanted a king, but the problem for Israel was that Saul was like Adam and like Israel. The problem was that Saul, like Israel, did what was right in his own eyes (cf. Judg. 17:6; 21:25).

The words of Samuel, that the kingdom would be taken from Saul and his family, begin to become a reality in the rest of 1 Samuel (chaps. 16–31). David is revealed to be a man after God's own heart, while Saul's rebellion against the Lord becomes even more apparent through his treatment of David. The dissolution of Saul's kingdom is set in motion immediately, for Samuel traveled to Bethlehem to anoint a new king from Jesse's children (chap. 16). The narrator emphasizes the surprising sovereignty of God, for the youngest son, David, who was not even at the meal, was chosen to be king, showing that Yahweh looks not on "outward appearance" but rather "on the heart" (16:7). When David was anointed as king, the Spirit of Yahweh "rushed upon" him (16:13), just as he did upon Saul at the outset of his kingship. Conversely, the Spirit now departed from Saul, and an evil spirit from Yahweh "tormented him" (16:14). Thereby David was brought into the court of the king, for his music was the means by which the evil spirit was chased away from Saul (16:15–23).

The story of David and Goliath is worthy of its fame. What is its role in the narrative? It demonstrates that David should lead Israel instead of Saul. Saul cowers with the rest of Israel's army and does not challenge Goliath.[22] David, even though he is a youth, acts boldly, trusting in Yahweh's name (17:32–37). David shows his leadership, scoffing that any uncircumcised Philistine "should defy the armies of the living God" (17:26; cf. 17:36). We see another pattern in the story, which reminds us of the conquest of Canaan. David did not triumph over Goliath because of superior weaponry; he slays him with a sling and a stone to show that the Lord "saves not with sword or spear" (17:47). The Lord made small, as Hannah predicted, one who was tall (*gābōah*) (17:4). Goliath "cursed David by his gods" (17:43). David, however, placed his trust entirely in the Lord. He came "in the name of the LORD of hosts" (17:45), showing that "the battle is the LORD's" (17:47). "The seed of the woman has arrived, and in David's first action as king he is a warrior, an anointed one who conquers and beheads a monstrous giant, whose speech echoes the serpent's voice."[23] Through David's victory the Lord will be glorified, with the result that "all the earth may know that there is a God in Israel" (17:46).

The narrator emphasizes that nothing can prevent David's ascent to the kingdom. No matter what machinations or forces Saul threw at David, he could not snuff out David's life.[24] Yahweh exalted the humble (David) and cast down the proud (Saul). The remainder of the narrative in 1 Samuel (chaps. 18–31) reflects the conflict between the offspring of the serpent (Saul) and the offspring of the woman (David), showing the triumph of the latter even through persecution. The ultimate triumph of David immediately surfaces in the narrative. Even Saul's son Jonathan, the rightful heir of the kingdom,

22. See Waltke, *Old Testament Theology*, 642.
23. Dempster, *Dominion and Dynasty*, 140.
24. Leithart (*A Son to Me*, 101) argues that we see a parallel between the lives of David and Joseph. Both went from suffering to glory.

sided with David, making a covenant with David (18:1–5). Saul, enraged with jealousy because David received more glory for military triumphs than he, tried to slay David (18:6–11). Saul had a foreboding of the future. He feared David, for Yahweh had departed from him but was with David as he was with Moses (18:12, 15). Therefore, David was wildly popular with the people (18:16) and "had success in all his undertakings, for the LORD was with him" (18:14). Saul hoped to kill David by intrigue, requiring the bride price of one hundred Philistine foreskins, thinking that they would slay David (18:20–29). But the plan backfired dramatically, for David killed twice the number of Philistines required, increasing his popularity. Moreover, now David was part of the royal family. The very thing Saul feared was becoming more of a reality (18:29).

Saul was bent on killing David, but again Jonathan (the heir to the throne!) interceded and persuaded Saul otherwise (19:1–7). Saul's insane jealousy struck him again, and he tried to pin David to the wall with a spear, but it missed its target (19:8–10). Saul tried to kill David in his own bed, but Saul's daughter Michal, who was also David's wife, took David's side and helped protect him (19:11–17). Saul's own family was thwarting his designs on David. David fled to Samuel for protection, but Saul again pursued him, first sending messengers and then coming himself to kill him (19:18–24). Saul was learning the hard way, and he never learned the lesson: he would never topple David. Both the messengers and Saul were seized by the Spirit and prophesied. Saul was so overcome that he stripped off his clothes and proclaimed God's words.

The narrative in 1–2 Samuel does not breathe an air of unreality. Yahweh protected David, but David continued to take precautions so that Saul could not kill him. The story in chapter 20 demonstrates that Saul's attitude toward David had hardened. When Saul realized that Jonathan was protecting David, he was so infuriated that he tried to kill his own son, convinced that Jonathan was supporting David as king (20:30–31). The only way to ensure Jonathan's reign was to kill David. Both Jonathan and David realized from that moment on that David could never sit at Saul's table again. Henceforth, David would be a fugitive. As a fugitive, David was now persecuted and on the run (21:10). He traveled to Gath in Philistia, but he feigned insanity when he realized that his life was in danger as the famous soldier who had killed many Philistines (21:10–15).

David and his men functioned as a kind of guerrilla kingdom in Israel, though David was not trying to displace Saul (22:1–4). Saul was irrationally consumed with the notion that David was trying to unseat him, seeing a conspiracy where none existed (22:5–23), which led to the slaughter of eighty-five priests and the annihilation of every man, woman, and child in Nob under the direction of Doeg the Edomite. Clearly, Saul was now allied with the serpent of Gen. 3, and, like Pharaoh and other enemies of Israel, he was destroying members of the people of God. David did not cower in his stronghold. He trusted in Yahweh and obeyed his directives (22:5). Under the Lord's direction he rescued the inhabitants of Keilah from the Philistines, even though his men did not want to risk such an attack, and he did not take vengeance on Keilah even when it was revealed to him that its people would hand him over to Saul (23:1–12).

Ultimately, Saul could not and would not triumph over David, for the Lord's rule cannot be overturned. The narrator summarizes the story aptly: "And Saul sought him every day, but God did not give him into his hand" (23:14). Saul's military and political power and his strategy were no match for the Lord. Indeed, at the crucial juncture where David was on the run, Yahweh comforts David with the words of Jonathan. Jonathan, as the heir to the throne, speaks the word of the Lord to David: "Do not fear, for the hand of Saul my father shall not find you. You shall be king over Israel, and I shall be next to you. Saul my father also knows this" (23:17). The promise of a Davidic reign would certainly become a reality. What a remarkable turn of events! The heir to the throne supported David instead of his father, and he acknowledged that David would serve as king rather than he, making a covenant with David to seal his loyalty to him (23:18). David still had his enemies. The Ziphites supported Saul and informed him of David's whereabouts (23:19–29). Saul pursued David and was remarkably close to catching him, for he was on the other side of the mountain, and David was fleeing from him. But just when it appeared that Saul would close his hand upon David, he had to leave to attend to a Philistine attack. The timing of the Philistine attack was no accident. No matter how close Saul got to David, he would never throw the net over him.

Saul was relentless, however. He functioned as David's Judas Iscariot, so to speak, doing all that he could to destroy him. When Saul discovered that David was in the wilderness of Engedi, the chase was on again (chap. 24). Saul relieved himself in a cave, unaware that David and his men were sitting in the back of the cave. David's men urged him to kill Saul, maintaining that Yahweh had arranged circumstances for him to do away with Saul (24:4). But David refused to slay Saul, since he was Yahweh's anointed king, and he only cut off the corner of his robe (24:4–7). After Saul left the cave, David remonstrated with him, providing proof that he could have killed him, showing that Saul's pursuit was unjust and irrational (24:8–11). David demonstrated that he was deserving of the kingship, for he did not take vengeance into his own hands. Instead, he appealed to Yahweh to "judge" between him and Saul (24:12, 15). For a moment, Saul recognized the truth, and the narrator records these crucial words from Saul's lips: "You are more righteous than I, for you have repaid me good, whereas I have repaid you evil. And you have declared this day how you have dealt well with me, in that you did not kill me when the LORD put me into your hands. For if a man finds his enemy, will he let him go away safe? So may the LORD reward you with good for what you have done to me this day. And now, behold, I know that you shall surely be king, and that the kingdom of Israel shall be established in your hand" (24:17–20). Even Saul acknowledged David's righteousness and his own evil, asking Yahweh to reward David for his goodness. Most important, Saul spoke the word of the Lord, recognizing that David would be the future king of Israel. In a moment of clarity Saul grasped the truth, acknowledging that David, as the offspring of the woman (see Gen. 3:15), would triumph. Or, to put it another way, God's kingdom cannot fail.

David would only be a worthy king if he pursued righteousness. If he surrendered to evil, his goodness would be compromised, making him unqualified to serve as king. In chapter 25 David was tempted to turn to vengeance, for he and his men had protected Nabal's flocks in the wilderness. When they asked Nabal for some reward, he rudely rejected their request, complaining that they were asking something for nothing. David was enraged and was prepared to kill Nabal and his entire house. But the Lord showed mercy to David, for Abigail, Nabal's wife, intercepted David before he reached Nabal. She apologized for the foolishness of her husband. Most important, she reminded David that he should not seek vengeance for himself (25:26). The crucial words of the story are spoken by Abigail:

> For the LORD will certainly make my lord a sure house, because my lord is fighting the battles of the LORD, and evil shall not be found in you so long as you live. If men rise up to pursue you and to seek your life, the life of my lord shall be bound in the bundle of the living in the care of the LORD your God. And the lives of your enemies he shall sling out as from the hollow of a sling. And when the LORD has done to my lord according to all the good that he has spoken concerning you and has appointed you prince over Israel, my lord shall have no cause of grief or pangs of conscience for having shed blood without cause or for my lord taking vengeance himself. And when the LORD has dealt well with my lord, then remember your servant. (25:28–31)

Abigail reminded David of the promise of God. He would make a "sure house" for David, and the Lord would repay enemies what they deserve. David must not take vengeance; he must leave it to the Lord to recompense evil. David recognized that the Lord sent Abigail to prevent him from executing evil (25:32–34). The greatness of David in contrast to Saul manifests itself here, for unlike Saul, he was open to correction. When Nabal died a few days later, David recognized what had occurred: "Blessed be the LORD who has avenged the insult I received at the hand of Nabal, and has kept back his servant from wrongdoing. The LORD has returned the evil of Nabal on his own head" (25:39). The words of Hannah's song and David's psalm were becoming a reality. Yahweh was lifting up the poor and humble and casting down the rich and proud.

The truth of Hannah's song was especially reflected in the conflict between David and Saul. Despite all of Saul's plots against David, David was being exalted as king, and Saul eventually would face judgment. The Ziphites stirred up again Saul's animus against David by informing him where David was hiding (chap. 26). David and his men came upon Saul's camp while he was sleeping. David and Abishai crept into the camp, and the Lord prevented anyone from waking. Abishai interpreted the event as a sign from God that he should slay Saul (26:8). David, however, refused to strike Yahweh's anointed, for to do so would be to incur guilt. He trusted the Lord to deal with Saul: "As the LORD lives, the LORD will strike him, or his day will come to die, or he will go down into battle and perish" (26:10). Again, the two songs that function as the envelope of the book were the signature of David's life. Yahweh would exalt and rescue David, and David did not have to turn to unrighteousness in order to advance himself. David and Abishai took Saul's spear and water jug to prove that they could have killed him had they wished to do so. Waking Saul up, David remonstrated again with Saul, showing that there were no grounds for Saul's pursuit. Saul admitted his error again, recognizing that the future lay with David. The key words of the narrative are reflected in David's self-defense before Saul: "The LORD rewards every man for his righteousness and his faithfulness, for the LORD gave you into my hand today, and I would not put out my hand against the LORD's anointed. Behold, as your life was precious this day in my sight, so may my life be precious in the sight of the LORD, and may he deliver me out of all tribulation" (26:23–24). Yahweh would shine his favor upon David because David trusted that the Lord would exalt him.

The final chapters of 1 Samuel (chaps. 27–31) record the last days of Saul. The Lord's promise of protection and exaltation did not preclude planning on the part of David. He decisively removed himself from Saul's sphere by escaping to the Philistines (chap. 27). He was out of Saul's reach and conducted raids on enemies, but he deceived Achish of Philistia into thinking that he was attacking his own compatriots. Saul, however, feared the Philistine army that was prepared to attack him (28:5). Yahweh had abandoned him, so he refused to answer Saul's inquiries (28:6–7). Saul was desperate, and so he sought out a medium (28:7–12), even though mediums were banned from the land by none other than Saul himself (28:3)! The medium succeeded in calling up Samuel, but his words to Saul were scarcely surprising, nor were they comforting. After all, Saul himself acknowledged to Samuel, "God has turned away from me and answers me no more, either by prophets or by dreams" (28:15). Samuel proclaimed the word of the Lord to Saul: "Why then do you ask me, since the LORD has turned from you and become your enemy? The LORD has done to you as he spoke by me, for the LORD has torn the kingdom out of your hand and given it to your neighbor, David. Because you did not obey the voice of the LORD and did not carry out his fierce wrath against Amalek, therefore the LORD has done this thing to you this day" (28:16–18). Yahweh was about to cut off the wicked in darkness and raise poor David up from the dust (cf. 2:8–9). Therefore, Saul was about to suffer the same fate as Hophni and Phinehas and to lose a great battle with the Philistines (28:19). A life that had begun gloriously was ending in ignominy and defeat. Any suggestion that Jonathan would serve as king is removed, for he is also killed in the battle in which Saul and Israel are roundly defeated by the Philistines (chap. 31).

What is the function of chapters 29–30 in the story? They explain why David could not come to the aid of Saul. We saw in chapter 27 that David was deceiving Achish, so David's intention almost certainly was to rescue Israel during the battle. But the other Philistine commanders sent him away, rightly discerning that there was no better way for David to earn Saul's affection than to come to his rescue (chap. 29). Even after David was sent away, however, he could have tried on his own to join the battle scene. But this possibility is ruled out by his return to Ziklag (chap. 30), for upon returning, he found that his city of residence had been plundered and his loved ones captured. An arduous journey and battle by David and his followers were necessary to reclaim what was theirs and to punish the Amalekites who attacked them. David showed that he was the rightful king of Israel, for he "strengthened himself in the LORD his God" when his own people wanted to stone him (30:6). He also showed his graciousness in sharing the spoils of victory with those who were too exhausted to make the entire trip, in contrast to the churlishness of some of his army (30:20–24). In any case, Yahweh had arranged circumstances such that David could not assist Saul. The doom of the latter was now sure. A new era had arrived with a king who was a man after God's own heart. Canonically, David points forward to Jesus Christ. Like David, Jesus suffered and was later glorified. And, as we will see, unlike David, he always did the Lord's will. David's obedience was remarkable, but it was not perfect, and thus it pointed forward to a king who surpassed him in righteousness.

David

The account of David's rule as king begins in 2 Samuel. David immediately demonstrates why it is right for him to reign as king. Apparently, the Amalekite lied about slaying Saul, though somehow he got Saul's crown (1 Sam. 31; 2 Sam. 1). He certainly expected a reward from David for killing Saul and bringing the crown to David. He didn't know David well, for his troops could have told the Amalekite how David would feel about killing the Lord's anointed. Instead of celebrating the death of Saul (and of Jonathan), David mourned (1:11–12), composing and singing a lament for the defeat that Israel had suffered (1:17–27). The Amalekite was put to death for admitting that he put Saul to death (1:13–15), showing that David was a righteous and just ruler. He did not countenance murder as a means of political advancement.

David's next step was under the supervision of the Lord. He consulted the Lord about which city he should travel to in Judah, and at Hebron he was anointed king over Judah (2:1–4). David commended the people of Jabesh-gilead for their kindness to Saul (2:5–6), showing that he did not want to divide Israel but to unify it. Nevertheless, the struggle was not over. Abner, Saul's uncle, put forward Ish-bosheth, Saul's son, as king (chap. 2). A struggle ensued for a number of years between Israel and Judah (chaps. 2–4), with David gradually growing stronger (3:1). Things clearly were turning David's way, for Abner and Ish-bosheth had a falling out over a concubine, and Abner transferred his loyalty to David (chap. 3). But the deal fell apart when Joab, the commander of David's army, murdered Abner (3:27). Again, David demonstrated his worthiness to serve as king when he repudiated the slaying of Abner and mourned his death (3:28–39), indicating that the evil was the responsibility of Joab and Abishai. The death of Abner, the general of Ish-bosheth's army, spelled the end of Ish-bosheth's cause (4:1). Two men, Rechab and Baanah, decided to speed things along and murdered Ish-bosheth while he was resting in his bed (4:2–7). Like the Amalekite, these men did not know David very well. They brought David Ish-bosheth's head, expecting commendation and a high place in his administration (4:7–12). David was not impressed. He executed them for such cold-blooded murder, showing that he had no desire to assume the kingship by murder and intrigue. He was, in accord with Hannah's song (1 Sam. 2:1–10) and his own song (2 Sam. 22), looking to the Lord to exalt him. He was a righteous king, and the Lord was his rock and fortress who would bring him victory and the kingdom. He had no need to turn to evil to advance himself.

Finally, the day came when the Lord exalted him and all Israel chose him to be king (chap. 5). They recognized that David had already functioned as a king in significant ways, and they ratified the Lord's words, "You shall be shepherd of my people Israel, and you shall be prince over Israel" (5:2).[25] David established Jerusalem as the capital city of his reign (5:5–9), which was significant because of its central location between the north and the south, and it was "independent of the tribes of Judah and Israel."[26] David's greatness was due to the Lord being with him, and not his own strength or wisdom (5:10). "David knew that the LORD had established him king over Israel, and that he had exalted his kingdom for the sake of his people Israel" (5:12). David's exaltation as king reflects the theme of Hannah's song and the psalm found in 2 Sam. 22. David's family prospered (5:13–16), though the reference to taking more concubines suggests future problems (5:13; cf. Deut. 17:17). As king, David prosecuted his battle against the Philistines by consulting the Lord (5:17–25). The Lord handed them over to David (5:19), and he "burst" upon them (5:20) and struck them down (5:24) in defeat. Clearly, David was prospering because he submitted himself to and trusted in the lordship of Yahweh.

David's God-centeredness is apparent in his desire to bring the ark to Jerusalem (chap. 6). David's joy in Yahweh is evident from the music that accompanied the transfer of the ark (6:5). But Yahweh is always the holy one of Israel. "Bringing the ark to Jerusalem is not just a matter of putting a religious stamp of approval on a regime."[27] Uzzah was struck dead because he touched the ark of the Lord (6:6–7). God's presence was specially manifested through the ark, for there he met with Israel (Exod. 25:20–22) and ruled over them. The Lord mandated that the Levites carry the ark (Num. 1:50). Furthermore, he warned Israel that "they must not touch the holy things lest they die" (Num. 4:15). The explanation for Uzzah's death is fuller in 1 Chronicles (15:13–15), showing that the ark was not transported in the prescribed way. Yahweh was not to be trifled with. David was both angry and afraid at what had happened (2 Sam. 6:8–10), and he refrained from taking the ark farther. But when he realized that the house of Obed-edom was blessed through the ark, he brought it up properly to Jerusalem (6:11–15). David was filled with rapturous joy, dancing and singing with joy to the Lord. His wife Michal, whom the narrator emphasizes was Saul's daughter, despised David for wearing only a linen ephod and dancing with such glee in public. Such actions lacked the dignity, she thought, fitting for a king. Indeed, there are a number of indications that David was functioning as a priest-king:[28] (1) he wears a "linen ephod" (6:14);

25. According to Rendtorff (*Canonical Hebrew Bible*, 110), the word *nāgîd* has a religious rather than political significance.
26. Ibid., 111.
27. Dempster, *Dominion and Dynasty*, 141.
28. See Hahn, *Kinship by Covenant*, 180–81; Gentry and Wellum, *Kingdom through Covenant*, 422.

(2) he sacrifices burnt and peace offerings (6:17–19); (3) he blesses the people as priests did (6:18; cf. Num. 6:24–26). The greatness of David surfaces here, for his joy was in the Lord, and he lived to praise him. It was God who appointed the poor and humble David to serve as king (6:21–22), and the arrogant Michal, who despised him, was humbled by never bearing a child. Therefore, the future king will not come from Saul's line.[29] So once again, we hear echoes of Hannah's song: the poor one has been exalted. David, as priest-king, desires to build the temple of the Lord.[30] Perhaps Scott Hahn is correct in arguing that David's priestly and kingly actions indicate that he represents Melchizedek.[31]

David's passion for Yahweh reaches its zenith in his desire to build a house for God's name (chap. 7). Nathan was sure that such a desire must be the Lord's will and encouraged David to move forward (7:3). But the word of the Lord surprised Nathan and David. The Lord said to David, "I do not really need a house. I have never asked anyone to build one for me, for it was my plan since the days of the exodus to move about with my people Israel in a moveable tent" (i.e., the tabernacle) (7:4–7). In other words, the Lord did not need David to advance his cause. In fact, it was precisely the opposite. It was the Lord who raised up David, exalting the one who was a country shepherd to "be prince over my people Israel" (7:8). Again, we see an allusion to the two songs that dominate the narrative (1 Sam. 2:1–10; 2 Sam. 22).

David's greatness is due to the Lord being with him "wherever [he] went" (7:9), so that his enemies were defeated. David ought not to think that he will make the Lord's name great by building him a temple. Instead, the Lord will make a "great name" for David (7:9). The promise of making his name great is the same promise that the Lord gave to Abraham (Gen. 12:2), which is one indication that the covenant promises with Abraham are becoming a reality through David.[32] The chapter began with David wanting to build the Lord a house, but the story dramatically changes. Instead of David erecting a home for the Lord, the Lord says that he will make a secure place for Israel so that "they may dwell in their own place and be disturbed no more" (7:10). A new day is coming when Israel will not be troubled (7:10–11). In fact, David will not build Yahweh a house, but the Lord "will make you a house" (7:11). In other words, a dynasty will be established so that David's son will succeed him as king (7:12). And this son (Solomon) will build the temple, and his kingdom will never end (7:13). If Solomon or his descendants sin, the Lord will discipline them, but he will never withdraw his "steadfast love" (7:14–15). In other words,

---

29. See Dempster, *Dominion and Dynasty*, 141.
30. So Hahn, *Kinship by Covenant*, 181.
31. Ibid., 192–93.
32. So Dumbrell, *Faith of Israel*, 87.

his covenant with David and his sons will endure perpetually. Individual kings will be disciplined, but the covenant will never be withdrawn.[33] Ultimately, a Davidic king will rule over Israel. "Your house and your kingdom shall be made sure forever before me. Your throne shall be established forever" (7:16).

This is a most remarkable passage. The Lord is pleased that David wants to build him a house, but the danger is that David will think that he has done great things for God. Therefore, the Lord focuses on what he has done for David, pledging to build him an enduring house. It is the Lord who lifts up and blesses and sustains. He is always David's rock, fortress, and deliverer. The Davidic covenant represents an expansion of the covenant with Abraham. The Lord will bring universal blessing to the world through the offspring of Abraham.[34] Now it is clear that this universal blessing will also become a reality through the offspring of David. Yahweh will bless the world through a king. Yahweh's lordship over the world will be expressed through the rule of a Davidic monarch. Matthew, of course, picks up this very theme in the first book of the NT. Jesus is "the son of David, the son of Abraham" (1:1). The offspring of the woman who will conquer the serpent (Gen. 3:15) will also be the offspring of David.

David is stunned and almost speechless because of the graciousness of the Lord (7:18, 20). He rightly exclaims, "Who am I?" and "What is my house?" in hearing that the Lord has promised such great blessings for him (7:18). Indeed, the Lord has given promises that relate to his family forever; this represents the *tôrâ*, the charter for all humankind (7:19).[35] In other words, the Lord has revealed that he will bless the world through a Davidic dynasty. David's heart welled up with praise, extolling the greatness of God and exclaiming, "There is none like you and there is no God besides you" (7:22). The exodus from Egypt, in which the Lord redeemed a people for himself, testifies that the Lord will never abandon his people, that Israel will be "your people forever" (7:23–24). David closes by praying that the Lord will fulfill what he promised, that he will build a house for David, just as he said, so that Israel will be blessed forever (7:27–29).

Hahn nicely summarizes the essential elements of the covenant with David insofar as they point to the NT and fulfillment in Jesus Christ:[36] (1) David's

---

33. Hahn (*Kinship by Covenant*, 198) fails to see this clearly and hence merges too closely the conditionality in the Mosaic and Davidic covenants.

34. For the connections to the covenant with Abraham, see Satterthwaite, "Samuel," 181; Hahn, *Kinship by Covenant*, 196.

35. See Leithart, *A Son to Me*, 201; Williamson, *Sealed with an Oath*, 129; Hahn, *Kinship by Covenant*, 183; Gentry and Wellum, *Kingdom through Covenant*, 399–401.

36. Hahn, *Kinship by Covenant*, 200–201. He sees these eight elements of the covenant of David fulfilled in Luke (pp. 218–19).

dynasty was promised via a covenant; (2) David was God's son (7:14); (3) he was the anointed one ; (4) David's rule was tied to Jerusalem, to Mount Zion; (5) his "monarchy was inextricably bound to *the Temple*";[37] (6) David ruled over twelve tribes, emphasizing the unity of the people of God; (7) the Davidic empire was international; and (8) David's house would last forever.

David praised the Lord, and therefore the Lord continued to exalt him, granting him victories over Philistia, Moab, the king of Zobah, the Syrians, and Edom (8:1–13). He also received tribute from foreign powers (8:12). The Lord was honoring the one who honored him. The distinctiveness of David's rule is summed up as follows: "And the LORD gave victory to David wherever he went. So David reigned over all Israel. And David administered justice and equity to all his people" (8:14–15). David was a wise and just king, and Yahweh had lifted the shepherd boy up from "the ash heap" (cf. 1 Sam. 2:8). David's graciousness is on display in his kindness to Mephibosheth (chap. 9). Typically, kings would wipe out potential threats to the throne, and Mephibosheth, as the son of Jonathan, even though he was lame, still functioned as such. But David remembered his covenant with Jonathan, and so he treated Mephibosheth like royalty by allowing him to dine at the royal table and by restoring to him the land of Saul. David realized that his kingship was established by the Lord, and that he did not need to turn to evil to secure his rule. Finally, when the Ammonites insulted David, they formed a broad coalition to defeat David and his army (chap. 10). But the entire coalition was crushed, so that David reigned in strength over his enemies.

David's life up to this point has been a remarkable account of his trust in and obedience to the Lord. An ominous note is struck, however, in 11:1.[38] David should have gone out to war, but instead he remained in Jerusalem. He spied Bathsheba bathing, called for her, and had sex with her (11:2–4). When he discovered that she was pregnant, he summoned her husband, Uriah, from the battle, trying to induce him to go home to sleep with Bathsheba so that his malfeasance would be covered up (11:5–13). Uriah, in striking contrast to David, was too noble for this. He did not allow himself to enjoy the pleasures of home while his fellow soldiers were on the field of battle. Even though David got him drunk and tried to persuade him to go home, he refused to do so. David was determined to hide his sin, and so he instructed Joab to place Uriah at the

37. Ibid., 201.
38. Hamilton overstates the point in saying that David "has been raised up as a new Adam in a new Eden, and tragically he falls prey to a new temptation that sets the nation on a path to a new exile from the place where God dwells" (*God's Glory in Salvation*, 173). It is better to say that David is analogous to a new Adam, and what we have is analogous to a new Eden because David, unlike Adam, was already a sinner.

front line of the battle, where he was most likely to be slain (11:14–25). The plan worked exactly as David had hoped, and Uriah was killed in the battle. Soon after, David took Bathsheba as his wife, and a son was born (11:27–28). But 1–2 Samuel have emphasized again and again that the Lord exalts the righteous and casts down the wicked. The cloud on the horizon appears in the last verse of the chapter: "But the thing that David had done displeased the LORD" (11:27).

The hammer blow is about to fall. Nathan recounted to David a parable about a rich man and a poor man, with the former taking the solitary lamb of the latter (12:1–6). David was properly enraged, but Nathan turned the tables on him by disclosing that David was the man in the parable (12:7). The Lord recounted all he did for David: anointing him as king, rescuing him from Saul, giving him a house and wives (12:7–8). Indeed, the Lord would have given him "much more" (12:8). David, by sinning, "despised the word of the LORD" (12:9). The consequences of David's sin fit the crime that he committed. He destroyed the house of Uriah; now conflict will sunder his house (12:10). He took another man's wife, and the Lord will see to it that another man will lie with his wives before the eyes of all Israel (12:11–12).

However, David's greatness surfaces even in this hour. Unlike Saul, he did not introduce a parade of excuses to justify his wickedness. He simply and humbly acknowledged, "I have sinned against the LORD" (12:13). The Lord granted him forgiveness, but the child born to Bathsheba was not spared (12:14–23). And yet there is mercy in the midst of judgment. Remarkably, the Lord blesses and loves the second son of Bathsheba and David, Solomon (12:24–25). One might think that any son of what began as an adulterous union would never be the one to succeed David. God's grace, however, is free and unpredictable. Solomon was specially loved by the Lord.

In the succeeding chapters of 2 Samuel, however, the judgment pronounced on David is unleashed (chaps. 13–20).[39] David's son Amnon fell "in love" with his half-sister, Tamar (13:1–19). Pretending to be sick, he arranged matters so that she would minister to him in his sickness. When she arrived to care for him, he raped her. Absalom, Tamar's brother, was enraged with Amnon, but he bided his time, waiting for the right moment to strike (13:20–39). After two years, Absalom got revenge for the rape of Tamar by killing Amnon. Absalom fled Israel and was absent for three years, but under Joab's influence he returned to the land (14:1–23).

Even after Absalom returned to Israel, David would not see him for two more years. Thus, when David finally consented to see his son Absalom, five

---

39. Satterthwaite ("Samuel," 181) points out that rape and civil war were present in Israel when they did not have a king in Judg. 17–21.

years had passed since they laid eyes on each other (14:24–33). In the interval, however, Absalom had come to resent David, plotting to overthrow his father. Absalom had natural advantages. He was incredibly attractive and handsome (14:25), and he used chariots and horses to display his importance (15:1). He insinuated himself into the affections of the people, claiming that the Davidic administration had no concern for justice, and that justice would become a reality only if he served as judge (15:2–6). Absalom launched his insurrection at Hebron, driving David out of Jerusalem (15:7–18). David once again was living the way he did when Saul was king, fleeing from an opponent who was trying to kill him. And the trust in Yahweh that David had in those days was evident as well. He left the ark in Jerusalem, resigning himself to the will of the Lord, trusting that the Lord would do what "seems good to him" (15:24–26). David also planned and prayed, sending Ahimaaz the son of Zadok and Jonathan the son of Abiathar to report to him any news (15:27–29). He also prayed that the Lord would make Ahithophel's counsel foolish (15:31), and he sent the counselor who would be the answer to that prayer, Hushai, back to Jerusalem (15:32–34), for the latter, he said, would "defeat for me the counsel of Ahithophel" (15:34).

Shimei, of the house of Saul, threw stones at David and cursed him as a man of blood, seeing Yahweh's vengeance upon him in the removal of his kingly power (16:5–8). Just as Abishai desired to slay Saul in the past, so he wanted to kill Shimei for his shameful treatment of the king (16:9). David, however, still relied upon the truths in Hannah's song (1 Sam. 2:1–10) and the final song of the book (2 Sam. 22). David replied that Shimei's curse might be from the Lord, and if the Lord was against him, then resistance would be futile, for no one would be blessed whom the Lord cursed (16:10). Furthermore, since David's own son had turned against him, it made sense for one from the tribe of Benjamin to do so (16:11). By absorbing the curse, the Lord might turn it into a blessing for David. "It may be that the LORD will look on the wrong done to me, and that the LORD will repay me with good for his cursing today" (16:12). Meanwhile, Ahithophel's counsel against David and in favor of Absalom was unerring (16:20–23). He counseled Absalom to have sexual relations with David's concubines "in the sight of all Israel" (16:22), fulfilling the prophecy of 12:11–12. This demonstrated that there was no turning back, that there would be no reconciliation between David and Absalom.

The tide began to turn in David's favor starting in chapter 17. The poor man who was hungry and empty was about to be exalted again. The proud and arrogant who had seized the kingdom were about to be humiliated. Both Ahithophel and Hushai gave counsel on how to conquer David and his men (17:1–13). In fact, the counsel of Ahithophel was superior, but Absalom and his men believed that the counsel of Hushai, the secret ally of David, was better (17:14). The narrator informs us why Absalom and his advisers ended up disbelieving the wise counsel of Ahithophel: "The LORD had ordained to defeat the good counsel of Ahithophel, so that the LORD might bring harm upon Absalom" (17:14).[40] Indeed, David's prayer that Yahweh would make Ahithophel's advice foolish had become a reality (15:31). Similarly, David's spies, Jonathan and Ahimaaz, escaped the clutches of Absalom and were able to report to David the advice from the palace (17:15–22). David's forces were careful to protect him by refusing to send him into the battle (18:1–4). Absalom, on the contrary, was undone in a most unusual way. His long hair was caught in a tree, and, hanging there helplessly, he was slain by Joab and his men (18:9–15). The wicked man had been humiliated and hung on a tree, and David, who was persecuted by his own son and fleeing like a fugitive, was again exalted. David returned as the gracious king, forgiving Shimei (19:16–23), showing kindness to both Mephibosheth and Ziba (19:24–30), and bestowing his kindness upon Barzillai for supporting him in his time of need (19:31–40). The tensions between Israel and Judah that would continually surface in Israel's history bubbled over, and Sheba from Benjamin drew Israel after him, but the rebellion was easily quashed (chap. 20).

The book of 2 Samuel concludes, then, with the kingdom safely in David's hands. The last chapter is significant. David fell into sin again and insisted on taking a census, trusting in the vastness of his army instead of in the Lord (24:1–2). Even Joab recognized that the king's desire to take a census was displeasing to the Lord (24:3). David recognized his sin, confessing it to the Lord and pleading for forgiveness (24:10). The Lord offered three options of judgment to David, who chose what is, according to von Rad, the most surprising one: three days of plague upon the land (24:11–14).[41] In doing so, he was casting himself upon the mercy of the Lord. The Lord sent a disease that struck down seventy thousand and threatened to wipe out Jerusalem (24:15–16). David, as king and mediator for the people, recognized that it was his sin that brought such devastation upon the people (24:17), and so he asked the Lord to inflict on him the punishment for Israel's sin: "Please let your hand be against me and against my father's house" (24:17). The means of forgiveness, however, could hardly be David himself. He was a righteous man, but he was also a transgressor and thus could not atone for the nation's sin. David's desire to atone for the nation's sin pointed to someone to come,

---

40. As von Rad (*Israel's Historical Traditions*, 315) notes, we see the theology of the writer at work here.
41. Von Rad, *Israel's Historical Traditions*, 318.

a priest and king more righteous than David. The prophet Gad instructed David to "raise an altar to the LORD on the threshing floor of Araunah the Jebusite" (24:18). The altar would be the means by which the plague would be turned away from Israel (24:21, 25). The place for the temple was purchased. As Leithart remarks, "The big story in the book of Samuel is the transition from tabernacle to temple."[42] Over the course of the Samuel narrative, Israel had moved from having a tabernacle to having a temple, from Shiloh as the center of worship to Jerusalem as the center of worship and the place where the temple would be built.[43] Israel had also moved from having judges to having a king.

Conclusion

In 1–2 Samuel we see the end of the period of the judges and the beginning of the kingship in Israel. Saul, as the first king, replicated the sin of Adam and of Israel. He began by trusting in the Lord, but then he turned away by failing to carry out the Lord's command. Therefore, the Lord did not reward him with a dynasty. Von Rad sums up the life of Saul "as the God-forsaken, driven from one delusion to the other, desperate, and in the end swallowed up in miserable darkness."[44] Instead, the Lord raised up David as a man after his own heart. The lives of Saul and David reflect Hannah's song (1 Sam. 2:1–10) and David's psalm (2 Sam. 22). Yahweh exalted and blessed the humble David, who trusted in and obeyed the Lord, whereas he brought to an end Saul, who turned to evil and pursued his selfish will. David's reign significantly reflected the justice and joy of a king who rules in the fear of God (2 Sam. 23:3–4). Leithart observes, "Saul's rise and fall is like an expanded retelling of the story of Adam, and if Saul was like the first Adam, David was a type of the Last Adam, called to replace the fallen king as the head of God's people, persecuted without cause by his rival, waiting patiently until the Lord gave him the kingdom."[45] Therefore, the Lord made an everlasting covenant with David (23:5), whereas Saul was thrust aside because of his wickedness (23:6–7). Under David Israel experienced to a great extent the blessing promised through the offspring of the woman (Gen. 3:15) and the offspring of Abraham (Gen. 12:1–3). For instance, David triumphed over his enemies, bringing peace and security to the land of

42. Leithart, *A Son to Me*, 26. Perhaps this is not the biggest story, for the promise of a Davidic dynasty probably is even more important.
43. Dempster, *Dominion and Dynasty*, 134. Hahn (*Kinship by Covenant*, 190–91) notes that the location was the place where Abraham offered Isaac.
44. Von Rad, *Israel's Historical Traditions*, 324.
45. Leithart, *A Son to Me*, 27.

Israel.[46] The dominion under foreign powers that was so typical of the days of the judges had ended. David and his men "finished the job that Joshua had started."[47] Yahweh was ruling over Israel through its anointed king, David. Indeed, David's rule extended beyond Israel. There is no clear indication, however, that faith in Yahweh accompanied David's rule beyond the borders of Israel. On the one hand, the blessing of Abraham promised to the whole world was not realized under David. On the other hand, Yahweh promised to extend the dynasty of David forever (2 Sam. 7). There would always be a son of David on the throne. The lordship of Yahweh would be extended through a son of David, through an anointed king.[48]

And yet David was not *the* king through whom the Lord would bless the whole world. Although his trust in and obedience to Yahweh were exemplary, the narrative also emphasizes his sin against Yahweh and the terrible consequences that were unleashed on the kingdom through his sin. David offered to atone for the nation's sin, but a better offering was needed to atone for Israel. David points forward to a better king, a king who always did the will of the Lord, Jesus the Christ. Just as David was persecuted by Saul, so too Jesus was persecuted by his enemies. Just as David did not turn to evil when he was mistreated, so too Jesus "continued entrusting himself to him who judges justly" (1 Pet. 2:23). "He is the True King, who rises like a sun and causes the vegetation of the land to flourish."[49] Finally, Jesus, unlike David, could offer himself for the forgiveness of sins because he was the sinless one, and therefore the blessing promised to the whole world through Abraham would become a reality through him. Jesus was not only the true king but also the "faithful priest" (1 Sam. 2:35).

---

46. For the significance of land in Samuel, see Bergen, *1, 2 Samuel*, 44.
47. Dempster, *Dominion and Dynasty*, 141. See also Dumbrell, *Faith of Israel*, 87.
48. Williamson (*Sealed with an Oath*, 131–32) maintains that the wording in chapter 23 also anticipates a future ruler through whom the promises will be realized.
49. Leithart, *A Son to Me*, 29.

10

1–2 Kings

Introduction

Like 1–2 Samuel, 1–2 Kings, though two books in English, should be considered as one book. What we have here is a theological history. "Theology and history are inseparable in Kings, not because of any sort of special pleading on the author's part but because the writer was convinced that historical effects were caused by theological principles that were heeded or ignored."[1] Reviewing the overarching story, we see that the Lord promised to bring in his kingdom through the offspring of the woman (Gen. 3:15), through the offspring of Abraham (Gen. 12:1–3). God promises to Abraham offspring, a land, and a blessing that encompasses the entire world. By the time we get to 1–2 Kings, Israel is teeming with people and it occupies the land. Indeed, 1–2 Samuel has added a new dimension to the old promise. There were hints in the five books of Moses that the blessing of Abraham would come to the world through a king (Gen. 17:6, 16; 49:10; Num. 24:17–19; Deut. 17:14–20).[2] What 1–2 Samuel has made clear is that this universal blessing will stream to the world through a king from David's line. The covenant with David (2 Sam. 7), which promises that a son from his line will rule, will be the means by which the covenant with Abraham becomes a reality.

We begin 1–2 Kings, then, with expectation, for it seems that worldwide blessing is just around the corner. Israel is in the land. The kingdom has been established under David. Israel apparently is on the cusp of being the vehicle by which blessing is extended to the entire world.[3] David's son is about to

1. House, *Old Testament Theology*, 250.
2. See Alexander, *Servant King*, 30.
3. See Hamilton, *God's Glory in Salvation*, 178.

build the temple where Yahweh will reside. In 1–2 Kings is recounted the story of what happened after the days of David. But the story is a surprising one. Instead of becoming a blessing to the world, Israel becomes entangled in evil, forsakes the ways and commands of the Lord, and suffers exile. The book of 1–2 Kings answers this question: "What happened to the Lord's promise to Israel, and what are the prospects for the future?"

One of the characteristics of 1–2 Kings is the interest in history that pervades the narrative, especially the history of kings. The book is aptly named, for what we find is scarcely a history "from below" in which the everyday life and social activity of the common people are related. Instead, the author focuses on history "from above," on the kings that ruled Judah and Israel. The fate of both Judah and Israel is encapsulated in the life of the kings who represented the people. It seems that both blessing and curse come to the people through the lives of the various kings. We can conclude, given that both Israel and Judah end up in exile, that the narrator is telling us as readers that the nation needs a better king, that the hope for the nation is a new and better David.[4] "First and Second Kings make it clear that no human king can lead God's people, not even the second David, Josiah."[5] Clearly, the NT picks up this theme, seeing Jesus as the true descendant of David, the one through whom the promises made to David and Abraham are fulfilled.

Thus, the history in this narrative is focused on the kings, those of Judah and those of Israel. Indeed, the narrator is careful to inform the readers about how long each king reigned and when his reign began. The chronology of the story clearly interests the writer, for not only are we told how long kings ruled but also the time period of their reign is always correlated with the history of the king in the north or the south. The reign of the kings of Judah, in other words, is never related in isolation from the reign of the kings of Israel, and vice versa. When a certain king ruled in Judah, we always know who was reigning in Israel, and we also are told the exact year when the king of Judah began his reign relative to the king in Israel. It is evident, then, that time and place matter to the narrator of the story. Clearly, the author selected and shaped the account to reflect what he wanted to teach his readers, for the story spans around four hundred years of history.

What we see in 1–2 Kings is a fall from a nearly paradisiacal state to exile.[6] The nation unravels and turns to false gods instead of trusting in the Lord.

---

4. For the centrality of the Davidic promise, see House, *Old Testament Theology*, 252–53. See also Childs, *Old Testament as Scripture*, 292–93.

5. Dumbrell, *Faith of Israel*, 90.

6. "The history ends with the loss of the land and the exile of the people. However, the threat of this disaster appears from the beginning of the history and connects the various reigns like a red thread" (Childs, *Old Testament as Scripture*, 288).

The curses of Deuteronomy are experienced by both Israel and Judah when they are thrust into exile.[7] Prophets and those who speak the word of the Lord play a central role in 1–2 Kings.[8] The narrative is threaded with the words of the prophets promising success if the people (and especially the kings) follow the Lord, and judgment if they turn away from the Lord's commands. I. W. Provan argues that the central theme is that Yahweh is the one and only true God. When Israel follows the Lord, it is blessed, but when Israel forsakes him, it is cursed, for Yahweh must be central in Israel's worship.[9] The narrator underscores in dramatic ways that the words of the prophets always come true. No king or enemy can thwart the word of the Lord. The focus is on judgment, given the nation's fall into sin, so that the terrible consequences predicted by the prophets become a reality. The book seems to end with despair, since both Judah and Israel are in exile, but we will see a ray of hope in the conclusion of the book. Indeed, the message of hope is woven into the warp and woof of the book, for the word of the Lord also promised a perpetual dynasty to David. That word cannot fail, so the history of Israel, according to the narrator, is not over. Even though the story of 1–2 Kings is the account of paradise lost, there is still hope for paradise regained.

An Anticipation of Paradise: 1 Kings 1–10

The first two chapters of the narrative, 1 Kings 1–2, often are identified as part of the succession narrative. Who will succeed David as king over Israel? Adonijah and Solomon stand in stark contrast with each other, for Adonijah grasps after the throne, scheming with his loyalists to succeed David. Solomon, on the other hand, does nothing. Others intervene to ensure that the kingdom will be given to him. Solomon was exalted by his father, just as the Lord Jesus Christ was exalted by his Father. Solomon did not use devious means to receive the kingdom; he was given the kingdom. Adonijah, on the other hand, "exalted himself" (1:5), and our suspicions about Adonijah are also raised because he seems to be Absalom reborn, for Adonijah "prepared for himself chariots and horsemen, and fifty men to run before him" (1:5; cf. 2 Sam. 15:1). Though two different Hebrew words are used, both Adonijah and Absalom are also praised for being "handsome" (1 Kings 1:6; 2 Sam. 14:25).

The narrator also ties Adonijah to Hophni and Phinehas, the two wicked sons of Eli, for just as Eli failed to reprove Hophni and Phinehas (1 Sam.

---

7. Deuteronomy clearly influences how the author interprets Israel's history. See ibid., 291–92.
8. For helpful comments, see House, *Old Testament Theology*, 250–51.
9. Provan, "Kings," 184–85.

3:13), so too David failed to correct Adonijah (1 Kings 1:6), with the result that Adonijah was self-absorbed and self-promoting. Another ominous sign appears in those who supported the crowning of Adonijah: Joab and Abiathar. No one doubted Joab's worth as a soldier and leader, but his ruthless murders of Abner (2 Sam. 3:27) and Amasa (2 Sam. 20:8–10) illustrated his viciousness. Abiathar was a descendant of Eli, and the Lord had promised that he would remove the priesthood from Eli's descendants (1 Sam. 2:27–36). However, those who supported Solomon's accession had a sterling reputation: Benaiah as one of David's mighty men, Zadok the priest, and Nathan the prophet (1 Kings 1:8, 26, 32, 38, 44). It is telling, therefore, that Adonijah "did not invite Nathan the prophet or Benaiah or the mighty men or Solomon his brother" to his coronation (1:10). The remainder of chapter 1 relates how Nathan executed a plan by which David would publicly install Solomon on the throne. Those who crowned Adonijah were worried, and so they dispersed to avoid retribution.

If chapter 1 narrates Solomon's accession to the throne, chapter 2 tells us how his kingdom was secured and established so that no threat to his reign remained. David on his deathbed gives final instructions to Solomon, emphasizing first of all that he must keep the commands and rules found in the Mosaic covenant (2:2–4). Only if Solomon remains faithful will his rule be secure. But then David turns to political matters in the kingdom, advising Solomon to be gracious to the sons of Barzillai the Gileadite, while exacting retribution on Joab and Shimei (2:5–9). Many interpreters are convinced that David's counsel represents a turn to evil, especially after his gracious forgiveness of Shimei earlier (2 Sam. 19:16–23).[10] I think it doubtful, however, that the narrator conceived of David's advice in this way. Instead, all of chapters 1–2 fit together, showing how the kingdom was rightly secured in Solomon's hands. We have already commented on Joab's malevolent character. When this is added to his siding with Adonijah, Joab's continued existence constitutes a threat to Solomon's reign. Hence, the narrator views Solomon's removal of Joab as an illustration of his wisdom and justice, not his vengeance (2:28–34). Similarly, the removal of Shimei (2:36–44) represents the wisdom and justice of Solomon, for Solomon granted Shimei an opportunity to preserve his life, but Shimei violated the conditions given to him. In addition, Solomon did not take action against Adonijah until the latter requested Abishag, who slept with David at the end of his life, as his wife (2:13–25). The narrator gives no indication that he disagrees with Solomon, who viewed such an action as an attempt by Adonijah to secure

10. See, e.g., Goldingay, *Israel's Gospel*, 561.

the kingdom. The execution of Adonijah removes the most prominent threat to the throne. Furthermore, Abiathar was deposed as a priest and sent home in fulfillment of the prophecy made to Eli (2:35–37). The narrator seems to approve what took place, for he concludes by saying, "So the kingdom was established in the hand of Solomon" (2:46). The narrator is not merely recording what happened; he places his imprimatur of approval on what Solomon did to secure the kingdom.

A warning signal appears, however, in Solomon's marriage to Pharaoh's daughter (3:1; cf. Deut. 17:17).[11] Nevertheless, Solomon began by following David's instructions. He loved Yahweh and obeyed him (3:3). Even in offering sacrifices on the high places, he was still devoted, albeit imperfectly, to Yahweh (3:4). Indeed, Solomon functions here as a priest-king like Melchizedek.[12] The Lord appeared to Solomon in a dream at Gibeon at the inception of his reign, summoning him to make his request in prayer. Solomon asked for wisdom to govern Israel so that he might do so in a way that pleased the Lord (chap. 3). We have an important connection and link with the wisdom tradition in the OT here. A just king will rule God's people with wisdom. Wisdom themes and the kingdom of God are not separated from each other; they are interrelated. Jesus Christ, as the sovereign of his people, fulfills this expectation, for as the wisdom of God, he rules over the church.[13] The Lord also blessed Solomon with riches, long life, and deliverance from his enemies, since he did not ask for such. What was crucial, however, the Lord tells Solomon, is that he "walk in my ways, keeping my statutes and my commandments" (3:14). For the narrator, the issue of obedience to Yahweh, to keeping covenant stipulations, is what will make or break Israel.

The reign of Solomon almost represents paradise in its blessing for the nation. What Israel needed was a king to rule with wisdom and justice (cf. Ps. 72) and in the fear of the Lord.[14] Solomon's wisdom was legendary, as is exhibited in the conflict between two prostitutes, one whose child died and one whose child lived, who quarreled over which of them was truly the mother of the living child (3:16–28). The narrator captures how Israel responded to Solomon: "And all Israel heard of the judgment that the king had rendered, and they stood in awe of the king, because they perceived that the wisdom of God was in him to do justice" (3:28). Life was practically idyllic, so that Israel was

11. Dumbrell calls it "an ominous anticovenantal political notice" (*Faith of Israel*, 91).
12. See Hahn, *Kinship by Covenant*, 199.
13. So also Alexander, *Servant King*, 88.
14. For indications that Solomon was a kind of "new Adam" who reigned in wisdom, fulfilling the creation mandate, see Beale, *Biblical Theology*, 66–73; Davies, "'Discerning between Good and Evil.'"

close to experiencing a new Eden.[15] The rule that God intended human beings to exercise over the world was virtually becoming a reality through a son of David, Solomon.[16] The kingdom was well organized (4:1–19), and there were ample provisions for Solomon's household (4:22–23, 26–28). The joy in Israel was palpable: "Judah and Israel were as many as the sand by the sea. They ate and drank and were happy" (4:20). Clearly, the promise to Abraham of countless offspring was becoming a reality. And Israel was living under Yahweh's lordship in the land, so that the land promises made to Abraham, Isaac, and Jacob were also coming to pass. "Solomon ruled over all the kingdoms from the Euphrates to the land of the Philistines and to the border of Egypt. They brought tribute and served Solomon all the days of his life" (4:21).[17]

Solomon's rule over the land was free from stress. It was remarkably peaceful and Edenic. Solomon "had dominion over all the region west of the Euphrates from Tiphsah to Gaza, over all the kings west of the Euphrates. And he had peace on all sides around him. And Judah and Israel lived in safety, from Dan even to Beersheba, every man under his vine and under his fig tree, all the days of Solomon" (4:25). The peace and the security of Israel were established under King Solomon, who, as we noted above, was particularly celebrated for his wisdom: "God gave Solomon wisdom and understanding beyond measure, and breadth of mind like the sand on the seashore, so that Solomon's wisdom surpassed the wisdom of all the people of the east and all the wisdom of Egypt" (4:29–30). The wisdom of Solomon was so extensive that people from all over came to learn from him (4:31–34). As Dempster says, "This epitomizes national security and prosperity similar to that predicted for the messianic ruler's reign in the latter days (Gen. 49:11–12; cf. Mic. 4:4)."[18]

What makes the land Edenic, however, is not fundamentally its prosperity and peace but rather the presence of Yahweh in the land. Therefore, the narrator emphasizes the building of the temple under Solomon's direction (chap. 5).[19] Just as the original garden of Eden was like a temple, so the land of Israel was like a new Eden with the temple at its center. As Jon Levenson

---

15. See Dempster, *Dominion and Dynasty*, 148.

16. So Hamilton, *God's Glory in Salvation*, 178–79.

17. "The nation, in Abrahamic promise terms, had become a great nation, now too numerous to be counted (3:8; 4:20). Israel now occupied the covenantal boundaries from the Euphrates to the border of Egypt (1 Kings 4:21) . . . and had achieved rest from her enemies all around (cf. 4:21)" (Dumbrell, *Faith of Israel*, 95).

18. Dempster, *Dominion and Dynasty*, 148.

19. Perhaps the story up to this point climaxes with the building of the temple (Brueggemann, *Theology of the Old Testament*, 211). For one perspective on temple theology, see Terrien, *Elusive Presence*, 161–226.

says, "The Temple was, in fact, a paradise."[20] Solomon, instead of David, was called upon to build the temple, for he was a man of peace (5:3–4). Solomon here anticipates the prince of peace, Jesus, who builds the new temple of the Lord—the people of the new covenant. The Lord granted Solomon "rest on every side" (5:4). Therefore, he intended to build a house for God's "name" (5:5). God's name plays a significant role in 1–2 Kings, and it is particularly associated with Jerusalem and the temple. This will be even more apparent as we consider shortly Solomon's prayer for the temple in chapter 8. God's name represents his character, his true nature and being. The temple being built for Yahweh's name shows the centrality of the Lord in Israel. Jerusalem is in the center of Israel, and at the center of Jerusalem is the temple, and the central theme of the temple is the presence of the Lord among his people.[21]

The narrator's interest in chronology surfaces in relationship to the temple. We are told how many years after the exodus from Egypt the building began, and also the year and month during Solomon's reign (6:1), and the writer further tells us the month and year in which the temple was finished, noting that it took seven years to complete (6:37–38). Levenson argues that the seven years allude to the seven days that it took to create the world (Gen. 2:1–3), suggesting ultimately that "the world is God's Temple, and in it he finds rest. . . . The Sabbatical experience and the Temple experience are one."[22] And yet the rest enjoyed by Solomon and the temple built by him are temporary, indicating that there is a greater rest and a greater temple to come.

The specifications for the temple are relayed in chapter 6. Intercalated is the description of Solomon's house (7:1–12), and then comes further description of the temple and its furnishings (7:13–51). No criticism of the splendor or length of time it took to build Solomon's house is implied. The narrative focuses on the beauty, size, and loveliness of both Solomon's house and the temple. The holiness of the temple is featured; no human tool was heard where the house was built (6:7). The temple is no talisman, for the Lord emphasizes that Solomon must keep his commands in order to enjoy the promise given to David (6:12). Yahweh will dwell with Israel and be faithful to them if they are obedient (6:13). The word "dwell" signifies that the uniqueness of the temple is found in the Lord's presence there, and his presence was especially found in the inner sanctuary, where the ark was placed (6:19). The inner sanctuary was a perfect cube overlaid completely with gold (6:20), signifying that this was consecrated space. "His presence is not gross and tangible, but subtle

---

20. Levenson, *Sinai and Zion*, 128. See also Alexander, *Eden to the New Jerusalem*, 44–45.
21. House (*Old Testament Theology*, 254) sees this as fulfilling the requirement of Deut. 12 that Israel worship at one central sanctuary.
22. Levenson, *Sinai and Zion*, 145 (see also pp. 142–44).

and delicate."[23] Two cherubim were stretched from end to end in the inner sanctuary (6:23–28; 8:6–7), just as cherubim guarded the divine presence in the tabernacle (Exod. 25:18–22) and in the garden of Eden (Gen. 3:24). The temple represents "the junction between heaven and earth, Zion, the Temple mount, is a preeminent locus of communication between God and man."[24]

The awesome holiness of the Lord is expressed by the ark and cherubim being placed in the inner sanctuary. The rule of Yahweh is also indicated, for he is "enthroned above the cherubim" (2 Kings 19:15; cf. 1 Sam. 4:4; 6:2; Pss. 80:1; 99:1).[25] The central reason for the idyllic nature of Solomon's reign was the presence of Yahweh and his lordship over the people. The people had rest and safety in the land when they and their king trusted in and obeyed the Lord. Hence, chapter 8 ends, "[Solomon] sent the people away, and they blessed the king and went to their homes joyful and glad of heart for all the goodness that the Lord had shown to David his servant and to Israel his people" (8:66).

Solomon celebrates the opening of the completed temple by bringing the ark into the building and by offering sacrifices and prayer (chap. 8). Solomon operates here (see also chap. 3) as both king and priest in terms of his prayer and in sacrifices,[26] anticipating again Jesus Christ, who serves as both king and priest. The God-centeredness of chapter 8 is striking. After the ark has been lodged in the temple and sacrifices have been offered, "a cloud filled the house of the LORD, so that the priests could not stand to minister because of the cloud, for the glory of the LORD filled the house of the LORD" (8:10–11). This language reverberates with the same terms used when Moses first set up the tabernacle (Exod. 40:34–35), showing that Yahweh was pleased with the building of the temple. The emphasis is on the presence of Yahweh with his people in the temple; his awesome glory was so stunning that the priests could not fulfill their duties.

Solomon in his prayer immediately picks up on this theme. The temple is a place where God dwells (8:12–13). The Lord especially dwells in the innermost sanctuary, which testifies to the truth that Yahweh "dwell[s] in thick darkness" (8:12), signifying both the graciousness and the mysteriousness of his presence. Yahweh's dwelling in the temple reflects his dwelling in heaven. Heaven is God's dwelling place, and the temple on earth functions as an earthly counterpart to a heavenly reality (8:30, 43). Obviously, there is no Platonic

---

23. Ibid., 125.

24. Ibid.

25. Ollenburger (*Zion*) argues that Zion represents fundamentally Yahweh's kingship. Thus, he says, Yahweh's reigning in Zion entails the security and protection of Israel as long as Israel trusts in him.

26. "Solomon plays a priestly role" (Dumbrell, *Faith of Israel*, 92).

theory of forms here! It is closer to what we find in the Lord's Prayer, where Jesus instructed his disciples to pray that the Lord's will be done on earth as it is in heaven (Matt. 6:10). So too, the Lord dwells on earth, in the inner sanctuary, just as he does in heaven.

The manifestation of Yahweh's name and character is communicated via the temple (8:16, 29; 9:3, 7). Solomon recognizes that Yahweh cannot be limited to or contained by the temple: "Behold, heaven and the highest heaven cannot contain you; how much less this house that I have built" (8:27). If the Lord is too immense for the heavens, then certainly he cannot be limited to the temple. And yet he has graciously condescended to put his name there (8:16, 20, 29, 43, 44, 48). The Lord has revealed himself to his people through the temple. His holiness is evident, for one cannot casually walk into his presence; rather, there are mandatory duties and the offering of requisite sacrifices. Yahweh is the awesome and terrible God who strikes down those who offend him. Truly there is no one like him; he is incomparable (8:23). But he is also a covenant-keeping God who has shown his gracious love to Israel by choosing them to be his people and heritage and by freeing them from Egypt (8:20, 23, 51, 53). Indeed, God is a promise-keeping God, one who is true to his covenantal promises. In the completion of the temple, Yahweh fulfilled what he promised to David (8:15–16). The fulfillment of the promise is not limited to the building of the temple, for the promise that the temple would be built is linked to the Davidic covenant, to the Lord choosing David and promising that the son who succeeds him would build the temple (8:20, 25).

From a canonical perspective, Solomon's building of the temple points forward to Jesus of Nazareth, who as the messianic king will build a new temple consisting of his people. But here the main theme is the fulfillment of the promises in Solomon's day. Solomon praises the Lord, exclaiming, "Blessed be the LORD who has given rest to his people Israel, according to all that he promised. Not one word has failed of all his good promise, which he spoke by Moses his servant" (8:56). Israel was not only in the land; it resided in the land with peace and joy, and the Lord's presence was established with his people via the temple.

Yahweh fulfilled his promises to Israel so that they would fear him all their days (8:40), and their fear would express itself in keeping his commands and rules (8:58, 61). Solomon recognizes, however, that Israel does not have the strength autonomously to do the will of the Lord. He prays that that Lord will not "forsake" his people, that he will "incline" their hearts to obey him (8:57–58). If Israel lives under Yahweh's lordship in this way, then "all the peoples of the earth may know that the LORD is God; there is no other" (8:60). Israel was not called upon to engage in a conscious mission to the nations.

Instead, when the nations witnessed Israel's obedience and blessing, they would be drawn to the Lord. Apparently, the nature of Israel's mission is such that the nations would "come and see" rather than Israel "go and tell."

At the inauguration of the temple Solomon prays that the Lord will keep his promises, so that a Davidic heir continues to reign on the throne (8:25–26). Since God has graciously condescended to place his name in the temple, Solomon prays that the Lord will specially attend to prayers offered toward the temple, particularly since the temple represents on earth God's heavenly dwelling place (8:28–30). In particular, Solomon requests that Yahweh will forgive his people. Various situations when Israel transgresses are contemplated, and Solomon asks the Lord to hear his people if they truly and humbly pray toward the temple. He prays that the Lord will condemn the wicked and vindicate the righteous (8:31–32), that Israel will be granted relief from their enemies if they repent (8:33–34, 44–45), and that drought, famine, and personal distress will be lifted when Israel turns to the Lord (8:35–40). Nor is the prayer restricted to Israel. If a foreigner comes to Israel "for your name's sake," having heard of God's "great name" and his "mighty hand," Solomon asks that the Lord will answer the foreigner's prayer so "that all peoples of the earth may know your name and fear you" (8:41–43). Here we have a glimpse of the universal blessing promised to Abraham (Gen. 12:1–3). It does not represent a mission to the nations, but it is a recognition that Yahweh is the God of the entire world, and that all people should fear and honor Yahweh as Lord.

The narrator gives the most attention to the situation that arises at the end of the book of 1–2 Kings, for both Judah and Israel are exiled for their sin. Solomon prayed about that very state of affairs (8:46–53), recognizing that all are sinners, and that Israel would sin against the Lord (8:46). If their sin was blatant and persistent, they would suffer exile (which again was the reality at the end of 1–2 Kings). But Solomon pleads that the Lord will have mercy on his people (and the narrator wants the readers to pray the same way, even though the temple has been destroyed), that he will forgive their sins and transgressions because they are the Lord's chosen inheritance, whom he rescued from Egypt. Israel's repentance must be genuine. They must "repent with all their mind and with all their heart" (8:48). Here is one of the most important texts in the book, which points to hope after exile. The exile that took place in 586 BC is not the last word.[27]

The building of the temple represents one of the most important events in the history of salvation, and this is signified by the Lord appearing to Solomon a second time after his prayer has been offered (chap. 9) and by the Lord

27. So also Dempster, *Dominion and Dynasty*, 154.

affirming that he has answered Solomon's prayer. Yahweh's dwelling in the temple represents a kind of new Eden, a new paradise, and it anticipates the new creation—the new heavens and new earth being God's temple in the future (see Rev. 21–22). Yahweh has set apart the temple for himself and put his name there forever (9:3). He admonishes Solomon, however, to keep his commands as David did, for by doing so his reign will be established in perpetuity (9:4–5). But if Solomon or his descendants abandon the Lord and turn away from him by worshiping other gods, the Lord will send Israel into exile. Israel will fall into disrepute, and the temple will be destroyed (9:6–9). The warning anticipates Israel's future fate, indicating that Israel would suffer exile because of their transgression, not because the Lord was too weak to deliver them from their enemies.

Chapter 10 returns to the theme of the idyllic nature of Solomon's reign. The queen of Sheba came for a visit and was astounded by Solomon's wisdom. All of her questions were answered (10:3), and his wisdom far exceeded her expectations, leaving her breathless (10:5–7). Typically, reports of someone's splendor are exaggerated, but not in this instance. Solomon's wisdom brought great prosperity and joy to Israel (10:7–8). The queen's visit "provided inspiration for the later prophetic vision that saw Gentile kingdoms coming into Jerusalem to receive wisdom and Torah from Yahweh's shrine."[28] Praise ultimately goes to God for Solomon's reign: "Blessed be the LORD your God, who has delighted in you and set you on the throne of Israel! Because the LORD loved Israel forever, he has made you king, that you may execute justice and righteousness" (10:9). The chapter concludes with lavish descriptions of Solomon's wisdom and riches, particularly calling attention to the abundant quantity of gold in Solomon's kingdom (10:2, 10–11, 14, 16–18, 21–22, 25). The gold present in the kingdom reminds the readers of paradise (cf. Gen. 2:11–12) and may point to God's presence with his people.[29] Israel was in the land, Yahweh was in the temple, and the nation was prospering. It seemed that universal blessing was just around the corner.

The Nation Unravels: 1 Kings 11–16

Paradise seemed imminent. Instead, Solomon and Israel turned toward evil and unleashed forces that split the kingdom and culminated in exile for both Judah and Israel. The problem is traced to Solomon's sex life: he "loved many foreign women" (11:1). Solomon had seven hundred wives and three hundred

28. Dumbrell, *Faith of Israel*, 94.
29. Alexander, *Eden to the New Jerusalem*, 46.

174

concubines (11:3), clearly violating Deut. 17:17: "He shall not acquire many wives for himself, lest his heart turn away." Some think Solomon was also guilty of acquiring too much silver and gold, which is indicted in the same verse in Deuteronomy. However, the narrator of 1–2 Kings does not accuse Solomon of excess in this matter. Solomon's riches are placed in the chapters that celebrate the glory of his reign (chaps. 1–10). Indeed, the narrator indicates that God gave him riches, specifically noting that Solomon neither asked for nor sought after wealth (3:11–13). But the same could hardly be said about his many wives. They are not mentioned in chapters 1–10, nor is it ever said that the Lord gave him many wives as a blessing. The writer emphasizes that Solomon's wives "turned" his heart away from the Lord (11:2, 3, 4, 8; cf. Exod. 34:11–16).

In his old age he worshiped other gods, including Ashtoreth and Milcom (11:5, 10), and he even built high places for sacrifices to Chemosh and Molech (11:7). David's sin with Bathsheba and murder of Uriah were egregious, but he never turned to other gods as Solomon did (11:32–33). Solomon violated the fundamental stipulation of the covenant in transgressing the first commandment of the Decalogue. Solomon brought upon himself the punishment that Yahweh threatened if one of David's sons turned to iniquity (2 Sam. 7:14). We have intimations here that Israel's expansion in the land will be short-lived because of Solomon's sin. The temporary glories that Israel enjoyed under Solomon point to a greater and more expansive fulfillment of the land promise, one that will encompass the entire creation.[30]

However, as we saw (2 Sam. 7), the covenant with David was irrevocable, and thus one tribe would be left for Judah despite Solomon's transgressions (1 Kings 11:11–13, 34, 36), testifying to the promise that David's dynasty would ultimately be the means by which Yahweh would rule the world and fulfill the promise to Abraham and Adam (see 11:39).[31] The kingdom would come, but now it was apparent that it would not be realized through Solomon. Indeed, the peace that characterized Solomon's reign was threatened; now enemies were on the horizon (11:14, 23). The most prominent was Jeroboam, whom Solomon sought to kill (11:28–40). Solomon's attempt to deprive Jeroboam of his life was futile, for the prophet Ahijah (11:29–31) prophesied that Jeroboam would rule over ten tribes of Israel. Ahijah delivered to Jeroboam an amazing promise from the Lord, that he would have a "sure house, as I built for David" (11:38) if he obeyed the Lord. As we will see, however, Jeroboam turned away from the Lord, and so his dynasty was short-lived.

30. See Williamson, "Promise and Fulfillment," 31–32.
31. For the collocation of the need for kings to obey to enjoy Yahweh's blessing and the irrevocability of the covenant with David, see Williamson, *Sealed with an Oath*, 133.

One of the prominent themes of 1–2 Kings is the fulfillment of prophecy. The word spoken through the prophets is irrevocable; it certainly comes to pass. The promise that ten tribes would abandon the Davidic king became a reality during the reign of Rehoboam, the son of Solomon. Inexplicably and foolishly, Rehoboam started his reign with bravado, threatening to make life harder for the people under his reign than it was under Solomon's (12:1–13). That was the spark needed to propel the ten tribes to crown Jeroboam as king (12:16–20). The narrator emphasizes that what occurred fulfilled prophecy: "So the king did not listen to the people, for it was a turn of affairs brought about by the LORD that he might fulfill his word, which the LORD spoke by Ahijah the Shilonite to Jeroboam the son of Nebat" (12:15). Rehoboam naturally was determined to fight to retain his rule over all twelve tribes, but he heeded the word of the prophet who instructed him to desist from fighting to retain the kingdom (12:24). The dissolution of the kingdom under Solomon, which the Lord threatened, had become a reality.

Jeroboam meanwhile wanted to secure the kingdom, fearing that he would be killed and the people would return to Rehoboam (12:26–31). Instead of trusting the divine promise to secure his dynasty, he improvised by establishing cultic worship in Bethel and Dan with an alternative priesthood and by making golden calves for Israel to worship. In doing so, he clearly violated the second commandment in the Decalogue and set a pattern for sin that culminated in the exile of Israel.[32] "Jeroboam's cult revives and perpetuates Aaron's Exodus 32 apostasy."[33] The curious incident with "the man of God" in chapter 13 follows to demonstrate afresh that God's word is effectual, that the judgment pronounced against Jeroboam most certainly will come to pass.[34] The prophet predicted that Josiah would defile the altar at Bethel where Jeroboam was making an offering, and that the altar would immediately be torn down (13:2–3). Jeroboam cried out against the man of God, commanding him to be arrested, but Jeroboam's outstretched hand was struck with leprosy (13:4), though it was restored shortly (13:6). The surety of the prophet's word was immediately evident, for the altar was torn down (13:5). A strange story ensues in which an old prophet summoned the man of God to come home and eat with him, even though the man of God was instructed not to eat bread or drink water in Bethel (13:11–32). The old prophet lied in inducing the man of God to come

32. House (*Old Testament Theology*, 257) says that he violated the first two commands of the Decalogue.
33. Dumbrell, *Faith of Israel*, 96. See also Dempster, *Dominion and Dynasty*, 150.
34. As Hamilton says, "The dramatic account in 1 Kings 13 serves as an illustration of the state of the whole nation. Israel received a clear word from Yahweh in the Torah. The man of God who denounces Jeroboam's altar also received a clear word" (*God's Glory in Salvation*, 180–81).

to his home. In the middle of the meal the elder prophet reproved the man of God for violating the Lord's word, for eating and drinking with him when the Lord prohibited it. As a result of his disobedience, the man of God would not be buried with his ancestors. As the man of God returned home, a lion attacked and killed him, fulfilling the word of the old prophet.

The narrator emphasizes that the only reason for the man of God's death was the prophetic word of the Lord. The lion was not hungry. He did not eat the man of God or the donkey! He simply stood in the road after killing the man of God. This bizarre story illustrates one of the main themes in 1–2 Kings: the prophetic word cannot be nullified; it will always come true. The narrator has no interest in why the older prophet lied or why he would call the man of God back to Bethel and thereby endanger his life. The point of the story is that the word of God is inviolable, that what the Lord proclaims will certainly take place. Therefore, the chapter ends with the assurance that the words that the man of God spoke "against the altar in Bethel and against all the houses of the high places that are in the cities of Samaria shall surely come to pass" (13:32).

The word proclaimed against Jeroboam immediately began to take effect (14:1–18). Jeroboam's wife tried to disguise herself in consulting the prophet Ahijah about the fate of her son. But even though Ahijah was blind, Yahweh revealed to him the identity of Jeroboam's wife and proclaimed the death of their son Abijam (not because of his own sin, but Jeroboam's). Yahweh showed favor to Jeroboam and installed him on the throne, but Jeroboam, contrary to David, abandoned the Lord and transgressed his commandments, making and worshiping idols instead. Therefore, the death of Abijam signifies the fate of Jeroboam's house: the Lord will cut off every person, so there will be no survivor. Indeed, Jeroboam's sin and leadership were so consequential that Israel will end up in exile because of his transgressions.

The narrator switches over to Judah (14:21–31) but immediately indicates that things were no better there. Judah was also guilty of idolatry (high places, pillars, Asherim), and male cult prostitutes were active in the land. The author hints that Judah will fare no better than Israel. The glory days of Solomon seem far away at this point in the story. Abijam, who succeeded Rehoboam, was an abject failure as well (15:1–8). The only reason why the Lord had mercy on Israel was "for David's sake" (15:4), so there was "a lamp in Jerusalem" (15:4). The narrator explains that David was fundamentally obedient, except in the case of Uriah the Hittite (15:5). The stability of the Davidic dynasty is contrasted with the instability of the dynasties in Israel, for in the latter there were ten dynastic changes.[35] Not all of David's descendants abandoned the

35. See Dempster, *Dominion and Dynasty*, 152.

Lord. Asa followed David's path by removing the male cult prostitutes and idols, even deposing his grandmother, Maacah, as queen mother because she was devoted to Asherah (15:11–13). Asa removed the image and burned it. The narrator says that Asa was "wholly true to the Lord all his days" (15:14), even though he allowed the high places to remain. In the midst of conflicts between Israel and Judah, the Lord fulfilled his promise to wipe out the house of Jeroboam (15:29–30). The problem in Israel, however, was that every king and every dynasty persisted in Jeroboam's sin (e.g., 15:34), and hence they were destined to meet the same fate as Jeroboam (16:1–7). Israel continued to sink toward oblivion. Omri was worse than those before him and did not forsake Jeroboam's sin (16:7, 26), and yet Ahab plunged the nation into even deeper evil, for he introduced Baal worship into Israel through his marriage with Jezebel (16:30–33).

Chapter 16 ends on a strange and seemingly unrelated note: "In his days Hiel of Bethel built Jericho. He laid its foundation at the cost of Abiram his firstborn, and set up its gates at the cost of his youngest son Segub, according to the word of the LORD, which he spoke by Joshua the son of Nun" (16:34). Actually, this verse is of immense significance, for the narrator reminds the readers that the word of the Lord always comes true, even if it is years and years before the prophecy is fulfilled, just as it took years for the prophecy of Joshua about Jericho to become a reality. Therefore, the worship of idols in Israel would have fatal consequences, even if many years away.

The Conflict with Baal Worship: 1 Kings 17–2 Kings 12

It seems fitting to consider 1 Kings 17–2 Kings 12 as a single section, for here the conflict with Baal worship comes to the forefront. Indeed, devotion to Baal was not confined to Israel, but also penetrated Judah. Israel and Judah had radically changed since the days of Solomon, when Israel lived in Edenic conditions in the land. Now the nation was turning away from Yahweh altogether and prostrating itself before Baal. But Yahweh always reigns as Lord, and therefore Baal worship could not and would not triumph. "Both Elijah and Elisha demonstrate that the Lord rules Israel, Judah, Syria, and the rest of the earth. Thus Yahweh deserves sole allegiance instead of being considered merely one among many religious options."[36] Those who gave themselves over to Baal would be judged, and those who remained faithful to Yahweh would triumph. The fight against Baal worship was not led by kings, for it was the

36. House, *Old Testament Theology*, 263.

kings who compromised. The Lord raised up prophets, especially Elijah and Elisha, to challenge the worship of Baal. As we have seen so often already in 1–2 Kings, the word of the Lord prevailed.

Baal was a storm god and a god of fertility.[37] Elijah appeared suddenly and spoke to Ahab (17:1), saying that there would be no rain or dew "except by my word" (17:1). Fertility came not from Baal but rather from Yahweh. Elijah was miraculously fed by the ravens (17:2–7), and he and the widow of Zarephath (and her son) were sustained by the flour and the oil that were miraculously replenished (17:8–16). This story was not simply meant for Elijah and the widow. Israel had rejected God's word (cf. Luke 4:24–26). But Yahweh provides for his own (even though the widow was a Gentile in Baal's territory),[38] for the Lord rather than Baal was the true source of nourishment. Death and life are in Yahweh's hands, and so when the widow's son dies, Elijah restores his life (17:17–23). The woman comes to realize, "Now I know that you are a man of God, and that the word of the LORD in your mouth is truth" (17:24). Israel too must realize that life is in Yahweh rather than Baal, that Elijah is Yahweh's spokesman, and that Elijah's words are from the Lord.

The contest between Yahweh and Baal reaches center stage in chapter 18. Ahab pursued Elijah assiduously during the three years of famine but could not find him, demonstrating Yahweh's sovereignty and rule. Ahab and Baal were not in control; Yahweh was. Elijah suddenly, at the Lord's direction, strode back into the picture, challenging Ahab and the prophets of Baal to a contest, saying that they must follow either Yahweh or Baal (18:21). Baal allegedly was the god of the storm, so Elijah constructed a contest in which the god who answered by fire and consumed the sacrifice on the altar would demonstrate his deity (18:23–24). The utter impotence of Baal is ridiculed by the narrator. No answer comes, even though Baal's prophets beg him to respond and lance themselves so that their blood flows (18:26, 28). Elijah mocked them, asking whether Baal was sleeping, relieving himself, or traveling (18:27). The difference between Yahwism and Baalism is clear. The final verdict on Baal is this: "There was no voice. No one answered; no one paid attention" (18:29). Clearly, the god of fire had no firepower. Elijah wanted there to be no doubt that Yahweh was God (18:30–35). So he poured water on the altar three times. No hidden spark could set this sacrifice ablaze. When Elijah prayed, Yahweh demonstrated that he was the true God, for the fire "consumed the burnt offering and the wood and the stones and the dust, and licked up the water that was in the trench" (18:38). The people's hearts were turned back (18:37), and

37. See ibid., 260.
38. Ibid.

they acknowledged that Yahweh was God (18:39). Elijah judged the prophets of Baal by putting them to death (18:40), and the Lord showed mercy to Israel by granting them rain (18:41–46).

The battle against Baal worship was not ended so easily. Jezebel threatened to kill Elijah after hearing about the execution of the prophets of Baal, and Elijah ran for his life (19:1–3). Elijah felt despair over the influence of Baal worship in Israel, thinking that he was the only one left devoted to Yahweh (19:10). He fled to Mount Horeb (19:8), where Yahweh had entered into covenant with Israel at Sinai (Deut. 5:2; 29:1), where Moses met Yahweh at the burning bush (Exod. 3:1), where Israel heard the words of the Lord out of the fire (Deut. 4:10, 15). Now Elijah was present to hear the Lord's word, a word of assurance that Yahweh had not abandoned his covenant with Israel. Nor does Elijah hear the Lord's voice out of a storm as Moses did on Sinai; the Lord was not in the gale-force winds or the earthquake or the fire but rather was present in a whisper (19:11–12). What is the significance of the Lord being present in a whisper? Perhaps there is the suggestion that Elijah should not be there, for the Lord had no new message to declare from the mountain and no new covenant to enact. Hence, Elijah is asked twice why he has come to Horeb when God has already spoken and has promised to preserve his people.[39] The whisper suggests that Baal worship was not going to be overthrown by a sudden upheaval, but rather that the Lord was quietly working to bring about its inevitable dissolution. The Lord would raise up Hazael as king of Syria to judge Israel for its devotion to Baal, Jehu to root out Baal worship in Israel, and Elisha to continue the prophetic resistance to Baal worship (19:15–16). Yahweh assures Elijah that Baal will not triumph: "Yet I will leave seven thousand in Israel, all the knees that have not bowed to Baal, and every mouth that has not kissed him" (19:18). The preservation of a remnant in Israel demonstrates that Baal worship will not triumph.[40] Yahweh is king, and he will preserve a people for himself. "The principle of election guarantees the survival of the people and of the divine promise"[41] (cf. Rom. 11:1–6). Elijah is virtually a new Moses in the story, reaffirming Israel's covenant with Yahweh at Sinai.[42]

The remainder of 1 Kings (chaps. 20–22) recounts the downfall of Ahab, signifying the beginning of the end for Baal worship in Israel in accord with the Lord's promise to Elijah. Chapter 20 is quite striking. Yahweh grants victory to Ahab over Syria, for the Syrians claim that their gods are greater, and

39. This interpretation was suggested by Joshua Greever.
40. On the remnant in the OT, see Rendtorff, *Canonical Hebrew Bible*, 705–13.
41. See Dempster, *Dominion and Dynasty*, 151.
42. Dumbrell, *Faith of Israel*, 98.

therefore the Lord gives Ahab victories in the hills and the valleys. But Ahab's true character manifested itself. As is typical in 1–2 Kings, the narrator communicates what is going on with a strange story about prophets (20:35–43). One prophet told a man to strike him by the word of the Lord, but the other refused to do so. The prophet predicted that a lion would immediately slay the man who refused to hit him, and what he prophesied came to pass. Again, the narrator is not interested in why a prophet would give such a bizarre command, nor does he defend, as we might expect, the reasonableness of the man who refused to hit his friend. Instead, the inexorable effectiveness of God's word is emphasized. What is prophesied will certainly take place. The prophet got another man to strike him and wound him, and he put a bandage on his head to disguise himself before Ahab. The prophet then invented a story to tell Ahab, informing the king that his life was on the line in guarding a man; but the man he was to guard got away, and so he had to pay a fine for letting him escape. The king replied that the judgment was just. The prophet forfeited his money by letting the man get away. But suddenly the prophet removed his bandage, so that Ahab recognized him as a prophet. And he pronounced judgment on Ahab. Since Ahab had preserved the life of Ben-hadad, whom the Lord "devoted to destruction" (20:42), the Lord would take Ahab's life, just as the man who refused to strike the prophet was slain. The narrator proclaims that disobedience to the Lord will lead to destruction.

Ahab was "vexed and sullen" (20:43) that judgment was coming, and he was "vexed and sullen" that Naboth would not give him his vineyard (21:3). Naboth followed the law of the Lord in refusing to hand over his inheritance (see Deut. 19:14; 27:17).[43] When Ahab did not get what he wanted, Jezebel swung into action, forming a kangaroo court that trumped up false charges against Naboth to put him to death (21:5–14). The injustice "worked," and Ahab gladly took possession of Naboth's vineyard. But while he was enjoying the vineyard, Elijah showed up, declaring that dogs would lick up Ahab's blood in the same place they licked up Naboth's. Ahab stood under judgment for selling himself to do evil (21:20, 25) and for worshiping the same idols as the Amorites (21:26). Because of Jezebel's role in encouraging Baal worship, the dogs would also lick up her blood as well (21:23), and the house of Ahab would be wiped out (21:21–24). Yahweh would demonstrate his lordship and judgment over all who worship Baal. Remarkably, Ahab repented at hearing such words, and the Lord showed him mercy, promising to bring the judgment in the days of Ahab's son instead of immediately (21:27–29).

43. So C. Wright, *Old Testament Ethics*, 90.

The power of the prophetic word and Yahweh's lordship over all things are featured in the account of Ahab's death (chap. 22). Jehoshaphat of Judah agreed to fight with Ahab against the Syrians. But Jehoshaphat did not want to fight without inquiring of the Lord. Ahab's prophets were more than willing to promise a splendid victory (22:6, 11–12), but Jehoshaphat recognized that they were false prophets rather than prophets of Yahweh. Ahab was reluctant to call upon a prophet of Yahweh, for he desired to hear pleasant words from his prophets instead of words of judgment. At Jehoshaphat's insistence, the prophet Micaiah was summoned, being encouraged by one of Ahab's bureaucrats to speak favorably like all the other prophets (22:13). Micaiah insisted that he must speak Yahweh's words (22:14), though he sarcastically promised Ahab victory (22:15). When he was asked to be serious, Micaiah prophesied that Ahab would die in the forthcoming battle (22:17).

Micaiah related a most astonishing scenario to explain how Ahab would be persuaded to go into battle and thereby meet his death (22:19–23). Micaiah pulled back the curtains on what was happening in the heavenly court so that those hearing would have insight into the Lord's purposes. In the heavenly court Yahweh asked who would deceive Ahab into going into battle so that he would meet his death. A messenger stepped forward, saying that he would speak lies through Ahab's prophets. Hence, the Lord decreed that Ahab would meet disaster through believing the words of the false prophets. The narrator is unconcerned about whether anyone would have ethical problems with Yahweh using false prophets to deceive Ahab. The concern of the author is quite different. Yahweh is Lord and king; his purposes will be established. No one can thwart his will or his word, and the judgment pronounced on Ahab because of his devotion to Baal will be carried out.

Perhaps there is a mitigating feature in terms of the ethical issue of Yahweh using false prophets to deceive Ahab. Micaiah tells Ahab what is going on behind the scenes, but Ahab did not believe him. Ahab imprisoned Micaiah, but Micaiah left no doubt about the import of his words. If Ahab returned alive, Micaiah was a false prophet as well (22:27–28). Ahab disguised himself in the battle, and Jehoshaphat wore royal robes, so the Syrians initially went after Jehoshaphat, for they wanted to kill the king of Israel (22:29–38). They could not find Ahab because he hid his royalty, but nothing can hinder the word of God. One man "drew his bow at random," and his arrow just happened, so it seems, to lodge into Ahab "between the scale armor and the breastplate" (22:34). Ahab died from the wound, and dogs licked up his blood, as had been prophesied. Yahweh is Lord, and Baal and his followers would not triumph, just as Elijah prophesied.

Baal worship was not yet rooted out of Israel. Jezebel was alive and kicking, and succeeding kings of Israel were still devoted to Baal. As 2 Kings opens, Ahaziah is sick and sends messengers to Baal in Ekron to see if he will recover (1:2). Yahweh is sovereign over all things, thus knowing what Ahaziah has done, so he sent Elijah to meet him to proclaim his impending death (1:3–4). If Ahaziah believed in anything, it was his own authority, so he sent three groups of fifty men to seize Elijah and bring him to the king (1:9). But the king had no authority over Elijah, nor does fire from heaven come from Baal. At Elijah's word, fire descended from heaven and killed two groups of fifty men who were trying to capture him. Elijah agreed to meet the king only when the third captain humbly requested him to come, and then Elijah clearly informed Ahaziah why he was going to die. By going to Baal for help, Ahaziah was denying that God was in Israel (1:3, 16), and his death at Elijah's word, just as we saw in 1 Kings 17, demonstrates that Yahweh alone is God.

As the conflict with Baal worship continues, Elijah's ministry comes to a close (chap. 2). What is the function of this chapter? The primary message seems to be that Elisha took on the mantle of Elijah's ministry. He asked for "a double portion of your [Elijah's] spirit" (2:9), and his prayer was answered, for he saw the chariots and horses whisk Elijah away. The "God of Elijah" was with him, for he was able to part the water of the Jordan just as Elijah did (2:14). The narrator recounts a collection of miracles from Elisha, though in some instances it is difficult to discern the significance of the miracles performed. Fundamentally, they confirm one of the central themes of 1–2 Kings: the inherent power of the prophetic word. Certainly, many of the miracles point forward to the miracles and kingdom work of Jesus of Nazareth.

Elisha's miracles anticipate the promised new creation where life on earth returns to and transcends life in Eden. Hence, water that was unfit for consumption was healed with salt (2:19–22).[44] Salt elsewhere designates God's covenant with his people (see Lev. 2:13; Num. 18:19). In a similar story, there is poison in the pot of stew, but Elisha puts flour in the pot, and the food becomes edible (4:38–41). The Lord's provision for his people, anticipating Jesus' feeding of the five thousand and of the four thousand, is evident when barley and grain are multiplied so that there is enough to feed one hundred men and have leftovers (4:42–44). In the same way, a widow of one of the prophet's companions was in debt, fearing that she would have to sell her children as slaves. She poured enough oil into jars, at Elisha's command, to pay her debts and sustain her life (4:1–7). The blessings of Elisha's miracles were not confined to Israel. The Shunammite woman recognizes that Elisha is a "man of God" (4:9), which is a common designation for prophets, but it is especially prominent in this chapter

44. Levenson (*Restoration of Israel*, 123–31) points out that the miraculous works of Elisha have a connecting theme, for Yahweh grants life where death threatens.

and is used of Elisha more than any of the other prophets.[45] She was unable to have children, and Elisha promised that she would have a son, to her astonishment (4:14–17). When the son was older, he suddenly had a hemorrhage or some problem with his head and died (4:18–37). After his death Elisha came to the son, laid on him, flesh on flesh, and restored him to life. Perhaps the miracle of the floating ax head should be placed here as well (6:1–7), for such tools were expensive and difficult to replace. In any case, all these miracles of Elisha demonstrate that he is a prophet of the Lord, that life and sustenance come from the Lord not Baal, and herald the coming of a new creation, a new heaven and new earth, where there is life, fullness, and joy.

The story of the bears mauling the boys who ridiculed Elisha (2:23–25) is strange to modern ears. The narrator, however, views this incident as an example of Elisha's prophetic power, for he curses the boys in the Lord's name. Indeed, the prophetic word is effective, for Elisha could not make the bears kill the young men, especially if he were in sin. Apparently, the ridiculing of Elisha was tantamount to a rejection of Yahweh. In contrast, we see in the ministry of Elisha that Yahweh's lordship is acknowledged outside of Israel. Both Elijah and Elisha anticipate here the spread of the gospel to all nations (cf. Luke 4:25–27). The Shunammite woman functions as one example (4:8–37), and Naaman as the other (chap. 5). A servant girl of Naaman informed him that he could be healed by Elisha. The king of Israel was concerned about a diplomatic and military disaster. Elisha, however, saw Naaman's request as a great opportunity, so that Naaman would "know that there is a prophet in Israel" (5:8). Naaman was outraged, however, by the treatment he received from Elisha, for Elisha did not even bother to greet him but instead informed him through a messenger to wash seven times in the Jordan to be cleansed. Naaman expected Elisha to do something more dramatic and took umbrage over the Jordan being the place of cleansing rather than the rivers of Damascus. But Naaman's servants convinced him to submit to "the word" of the prophet, and he was cleansed (5:14). The main point of the story follows when Naaman confessed, "Behold, I know that there is no God in all the earth but in Israel" (5:15). Here we see one of the major themes of 1–2 Kings: the word of the prophets demonstrates that Yahweh is the one and only true God. Baal or any other competitor is to be rejected.

45. So Moses (Deut. 33:1; Josh. 14:6; 1 Chron. 23:14; 2 Chron. 30:16; Ezra 3:2; Ps. 90:1); unnamed prophet (1 Sam. 2:27); Samuel (1 Sam. 9:6, 7, 8, 10); Shemaiah (1 Kings 12:22; 2 Chron. 11:2); unnamed (1 Kings 13:1, 4, 5, 6, 7, 8, 11, 12, 14, 21, 26, 29, 31; 2 Kings 23:16, 17); Elijah (1 Kings 17:24; 2 Kings 1:9, 10, 11, 12, 13); unnamed (1 Kings 20:28); Elisha (2 Kings 4:7, 9, 16, 21, 22, 25, 27, 40, 42; 5:8, 14, 15, 20; 6:6, 9, 10, 15; 7:2, 17, 18, 19; 8:2, 4, 7, 8, 11; 13:19); David (2 Chron. 8:14; Neh. 12:24, 36); unnamed (2 Chron. 25:7, 9).

Three other stories feature Elisha's prophetic abilities. When Gehazi took money and clothing from Naaman and tried to hide them from Elisha, Elisha knew what Gehazi did, and the latter was struck with leprosy (5:19–27). Elisha also knew the battle plans of the Syrians from his bedroom (6:8–23). When the Syrians came to Dothan to seize Elisha, his servant feared for his life. But Elisha prayed that his eyes would be opened, and then he saw that "the mountain was full of horses and chariots of fire all around Elisha" (6:17). The Lord struck the army with blindness, and Elisha led them to Samaria, where, after the Lord opened their eyes again, Elisha fed them and sent them home. Finally, a great famine struck Samaria, and the king irrationally blamed Elisha (6:24–7:20). When all hope of sustenance seemed lost, Elisha prophesied that plentiful food would be available the next day for virtually nothing. The captain who attended the king exclaimed that such a state of affairs could scarcely come to pass even if the Lord made "windows in heaven" (7:2). Elisha prophesied that the man would see the Lord bring about this amazing provision but would not be able to eat any of the food. And so it came to pass, for the man was trampled when the people of Israel rushed to consume the food that the Syrians left behind. What is the point of these stories? The common thread seems to be that Israel can trust the word of the Lord. As the covenant Lord, he will take care of his people. Unlike Gehazi, they do not need to violate God's word in order to satisfy material needs. Instead, they can rest in the Lord as Elisha did when the Syrians came to attack him. And they can trust even in the most extreme situations that the Lord will provide for their needs. Hence, they should not turn to Baal or any other god for provision.

The struggle against Baal was not over. Jehoshaphat aligned himself with Ahab's son Joram (see 3:1),[46] which opened the door in subsequent years, though not through Jehoshaphat himself, to Baal worship in Judah. Jehoshaphat's son Jehoram married Ahab's daughter and "walked in the ways of the kings of Israel, as the house of Ahab had done" (8:18). That almost certainly means that he promoted and participated in Baal worship. The judgment upon Israel for its sin would be inflicted by Hazael of Syria (8:12), but Judah was spared from losing the Davidic line altogether because of the Lord's covenant with David (8:19). Nevertheless, its political power was weakened because of its sin (8:20–22). Ahaziah succeeded Jehoram in Judah, but he followed the ways of Ahab and Baal worship as well (8:26–27). The infection in Judah was not going away. Now both the northern and the southern kingdoms were pursuing Baal worship. The Lord raised up Jehu to rid both the north and the south, both

---

46. He is also called Jehoram. We should note that Jehoshaphat also names one of his sons Jehoram.

Israel and Judah, of sin (9:1–3). He wiped out the house of Ahab, so that it ceased to exist (9:8–10), slaying Joram and dumping his corpse in the field of Naboth in fulfillment of prophecy (9:22–26). At the same time, Jehu put to death Ahaziah, the king of Judah (9:27–29). The foundation of Baal worship was Jezebel, and Jehu had her thrown from a window, and dogs ate her flesh in fulfillment of Elijah's prophecy (9:30–37; cf. 1 Kings 21:23).

Even though Baal worship was entrenched in Israel and Judah, and the house of Ahab looked impregnable, the word of the Lord could not fail. Out of fear of Jehu, Ahab's seventy sons were slain (10:1–9). The emphasis on the fulfillment of prophecy is evident (10:10–11). Similarly, all the relatives of Ahaziah were slain (10:13–14), presumably because they were sympathetic to Baal worship. The removal of Baal worship was imminent, for Jehu wiped out all those sympathetic to Ahab in fulfillment of Elijah's prophecy (10:18). Then, at a great feast, he proceeded to slaughter all those belonging to Baal (10:18–27), and the narrator concludes, "Thus Jehu wiped out Baal from Israel" (10:28). What the Lord prophesied to Elijah in 1 Kings 19 had become a reality.

The crisis was not over in Israel, for Athaliah, who may have been a daughter of Jezebel (cf. 2 Kings 8:26), put to death the entire royal family in Judah (11:1–3). She did not realize that Jehosheba had spared Joash the son of Ahaziah. The house of David was almost entirely destroyed. Clearly, Athaliah was the offspring of the serpent attempting to snuff out the offspring of the woman promised in Gen. 3:15.[47] But nothing and no one can succeed against the Lord, and so Joash was preserved. After six years Jehoiada carried out his plan to install Joash as king and put Athaliah to death (11:4–20). Finally, Judah was cleansed of Baal worship (11:17–18). Judah was dedicated afresh to the Lord, so there was joy in the land and quiet in the city (11:20). The high places remained under Joash (12:3), but he was careful to repair the temple (12:4–16).

Exile: 2 Kings 13–25

The extirpation of Baal worship may have suggested that Israel and Judah were about to experience a new day of devotion to the Lord, but despite some short periods where love for Yahweh blossomed in Judah, the trajectory was on a downward slope. Jehoahaz took up the kingdom in Israel and, like so many before him, followed the pattern of Jeroboam the son of Nebat (13:1–2). Therefore, Hazael of Syria began to triumph over him because of the Lord's anger (13:3). The difficult times provoked Jehoahaz to seek the Lord, and the

---

47. Dempster (*Dominion and Dynasty*, 152) rightly compares her action to Pharaoh's attempt to wipe out Israel.

Lord provided some relief from Syrian oppression, but even then the people continued in their idolatrous ways (13:4–7). Even though Israel sinned, Yahweh showed them remarkable mercy and patience (13:23). Such grace was rooted in the covenant made with their ancestors.

Amaziah had a mixed record as a king of Judah, and accordingly he won victories and suffered defeats (14:1–14, 17–20). Again, what is featured is the mercy of the Lord. Jeroboam II became king of Israel, and he practiced evil like the other kings of Israel who preceded him (14:23–24). But Jonah prophesied, testifying to the grace of the Lord, that Israel's territory would be expanded under Jeroboam (14:25). Eventually, the Lord sent Israel into exile, but the narrator wants to focus on the patience and incredible love of the Lord. He came to Israel's aid in the days of Jeroboam II (14:26–27). Azariah and Jotham were fundamentally good kings for Judah (15:1–7, 32–38), but things began to fall apart for Israel as one ruler followed another and all of them were evil (15:8–31). King Tiglath-pileser of Assyria began to gobble up some of Israel's land. The poison in the north flowed down to the south, for when Ahaz took the reins of Judah, he turned the nation toward evil (chap. 16). The evil of Ahaz was shocking, so much so that he burned his son as an offering, following the practices of the pagan nations (16:3). When political pressure came from Israel and Syria, Ahaz turned to Tiglath-pileser of Assyria for protection (16:5–9) instead of trusting in the Lord. So impressed was Ahaz with Assyria that he made a replica of its altar and substituted it for the altar of the Lord (16:10–15).

The last days of Israel as an independent country are related in chapter 17. Israel continued to sin against the Lord and was carried into exile by Assyria. The narrator reflects extensively in this chapter on why Israel suffered such a fate. The fundamental problem was not political but religious. Israel "sinned against the Lord their God" (17:7); they followed the pattern of pagan nations (17:8); they built high places and erected pillars and Asherim (17:9–11) and worshiped false gods (17:12). They were graciously warned by prophets to turn from their evil, but they were stubborn and resistant to the Lord's counsel (17:13–15), turning toward Baal worship instead (17:16), even offering their children as sacrifices (17:17). Jeroboam the son of Nebat got Israel off on the wrong foot right from the beginning (17:21–23). In terms of the story line of Scripture as a whole, Israel suffered the curses of the covenant (Lev. 26; Deut. 27–28), which Moses predicted they would experience if they violated covenant stipulations. Indeed, we saw in Deuteronomy that Moses predicted that Israel would commit apostasy and depart from the Lord. They did not submit to him as their covenant Lord, and hence they suffered what the Lord threatened. After Israel went into exile, the land was populated both with natives of Israel and people from other nations (17:24–41), so that the north was compromised by syncretism.

While Israel was imploding, a bright spot appeared on the horizon for Judah. Hezekiah turned Judah back to Yahweh in a dramatic way (chaps. 18–20). Idols were repudiated (18:4). Hezekiah kept the Lord's commands, for he trusted in the Lord (18:5–6). Hence, the Lord was with him (18:7), for the Lord always defends one who lives to honor his name. Hezekiah defeated the Philistines (18:8) and rebelled against Assyria (18:7). The Assyrians had no doubt that they would capture Jerusalem, ridiculing the idea that the Lord would deliver Israel from their hand (18:19–37), for the gods of other nations had been unable to withstand the might of the Assyrian superpower. However, the Lord promised to spare Jerusalem from Assyria's hand in order to thwart Assyria's pride (chap. 19). Hezekiah prayed that God would deliver Jerusalem (19:15–19), and Yahweh answered his prayer (since Assyria had mocked the "the Holy One of Israel" [19:22]), by striking dead 185,000 Assyrians (19:35–37). God's name was honored by this deliverance, and he also vindicated the Davidic king (19:34). The deliverance under Hezekiah signifies that the Lord will ultimately rescue his people.

The end of Hezekiah's life was mixed. On the one hand, Yahweh healed him of his sickness (chap. 20), signifying that he would spare Jerusalem "for my own sake and for my servant David's sake" (20:6). Jerusalem and Judah would not suffer exile under Hezekiah, as Israel did when faced with the Assyrian superpower. But Hezekiah's reign ended on a dismal note. He invited the Babylonians to his palace, showing them all his wealth. Isaiah predicted that Judah in the future would be exiled to Babylon (20:17). Hezekiah's callousness is evident, for he was unconcerned because the exile would not occur in his day. Dumbrell rightly says that Hezekiah represents Judah as a whole. "Hezekiah seems a paradigm for Judah, suffering a sickness that should have led to death (20:1–7). He was restored (20:8–11) only to resort in the future to foreign assistance for salvation."[48]

And into exile Judah would go, and Hezekiah's son and successor, Manasseh, played a significant role in the downfall of Judah. Manasseh's reign (chap. 21) can be summarized as a blatant and egregious violation of the covenant stipulations of the Sinai covenant. He restored idol worship with a vengeance (21:3), installing foreign altars in the temple where the Lord's name was to be specially honored (21:4; cf. 21:5, 7). The depth of his evil is apparent, for "he burned his son as an offering and used fortune-telling and omens and dealt with mediums and with necromancers. He did much evil in the sight of the

---

48. Dumbrell, *Faith of Israel*, 101.

Lord, provoking him to anger" (21:6). Exile would be avoided if God's people abided by the provisions of the Mosaic covenant (21:8–9), but Manasseh's horrendous evils guaranteed punishment and exile (21:10–16). His son Amon followed the same pattern (21:19–22).

Along came Josiah, a brief shining light (chaps. 22–23), but it was too late for Judah to survive. Josiah was a worthy successor to David, exemplifying what the Davidic kingdom should be. Josiah repaired the temple, and in the process the book of the law was discovered, which contained the covenant obligations for Judah. When the book was read to Josiah, he understood the danger (22:13). One of the central themes of 1–2 Kings is the inviolability of God's word. The Lord will judge his people when they transgress his prescriptions. When Huldah the prophetess was consulted, she was not the bearer of good news. Disaster was destined for Judah because they had forsaken their king and turned to other gods (22:16–17). God's wrath was about to be poured out on Judah, and yet Josiah himself would die in peace, for he humbled himself before the Lord, wept over the sins of the nation, and longed for the Lord's will to be done (22:18–20).

Josiah, instead of being deterred by the word of judgment, was spurred to action, reforming the nation with zeal (chap. 23). The book of the covenant was read publicly in the temple, and the people pledged to be devoted afresh to their covenant Lord (23:1–3). Cult objects for other gods were burned, and idolatrous priests were deposed (23:4–7, 11–12). Josiah defiled the cultic places where idolatrous offerings were sacrificed (23:8–10). He even went so far as to destroy the cultic places established by Solomon (23:13). The prophecy made by the man of God (see 1 Kings 13) was fulfilled inasmuch as Josiah tore down the altar at Bethel (23:15). The narrator makes a special point to remind readers that in doing so, Josiah fulfilled an ancient prophecy (23:16–18). Remarkably, Josiah's reforms even reached to the northern kingdom (23:19–20). Josiah celebrated Passover and purged Judah and Jerusalem of sorcery (23:21–24).

Unfortunately, Josiah's reforms were not enough to spare Judah. The Lord's wrath was still impending on the nation (23:26–27). After his death, Josiah's sons succeeded him and turned again to evil (23:32, 37). The days of exile under Nebuchadnezzar were at hand. The narrator remarks, "Surely this came upon Judah at the command of the Lord, to remove them out of his sight, for the sins of Manasseh, according to all that he had done, and also for the innocent blood that he had shed. For he filled Jerusalem with innocent blood, and the Lord would not pardon" (24:3–4). Nebuchadnezzar besieged Judah three different times, for the nation kept rebelling. Finally, he burned the temple and took the city. The blinding of Zedekiah and the slaughtering of his sons represented the devastation wrought by their captors (25:6–7), as did the removal of temple objects to Babylon (25:13–16). Judah suffered exile for its covenantal violations. "The judgment of the exile had been foreshadowed in Deuteronomy 29:1–30:10, in the prophetic poetry of Deuteronomy 32, and again in the last words of Joshua 23–24."[49]

Conclusion

The book of 1–2 Kings began on a bright note. The reign of Solomon seemed like a return to paradise; the worldwide blessing promised to Abraham was just around the corner. What we see in 1–2 Kings is a slow devolution, beginning with Solomon. The Edenic-like paradise under Solomon was now a distant memory. Israel, like Adam, was in exile.[50] And as David Freedman points out, the story has not progressed beyond Babylon since the days of Genesis; it began in Babylon (Gen. 11:1–9), and now Israel is in Babylon again.[51] The promise of Abraham seemed further away than ever. Israel was in exile and in danger of losing its distinctiveness among the nations. Every element of the promise to Abraham (land, offspring, blessing) was endangered. One of the fundamental themes of the narrative is the efficacy of God's word. That which the covenant Lord speaks will most certainly come to pass. It may take time, and it does take time, because of God's mercy, but ultimately he punishes those who abandon him. Both Israel and Judah were in exile because of their blatant failure to keep covenant stipulations. The future looked bleak.

And yet, remarkably enough, there was hope.[52] The book ends with Jehoiachin's release from prison and his dining at the king of Babylon's table (25:27–30). What happened to Jehoiachin seems almost trivial. But the narrator sees hope in this turn of events. The Davidic king survived, and he was, in a sense, thriving in exile.[53] And we remember a major theme in 1–2 Kings: the reliability of God's word. And we know that the Lord promised that the dynasty with David would not end. He has preserved a "lamp" for David.[54] The Lord is king, and he will fulfill his promises. Nothing can thwart his word. The offspring of the woman will triumph over the serpent through a son of David. No matter how improbable that hope seems, it will not be thwarted.

49. Ibid., 104. Dumbrell goes on to say, "The reader cannot escape the conclusion that Yahweh was justified in his judgment, that his people were amply prepared for it, and that they should accept the blame."
50. So Freedman, *Unity of the Hebrew Bible*, 8.
51. Ibid., 9.
52. House, *Old Testament Theology*, 269.
53. Against Dumbrell, *Faith of Israel*, 104. Rightly Dempster, *Dominion and Dynasty*, 155–56.
54. For a convincing defense of this reading, see Provan, "Kings," 185–87.

Just as the Lord fulfilled his promise to judge his people, so the ending of 1–2 Kings promises that the Lord has not forgotten his covenant. The conclusion of the narrative whispers hope instead of shouting it. Still, the history of Israel shows the power of sin, indicating that salvation and deliverance would be a miracle. Israel, on its own, lacks the resources to do the will of the Lord.

11

1–2 CHRONICLES

Introduction

The books of 1–2 Chronicles, which, as is the case with 1–2 Samuel and 1–2 Kings, are actually one book, cover the same general period of time as 1–2 Kings. In some passages 1–2 Chronicles rehearses the identical story with the same words found in 1–2 Samuel and 1–2 Kings. But differences between Chronicles and Samuel and Kings are also evident. The Chronicler often adds distinctive material to stories drawn from Samuel and Kings. The Chronicler's perspective and theology are set forth by the selection, adaptation, arrangement, and inclusion of various stories and traditions. It would be a mistake to limit ourselves to what the Chronicler added, as if only what is distinctive to this narrative should be taken into account in conveying the theology of the work. Both tradition and redaction must be included in the Chronicler's theology. Still, I will focus a bit more on what is distinctive in Chronicles without neglecting what is shared in common with Samuel and Kings. Hence, the common material will be treated in a more abbreviated fashion.

Chronicles focuses in many ways on the kingship and the priesthood. The rule of Yahweh is exercised through the Davidic king and the priests and Levites.[1] When Israel is obedient to the Lord, the nation will be blessed, but when they forsake the worship and praise of the Lord and abandon him for other gods, the nation will be cursed. Childs nicely summarizes the major purpose of the book: "The author was attempting to interpret to the restored community in Jerusalem the history of Israel as an eternal covenant between God

---

1. For the notion that Chronicles was written to defend the Davidic monarchy, see Freedman, "The Chronicler's Purpose."

and David which demanded an obedient response to the divine law. On the basis of past history he sought repeatedly to draw the lesson that Israel prospered when obedient but courted God's wrath and destruction of the nation through disobedience. In spite of continual warnings from the prophets, Israel abandoned God's law and suffered the consequences. . . . However, after the judgment, God once again restored his people who continue to stand under the same divine imperatives."[2] The covenant with David is one that will not be revoked. Even when Israel sins and suffers the worst punishments imaginable, even exile from the land, the Lord will still fulfill his promises. Hope is not quenched for a new generation of Israel.

The Genealogy

The genealogy that opens the book (1 Chron. 1–9) is quite off-putting to modern readers, and yet attention to its larger structure uncovers some of the theology of the Chronicler. The genealogy goes back to Adam (1:1), showing that the implication of what is taught here embraces the whole world.[3] Still, the Chronicler focuses on Israel, particularly the fate of Judah, for it is through Judah that blessing will come to all. The story of Judah is connected to the history and story of the whole human race.[4] The role of Abraham as the father of many is also introduced in chapter 1 (1:27–54). The writer does not emphasize the blessing of Abraham, but since chapter 2 sets forth the sons of Israel, it is difficult to believe that the blessing of Abraham was not in mind. The selectivity in the genealogy reflects the Chronicler's interest. For instance, the genealogy of the tribe of Judah is set forth in some detail (2:3–4:23). The genealogy of David and his sons is placed in the middle of this section (3:1–24), receiving particular attention. The hope of a future kingdom for Israel comes from David and his line. Significantly, the narrator includes those in David's line since the time of the Babylonian exile (3:17–24), suggesting thereby that the covenant hope pledged to David still persisted. The narrator believed that the promises given to David for Israel were not nullified and would still be fulfilled,[5] for God's word in the Scriptures is effective.[6]

2. Childs, *Old Testament as Scripture*, 644.
3. So Selman, "Chronicles," 189.
4. See Dumbrell, *Faith of Israel*, 324–25; Kelly, *Retribution and Eschatology*, 177–78.
5. Against those who see little interest in messianism in the work (e.g., Ackroyd, *The Chronicler*, 71–72, 267–68). Japhet (*Ideology*, 358, 387–93) sees little interest in the covenant with David and no interest in eschatology. For a more convincing analysis, see Kelly, *Retribution and Eschatology*, 143–67.
6. On the centrality of God's word in Chronicles, see Selman, "Chronicles," 189–92.

The genealogies of the northern tribes (7:1–40) and the Transjordan tribes (5:1–26) are brief by comparison. In fact, it is only here in the book that the author mentions that the northern tribes went into exile under Assyrian power (5:25–26), explaining that they defected from Yahweh and worshiped other gods. Still, the focus is elsewhere. The tribes of Simeon (4:24–43) and Benjamin (8:1–40) receive more attention. Perhaps Simeon and Benjamin are examined in more detail because they were closely related to Judah, for Simeon basically lived within the tribe of Judah, and some of the tribe of Benjamin stayed with the Davidic king when the northern and southern kingdoms split.

What is certainly an anticipation of things to come in 1–2 Chronicles is the focus on the tribe of Levi (6:1–81), with particular attention given to the sons of Aaron and the Gershonites, Kohathites, and Merarites. Proper worship and conformity in cultic matters to the will of Yahweh are required. The centrality of worship is evident when the genealogy is interrupted with this comment: "These are the men whom David put in charge of the service of song in the house of the LORD after the ark rested there. They ministered with song before the tabernacle of the tent of meeting until Solomon built the house of the LORD in Jerusalem, and they performed their service according to their order" (6:31–32). The importance of atonement is also communicated in the midst of the genealogy: "But Aaron and his sons made offerings on the altar of burnt offering and on the altar of incense for all the work of the Most Holy Place, and to make atonement for Israel, according to all that Moses the servant of God had commanded" (6:49). Israel's praise of and relationship with Yahweh are impossible unless the rules and stipulations of the cult are observed. Significantly, the genealogy continues with those who returned after the exile to Babylon (9:2–34). Once again the narrator signals that there is hope for Israel—the glory days are not over with the passing of David and Solomon.[7] The author also focuses on "the priests, the Levites, and the temple servants" (9:2) in describing those who returned from exile. Furthermore, other tribes joined Israel in Jerusalem (9:3), indicating that the return holds out promise for all Israel.[8] The land is still an important theme for the Chronicler.[9] One of the major themes of Chronicles is "all Israel."[10] The author uses the phrase forty-seven times to denote the universality of the people of God. The narrator does not emphasize the division of Israel and Judah but instead emphasizes that the true people of God are united around the Davidic king and the temple

7. "The message to all Israel is that there can still be a glorious future" (Dumbrell, *Faith of Israel*, 326).

8. So also Waltke, *Old Testament Theology*, 756.

9. Rightly Kelly, *Retribution and Eschatology*, 179–82.

10. See Japhet, *Ideology*, 209–17. See also her further discussion (pp. 217–84).

in Jerusalem. The focus on the temple is quite noticeable in chapter 9. Those who return are devoted to the house of God (9:11, 13) and were entrusted as gatekeepers to the Lord's house (9:21–27). Indeed, the author specifies those who were responsible for the utensils, food, and goods for the temple so that everything was carried out properly (9:28–33). There is a future for "all Israel," both south and north, if they give themselves to the Lord.[11]

Saul and David

The reign of Saul is covered in an abbreviated fashion in 1 Chronicles. The detailed story in Samuel recounting how Saul pursued David and how David eventually succeeded Saul as king is mainly passed over. The reason for Saul's rejection is presented in a short summary statement: "So Saul died for his breach of faith. He broke faith with the LORD in that he did not keep the command of the LORD, and also consulted a medium, seeking guidance. He did not seek guidance from the LORD. Therefore the LORD put him to death and turned the kingdom over to David the son of Jesse" (10:13–14). What interests the writer is the reign of David and the promise that an heir of David would serve as king forever. Perhaps he emphasizes David's rise after Saul to encourage Israel that they too can rise again after the exile.[12] Along the same lines, the narrator reveals no independent interest in the kings of Israel in the north or in the history of the northern kingdom. For instance, Elijah is mentioned only once in the book, and Elisha does not appear at all. This is scarcely surprising because these two prophets focused their ministry on the northern kingdom. In fact, Elijah's name appears only because he wrote a letter to Jehoram, king of Judah (2 Chron. 21:12). The kings of Israel and the fate of the northern kingdom crop up in the story only when they intersect with the history of Judah. Clearly, the Chronicler concentrates on David and the history of Judah.

The Chronicler skips over the struggle with Ish-bosheth for the throne, and emphasizes that "all Israel" and "all the elders of Israel" (1 Chron. 11:1, 3) anointed David as king. Indeed, Israel was drawn to David even before he was crowned as king. Even some from the tribe of Benjamin joined with David (12:2, 16), along with Gadites (12:8, 14) and those from the tribe of Manasseh (12:19), such that those with David were "a great army, like an army of God" (12:22). The author lovingly recounts, when the time came to anoint David as king, how many from each tribe came to Hebron to crown him (12:23–40).

11. See Kelly, *Retribution and Eschatology*, 182–84.
12. See Ackroyd, *The Chronicler*, 68.

The unity of Israel is of great importance to him, as is clear from 12:38: "All these, men of war, arrayed in battle order, came to Hebron with full intent to make David king over all Israel. Likewise, all the rest of Israel were of a single mind to make David king." David's role as the "shepherd" and "prince" over Israel is featured (11:2). Indeed, "all Israel" went to Jebus with David; the city was conquered and became the center of David's reign (11:4–9). Jerusalem was important not only for political reasons; it will also be the place where the temple is built and Yahweh is worshiped in Israel. The Chronicler believes that the promises made will be fulfilled to "all Israel."[13] From a NT perspective, these promises for Israel are fulfilled in Jesus Christ. He is the true son of David who rules over the true people of God made up of Jews and Gentiles.

David's wisdom as a leader is featured. Before making a decision, he wisely consulted with others (13:1). David wanted to bring the ark to Jerusalem, but before doing so, he sought the advice of "all the assembly of Israel" and sent invitations to "our brothers who remain in all the lands of Israel, as well as to the priests and Levites in the cities that have pasturelands, that they may be gathered to us" (13:2). It was crucial to David that the people be united in worshiping the Lord, and his plan succeeded: "All the assembly agreed to do so, for the thing was right in the eyes of all the people" (13:4). The emphasis on unity is quite astonishing: "So David assembled all Israel from the Nile of Egypt to Lebo-hamath, to bring the ark of God from Kiriath-jearim. And David and all Israel went up to Baalah, that is, to Kiriath-jearim that belongs to Judah, to bring up from there the ark of God" (13:5–6). The rest of the chapter relates the death of Uzzah, caused by his illicit touching of the ark, for proper procedure relative to the cult is of special importance to the Chronicler.

David's success as a leader stands in contrast to Saul. The narrator emphasizes that the Lord put Saul to death and turned the kingdom over to David because Saul failed to seek the Lord's guidance (10:13–14). When David faced the Philistines, he inquired of the Lord every step of the way (14:10, 14). Contrary to Saul, he "did as God commanded him" (14:16), and hence "the LORD brought the fear of him upon all nations" (14:17). One of the central themes of Chronicles is that obedience brings blessing while disobedience leads to terrible consequences.[14] Furthermore, David learned from the incident with the ark (chap. 15). Only the Levites could carry the ark (15:2, 12; cf. Deut. 10:8). The disaster with Uzzah occurred "because you did not carry it the first time, the LORD our God broke out against us, because we did not seek

13. Perhaps the Chronicler's use of "all Israel" indicates a redefinition of true Israel, as is proposed by Joshua Greever.
14. See Childs, *Old Testament as Scripture*, 652–53.

him according to the rule" (15:13; cf. Num. 1:50; 4:15). So "Levites carried the ark of God on their shoulders with the poles, as Moses had commanded according to the word of the LORD" (15:15). The Chronicler was not devoted to following pedantic rules for their own sake. The ark represented the rule of Yahweh, "who sits enthroned above the cherubim" (13:6). Since Yahweh is the great king and ruler, he is to be treated as the holy one of Israel.

One of the major themes in Chronicles surfaces here. Yahweh as the great king and redeemer should be praised.[15] Therefore, care was taken to appoint singers and musicians to praise him skillfully (15:16–24; 16:4–6; cf. 16:41–42), which was a special responsibility of the Levites. David, with his linen ephod, functioned as a priest-king in bringing up the ark (15:27), for not only did he present offerings but also he gave the people a priestly blessing (16:2). The purpose of the music and the offerings, of course, was to offer Yahweh praise, and so a hymn of praise is included in the midst of the narrative (16:8–36). The theme of the song is that Yahweh is to be praised and thanked as the covenant God of Israel and as the King of the entire world. Yahweh made a covenant with Abraham and his descendants (16:15–22), and he fulfilled it by liberating his people from Egyptian bondage (16:13–14).[16] Because of Yahweh's greatness, Israel must "ascribe to the LORD the glory due his name; bring an offering and come before him! Worship the LORD in the splendor of holiness" (16:29). The note of praise, exultation, and unrestrained joy pulsates through the psalm. Those whom the Lord saves bless his name and are filled with inexpressible joy (cf. 1 Pet. 1:8). The kingdom of the Lord is a major theme in Chronicles, and that kingdom will reach its intended goal through the rule of a Davidic king.[17]

The covenant with Abraham, however, is not the only one that the Lord made. Chapter 17 recounts the covenant made with David, which is also relayed in 2 Sam. 7. The covenant with David promises him a dynasty that will not come to an end. Individual kings may be disciplined for violating the Lord's will, but the covenant itself is irrevocable; it will finally be fulfilled. Chapters 18–20 recount Davidic victories over his enemies along the same lines that we see in 2 Samuel. The obedient king who trusts in the Lord is blessed with triumph over all his enemies. Even though Chronicles bypasses David's sin with Bathsheba and murder of Uriah, his sin of counting the people in the census is narrated (chap. 21). The faults of Solomon are omitted. The Chronicler is not suggesting that David and Solomon were without fault, since, as we saw, David's sin regarding the census is duly noted. Rather, the Chronicler focuses on their strengths and

15. The God-centeredness of Chronicles is also evident from the emphasis on seeking Yahweh. See C. Berg, "'Seeking Yahweh.'"
16. The Lord's "salvation" and "marvelous works" likely refer to liberation from Egypt.
17. Kelly, *Retribution and Eschatology*, 211. See also Japhet, *Ideology*, 308–20.

godliness to give hope to the nation, for the covenant with David promises that a future king is coming who will reflect all the virtues of David and Solomon and more.[18] From a canonical perspective, Jesus as the Christ fulfills this expectation.

David's sin relative to the census is included because we learn from the account where the temple will be built. David's sacrifice ended the plague that fell upon Israel (21:28), and thereby this became the spot on which the temple would be erected (1 Chron. 22:1; 2 Chron. 3:1), and offerings would be sacrificed for the atonement of the sin of the people. Certainly, such sacrifices find their ultimate fulfillment in the atoning work of Jesus Christ, which accomplishes forgiveness of sins.

The Temple

The temple plays a central role in Chronicles. "The cult becomes the central vehicle through which Israel's relationship to Yahweh is celebrated and presented."[19] In 1 Chronicles the narrator notes that David furnished provisions for the temple (22:2–5, 14–16), for he himself could not build it because he was a warrior (22:7–8). Solomon, as a man of peace, would erect the temple (22:9–10). Solomon's success was dependent upon his obedience (22:12–13) and his seeking of the Lord (22:14). David organized effectively, preparing for the day when the temple would be built. He organized the Levites into larger groups in which they would care for the Lord's house, serve as officers and judges, and function as gatekeepers and musicians (23:3–5). The duties of the Levites were changing because the tabernacle was being retired from use (23:26), and so they were given various responsibilities to help with temple worship (23:29–30). David also organized the priests, the sons of Aaron, so that all of them could serve at the requisite time (chap. 24), ensuring also that musicians were installed so that the Lord's praises would be regularly sung (chap. 25). The Chronicler does not just commend singing, for "in the choral service in particular the cult has a forward-looking character, as it expresses praise for Yahweh's universal kingship, petition for the covenant people, and the assurance of deliverance from enemies."[20] Brian Kelly also notes that singing in Chronicles is linked with sacrifice and with Yahweh's powerful appearance among his people, and thus they anticipate God's future work among his people.[21]

18. See Waltke, *Old Testament Theology*, 760.
19. Dumbrell, *Faith of Israel*, 327.
20. Kelly, *Retribution and Eschatology*, 169–70.
21. Ibid., 171–75.

Fittingly, David's last words relate to the building of the temple and the succession of Solomon to the throne (chaps. 28–29). The solemnity of the occasion is signaled by David assembling officials for the speech (28:1). He explained that he desired to build the temple, but Solomon as a man of peace was appointed to do so. What is imperative is that Solomon seek the Lord and keep his commands (28:7–9). David passed on to Solomon the plan for the temple in some detail, a plan that David himself received from the Lord (28:11–19). Using words that remind us of the admonition to Joshua before he entered the land of promise, David exhorts Solomon, "Be strong and courageous and do it. Do not be afraid and do not be dismayed, for the LORD God, even my God, is with you. He will not leave you or forsake you, until all the work for the service of the house of the LORD is finished" (28:20). David closed his farewell address by recounting the wealth that he had furnished for the building of the temple (29:1–5). The people also gave generously to fund the house of the Lord (28:6–9).

David's last words are God-centered (29:10–20). He praises the Lord for his sovereignty and rule over all.[22] "Yours, O LORD, is the greatness and the power and the glory and the victory and the majesty, for all that is in the heavens and in the earth is yours. Yours is the kingdom, O LORD, and you are exalted as head above all. Both riches and honor come from you, and you rule over all. In your hand are power and might, and in your hand it is to make great and to give strength to all" (29:11–12). Because the Lord is the great King, people "praise your glorious name" (29:13). The temple was erected to communicate to Israel the majesty and beauty of the Lord. Nor could Israel take credit for the gifts they gave, "for all things come from you, and of your own have we given you" (29:14). David prays that the people and Solomon will remain faithful to the Lord, and that Solomon will complete the temple (29:18–19). He closes by blessing the Lord (29:20), and the people offered sacrifices and ate in the Lord's presence with joy when Solomon was installed as king (29:21–22). Nothing is said about the rebellion of Absalom in David's reign or about Adonijah's attempt to secure the kingship.

As 2 Chronicles opens, the Chronicler focuses in Solomon's reign on the building of the temple. Apart from the activity that relates to the temple, we are told very little about Solomon, though his riches and wisdom are also celebrated (chaps. 8–9). His turn toward idolatry at the end of his life, which is set forth in 1 Kings, is excluded from the narrative. The concentration on the temple reveals how central and significant the temple is for the narrator. The kingdom was secured in Solomon's hands because "the LORD his God

---

22. On the Chronicler's view of divine sovereignty, see Japhet, *Ideology*, 42–47.

was with him and made him exceedingly great" (1:1). Solomon's reign was over "all Israel" (1:2). The narrative emphasizes Solomon's wisdom and riches, which were a gift of God. His fundamental purpose as king was to build the temple (chap. 2), in which he would honor the Lord by building "a house for the name of the LORD my God" (2:4). The temple was built not to call attention to itself but rather to testify to the greatness of the Lord. Solomon remarks, "The house that I am to build will be great, for our God is greater than all gods" (2:5), though he also recognizes that no building can contain the Lord, whose greatness transcends any human abode (2:6). The author recounts Solomon's preparation to build the temple (chap. 2), the actual building of the temple (chap. 3), and the furnishings of the temple (chap. 4).

The dedication of the temple was a magnificent spectacle. The inclusion of the whole of Israel is particularly emphasized in the induction of the ark into the temple: "Solomon assembled the elders of Israel and all the heads of the tribes, the leaders of the fathers' houses of the people of Israel, in Jerusalem, to bring up the ark of the covenant of the LORD out of the city of David, which is Zion.[23] And all the men of Israel assembled before the king at the feast that is in the seventh month. And all the elders of Israel came, and the Levites took up the ark" (5:2–4). Sacrifices without number were offered, and the Levitical singers praised the Lord with both their voices and instruments (5:6–13), celebrating in particular the gracious love of the Lord. Suddenly the temple was filled with the cloud, just as the tabernacle had been, and the glory of the Lord's presence was so awesome in the temple that the priests could not stay to minister (5:13–14). The temple reflected the glory of God and the presence of God with his people, for the Lord had chosen specially to put his name in Jerusalem and in the temple (6:5–6; 7:16). The temple represents Yahweh's presence and his rule over his people, and it points forward to Jesus as the true temple and the presence of God in the new creation, for in the world to come, as we will see in Rev. 21–22, the whole world will be God's temple.

Solomon's inaugural prayer (6:12–42), found also in 1 Kings 8, indicates the centrality of the temple in Israel's life. When Israel invokes the Lord, asking for his grace in repentance relative to the temple, the Lord will hear and forgive and act. Solomon's prayer concluded with a lightning strike, as fire came down from heaven and consumed the offerings (7:1). The awesome glory of the Lord filled the temple, and the people fell to the ground in praise of the Lord for his gracious goodness (7:2–3, 6). Israel was full of joy, and the Lord affirmed that he would answer Solomon's prayer regarding the temple (7:10–12). But if Israel departed from Yahweh's commands and turned toward idols, then the

---

23. On Zion theology in the OT, see Rendtorff, *Canonical Hebrew Bible*, 575–85.

people would be sent into exile and the temple would be destroyed (7:19–22). The temple was not a magical talisman that would protect Israel even if they departed from the Lord. Indeed, the narrator anticipates the close of the book, where the temple was destroyed and the nation goes into exile because of its apostasy from the Lord.

The Downward Trajectory under Judah's Kings

The unity of all Israel was fractured under Rehoboam's rule, as he unwisely paid heed to impetuous youth instead of listening to the seasoned words of his elders (2 Chron. 11). As a result, the north stood under the authority of Jeroboam the son of Nebat and the south under Rehoboam. The narrator distinctively emphasizes those among the Levites and priests who joined Rehoboam, since Jeroboam instituted a deviant priesthood and sacrifices (11:15): "And the priests and the Levites who were in all Israel presented themselves to him from all places where they lived. For the Levites left their common lands and their holdings and came to Judah and Jerusalem, because Jeroboam and his sons cast them out from serving as priests of the LORD" (11:13–14). Despite his sins and weaknesses (chap. 12), Rehoboam faithfully maintained the sacrifices and priesthood ordained in the law. Rehoboam's faithfulness had an impact on all Israel: "And those who had set their hearts to seek the LORD God of Israel came after them from all the tribes of Israel to Jerusalem to sacrifice to the LORD, the God of their fathers" (11:16). Those who truly belonged to the Lord in the north realized that the only legitimate place to offer sacrifices was in Jerusalem.

The distinctiveness of the Chronicler is apparent in what he includes about Abijah. In Kings Abijah (where he is called "Abijam") is not given a flattering portrait and is characterized as fundamentally unfaithful to Yahweh and his ways (1 Kings 15:1–8). But the picture in 2 Chronicles is remarkably different. The narrator focuses on an occasion when Abijah and Jeroboam were joined in battle, relaying the speech Abijah gave on that occasion. He begins by pointing out that the Lord made a perpetual covenant with David and his heirs (13:5), while Jeroboam rebelled against authority (13:6). Furthermore, Jeroboam established worship of the golden calves (13:8). The concern for the cult, so characteristic of Chronicles, manifests itself in Abijah's words: "Have you not driven out the priests of the LORD, the sons of Aaron, and the Levites, and made priests for yourselves like the peoples of other lands? Whoever comes for ordination with a young bull or seven rams becomes a priest of what are no gods" (13:9). By way of contrast, Abijah emphasizes that the cult is being

201

observed properly and according to the Lord's will in his kingdom (13:10–11), and hence God is with them in the battle (13:12), and as a result they won a significant victory over Jeroboam (13:13–20).

Abijah's successor, Asa, started well as king of Judah, following the regulations of the Torah. Once again, cultic interests dominate: "He took away the foreign altars and the high places and broke down the pillars and cut down the Asherim and commanded Judah to seek the LORD, the God of their fathers, and to keep the law and the commandment. He also took out of all the cities of Judah the high places and the incense altars. And the kingdom had rest under him" (14:3–5). Asa trusted the Lord in a battle with the Ethiopians and won a great victory (14:9–15). The prophet Azariah encouraged Asa to seek the Lord ardently (15:1–7), and Asa responded by removing idols and repairing the altar in the temple (15:8), even deposing his grandmother Maacah from being queen mother (15:16). The narrator notes that many from the north supported Asa in this venture: "And he gathered all Judah and Benjamin, and those from Ephraim, Manasseh, and Simeon who were residing with them, for great numbers had deserted to him from Israel when they saw that the LORD his God was with him" (15:9). Asa enacted a covenant whereby Israel pledged to seek the Lord (15:12–15). However, at the end of his life Asa departed from seeking the Lord and trusting him, relying instead on the Syrians (chap. 16). When Hanani the prophet rebuked him, Asa put him in prison and abused the human rights of others as well (16:7–10). At the end of his life Asa contracted a disease in his feet, and the narrator informs us that he did not seek the Lord but instead trusted in his own physicians (16:12). It seems that Asa functions as a parable of Judah, which started well and trusted in the Lord but later departed from him and thereby suffered the consequences.

Jehoshaphat, the successor to Asa, is presented in very positive terms: "The LORD was with Jehoshaphat, because he walked in the earlier ways of his father David. He did not seek the Baals, but sought the God of his father and walked in his commandments, and not according to the practices of Israel" (17:3–4); and, "His heart was courageous in the ways of the LORD. And furthermore, he took the high places and the Asherim out of Judah" (17:6). He sent officials and Levites to teach the Torah in the cities of Judah (17:7–10), and he saw to it that justice was enforced throughout the land (19:5–11). Nonetheless, Jeshoshaphat was also flawed, for he aligned himself with Ahab by marriage and helped the latter in battle (chap. 18), and so he was rebuked by the prophet Jehu (19:2). However, his battle with the Moabites, Ammonites, and Meunites is paradigmatic for the author (chap. 20). The overwhelming odds set against Jehoshaphat frightened him, and his fear provoked him to seek the Lord and to fast (20:2–3). Judah gathered together to seek the Lord's help. Jehoshaphat acknowledged to the Lord, "You rule over all the kingdoms of the nations. In your hand are power and might, so that none is able to withstand you" (20:6). The sovereign Lord had made a covenant with Israel through Abraham to give Israel the land (20:7), and Jehoshaphat was applying Solomon's prayer (chap. 6) for the Lord's help from the temple (20:8–11). Jehoshaphat confessed that the nation was powerless, but the Lord promised to rescue Judah (20:12–15). In response, the nation praised the Lord and worshiped him (20:18–19). Remarkably, Judah entered into battle by singing the Lord's praises and won a great victory (20:21–24), and they returned with praise to Jerusalem (20:28). Jehoshaphat's victory serves as a lesson for Israel in the Chronicler's day. They had returned from exile, but life in the land was tough. But just as Jehoshaphat was helped when he was weak, so Israel would prosper again if they trusted in the Lord, sang his praises, and followed his will. Since the Lord is sovereign over all nations, he will restore Israel again if they devote themselves to him.

Unfortunately, the next king, Jehoram, allied himself with Baal worship and the kings of Israel (chap. 21). Because of his idolatry he died in agonizing pain, as his bowels came out. The next chapters represent what we also see in Kings. Ahaziah and Athaliah turned Judah to Baal worship, and the latter almost extinguished the line of Judah in Israel (chaps. 22–24). But the Lord promised that the offspring of Israel would not be wiped out, and the line was preserved through Joash. Joash was devoted to the house of the Lord during the days of Jehoiada and even repaired the temple, but after Jehoiada's death he turned against the Lord and his temple, even murdering Zechariah, Jehoiada's son. As a result, Joash was murdered by his own servants.

Amaziah, like Jehoshaphat (chap. 25), functions as an example for the nation that has just returned from exile. He began by trusting the Lord and keeping his commands, so that, in accord with the Mosaic law, he did not put to death the children of those who killed his father (25:4). He also responded to the admonition of the prophet who exhorted him not to fight the battle with troops from the northern kingdom of Israel (25:7–8). Amaziah initially complained about allowing the troops to leave, since he had spent a considerable sum on them, but the man of God replied, "The LORD is able to give you much more than this" (25:9). Amaziah believed this promise and won a significant victory over Edom. Again, the Chronicler is promising the same thing to his generation. If they trust in the Lord and refuse to compromise by forging alliances with those contaminated by idolatry, the Lord will be more gracious to them than they could imagine. Actually, Judah went into exile because they followed the same path as Amaziah. After he won a significant victory over Edom, he irrationally and inexplicably worshiped the gods of Edom (25:14). When reproved by a prophet, he, unlike David, did not soften his heart and repent (25:15–16), and so the prophet declared that the Lord would destroy him. Subsequently, Judah was decisively defeated by Israel, and Amaziah was put to death through a conspiracy (25:17–28). In the same way, Judah suffered exile because it forsook the Lord, and it would advance in the future only by keeping his commands.

Uzziah followed the same pattern, though politically and militarily he was much stronger than Amaziah (chap. 26). He began by seeking the Lord and prospered. But his own success was his undoing: "But when he was strong, he grew proud, to his destruction. For he was unfaithful to the LORD his God and entered the temple of the LORD to burn incense on the altar of incense" (26:16). With the Chronicler's interest in the cult, we know that the malfeasance of Uzziah was deplorable. Indeed, eighty priests pursued him to rebuke him, but he refused to heed their warnings until he was struck with leprosy, remaining a leper until the day he died.

His successor, Jotham, is commended for following the Lord (chap. 27), but Ahaz is a different story (chap. 28). He pursued idols with a vengeance and even offered his sons to secure the favor of the gods. As a result, Ahaz was subjugated to Tiglath-pileser. Perhaps the most egregious thing for the author was that "Ahaz gathered together the vessels of the house of God and cut in pieces the vessels of the house of God, and he shut up the doors of the house of the LORD, and he made himself altars in every corner of Jerusalem" (28:24). Hezekiah did not turn out like his father (chaps. 29–32), but rather he followed the Lord as David did (29:2). The narrator focuses on his concern for the temple and the role of priests and Levites: "In the first year of his reign, in the first month, he opened the doors of the house of the LORD and repaired them. He brought in the priests and the Levites and assembled them in the square on the east and said to them, 'Hear me, Levites! Now consecrate yourselves, and consecrate the house of the LORD, the God of your fathers, and carry out the filth from the Holy Place'" (29:3–5). Hezekiah made a covenant with the Lord, and the Levites consecrated themselves to cleanse the temple (29:10–19). Requisite sacrifices were offered according to the law to secure atonement for the people (29:20–24). The Levites were stationed to play instruments and to sing, and the assembly worshiped the Lord and sang his praises (29:25–30) and offered sacrifices of joy and consecration (29:31–33).

In addition, Hezekiah celebrated Passover a month late (chap. 30), promising mercy if the nation returned to the Lord. The importance of "all Israel" surfaces in the account. "So the couriers went from city to city through the country of Ephraim and Manasseh, and as far as Zebulun, but they laughed them to scorn and mocked them. However, some men of Asher, of Manasseh, and of Zebulun humbled themselves and came to Jerusalem" (30:10–11).

We see here the theme that a remnant will pay heed to the things of the Lord (30:12). The Chronicler clearly was interested in things being done in accord with the law, but many had not cleansed themselves to participate in Passover, and yet they were permitted to partake, and the Lord answered Hezekiah's prayer that they be forgiven (30:17–20). The experience of Israel was almost Edenic at the Passover: "The whole assembly of Judah, and the priests and the Levites, and the whole assembly that came out of Israel, and the sojourners who came out of the land of Israel, and the sojourners who lived in Judah, rejoiced. So there was great joy in Jerusalem, for since the time of Solomon the son of David king of Israel there had been nothing like this in Jerusalem. Then the priests and the Levites arose and blessed the people, and their voice was heard, and their prayer came to his holy habitation in heaven" (30:25–27). The narrator believes that such joy will belong to Israel again if they turn to the Lord in obedience and abandon false gods. In response, "all Israel" went out and destroyed idols in the land (31:1). The priests and Levites were appointed to serve in their divisions, just as David structured them, so that sacrifices and praise would be offered (chap. 31; cf. 1 Chron. 23–25), and contributions and tithes were brought so that they could perform their ministry. Just as we find in Kings, Hezekiah and Jerusalem were spared from the Assyrians because they trusted in the Lord (chap. 32), though the Lord uncovered the pride in Hezekiah's heart, and thus the day of exile was at hand.

Manasseh was Ahaz's duplicate, only worse (chap. 33). He pursued idolatry with a vengeance, even building altars in the Lord's house, where his name dwelt (33:4). He burned his sons in fire and turned to fortune-tellers and mediums instead of trusting in the Lord (33:5–6). Indeed, "The carved image of the idol that he had made he set in the house of God, of which God said to David and to Solomon his son, 'In this house, and in Jerusalem, which I have chosen out of all the tribes of Israel, I will put my name forever'" (33:7). As a result of his sins, Manasseh was brought to Babylon. The Chronicler adds a dimension that is missing in Kings. When Manasseh was in Babylon, he repented and asked the Lord for mercy, and the Lord answered and restored him to Jerusalem (33:12–13). Given the extent of Manasseh's sins, the Lord's mercy is nothing short of astonishing.[24] Surely the Chronicler wants his readers to see such as hope for his generation. If the Lord showed mercy to Manasseh,

24. For an appraisal that takes into account the theme of mercy and rightly locates the reward/punishment theme in the work to the blessings/curses of the Mosaic covenant, see Kelly, *Retribution and Eschatology*, 29–110; for a less satisfying reading, see Japhet, *Ideology*, 117–51. For an interpretation that fails to see the complexity in the Chronicler's theology, see North, "Theology of the Chronicler," 372–74.

then there is hope for the Chronicler's day as well.[25] Manasseh's repentance was not abstract. It led to concrete actions: "And he took away the foreign gods and the idol from the house of the LORD, and all the altars that he had built on the mountain of the house of the LORD and in Jerusalem, and he threw them outside of the city. He also restored the altar of the LORD and offered on it sacrifices of peace offerings and of thanksgiving, and he commanded Judah to serve the LORD, the God of Israel" (33:15–16). Despite Manasseh's repentance, Judah was near the end now. His son Amon pursued evil and did not humble himself as Manasseh did (33:21–23).

The history of Judah certainly was not a straight-line trajectory downward. Perhaps the best king of them all appeared on the scene shortly before the nation's dissolution. Nothing negative is said about Josiah (chaps. 34–35), for "he did not turn aside to the right hand or to the left" (34:2). He is a fitting inhabitant of David's throne, and he vigilantly rooted idolatry out of Jerusalem and Judah (34:3–5). Indeed, his reform program even reached the northern kingdom (34:6–7). He ordered repair of the Lord's house as well (34:8–13). The book of the law was discovered, which certified that the nation would suffer the curses of the covenant for forsaking the Lord, and Huldah confirmed this prognosis (34:14–25). Because of his humility, Josiah would be spared from seeing such punishment (34:27–28), and he made a covenant to devote himself and Judah completely to the Lord (34:30–33). Like Hezekiah, Josiah celebrated Passover (chap. 35). Given the interest of the Chronicler, we are not surprised to learn that Josiah instructed the Levites to put the ark in the temple and to follow the prescriptions laid down by David and Solomon (35:3–6, 10). The offerings were brought and performed according to the rule of the law of Moses (35:11–14). Similarly, the singers and gatekeepers performed the duties prescribed by David (35:15).

But Josiah's reign was a short-lived interval. His children who succeeded him turned to evil (chap. 36), and the nation went into exile. The reason for the exile and the central problem with the people is communicated in these important words:

All the officers of the priests and the people likewise were exceedingly unfaithful, following all the abominations of the nations. And they polluted the house of the LORD that he had made holy in Jerusalem. The LORD, the God of their fathers, sent persistently to them by his messengers, because he had compassion on his people and on his dwelling place. But they kept mocking the messengers of God, despising his words and scoffing at his prophets, until the wrath of the LORD rose against his people, until there was no remedy. Therefore he brought

25. So also Dumbrell, *Faith of Israel*, 330–31.

up against them the king of the Chaldeans, who killed their young men with the sword in the house of their sanctuary and had no compassion on young man or virgin, old man or aged. He gave them all into his hand. And all the vessels of the house of God, great and small, and the treasures of the house of the LORD, and the treasures of the king and of his princes, all these he brought to Babylon. And they burned the house of God and broke down the wall of Jerusalem and burned all its palaces with fire and destroyed all its precious vessels. (36:14–19)

But exile is not the final word in the book. The author concludes with the decree of Cyrus, in fulfillment of the promise made through Jeremiah, that those in Babylon may return to Jerusalem and build a house for the Lord (36:22–23). "The Chronicler wishes to emphasize that the conditions for achieving a fuller measure of restoration now exist."[26] The invitation to "go up" (36:23) "functions as an appeal to the Chronicler's own community, which stands typologically in the same situation as the original returnees."[27] The Lord was not finished with Israel or the temple. His covenant promises were still trustworthy. There was a future for the people of Israel despite their persistent unfaithfulness.

Conclusion

Chronicles is fundamentally a book of hope. Israel has returned from exile, but the promises of the Lord were not yet fulfilled in their entirety. The second exodus would be fulfilled in a deeper way in the future. God made an irrevocable covenant with David, and his dynasty would last forever, even though there was no king presently on the throne. "In the Chronicler's time, although the dynasty had ceased to function, Yahweh's rule is secure, as is Israel's final place. Worship in the temple was designed to remind the community of Yahweh's universal rule."[28] And, "The message of Chronicles is that the kingdom of God will come and that the second exodus will occur."[29] Israel's history shows, however, that no particular king or generation would experience that blessing if they did not keep the Torah and walk in God's ways. Israel and Judah originally went into exile because they failed to do the Lord's will. Yahweh is the covenant King of Israel, and he must be obeyed as its covenantal Lord. Israel must not forsake him; they must cling to him in covenantal love and obedience. The Lord is present with his people in the

26. Kelly, *Retribution and Eschatology*, 189.
27. Ibid.
28. Dumbrell, *Faith of Israel*, 332.
29. Ibid.

temple, and devotion to him means that Israel must follow the regulations set forth for how Yahweh is to be worshiped. The priests and Levites must serve according to the mandate of Torah. Subsequently, they followed the regulations laid down by David. What it means to have Yahweh at the center of existence is to praise him and glorify him as King and Lord. The author is confident that a new day is dawning for Israel, and they will experience the loveliness of the Lord's presence if they obey and follow him. The NT message is that such obedience is the result of the new covenant that the Lord enacts with his people, a covenant enacted through the death and resurrection of Jesus Christ.

12

EZRA-NEHEMIAH

Introduction

In the Hebrew canon of Scripture Ezra and Nehemiah are one book. I am not following the MT order in this book, but Ezra and Nehemiah are placed together in the order that has come down to us in English Bibles as well. In addition, the books themselves link together the work of both Ezra and Nehemiah.[1] "Nehemiah participates with Ezra in the instruction of the people, and conversely Ezra shares in the dedication of the wall built by Nehemiah (Neh. 12:27). Clearly the narrator(s) envisions the political and religious work of the two men as functioning together in the reconstitution of the community."[2] Scholars differ as to whether Ezra-Nehemiah should be understood as the prelude to Chronicles or be interpreted as a sequel. If one follows the Hebrew order for the canon, we have the former, while the Greek order points to the latter. I suggest that the matter of order is not decisive. Insights and connections can be drawn legitimately whichever order is adopted. My purpose is not to speak against the Hebrew order. I simply want to point out that the Greek order makes very good sense here. Ezra, in fact, picks up with the very words that conclude Chronicles (2 Chron. 36:22–23; Ezra 1:1–4) and expands on them.

In other words, the story and account in Chronicles continue in Ezra and Nehemiah, so that historically Ezra and Nehemiah fit nicely after Chronicles, recounting some historical events that occurred after Cyrus's decree. Placing Ezra and Nehemiah together also makes sense. The books overlap in terms of time period, and Ezra plays a role in both books. Thematically, they fit together

1. So Childs, *Old Testament as Scripture*, 634–35; House, *Old Testament Theology*, 512–13.
2. Childs, *Old Testament as Scripture*, 635.

as well, for both works devote attention to rebuilding, whether it relates to the temple or the city. The issue before Israel is not only whether they will do the requisite work but also whether they will be devoted to Yahweh's lordship, whether they will do his will. Israel has returned from exile, and the question is what its future will be. Will Israel be devoted to the Lord and pursue his purposes, or will they again sink into syncretism and sin? These two books, by recounting some of the history of Israel after the exile, are designed to encourage Israel to be faithful to its covenant with Yahweh, to focus on the Lord's priorities, and to refrain from aligning itself with those who are not faithful to the Lord.

Rebuilding the Temple in the Midst of Opposition

The story begins with the return from exile, which both Ezra and Nehemiah pick up (Ezra 1; Neh. 7). Cyrus, the king of Persia, decreed in 538 BC that Israelites could return to Israel and build a temple in Jerusalem (Ezra 1:1–3). Furthermore, he mandated that inhabitants of the region assist the Jews in building the temple (Ezra 1:4). One of the themes of both Ezra and Nehemiah surfaces here. Consistently throughout the books God sovereignly works through kings to carry out his will and to do good to the Jewish people (cf. Ezra 4; 6–8; Neh. 1).[3] The Jews responded by giving generously to support the building of the temple, while Cyrus returned the vessels taken from the temple by Nebuchadnezzar (Ezra 1:5–11). The earthly temple represents the heavenly temple, and thus the rebuilding of the temple signals the reign of the Lord over Israel and the restoration of the Lord's favor upon his people (see 1 Kings 8; 2 Chron. 6). Before the temple was built, the altar where sacrifices were offered was restored and the feast of Booths was celebrated (Ezra 3). The laying of the foundation of the temple provoked praise and weeping (Ezra 3:10–13)—praise because it was a new beginning, weeping because the foundation was nothing like the old temple. Still, the people saw the foundation as an indication of God's grace and covenant love for his people (Ezra 3:11).

A fundamental theme of Ezra-Nehemiah is the danger of syncretism, for Israel suffered exile because it did not exclusively worship Yahweh but also participated in worship of other gods. The desire of Israel's enemies sounds innocent enough and seems even to indicate a catholicity of spirit: "Let us build with you, for we worship your God as you do, and we have been sacrificing to him ever since the days of Esarhaddon king of Assyria who brought us

---

3. See Childs, *Old Testament as Scripture*, 633; Waltke, *Old Testament Theology*, 796–97; Kidner, *Ezra and Nehemiah*, 20–21; Kelly, "Ezra-Nehemiah," 196.

here" (Ezra 4:2). The sharp rejection of this offer (Ezra 4:3) might seem to be uncharitable, but the narrator clearly approves of the rebuff. Such compromise would contaminate and ultimately undermine the worship of Yahweh.

The adversaries of Israel turned to another tack when repelled. They discouraged and frightened the people so that the temple was not built during the rest of Cyrus's reign and did not begin again until the second year of the reign of Darius (522–486 BC) (Ezra 4:24), which would mean that construction commenced around 520 BC, though was not completed until 516 BC. The Jewish opponents, then, hindered the construction of the temple for some fifteen years. The chapter takes a surprising turn, for the author shifts from the building of the temple to opposition to the Jews in the reigns of Ahasuerus (486–464 BC) (Ezra 4:6) and Artaxerxes (464–423 BC) (Ezra 4:7–23). The resistance under Artaxerxes was not to the building of the temple but rather to the rebuilding of the walls of Jerusalem. Artaxerxes prevented the Jews from building the city because it had a reputation for sedition and rebellion. This matter of rebuilding the city is picked up in Nehemiah. Why does the narrator include, while recounting the resistance to the building of the temple in the 500s, opposition to the Jews in the next century? His point seems to be that there is a pattern and perpetuity to this opposition. Picking up the story line from Genesis, we see the offspring of the serpent still trying to crush and destroy the Jews. The temple represented God's dwelling place—God's Eden on earth, so to speak—and so it was resisted by those who sided with evil.

The opposition to the temple, however, did not succeed, as Ezra 5–6 clarifies. The prophets Haggai and Zechariah encouraged the people to build, and Jeshua and Zerubbabel, representing the priest and the king, spearheaded the building (5:1–2). Tattenai objected to the rebuilding, but the Jews appealed to the decree of Cyrus to justify the project (5:3–17). Darius investigated the matter and found that Cyrus had indeed decreed that the temple should be rebuilt (chap. 6). Darius not only concurred with the building of the temple but also provided funds for it from the royal treasury (6:3–4)! Not only was Tattenai mandated to refrain from his opposition but he was also required to pay for and furnish the necessary supplies for the temple (6:5–13). Hence, the temple was completed in 516 BC (6:14–15). Even though Israel faces enemies throughout its history, the Lord will cause Israel to triumph if they are faithful to him. He will sovereignly accomplish his will through rulers and political functionaries, for he is the King of the universe. Israel responded with joy and celebration and great praise (6:16–22). Ezra insisted that the cult function according to the will of God. Hence, the priests and Levites served in their divisions according to the Mosaic law (6:18). The Passover was observed, and the priests and Levites observed purity regulations (6:20). The writer sees an anticipation of paradise: "It [Passover] was eaten by the people of Israel who had returned from exile, and also by every one who had joined them and separated himself from the uncleanness of the peoples of the land to worship the LORD, the God of Israel. And they kept the Feast of Unleavened Bread seven days with joy, for the LORD had made them joyful and had turned the heart of the king of Assyria to them, so that he aided them in the work of the house of God, the God of Israel" (6:21–22). Israel's joy was attributed to the sovereign Lord, who worked so that the king had favor on Israel (cf. Prov. 21:1).

The Reform Work of Ezra

From 515 BC, the book of Ezra leaps to 458 BC in chapter 7, when Ezra, furnished by Artaxerxes with gifts and provisions for the temple, made a four-month trip from Babylonia to Jerusalem. The narrator emphasizes in chapters 7–8 that the hand of God was on Ezra and those who traveled with him (7:6, 9, 28; 8:18, 22, 31), for such a journey was dangerous and long, but such favor is limited to those "who seek him" because "the power of his wrath is against all who forsake him" (8:22). The success of the journey is attributed to God, but it would not have taken place apart from Ezra's devotion to the Lord. The hand of the Lord being on Ezra is also due to his being "skilled in the Law of Moses" (7:6) as a scribe. We read in 7:9 that Ezra made it to Jerusalem because God's "good hand . . . was on him," but 7:10 explains further: "For Ezra had set his heart to study the Law of the LORD, and to do it and to teach his statutes and rules in Israel." Ezra's success is explained in terms of his faithful teaching and obedience of the law. Ezra is not presented merely as an intellectual. He studied, obeyed, and taught. The order is crucial. Before Ezra taught the law, he himself obeyed it. There is no abstract or merely intellectual interest in the Torah.

The focus of the trip is on provisions for the temple, so we are not surprised to read that along with ordinary Israelites "priests and Levites, the singers and gatekeepers, and the temple servants" traveled to Jerusalem (7:7). Personnel for temple ministry were particularly important. Indeed, Ezra brought money from the king for the temple and solicited further offerings as well (7:15–16). The money was provided to offer requisite sacrifices (7:17). The provisions from Artaxerxes were lavish indeed: "And whatever else is required for the house of your God, which it falls to you to provide, you may provide it out of the king's treasury" (7:20; cf. 7:21–23). Indeed, Artaxerxes instructed Ezra to teach the people divine law, to appoint justices and officials to enforce it, and to punish those who violated it (7:25–26). The sovereign work of the Lord for the good of his people and his house was celebrated by Ezra: "Blessed be the LORD, the God of our fathers, who put such a thing as this into the heart of the king, to beautify the house of the LORD that is in Jerusalem, and who extended to me his steadfast love before the king and his counselors, and before all the king's mighty officers" (7:27–28).

The Lord had shown his favor to Israel, but the danger that the nation faced was compromise and syncretism.[4] Israel went into exile in the first place because it violated covenant stipulations, and the faithlessness of Israel cropped up again, for many within Israel had married foreign women—those who worshiped other gods (chaps. 9–10). Intermarriage with foreigners who worshiped other gods was forbidden in the Torah (see Exod. 34:16; Deut. 7:3–4; cf. Josh. 23:12). What was particularly galling to Ezra was that the sin was especially prominent among "the officials and chief men" (9:2). Ezra turned to the Lord in prayer, confessing the sins of Israel before him (9:6–15). It was Israel's sin that led to their exile in the first place, and Ezra feared the consequences of such sin. Israel's return from exile is clearly not viewed as the fulfillment of all that the Lord promised for his people. The present state of Israel is ambiguous. On the one hand, they are still viewed as slaves and captives (9:7, 9); on the other hand, the Lord has shown his grace to Israel and given them "a little reviving in our slavery" (9:8). The Lord had been faithful to his covenant promises so that Israel survived as a remnant, so that the temple had been rebuilt and they lived in the land again (9:9). But their old nemesis (their sin!) had arisen, for Israel failed to keep covenant stipulations and flouted the mercy granted to them (9:13). If they failed to act, the remnant could be removed from their midst (9:14–15). Israel responded in repentance by breaking off the marriages to foreign wives (chap. 10).

For the narrator, the saving promises granted to Israel would become a reality only if Israel separated from the nations. The temple signified God's special presence with Israel, but the presence of the temple was worthless if Israel did not live as a holy people, if they were no different from the nations, if they did not worship and obey Yahweh as their sovereign and their God. There was hope for Israel, for they had returned from exile and rebuilt the temple. But if Israel turned away from Yahweh, they would experience a curse rather than a blessing.

Rebuilding Jerusalem

The book of Nehemiah addresses, from a slightly different angle, many of the same themes that we see in Ezra. Instead of the building of and furnishing of

4. See Kelly, "Ezra-Nehemiah," 197.

the temple, the focus is on the rebuilding of Jerusalem, though the latter, as we saw, comes up in Ezra as well. Nehemiah wept, mourned, fasted, and prayed when he heard that Jerusalem's wall was torn down and its gates destroyed (1:3–4), for this news was not received as merely a political report of the fortunes of Jerusalem. Rather, Nehemiah concluded that such a state of affairs indicated that Israel had sinned against Yahweh. Hence, he responded in prayer, confessing to the covenant God the sins of Israel in that they did not observe the commands given by Moses (1:5–7). Moses predicted that Israel would go into exile if they strayed from the Lord, but that the Lord would have mercy if they repented and would bring them back to the land (1:8–9). Nehemiah prayed that the Lord would grant him success, since the Lord had redeemed Israel as his own people at the exodus (1:10–11). Specifically, Nehemiah, as the king's cupbearer, wanted to secure a sabbatical from his work so that he could attend to the problem of Jerusalem. Certainly, one of the themes that stands out in the book is Nehemiah's initiative and hard work. But the book is misunderstood if it is read fundamentally in terms of the "can do" attitude and strategic thinking of Nehemiah. The whole process began with prayer, with Nehemiah entreating the Lord to grant him mercy before the king. Indeed, prayer is sprinkled throughout the book at key points, as we will see when we rehearse the narrative. Thus, when Nehemiah asked Artaxerxes if he could make a trip to Jerusalem, he quickly prayed before making the request (2:4), for he realized that the entire venture depended upon the Lord's favor.[5]

However, Nehemiah did not believe that the Lord's sovereignty and favor precluded human initiative, but rather that they undergirded and supported what human beings accomplish. In any case, when the king asked Nehemiah what he wished to do about the state of the city of Jerusalem, Nehemiah responded with a well-thought-out proposal (2:5–8), though the king's favorable response to Nehemiah was because "the good hand of my God was upon me" (2:8). Another theme that surfaces in the narrative is the intense opposition to the rebuilding of the wall. Here we see another version of the conflict that has its origins in the early chapters of Genesis. The offspring of the serpent resist the offspring of the woman. Israel is the people of God, and Jerusalem is the place of his dwelling. Sanballat and Tobiah are "displeased . . . greatly that someone had come to seek the welfare of the people of Israel" (2:10). Nehemiah continued to carry out his plan to rebuild Jerusalem's walls (2:12–18). Opponents derided the work, describing it as rebellion against Artaxerxes, but Nehemiah did not compromise with them, maintaining that they did not belong in Jerusalem (2:19–20).

5. On the centrality of prayer in Ezra-Nehemiah, see Kidner, *Ezra and Nehemiah*, 24–26.

As the wall was rebuilt, opposition continued (chap. 3). The opposition tried ridicule (4:1–3) and intimidation (4:7–8; 6:6) with the threat of physical attack (4:11), arguing that Nehemiah was starting a political rebellion (6:7). Apparently, prophets were even hired to proclaim messages to Nehemiah that would push him toward cowardice and undermine his leadership (6:10–14). Nehemiah encouraged the people to work steadily despite their adversaries, and he was undaunted by the threats of his enemies. As noted earlier, Nehemiah's strategy was not merely a secular program of hard work and organization; he prayed that the Lord would frustrate their adversaries and turn their evil back upon them (4:4–5; 6:14) and would give him strength to finish the task (6:9). Not only did Nehemiah set a guard to protect the builders while putting up the wall but he also prayed for the Lord's protection (4:9), and the Lord answered his petition (4:15). We also see in chapter 4 that Nehemiah wisely administered the situation so that those who worked would be protected. The people worked with their weapons at hand and were ready to fight if necessary (4:14).

After the wall was built, Nehemiah ensured that procedures were in place to keep the city safe (7:1–3) and made plans to repopulate Jerusalem (chaps. 7; 11). In particular, it was important that priests, Levites, gatekeepers, and temple servants were in Jerusalem. We see concerns very similar to Chronicles here. Levites were appointed "to praise and to give thanks, according to the commandment of David the man of God, watch by watch" (12:24). Similarly when the wall was dedicated, "they sought the Levites in all their places, to bring them to Jerusalem to celebrate the dedication with gladness, with thanksgivings and with singing, with cymbals, harps, and lyres" (12:27). The wall did not exist for its own sake. Ultimately, the purpose was to offer up praise and thanks to God. Jerusalem was intended to be a place of praise, and thus Israel celebrated the dedication of the wall with joy (chap. 12; cf. 12:46). Dedication to the Lord was primary, so "the priests and the Levites purified themselves, and they purified the people and the gates and the wall" (12:30). They celebrated with choirs and praised the Lord in song and offered sacrifices (12:42–43).

Living in the Fear of Yahweh

Nehemiah's fundamental message fits with what we see elsewhere in the OT. Israel's primary problem was not the opposition of its enemies; rather, it was their own lack of devotion and commitment to Yahweh, for they were called to live under his rule. The officials and nobles, for instance, were enriching themselves at the expense of the common people by taking interest from them (chap. 5), a practice contrary to the Torah (see Exod. 22:25; Lev. 25:36–37; Deut. 23:19–20). The people were struggling to make it financially and were suffering from a lack of food (5:2). Hence, they were mortgaging their possessions to get food (5:3) and were even selling their children into slavery (5:5).[6] Nehemiah was outraged by such injustice, reproving boldly the leaders for such blatant evil. He demanded that they return to the people their possessions and cease from exacting interest (5:11). The officials responded rightly and carried out Nehemiah's instructions (5:12–13). Nehemiah functioned as a model for the nobles, for when he served as governor, he provided for the people at his own expense, not enriching himself by virtue of his leadership position (5:14–19). The root issue in the matter is expressed in Nehemiah's rebuke to the officials: "Ought you not to walk in the fear of our God to prevent the taunts of the nations our enemies?" (5:9). The perpetration of evil is always traced to one's defective relationship to God, demonstrating that God is not central in one's affections.

Devotion to Yahweh expresses itself in obedience to the Torah. Chapter 8 recounts an event in which Israel gathered as the people of God and Ezra read the Torah, as the Torah itself mandates (see Deut. 31:11; cf. Deut. 17:19). Others assisted Ezra so that the law was understood when it was read (8:7–8). The people wept when hearing the law, presumably because they realized how seriously they had violated the stipulations of the covenant (8:9–11). Still, the priests, scribes, and Levites encouraged the people to be joyful instead of grieving, for this was a day of renewed commitment to the Lord. The people celebrated the feast of Booths with great joy (8:14–18; cf. Lev. 23). All of this was part of a covenant renewal ceremony in Israel. The people of Israel would be great only if they were dedicated to the Lord and gave themselves entirely to him. They were at a low ebb in their history because they had forsaken his lordship. The covenant renewal was a day of joy but also a day of fasting and confessing of sins, of reading the Torah and of worshiping the Lord (9:1–3). Contrary to many commentators and a long critical consensus, we should not understand the law in legalistic terms here.[7] The Levites led worship so that the people would stand up and praise and bless the Lord (9:4–5). The heart and soul of what Nehemiah was calling for was praise and honor and glory to Yahweh through the obedience of the people.

The history of the Lord's covenant relationship with Israel is then rehearsed. Yahweh is the Lord not only of earth but also of heaven, and thus

6. For a helpful discussion of slavery in Israel, see Goldingay, *Israel's Life*, 458–75. Goldingay argues that the Western notion of slavery did not exist in the OT, and that what we find in the OT is closer to what we call serfdom than it is to slavery.
7. Rightly Childs, *Old Testament as Scripture*, 636.

he is the Lord of all (9:6) as the creator and preserver of all things. The Lord graciously chose Abraham and brought him from Ur to Canaan (9:7), making a covenant with him and fulfilling it by freeing Israel from Egyptian bondage (9:8–11). The redemption accomplished is God-centered, for as Ezra says to the Lord, in saving Israel, "you made a name for yourself" (9:10).[8] The Lord led them in a pillar of cloud and fire (9:12), revealing his will to them with the commands given at Sinai (9:13–14). He provided for them in the wilderness (9:15), but Israel refused to obey and did not enter the promised land (9:16–17). Nevertheless, the Lord was gracious and merciful and did not forsake Israel despite its apostasy (9:17), even when they made golden calves to worship (9:18–19). The Lord was faithful to his covenant, making Israel as numerous "as the stars of heaven" (9:23), instructing them through the Spirit, sustaining them in the wilderness, and giving them the land that he promised (9:20–25). But Israel was unfaithful to the covenant, rejecting the Lord's law and slaying the prophets (9:26). In the days of the judges the Lord handed Israel over to their enemies but showed mercy when they repented (9:27–29). The Lord promised that Israel would live in the land if they obeyed (see Lev. 18:5), but they failed to obey, and so the Lord sent the nation into exile (9:29–30). And yet the Lord will never abandon his people: "In your great mercies you did not make an end of them or forsake them, for you are a gracious and merciful God" (9:31). Therefore, Israel called upon the Lord to remember them again in their distress because he had made a covenant with them and had not destroyed them (9:32). The Lord's punishments have been righteous, and Israel has been stubborn and lawless (9:33–35). Hence, even though they are in the land, they are still slaves because their labor goes to kings who rule over them (9:36–37).

As a result, the people made a covenant to serve the Lord and to give themselves to him entirely (9:38). The substance of the covenant was a pledge to be faithful to covenant obligations: "The rest of the people, the priests, the Levites, the gatekeepers, the singers, the temple servants, and all who have separated themselves from the peoples of the lands to the Law of God, their wives, their sons, their daughters, all who have knowledge and understanding, join with their brothers, their nobles, and enter into a curse and an oath to walk in God's Law that was given by Moses the servant of God, and to observe and do all the commandments of the LORD our Lord and his rules and his statutes" (10:28–29). They would not intermarry with foreigners, would refrain from commerce on the Sabbath and from taking interest, and would bring in the firstfruits and tithes (10:30–39; cf. 12:47).

8. The LXX identifies Ezra as the speaker.

The covenant that Israel made focuses on its distinctiveness, its separation from pagan nations. Israel had been contaminated by syncretism, and both Ezra and Nehemiah are concerned about the purity of the people. Hence, we are not surprised to read the regulation, in dependence upon Deut. 23:3–5, that Moabites and Ammonites should never enter the Lord's assembly (13:1–2).[9] The people responded in covenant obedience (13:3). The significance of Tobiah being an Ammonite (2:10, 19; 4:3, 7; 6:1, 12, 14, 17, 19) becomes clearer to us. Not only was he an enemy of Nehemiah in the book but also he stood in line with those like Balaam who were historic enemies of Israel (13:2). Nehemiah was outraged to learn that the priest Eliashib, a relative of Tobiah, had taken a storage chamber for grains and other offerings given to priests in the courts of the Lord and had put Tobiah in the chamber (13:4–7). Nehemiah, representing how Israel should respond to evil, threw his furniture out of the chamber, cleansed it, and brought back the goods that belonged there (13:8–9). Nehemiah also discovered that the Levites were not being provided for with tithes, and he remedied that situation as well (13:10–13). He also stopped the practice of those who were trading on the Sabbath (13:15–22). Israel had just made a covenant recently to keep the Sabbath, but they were now violating it in an egregious way. Nehemiah was a model of one who lived for the honor of God and the glory of his house (13:14, 22), and the Lord would reward Israel if they followed his pattern and would spare them from judgment.

Remarkably, after all that Israel had been through, some in Israel were also intermarrying with pagan nations, even after making a covenant in which they renounced that very practice (13:23–24). Some "could not speak the language of Judah" (13:24). They had forgotten their heritage and were scarcely different from the pagan nations. Nehemiah, according to the narrator, was not guilty of having a temper tantrum in cursing them and pulling out their hair and administering physical punishment (13:25). Instead, he called them to renew their oath to the Lord. He reminded them of Israel's history. Solomon started the slide into exile through his marriages to pagan women (13:26). Such behavior is nothing less than covenant treachery (13:27), threatening Israel with exile again. Not only was Eliashib's family related to Nehemiah's old enemy Tobiah the Ammonite but also Eliashib's son apparently married the daughter of Nehemiah's other enemy, Sanballat the Horonite (13:28; cf. 2:10, 19; 4:1, 7; 6:1–2, 5, 12, 14). The compromise with paganism was deeply entrenched in Israel, and Israel, like Nehemiah, must chase those who do such away from the Lord's house (13:14). The concern for purity shines through:

9. We have already seen that Ruth is an exception, which perhaps means that the rule does not apply if a Moabite joins Israel.

"Remember them, O my God, because they have desecrated the priesthood and the covenant of the priesthood and the Levites" (13:29). But Nehemiah was in another category: "Thus I cleansed them from everything foreign, and I established the duties of the priests and Levites, each in his work; and I provided for the wood offering at appointed times, and for the firstfruits" (13:30–31). Nehemiah lived for the honor and glory of God, and thus longed to see his holiness preserved. The book ends with one of the many "remember" prayers in the book: "Remember me, O my God, for good" (13:31; cf. 5:19; 6:14; 13:14, 29). These prayers of remembrance will certainly be answered in the affirmative. The Lord of the covenant will bless those who are loyal to him and punish those who oppose him. But such prayers are not only for Nehemiah; they apply to all those who devote themselves to the covenantal Lord by zealously preserving his honor and by keeping his commands. Thereby Israel lives under Yahweh's lordship.

Conclusion

Where do Ezra and Nehemiah put us in terms of the story? Israel has returned from exile. The temple is rebuilt, and the walls of Jerusalem are erected, and yet the nation is very weak. "If Ezra is a second Moses, he, like the first Moses, has not produced and cannot produce a change in the heart of the people."[10] Both books acknowledge the return, but also they admit that Israel is under the tutelage of other powers. "The exile continues even though Israel is in the land."[11] They are not enjoying true freedom and joy in the land. Why are they so weak? Because they have not obeyed Yahweh as covenant Lord. They must heed the covenant stipulations in the Torah given by Moses. The temple worship must be carried out as the Lord mandates, and Israel must purify itself from uncleanness. Israel has compromised with pagans to prosper financially and to enjoy sexual relations with women from cultures where other gods are worshiped. They must renew their covenant with the Lord, for the Lord, despite all of Israel's sin, has not abandoned Israel. He will fulfill his covenant promises, but only to a people who are submissive to his will.

10. Dempster, *Dominion and Dynasty*, 224.
11. Ibid.

13

ESTHER

Introduction

The book of Esther is one of the most delightful narratives in the Scriptures, though it also strikes contemporary readers as vengeful and unforgiving, about which I will comment in due course. The theology of the book is communicated through the narrative account, which tells of how Esther became the queen of King Ahasuerus, who reigned 486–464 BC. The theme of the book is God's sovereign work in preserving the Jewish people from annihilation.[1] Yahweh reigns over his people and preserves them, even when they live in the midst of pagan oppressors. The narrator, however, tells the story in an unusual way, for God is never mentioned in the book. The omission is deliberate, for there are a number of points in the book where God's role in the story almost begs to be introduced but he remains unmentioned.[2] "God is present even when he is most absent; when there are no miracles, dreams or visions, no charismatic leaders, no prophets to interpret what is happening, and not even any explicit God-talk. And he is present as deliverer."[3] The story, from a canonical perspective, functions as an elaboration of Gen. 3:15. The offspring of the serpent attempt to destroy and wipe out the offspring of the woman.[4] God sees to it, however, that the attempt to obliterate his people is frustrated, so that the offspring of the serpent end up being crushed by the offspring of the woman.

1. See Keys, "Esther," 198–200.
2. See House, *Old Testament Theology*, 496; Dumbrell, *Faith of Israel*, 299; B. Webb, *Five Festal Garments*, 121.
3. B. Webb, *Five Festal Garments*, 124.
4. See Dempster, *Dominion and Dynasty*, 223.

220

Mordecai and Esther function for the author like Joseph and Moses, whom the Lord used to rescue Israel from annihilation.[5]

The Story

The story begins with the demotion of Queen Vashti because of her refusal to obey King Ahasuerus's command that she display her beauty before his guests (chap. 1). The narrator betrays no interest in moralizing over the king's behavior or the queen's refusal to do what the king demanded. The point of the story is that God was secretly and unobtrusively working in human affairs, for by this means the pathway was opened for Esther to replace Vashti as queen (chap. 2). Esther was now in position to advocate for the Jews at the crucial hour. Following Mordecai's command, she had not revealed that she was Jewish, which is another way of saying that she had not disclosed that she worshiped Yahweh (2:10, 20). The author, by twice reflecting on Esther being Jewish, foreshadows a theme that will play a central role in the story. Another significant foreshadowing closes chapter 2 (2:21–23). Mordecai discovered that two of King Ahasuerus's officials were plotting to murder the king. He relayed the plan to Esther, who informed the king, and the perpetrators were executed. The incident was duly recorded in the king's records.

The opposition to the Jews appears on the scene in the person of Haman (chap. 3). Haman was an Agagite, which means that he was a descendant of Agag of Amalek (1 Sam. 15).[6] Amalek fought against Israel in the wilderness when it was weak and exhausted (Exod. 17:8–16). Therefore, they were counted as perpetual enemies of Israel and were to be destroyed (Deut. 25:17–19). Haman, as we will see, is a fitting descendant of his ancestors, reflecting the proverb "Like father, like son." He was hungry for power and relished servants who bowed down and paid him homage (3:2). Mordecai, however, refused to "bow down or pay homage" (3:2), in violation of the king's decree (3:3). Mordecai informed his fellow servants that his reason for refusing to bow down was "that he was a Jew" (3:4). Here is one of those occasions in the book where we expect Yahweh to be mentioned. It might seem that Mordecai was rather recalcitrant and stubborn, but the narrator apparently believes that Mordecai was right and justified, though he never explains why, leaving us to

5. House, *Old Testament Theology*, 494.
6. See Childs, *Old Testament as Scripture*, 605. Mordecai was a descendant of Saul, who infamously refused to destroy all the Amalekites when commanded to do so (1 Sam. 15). Mordecai, of course, in his resistance to the Amalekites stands in a very different position from Saul. See Dempster, *Dominion and Dynasty*, 222.

read between the lines.[7] It seems that bowing down to Haman would violate his devotion to Yahweh as the God of Israel. The Lord was Mordecai's king and sovereign, not Haman.[8] When Haman discovered what Mordecai was doing, he became enraged. And in finding out the reason, he was not satisfied to kill only Mordecai. He engineered a plot by which he would wipe out all the Jews in the empire (3:5–15). He charged the Jews with disloyalty to the empire (3:8), promising to give ten thousand talents of silver to the king's treasury if the Jews were wiped out (3:9–11). Haman functioned as a successor to Cain, Pharaoh, and the other enemies of the Jews who desired to annihilate them, revealing himself to be the offspring of the serpent. As an enemy of the covenant people, as one who cursed them, he himself was destined to be cursed (see Gen. 12:2–3).[9]

Mordecai and the Jews, upon hearing the news, fasted and mourned (4:1–4). Such activities almost certainly were accompanied by prayer for the nation, but the author continues his studied and intentional neglect of mentioning God explicitly, though that should not be interpreted to say that the author has a secular point of view. Mordecai asked Esther to intercede before the king for the Jewish people (4:8–10), but Esther hesitated because she faced a death penalty if she entered the king's presence unbidden (4:11). Mordecai struck back, affirming that Esther and her family, even though they were in the palace, would not escape Haman's plot, for they too were Jews (4:12–13). The hidden sovereignty of the Lord creeps into the story again, for Mordecai suggested that Esther was appointed as queen "for such a time as this" (4:13). And if she did not act, then "relief and deliverance will rise for the Jews from another place" (4:14). The vagueness of the expression is striking. The author could have easily said that the Lord would provide another means by which the Jews would be delivered. Instead, he refers to the deliverance allusively and mysteriously to provoke the reader to ask about the source of the rescue. Remarkably, Mordecai was convinced that the Jews would be delivered. That was not the question. The issue was whether Esther would fulfill her responsibility at her appointed time in history. Esther rose to the occasion, fasting for three days before going in to the king (4:16),[10] and she gave herself into the Lord's hands without mentioning him, exclaiming, "If I perish, I perish" (4:16).

7. It is possible as well that there is a subtle critique of both Esther and Mordecai. For discussion of this matter, see B. Webb, *Five Festal Garments*, 119–20. It seems unlikely to me, however, that the narrator saw any problem with their behavior or actions.
8. Against Waltke (*Old Testament Theology*, 767), who thinks that Mordecai was simply guilty of pride.
9. Rightly B. Webb, *Five Festal Garments*, 127.
10. Waltke (*Old Testament Theology*, 767) wrongly reads Esther's fast as not conforming fully to the Lord's will. For a more convincing reading, see House, *Old Testament Theology*,

Esther summoned up the courage to go into the king's presence and make her request, and the king spared her life (chap. 5). Her first request was that the king and Haman attend a feast that she prepared, and somewhat mysteriously, instead of voicing her petition at the first feast, she asked that they both attend another feast the next day. The delay proves to be decisive for the outcome of the story, confirming the Lord's providence in all that happens. Haman left the feast joyfully because he was the only person outside of the royal couple invited to the feasts. Still, he was outraged when Mordecai "neither rose nor trembled before him" (5:9). He remedied the situation by building a gallows upon which to hang Mordecai (5:13–14). Everything seemed to be shaping up for Haman. He spent the evening boasting about "the splendor of his riches, the number of his sons, all the promotions with which the king had honored him, and how he had advanced him above the officials and the servants of the king" (5:11).

Haman seemed to be headed to the zenith of his career. Little did he know that the nadir was at hand. The narrator signals the change with a seemingly insignificant detail, "On that night the king could not sleep" (6:1), and he called for some reading material, perusing the account of how Mordecai saved his life from conspirators. He learns that nothing had been done to honor him for his act of loyalty (6:2–3). Again, God is not mentioned, but this seemingly chance event reveals that he is the central character in the story. Indeed, right at that moment Haman appeared in the court, intending to bring charges against Mordecai (6:4–5). But the king spoke first, asking Haman what should be done for a man whom the king desired to honor (6:6). One quality that Haman did not lack was self-confidence, so he assumed that the man in view was himself, and thus he suggested that the man be paraded through the streets on a royal steed in a manner befitting a king (6:6–9). Even worse for Haman, the king selected him to escort Mordecai through the streets (6:11). The reversal of fortunes had begun, and the Jews would be exalted, and those who opposed them would be dishonored (6:13). The special place of the Jews was recognized even by Haman's friends (6:14), and no one who opposed them would triumph over them.[11] God rules over history, and he will exalt his people and destroy his enemies.

The second feast requested by Esther was held, but her request at the banquet was hardly what the king expected. She asked that her life and the lives of her people be spared (7:2–4). The king was enraged, particularly when he

493. Indeed, the reference to fasting shows that God is not absent from Esther (see B. Webb, *Five Festal Garments*, 122).

11. House, *Old Testament Theology*, 494; B. Webb, *Five Festal Garments*, 123.

discovered that Haman was the mastermind of the plot (7:5–6). Not only had Haman planned to kill the queen but also he also intended to hang Mordecai, who had rescued the king from conspirators (7:9). It looked very much like Haman was part of the plot to destroy the king, and so he was hanged by the king (7:10). Esther still needed to take steps to avert the planned massacre of the Jews, orders for which had been sent out by official royal missives (chap. 8). The "king allowed the Jews who were in every city to gather and defend their lives, to destroy, to kill, and to annihilate any armed force of any people or province that might attack them, children and women included, and to plunder their goods, on one day throughout all the provinces of King Ahasuerus, on the thirteenth day of the twelfth month, which is the month of Adar" (8:11–12). Many even became Jews at that time because of fear of the Jewish people (8:17), showing that salvation was open to those outside Israel as well, that it was not limited to the Jewish people.[12]

The book concludes with the Jews defending themselves and triumphing over their enemies by slaying those who wanted to kill them (chaps. 9–10). Hence, the steps taken to destroy the Jews were reversed. The lot ("Pur") that was cast to determine the day on which the Jews would be killed had fallen in the Jews' favor. Hence, the days that were intended for their destruction by lot ("Purim") became the days of their triumph. "Reversal seems the most important structural theme in Esther."[13] As Sandra Berg points out, Purim in the book indicates that the fasts for Israel's protection have turned into feasts.[14] This fits with the message of the entire book. As the book of Proverbs says, the decision of the lot belongs to the Lord (16:33), and Purim reminds the readers that God sovereignly, through the ordinary circumstances of human life, protected his people. Joyce Baldwin says, "Even when the dice had fallen the Lord was powerful to reverse its good omen into bad, in order to deliver his people."[15] Thus Purim, like Passover, celebrates the salvation of the Jewish people, the preservation of God's chosen ones.[16] The killing of enemies seems savage and brutal to many modern Westerners, but the narrator clearly believed that they deserved destruction, that the Jews acted in self-defense, that there was an implacable and irreparable conflict between the Jews and their enemies, and that either one or the other would be destroyed.[17] Such a

---

12. So House, *Old Testament Theology*, 495.
13. Dumbrell, *Faith of Israel*, 300. See S. Berg, *Book of Esther*, 104–6.
14. S. Berg, *Book of Esther*, 31–47.
15. Baldwin, *Esther*, 23.
16. So Dumbrell, *Faith of Israel*, 300.
17. Rightly House, *Old Testament Theology*, 492. Against Waltke (*Old Testament Theology*, 767–68), who thinks that the Jewish attack on their enemies was wrong. The narrator hardly holds Waltke's view, for the celebration of Purim points in the opposite direction. There is no

perspective reflects, as noted earlier, the conflict between the offspring of the woman and the offspring of the serpent.

A Final Word

The message of Esther is not difficult to understand. Even though God is never mentioned, Yahweh is King, and the Jews are his people. No plot to annihilate them will ever succeed, for Yahweh made a covenant with Israel and will fulfill his promises to them. The serpent and his offspring will not perish from the earth until the final victory is won, but they will not ultimately triumph. The kingdom will come in its fullness. The whole world will experience the blessing promised to Abraham.

---

subtle criticism of what the Jews did on this occasion. Remarkably, Waltke fails to see that the omission of God is deliberate by the narrator, and that it should not be interpreted to say that the Jews were not seeking God, though he rightly sees the importance of the theme of providence in the book (p. 769). Waltke's judgment is surprising, since he rightly sees that the conflict between Mordecai and Haman is a reprise of 1 Sam. 15 (pp. 769–70).

INTERLUDE

A Synopsis of
THE STORY OF POSSESSION, EXILE, AND RETURN

The story from Joshua to Esther takes many turns. First, we should remind ourselves of where we left off in the Pentateuch. God created Adam and Eve to rule the world for his glory, but they rebuffed his lordship and sinned, and their sin led to death. Still, God promised victory over the serpent through the offspring of the woman. The conflict between these offspring begins immediately, and it seems that the serpent is winning, for the world turns to evil at both the flood and the tower of Babel. God always reigns, however, judging and punishing those who have given themselves over to evil. Noah and Abraham stand out, by virtue of God's grace, as offspring of the woman. God chooses Abraham and promises him land, offspring, and worldwide blessing. By the end of the Pentateuch the promise of offspring is being fulfilled, with many twists and turns along the way. And the Lord delivered Israel from Egypt and brought them to the edge of Canaan, and so the second element of the promise is about to be fulfilled.

The wilderness generation refused to trust in Yahweh's power and to submit to his lordship, and thus they did not possess the land. The generation under Joshua, however, followed the Lord's directives and possessed the land by disinheriting the Canaanites. Joshua apportioned an inheritance to each of the tribes. Now, two out of three of the promises to Abraham were fulfilled. Israel was a large nation, dwelling in the land. Worldwide blessing seemed to be just around the corner.

Unfortunately, there was a worm in the apple. The book of Judges relates how often Israel failed to abide by the stipulations of the covenant. Again and again they did not submit to their covenant Lord and King. When they got into trouble, they repented and turned to the Lord, and he sent them saviors/judges who rescued them from their enemies, showing the Lord's mercy and grace and patience. Still, when outside trouble ceased, Israel turned again toward idolatry. The book of Judges locates the problem in Israel's lack of a king, for "everyone did what was right in his own eyes" (17:6; 21:25). Two sordid stories conclude Judges (chaps. 17–21), such that readers might be forgiven for wondering if it is Israel who is the offspring of the serpent!

Bright spots still existed in Israel. The story of Ruth shines the light on some who are righteous and godly in Israel. There are still some who have not given themselves over to a selfish will; there are some who honor Yahweh as King. Ruth concludes with genealogy. Her child, Obed, is in the line that will lead to David the king. There had been hints from the beginning that a king would triumph over the serpent and his offspring. Kings would come from the family of Abraham and Jacob (Gen. 17:6, 16; 35:11). Judah's hand would be on his enemies' necks (Gen. 49:8), which suggests that his tribe will crush the offspring of the serpent. The "scepter" will belong to Judah, and the peoples will obey him (Gen. 49:10). Balaam prophesied that a scepter and a star would arise from Jacob and crush Moab's forehead (Num. 24:17). Moab likely stands here for all the enemies of Israel, and the crushing of Moab again resonates with Gen. 3:15. Now we see from Ruth the genealogy of this king. As we read Israel's story, surprises await around every corner, since Ruth is a Moabite. The intractability and sheer stubbornness and evil of human beings, and particularly the Lord's chosen people, are evident. And yet nothing and no one will triumph over the Lord. His kingdom will come, and his people will enjoy fellowship with him. They will see the King in his beauty.

The account in 1–2 Samuel relates the story of how Israel came to have a king, or more specifically, how David came to be king. The story begins with Samuel as the last of the judges, but the nation longed for a king. Saul was appointed as king, and he began his reign with humility and tremendous promise. But Saul replicated in his own life the story of Adam and Israel. He became his own sovereign and took matters into his own hands. Instead of obeying the Lord, he rationalized his sin, turning toward evil, and therefore he was rejected as king. The Lord raised up David to be king instead. David was harassed and persecuted by Saul, but he was a remarkable example of a man who put his life in God's hands, trusting the Lord instead of relying on his own devices. Hannah's song became a reality in David's life. David as the man who suffered was also exalted. Yahweh put down the rich and exalted the poor. Already, we see how David's life anticipates and corresponds to the life of Jesus, for suffering precedes glory.

Yahweh made a covenant with David that his dynasty would never end; his sons would reign forever (2 Sam. 7). The triumph over the serpent would come through one of David's sons. The worldwide blessing pledged to Abraham would become a reality through a king. But the worldwide blessing would not take place through David, for, despite all his greatness, he was flawed as well. At the height of his power he turned toward evil by committing adultery with Bathsheba and murdering her husband. The promise was not withdrawn from David, but it is evident that worldwide blessing will not become a reality through him.

When 1–2 Kings opens, it seems that worldwide blessing may become a reality through Solomon, David's son. He is a man of peace and is devoted to Yahweh. He builds a temple for the Lord, so that Yahweh can dwell in the midst of the people. The goal of God's kingdom, after all, was that human beings enjoy fellowship with him, so that they would revel in his presence. Solomon, however, stumbles badly, yielding to idolatry as he grows older. The covenant with David is not withdrawn, but Israel splits in two, with ten tribes forming a confederation in the north (Israel) and two tribes devoted to the Davidic dynasty in the south (Judah). The narrator of 1–2 Kings rehearses the history of both kingdoms. In Judah some kings serve and obey the Lord, but the picture in the north is unrelievedly negative. In any case, the trajectory for both kingdoms is a downward one. Hence, the north is taken into exile by Assyria in 722 BC, and the south by Babylon in 586 BC. The great promise of the Lord's kingdom reaching the ends of the earth was not becoming a reality at all. Things were moving backward.

Now Israel was not in the land again, and they certainly were not free. Hundreds and hundreds of years had passed since the promise was made to Abraham, and the promises seemed as far away as ever. But the promise was not revoked or canceled. The release of Jehoiachin in 2 Kings 25 indicates that the Lord has not written off Israel or the Davidic dynasty. Still, the history of Israel demonstrates the titanic power of sin. Winning victory over the serpent was no trivial matter. Something supernatural had to happen, something that was not dependent on the strength or piety of human beings.

The history in 1–2 Chronicles is quite similar to what we find in 1–2 Kings. The Chronicler emphasizes the Davidic dynasty. The Lord will fulfill his promises to David even though Israel is in exile. Furthermore, the temple occupies a central place in Chronicles. Yahweh is present with his people through the temple. If Israel wants to enjoy his presence, they must worship the Lord the way he has instructed. Priests and Levites must do what the Lord has commanded, and the nation as a whole must keep the Torah. No blessing will come to pass for a nation that violates Yahweh's will.

Ezra and Nehemiah reflect on Israel's return from exile. The building of the temple and the rebuilding of Jerusalem take center stage. The temple's role in the OT can hardly be exaggerated, for Yahweh was specially present with his people in the temple. Furthermore, Jerusalem was the center of Israel, the city of the great king. If Israel is to be the people of the Lord, they must be devoted to the temple and Jerusalem. We see in Ezra-Nehemiah that the people faced significant opposition in the rebuilding of both the temple and Jerusalem. But Yahweh reigns over all. His kingdom cannot fail. He moves the hearts of kings and government officials so that both the temple and Jerusalem are rebuilt. Those who oppose Israel are the offspring of the serpent. Israel must not compromise or join with those who are not part of the Lord's people. They must cleanse themselves from sin and live according to the Torah. As we saw in Chronicles, Israel would not experience blessing if they transgressed Yahweh's will. God's saving promises will certainly be fulfilled, and yet no generation that refuses to follow Yahweh will experience the realization of such promises.

The book of Esther is also written after the return from exile. Here we see Israel under Persian rule, and the offspring of the serpent, Haman, wants to destroy Israel. Like Pharaoh, he wants to put every Jewish person to death. Although God is never mentioned in the book, he is actually the central character. The sovereignty of God runs like a thread through the entire book. Israel was saved not because of the courage of Mordecai and Esther, though, of course, the Lord used them to accomplish his purposes. God would deliver Israel another way even if Esther did not act (Esther 4:14). There was never any question about whether God would save his people. The book of Esther reminds Israel that Yahweh's promises have not been revoked. Israel was at a low ebb, like their days in Egypt. But just as Yahweh rescued Israel from Pharaoh's plots, so he delivered them from Haman's attempted genocide. The promise of a Davidic king who will rule the world for God has not been withdrawn. Just as Israel waited in Egypt for Yahweh to act, so they must wait again. But they must be like Esther and Mordecai, who were obedient to what the Lord called them to do.

Part 3

ISRAEL'S SONGS
AND WISDOM

14

JOB

Introduction

The book of Job introduces us to the OT Wisdom literature.[1] Does the Wisdom literature fit with the kingdom of God being central in the Scriptures?[2] Many would say no. Certainly, wisdom does not advance the story line of the Bible. We have to look at each wisdom book individually, but I will argue in due course that every wisdom book emphasizes the fear of the Lord, and fearing the Lord is what it means to live under Yahweh's lordship. The Wisdom literature asks what it looks like specifically in everyday life to live under the rule of God. The wisdom books, of course, differ from one another and cannot be mushed together as if they all say exactly the same thing. It has long been recognized that Job and Ecclesiastes are quite different from Proverbs. The diversity of these writings is evident, and yet I will also argue that the diversity does not rule out unity.

The book of Job actually fits quite well with the major thesis of the present work. Dempster captures one of the major themes of Job: "God rules the world and . . . this rule is of a different order from what one might expect."[3] Job partially represents a qualification of the message of Proverbs, for the latter book often emphasizes that one reaps what one sows, so that those who live righteously will be rewarded. Actually, a careful reading of Proverbs demonstrates that even in Proverbs the message is more complex. There are proverbs

1. For a standard introduction, see Crenshaw, *Old Testament Wisdom*. See also von Rad, *Wisdom in Israel*; Perdue, *Wisdom and Creation*.
2. For an introduction to the issues, see Schultz, "Unity or Diversity?" Schultz rightly argues that the theology of the wisdom books is complementary rather than contradictory.
3. Dempster, *Dominion and Dynasty*, 202.

that moderate and nuance the theme that righteousness is its own reward.[4] Still, the basic message of Proverbs emphasizes reward for righteousness and punishment for wickedness, and Job stands forth as an important qualification of what Proverbs teaches. The righteous are not invariably spared from suffering; indeed, they sometimes suffer in agonizing and inexplicable ways.

True wisdom recognizes that life is complex and defies simplistic answers as to why there is suffering in the world. Monolithic answers that neglect complexity masquerade as wisdom but are fundamentally foolish. Even though life has mysteries that baffle us, we are still called upon to fear the Lord and do his will. The bulk of Job is devoted to the dialogue between Job and his friends (chaps. 3–37). The prologue and epilogue (chaps. 1–2; 42:7–17) frame the book, and Yahweh's encounter with Job functions as the climax (38:1–42:6). In setting forth the theology of the book, I will consider first the role of the prologue and epilogue, then the dialogue between Job and his friends, and finally Job's encounter with Yahweh.

Prologue and Epilogue

The narrator begins by featuring Job's righteousness in emphatic terms: "There was a man in the land of Uz whose name was Job, and that man was blameless and upright, one who feared God and turned away from evil" (1:1). Furthermore, Job fits the paradigm of the book of Proverbs, where righteousness brings great rewards. He was incredibly wealthy and was blessed with seven sons and three daughters (1:2–3). Indeed, Job interceded for his children, offering burnt offerings for them in case they sinned (1:4–5). The prologue, however, introduces readers to another level of reality, to events that were taking place in the heavenly realm. If readers are to acquire wisdom about life, they must not limit themselves to what happens in the earthly sphere.

When the curtains on the heavens are pulled back, a most remarkable conversation between Yahweh and Satan takes place, a conversation hidden from Job. Satan appears as one of the sons of God before Yahweh, and the Lord boasts in the righteousness of his servant Job, using the emphatic language about his righteousness that appeared in 1:1 (1:6–8). Satan, like the serpent in Gen. 3, offers another interpretation. Job feared the Lord, according to Satan, because it brought him prosperity and protected him from harm (1:9–10). If the Lord, however, removed Job's protection and took away the gifts that he enjoyed, then Job would curse the Lord (1:11). The Lord granted Satan's

4. See the discussion of Proverbs below.

request, allowing Satan to take away Job's possessions but forbidding him to touch his person (1:12). Job's world came tumbling down in a hurry; in a single day he lost his oxen, donkeys, sheep, camels, servants, and, most important, his children (1:13–19). Job's response is stunning: "Job arose and tore his robe and shaved his head and fell on the ground and worshiped. And he said, 'Naked I came from my mother's womb, and naked shall I return. The LORD gave, and the LORD has taken away; blessed be the name of the LORD'" (1:20–21). Both grief and worship flowed from his heart. He acknowledges the Lord's sovereignty and goodness (1:22), praising God's name despite the evil that he has experienced.

Chapter 2 represents the second round in Satan's attacks against Job. Again the Lord boasts about Job in the heavenly council, reiterating his blamelessness, even though Satan incited the Lord against him (2:3). Satan again counters the Lord's boast, arguing that Job would curse the Lord if he suffered physically (2:4–5). The Lord responds by permitting Satan to strike Job's body, though he must spare Job's life (2:6). Satan inflicts Job with something like boils all over his body (2:7). Job's wife counsels him to "curse God and die" (2:9), but Job reproves her, saying that one must receive both good and evil from God, thereby keeping himself from sin (2:10). Job's friends then arrive to comfort him in his suffering (2:11–13).

The prologue provides a window into wisdom, disclosing one of the reasons for Job's suffering. Job and all human beings live their lives before heavenly beings, and they either bring praise to the Lord or vindicate Satan's claim that human beings live only for themselves. "God's honour is at stake. Can a human being love God for God's sake?"[5] Job's faith in his suffering, unbeknownst to him, brings glory to God as he trusts God in his agony. Even though the heavenly council is revealed to readers, it is still the case that the rationale for suffering is not clearly comprehended by human beings. The mystery of why the Lord allows evil is not lifted entirely. The prologue indicates that suffering in faith brings honor to the Lord, but such a revelation does not answer every question, nor does it intend to do so.[6] The mystery of evil reveals itself in the conversations between Satan and the Lord. These brief dialogues show that the evil inflicted upon Job was Satan's idea, and that Satan, not the Lord, directly afflicted Job. And yet Job knows nothing about Satan's involvement. He attributes the suffering that came upon him to the Lord, and he is not wrong, for twice the author affirms that he did not sin in assigning his sufferings to

5. Childs, *Old Testament as Scripture*, 537. See also Waltke, *Old Testament Theology*, 931; von Rad, *Wisdom in Israel*, 208.
6. Fyall (*Now My Eyes Have Seen You*, 36–37) rightly suggests that Satan's main goal is to cast aspersions on God's name in questioning Job's righteousness.

the Lord (1:22; 2:10). Surely Job would be guilty of horrendous sin if he attributed to the Lord what Satan did. The view of the narrator is complex. On one level, the evil inflicted comes from Satan, and yet the Lord granted Satan permission to strike Job, and so ultimately the Lord willed the evil to occur. Nevertheless, the Lord's purposes and motivations must be distinguished from Satan's. Satan wanted Job to fail and to be destroyed by evil. The Lord allowed Job to suffer in order to show the heavenly council the beauty and radiance of his faith. Again, the narrator scarcely intends to answer all questions about suffering, but he does teach that suffering brings glory to God, and that God has reasons for suffering that, though not fully comprehensible to human beings, exculpate him from evil.

The epilogue (42:7–17), like the prologue, sheds light on the dialogue (chaps. 32–37) and the Lord's encounter with Job (38:1–42:6). The author clarifies that Job's words in the dialogue were fundamentally right, and his friends had not spoken rightly about the Lord (42:7). Job's sufferings, then, did not come because he had sinned. The prologue's assessment of Job's righteousness is reaffirmed, and therefore the perspective of the friends, that Job was receiving recompense for the evil he did, is rejected. The Lord brought suffering into Job's life for his own wise purposes. One of those purposes, it seems, was to display Job's devotion to Yahweh even in the midst of his pain. Job functions as mediator for his friends, praying for them so that their sins will be forgiven and they will be spared from the Lord's wrath.

The epilogue also confirms that Yahweh was sovereign over the evil that Job experienced. The narrator does not separate Yahweh from Job's suffering, speaking almost shockingly of "all the evil that the LORD had brought upon him" (42:11). And yet we must remember the perspective of the prologue, where Satan's role in the suffering is also explicated. Still, the sovereign hand of Yahweh in Job's sufferings is underscored. The narrator does not resort to the strategy of saying that the Lord helplessly watched Satan torment Job. Yahweh is not evil, but Job's suffering was due to his sovereign will. The epilogue concludes with Job's wealth being restored and the birth of seven sons and three daughters. What are we to make of this conclusion? It would contradict the message of the entire book to interpret its conclusion as saying that those who suffer will eventually experience blessing in this life. The latter view was the theology propounded by Job's friends. We should reject the idea that we have a clumsy later editor who failed to understand the point of the dialogues. Instead, the narrator teaches that ultimately it will be well for those who are righteous and suffer. We have a peek here into the eschatology of the narrator. Suffering is not the last word for those who belong to Yahweh. They will be finally vindicated, and so there is a hint here of future life with Yahweh.

The Dialogues

The beauty of Job (and his anguish) is artfully conveyed through the dialogical debate between Job and his friends. The dialogues progress to a conclusion of sorts, and so I will sketch in briefly here the story and theology of chapters 3–31. Job begins (chap. 3) with a cry of agony, lamenting that he was ever born, wishing that he had died at birth instead of living such a miserable life. The question "Why?" pervades the chapter, captured well by 3:20–22: "Why is light given to him who is in misery, and life to the bitter in soul, who long for death, but it comes not, and dig for it more than for hidden treasures, who rejoice exceedingly and are glad when they find the grave?" Eliphaz has a ready-made answer to Job's bitter lamentation (chaps. 4–5). Job's confidence should be in God because those who trust in him will not perish but prosper. Those who sow evil will reap it (4:8). Fools who reject Yahweh suffer hunger and loss of children (5:3–5). If Job suffers, Eliphaz suggests, God is disciplining him so that he would seek God (5:8–27). If he turns to God, he will be delivered from his afflictions and enjoy peace once again.

Eliphaz, Job exclaims, has not come close to understanding the depth of Job's suffering. "The arrows of the Almighty" have been shot into Job, and he is experiencing "terrors" from God (6:4). Job's friends have failed to hear the cry of his heart. They treat his suffering as if it were a subject for academic discussion instead of empathizing with him in his distress (6:14–30). So Job has not changed his mind. He still wants God to kill him (6:8–9), for Job is a man of flesh and blood, not a stone that is impervious to pain (6:11–12). In any case, Job insists that his suffering is not due to his sin. He confesses, "I have not denied the words of the Holy One" (6:10). In chapter 7 Job turns from his friends to God, reflecting on the brevity and misery of life. Job wonders why God does not just leave him alone. Why does God afflict him so that it is even hard to swallow his spit (7:19)? Ultimately, Job's questions and longings can only be answered by God himself. Bildad immediately seizes upon Job's words, which suggest that God "pervert[s] justice" (8:3), launching into an attack upon Job's integrity. Job's children died because they sinned (8:4). If Job repents and seeks God, then God will restore him (8:5–7). Bildad appeals to tradition to support his theology, saying that this is what the ancients have taught (8:8–10). Those who forget God will be cut down and wither (8:12–13), while the righteous will exult with joyful laughter (8:20–21).

Job again goes straight to God. He wants to present his case, so to speak, before God in court (chap. 9). But, says Job, it cannot be done. God is the awesome and mighty creator who levels mountains and made the constellations. His work is beyond the comprehension of human beings. He "does great things beyond searching out and marvelous things beyond number" (9:10). Job cannot require this awesome God to come to a court hearing (9:32–33). Indeed, God is crushing him and increasing "his wounds without cause" (9:17). He takes Job's breath away and "fills [him] with bitterness" (9:18). Even if Job's case in the courtroom were flawless, God is so powerful and wise that he would make Job look guilty (9:20). Still, Job insists that he is "blameless" (9:21). There is not justice with God. "He destroys both the blameless and the wicked" (9:22).[7] Indeed, God allows the wicked to reign on earth (9:24).

In chapter 10 Job continues his complaint, which really consists of what he would say to God in the courtroom. He wonders why God condemns him (10:2–3). Does God feel his anguish and pain? "Have you eyes of flesh? Do you see as man sees?" (10:4). Christian readers cannot help thinking of the incarnation here, but Job did not have access to that truth. Job wonders why God pursues his sin when God knows that he is righteous (10:6–7). Of course, Job is not saying that he never sinned. As von Rad says, "Job asserts in the first place that he is unaware of having committed such a grievous sin as could explain the severity of his suffering. It is also clear that with this assertion he is not intending to declare that he is absolutely sinless."[8] Why is God inflicting all this pain on Job, since he created Job in the first place (10:8–13)? Job just wants God to leave him alone and let him die instead of attacking him like a marauding army (10:14–22). Zophar is outraged by Job's words against God (chap. 11). He is shocked that Job sees himself as being "clean in God's eyes" (11:4). Actually, argues Zophar, Job is getting less than he deserves (11:6). Job can hardly claim to understand the things of God (though apparently Zophar does!), and what he must do is repent, and then God will restore him and life "will be brighter than noonday" (11:17), while the wicked will be destroyed (11:20).

Job is exhausted and is frustrated with his friends. The things they say that are true he already agrees with, for he knows that the wicked will finally be punished as well (12:1–3), but he is probing at a deeper level. Job's point is that the wicked, who ignore God, often prosper, and that is evident to anyone who takes a sober and clear look at the world (12:6–11), and thus his friends apparently lack wisdom. Clearly, God is sovereign over all that happens; he takes away wisdom from the wise and casts down nations that are great (12:13–25). Job affirms all this (13:1–2). But his friends have distorted the truth as well, even while claiming to speak the truth for God (13:3–12). In defending God,

7. The shocking feature here is that Job questions God's justice. See Rendtorff, *Canonical Hebrew Bible*, 344; Perdue, *Wisdom and Creation*, 152.
8. Von Rad, *Wisdom in Israel*, 218.

they have actually misstated what God would say. They "whitewash with lies" and are "worthless physicians" (13:4). Silence would be their wisdom (13:5). Their "maxims are proverbs of ashes," and their "defenses are defenses of clay" (13:12). What Job wants is a meeting with God in the courtroom, where he can argue his case before him (13:15–28), but God must remove his terror from Job so he can speak. Job wants to know what sins warrant such punishment, but he will continue to hope in God even if God puts him to death (13:15), hinting that there may be future vindication for Job.

In chapter 14 Job reflects on the evanescent nature of life. He compares human life to that of a tree: even the stump of a tree may send out shoots and live again, but once extinguished, human life is over. And yet Job also expresses hope for future life, for a day when he will be renewed and live in fellowship with God (14:14–17). The chapter slips back, though, to the futility of life, in which human beings do not know the honor bestowed on their children and are caught up in their own pain (14:18–21). Job's words provoke Eliphaz to answer vigorously (chap. 15). Job's words are nothing more than hot air (15:2–3). Job's sin has influenced his theology, such that he is "doing away with the fear of God" (15:4–5). Job arrogantly puts himself above his ancestors and contemporaries, thinking that he knows more than they do, and that he is pure before God (15:7–16). Job has it all wrong; the wicked suffer agony throughout their lifetime (15:17–35). Eliphaz merely repeats the same theology, asserting it with dogmatism.

Job has no use for the words of his friends (16:1–6). His issue is with God. God, he says, has "worn me out" (16:7) and "shriveled me up" (16:8). The language is shockingly vivid: "[God] has torn me in his wrath and hated me; he has gnashed his teeth at me" (16:9). It is God who handed him over to the wicked (16:10–11). The enmity of God is portrayed in graphic terms: "I was at ease, and he broke me apart; he seized me by the neck and dashed me to pieces; he set me up as his target; his archers surround me. He slashes open my kidneys and does not spare; he pours out my gall on the ground. He breaks me with breach upon breach; he runs upon me like a warrior" (16:12–14). "Here," notes von Rad, "is a new tone which has never been sounded before."[9] But despite all this, Job does not forsake God.[10] He continues to argue the case for his innocence (16:18–22), insisting, "Even now, behold, my witness is in heaven, and he who testifies for me is on high" (16:19). Job still expects to be vindicated.[11] Job is ready for death, resigned to the inability of his friends

---

9. Ibid., 217.
10. See ibid., 220.
11. See Dumbrell, *Faith of Israel*, 257; House, *Old Testament Theology*, 433–34.

to comprehend what is truly happening to him (chap. 17). Bildad, instead of becoming wise, feels insulted (18:1–3), and he repeats the mantra that terrors and punishments are the lot of those who are evil (18:4–21).

The counsel of Job's friends continues to torment instead of comfort him (19:1–5). Job continues to address God boldly, claiming that God has wronged him and that justice eludes him (19:6–7). God, he says, has plunged him in darkness (19:8) and "has stripped from me my glory" (19:9). "He breaks me down on every side" and has "uprooted my hope like a tree" (19:10). God has made Job his enemy (19:11) and, like an army, is laying siege to Job (19:12). The consequence is that Job has no friends left. His brothers, relatives, wife, and even his servants find him repulsive (19:13–19). Why can his friends not show him mercy, since God has chosen not to do so (19:21–22)? Von Rad observes, "What concerned Job above all else was the credibility of God. . . . He can live and breathe only if it is this Yahweh who reveals himself to him."[12] Just when it looks as if Job will collapse in despair, a message of hope appears: "I know that my Redeemer lives, and at the last he will stand upon the earth. And after my skin has been thus destroyed, yet in my flesh I shall see God, whom I shall see for myself, and my eyes shall behold, and not another. My heart faints within me" (19:25–27).[13] It seems that Job has come to believe that vindication will come for him after life ends.[14] This theme of future vindication has appeared in the account now three times. This seems to confirm the interpretation offered for the epilogue. The final vindication is not necessarily in this life; it will come in the future. Zophar responds with the same old line that the wicked suffer for their sin (chap. 20), giving no evidence of having listened to Job.

Job directly refutes the theology of his friends in chapter 21. He asks, "Why do the wicked live, reach old age, and grow mighty in power?" (21:7). Often they prosper so that their children multiply, their houses are safe, their flocks are fruitful, and they rejoice in blessing (21:8–13). All the while they reject God and his ways (21:14–15). It is not enough that God punishes the children of the wicked, for then the evildoers themselves get away with their iniquity (21:19–21). Everyone knows, exclaims Job, that the wicked often prosper and go to their death in comfort (21:28–33). Obviously, Job is unconvinced of his own evil by his friends, so Eliphaz mounts a direct attack on him (chap. 22). According to Eliphaz, Job had ripped away the clothes of the poor (22:6), withheld food and drink from the hungry and thirsty (22:7), and oppressed

---

12. Von Rad, *Wisdom in Israel*, 221–22.

13. In support of the view that the redeemer is God, see Fyall, *Now My Eyes Have Seen You*, 47–49.

14. This interpretation is sharply contested, but for support, see ibid., 49–52.

widows and orphans (22:9). That is why Job is suffering pain, so if he repents and turns to God, he will experience relief (22:10–30).

The dialogue has reached the third round with Eliphaz's response to Job, but in this third round Bildad's words are very brief (chap. 25), and Zophar does not reply at all. Indeed, in chapter 23 Job ignores what Eliphaz said. His questions are for God. He wants to find God and to present his case before him so that his righteousness will be vindicated. Job is convinced that "when he has tried me, I shall come out as gold" (23:10). He insists, "My foot has held fast to his steps; I have kept his way and have not turned aside" (23:11). The confusing thing, claims Job, is to understand what God is doing (chap. 24). Often the wicked oppress the poor, and there is no indication that God cares or helps those being mistreated. The land of the poor is taken from them (24:2); the possessions of widows and orphans are stolen (24:3); the poor shiver with cold and hunger (24:7–10) and work for the rich (24:5–6, 11). And God does nothing about it (24:12). The wicked commit murder, adultery, and theft (24:14–16). Yes, they end up dying, but their time on earth is sweet, and God sustains them during their earthly sojourn (24:22–24). Bildad seems to have lost track of the conversation, and simply insists that human beings cannot be right with God (chap. 25).

Job has left his friends far behind. Their failure to answer demonstrates that they cannot refute him.[15] Job sums up his case in the next six chapters (chaps. 26–31). His friends are worthless counselors (26:2–4), for they have not really reflected on who God is. God's majesty as the sovereign creator is emphasized, for he sees into Sheol (26:6), stretches out the heavens (26:7), and rules in the heavens, even over hostile powers (26:8–13). Job concludes, "Behold, these are but the outskirts of his ways, and how small a whisper do we hear of him! But the thunder of his power who can understand?" (26:14). Job reminds his friends that they have a very limited knowledge of God, and the words uttered here relate to Job as well. As we will see, some of his accusations against God constituted attempts to understand and domesticate the inscrutable.

Chapter 27 is difficult to interpret. It seems that Job suddenly subscribes to the theology of his friends! He appears to argue that the wicked are punished for their transgressions in a way that would be compatible with his friends' theology. Some have wondered if the speech could actually represent the last words of Zophar or if perhaps Job is simply quoting dismissively a theology that he rejects, but there is no textual basis for these interpretations. I suggest that the best solution to this difficulty is that Job thinks here of the ultimate and future judgment of the wicked. There are hints, as we have

---

15. So Childs, *Old Testament as Scripture*, 535.

seen, throughout the book that Job will be vindicated in the future. We have also seen some evidence that Job partially agrees with the theology of the friends. There is indeed punishment for the wicked! The friends, however, wrongly concluded that joy and sorrow during this life reflect one's godliness or lack of it. The narrator of the story was not a modern nihilist. He believed in a future judgment, but one must beware of imposing the future on the present.

Chapter 28 plays a central role in the story; it "is a metaphor of the entire book."[16] The book of Job is part of the wisdom tradition in the OT, and here Job reflects on the nature of wisdom. He begins by considering mining (28:1–11). Mining is a fascinating enterprise, for precious gems and rocks must be discovered and excavated. The skill and imagination required to unearth gems are uniquely human qualities, testifying to the creation theme that the Lord made human beings as the crown of creation (see Gen. 1:26–27), with human beings ruling over the "bird of prey" and the "falcon," and "the proud beasts" and "the lion" (28:7–8). The imagination, creativity, and intelligence of human beings should not be equated with wisdom (28:12–28). Wisdom cannot be found through digging, nor can it be purchased with gold or jewels. Indeed, wisdom cannot be gained simply through observing the created order. It is concealed from those who scan the world to gain understanding. Only God knows what wisdom is. Wisdom is fundamentally God-centered. It is not discoverable simply by observing the world and using human intelligence (28:23–27). The God-centeredness of wisdom is captured by the climactic ending to the chapter: "Behold, the fear of the Lord, that is wisdom, and to turn away from evil is understanding" (28:28). What is remarkable here is that the heart of wisdom concurs with what we read in Proverbs (1:7; 9:10) and Ecclesiastes (12:13). Those who are wise are rightly related to the Lord. They stand in awe of him and consequently do his will. According to Job, wisdom does not mean that one has a nicely packaged answer to suffering (chaps. 26; 38–42). Suffering has an irrational character that evades the intelligence of human beings, but human beings must understand their responsibility as creatures. They are to fear and honor the Lord. They are to submit to his lordship, even if they do not understand why they are suffering.

Job finishes his address with a peroration (chaps. 29–31). First, Job remembers the good old days when God's light shone upon him (chap. 29). He was rich and respected, and he helped those who were weak and poor. Others looked to Job for assistance and support. But now the tables have turned (chap. 30). Now Job is mocked and ridiculed by those who are on the margins of society

16. Fyall, *Now My Eyes Have Seen You*, 66.

(30:1–14). His prosperity is gone (30:15), he suffers agonizing pain (30:16–17), and God is against him and does not help him (30:20–23). Job cries for help but he is utterly alone, and so he is plunged into sorrow (30:24–31). Job concludes with a ringing affirmation of his righteousness (chap. 31). Job did not lust after virgins (31:1–4), nor has he committed adultery (31:9–12); he has lived with integrity (31:5–8) and has treated his slaves with justice (31:13–15). He has cared for the poor and supplied their needs (31:16–22). Nor has Job put his trust in riches (31:24–25) or worshiped the sun (31:26–28). What is striking is how God-centered Job's righteousness is. He lives in the presence of God every moment (31:4), knowing that God will judge (31:14). Idolatry would be "false to God above" (31:28). Job has neither rejoiced in the ruination of nor pled for the death of his enemies (31:29–30), and he has assisted the traveler in need (31:31–32). Job has confessed his sins (31:33), and so he cries out for the Almighty to hear his case (31:35–40).

The dialogues have ended, except for the contribution of Elihu. We know from the epilogue that the friends have spoken wrongly and misunderstood the case of Job. The structure of the dialogue suggests also that the friends are deceived. Job continues to prosecute his case, but the friends cannot keep up with him, so that Bildad's final words are remarkably short (chap. 25), and Zophar does not even manage a final reply. In addition, Job's final words (chaps. 26–31) constitute a ringing peroration that sums up his position and emphasizes his righteousness. Indeed, the prologue, epilogue, and dialogues stress Job's blamelessness. True wisdom does not offer simplistic formulas about human life but rather recognizes life's complexity, ambiguity, and irrationality. Yahweh's lordship over the world is not perceptible to human beings. It must be embraced by faith, for the evil perpetrated in the world calls into question God's righteousness. The notion that suffering is always due to personal sin is categorically rejected by Job. It might seem that God's rule over the world would manifest itself in a way that is discernible to human beings, but Job teaches us that true wisdom, which is marked by fear of the Lord and honoring him, does not lend itself to such a pat answer.

Elihu's Contribution

Elihu's role in the book is difficult to determine (chaps. 32–37). Nothing is said in the epilogue about whether he was right or wrong in terms of his advice. Nor does Job answer him. His speech is immediately followed by the words of the Lord (38:1–42:6). Apparently, the narrator expected readers to discern the import of Elihu's contribution by the clues given in the rest of the book.

Some dismiss Elihu entirely, seeing him as saying the same thing as the friends.[17] Others think that Elihu is fundamentally right in his criticism of Job.[18] I will argue here that Elihu represents a transitional figure in the book. His dialogue appears structurally between the speeches of Job's friends and the speeches of the Lord because he is partly right and partly wrong. Insofar as he shares the view of the friends, he misspeaks; but insofar as he communicates the Lord's perspective, he speaks God's word to Job.

Elihu is angry because Job justifies himself rather than God (32:2), and we will see from the Lord's speech that there is truth and validity in Elihu's objection here. Furthermore, Elihu recognizes that the three friends have not given a persuasive answer to Job (32:3, 12, 15), and Elihu promises to give an answer different from that of the friends (32:14). Job should have no fear of conversing with Elihu, for he is mortal just like Job (33:6–7). Elihu rightly sees a problem in Job's defense in that he has reckoned God to be his enemy (33:10–11). Job has veered from the truth, for God's majesty is beyond human comprehension (33:12).

But Elihu himself veers off into error, basically repeating the view of Eliphaz in chapters 4–5, where Job's suffering is considered to be discipline for his sin (33:14–35:16). Indeed, Elihu ends up sounding just like Job's friends. Job is a scoffer (34:7), and he "revels in company with evildoers and walks with wicked men" (34:8). Elihu rightly sees that Job has erred in suggesting that God actually does what is wicked (34:9–32). But Elihu's response is over the top, for he places Job with the wicked: "Would that Job were tried to the end, because he answers like wicked men. For he adds rebellion to his sin; he claps his hands among us and multiplies his words against God" (34:36–37; cf. 35:16). And he seems to relapse into the simplistic theology of the friends in his words against Job (36:1–21).

But Elihu's response is ambiguous and complex. Some of his words are flawed, while others accurately convey divine truth. Elihu begins to contemplate God's power (36:22), recognizing the greatness of God: "Behold, God is great, and we know him not; the number of his years is unsearchable" (36:26). He especially sees the power and mystery of God in creation (36:27–33). God's majesty is unleashed in the thunderstorm when lightning blazes and thunder shakes the earth (37:1–5). The point is that God "does great things we cannot comprehend" (37:5). The Lord's rule over the world exceeds human understanding, but rule he does. He sends snow and unbearable cold into the world (37:6–10). The weather takes place by his command and guidance (37:11–12). God's encounter with Job is imminent, and Elihu's words anticipate the words

17. See, e.g., Waltke, *Old Testament Theology*, 939.
18. Apparently Dempster, *Dominion and Dynasty*, 204.

of God. Job should consider God's "wondrous works" (37:14). He does not and cannot understand God's sovereign control over clouds and storms (37:15–16). Job cannot "spread out the skies" the way God does (37:18). "God is clothed with awesome majesty" (37:22), and he is not subservient to or mastered by human beings. "The Almighty—we cannot find him; he is great in power; justice and abundant righteousness he will not violate" (37:23). Job has erred in questioning God's justice, as if he has the gravitas and insight to pronounce on God's ways. Elihu, then, has seen part of Job's problem, but Elihu's flaw is that he is between two worlds. He has one foot in the camp of the friends and one foot in God's camp. A more clarifying word is needed, and it is coming.

God's Response to Job

The climax of the book arrives when God encounters Job and speaks to him (38:1–42:6), "for the divine speeches are the key to understanding the book as a whole."[19] Job has been asking for a meeting with God, and he gets one. The Lord appears out of the whirlwind and immediately rebukes Job: "Who is this that darkens counsel by words without knowledge?" (38:2). God's commendation of Job's words in the epilogue must be balanced by the rebuke that Job receives here.[20] Job was right in contending that he did not suffer because of his sin, but it does not follow that everything that Job said was on target. Yahweh poses a series of biting questions to Job. Was Job present when he created the world, and did he consult with Job in establishing the world (38:4–11)? Robert Fyall argues that the sea here is conceived of as a mythological chaotic force subdued and controlled by Yahweh.[21] Does Job command the dawn to take hold of the world (38:12–15), so that he knows the depths and heights of the earth, plumbing "the springs of the sea" (38:16) and comprehending both light and darkness (38:16–20)? Why all these questions? Certainly, Yahweh reproves Job for claiming to understand reality, for he sarcastically interrupts his own questions to say to Job, "You know, for you were born then, and the number of your days is great" (38:21).[22] The Lord continues to query Job, asking whether Job understands and controls the weather so that snow, rain, and freezing weather are within the purview of his comprehension and power (38:22–30, 34–35, 37–38). In addition, does Job lead out the stars each night as the Lord

---

19. Fyall, *Now My Eyes Have Seen You*, 25–26.
20. Childs (*Old Testament as Scripture*, 533–34) rightly argues that these two competing themes are not necessarily at odds with each other.
21. Fyall, *Now My Eyes Have Seen You*, 92–98.
22. See Childs, *Old Testament as Scripture*, 539.

does? Does he rule over the heavens (38:31–33)? Does he grant human beings understanding (38:36) and provide food for lions and ravens (38:39–41)?

The battery of questions from the Lord continues unabated. Does Job know when mountain goats and deer give birth and give them strength to prosper (39:1–4), and what does he know of the freedom of the wild donkey (39:5–8), or can he control the strength of the wild ox (39:9–12)? The ostrich has amazing speed, but "God has made her forget wisdom" (39:17) so she does not care for her young (39:13–18).[23] How does Job explain the might and majesty and bravery of the horse (39:19–25), or does he have anything to do with the soaring hawk and eagle (39:26–30)? All of these questions, of course, are designed to show Job his finitude and smallness. The sovereign Lord created and runs the world. Job, as a mere creature, scarcely understands the world, nor does he ordain what happens. Fyall says about these examples, "Chapter 39 especially deals with untamed nature and shows not so much that animals are evil, but that animal life is shot through with a savagery which mirrors ultimate cosmic evil."[24] Given Job's limited comprehension, the Lord asks, "Shall a faultfinder contend with the Almighty? He who argues with God, let him answer it" (40:2). Job apparently thinks that he knows enough to tell God about justice, so God asks him for a full dissertation. Job confesses his smallness and stupidity: "Behold, I am of small account; what shall I answer you? I lay my hand on my mouth. I have spoken once, and I will not answer; twice, but I will proceed no further" (40:4–5). Fyall rightly says, "We are being forced to the conclusion that there is far more mystery at the heart of providence than we have yet understood and that this sense of mystery is fundamental to all true worship"; and, "This means that the created universe in itself can provide no real answer to the problems of evil and suffering."[25] When one looks at the created world, one sees beauty, patterns, and wisdom, but at the same time one sees irrationality and absurdity.

Still, the Lord is not done, challenging Job again from the whirlwind (40:6–7). The Lord's fundamental complaint with Job is immediately voiced: "Will you even put me in the wrong? Will you condemn me that you may be in the right?" (40:8). Job is not suffering for his sins, nor is he being disciplined for his sins, but he has gone astray in questioning God's justice and righteousness. In effect, Job has made himself lord of the world by telling God what is wrong with its government. God is telling Job that if he is lord, then he should use his

23. The ostrich is stunning and beautiful, and yet God has made it a certain way, so that it lacks wisdom. The focus on what God has done here is instructive (so Fyall, *Now My Eyes Have Seen You*, 78).

24. Ibid., 130.

25. Ibid., 79.

lordship to bring down the proud from their thrones (40:9–14), that he should use his power to cast evil out of the world. Next the Lord queries Job about Behemoth (40:15–24). Though a number of proposals have been put forward regarding the identity of this creature, Duane Garrett rightly says that none of the identifications fit. "Behemoth appears to be a kind of composite animal that represents the strength, domain, and independence of the animal world. It is wild, powerful, and free. Behemoth is not a supernatural creature, but it is more than one natural animal. It is a kind of conceptual being, a representative of animal wildness."[26] Garrett suggests that the human race may be in view here, or perhaps more likely the point is that Job cannot tame or domesticate "all the wildness and ferocity of the animal world."[27] Or possibly Behemoth here stands for Death, for Mot the god of Death.[28]

The final creature is Leviathan (chap. 41). "God is revealing to Job the nature of his adversary."[29] He is no plaything and cannot be captured by human beings, and no human being is a match for him. And if no one can handle Leviathan as a creature, then neither can anyone domesticate God. "Who then is he who can stand before me? Who has first given to me, that I should repay him? Whatever is under the whole heaven is mine" (41:10–11). Yahweh is the Lord of the universe. Even if human beings do not and cannot understand the whys and wherefores of suffering, Yahweh is still the Lord of all. Human beings cannot conquer Leviathan, but God can. There is no creature comparable to Leviathan on earth. "On earth there is not his like, a creature without fear. He sees everything that is high; he is king over all the sons of pride" (41:33–34).[30]

Who is Leviathan? Garrett rightly argues that the reference is to Satan.[31] "Much of this could be taken as a hyperbolic description of the crocodile or whale, but further description makes even this interpretation unfeasible. Leviathan breathes fire! Smoke comes out of his nostrils and sparks fly when he sneezes. His breath can kindle coals (41:18, 21). It is pointless to try to explain this as merely a metaphorical way of saying the Leviathan is ferocious; every other fierce creature is described in terms that although sometimes exaggerated are nevertheless recognizable and within the realm of nature. Leviathan is supernatural; Leviathan is a dragon."[32] That Leviathan can stand for a demonic

26. Garrett, *Job*, 90.
27. Ibid., 89.
28. So Fyall, *Now My Eyes Have Seen You*, 126–37.
29. Ibid., 163.
30. The incomparability of Leviathan also points to a reference to Satan (see ibid., 168).
31. Garrett, *Job*, 90–92. See the extensive defense for a reference to Satan in Fyall, *Now My Eyes Have Seen You*, 139–74. Dempster (*Dominion and Dynasty*, 205) sees this as a possibility.
32. Garrett, *Job*, 90–91. See also Fyall (*Now My Eyes Have Seen You*, 165), who says that the fire delineates "the god-like pretensions of Leviathan."

creature is confirmed by other references (Job 3:8; Isa. 27:1; Ps. 74:13).[33] "The natural imagery does not imply that Leviathan is a natural creature, rather it shows the palpable nature of the evil he embodies."[34] One answer to the problem of evil is finally given to Job. Job must realize his finiteness and trust in the Lord. The world was created and is sustained by the sovereign Lord, not Job. Even the demonic forces unleashed in the world are finally under God's sovereign hand. Job may not perceive how this is so, but is this any great surprise, given that he does not even understand how the natural world operates? Fyall says about Satan's role in evil, "Even now—and this is part of the mystery of providence—he cannot act except with God's permission."[35] Garrett rightly captures the Lord's message to Job:

> God's answer is this: "I am the only one who can manage all the chaotic forces of life and who can bring about the ultimate triumph of righteousness, and I know what I am doing. If this has meant some suffering on your part, you must understand that this does not mean that I am unfair or that you have the right to challenge my justice. I will do what must be done to defeat Leviathan and all the powers of chaos and evil. This may sometimes require suffering on the part of the righteous, but I will bring all things to a just conclusion. Your role is simply to trust in my wisdom and goodness."[36]

Or as von Rad says, Job "now knows that his destiny, too, is well protected by this mysterious God."[37] Job recognizes the sovereign power of the Lord and acknowledges that he spoke of matters beyond his comprehension (42:2–3). Job does not have the capacity to rule the world or to inform God about how it should be run. Now that Job sees God and enjoys his presence, he repents (42:5–6). What makes life worth living is not the absence of suffering but rather a relationship with the living God.[38] It is seeing the King in his beauty. The restoration of Job does not contradict the message of the book. It is God's gracious gift, and it shows on the earthly plane that Job is vindicated by God.[39]

33. See Fyall, *Now My Eyes Have Seen You*, 139–56, 168. Fyall also sees allusions to the same in 7:12–14; 9:8, 13; 26:12–13; 28:8. This is not to say that Leviathan is always demonic (cf. Ps. 104:26), but Fyall argues that even in Ps. 104:26 Satan is seen as Yahweh's "plaything," given Yahweh's power (p. 170). See also Hamilton, *God's Glory in Salvation*, 198–99. For another view of Ps. 74:12, see Levenson, *Persistence of Evil*, 54–55.
34. Fyall, *Now My Eyes Have Seen You*, 159.
35. Ibid., 183.
36. Garrett, *Job*, 92.
37. Von Rad, *Wisdom in Israel*, 225.
38. Viberg ("Job," 202) says that Job is not centrally about suffering but rather is about Job's personal relationship with God.
39. Fyall, *Now My Eyes Have Seen You*, 182, 184.

Conclusion

Job is a rich and complex book. Job's friends have a comfortable and cookie-cutter theology. According to them, Job suffers because he has sinned, but the book contradicts such a conclusion. Job suffers even though he is righteous. For Job, such suffering is baffling, and he ends up calling God's justice into account, for even though he rejects the theology of his friends, he is still infected with it to some degree. Someone must be to blame, and he begins to think that this someone is God himself. Wisdom recognizes, however, that the fear of the Lord is the root of all understanding (chap. 28). Those who are wise realize that they cannot discover wisdom on their own. Wisdom must be revealed to them. When the cover is drawn back, the role of Satan in the evil that takes place in the world is revealed (chaps. 1–2; 41). A great contest between God and Satan is underway (once again, Gen. 3:15), and Satan wants to annihilate all that is holy. "The story of Job is an outcropping of that great struggle begun in Genesis 3:15."[40] And yet, God reigns over Satan and Leviathan as well. Human beings are no match for Satan, but God is. The evil unleashed on the world by Satan does not transpire apart from God's will. As the sovereign creator of all, he rules over the forces of insanity and evil as well. In the great cosmic conflict he is Lord. It does not follow, of course, that a completely satisfying explanation for the presence of evil is given. The book of Job teaches that God is sovereign and just, but it does not explain why God allows such evil in the world in a way that answers all questions. It leaves us instead with the questions with which God confronts Job in chapters 38–41. It leaves us with the truth that God as creator and Lord of the world knows what he is doing. As human beings, we are not given all the answers. "All is under God's will in spite of the dark mystery that often surrounds his ways."[41] Instead, we are called upon to trust him and to rest in the truth that he will make all things right in the end. We fear the Lord by obeying him even when we do not understand what is happening. From a canonical perspective, the evil unleashed by Satan and humanity in the world will be conquered by one who overcomes evil not through warfare but through suffering. He conquers the power and mystery of evil by letting it do its worst to him and then triumphing over it. What sustains through suffering is a relationship with a loving, just, and mysterious God. This God has taken on flesh and evil has done its best to destroy him, but he has conquered demons and death.

40. Ibid., 189.
41. Ibid., 161.

15

PSALMS

Introduction

Although the Psalter contains psalms of both lament and praise, the psalms are fundamentally a call to praise the Lord.[1] Therefore, the psalms are God-centered, rejoicing in or anticipating the salvation that the Lord has wrought. The psalms capture the sorrows and joys that punctuate the experience of both individuals and the people of God. They are richly experiential, demonstrating that the relationship with the sovereign Lord is profoundly personal, expressing intense sorrow and overflowing joy. They testify that ultimately, though only partially and provisionally in the present age, one's relationship with the Lord is marked by fervent joy. As Gerald Wilson points out, even in the shape of the Psalter there is a movement from lament to praise, so that laments are more common in the first part of the Psalter, and praise concludes it.[2] "Praise," Wilson says, "constitutes another reality in which the presence of God has become so real that anger has no point, pain has no hold, and death lacks all power to sting."[3] It is significant that the psalms are musical and poetic, for music reaches the depths of the heart. Profound joy and stabbing sorrow are portrayed best through poetry set to music. What it means to live under Yahweh's lordship, both corporately and personally, is to lift one's voice to him, whether in joy or sorrow. Viewing the Psalter in relation to the story line of the Scriptures, we see that triumph over the serpent and the blessing of Abraham produce praise in the people of the Lord. As Clinton McCann says,

1. Rightly Childs, *Old Testament as Scripture*, 514.
2. G. Wilson, "Shape of the Book of Psalms," 138–39.
3. Ibid., 139.

"The central affirmation of the Psalter is that the Lord reigns!"[4] And because he reigns, his people praise him. "Praising God is the goal of human life, the goal of every living thing, the goal of all creation!"[5]

Here we will consider the book of Psalms in its final form,[6] and so the superscriptions will be integrated as part of the individual books within the Psalter to be studied.[7] The five books of the Psalter (Book 1: Pss. 1–41; Book 2: Pss. 42–72; Book 3: Pss. 73–89; Book 4: Pss. 90–106; Book 5: Pss. 107–150) function as a paradigm for unlocking the book as a whole, though other studies have usefully and fruitfully unpacked the psalms from other perspectives.[8] Perhaps the five books of the Psalter are meant to mirror the five books of the Pentateuch, as many Jewish interpreters have argued. Doxologies conclude each book of the Psalter, and royal psalms are near the beginning (Ps. 2) or conclude some books (Pss. 72; 89).[9] Here I will comment on the psalms in the order in which they occur, and I will attempt to see connections in the order given.[10] The reading offered of the psalms here is not only historical but also canonical, so that the psalms are also read as a witness to the revelation of God in Jesus Christ.

Clearly, some of the psalms invite further study as mini-collections. Book 3 (Pss. 73–89) particularly seems to fit the time of Israel's exile, where we find many psalms of Asaph (Pss. 73–83; cf. Ps. 50) and some psalms from the sons of Korah (Pss. 84; 85; 87; 88). Psalms 93–100 focus on the Lord's reign over Israel and the entire world. So also the psalms designated as the Psalms of Ascent clearly belong together (Pss. 120–134), and the Psalter ends, significantly, with a ringing call to praise the Lord (Pss. 146–150). Psalms from the sons of

---

4. McCann "Psalms as Instruction," 123.

5. Ibid., 124.

6. The hypothesis, accepted by many now, is that the final form represents "purposeful editorial activity, and that its purpose can be discerned by careful and exhaustive analysis" (G. Wilson, "Purposeful Arrangement of Psalms," 48). Wilson's work has been programmatic in this regard; see G. Wilson, *Editing of the Hebrew Psalter*; idem, "Shape of the Book of Psalms," 129–42. See also the intriguing essay by John Walton titled "Psalms: A Cantata about the Davidic Covenant." Walton certainly sees the Davidic character of the psalms, and he may be correct in seeing Book 1 as focusing on the time before David became king. But if the titles of Pss. 50–60 are ancient and accurate, as I believe they are, then Book 2 does not refer to David's reign as king, since many of the psalms in this section take place in a time in which Saul is trying to slay David.

7. In critical scholarship the consensus view is that the psalm titles are inauthentic and late (see Childs, *Old Testament as Scripture*, 509). Still, as Childs notes (pp. 520–21), the seventy-three titles that ascribe psalms to David give the psalms in their final form a Davidic stamp. Waltke (*Old Testament Theology*, 872–74) defends their antiquity and authenticity. See also Kidner, *Psalms 1–72*, 32–33.

8. Note that the book of Psalms follows the same order and sequence in the MT and the LXX. See Mitchell, *Message of the Psalter*, 16–17.

9. See G. Wilson, "Shaping the Psalter," 73.

10. Howard (*Psalms 93–100*, 3) points out that Franz Delitzsch pursued this approach starting in 1846. For a history of scholarship on this matter, see ibid., 2–19.

Korah are also collected together (Pss. 42–49). It is striking that seventy-three of the psalms are attributed to David, pointing toward the Davidic and kingly character of the final form of the book. James Hamilton's reading of Psalms seems convincing.[11] Books 1–2 focus on David's life, but Book 3 relays the discouragement that Israel feels because Davidic kings no longer reign. Book 4 begins by reflecting on the time of Moses, reminding Israel that Yahweh will fulfill his promises just as he did at the exodus and in the life of the historical David. So, Book 4, like Isaiah and other prophets, points to a new exodus. Book 5 celebrates with praise the salvation that will come from a new David, with the Psalms of Ascent celebrating the truth that the exile will end and Israel will experience the blessing promised to Abraham.

Book 1

Book 1 (Pss. 1–41) begins with Pss. 1–2, featuring major themes in the book.[12] Psalm 1 sets the scene for the book of Psalms,[13] indicating that the psalms represent the word of God for human beings.[14] The wise refuse to find their fellowship and joy with the wicked. Instead, their delight and joy are in the Torah. Many scholars have pointed out that Ps. 1 introduces a wisdom theme that informs the entire Psalter.[15] Thus, the psalms also function as a medium for instruction, so that those who meditate on them grow in wisdom.[16] There is a close connection, then, between wisdom and hymnic traditions, suggesting that they should not be segregated from each other. Those who meditate on the Torah will have a stability that will weather every storm, whereas the wicked will perish in the judgment.[17] The psalms conclude with a rousing note of praise (Ps. 150), and if we put Ps. 150 with Ps. 1, we realize that those who love the Torah will be those who will praise the Lord with dancing and "loud clashing cymbals" (150:5).

Psalm 2 introduces another major theme of the book.[18] Here we see the wicked in Ps. 1 portrayed from another perspective. They rage against the

11. Hamilton, *God's Glory in Salvation*, 278–79.

12. The programmatic nature of Pss. 1–2 is suggested by the lack of a title. See Childs, *Old Testament as Scripture*, 516.

13. See ibid., 512–13.

14. So G. Wilson, "Shaping the Psalter," 74.

15. See, e.g., ibid., 80.

16. See McCann, "Psalms as Instruction," 117–28. As McCann (p. 121) notes, the emphasis upon the psalms as instruction is not new. It is found clearly in John Calvin's work.

17. Childs (*Old Testament as Scripture*, 513) notes that the prayers of Israel are "a response to God's prior speaking" in the Torah. Cf. Deut. 30; Josh. 1.

18. It is now common to see Pss. 1–2 as introducing the book. See, e.g., Mays, "Context in Psalm Interpretation," 16.

dominion of the Lord and the anointed king of Israel (2:1). Instead of "meditating" (*hāgâ*) on the Torah (1:2), they "meditate" (*hāgâ*) on what is vain (2:1), longing to throw off the shackles of the rule of Yahweh and his anointed (2:2–3). Those who refuse fellowship with the wicked are "blessed" (1:1), just as those who take refuge in Yahweh are "blessed" (2:12).[19] The resistance put up by the wicked will fail, for Yahweh has installed the Davidic king, his son, in Zion (2:6–7). Jamie Grant argues that the faithful king who pleases the Lord is one who meditates and does the Torah per Deut. 17:18–20.[20] Childs suggests that Psalm 2 "was placed in such a prominent place . . . to emphasize the kingship of God as a major theme of the whole Psalter."[21] The promise to Abraham that all nations will be blessed through him will become a reality through the Davidic king, for "the ends of the earth" will be his "possession" (2:8).[22] Only those who "serve the LORD" and "kiss" the anointed "Son" (2:11–12) will escape judgment. Royal psalms (see Pss. 72; 89; 132) "witness to the messianic hope which looked for the consummation of God's kingship through his Anointed One."[23] Grant argues that Pss. 1–2 together look forward, so that "the introduction to the Psalter presents an eschatological hope for a new leader who would be the fulfillment of the Law of the King."[24] James Luther Mays remarks, "The Psalter can be read as a Davidic, messianic book of prayer and praise."[25] And he notes that the "pairing" together of Pss. 1–2 "says that all the psalms dealing with the living of life under the Lord must be understood and recited in the light of the reign of the Lord and that all psalms concerned with the kingship of the Lord are to be understood and recited with the torah in mind."[26]

The final form of the Psalms suggests that what is said about the king will be fulfilled in the future.[27] Canonically, the one who fully and completely delighted in the Torah was Jesus of Nazareth. He also fulfills the messianic destiny of Ps. 2, for he was installed as the reigning Lord and Christ at his resurrection (Acts 13:33; Heb. 1:5). The blessing promised to the world will become a reality through his reign. The lordship of Yahweh is central to both

19. As Grant (*King as Exemplar*, 61) points out, there is an inclusio here since the blessing commences Ps. 1 and concludes Ps. 2. For other themes and words that tie the two psalms together, see ibid., 61–65.
20. Grant, *King as Exemplar*.
21. Childs, *Old Testament as Scripture*, 516.
22. Childs (ibid.) rightly sees a messianic theme in the psalm.
23. Ibid., 517.
24. Grant, *King as Exemplar*, 67.
25. Mays, *Psalms*, 18.
26. Mays, "Torah-Psalms in the Psalter," 10.
27. Ibid.

Ps. 1 and Ps. 2. Those who submit to Yahweh's lordship keep the Torah, and they also place themselves under the reign of the Lord's anointed king.

If Ps. 2 focuses on the Davidic king, Books 1–2 focus on David. Virtually all of the psalms in Book 1 are Davidic, and Ps. 72:20 closes Book 2 by saying that the psalms in this book constitute "the prayers of David," signaling that these psalms have a messianic cast. Patrick Miller observes, "There is nothing that excludes or prohibits reading most of the psalms in the first half of Book 1 of the Psalter as coming from the mouth of the king."[28] Psalms 3–7 are prayers asking for deliverance, focusing on opposition to David. The foes mentioned in Ps. 2 gather against David and try to destroy him, and we discover in Ps. 3 that even David's son Absalom belongs with those who rage against the Lord's rule. Hence, David calls upon the Lord to arise and judge the wicked and to vindicate the righteous (3:7; 7:6; 9:19; 10:12).[29] These psalms illustrate the truth of Ps. 2: the wicked chafe at and try to overthrow the rule of David as God's anointed.

Tucked into the middle of these psalms is Ps. 8, a creation psalm, reflecting on the role of human beings in the created order. Clearly, the psalmist is thinking about Gen. 1:26–27, where human beings are the crown of creation and were made to rule over the world. David reflects on the role the Lord gave to human beings: "You have given him dominion over the works of your hands; you have put all things under his feet" (8:6). Who are human beings? They were created to rule the world for God, and in their ruling the Lord's majestic name resounds throughout the earth. Given the placement of this psalm, it seems justified to conclude that this rule of human beings is manifested in the rule of David, the anointed one. The call for human beings to display God's majesty by ruling the world will become a reality through David and his heirs. The NT sees Ps. 8 fulfilled in Jesus Christ (Heb. 2). The risen Christ is exalted as the messianic king because of his suffering and death, even though everything in the created world is not yet subject to his reign. Human beings will rule over the world only if they belong to Jesus, and they will share his future reign with him.

Many of the themes in the psalms are repeated. It seems that Pss. 11–18 particularly emphasize that the Lord will vindicate and extend his salvation to the righteous. The wicked may tell David to flee (11:1), but why should he, when the Lord has installed him as the anointed king (2:6–7)? The Lord reigns, and he will "rain coals on the wicked" (11:4, 6). The wicked strut along proudly (Ps. 12), so David wonders how long he must wait for the Lord's salvation (Ps.

28. Miller, "Beginning of the Psalter," 89.
29. For intertextual themes that link together Pss. 7–10, see G. Wilson, *Psalms*, 236–37.

13). The fool refuses to acknowledge that God is everywhere on earth (Ps. 14), and thus David longs for the day when the Lord will save his people.

It seems that there is a ring structure in Pss. 15–24, with Ps. 15 and Ps. 24 forming the "outer ring," and Ps. 19 being the "center."[30] Who will be able to live in God's presence and in his tabernacle (Ps. 15)? Only those who are righteous and innocent. "Delight in the torah and obedience to it stand at the beginning and end of this collection in the torah entrance liturgies."[31] Only those who trust in the Lord will be preserved by him (Ps. 16). Miller also rightly sees in these psalms the centrality of the king, which fits with the programmatic nature of Pss. 1–2. The righteous king is one who meditates on and obeys the law.[32] If all people are evil (Ps. 14), then the righteousness of Ps. 15 is true finally only of the Christ, which fits with 16:9–11 being a prophecy of Christ's resurrection.[33] David asks for vindication since he has trusted in the Lord (Ps. 17), and he exults in God since the Lord has rescued him from all his enemies (Ps. 18). David emphasizes that the Lord rescued him because of his righteousness (17:2–5; 18:19–25),[34] which points forward to the righteousness described in Ps. 24.[35] This cluster of psalms emphasizes that the Lord saves the righteous. He will exalt his anointed one who trusts in and obeys him (Ps. 2), but David ultimately fails in this area, so these psalms are ultimately fulfilled in Jesus Christ. The forward thrust fits with the psalm that speaks of the Lord's "steadfast love to his anointed, to David and his offspring forever" (18:50). The psalmist sees in David's victories promises of a final and definitive victory through David's offspring. Psalm 19 celebrates the glory of God in creation and in the Torah. Perhaps there is the suggestion that the glory of God in the heavens will reach the earth when the Torah is kept, which hearkens back to the message of Ps. 1.[36] "The idea of seeking refuge in Yahweh is central to a proper understanding of Pss 20 and 21."[37] And in the prayer of the king in Ps. 20 we have an allusion to Ps. 2:8, where Yahweh speaks of giving the king

30. Miller, "Beginning of the Psalter," 86; idem, "Kingship, Torah, Obedience, and Prayer," 127; see also Grant, *King as Exemplar*, 73.

31. Miller, "Kingship, Torah, Obedience, and Prayer," 127.

32. Ibid., 128.

33. Mays says about Ps. 15, "Christians come to worship in the confidence that God has made Jesus Christ our righteousness" (*Psalms*, 86).

34. Self-righteousness is not in view here. David has fulfilled the requirements of Deut. 17:18–20 (so Grant, *King as Exemplar*, 81–83), which is not the same thing as claiming sinlessness. Finally, the limited righteousness of David points to the perfect righteousness of the Christ (so Kidner, *Psalms 1–72*, 25).

35. So Miller, "Kingship, Torah, Obedience, and Prayer," 129.

36. For links between Ps. 18 and Ps. 19, see Grant, *King as Exemplar*, 97–99; Mays, "Torah-Psalms in the Psalter," 11.

37. Grant, *King as Exemplar*, 107.

rule over the nations.[38] Psalm 19's central role in Pss. 15–24 suggests that the king who is victorious trusts in Yahweh and keeps his Torah.[39]

The tone of Ps. 22 represents a dramatic change. The psalm alternates between a sense of God-forsakenness (22:1) and expressions of trust and confidence in God. Here the enemies of Ps. 2 conspire to destroy David. They are like ferocious bulls, lions, and dogs poised to ravage their victim (22:11–16, 20–21). David calls on the Lord who had forsaken him to deliver him. The psalm veers sharply in a new direction starting in 22:22. Here David pledges to exalt and praise the Lord in the congregation. The deliverance points beyond David: "All the ends of the earth shall remember and turn to the LORD, and all the families of the nations shall worship before you. For kingship belongs to the LORD, and he rules over the nations. All the prosperous of the earth eat and worship; before him shall bow all who go down to the dust, even the one who could not keep himself alive" (22:27–29). These promises exceed the horizon of David's experience and hearken back to the universal promises given to Abraham. "From a Christian perspective, one also finds in the Psalms revelation into the suffering of the Messiah."[40] Canonically, this promise is realized in Jesus of Nazareth, whom God forsook at the crucifixion (Matt. 27:46) and delivered in the resurrection (Heb. 2:12; cf. Ps. 22:22) so that the promises of universal blessing would be realized through him.[41]

Psalm 23 belongs in the same orbit as Ps. 22. The Lord will set a table of triumph before David in the presence of his enemies. Since the Lord is his shepherd, he does not fear when times are dark. Remarkably, the NT sees Jesus as the shepherd of God's people (John 10). He will shepherd God's people to springs of life (Rev. 7:17). The rule of God is paramount in the Psalter, as is evident from Ps. 2. In Ps. 24 the Lord is celebrated as the king of glory, but only those who have clean hands can ascend to his hill and stand in his holy place. Clearly, David (see Ps. 15) represents one who lives with such integrity, but David defiled his hands by committing adultery with Bathsheba and murdering Uriah. The only one who can enter into the Lord's temple with clean hands, then, is the Lord Jesus Christ.

If Ps. 24 emphasizes that only those with clean hands may "ascend the hill of the LORD" (24:3), David in Ps. 25 pleads for forgiveness of his sins on the basis of Yahweh's "steadfast love" and "goodness" (25:7). He prays, "For your name's sake, O LORD, pardon my guilt, for it is great" (25:11). David will be delivered from his enemies only if the Lord acts on his behalf. The

38. Miller, "Kingship, Torah, Obedience, and Prayer," 132.
39. See Grant, *King as Exemplar*, 113; Miller, "Kingship, Torah, Obedience, and Prayer," 128.
40. Sheppard, "Book of Psalms," 155.
41. I understand Ps. 22:22 to imply victory over death, i.e., resurrection.

same is true for Israel, and therefore David does not pray only for himself but climaxes and concludes the psalm with the request that the Lord "redeem Israel . . . out of all his troubles" (25:22).[42] Psalm 26 also calls for redemption and deliverance (26:9, 11), but David emphasizes his integrity and godliness, which is quite a striking contrast to and stands in tension with his plea for forgiveness of sins in Ps. 25, since his sin was "great" (25:11). But in Ps. 26 David seems to say that his obedience is great. There is a sense in which both are true. David's sin with Bathsheba and Uriah was egregious, and yet David on the whole was remarkably devoted to the Lord.[43] Again, in a christological reading of the text, Jesus Christ was the only one who perfectly embodied the integrity set forth in Ps. 26.

One of the themes often broached in Book 1 is the Lord's "holy hill" (2:6; 3:4; 15:1; "hill" in 24:3). Who can stand in his presence—in his "tent" (15:1) or his "holy place" (24:3)? David will "bow down toward your holy temple" (5:7; cf. 11:4; 18:6), and God sends assistance from his "sanctuary" (20:2).[44] There is no joy greater than abiding in the Lord's presence. Psalm 27 expresses this beautifully: "One thing have I asked of the LORD, that will I seek after: that I may dwell in the house of the LORD all the days of my life, to gaze upon the beauty of the LORD and to inquire in his temple" (27:4). David is convinced that the Lord will be his "light" and "salvation" and will "hide" him "in his shelter" and "cover" him in "his tent" (27:1, 5). It is sometimes difficult to determine whether the temple is heavenly or earthly, but the ambiguity itself is significant. "What we see on earth in Jerusalem is simply the earthly manifestation of the heavenly Temple, which is beyond localization. The Temple on Zion is the antitype to the cosmic archetype. The real Temple is the one to which it points, the one in 'heaven,' which cannot be distinguished sharply from its earthly manifestation."[45]

If we link Ps. 27 to Ps. 26, we see that the message is that the Lord will deliver the one who is godly and waits for him. In Ps. 28 David prays that the Lord will hear him from "his most holy sanctuary" (28:2) and deliver him while judging the wicked. David prays as the king, asking the Lord to "save your people and bless your heritage" (28:9). We have already noted that many psalms end with a call to save or a promise that the Lord will bless Israel, even if the rest of the psalm is about David (see 3:8; 5:11–12; 14:7; 18:50; 22:31;

---

42. Childs (*Old Testament as Scripture*, 519–20) rightly points out that even the psalms that speak of an individual in the final form of the Psalter also have a corporate reference.

43. The righteousness described here is not self-righteousness (so Mays, *Psalms*, 129–30).

44. For a helpful survey on the role of the sanctuary in Psalms, see Kraus, *Theology of the Psalms*, 73–84.

45. Levenson, *Sinai and Zion*, 140.

25:22; 28:9). Psalm 29 shares this feature, concluding with the words "May the LORD give strength to his people! May the LORD bless his people with peace" (29:11). The majority of psalms in Book 1 focus on the call for the Lord to deliver David, and since David was the king, the call to save Israel at the end of many psalms is fitting. The rescue of David cannot be separated from salvation for Israel. The life of David points to and is fulfilled in Jesus, for as the Christ, his triumph over sin and death wins the victory for his people. Returning to Ps. 29, the prayer for strength and peace for Israel occurs in the context of a creation psalm (cf. 19:1–6). Psalm 29 depicts a storm that summons all to "ascribe" "glory and strength" to the Lord (29:1). As the storm is unleashed, those "in his temple" cry "Glory!" (29:9). The Lord's rule over the storm reveals his kingship: "The LORD sits enthroned over the flood; the LORD sits enthroned as king forever" (29:10). The Lord of creation is also Lord over his people, and he is able to protect them.

We have noted the recurrent emphasis on the Lord's holy hill, sanctuary, tent, and temple in the psalms, and the superscription of Ps. 30 says that it is "a song at the dedication of the temple." Even if Psalms scholar Sigmund Mowinckel (1884–1965) exaggerated or misinterpreted in some respects the cultic dimension of the psalms, he was surely right in seeing it as quite prominent in the book. Here the temple theme is joined to a song of praise for Yahweh's deliverance of David. The Lord's residence with his people is inseparable from his protection of his people, and thus the temple becomes the place where he is praised. "In the Temple, instead of want, they found surfeit; instead of abandonment, care; instead of pollution, purity; instead of victimization, justice; instead of threat, security; instead of vulnerability, inviolability; instead of change, fixity; and instead of temporality, eternity."[46] If Ps. 30 rejoices in Yahweh's salvation, Ps. 31 pleads for it. David "commits" his "spirit" to the Lord (31:5), just as Jesus did at his death (Luke 23:46). The psalm concludes with a call for the people of God to love him and to be strong in waiting for his deliverance (31:23–24).

In the light of the fact that Ps. 32 emphasizes the blessing of those who confess their sins, how does Ps. 32 relate to Ps. 31? It seems that the relationship is this: the Lord delivers his people by forgiving their sins if they confess them to him. Those who confess their sins are then counted as "righteous" and are full of joy (32:11) and blessing (32:1)! The end of Ps. 32 and the beginning of Ps. 33 are closely stitched together. Psalm 32 concludes with the words "Be glad in the LORD, and rejoice, O righteous, and shout for joy, all you upright in heart!" (32:11), and Ps. 33 opens with "Shout for joy in the LORD, O you

46. Levenson, *Restoration of Israel*, 94.

righteous! Praise befits the upright" (33:1). Those whom the Lord saves and forgives are full of joy. Psalm 33 emphasizes the Lord's creation of the world (33:6–9) and his sovereignty (cf. Ps. 2): "The LORD brings the counsel of the nations to nothing; he frustrates the plans of the peoples. The counsel of the LORD stands forever, the plans of his heart to all generations" (33:10–11). Israel can be confident of victory, then, not because of its own strength but rather because Yahweh is a mighty king, and hence they are called to wait upon and trust in him (33:20–22).

Many of the psalms are about David's need for deliverance, as he was constantly in danger. Psalm 34 reflects on the peril that David faced when he was fleeing from Saul and escaped to the Philistine king. David praises the Lord because he "sought the LORD, and he answered me and delivered me from all my fears" (34:4). Those who suffer will be rescued from all their afflictions by the Lord. Their bones will not be broken (34:20), and they will be redeemed (34:22). Just as the Lord delivered David from Saul and his enemies, so he delivered Jesus the Christ. His bones were not broken (John 19:33–36), and he was liberated from death by the resurrection. If Ps. 34 thanks the Lord for his deliverance, Ps. 35 asks the Lord to deliver David and to judge his enemies. David's vindication will not be established if his enemies prosper. Here we have what are known as imprecatory psalms (see also Pss. 69; 109; 137).[47] If Ps. 35 is a call to judge the wicked, Ps. 36 reflects on the contrast between the righteous and the wicked. The righteous enjoy the Lord's gracious love, and they "feast on the abundance of your house" and "drink from the river of your delights" (36:8). "These verses epitomize the paradisiacal elements of the temple experience—divine presence, abundant food and drink in the temple, and the experience of seeing God as an image of divine light."[48] Ultimately, the prayer voiced in Ps. 35 will be answered (Ps. 36:12), and believers will enjoy God's presence forever.

The contrast between the righteous and wicked continues in Ps. 37. The wicked may prosper in the short term, but not in the long term. Ultimately, the righteous will inherit the land. Therefore, they are called upon to trust in the Lord, to wait upon and find their delight in him. Psalm 38 helps us understand who the righteous are who will inherit the land according to Ps. 37. What is striking is that David confesses his sin, and thus he does not seem to be righteous enough to stand in Yahweh's sanctuary (cf. Pss. 15; 26). But it is precisely because he admits his sin and turns to the Lord for forgiveness

47. For an excellent discussion of how these psalms relate to today, see Waltke, *Old Testament Theology*, 878–80.
48. M. Smith, "Book for Pilgrims," 162.

that he is considered "good" (38:20) (see on Ps. 32 above). Similarly, in Ps. 39 David tries to restrain his tongue but finds it impossible to do so. He recognizes the brevity of life and his sinfulness, and he confesses that his hope is in God for the forgiveness of his sins and for living out his days on earth. Psalm 40 continues the emphasis upon the Lord's deliverance, which leads David to sing a new song. In the NT Hebrews picks up the language of 40:6–8, seeing Jesus as the one who has fully carried out the will of God and as displacing the old covenant sacrifices with the new covenant established upon the basis of Jesus' once-for-all sacrifice (Heb. 10:5–10). The theme of deliverance continues in Ps. 41, with the righteous David contrasted with his enemies, for a close friend has turned against him (41:9; cf. John 13:18). The tension that we have seen in many psalms surfaces here again. David remains because of his "integrity" (41:12), and yet he calls upon God to be gracious to him because of his sin (41:4). The psalmist likely believes that those who turn to the Lord for forgiveness are righteous, but in light of the canon as a whole, the only true son of David who lived without fault was Jesus of Nazareth.

Book 2

In Book 1 the name "Yahweh" is most often used for God, but in Book 2 "Elohim" takes center stage. Book 2 begins with psalms from the sons of Korah (Pss. 42–49).[49] Psalms 42–43 are likely one psalm and introduce Book 2. The psalms address the situation of one who is separated from the temple, one who longs to praise God in the sanctuary.[50] This separation from God's presence produces despair, for the great longing and thirst is to be in God's presence. As Mark Smith comments, "The pilgrimage was like visiting paradise and temporarily recapturing the primordial peace and enriching relationship with God."[51] This refrain marks Pss. 42–43: hope in God, for he will save his people, and they will praise him again with joy. It is illuminating at this juncture to consider how Book 2 ends, with a psalm of Solomon (Ps. 72).[52] Here Solomon prays that the hope expressed in Pss. 42–43 would become a reality through "the royal son" (72:1). Then the people will prosper and enjoy peace. The universal blessing to Abraham will become a reality: "May he have dominion from sea to sea, and from the River to the ends of the earth" (72:8), and "May people

---

49. Hamilton (*God's Glory in Salvation*, 284) argues that Pss. 42–50 represent the events of 2 Sam. 7–10, when the ark was brought into Jerusalem.
50. McCann ("Books I–III," 102–3) maintains that Israel's experience of exile is in view here.
51. M. Smith, "Book for Pilgrims," 161.
52. Williamson (*Sealed with an Oath*, 140) thinks that it is a psalm David uttered at Solomon's coronation.

be blessed in him, all nations call him blessed!" (72:17). And the prophecy of the serpent being crushed would come true. For all peoples and kings will serve him, and his "enemies would lick the dust" (72:9). When this prophecy becomes a reality, then the Lord's name would be blessed forever, and "the whole earth" would "be filled with his glory" (72:19). The whole earth would become God's temple over which he reigned and in which he lived. Psalm 72 concludes by identifying the psalms in Book 2 as Davidic, for they will be fulfilled through a Davidic heir.

The call to hope in God, stressed in Pss. 42–43, is accentuated by the message of Ps. 44. The poets recall the days when Yahweh, by his own might, won victories for the sake of his people. He was Israel's king, and since he triumphed over Israel's foes, he received praise: "In God we have boasted continually, and we will give thanks to your name forever" (44:8). But God has forgotten Israel, and now they are delivered into the hands of their enemies. One would think that Israel's setbacks could be attributed to their sin, but not in this instance. Israel has been faithful to the Lord and yet is being handed over as sheep to be slaughtered (44:22; cf. Rom. 8:36). So God is summoned to "awake," to "rouse" himself, and to "rise up" and "come to our help" (44:23–26). These pleas express hope in God despite the suffering endured by Israel.

Psalm 45 represents the answer to the plea voiced in Ps. 44 (cf. Ps. 72). Israel will be delivered by a king who "ride[s] out victoriously for the cause of truth and meekness" (45:4), whose arrows will sink into the hearts of his enemies, so that he will rule over all. His victory will be due to his righteousness, and it should be enough to win over a wife from a foreign country.[53] Canonically, the ideal king sketched in here is not King Arthur of medieval England, but King Jesus. Hebrews sees proof in this psalm for his deity (Heb. 1:8–9), and the "daughter" in the psalm finds its fulfillment in the salvation of the church, which includes the Gentiles (Eph. 5:32; Rev. 19:9; 21:1). If Ps. 45 focuses on the king in his beauty who will bring victory to his people, Ps. 46 fixes our gaze on "the city of God, the holy habitation of the most High" (46:4). God lives in the midst of his people, and therefore they need not fear even if the entire world threatens to implode. "There is a river" that will satisfy every thirst (46:4).[54] God will be exalted as king and will triumph over the nations; he is the fortress of his people.

The victory of the Lord as king is also featured in Ps. 47. He is "a great king over all the earth" (47:2). The nations are therefore subjugated to Israel,

53. Superficially, marrying a foreign wife contradicts the message of Ezra-Nehemiah, but the psalmist assumes that the king's wife will give her allegiance to Yahweh.
54. Cf. the river that flows from the temple (Ezek. 47:1–12; Joel 3:18).

for "God is the King of all the earth" (47:7) and "reigns over the nations" (47:8). Hence, Israel will burst forth with exuberant praise. The loveliness of the city of God continues to be a theme in Ps. 48. God is a "fortress" (cf. Ps. 46) because he dwells in the city.[55] Foreign kings were routed, for the city of God will be established forever, and God will be praised in his temple.[56] Those who walk around Zion will recount God's praises forever. The NT makes it clear that the heavenly city and the new temple represent the new heaven and the new earth (Rev. 21–22), not a literal building or a literal Jerusalem. The psalms about the city of God point to the renewed universe, the new creation, as the place of God's dwelling. The last psalm in the collection from the sons of Korah emphasizes that the proud and rich do not have a lasting destiny (Ps. 49). Only those who belong to Yahweh will be ransomed and redeemed by him. Psalm 49 fits with the preceding ones in stressing that those who belong to the Lord will finally triumph.

Even though Ps. 50 is not from the sons of Korah, it fits nicely with Ps. 49, for the theme is that God as king will judge the wicked. The judgment will come from "Zion, the perfection of beauty" (50:2). Those who are faithful will be rewarded, but the wicked will not avert judgment simply because they offer sacrifices. What it means to know God is to call upon him for help and to praise him for receiving it. Those who "forget God" will be torn to pieces (50:22). What it means to forget God is explicated by Ps. 51. David has sinned grievously by committing adultery with Bathsheba and murdering Uriah, but he has not forgotten God, for he profoundly and from a "broken and contrite heart" (51:17) asks God to forgive him. David as the king longs to see God "do good to Zion" and to "build up the walls of Jersualem" (51:18). The wicked, who will be judged (cf. Ps. 50) and broken down by God, are like Doeg (Ps. 52), for Doeg practiced evil without regret. Only those who make God their "refuge" will be like David, "a green olive tree in the house of God" (52:8). We note again that those who are in God's house are protected from harm. By contrast, the wicked (Ps. 53), like Doeg (Ps. 52), live as if God does not exist (53:1). But a day of terror is coming for the wicked when "salvation for Israel" comes "out of Zion" (53:6). The wicked who forget God, such as the Ziphites who plot to kill David, are trying to destroy David (Ps. 54), but the Lord will uphold his life.

The treachery of David's close friends brings intense pain (Ps. 55), but he gives himself to the Lord, knowing that they will be judged. The same

---

55. See Mays, *Psalms*, 190.
56. On the significance of Ps. 48, where Mount Zion is exalted above all, see Goldingay, *Israel's Faith*, 240–41.

theme is struck in Ps. 56, but here the attack of the Philistines against him is contemplated. David puts his trust in the Lord, who will deliver him from death. Even though Ps. 51 recounts David's confession of his sin relative to Bathsheba and Uriah, the psalms beginning with Ps. 52 seem to reflect on the time period before he became king. Psalm 57 fits such a narrative, for here David reflects on his eluding Saul in a cave. The psalm beats with exultation, for David praises God exuberantly for rescuing him from Saul's designs, and hence David praises God for his "steadfast love" and "faithfulness" (57:10). Indeed, David's deliverance brings praise to God as the divine king, as the refrain in 57:5, 11 attests: "Be exalted, O God, above the heavens! Let your glory be over all the earth!"

Psalm 58 remains in the same orbit as the preceding psalms, but here David reflects on the injustice and unrighteousness of the wicked and asks God to judge them. Ultimately, there is justice so that the wicked will be recompensed for their evil, and the righteous rewarded. In Ps. 59 Saul's attempt to destroy David is once again center stage. David prays God will sap the strength of his enemies so that they will fall and be consumed by his wrath. The purpose of the judgment is "that they may know that God rules over Jacob to the ends of the earth" (59:13). Meanwhile, David will sing God's praises. David's battle with his enemies forecasts the opposition to Jesus that culminated in his death, but God vindicated him by raising him from the dead, which spells victory over and judgment of Satan and the Lord's enemies.

Psalm 60 moves forward in history to the day when David is king and faces enemies in battle. Israel has been defeated in battle, and God has rejected them (cf. Ps. 44), but David asks God to intervene and to grant victory, and he receives a promise from God that he will grant victory over their foes. David asks in Ps. 61 that his reign as king will be preserved, and that he "may be enthroned forever before God" (61:7). The theme of God functioning as David's protection continues to be advanced in Ps. 62, and in this psalm David confesses that God alone is his fortress and refuge. Since God is David's only hope, he seeks God "earnestly" (63:1). The temple theme returns; David has seen God's "power and glory" in the sanctuary (63:2).[57] Nothing in life can be compared to sweet fellowship with God. This God will destroy David's enemies and uphold him as king (Ps. 64).

Psalm 65 steps back a bit from the conflict and is more reflective in tone. David praises God for hearing his prayer and for atoning for his sins. The ultimate goal is relationship with God, which is realized in the temple: "Blessed is the one you choose and bring near, to dwell in your courts! We shall be

57. See M. Smith, "Book for Pilgrims," 162.

satisfied with the goodness of your house, the holiness of your temple!" (65:4). God's goodness and blessing are experienced in the land. The rains water the earth and grain is provided for sustenance, and David says to the Lord, "You crown the year with your bounty," and he exults that "the pastures of the wilderness overflow" (65:11–12). Psalm 66 also praises God for his goodness. The God-centeredness that is characteristic of the psalms is expressed in the shouting of joy to God, in singing to "the glory of his name" (66:1–2). God is particularly praised for the exodus, for liberating his people from bondage.

Psalms 65–66 reflect on God's goodness to Israel, the abundant blessings vouchsafed to his people. The universal vision of the OT emerges in Ps. 67. Here the psalmist, picking up on the priestly blessing of Num. 6:24–26, asks that God would continue to bless Israel and make his face shine upon them (67:1). But this blessing was never intended to be for Israel alone; God's "saving power" should be disseminated "among all nations" (67:2). God's reign over the whole earth will be realized when "all the peoples praise" him (67:3), when "the nations" are "glad and sing for joy" (67:4). The physical blessing of Israel (see Ps. 65) is not to be turned inward, for God's purpose is that "all the ends of the earth fear him" (67:7), just as he promised to Abraham.

Psalm 68 describes a procession (68:24–27) to the temple, where the ark, representing God's royal rule, was installed.[58] The procession celebrated the victory that God granted Israel over their enemies so that Israel sang God's praises. David reflects on the exodus, where nature convulsed and God triumphed over his enemies. The sovereign Lord who "rides in the heavens" is "awesome" in "his sanctuary" (68:35). In Ps. 69 David is in great distress and about to sink into oblivion. He beseeches God to save him in his hour of extremity, confessing his sin and acknowledging the hostility of those who despise him. Indeed, David was suffering reproach because of his zeal for the Lord, because he lived to bring honor to his king. Hence, he prays that his enemies will be punished by the Lord for their opposition and is confident of final salvation. When all has been said and done, "God will save Zion and build up the cities of Judah" and "those who love his name shall dwell in it" (69:35–36). David's sufferings point forward to those of the Christ (69:9; cf. Rom. 15:3), as does the drink offered him (69:21; cf. Matt. 27:34, 48). The punishment of the wicked is also applied to the enemies of Jesus (69:22–23; cf. Rom. 11:9–10). In Ps. 69 David prays for deliverance from enemies, while in Ps. 70 he urgently prays that God will help him and rescue him from his opponents. Psalm 71 is quite similar, with David asking particularly that the

---

58. There is a close link between Yahweh residing in the temple and his rule over all (see Brueggemann, *Theology of the Old Testament*, 655–61).

Lord will continue to sustain and keep him during his old age. We noted above that Book 2 ends with a messianic psalm, forecasting the fulfillment of the promises made to Abraham through a Davidic king. The royal dimension of the psalms shines through in the first two books of the Psalter. The theme of the kingdom, which is the burden of this book, plays a major role in the psalms.

Book 3

Books 1–2 emphasize God's deliverance of Israel, especially of David as the king of Israel. Book 3 (Pss. 73–89), however, seems to correlate best with Israel's exile.[59] The collection consists of psalms of Asaph (Pss. 73–83), several psalms from the sons of Korah (Pss. 84–85; 87–88), one psalm of David (Ps. 86), and one by Ethan the Ezrahite (Ps. 89). Community laments dominate this section, showing that "Book III has been decisively shaped by the experience of exile and dispersion."[60] McCann observes, however, that the laments "do not occur consecutively. Instead, they are interspersed with psalms which grasp for threads of hope amidst the experience of exile and dispersion by celebrating God as judge of all the earth or by rehearsing God's past deeds on Israel's behalf despite Israel's faithlessness."[61]

Psalm 73 launches Book 3, and Asaph envies the prosperity of the wicked upon seeing their health, happiness, and prosperity. Surely Asaph's experience matched Israel's experience in exile, where seeing Babylon's glory must have been quite dispiriting. Such envy, however, is ignorant and beastlike. Asaph saw the true state of things in God's temple when he entered "the sanctuary of God" (73:17). Then he saw that the glory of the wicked was evanescent, that they would ultimately perish. Indeed, Asaph realized in the temple that nothing could compare to fellowship with God: "Whom have I in heaven but you? And there is nothing on earth that I desire besides you. My flesh and my heart may fail, but God is the strength of my heart and my portion forever" (73:25–26).[62] Psalm 73, then, is paradigmatic for this entire section, as is the closing psalm, Ps. 89 (which we will examine below). No matter how dire the circumstances, no matter how prosperous Israel's enemies are, ultimately they will perish, and those who know God will be received into "glory" (73:24).

59. See Dempster, *Dominion and Dynasty*, 196.
60. McCann, "Books I–III," 96.
61. Ibid.
62. For the future hope envisioned here and in Ps. 49 and its connection to fellowship in the temple, see the fascinating and illuminating discussion in Levenson, *Restoration of Israel*, 82–107.

Psalm 74 returns to the dismal state of Israel. God's wrath has been dispensed against the "sheep of [his] pasture" (74:1). The sanctuary is devastated, and everything is in ruins. "They set your sanctuary on fire" (74:7) and "burned all the meeting places of God in the land" (74:8). No prophet is present to interpret what is happening. But God is still King, and he cannot allow his name to be besmirched forever. The same God who delivered Israel at the exodus will not forsake his people. He "crushed the heads of Leviathan" at the exodus (74:14),[63] and the exodus functions as a pattern and precursor of future salvation. The psalmist calls upon the Lord to arise and to remember his covenant. Ultimately, this prayer is fulfilled in Jesus of Nazareth, who accomplished a new exodus and crushed Satan's head by virtue of his death and resurrection.[64] Psalm 75 is a song of praise that confesses that the Lord will judge the wicked and vindicate his people. Psalm 76 is rather similar to Ps. 75, but it emphasizes that the Lord has "established" "his abode" "in Salem, his dwelling place in Zion" (76:2). Yahweh is known in a certain place, Zion, and with a certain people, Israel. The King is seen in his beauty in Jerusalem. Asaph goes on to reflect on the exodus, where God triumphed over his enemies.

Psalm 77, however, returns to the sorrow and devastation expressed in Ps. 74. The troubles of Israel are so great that Asaph cannot even speak. He wonders whether the Lord will ever show favor again, whether he has withdrawn his steadfast love forever. But then he muses upon the exodus, finding in it strength to endure present suffering. If God delivered his people formerly, he will do so in the future. As he led his "flock by the hand of Moses and Aaron," so he will do again (77:20). He will raise up a new shepherd-king for Israel. Psalm 78 reviews Israel's history from the exodus to the time of David. The theme is God's faithfulness and Israel's unfaithfulness. Despite the Lord's stunning power in liberating them from Egypt and his faithfulness in satisfying their needs in the wilderness, Israel rebelled against him continually. But the final word of the psalm is God's faithfulness. Psalm 77 ended with God as a shepherd leading his people through Moses and Aaron. The theme of God as the shepherd of Israel is picked up again in Ps. 78:52. God raised up a new shepherd for his people: "He chose David his servant and took him from the sheepfolds; from following the nursing ewes he brought him to shepherd Jacob his people, Israel his inheritance. With upright heart he shepherded them and guided them with his skillful hand" (78:70–72). Israel can take hope, for God has not abandoned them. His sanctuary is in Mount Zion (78:68–69) and his

63. As Kline (*Kingdom Prologue*, 181) says, the demonic nature of Egypt's opposition is thereby communicated.
64. Beale (*Biblical Theology*, chap. 8) rightly argues that the resurrection represents the inauguration of the new creation.

king will reign. Even after the days of David, therefore, Israel should be full of hope. God will fulfill his promise to shepherd and reign over his people with a new David.[65]

The hope engendered by David's reign is important because Ps. 79 recalls the themes of Pss. 74 and 77. The nations "have defiled your holy temple; they have laid Jerusalem in ruins" (79:1). The blood of Israelites has been spilled in the city, and foreigners mock them. Asaph asks God to show mercy and to punish the nations that have visited their wrath on Jerusalem. We see a fundamental prayer of the psalms: "Help us, O God of our salvation, for the glory of your name; deliver us, and atone for our sins, for your name's sake!" (79:9). God should save his people for the sake of his great name and his reputation among the Gentiles. The psalm concludes with a theme that has been prominent in Book 3. Israel is God's flock: "But we your people, the sheep of your pasture, will give thanks to you forever; from generation to generation we will recount your praise" (79:13).

Psalm 80 picks up where Ps. 79 leaves off: "Give ear, O Shepherd of Israel, you who lead Joseph like a flock! You who are enthroned upon the cherubim, shine forth. Before Ephraim and Benjamin and Manasseh, stir up your might and come to save us!" (80:1–2). God is Israel's shepherd and king. Israel is God's vine that he planted when they were rescued from Egypt, and Asaph pleads for God to look with favor on that vine. Days of tears and defeat have come, but God can make all things new. So the refrain of the psalm is this appeal to God: "Restore us . . . ; let your face shine, that we may be saved!" (80:3, 7, 19). Israel is suffering under the hand of enemies. Psalm 81 clarifies that this suffering is due to Israel's sin. The Lord longs to fill them with good things and will do so if they turn from evil. Psalm 82 puts the spotlight on evil in Israel, for the judges are not executing justice, and thus society is imploding. Psalm 83 represents the last psalm of Asaph, and he pleads again for God to speak, to judge the nations that are despoiling Israel. Thereby, they will "know that you alone, whose name is the LORD, are the Most High over all the earth" (83:18).

The psalms from the sons of Korah are filled with a longing for the courts and the temple of the Lord (Ps. 84). Such a longing fits a time of exile and dispersion, where Israel cannot enjoy God's sanctuary. The psalmist longs deeply for the loveliness and beauty that come from fellowship with God in his "dwelling place" (84:1–2). What a joy it is to sing praise in his presence,

---

65. Against McCann ("Books I–III," 99), who sees a "rejection of the Davidic/Zion theology." McCann also speaks of a "reorientation" (p. 99) and rightly says that the hope is not abandoned (p. 100). He still seems to imply, however, that a personal Davidic ruler might not be forthcoming.

even to be a lowly doorkeeper in the courts of the Lord. He asks the Lord to look with favor on the anointed king and show his favor to Israel. Psalm 85 could be construed as the answer to the request for favor in Ps. 84. The sons of Korah recall how the Lord forgave his people in the past and ask him to restore and revive the nation again. They are convinced that the Lord will again show his faithfulness, steadfast love, and salvation to Israel. A new day is coming.

The only psalm of David in this section follows (Ps. 86), perhaps to emphasize the need for the Lord to show favor to the anointed king. David pleads with the Lord to show him grace and save him from his distress. Such a great deliverance will bring glory to God: "All the nations you have made shall come and worship before you, O Lord, and shall glorify your name" (86:9). The universal promises made to Abraham will be fulfilled through a Davidic king. The Lord's glory over the nations is expanded upon in Ps. 87. The springs of life are in Zion—the mountain of God—the city of his residence.[66] Hence, those from other nations who enjoy life do so because they are born in Zion.

The joy and confidence of Pss. 84–87 are swept out the door when it comes to Ps. 88. The psalm is written in the first person, but it speaks of the state of Israel: troubled, enervated, depressed, friendless, grieving, and most of all separated from the Lord. Psalm 89 closes Book 3 and is remarkably similar in some ways to Ps. 73. The psalmist remembers the Lord's covenant with David—the promise that his dynasty will never end. He recalls the Lord's great victories, his crushing of Rahab (89:10), and the promise that the same victories will be given to David (89:23). The serpent will be crushed beneath David's feet. If David's heirs stray from God's covenant, they will be disciplined, but God will never revoke his covenant with David. But, says the psalmist, what has happened? The covenant seems to have been nullified. Israel has been defeated and is full of shame, and it looks as if God's promises will not come true. So the psalm concludes with a cry to God to remember his covenant and to act for the sake of his people so that the promises made to David become a reality and their exile becomes a distant memory.

Book 4

Book 4 of the Psalter consists of Pss. 90–106. If Book 3 emphasizes Israel's exile and suffering, Book 4 focuses on the Lord's sovereignty and his promise to bless Israel. Yahweh's promise has not been withdrawn, and the sovereign

66. On the role that Psalm 87 plays in the fulfillment of God's promises, see Gentry and Wellum, *Kingdom through Covenant*, 449–54.

Lord will fulfill his promise to redeem Israel, and hence they should exult in, praise, and bless the Lord.[67] Book 4 represents the promise of a new exodus, a new act of redemption for Israel. McCann thinks that Book 4 is the center of the Psalter and contains its principal theme: "The Lord reigns."[68]

Book 4 begins with the only psalm of Moses (Ps. 90), which bridges the pessimism of Book 3 with the optimism of Book 4.[69] Moses reflects on the brevity and evanescence of human life and its futility because of sin. Hence, those who are wise will number their days, pondering how quickly one's sojourn on earth passes. But the Lord is the everlasting God, and human life is meaningful if one is satisfied with the Lord's "steadfast love" so "that we may rejoice and be glad all our days" (90:14). Moses prays that God's power will be shown to forthcoming generations, and that the Lord will "establish the work of our hands" (90:17). The Psalter is shaped so that the redemption accomplished for Moses' generation would be realized again in a new exodus. Psalm 90 begins by saying that the Lord has "been our dwelling place in all generations" (90:1), and Ps. 91 picks up this theme, referring to the one "who dwells in the shelter of the Most High" (91:1). Those who trust in the Lord are told that they are protected ultimately from every evil "because you have made the LORD your dwelling place" (91:9). The prayer of Ps. 90 will be answered, for those who make the Lord their refuge will be satisfied "with long life" and "salvation" (91:16).[70] Psalm 92 is a Sabbath song that celebrates the goodness and faithfulness of the Lord, who grants triumph over one's enemies. The righteous are satisfied with God's goodness, for they enjoy the wonder of his presence in the temple: "They are planted in the house of the LORD; they flourish in the courts of our God" (92:13). The concerns that mark Ps. 90 are answered to a considerable degree in Ps. 92.[71] Israel will return to the land, worship Yahweh in his temple, and exult in his grace.

67. Wilson rightly emphasizes that in response to Book 3, Book 4 teaches that Yahweh reigns and is Israel's only hope; however, Wilson underestimates the promise to fulfill the Davidic covenant in Book 5, concluding that the Davidic covenant has failed (cf. Pss. 110; 132). See G. Wilson, "Shape of the Book of Psalms," 140; idem, *Editing of the Hebrew Psalter*, 213, 215, 222; idem, "Use of Royal Psalms." Note the unpersuasive attempt by Wilson (*Editing of the Hebrew Psalter*, 225) to explain Ps. 132 as if it is a foreign part of the Psalter that was retained. McCann ("Psalms as Instruction," 123) also separates too sharply the Lord's reign from the reign of the Davidic king. On the idea that the reign of the Lord should not be separated from the reign of his anointed one, see Grant, *King as Exemplar*, 34–37; Howard, *Psalms 93–100*, 201–2; Mitchell, *Message of the Psalter*, 78–81. Mays (*Psalms*, 17–18) rightly argues that Pss. 110; 132 represent a renewal of hope for a Davidic king.
68. McCann, "Psalms as Instruction," 123.
69. So Howard, *Psalms 93–100*, 168–69.
70. So also Sheppard, "Book of Psalms," 151; Howard, *Psalms 93–100*, 170.
71. Howard, *Psalms 93–100*, 170.

Psalms 93–100 are often identified as royal psalms, for they celebrate the Lord's kingship, which we have seen is a major theme in the Psalter.[72] Human beings cannot bring salvation; "these psalms counsel the hearer to find refuge in YHWH who alone is eternal and able to save."[73] Only the Lord can rescue Israel from exile.

Psalm 93 begins with the signature phrase of these psalms: "The Lord reigns" (93:1). As the mighty one, he is stronger than any flood or disaster that threatens God's people. The theme of the temple continues as well, for "holiness befits" the "house" of the reigning king (93:5). This mighty God is one of vengeance and justice who will judge the wicked and vindicate the righteous, according to Ps. 94. Psalm 95 is a call to come into God's presence in his temple and to sing his praise because he is creator and Lord and king, and Israel is his flock,[74] but Israel must ensure that they do not harden their hearts as the wilderness generation did.[75] Those who harden themselves against the Lord will not enjoy the new exodus.

Psalm 96 is a song of praise to the Lord, for he is the one true God and is exalted above all other "gods." This God is to be worshiped in the temple through offerings, and his glory is to be proclaimed to all nations, for he is the judge of the entire world. The Lord's reign over the entire world is also featured in Ps. 97, and hence all are summoned to praise and worship this one who judges the earth by fire and storm.[76] The Lord's judgment and reign over the entire world continue in Ps. 98. Indeed, Ps. 98 is remarkably similar in many respects to Ps. 96.[77] Clearly, Yahweh is not a tribal or localized deity, since he judges all, and yet at the same time he has shown his love and salvation to Israel as his people. We have a hint here that the new exodus will embrace all nations and will not be limited to Israel.

Yahweh is the sovereign one, for Ps. 99 begins with the words "The LORD reigns" (99:1). He is "enthroned upon the cherubim" in the temple (99:1) and should be worshiped "at his holy mountain" (99:9).[78] Yahweh is holy and awesome, judging and avenging those who violate his will. Hence, people must exalt and praise Yahweh as the holy one. Psalm 100 is an exuberant song of praise that is to be sung as his people enter into the temple, as they "enter into his gates with thanksgiving and his courts with praise" (100:4). Israel

72. See ibid., 21.

73. G. Wilson, "Shaping the Psalter," 76.

74. As Howard (*Psalms 93–100*, 176) points out, Ps. 95 is closely related to Ps. 100, and the two seem to function as an inclusio.

75. Howard (ibid., 120–21) sees a link with Ps. 94 in the emphasis on God's people.

76. For the many links between Ps. 96 and Ps. 97, see ibid., 141–44.

77. See ibid., 178–79.

78. As Ollenburger (*Zion*, 50) notes, the presence of Yahweh is closely linked with Zion here.

praises the Lord because of his great love.[79] If we consider these royal psalms in Book 4, and if we see them as a response to the exile depicted in Book 3, we learn that Yahweh can and will fulfill his promises to Israel and David because he reigns over all, and nothing can ultimately thwart his will.

David considers his calling as the king in Ps. 101. He has the responsibility to ensure that wickedness is not honored in his kingdom, so that the righteous are shown favor but the wicked are rooted out. The psalm looks forward ultimately to the reign of Jesus Christ, where evil will be a distant memory and righteousness will be rewarded. The psalmist is in great distress in Ps. 102, fearing that his life is about to be extinguished as his enemies oppress him. But the Lord reigns over all, and his purposes for Zion will not be frustrated. The Lord will not forget his people: "Nations will fear the name of the LORD, and all the kings of the earth will fear your glory" (102:15).

The sovereignty of the Lord continues to be celebrated in one of the greatest of the psalms, Ps. 103. "The LORD has established his throne in the heavens, and his kingdom rules over all" (103:19). Israel is summoned to bless the Lord because he has forgiven their sins and healed them of their diseases. The merciful and gracious God of the exodus is still Israel's God, and he will bless Israel in coming generations by keeping his covenant and showing them his steadfast love. He will have mercy on them again. Psalm 104 is a nature psalm in which the psalmist praises the Lord for creating and sustaining the world. Wisdom and creation themes merge here, for when the psalmist considers the world that the Lord created, he confesses, "In wisdom you made them all" (104:24). The beauty and the wonder of creation provoke the psalmist to pen, "May the glory of the LORD endure forever; may the LORD rejoice in his works" (104:31).

Book 4 closes with two psalms about the history of Israel (Pss. 105; 106). Psalm 105 is a call to praise Yahweh for keeping his covenant with Israel. The story from Abraham until possession of the land is rehearsed. Despite ups and downs along the way, the Lord fulfilled his covenant promise to Israel so that they entered the land. The purpose for Israel's redemption was so that they would do the Lord's will and keep his Torah. This psalm is placed here to remind Israel that Yahweh keeps his promises, and that they are called upon to do his will. Psalm 106 tells the story of Israel from another perspective. Here the persistent unfaithfulness and sin of Israel are featured. The Lord intervened and saved his people repeatedly—for his name's sake (Ps. 106:8)—and yet they continued to stray from him after being delivered and hence fell into a pattern where the Lord saved them and then judged them for their waywardness. The

79. Both Ps. 99 and Ps. 100 refer to God's name, and the people of God receive attention in both. See Howard, *Psalms 93–100*, 165.

psalmist does not rehearse this narrative fundamentally to discourage Israel because of its constant unfaithfulness; rather, the account emphasizes the mercy of God, how he delivered his people again and again. Therefore, the psalm ends, and Book 4 concludes, with a cry for the Lord to save his people again: "Save us, O LORD our God, and gather us from among the nations, that we may give thanks to your holy name and glory in your praise" (106:47). Book 4 emphasizes Yahweh's sovereignty—his salvation of his people and his judgment of those who scorn him. Yahweh is faithful to his covenant and is merciful and gracious, as Exod. 34:6–7 says, and therefore he will show mercy again to Israel and save them.[80] The covenant made with David (see Ps. 89) will be fulfilled by the Lord. Israel will rise again.

Book 5

Book 5 picks up where Book 4 left off. Israel must give thanks to the Lord, for he has redeemed them (Ps. 107). The fifth book is marked by praise, by the call to praise Yahweh.[81] The first four books end with a doxology, but Book 5 ends with five psalms (Pss. 146–150) that are doxological, for Israel can be assured that Yahweh will answer their prayers, save them, and fulfill his covenant promises. Indeed, the author begins (weaving Book 5 with Book 4) by emphasizing the return from exile, God's people being gathered from every nation. The psalmist sketches in examples of those who have been rescued: those lost in the wilderness, prisoners, those suffering because of their foolishness, and those in peril at sea because of storms. The variety of examples instructs Israel that when they cry to Yahweh, he will rescue them.[82] In Ps. 108 David sings Yahweh's praises because of his covenant love. Yahweh will answer Israel's prayers and give help against enemies so that Israel will triumph.[83] What stands in the way of Israel's triumph? The enemies of David and Israel. David recounts in Ps. 109 his enemies, asking God to have mercy on him and to punish those who oppose him. Psalm 110, much like Ps. 2, reflects on the rule of the anointed king—the offspring of David who will also be David's lord. The Lord has promised that he will rule over his enemies, answering the petition of Ps. 109. This one is a priest-king who will triumph over his enemies, crushing them under his feet (cf. Gen. 3:15). Jesus Christ fulfills Ps. 109 and Ps. 110,

---

80. So Ps. 106 represents an answer to Moses' petition in Ps. 90. See Zenger, "Fifth Book of Psalms," 79n8.

81. See ibid., 77–78.

82. Zenger (ibid., 88–89) sees Ps. 107 and Ps. 145 as the framework before the closing psalms, 146–150.

83. In support of taking Pss. 108–110 together, see ibid., 89–91.

for his enemies betrayed him and killed him, but the Lord raised him from the dead and seated him at his right hand as the priest-king. The promise of the new exodus and final salvation will be realized through him.

Psalm 111 praises the Lord for his saving work, particularly remembering the exodus, which surely functions as an anticipation for the days to come. Indeed, it could be argued that the praise songs that predominate after Ps. 110 are a response to the salvation promised through the Davidic king in Ps. 110.[84] Psalm 111 also has a wisdom theme, for the psalmist notes that "the fear of the LORD is the beginning of wisdom" (111:10). Those who live righteously, who fear the Lord and keep his commands, will be rewarded (Ps. 112).

Psalms 113–118 are often referred to as the Hallel psalms, sung by Israel on the night of Passover. Psalm 113 is a beautiful song of praise. "Blessed be the name of the LORD from this time forth and forevermore! From the rising of the sun to its setting, the name of the LORD is to be praised!" (113:2–3). The transcendent Lord also cares for his people, raising them from the dust and promising them rule. The supreme example of raising Israel from the ash heap is the exodus (Ps. 114). "Judah became his sanctuary, Israel his dominion" (114:2). The God who rescued Israel in the past will have mercy on them again. Israel can be confident of future deliverance, for they worship the one true God, to whom belongs all the glory, instead of idols (Ps. 115). Therefore, Israel is summoned to trust in the Lord. Psalm 116 is a psalm of individual praise, for one who was near death was rescued by the Lord, for as Ps. 115:17 says, "The dead do not praise the Lord." Because of such deliverance from death, the psalmist gives thanks to the Lord and pays his vows "in the courts of the house of the LORD, in your midst, O Jerusalem" (116:19). Jesus sang these psalms with his disciples on Passover eve, and he surely saw in Ps. 116 a promise that God would raise him from the dead and would deal bountifully with him.

Psalm 117 calls upon all nations to praise the Lord because of his steadfast love and covenant faithfulness. In Ps. 118 the psalmist praises the Lord for his steadfast love when he encountered enemies trying to destroy him with an intense onslaught. The psalmist bursts forth in praise for his victory, rejoicing because "I shall not die, but I shall live" (118:17). The nations rejected this Davidic leader, but the Lord had established him as the cornerstone of the building. The NT sees this psalm as fulfilled in Jesus Christ. Although his contemporaries rejected him as the builder of God's new temple, God raised him from the dead and made him the cornerstone of the entire building. The people of God now take their shape from Jesus Christ as Messiah and Lord (cf. Matt. 21:42–43 pars.; Acts 4:11; Eph. 2:20–21; 1 Pet. 2:6–8).

84. So Zenger, "Fifth Book of Psalms," 91; J. Kim, "Royal Psalms," 155.

Psalm 119 is a sustained meditation upon the joy of keeping God's law and a prayer that the psalmist will be empowered to do so.[85] It fits nicely with themes found in Ps. 1 and Ps. 19:7–14. Erich Zenger maintains that Ps. 119 "is a prayer for a life according to Torah which is a precondition for the advent of the universal reign of the God of the Exodus and of Zion celebrated in the fifth book of psalms."[86] Such a theme fits with what we have seen elsewhere in the Psalter. The Lord's reign over the world will become a reality when a king arises who observes the Torah.[87] The NT, of course, finds Jesus Christ to be the fulfillment of this theme.[88]

Psalms 120–134 are collected together as the Psalms of Ascent. Thus, these psalms consider a pilgrimage to the temple, where a journey is made to enter the presence of the Lord—Mount Zion—with the congregation.[89] "These pilgrimage songs are probably placed here to show that the reason for return from exile is to go up to Mount Zion to hear the Torah in all its wonder and to worship the Lord."[90] It is in Zion where the Lord dwells with his people, blessing and protecting them. "The joy of the occasion of going to God's house was well-founded. The pilgrims' experience of the temple was all-encompassing. It saturated the psalmists' senses with all kinds of wonders, abundant food and incense, music and singing, gold and silver, palm trees, water, and cherubim. This joyful experience was an experience of both awe and holiness in the presence of God."[91] Philip Satterthwaite argues that the theme of the mini-collection is the restoration of Zion.[92] In terms of the canon, these psalms anticipate the end of redemptive history, where the Lord will dwell with his people in the new Jerusalem, the heavenly city.

The first of the Psalms of Ascent (Ps. 120) laments life outside of the people of God, life away from the temple. Jerusalem is a place of peace, but those outside of it live for war and will face judgment. Probably the hills in Ps. 121 refer to Mount Zion, reflecting the theology of 1 Kings 8. The Lord will grant help from Mount Zion and will protect his people from all evil. Psalm 122 reflects on the joy of traveling to the Lord's house and to

85. For links between Ps. 118 and Ps. 119, see Grant, *King as Exemplar*, 175–80.
86. Zenger, "Fifth Book of Psalms," 98.
87. See Mays, "Torah-Psalms in the Psalter," 11.
88. The NT reading fits with Zenger's reading of Book 5, where he sees "an eschatological-messianic perspective" ("Fifth Book of Psalms," 98), though Zenger does not emphasize the Messiah to the same degree that I do.
89. For a helpful entrée to the Psalms of Ascent, see Mays, *Psalms*, 385–87.
90. Dempster, *Dominion and Dynasty*, 200. See also Satterthwaite, "Songs of Ascents," 114–15.
91. M. Smith, "Book for Pilgrims," 162.
92. Satterthwaite, "Songs of Ascents," 107.

Jerusalem.[93] The Lord exercises his rule over the earth through the house of David in Jerusalem. Jerusalem represents the place of God's presence and his rule over the world, so peace on earth will come only through Jerusalem. From the NT perspective, such peace has been realized through Jesus of Nazareth, who reigns over the new Jerusalem, the heavenly city, and brings peace to his people.

Satterthwaite argues that Ps. 123 returns to the themes of Ps. 120, "sounding a note of alienation, of hostility which has to be endured."[94] The enthronement of the Lord in the temple reflects a greater reality: his enthronement in the heavens (Ps. 123:1). The psalmist pleads with the Lord, asking him to show mercy to Israel. The theme of hostility against Israel continues in Ps. 124.[95] Indeed, the Lord, as Ps. 124 confesses, has shown mercy to Israel, for if he had not, Israel would have been swallowed up and destroyed by the nations; but the maker of "heaven and earth" has helped his people (124:8). Psalm 125 sounds out themes that are similar to Ps. 124. Mount Zion, where the Lord dwells, is immovable and impregnable. So too, those who trust in the Lord will never be defeated. The "scepter of wickedness" (125:3) will never reign over those who are righteous, and so Israel may be confident of final victory.

The promise of Ps. 125 is confirmed by Ps. 126. When Israel was in exile, far from Zion, they longed for the day when they would be restored to the land. The day of restoration was so delightful that it was like dreaming. The psalmist prays that just as Yahweh delivered Israel in the past and made it glad, he will do so again in the current generation.[96] Indeed, Israel cannot accomplish its own salvation; the house must be built by the Lord (Ps. 127). He must provide the children to protect the city, which includes the building of the temple as well, fitting with the restoration theme of the Psalms of Ascent.[97] Psalm 128 recounts the joy and peace of those blessed by the Lord from Zion.

Israel has often been the subject of oppression and attack, but the Lord has defeated and will ultimately defeat the wicked (Ps. 129). What is Israel's fundamental need? Forgiveness of sins. Therefore, the psalmist prays that the Lord will pardon Israel for its iniquities and show mercy to his people (Ps. 130) and restore Israel.[98] Israel must hope in the Lord, trusting him for final

93. Satterthwaite (ibid., 118) sees Ps. 122 as the "climax" of Pss. 120–122.
94. Ibid., 119.
95. Ibid., 120.
96. See ibid., 122.
97. Dempster (*Dominion and Dynasty*, 201) rightly argues that the house here is not just individual but relates to the Davidic dynasty and the temple. So also Satterthwaite, "Songs of Ascents," 115.
98. Satterthwaite ("Songs of Ascents," 124–25) rightly argues that forgiveness and redemption are requested so that Israel would be restored.

redemption. Such hope is described in Ps. 131 as the trust and peace that a weaned child has with his or her mother (Ps. 131).

Israel's hope for forgiveness of sins and future restoration comes from the covenant made with David, where the Lord promised him an eternal dynasty (Ps. 132). The rule of the Davidic king will come from "Zion," the Lord's "dwelling place" (132:13). Ultimately, Jesus is the "horn" that will "sprout for David," and he is the one who kept God's "covenant" and "testimonies" (132:12) so that the promises made to David become a reality through him. The praise that marks Book 5 is due to the promise that Yahweh will fulfill his covenant with David for the sake of the whole world. Psalm 133 celebrates the unity of the people of God and the refreshment that such unity brings. That unity is found through the priesthood of Aaron and worship in the temple in Jerusalem.[99] Psalm 134 represents the end and climax of God's saving work for his people. In the Lord's house they are to bless the Lord's name: "Lift up your hands to the holy place and bless the LORD!" (134:2). The psalmist then prays that this vision for the future will become a reality.[100]

The Psalms of Ascent have concluded, but Ps. 135 continues themes from Ps. 134. The "servants of the LORD" (135:1; cf. 134:1) are to praise the Lord's name "in the courts of the house of the LORD" (135:2; cf. 134:1). The psalmist celebrates that the God who created all things elected and redeemed Israel, and hence Israel must praise him. Psalm 136 runs along the same arteries, where a refrain praises the Lord for his steadfast love and for his mercies shown in both creation and redemption. Psalm 137 reflects on Israel's experience in Babylon, where they were absent from Zion and Jerusalem and were cast down with sorrow. The psalmist concludes by asking the Lord to take vengeance on Edom and Babylon. The Lord has not forsaken Israel in Babylon. Psalm 138 records a song of David in which he praises the Lord for rescuing him from his enemies and for preserving his life. Just as the Lord preserved David, he will fulfill his purpose for Israel.[101] How does Ps. 139 fit with Ps. 138? Here the psalmist stands astonished at the Lord's majesty. He knows everything that happens to a person before it occurs (139:1–6), and never forsakes his own (139:7–12). He is always with his people. No matter how dark the situation, the Lord shines his light in the midst of such darkness and will hold up his own. After all, he is the creator God, who formed each one in the womb

99. See ibid., 126.
100. J. Kim ("Royal Psalms," 155–56) notes that Ps. 132, which emphasizes the fulfillment of the Davidic covenant, is followed by doxological psalms. He also thinks that Ps. 133 intervenes because it shares the theme of Zion with Pss. 132; 134 (p. 156).
101. So Ps. 138 may function as an answer to the problem in Ps. 137 (Zenger, "Fifth Book of Psalms," 96).

of his or her mother (139:13–18). Since the Lord guards his people with his knowledge and presence, they can be assured that he will fulfill his purpose for Israel. If he cares for each person so intimately, he also cares for Israel as a whole. The hatred for enemies, then, reflects God's perspective on those opposed to him (139:19–22). The psalmist prays that he will continue to walk in God's way (139:23–24).

David prays, as the anointed king, for deliverance from enemies in both Ps. 140 and Ps. 141. His enemies are children of the serpent (140:3; cf. Gen. 3:15), but they will be defeated, and "the righteous shall give thanks to your name; the upright shall dwell in your presence" (140:13). David prays for deliverance and mercy in Ps. 142, for he is utterly alone and abandoned. The Lord is his only refuge, and he is confident that God "will deal bountifully with me" (142:7). Psalm 143 follows in the same train as the previous psalms. David pleads for mercy and deliverance. He acknowledges and confesses his sin (143:2), asking God to "preserve" him "for your name's sake" and "in your righteousness" (143:11). Victory will come only through the forgiveness of sins. Israel is not righteous enough to enjoy salvation.

Human life, Ps. 144 attests, is brief, and since human beings are ephemeral and weak, David's reign and triumphs come from the Lord. He asks, as the Davidic king, that the Lord will bless Israel. Jinkyu Kim argues that Ps. 144 as a messianic psalm is followed, as was the case in Ps. 110 and Ps. 132 (also messianic psalms), with doxological psalms.[102] Seeing Yahweh conquer his enemies and vindicate his people through a son of David evokes praise, as the people see the King in his beauty. Psalm 145 is in some respects quite like Ps. 103, and clearly it is one of the great praise psalms in the Psalter. Yahweh is extolled and praised for his greatness and splendor and mighty works. "They shall pour forth the fame of your abundant goodness and shall sing aloud of your righteousness" (145:7). God's character as disclosed in Exod. 34:6–7 is celebrated here (145:8).[103] The Lord's sovereignty is also featured: "They shall speak of the glory of your kingdom and tell of your power, to make known to the children of man your mighty deeds, and the glorious splendor of your kingdom. Your kingdom is an everlasting kingdom, and your dominion endures throughout all generations" (145:11–13). All depend upon the Lord for life, and "he fulfills the desire of those who fear him" (145:19), whereas the wicked will be destroyed. The kingdom will arise again through a coming son of David, and the Lord will act on behalf of Israel again, particularly by forgiving their sins.

102. J. Kim, "Royal Psalms," 155–57.
103. On the use of Exod. 34:6–7 in the OT, see Hamilton, *God's Glory in Salvation*, 133–37.

The book of Psalms fittingly ends with five psalms of praise (Pss. 146–150). In Ps. 146 Yahweh is praised as the helper of the weak, for he gives sight to the blind and exalts the poor and liberates prisoners. God is praised for his reign, which never ends. In Ps. 147 Yahweh is praised for building up Jerusalem. The one who created the stars also attends to the wounds of the brokenhearted. As the creator of all, he takes pleasure not in the strength of human beings but rather in those who trust him for deliverance. He has shown special favor to Israel in giving them the Torah. The Lord is to be praised exuberantly, according to Ps. 148. All the works of creation—sun, moon, stars, fire, hail, snow—praise the Lord as they carry out God's will. Animals and human beings also bring praise to the Lord. The Lord is praised for his name—his unique character. And Israel also praises him particularly, for a Davidic king—a horn—has been raised up by Yahweh. Israel is to praise God joyfully and should take vengeance on its enemies (Ps. 149). The centrality of Yahweh is confirmed by the emphasis on praise, for praise expresses joy and love for God better than any other activity. Hence, Ps. 150 concludes Book 5, and the Psalter, by calling all of creation to praise Yahweh. Books 1–4 of the Psalter conclude with praise to God, and indeed, the last psalm is devoted entirely to his praise.[104] He is to be praised for his saving love and his intrinsic excellence. Praise is to be expressed with human creativity, with music and instruments that redound to his glory. All of creation was created to give praise to Yahweh, and so the Psalter ends, "Let everything that has breath praise the LORD! Praise the LORD!" (Ps. 150:6). Book 5 ends with praise, for God will free his people through a Davidic king. The new exodus will become a reality, and Israel will be forgiven their sins.

Conclusion

This study of Psalms seems to confirm the notion that the arrangement of the Psalter is intentional. Books 1–2 focus on David and his reign. Book 3 considers Israel and exile, and Israel wonders if Yahweh will fulfill the promises made to David and restore the people to the land. Books 4–5 answer that question. Yahweh will restore Israel again, and he will raise up for them a new David, which the NT identifies as Jesus of Nazareth. He will save his people by forgiving their sins. The new exodus and the reign of God will not be limited to Israel. God's rule will extend over the entire earth. Book 5 is full of praise to the Lord for his kingdom promises and for his saving faithfulness. From Ps. 1

---

104. So Childs, *Old Testament as Scripture*, 512.

to Ps. 150 Yahweh's faithfulness to his promises is featured. His kingdom will come. The world will be blessed. Yahweh reigns over all, and the world will see the King in his beauty, and they will enjoy Yahweh's presence in his temple, gazing upon and reveling in his loveliness. Praise is the glad response to Yahweh's saving love, showing the God-centered vision of the book of Psalms.

16

PROVERBS

Introduction

With the book of Proverbs, we return to Wisdom literature. Proverbs does not have a narrative framework but rather sets forth, mainly in maxims and proverbial statements, the way of wisdom. As von Rad remarks, "No one would be able to live even for a single day without incurring appreciable harm if he could not be guided by wide practical experience."[1] Bruce Waltke says, "The possession of wisdom enables humans to cope with life."[2] James Crenshaw says, "The goal of wisdom was the formation of character and to make sense of life's anomalies."[3] Our concern here is not with how the book reached its final composition. It is obvious from the content of the book that different hands played a role in the process: chapters 1–9 consist of discourses; the material in 10:1–22:16 is identified as the proverbs of Solomon; 22:17–24:22 introduces the thirty "sayings of the wise"; 25:1–29:27 relays further proverbs of Solomon copied by Hezekiah's scribes; 30:1–31 contains the words of Agur; 31:1–9 contains the proverbs of King Lemuel; and 31:10–31 concludes the book with a tribute to a noble wife. The theme of the noble wife functions as an inclusio with chapters 1–9, where Woman Wisdom is contrasted with Woman Folly, for the noble wife is one who fears the Lord (31:30) and is wise (31:26).[4] Our concern here is with the final form of Proverbs and the message of the book as a whole. The international character of wisdom is evident, for the proverbs in 22:17–24:22 are derived from, with some adaptations, the wisdom

---

1. Von Rad, *Wisdom in Israel*, 3.
2. Waltke, *Book of Proverbs*, 76–77.
3. Crenshaw, *Old Testament Wisdom*, 4.
4. So Dumbrell, *Faith of Israel*, 263.

of Amenemope (twelfth century BC).⁵ Dependence upon wisdom traditions from other countries has contributed to the view among some scholars that Proverbs reflects secular wisdom, particularly since many of the proverbs relay observations on life and do not seem to reflect a religious standpoint.⁶

For the sake of discussion, I have split Proverbs into the various categories, such as God-centered, wisdom, riches, and speech. It must be acknowledged at the outset that the various categories overlap. For instance, one's speech, riches, poverty, and so forth all relate to God. In the same way, all the categories could be placed under wisdom. In the same way, proverbs about the future in many instances are not clearly differentiated from proverbs about riches and poverty. Still, as long as we acknowledge that the various topics here are rough-hewn, the subjects examined are one way to consider the theology of Proverbs.

God-Centered

Certainly, many proverbs make observations about everyday life without mentioning the Lord and the faith of Israel, nor does Israel's covenant with the Lord receive attention in the book. I will argue here, however, that all of the proverbs, even the seemingly secular ones, are integrated into a Yahwistic framework in the book. Waltke rightly argues that wisdom is not ultimately "within the creation."⁷ The book of Proverbs is not a secular work, for in Israel no realm of life was secular, for "the teachers were completely unaware of any reality not controlled by Yahweh."⁸ Even if Yahweh is not mentioned, there was no arena of life in Israel where he was absent.⁹ Even the prosaic details of life cannot be separated from Yahweh, nor does the book of Proverbs, considered as a whole (in its final canonical form), support a secular/sacred split.¹⁰ "It would be madness to presuppose here some kind of separation, as if in one case the man of objective perception were speaking and in the other the believer in Yahweh."¹¹

5. But as von Rad (*Wisdom in Israel*, 193) notes, the distinctiveness of Israel's faith is indicated by the insertion of trust in Yahweh in 22:19.
6. For a short entry into the issue, see Childs, *Old Testament as Scripture*, 549–50; see also von Rad, *Wisdom in Israel*, 9–10.
7. Waltke, *Book of Proverbs*, 81. His entire discussion on pp. 81–83 supports the notion that wisdom cannot be obtained apart from divine revelation.
8. Von Rad, *Wisdom in Israel*, 64. See also Crenshaw, *Old Testament Wisdom*, 82–83; House, *Old Testament Theology*, 440; Garrett, *Proverbs, Ecclesiastes, Song of Songs*, 54–55.
9. "Sapiential imagination is especially at work in envisioning God, for the sages locate God at the center of their historical and linguistic world of space" (Perdue, *Wisdom and Creation*, 55).
10. See Childs, *Old Testament as Scripture*, 553–56; von Rad, *Wisdom in Israel*, 60–64.
11. Von Rad, *Wisdom in Israel*, 62.

Proverbs belongs to the wisdom tradition in Israel, and the book unpacks what it means to live wisely. Such wisdom, however, must not and cannot be understood in secular terms. The book relays its purpose at the outset: it was written so that readers might gain prudence, wisdom, and insight (1:2–6). But what is fundamental and determinative for wisdom is conveyed by 1:7, "The fear of the LORD is the beginning of knowledge." Indeed, the fear of the Lord plays a central role in the entire book. The fear of the Lord means that he is supreme in one's life, that all of life is ordered by one's relationship with him.[12] The discourses that open the book contrast wisdom with folly (chaps. 1–9). Dumbrell notes that the "fear of the Lord" in 1:7 and 9:10 functions as the framework for the discourses that introduce the book.[13]

What is striking about wisdom is that it is publicly accessible. It "cries aloud in the street" and "raises" its voice "in the markets" (1:20) and speaks "at the entrance of city gates" (1:21). We see from the subsequent verses that wisdom "calls" and stretches out its hands (1:24), imploring the simple to be wise. Those who listen to reproof and accept wisdom's words will have security (1:33). Significantly, those who repudiate wisdom "did not choose the fear of the LORD" (1:29). Wisdom means that one lives rightly (1:8–19), but it is profoundly theological and God-centered, for "the wisdom movement directed its attention to what creation itself implied for human conduct."[14] In some ways, Proverbs can be understood as an unpacking of the fifth commandment, which calls upon children to obey their parents. The father in Proverbs (see the introductory role of chaps. 1–9) urges his son to obey him. But to obey one's parents is to fear the Lord. To follow the instruction of parents is to live under Yahweh's lordship.

The search for wisdom is elaborated in Prov. 2. Those who gain wisdom long for it, cry out for it, and search for it as one searches for silver and gold (2:1–4). And yet those who gain wisdom do not merely have discernment regarding how to live everyday life; true wisdom means that they "understand the fear of the LORD and find the knowledge of God" (2:5). In other words, those who are truly wise both know and fear God, and it is from his mouth that wisdom comes (2:6). Indeed, wisdom should not be separated from Torah.[15] The "commandments" that the father exhorts his son to receive almost certainly

---

12. See ibid., 66–67. I think, however, that von Rad underestimates the emotional dimension of fearing the Lord.

13. Dumbrell, *Faith of Israel*, 265. And House (*Old Testament Theology*, 446) shows how fear of the Lord informs Prov. 10–24.

14. Dumbrell, *Faith of Israel*, 273.

15. See also Schultz, "Unity or Diversity?" 296–98; G. Wilson, "'Words of the Wise,'" 183–89. There are a number of connections to the Decalogue in Exod. 20:1–17 (House, *Old Testament Theology*, 444).

include the commands in the Torah (2:1).[16] In 3:1 the son must recall his father's "teaching" (*tôrâ*), and he must keep his "commandments." The promise of long life (3:2) as a result of obedience reflects the teaching of Torah. The relationship of wisdom to Torah is also reflected in 4:4, 10, where those who keep the father's commands are promised life. Similarly, the Torah promises life to those who keep its statutes (see Lev. 18:5). So also the "commandment" of the father and the "teaching" (*tôrâ*) of the mother are put together in 6:20. The close relationship to the Mosaic Torah is immediately evident, for we find in Deuteronomy the Lord's commands are to be bound "as a sign on your hand, and they shall be as frontlets between your eyes" (Deut. 6:8), while in Proverbs such teaching is to be bound to one's heart and neck (Prov. 6:21).

In Proverbs the instruction of mother and father will speak to the son everywhere he goes: "When you walk, they will lead you; when you lie down, they will watch over you; and when you awake, they will talk with you" (6:22). In Deuteronomy we read, "You shall teach them diligently to your children, and shall talk of them when you sit in your house, and when you walk by the way, and when you lie down, and when you rise" (6:7). Clearly, the proverbial teaching reflects the Torah ideal. The Deuteronomic flavor of Proverbs is also evident in the words "For the commandment is a lamp and the teaching a light, and the reproofs of discipline are the way of life" (6:23). Perhaps chapter 30 is even more explicit, where 30:5–6 shows "that God has already made himself known truthfully in his written word. His self-revelation must be obeyed and not falsified by additions."[17] Waltke rightly says that wisdom to live life successfully requires comprehensive knowledge, and such exhaustive knowledge is available only by revelation.[18]

The same phenomenon crops up in chapter 7. The son is told to keep his father's "words" and to "treasure up my commandments with you" (7:1). But the relationship to Torah is even clearer in 7:2 in the words "keep my commandments and live" (cf. 13:13–14; 19:16; see also Lev. 18:5; Deut. 4:40; 5:33; 8:1, 3; 11:8–9). And the relationship to Deut. 6 is communicated in the words "bind them on your fingers; write them on the tablet of your heart" (7:3). Deuteronomy also emphasizes that the words written on the stony tablets are to be imprinted on Israel's heart (Deut. 6:6; 11:18; 30:14). Several proverbs near the end of the book also underline the importance of keeping the law (28:4, 7, 9). Proverbs 29:18 says, "Blessed is he who keeps the law." Indeed, this verse is quite interesting, for a link is forged between Torah and prophecy, suggesting

16. The book of Sirach (24:1–23) makes the connection between wisdom and Torah explicit.
17. Childs, *Old Testament as Scripture*, 556.
18. Waltke, *Book of Proverbs*, 78–80.

perhaps that the latter is an expansion of the former. To sum up, the parallels adduced here between wisdom and Torah demonstrate that wisdom is not a secular enterprise; rather, it is irrevocably tied to devotion to Yahweh and to the commands revealed in the Torah.

The importance of "the fear of the LORD" is not restricted to the introduction. This phrase occurs quite regularly in the book, punctuating the truth that such fear is fundamental to wisdom.[19] So we read in Prov. 9:10, "The fear of the LORD is the beginning of wisdom, and the knowledge of the Holy One is insight." The word "beginning" here does not bear the idea of a starting point that is left behind. Instead, the fear of the Lord is the origin and fountainhead for all wisdom, and one who pursues wisdom never leaves such fear behind. The fear of the Lord is often tied to life in Proverbs, so that fear of the Lord "prolongs life" (10:27), produces "a fountain of life" (14:27) and "riches and honor and life" (22:4), and "leads to life" (19:23). Such fear also leads to "strong confidence" (14:26), is the heart of wisdom (15:33), causes one to hate and turn away from evil (8:13; 16:6), frees one from envy of the wicked (23:17), and is better than prosperity (15:16).

Nor is the God-centered vision of Proverbs restricted to keeping the Torah or to places where the phrase "fear of the Lord" occurs. One can hardly read the book as a whole and fail to see the theocentric dimension of the work. How tempting it is to fear people, but those who trust in the Lord find safety (29:25; cf. 16:20). Finding a good wife is ultimately a gift from the Lord (18:22; 19:14). Human actions are not carried out on a neutral stage, for the Lord observes all that occurs (15:3, 11; 20:12). Justice, then, accords with the Lord's will, for only "those who seek the LORD" understand what justice is (28:5). Punishment is not merely cause and effect; it stems from a personal God. He tests hearts (17:3) and hates and punishes those who practice evil (11:21; 15:8, 9, 25, 26, 29; 16:5; 17:15; 21:10, 27; 22:12).[20] Moving someone's landmark does not escape God's notice, and he will intervene on behalf of the one cheated (23:10–11).[21] Conversely, those who practice righteousness and justice will be rewarded by the Lord (12:2; 15:29; 16:20; 18:10; 21:3), and the Lord delights in those who pursue goodness (11:20). Those who fear Yahweh are humble (3:34; 11:2; 15:33; 18:12; 22:4), acknowledging that they are not free from sin

19. On this phrase, see ibid., 100–101.
20. See ibid., 74–76.
21. See von Rad, *Wisdom in Israel*, 90–94. He writes, "If experience taught the awareness of orders, then it was teaching ultimate truths, truths about God. Correspondingly, the expression 'inherent laws,' which is sometimes used, can only be employed in a restricted sense. In the long run, it was always Yahweh himself with whom man saw himself confronted, and in him the indirectness of the apparently neutral events was again superseded" (p. 92).

(20:9). Such humility manifests itself in a willingness to confess one's sins and to forsake them (28:13).

Rather striking is the emphasis on the sovereignty of God in Proverbs.[22] Those who fear the Lord and obey him submit to him as ruler and king. His sovereignty has already been touched on, but it should be underscored. We noted above that the Lord punishes the evil and rewards the good, and retribution for those who do evil and blessing for those who practice righteousness can be meted out only by one who is sovereign, by one who rules over history and can dispense justice. God's sovereignty is pervasive and universal, and it is not limited to judgment and reward. He is the king who rules over kings, even controlling the thoughts and inclinations of kings: "The king's heart is a stream of water in the hand of the LORD; he turns it wherever he will" (21:1). The Lord reigns over all human beings because he is the creator (20:12). The life of human beings, in a way that surpasses human comprehension, is planned by the Lord: "A man's steps are from the LORD; how then can man understand his way?" (20:24). Proverbs advocates wisdom and discretion and prudence, but human intelligence can never match or defeat the Lord: "No wisdom, no understanding, no counsel can avail against the LORD. The horse is made ready for the day of battle, but the victory belongs to the LORD" (21:30–31). If the Lord has ordained victory for an army, it will conquer even if its troops and armaments are no match for its adversaries. Given the Lord's sovereign rule, we understand why "the name of the LORD is a strong tower" that gives safety to the righteous (18:10).

The sovereignty of the Lord is ultimate, but Proverbs nicely correlates this with human initiative and choices. Human planning, as all of Proverbs demonstrates, is part of what it means to live wisely. Fools plunge ahead with no forethought or consideration. Thus, human planning and strategizing are commendable (16:1, 9; 19:21). None of these proverbs criticize a careful assessment of future possibilities or the decision to pursue a particular direction. What Proverbs emphasizes, however, is that ultimately what will come to pass is what the Lord decides, not what human beings plan. "God is there precisely in the incalculable element, and at a single stroke which you have scarcely noticed, he has taken the whole affair out of your hands."[23] So, a human being may plan, "but the answer of the tongue is from the LORD" (16:1), and "the LORD directs his steps" (16:9), and it "is the purpose of the LORD that will stand" (19:21).[24] Thus, we are told, "Commit your work to the Lord, and your plans

22. See Waltke, *Book of Proverbs*, 70–71.
23. Von Rad, *Wisdom in Israel*, 100.
24. See ibid., 101.

will be established" (16:3). As human beings, we are quite convinced that we are right and blameless, but the Lord knows all, and he "weighs the spirit" (16:2), revealing what is truly in our hearts. There are no exceptions to the Lord's sovereignty. If he controls the hearts of kings (21:1), the most powerful persons in the ancient world, then he controls the hearts of all. Even those who are evil do not ultimately outfox the Lord, for he "has made everything for its purpose, even the wicked for the day of trouble" (16:4).[25] Indeed, the smallest things in life, even the seemingly random events—that is, so-called secular events, such as how the casting of a lot turns out—are determined by the Lord (16:33).

Von Rad nicely summarizes the stance of wisdom: "Do not hesitate to summon up all your powers in order to familiarize yourself with all the rules which might somehow be effective in life. Ignorance in any form will be detrimental to you; only the 'fool' thinks he can shut his eyes to this. Experience, on the other hand, teaches that you can never be certain. You must always remain open for a completely new experience. You will never really become wise, for in the last resort, this life of yours is determined not by rules but by God."[26]

Wisdom

Proverbs is fundamentally about wisdom, and wisdom, as we have seen, is God-centered, focusing on fear of the Lord. Wisdom means living under his sovereign rule in the particulars of daily life. Hence, as was noted above, all the topics discussed here could be placed under wisdom. The contrast between wisdom and folly takes center stage from the beginning of Proverbs. As noted above, wisdom is in the public venue, calling people to submit to its authority (1:20–33). "Wisdom goes in search of people in their customary pursuits and offers them instruction for life so that their various activities, from marriage to business deals," may assist them "to live in harmony with the world and experience success."[27] The public character of wisdom is picked up again in 8:1–5, for wisdom calls out to all. Both Woman Wisdom and Woman Folly (chap. 9) have prepared a feast, inviting all and sundry to come and partake of what they have prepared. Lady Wisdom is not a hard taskmaster, for she invites the simple and foolish to become wise, to attend to what she teaches. Those who pay heed to wisdom will enjoy a long life (9:11), while those who turn aside to folly will end up in Sheol (9:18).

Dame Folly is closely connected in these introductory chapters with turning aside to apostasy, to having sexual relations with a prostitute (2:16–19;

25. On this verse, see Perdue, *Wisdom and Creation*, 106–7.
26. Von Rad, *Wisdom in Israel*, 106.
27. Dumbrell, *Faith of Israel*, 270.

5:1–23; 6:24–35; 7:1–27).[28] The one who has wisdom as a "sister" (7:4) and calls out to wisdom (2:3) will not be seduced by the sexual pretensions of a forbidden woman who promises deliciously ecstatic delights (5:3, 20; 6:24–25; 7:10, 16–18). Adultery forsakes the covenant made with God (2:17) and is suicidal, for it leads to death and destruction (2:18–19; 5:4–5, 11, 14; 6:27–29, 32–33; 7:22–23, 26–27). Therefore, one must "not desire her beauty in your heart" and must not be won over by "her eyelashes" (6:25).[29] Instead, one must "drink water from your own cistern" (5:15) and "rejoice in the wife of your youth" (5:18). One must be captured by one's wife's beauty, "a lovely deer, a graceful doe. Let her breasts fill you at all times with delight; be intoxicated always in her love" (5:19). Proverbs does not denounce sexual pleasures but rather embraces them within the confines of marriage.[30] Sexual desire must be channeled within the riverbanks of marriage. Being entranced with one's wife versus falling prey to an adulteress illustrates paying heed to wisdom or to folly. Those who turn aside to an adulteress testify to their utter folly, to their refusal to pay attention to the clarion call of wisdom in the public square.

What it means to be a fool is to refuse to listen to correction, to be fanatically insistent on living on the basis of one's own wisdom instead of trusting in the Lord (3:5–6). Turning aside to folly is truly a kind of insanity because it is inherently destructive. The delights that attend following wisdom stagger us because they promise joys never-ending. "Blessed is the one who finds wisdom, and the one who gets understanding, for the gain from her is better than gain from silver and her profit better than gold. She is more precious than jewels, and nothing you desire can compare with her. Long life is in her right hand; in her left hand are riches and honor. Her ways are ways of pleasantness, and all her paths are peace. She is a tree of life to those who lay hold of her; those who hold her fast are called blessed" (3:13–18).

Heeding Dame Folly can only be explained in terms of stubbornness and blindness, for fools or "scoffers" (lēṣîm [1:22; 3:34]) or the "simple" (pĕtāyim [1:22]) are enshrouded in darkness (4:19) though they have great dreams for the future (17:24).[31] They are convinced of their own intelligence (26:12; 28:26) and the rightness of their path (12:15), and they refuse to heed correction from their parents (15:5) or from anyone else (1:7, 22; 9:7; 15:12). And so they only

28. Waltke says that the woman portrayed is a prostitute in that she has "no intention of a binding or enduring relationship" (Book of Proverbs, 124). See his entire discussion of the matter (pp. 119–25).
29. See Crenshaw, Old Testament Wisdom, 14, 78–79.
30. Here we can compare Proverbs to Song of Songs.
31. Various words are used to describe the fool: "evil" (rāšāʿ), "stupid" (kĕsîl), "fool" (ʾĕwîl), "sinner" (ḥāṭāʾ). I do not intend to delve into the differences between these terms here, though I note below that the "simple" are amenable to change, while fools are not.

like to air their own opinions instead of learning from others (18:2). Their mouths gush "folly" (15:2, 14; cf. 10:21). Folly and evil are entertaining to the deluded (10:23; 15:21), and they ridicule godly devotion (14:9) and are full of pride and arrogance (21:24). They are easily ensnared in quarrels (20:3) and are quick to let their annoyance be known (12:16; 14:29; 29:11). Arguments with scoffers and fools are useless (9:8; 13:1; 26:4; 29:9), unless one plays the fool's game in order to expose their folly (26:5), for they do not even listen before giving answers (18:13) and have no category for learning (14:15). A fool ends up ruining his or her own life, all the while blaming God for the downfall: "A person's own folly leads to their ruin, yet their heart rages against the LORD" (19:3 NIV). Being a fool or a scoffer is irremediable.[32] But one who is "simple" can turn from gullibility and can become wise (19:25), if one is willing to listen to Woman Wisdom (1:4; 8:5; 9:4, 6; 19:25; 21:11).[33]

What is fundamental to wisdom is fearing the Lord, and those who listen to and pay heed to Woman Wisdom instead of Woman Folly gain discretion. The importance of listening and learning is apparent in the introductory discourse chapter, where the father repeatedly exhorts his son to listen and be attentive to his teaching (2:1–4; 3:1; 4:1–7, 10, 20–21; 5:1–2; 7:1–2). This is captured nicely in 4:7: "The beginning of wisdom is this: Get wisdom, and whatever you get, get insight." And we read in 19:20, "Listen to advice and accept instruction, that you may gain wisdom in the future" (cf. 13:1; 17:24; 18:15). Those who become wise are humble and teachable.

Wisdom should not be equated with intellectual giftedness or philosophical brilliance. Wisdom expresses itself in the way one lives. Human beings do not have the capacity to acquire wisdom on their own, for that would require ascending to heaven (30:1–4), and thus those who are wise put their trust in the words revealed by God (30:5–6). Here we have another indication that wisdom and Torah are not polarized. Wisdom expresses itself in concrete ways in the warp and woof of life. Those who are wise refrain from anger (29:8), their speech is gracious, and they are faithful in their marriages and diligent in their work.[34]

What is remarkable about wisdom is that it becomes stitched into the character of those who receive it. Wisdom is not merely some external feature that is true of one's life; it is constitutive of one's life and existence. One becomes wise. If one longs for wisdom, "wisdom will come into your heart, and knowledge will be pleasant to your soul" (2:10). Wisdom becomes part of the fabric of one's character. Living wisely is not merely an obligation,

32. See von Rad, *Wisdom in Israel*, 64–65.
33. In defense of the idea that "fools" and "scoffers" are hopeless, while the "simple" can change, see Waltke, *Book of Proverbs*, 111–14.
34. These topics are touched on both above and below.

something that must be done. Wisdom becomes "pleasant," desirable, and attractive. When wisdom becomes an internal reality, "discretion will watch over you, understanding will guard you" (2:11). Wisdom becomes an internal radar that detects and rejects evil. Fools "rejoice in doing evil and delight in the perverseness of evil" (2:14), but the wise find their delight in goodness. Hence, "the integrity of the upright guides them" (11:3), and "righteousness guards him whose way is blameless" (13:6).

What is said here about wisdom is quite similar to the promise of a new covenant in Jer. 31:31–34. The wise have become righteous; they are transformed internally, and so they sense the right course of behavior. It is second nature to them. "Wisdom is pleasure to a man of understanding" (10:23).

Another theme, one that OT scholars have often pointed out, is the relationship of wisdom to creation.[35] The close relationship between wisdom themes and creation is understandable, for many wisdom sayings reflect on the created world, observing what takes place in the world God made.[36] The links between wisdom and creation, as we saw with wisdom and Torah, are another indication that wisdom is integral to OT theology, that it is not segregated from the message of the OT as a whole. The Lord's wisdom in making the world is affirmed: "The LORD by wisdom founded the earth; by understanding he established the heavens; by his knowledge the deeps broke open, and the clouds drop down the dew" (3:19–20). The Lord's wisdom in creation is particularly celebrated in 8:22–31.[37] The wonders of creation are set forth in these verses, and what the writer emphasizes is that wisdom was God's "partner" and "companion" at every step. The complexity and beauty of the created world testify to God's wisdom. Wisdom is publicly available, as we have seen, but it also belongs to God and was his partner, so to speak, in creation.[38]

Wisdom and Speech

Wisdom translates into daily life, showing itself especially in speech.[39] "Rash words are like sword thrusts" that cut and murder others, while "the tongue of the wise brings healing" (12:18). Wise words do not wound and destroy;

35. Wisdom is not a hypostasis but rather a personification (Childs, *Old Testament as Scripture*, 554; Dumbrell, *Faith of Israel*, 271). Wisdom in chapters 1–9, as Waltke (*Book of Proverbs*, 86–87) argues, is virtually equated with the words addressed by the father to the son. This link demonstrates that wisdom is personified, not an actual hypostasis.
36. See Perdue, *Wisdom and Creation*, 35.
37. For an insightful discussion of wisdom in Prov. 8, see von Rad, *Wisdom in Israel*, 149–66.
38. See Dumbrell, *Faith of Israel*, 267.
39. For an excellent study on the effect of words in Proverbs, see Kidner, *Proverbs*, 46–49.

they seek to build up and bring comfort and health to others. The lips of wise persons "feed" others and promote knowledge, giving them sustenance for their earthly sojourn (10:21, 31; 15:7). Fools speak before they think, pouring words out of their mouths like a torrent (29:20), but those who are wise do not believe that authenticity means saying everything on one's mind (21:23). They restrain the impulse to blurt out their thoughts (13:3; 17:27; 29:11). "When words are many, transgression is not lacking, but whoever restrains his lips is prudent" (10:19). The wise listen and ponder before giving a reply (15:28; 18:15). Since fools lack self-restraint, their mouths walk into quarrels (15:18; 18:6). They belittle their neighbors when they should remain silent about the faults of those who live nearby (11:12). Those who are wise keep a promise and do not disclose secrets, but fools find gossip to be delicious and spread abroad slanders about others (11:9, 13; 16:28; 17:9; 18:8). Fools are not truthful in their speech but instead propagate lies (12:22). The wise, however, are honest and gentle in their speech (15:4; 24:26). Instead of speaking aggressively and rudely, they respond to confrontation with grace and judiciousness and hence turn aside wrath (15:1; 16:23, 24; 25:15).

Wisdom and Riches/Poverty[40]

It has often been observed that the book of Proverbs presents a sharp contrast between the rich and the poor, those who work hard and those who are lazy. The former enjoy prosperity, and the latter endure poverty. The proverbs about the rich and the poor are, of course, generalizations, and so they must not be interpreted as if there are no exceptions. Many proverbs represent maxims that apply in some circumstances but should not be understood to apply to every situation. In reading proverbs about riches and poverty, we clearly see that a diversity of situations is addressed.[41] No single proverb about riches and poverty can handle the complexities of life.[42] Childs wisely comments on the role of proverbs: "The significance of the proverb does not lie in its formulation of timeless truths, but in the ability of the wise man to use the proverb in discerning the proper context by which to illuminate the human situation."[43] The depth and breadth relative to poverty is evident from the many proverbs on the topic.

40. See the discussion in Perdue, *Wisdom and Creation*, 113–15; also important is Van Leeuwen, "Wealth and Poverty."
41. For a helpful and rounded discussion of poverty in the OT, see C. Wright, *Old Testament Ethics*, 168–80, which shows that much poverty is attributed to oppression in the OT.
42. See von Rad, *Wisdom in Israel*, 126; House, *Old Testament Theology*, 448.
43. Childs, *Old Testament as Scripture*, 557.

Some people are poor because of laziness, and sluggards are described with dark humor.[44] They make wild excuses: they cannot go outside because there are lions in the street (22:13; 26:13). They are so lacking in initiative that they cannot summon up the energy to feed themselves (12:27; 19:24; 26:15). Instead of learning from the ant about planning and industry, they yearn for more sleep (6:6–11; 19:15; 20:13; 24:30–34; 26:14), and so they do not work at harvest time (20:4). They have a craving for many things but do nothing productive to satisfy their desires (12:11; 13:4; 21:17, 25–26; 28:19); instead, they satisfy their gluttonous desires when they should be laboring (10:4; 23:20–21). Everything is an obstacle to them instead of an opportunity (15:19), and they constantly beg others for help (30:15) but are unwilling to help others (28:22). Sluggards may think they do not cause any harm, but their failure to work impoverishes themselves and others (18:9). Clearly, according to Proverbs, some are poor because of their laziness and unwillingness to invest themselves in work.

Often those who are rich have prospered because of their hard work and discipline. God gave human beings an appetite to provoke them to work (16:26). Instead of frittering away their time, they labor for the harvest (10:5; 12:11, 27; 28:19), investing time, energy, and forethought in their work (27:23–27). They do not attempt to gain wealth through get-rich-quick schemes; instead, patiently and slowly they increase their wealth by laboring day after day (20:21; 21:5). Investing in the future is not considered to be greedy; rather, it constitutes evidence of wisdom and thoughtfulness. It is common sense to complete needed work outside before one works on one's house (24:27). The rich do not hoard money (22:9) or charge interest to improve their financial standing (28:8); they give generously to the poor. Riches are not viewed from a secular perspective, as if all those who work hard will certainly become rich. One must work hard to prosper, but it is ultimately the Lord's blessing if one becomes rich, a gift from his hand (10:22). Hence, one must not place one's trust in riches (11:28).

Proverbs does not commend a mechanistic view of life, as if gaining riches is necessarily a sign of the Lord's favor.[45] Some proverbs comment on the security that comes from riches. The rich enjoy life (15:6) and have power over the poor (22:7), their riches are their "strong city" (10:15; 18:11), bringing friends (19:4) and guaranteeing an inheritance for the future (13:22). Such observations do not necessarily mean that riches are automatically a boon. Indeed, anyone who "trusts in his riches will fall" (11:28). The book of Proverbs recognizes that some who are rich gain their wealth unrighteously. For instance, bribes

---

44. See the excellent little vignette on the sluggard in Kidner, *Proverbs*, 42–43.

45. Goldingay (*Israel's Life*, 483) rightly remarks that the view of wealth in Proverbs is "complex," and thus simplistic construals of what Proverbs says about riches and poverty must be rejected (see also p. 488).

may help a person get ahead (17:8; 18:16; 21:14), but the end does not justify the means, for accepting a bribe "pervert[s] the way of justice" (17:23). One may become rich by robbing the poor (22:22), by financial chicanery (16:11), or by oppressing the poor in order to gain more wealth (11:26; 22:16). One's riches do not guarantee security when a day of judgment arrives (11:4). Some have read the book of Proverbs as if it teaches that those who are wealthy enjoy the Lord's favor. Such a reading is superficial because the book also recognizes that the rich may have come upon their wealth unscrupulously, or they may wrongly trust in their wealth.

Along the same lines, those who are poor are not necessarily sluggards and lazy. Proverbs should not be read as if it endorses a one-dimensional view of poverty and riches. We must beware of selectively citing a few proverbs to establish a case, for the book of Proverbs represents observations that capture a slice of life but do not claim to represent exhaustively all of reality. Some of those who are poor are such because of laziness, and yet such a judgment is not a complete picture. The poor may suffer from want because of oppression (14:31), and the possibility of prosperity may be "swept away through injustice" (13:23). "There are those whose teeth are swords, whose fangs are knives, to devour the poor from off the earth, the needy from among mankind" (30:14). Those who mock the poor actually mock God, who created both the rich and the poor (17:5; 22:2). "A righteous man knows the rights of the poor; a wicked man does not understand such knowledge" (29:7). The rich are in danger of thinking that they are more godly than the poor simply because they have been blessed with abundance. One may remain poor and live a life of integrity in contrast to one who is rich but crooked (28:6). "Better is a poor person who walks in his integrity than one who is crooked in speech and is a fool" (19:1). A "poor man is better than a liar" (19:22). A poor person may be more righteous than the rich. "A rich man is wise in his own eyes, but a poor man who has understanding will find him out" (28:11), though even the poor may mistreat others who are poor (28:3). Indeed, those who are poor may enjoy more happiness than the rich. One may fear the Lord and have little to live on, while others may be prosperous but live in a house full of strife and hatred (15:16–17; 17:1). "Better is a little with righteousness than great revenues with injustice" (16:8). The rich must not think that the poor deserve their fate, but instead should give generously to assist them (22:9; 28:27).

The book of Proverbs, then, conveys a balanced perspective on riches and poverty, the wealthy and the indigent. It recognizes that those who are wealthy often gain riches because of their hard work and discipline, while the poor may be so because of laziness and unwillingness to work. However, riches may be gained through injustice, and those who are poor may be victims of oppression or difficult circumstances. Hence, deriding the poor constitutes a defiance of God as creator. Those who are financially prosperous should be eager to assist the poor. Wealth is not celebrated as the greatest good in Proverbs; it is better to fear the Lord and to pursue wisdom. The stance of Proverbs on wealth is captured well in 23:4–5: "Do not toil to acquire wealth; be discerning enough to desist. When your eyes light on it, it is gone, for suddenly it sprouts wings, flying like an eagle toward heaven." Wealth is a blessing from God, but one must not pursue it ardently, for it is temporary and evanescent. Perhaps the prayer in 30:7–9 best captures the stance toward riches and poverty in Proverbs: "Two things I ask of you; deny them not to me before I die: Remove far from me falsehood and lying; give me neither poverty nor riches; feed me with the food that is needful for me, lest I be full and deny you and say, 'Who is the LORD?' or lest I be poor and steal and profane the name of my God." Too much wealth may lead to self-satisfaction, so that one ceases to trust in the Lord and relies on riches instead. Conversely, extreme poverty may have a similar effect, causing one to become desperate and turn to sin to support oneself.

The King

Many topics in Proverbs could be investigated, but what it says about kings is instructive for understanding the book. In some contexts the king is portrayed as a paragon of righteousness. A cluster of proverbs in chapter 16 illustrates the point. "An oracle is on the lips of a king; his mouth does not sin in judgment" (16:10). Clearly, an ideal king is in view here, one who pursues the way of righteousness and wisdom. Proverbs 16:12–13 is quite similar: "It is an abomination to kings to do evil, for the throne is established by righteousness. Righteous lips are the delight of a king, and he loves him who speaks what is right." We immediately think of exceptions to what is found here, but the proverbs address a situation where the king is righteous, where evil is detestable, and truth and integrity are celebrated. We must think along the same lines when we read, "A king's wrath is a messenger of death, and a wise man will appease it. In the light of a king's face there is life, and his favor is like the clouds that bring the spring rain" (16:14–15; cf. 19:12; 20:2). Since authority is so often exploited for evil ends, the wrath of the king may not summon up thoughts of beauty and truth. The writer, however, clearly thinks of wrath that is justified and righteous.

Righteous kings are also in view in 20:8: "A king who sits on the throne of judgment winnows all evil with his eyes" (cf. 20:26; 25:5). We may respond to a proverb such as this by thinking, "Where is the king who does this?" But the writer thinks of the ideal king, for the king's responsibility is to enforce justice, and hence a wise person lives to please the king, for his approbation represents the favor of the righteous. Therefore, "He who loves purity of heart, and whose speech is gracious, will have the king as his friend" (22:11). It follows, then, that those who truly fear the Lord, who walk in the way of wisdom, will also fear the king. "My son, fear the LORD and the king" (24:21). It is remarkable how closely aligned the king is with Yahweh here, and this is apparent in other proverbs as well. "It is the glory of God to conceal things, but the glory of kings is to search things out" (25:2). Kings have almost a godlike ability to unearth what God has hidden. The godlike stature of the king is also apparent in another proverb: "As the heavens for height, and the earth for depth, so the heart of kings is unsearchable" (25:3). Elsewhere what is unsearchable is ascribed to God (Job 5:9; 9:10; Ps. 145:3; Isa. 40:28), and here the heart of the king is put in the same category. It seems that no ordinary king is in view. The proverbs in the book are mainly ascribed to King Solomon (1:1; 10:1; 25:1). No human king fulfills the ideal king described here, for all kings, to one extent or another, practice injustice. If Proverbs is viewed from a canonical perspective, the ideal picture of the king points to a future king—a king who fulfills the promise of the covenant with David. The righteousness, wisdom, and godlike stature of the king point to Jesus of Nazareth. The righteousness and wisdom and godly rule described in Proverbs are fulfilled in Jesus Christ.

It must also be pointed out that the book of Proverbs recognizes that kings may do what is evil. Some might suspect that Solomon, being a king, wrote only positive things about kings, or that the final editor of the book excluded any negative perspectives on kings. We read in 29:12, however, "If a ruler listens to falsehood, all his officials will be wicked." Here is a clear acknowledgment that leaders may turn to evil, and that such a turn will have deleterious consequences for the kingdom as a whole. Along the same lines, we read, "By justice a king builds up the land, but he who exacts gifts tears it down" (29:4). The issue facing kings is whether they will follow justice or evil. If they choose the latter course, their kingdom will implode. Similarly, "If a king faithfully judges the poor, his throne will be established forever" (29:14). The possibility that a king will not fulfill this injunction, that he would mistreat the poor and thereby undermine his dynasty, is implicit in the proverb. In the same way, "A wise king winnows the wicked and drives the wheel over them" (20:26). Again, there is the suggestion by implication that not all kings are wise, that some, instead of judging the wicked, promote those who are evil to positions of leadership. Other verses are more explicit. "Like a roaring lion or a charging bear is a wicked ruler over a poor people. A ruler who lacks understanding is a cruel oppressor, but he who hates unjust gain will prolong his days" (28:15–16). Some rulers are like rapacious animals, savaging their people instead of nurturing them. King Lemuel's mother admonished him about the course that should be pursued by kings (31:1–9). They are to uphold "the rights of all the afflicted" (31:5) and "defend the rights of the poor and needy" (31:9). But if kings live a dissolute life and pursue pleasure, they will abandon their stewardship over the people and abuse them instead of treating them justly.

Wise Observations about Life

Many proverbs simply make wise observations about life. This does not mean that Proverbs is a secular book disconnected from the lordship of Yahweh. Indeed, such reflections on life are tied to creation—the world Yahweh has made. There was no sacred/secular split in Israel. What was observed in daily life was inseparably connected with the world Yahweh had formed, for wisdom draws on creation traditions. It is regularly acknowledged today that there is no such thing as neutral observation, that our perspectives on life are shaped and constrained by our worldview. So too in Proverbs. The maxims are not just neutral reflections on life. They contain as well an implicit exhortation, pointing to a way to live wisely in the world.

Often observations are made about life to provoke readers to acquire wisdom. A person who first defends a case seems to be completely right, until one hears the other side (18:17). People claim to be faithful and loyal, but actually that quality is quite rare (20:6). Visiting a neighbor too often may cause that person to hate you (25:17). When dickering over the price of an item for sale, a buyer may claim that it is worthless, but then, after buying it, brags about the purchase (20:14). Those who are blessed with skill and expertise in their work will receive honor and fame for their work (22:29). Only the heart of a person knows its joy or grief (14:10), and even those who are laughing may be covering up sorrow that stabs the heart (14:13). A desire that fails to materialize may cause one to become heartsick, whereas a desire fulfilled is like a "tree of life" (13:12). Those who are cheerful enjoy life because of their positive attitude (15:15), and their joy gives them strength to endure sickness and adversity (17:22; 18:14). Giving an apt answer to help another brings great joy (15:23), for a good word may bring comfort to those who are anxious (12:25; cf. 15:30). Alternatively, singing glad songs when another is grieving violates love (25:20). Those who pursue plans without seeking counsel often fail because they did not seek out wisdom (11:14; 15:22; 20:18). The poor must be diplomatic in social contexts, but the rich can get away with answering rudely (18:23). Someone who has no oxen is spared the effort of cleaning up a manger, but at the same time one loses the benefit of "the abundant crops" that come from having an ox to work the land (14:4). One must weigh costs and benefits in every situation. Those who make friends with the wise become wise themselves (13:20). If one thinks wisely about life, one can avoid much trouble. For example, people should not meddle in the quarrels of others (26:17), nor should anyone deceive a neighbor and then claim that it was a joke (26:18–19). Similarly, strife and quarrels will die out if there is no gossip to feed them (26:20–21).

Other observations clearly stem from a God-centered worldview. One can even see in children whether they are "pure and upright" (20:11). Righteousness leads to the prosperity of a nation, but sin brings reproach (14:34). Envy consumes a person and is inherently self-destructive (14:30). Some human beings are blessed with a supreme confidence in their ethical probity, when in fact they are defiled by evil (30:12). Those who boast in their own intellectual abilities are actually fools (26:12). An adulteress, for instance, may defend her conduct with an aplomb that is unnerving (30:20). So too, a woman may be beautiful, but if she lacks "discretion," her beauty is tarnished (11:22). It has often been noted, "Pride goes before destruction, and a haughty spirit before a fall" (16:18; cf. 18:12). Often, a person whose life disintegrates because of bad choices or behaviors blames others: "When a man's folly brings his way to ruin, his heart rages against the LORD" (19:3). Living in the desert is preferable to marriage to a wife who constantly quarrels (21:19; cf. 21:9; 25:24). Surely, the converse is true. A woman married to a cantankerous and angry man suffers daily.

The Future

What it means to be wise is to consider the future, and those who live wisely will be rewarded, and the consequences will be pleasing. Proverbs "never criticizes man's search for happiness and fulfillment. . . . It simply presupposes this search as a fact. . . . This desire to survive without coming to grief . . . is planted deep within man and is accepted without question."[46] Since proverbs are generalizations and not promises, there certainly will be exceptions to what is observed, for proverbs relay what *typically* occurs. Decisions in life have consequences, and there are rewards for those who pursue wisdom and righteousness. "The reward for humility and fear of the LORD is riches and

46. Von Rad, *Wisdom in Israel*, 81.

honor and life" (22:4). Those who live righteously will experience good (12:21; cf. 11:31; 12:27). The righteous will be delivered from death and typically will live a long life (3:2; 10:2; cf. 3:16), for they are recompensed on earth for their goodness (11:31), but the wicked will die (12:28; 14:12). The wicked will be forgotten, and their prosperity will be short-lived (10:7, 25; 14:32; 19:16). The righteous will be blessed, but the wicked will be cursed (3:33). And the proud will be humiliated, while the humble will be honored (29:23; cf. 14:14). Those who live righteously will find deliverance, whereas the wicked will suffer the consequences (28:18; cf. 11:8; 14:11; 21:7; 24:16; 28:10). Injustice will lead to "calamity" (22:8; cf. 13:15), and those who curse their parents will find their lamp extinguished (20:20). Those who "fear the LORD and the king" will be preserved, but "disaster" and "ruin" will come upon those who resist their authority (24:21–22). The righteous should not worry and fret about the wicked, "for the evil man has no future; the lamp of the wicked will be put out" (24:20; cf. 13:9). Similarly, for those who obtain wisdom, "there will be a future, and your hope will not be cut off" (24:14); but those who turn to folly will pay for it: "One who wanders from the way of good sense will rest in the assembly of the dead" (21:16). Nor should what happens be viewed as mechanical cause and effect. "The Righteous One observes the house of the wicked; he throws the wicked down to ruin" (21:12). The dire consequences of a life devoted to evil are God's judgment upon the wicked, his personal repayment for their sin. The wicked will experience wrath (11:23).

Interestingly, Proverbs hearkens back to Eden (Gen. 2:9; 3:17, 22, 24) with four references to the "tree of life" (Prov. 3:18; 11:30; 13:12; 15:4).[47] At one level the focus is on earthly life, for "a gentle tongue is a tree of life" (15:4), and even the fulfillment of a desire is said to be a "tree of life" (13:12). But there may also be an intimation here that the life transcends present existence. Hence, those who speak gently experience life that is akin to what is found in paradise, and desires are truly fulfilled in a life which conquers death. Similarly, those who acquire wisdom find it to be a "tree of life" (3:18) and will enjoy "long life" (3:16), suggesting perhaps life beyond this life.

Wisdom says, "Whoever finds me finds life" (8:35). Life is also the fruit of wisdom (11:30). Other texts on death and life are instructive. Wisdom "is your life" (4:13). One who turns aside to an unfaithful woman "sinks down to death" and will not "regain the paths of life" (2:18–19; cf. 5:5–6; 6:26; 7:23). Keeping the father's commands will lead to "length of days and years of life" (3:2; cf. 4:22; 6:23; 10:17; 13:14; 19:16); "the years of your life" will be "many" if one obeys (4:10). So too righteousness leads to life (12:28; 16:31; 21:21). The

47. See Perdue, *Wisdom and Creation*, 82.

fear of the Lord brings great blessing, for by it "your days will be multiplied, and years will be added to your life" (9:11; cf. 10:27; 14:27; 19:23; 22:4). The focus in these texts is on a long life on earth, a fruitful productive life during one's earthly sojourn. Waltke believes that some of the sayings refer to "eternal life."[48] In some instances the reference is "to abundant life in fellowship with God, a living relationship that is never envisioned as ending in clinical death in contrast to the wicked's eternal death."[49] He sees an explicit promise of life in the future in 12:28; 14:32.[50] Proverbs 14:32 seems especially significant, for "the righteous finds refuge in his death." And 15:24 seems to promise that the prudent will not experience Sheol.[51] Even if one were to disagree with Waltke,[52] typologically and canonically the NT takes what the OT says about life on earth and applies it to life in the age to come.

The role of the land in the book, though not a major one, is also of interest. Proverbs focuses on the reward or punishment for the individual: "The upright will inhabit the land . . . ; but the wicked will be cut off from the land, and the treacherous will be rooted out of it" (2:22). Similarly, "The righteous will never be removed, but the wicked will not dwell in the land" (10:30). The tree of life and the land in Proverbs both relate to life on earth, to blessing in the here and now. The NT picks up these themes typologically and relates them to an eternal future, to life that never ends.

The "future" ('aḥărît) should also be considered in Proverbs. Those who turn aside to adultery find that the "end" ('aḥărît) "is bitter as wormwood" (5:4; cf. 5:11). The way that seems right to a person may, in the "end" ('aḥărît), lead to death (14:12; 16:25). The same term can be used in a less final sense, as when "the end ['aḥărît] of joy may be grief" (14:13). We are also told that those who pay heed to wisdom will experience a happy future (19:20), which certainly refers to this life but may contain a hint about life to come. Those who fear the Lord are promised, "Surely there is a future, and your hope will not be cut off" (23:18; 24:14). Along the same lines, the righteous are assured that the wicked will not finally prosper: "The evil man has no future; the lamp of the wicked will be put out" (24:20). In some contexts, then, the "future" ('aḥărît) seems to be similar to "the tree of life" and "the land," pointing to the reward in this life that belongs to those who pursue wisdom, but once again the NT moves the theme into another sphere, seeing a reward or repayment that lasts forever.

48. Waltke, Book of Proverbs, 105.
49. Ibid.
50. Ibid., 106.
51. Ibid., 634.
52. Most OT scholars do not see a hope beyond the grave in Proverbs. For a middle position, more restrained than Waltke's but one that sees a hint of future life, see Kidner, Proverbs, 54–55.

The New Testament and the Book of Proverbs

Here I sketch in briefly the relationship of Proverbs to the final and definitive revelation in Jesus Christ.[53] What is personified as wisdom in Proverbs reaches its fullest and final fulfillment in Jesus Christ. Wisdom does not represent Christ in 8:22, for it is pictured as something created. But typology always involves escalation, so that Christ fulfills and exceeds what is said about wisdom in Proverbs, since he is the wisdom of God (1 Cor. 1:24, 30; cf. Col. 2:3) and is wiser than Solomon (Matt. 12:42). Proverbs emphasizes that consequences stream from what we do, whether good or evil. The earthly riches in Proverbs point to spiritual riches in Christ—to every spiritual blessing in the heavenly places (Eph. 1:3). Also in the NT the consequences are eternal. Those who are righteous will enjoy eternal life, whereas the wicked will be judged eternally. We have also seen that Proverbs sometimes refers to the actions and integrity of kings as if they are perfect. Such perfection is found ultimately in Jesus Christ as the king of his people. He is the righteous one who was rewarded for his obedience. He, above all others who ever lived, feared the Lord. He is greater than Solomon, for he will rule the universe with the wisdom of God.

Conclusion

Does Proverbs fit with the theme of God's rule over his people, with the lordship of Yahweh? It certainly does. We have seen above that the wisdom traditions in Proverbs are connected to creation and Torah. Wisdom must not be segregated from what we find elsewhere in the OT. Indeed, the heart and soul of wisdom is the fear of the Lord, which is a major theme in Deuteronomy. Furthermore, we saw a number of links between wisdom and Torah in Proverbs. Those who do not fear Yahweh are not wise; the wise live under Yahweh's lordship. Proverbs unpacks what the fear of the Lord looks like in everyday life, applying wisdom to the practical realities of human existence. But life under Yahweh's lordship is not an abstraction. Fearing the Lord is related to the everyday circumstances of human life. If Psalms emphasizes praising the Lord, Proverbs focuses on fearing him. These are two different perspectives on the same reality. Only those who fear the Lord will praise him, and those who praise him will fear him. Proverbs points to Jesus Christ, who is wiser than Solomon and rules the world with a wisdom greater than his.

53. See Waltke, *Book of Proverbs*, 126–33.

17

ECCLESIASTES

Introduction

Waltke says, "The book of Ecclesiastes is the black sheep of the canon of biblical books. It is the delight of skeptics and the despair of saints."[1] It is typical for scholars to read the message of the book in bleak terms, but Waltke rightly says that "the view that Qoheleth lost faith in God's justice and goodness depends on proof texting and not on interpreting the book holistically."[2] If Proverbs focuses on the regularities of life, Ecclesiastes concentrates on the anomalies. I should add immediately that such a dichotomy between Proverbs and Ecclesiastes is too rigid, for Proverbs, as noted above, has often been interpreted simplistically. A careful reading of Proverbs demonstrates that Solomon and the other proverb writers were well aware that those who worked hard did not always get rich, that the poor were often victims of injustice, and that tragedies struck the righteous and not just the wicked. Nevertheless, the popular perception of Proverbs exists for a reason, for the book often emphasizes that good comes to those who do good. Ecclesiastes gazes at another dimension of reality and reflects on the irrationality and perverseness of life under the sun. Both Proverbs and Ecclesiastes are part of what is called Wisdom literature, but their profoundly different emphases demonstrate that wisdom cannot be captured by a simple formula. Wisdom perceives what ordinarily happens in life, and it attempts to discern and understand the mysteries and injustices of human existence. Ecclesiastes probes the latter. House rightly emphasizes

1. Waltke, *Old Testament Theology*, 946.
2. Ibid., 953. Waltke provides a helpful survey of skeptical approaches (pp. 953–54). For a survey of a variety of interpretations, see Garrett, *Proverbs, Ecclesiastes, Song of Songs*, 271–77.

that Ecclesiastes must be read as part of the canon, noting that apart from the canon a multiplicity of interpretations can be defended, from existentialism to pessimism.[3]

What is striking about Ecclesiastes, as we will see, is the recognition that the injustice and evil that characterize human existence seem to be senseless. Many have understood the book to contradict the message of the remainder of the OT. Typically, the OT forecasts hope and promise for the future, but, it is argued, Ecclesiastes offers no such hope. Instead, none of us know what is coming our way. Life is perplexing, maddening, frustrating, and ultimately inexplicable. I suggest, however, that such a reading of Ecclesiastes should be rejected.[4] What I call the "despairing" interpretation spies out part of what the book teaches, and often it is defended by severing the conclusion of the book from the body. My purpose is not to excavate the history of the composition, for the goal here is to investigate Ecclesiastes as it has come down to us, to explain the final and canonical form of the text. The text as we have it does not contradict what the OT teaches elsewhere. Indeed, the conclusion of the book functions as the hermeneutical lens by which the whole of the book should be read: "The end of the matter; all has been heard. Fear God and keep his commandments, for this is the whole duty of man. For God will bring every deed into judgment, with every secret thing, whether good or evil" (12:13–14). The theme of Ecclesiastes, then, accords with what we have seen in two other wisdom books: Job and Proverbs. The fundamental requirement is to fear God. It "is a dominant note of this book."[5] Ecclesiastes does not depart from the God-centered perspective of Job and Proverbs but rather affirms it. The book does not counsel despair or teach that since life is meaningless under the sun our actions are inconsequential. As House remarks, there are "hints about the afterlife" in the book.[6] Those who interpret Ecclesiastes nihilistically fail to reckon with the framework and perspective provided by the author. They detach the conclusion from the rest of the book, neglecting to see how the conclusion fits with what Ecclesiastes teaches elsewhere.

Ecclesiastes 12:13–14, in other words, is intended to sum up the message of the book. Fearing God is not an abstract reality; it leads to observing his commandments, to doing his will. Ecclesiastes should not be interpreted as if it undermines obedience. Indeed, a future judgment is envisioned where the actions of human beings are assessed, so that those who do good are rewarded

---

3. House, *Old Testament Theology*, 470–71. See also Farmer, *Who Knows What Is Good?*, 6.

4. For a reading that accords with what is argued here, see Garrett, *Proverbs, Ecclesiastes, Song of Songs*, 277–78; Schultz, "Ecclesiastes."

5. Waltke, *Old Testament Theology*, 959.

6. House, *Old Testament Theology*, 480.

and those who do evil are punished.[7] The message of the book, then, is not that life is ultimately absurd and meaningless. Reverence for God is the primary responsibility of human beings, and whether or not one obeys God's commands does make a difference.[8] Indeed, the focus on "commandments" brings Ecclesiastes into the circle of Torah piety[9] and also fits with the teaching of Proverbs, where, as we saw, wisdom and Torah are compatible. Like Proverbs, Ecclesiastes sketches in what it looks like to live under Yahweh's reign. The absurdity of life is not due to events that lie outside God's control. As Roland Murphy says, even if mysterious, "everything happens because of the Lord's action. . . . God is portrayed as intimately involved in all that occurs."[10] And as Daniel Fredericks notes, the Preacher presents "a sovereign, predetermining God who acts in ways fully calculated, yet not calculable."[11] Since God is sovereign and wise, human beings must stand in awe of him and obey him.

I suggest that the conclusion matches the truth of what is taught in the entire work.[12] The book comes from "the Preacher" (12:9, 10; cf. 1:1, 2, 12; 7:27; 12:8),[13] who probably is Solomon, for he is "the son of David, king in Jerusalem" (1:1; cf. 1:12).[14] By referring to Solomon, the book is given authoritative status.[15] The riches, wisdom, and wives clearly point to Solomon (2:4–10), for he "surpassed all who were before in Jerusalem" (2:9). Indeed, no one will ever be richer or wiser than he: "For what can the man do who

7. See Childs, *Old Testament as Scripture*, 588.

8. See Dempster, *Dominion and Dynasty*, 207.

9. "Clearly no sharp distinction between wisdom and law was being suggested by the epilogue" (Childs, *Old Testament as Scripture*, 586).

10. Murphy, *Ecclesiastes*, lxvi. Murphy says that "determinism" is fitting if it "means the sovereign disposition of all things by the divinity. . . . But it is a determinism of an unusual kind because it does not exempt human beings from responsibility. Israel never engaged in any theoretical discussion concerning the reconciliation of these contraries. . . . The OT affirms equally determinism and human responsibility, or in other words, freedom of the will" (pp. lxvi–lxvii). I disagree with Murphy, though, when he says that there is no "personal relationship with God" in the book (p. lxviii).

11. Fredericks, *Coping with Transience*, 37. For the notion that the picture of God in Ecclesiastes coheres with OT theology, see De Jong, "God in the Book of Qohelet."

12. Some scholars think that the narrator who introduces and closes the book in the prologue and epilogue critiques what is found in the body of the book (see Longman, *Book of Ecclesiastes*, 31–39). But this view should be rejected. See the decisive arguments in Waltke, *Old Testament Theology*, 949–51. See also Farmer, *Who Knows What Is Good?*, 197.

13. In terms of structure, I agree with those who see Ecclesiastes as proverbial without a clear overall structure. See Childs, *Old Testament as Scripture*, 587.

14. Most modern scholars doubt that Solomon is the author. It is not my purpose here to defend Solomonic authorship, but for one such defense, see Garrett, *Proverbs, Ecclesiastes, Song of Songs*, 254–67. For another view, see Waltke, *Old Testament Theology*, 947–49. For a messianic reference, see Perrin, "Messianism in the Narrative Frame?"

15. So Childs, *Old Testament as Scripture*, 584.

comes after the king? Only what has already been done" (2:12). In any case, the contents of the book derive from the Preacher's wisdom and knowledge (12:9), and what he wrote in the book were "words of truth" (12:10). What is collected here belongs to "the words of the wise" (12:11). "His sayings are not just pessimistic emotions, but designated as part of Israel's wisdom."[16] The conclusion of Ecclesiastes does not repudiate the rest of the book; it is part of biblical wisdom. Since the book comes from God as the shepherd, the author "legitimates Ecclesiastes as divine wisdom and rules out any merely private interpretation."[17] Understanding what the book teaches is part of what it means to fear God.[18]

The Futility of Life under the Sun

So what do we find in the remainder of the book? One of its major themes is the vanity and futility of human life.[19] The word "vanity" (*hebel*) occurs thirty-seven times in the book, signifying the futility and meaninglessness of human existence. The slogan functions as an envelope for the book, both opening it (1:2) and closing it (12:8).[20] The Preacher draws on creation here, and although

16. Ibid., 585. Against Longman (*Book of Ecclesiastes*, 277–81), who argues that 12:9–12 does not commend the teaching of Qohelet. Murphy rightly says, "The laudatory tone of vv 9–11 is unmistakable. The warning of 12:13 is to be seen as an approval of 'these'—namely the previous wisdom writing among which the book of Ecclesiastes is included" (*Ecclesiastes*, lxi). But against Murphy (p. 126), I believe that 12:13–14 coheres with the remainder of the book.

17. Childs, *Old Testament as Scripture*, 586.

18. "True wisdom will accept that our experience of a fallen world and the evil within is soon to pass. The book may then be read as a positive assessment of faith that is able to look beyond such limitations, and to conclude as it does that the duty of humankind is to fear God and to keep God's commandments" (Dumbrell, *Faith of Israel*, 285). See also Fredericks, *Coping with Transience*, 78–90.

19. A. Wright finds a careful structure in the book such that 1:12–6:9 stresses "the vanity of various human endeavors" and 6:10–11:6 "man's inability to understand the work of God" ("Riddle of the Sphinx," 324). According to Wright, 1:2–11 and 11:7–12:8 are two poems that introduce and conclude the book (pp. 333–34). See Wright's entire argument (pp. 313–34). See also idem, "Riddle of the Sphinx Revisited"; idem, "Additional Numerical Patterns in Qoheleth."

20. So also Dumbrell, *Faith of Israel*, 284; Waltke, *Old Testament Theology*, 955. The term *hebel* denotes the "absurdity" of life under the sun (Murphy, *Ecclesiastes*, lix; Waltke, *Old Testament Theology*, 956). When I use the term "irrational" with reference to Ecclesiastes, I am using it as a synonym of absurdity, not to convey the idea that life is ultimately without meaning (see Fox, *Qohelet and His Contradictions*, 29–51). Fredericks (*Coping with Transience*, 11–32) argues that the term *hebel* focuses on the transience of life (see also Perdue, *Wisdom and Creation*, 206–7), but such a definition, though partially true, does not fully account for the frustration that permeates the book. DeRouchie ("Shepherding Wind") argues that *hebel* means that life is an enigma. Caneday ("'Everything Is Vapor'") believes it refers to that which is insubstantial, transient, and evil. Both DeRouchie and Caneday reject the translation of *hebel*

the absurdity in the world is inexplicable at one level, at another level there is an explanation: the fall into sin described in Gen. 3.[21] Another favorite expression to convey the absurdity of life is "striving after wind" (1:14; 2:11, 17, 26; 4:4, 6; 6:9), which often is parallel with "vanity."[22] "Striving after wind" nicely pictures the futility of human life, for no one can grasp the wind.

Another key phrase in Ecclesiastes is "under the sun," which occurs twenty-nine times in the book. The phrase denotes life on earth—life in this world. Speaking of the dead (9:5), the author writes, "Their love and their hate and their envy have already perished, and forever they have no more share in all that is done under the sun" (9:6). It is clear from this text that "under the sun" refers to existence in this world. We are told that "there is nothing new under the sun" (1:9), that "everything . . . done under the sun . . . is vanity and striving after the wind" (1:14), and that, regarding toil, "there was nothing to be gained under the sun" (2:11; cf. 1:3).[23] The phrase "under the sun," then, denotes a limited perspective in which life is considered from an earthly standpoint.[24] It confirms "that the meaning of life cannot be ascertained solely through experience and observation."[25] The latter is a mistake that one might make in reading Proverbs, although, as noted earlier, Proverbs itself does not teach such a mistaken view. Kathleen Farmer rightly suggests that the term implies "an interest in the question of the existence of some form of afterlife."[26]

Why is life vain? Solomon, as the Preacher, illustrates its vanity in a multitude of ways. For instance, the uselessness of human labor is contemplated (1:3–11). The fundamental structures of the world remain unchanged, and the cycle of nature repeats itself over and over, and hence there is nothing truly new in

---

as "meaningless" or "futility" because they believe that such a meaning supports the notion that the book is one of ultimate despair. Space does not permit a full discussion of the meaning of *hebel* here. I think that the context of the book indicates that *hebel* is a wide-ranging term, and that the notions of absurdity, futility, and meaninglessness are part of its meaning. Nevertheless, the author is not teaching that life is ultimately meaningless or futile. His point is that life under the sun is meaningless, futile, absurd, an enigma, and transient; that is, we cannot make sense of life by observing what takes place on earth. But it does not follow from this that Ecclesiastes is teaching that life itself is ultimately meaningless and absurd. His point is that we cannot discern a pattern from the events of history.

21. So B. Webb, *Five Festal Garments*, 104. See also Garrett, *Proverbs, Ecclesiastes, Song of Songs*, 278–79.

22. See Waltke, *Old Testament Theology*, 957.

23. His toil was "under the sun" (2:18), and "all the toils of my labor under the sun" (2:20). See also 2:22.

24. See Dumbrell, *Faith of Israel*, 288–89.

25. House, *Old Testament Theology*, 471.

26. Farmer, *Who Knows What Is Good?*, 206. She also says that there is an implication "that a distinction can be made between what happens (under the sun) and what happens elsewhere" (p. 206).

human existence. Toil is futile also because the fruit of one's toil is temporary, and one leaves riches to heirs who may end up being fools (2:18–19). Work brings "vexation," and "even in the night [one's] heart does not rest" because a laborer worries about profitability (2:23). Others work constantly, but they do not even have an heir, and they find no satisfaction in their wealth (cf. 6:7), never contemplating why they are working so hard (4:7–8).

Indeed, human toil and even "skill" derive from competition, from the desire to be approved for one's abilities, and hence labor has its roots in "envy" (4:4). But what a useless life it is for those who have "two hands full of toil" (4:6) and strive after the wind, since they will never obtain happiness by incessant labor. Ecclesiastes does not disagree with the emphasis in Proverbs on working hard, for a "fool" who refuses to work will end up in self-destruction (4:5), but a wise person achieves a balance of both work and relaxation (4:6) and does not fall prey to the illusion that work will bring joy. Still, life is full of absurdity and perplexity. A poor person who is wise may replace a foolish king, but the poor person who becomes king will be forgotten as well (4:13–16). Nothing done on earth lasts.

Vanity and striving after wind are also the portion of those who pursue pleasure to escape the meaninglessness of existence under the sun (2:1–12). Solomon becomes Exhibit A of such an approach to life because he had enough wealth to seek pleasure without limitation (2:11). There are only "a few days" of life "under heaven" (2:3), and one may seek to escape the emptiness of life through hedonism. Solomon did not forsake wisdom in pursuing pleasure (2:3). No, this was a pursuit of the joys of the flesh guided by discretion and informed by understanding. Solomon built majestic parks and gardens, had numerous slaves to do his bidding, enjoyed riches to an unparalleled degree, was entertained by the finest musicians and singers in Israel, indulged in the joys of sexual intercourse with countless women, and stimulated his pleasure with wine. In short, "Whatever my eyes desired I did not keep from them. I kept my heart from no pleasure, for my heart found pleasure in all my toil, and this was my reward for all my toil" (2:10). And yet the path of hedonism did not ultimately satisfy. The emptiness of life was not chased away by life's pleasures. Indeed, the absurdity of life was even more evident, for, after satisfying every desire of the heart, it was plain to him that pleasure does not remove the ennui of life.

If pleasure does not yield satisfaction, then perhaps the answer is to be found in wisdom—the ability to negotiate life with prudence and understanding. The Preacher affirms that wisdom is preferable to folly (2:13–14), agreeing here with the book of Proverbs. Fools have no idea where they are heading and live shrouded in moral darkness, but the wise consider what is ahead and live morally, and hence they may live longer than fools because of their insight (7:11–12; cf. 9:18; 10:10). As Murphy says, "Folly is never a viable option for Qoheleth."[27] And yet there is still an emptiness and absurdity in life under the sun even for those who are wise. The wise perceive the meaninglessness of life under the sun and see more clearly than fools the sorrow and grief and frustration in human existence (1:13–18). The wise realize that "it is an unhappy business that God has given to the children of man to be busy with" (1:13), and that there are many things in life that cannot be amended or corrected (1:15). What's more, fools can undermine the labors of the wise in short order (10:1). Those who are wise realize that the advantage of being wise on earth is short-lived, for both the wise and fools die and are forgotten (2:15–17). Indeed, a wise person who is not rich or famous may because of his prudence rescue a city, and yet his work on behalf of the city may be completely forgotten (9:13–18).

One of the fundamental themes of Ecclesiastes is the irrationality of life under the sun. It is captured by 2:17: "So I hated life, because what is done under the sun was grievous to me, for all is vanity and a striving after wind." The Preacher laments the injustice that marks human existence. Indeed, injustice thrives in places that are reputed to be places of righteousness (3:16). It is important to see here that the injustice under the sun during the present era does not rule out a final judgment,[28] for the Preacher immediately says, "God will judge the righteous and the wicked, for there is a time for every matter and for every work" (3:17). Here the Preacher anticipates the conclusion to the entire work (12:13–14), demonstrating that the conclusion is in accord with what the book teaches elsewhere. Still, what the Preacher emphasizes in chapter 3 is the "insanity" of human life, for it is not perceptible that human beings have any advantage over animals (3:19–21; cf. 6:12). Both humans and animals return to the dust, signifying the futility of human existence (cf. 9:1–3).

No one can accuse the Preacher of gazing only at the sunny side of life. He considers the oppressed, who are filled with grief and find no comfort (4:1). Their oppressors are unrelenting because they enjoy power over the weak and disenfranchised (cf. 5:8–9). The Preacher concludes that it is better to be dead than alive, and never being born is the best of all (4:2–3). After all, we see those who are evil prosper because of their wickedness, while those who are righteous perish because of their righteousness (7:15; cf. 8:14). Life is unpredictable and unfair: "Again I saw that under the sun the race is not to the swift, nor the battle to the strong, nor bread to the wise, nor riches to

27. Murphy, *Ecclesiastes*, lxii.
28. See also Garrett, *Proverbs, Ecclesiastes, Song of Songs*, 272.

the intelligent, nor favor to those with knowledge, but time and chance happen to them all. For man does not know his time. Like fish that are taken in an evil net, and like birds that are caught in a snare, so the children of man are snared at an evil time, when it suddenly falls upon them" (9:11–12). No one can calculate the day of death, nor does one know whether tragedy or triumph is around the corner.

Human beings do not manage their lives; life manages them. The famous poem on time (3:1–8) emphasizes that human beings must respond to life as it occurs.[29] We must plant during planting season, and we will cry at death and rejoice at birth. When it is a time for war we fight, and when it is a time for peace we celebrate. Human beings are fundamentally helpless to change the world. "Consider the work of God: who can make straight what he has made crooked?" (7:13). The answer, of course, is "no one," for no one can unbend what God has bent. Indeed, "No man has power to retain the spirit, or power over the day of death" (8:8). The grim reaper comes, and we are powerless to stop it. As Leo Perdue says, "Denied the comprehensive knowledge of the cosmic and historical components of time and the course of divine events—in the past, present and future—humanity is trapped in an opaque, mysterious, and ambiguous present, unaware of what may or may not happen."[30]

The Preacher often contemplates the incongruity between wealth and happiness, for wealth seems to guarantee fulfillment but does not necessarily bring it: "He who loves money will not be satisfied with money, nor he who loves wealth with his income; this also is vanity" (5:10). More money means more friends who consume one's substance; and wealth occupies the mind, depriving the rich of sleep (5:11–12). A person's assets can be lost suddenly "in a bad venture" (5:14), with hard-earned gains vanishing so that nothing is left for one's progeny, and thus all the labor is "for the wind" (5:16). Similarly, a person may be blessed with enormous affluence and yet fail to enjoy the fortune amassed (6:1–2). The Preacher muses over how absurd life can be. One may have a hundred children and live a long life, but it is all for naught if one does not enjoy "life's good things" (6:3). A "stillborn child is better off than he" (6:3) because it finds rest immediately (6:5).

Sometimes the Preacher sounds as if he thinks that death is better than life, as was noted above (4:2–3; 6:3). We must recognize that the book is proverbial, and so maxims that celebrate death must be qualified by other statements elsewhere.[31] We already saw in Proverbs the danger of overextending the meaning

29. See Dumbrell, *Faith of Israel*, 289.
30. Perdue, *Wisdom and Creation*, 217.
31. Murphy (*Ecclesiastes*, lxvii) says that the sayings on the preferability of death are "very narrow cases."

of any single proverb. The Preacher recognizes the wonder and beauty of life (more on this below): "But he who is joined with all the living has hope, for a living dog is better than a dead lion. For the living know that they will die, but the dead know nothing, and they have no more reward, for the memory of them is forgotten. Their love and their hate and their envy have already perished, and forever they have no more share in all that is done under the sun" (9:4–6). The Preacher communicates the preciousness of life, and yet its futility is also captured by the reality of death. We must not overinterpret what the Preacher says about death, as if he denies any future life. He speaks of life "under the sun," acknowledging that human beings have no glimpse into the future on the basis of their own wisdom.

Fearing God

One of the central themes of Ecclesiastes is that life is puzzling, perplexing, unpredictable, unjust, and maddening. There are no formulas that apply to every situation. Too often evil triumphs, and good languishes under the sun. The Preacher, however, does not leave readers with that message. Even though life is futile and a striving after wind, human beings should still fear God, for he will assess the life of each one. Nor is this message confined to the conclusion of the book.[32] In the midst of musing on how maddening life is, the Preacher unexpectedly says, "Though a sinner does evil a hundred times and prolongs his life, yet I know that it will be well with those who fear God, because they fear before him. But it will not be well with the wicked, neither will he prolong his days like a shadow, because he does not fear before God" (8:12–13). Ultimately, one's fear of God will be rewarded, even though one cannot see how this is so during this futile life under the sun.[33] Life is baffling and beyond human comprehension, but the mysteries of existence should not lead people to atheism, agnosticism, or despair. Instead, God's purpose is to humble human beings: "I perceived that whatever God does endures forever; nothing can be added to it, nor anything taken from it. God has done it, so that people fear before him" (3:14). Human beings must recognize that they are not masters of the universe. They cannot supplement what God has done or reverse what he has ordained. They are to acknowledge his greatness and fear him. The centrality of fearing God also emerges in 5:1–7, where the

32. Rightly Childs, *Old Testament as Scripture*, 586. See also Murphy, "Qoheleth and Theology?," 31–32.
33. See Waltke, *Old Testament Theology*, 961.

Preacher instructs his readers to be reverent before God and not to pour out words before him like a fool.

Part of what it means to fear God, according to the Preacher, is to be wise—a theme that resonates with what we find in Proverbs. Those who are wise realize that "two are better than one" (4:9) because there is help, warmth, and protection in numbers (4:10–12). Prudence manifests itself in industry, hard work, and planning (11:1–6). Once again the parallels with Proverbs are obvious, suggesting again that those who put Ecclesiastes and Proverbs in polarized camps overestimate the differences between them. Wisdom perceives the evil in human beings, recognizing that all are sinners, and hence does not take too seriously criticism by others (7:20–22, 25–29). Even though life is full of vanity, folly must be avoided (10:2–3, 12–16). In particular, a land is destined for disaster if the king is a fool (4:13; 5:9; 10:16), but that land is blessed that has a wise and just king (10:17).

The wise ruminate about the day of death often, for pondering the end of life provokes people to live wisely in the present (7:1–6). The book closes with an admonition to remember God as creator before senility sets in and one is unable to think clearly about life. There is the recognition that the spirit of human beings will "[return] to God who gave it" (12:7), and that a day of judgment is coming in which God will judge people for their actions (11:9).

Enjoying Life

Another central theme, one that punctuates the book of Ecclesiastes repeatedly, plays a significant role in the book. Thus far we have seen that human beings must fear God and obey him, even though life under the sun is futile, irrational, absurd, and meaningless. No one can chart out his or her life and predict how it will turn out under the sun. So what should one do in the meantime? The Preacher advises, "There is nothing better for a person than that he should eat and drink and find enjoyment in his toil. This also, I saw, is from the hand of God, for apart from him who can eat or who can have enjoyment?" (2:24–25). The Preacher is not counseling readers here to live an unrestrained, hedonistic life; rather, he is saying that human beings must live one day at a time and enjoy each day for the pleasures it brings.[34] This is not an isolated theme, for the Preacher revisits it in 3:11–13:[35] "He has made everything beautiful in its

34. Rightly Waltke, *Old Testament Theology*, 961–63. See also Fredericks, *Coping with Transience*, 64–77; Whybray, "Qoheleth." Whybray rightly sees the emphasis on joy, but he exaggerates it. See the next note.
35. The theme of joy could be exaggerated and must be correlated with other themes in the book (so Garrett, *Proverbs, Ecclesiastes, Song of Songs*, 273), but Murphy goes too far in

time. Also, he has put eternity into man's heart, yet so that he cannot find out what God has done from the beginning to the end. I perceived that there is nothing better for them than to be joyful and to do good as long as they live; also that everyone should eat and drink and take pleasure in all his toil—this is God's gift to man." God has so designed life that human beings see the glory and beauty of God in the world he created. But life in the world also eludes human comprehension, such that there is no evident pattern or plan in history. Vanity and futility and absurdity characterize human life. Instead of trying to figure out how everything fits together, human beings should take pleasure in God's gifts. There is a humility in accepting each day from God's hand and thanking him for the joys that he grants.[36]

Similarly, 3:16–22 is one of the bleakest passages in the book, emphasizing the vanity of life. But the Preacher again concludes by saying, "So I saw that there is nothing better than that a man should rejoice in his work, for that is his lot. Who can bring him to see what will be after him?" (3:22). Life cannot be domesticated by human intelligence, and one should avoid trying to figure everything out, since answers to all of life's follies are not available. Instead, we should take one day at a time and enjoy life if it is good. The same theme emerges in 5:18–20. Despite the absurdity of life, if God grants joy in one's work, then one should not attempt to unravel the whys and wherefores of what happens on earth, since such is hidden from human beings. Instead, one should find joy in what God gives each day, giving thanks for the good things granted.[37]

The Preacher is scarcely saying, given the rest of the book, that every day is a good one in which one finds joy. This is clear from 7:14: "In the day of prosperity be joyful, and in the day of adversity consider: God has made the one as well as the other, so that man may not find out anything that will be after him." The Preacher's thesis is that when days are good, one should rejoice and enjoy life. But there are also days of adversity and trouble. God

the other direction in saying that Qohelet offers only "resigned conclusions" ("Qoheleth and Theology?," 32).

36. The Preacher emphasizes that if one experiences joy, it is a gift of God (so Whybray, "Qoheleth," 88).

37. Longman (*Book of Ecclesiastes*, 168–69) argues that what Qohelet says about joy does not cohere well because of his contrary comments about joy in 7:4; 2:1–2, 10. Against Longman, the comments about joy in chapter 2 and chapter 7 are directed against those who think that they can find fulfillment in pleasure, but this is quite distinct from what Qohelet teaches in 5:18–20 and the other passages about joy. The texts that counsel joy also affirm that no one under the sun can discern the meaning of life by observing the world. Suffering and absurdity characterize human existence. And yet in the midst of this fallen and crazy world there are days of joy—days when one enjoys one's work and food and marriage. Qohelet simply says, "Thank God for days like that. They are a gift, but they will not last forever." For an analysis of this theme, see Fox, *Qohelet and His Contradictions*, 53–77.

sovereignly stands behind both. He is king over all that happens, but he has structured history and human life so that human beings cannot unravel the secrets of existence. "Qohelet argues that God keeps us ignorant about the future in order to convince us that we cannot manipulate God in that way. That is the essence of what it means to 'fear' God: to recognize that God's favor cannot be controlled by anything we humans do."[38] Farmer rightly says that we have here a theology of grace.[39]

It is important to note how pervasively the Preacher summons the readers to enjoy life:

> And I commend joy, for man has no good thing under the sun but to eat and drink and be joyful, for this will go with him in his toil through the days of his life that God has given him under the sun. When I applied my heart to know wisdom, and to see the business that is done on earth, how neither day nor night do one's eyes see sleep, then I saw all the work of God, that man cannot find out the work that is done under the sun. However much man may toil in seeking, he will not find it out. Even though a wise man claims to know, he cannot find it out. (8:15–17)

No one can discover or unearth God's plan by scrutinizing life "under the sun." During the limited span of human life, then, humans should fear God and rejoice in the good things that God has given them. As noted before, this is not a counsel of hedonism. Instead, it is a recognition of finiteness and a stance of humility and gratefulness. When one is blessed with good days, one should not be perturbed by trying to sort out the injustices of human existence.

Certainly we are not blind to the futility of life, nor is the Preacher saying that we are not grieved by sorrow. And yet we should also gratefully receive good gifts when they are given (cf. 9:7–9). When life is good, we should rejoice in it, acknowledging God's beneficence. The Preacher realizes that good days on earth are not forever. Young persons should remember their creator before days of decrepitude arrive (11:7–8; 12:1–8). The years of youth and vigor are to be enjoyed if possible, but the wise person recognizes that life is short, that fearing God is most important. Here the themes of Ecclesiastes are nicely tied together. Life is full of vanity and absurdity, and yet one should also find joy in good days when they come. In the midst of a life that exceeds human comprehension, God should be feared and trusted, for ultimately he will reward those who fear and obey him. Such fear of God is the path of wisdom, as also Job and Proverbs affirm.

38. Farmer, *Who Knows What Is Good?*, 177. We should say that this is part of what it means to fear God rather than the essence of what fearing God means.
39. Ibid.

Conclusion

Ecclesiastes is part of the wisdom tradition in Israel. The book is similar to Job in that it focuses on the vanity and absurdity of life. Life baffles us with its irrationality, unfairness, and capriciousness. The created world since the sin of Adam and Eve is full of thorns and thistles (Gen. 3:17–19). The world has been subjected to futility (Rom. 8:18–25). The Preacher emphasizes that there are no pleasures under the sun that finally satisfy, and there is no wisdom available that will unlock all of life's secrets. God rules over all, but much is hidden from the gaze of human beings. Still, Ecclesiastes fits with the wisdom tradition of both Job and Proverbs, for the Preacher's final advice is that human beings should fear God and keep his commands. Instead of attempting to unravel the puzzles of human existence by trying to discern why one thing happens rather than another, human beings must give themselves entirely to God. They must live under his lordship. And when God grants joy and food, then one should give thanks to him and enjoy his gifts. In other words, Ecclesiastes says take one day at a time and do not worry about tomorrow (cf. Matt. 6:25–34). Chapters 11–12, however, warn against a misunderstanding. The Preacher does not call for hedonism, for a day of judgment is impending, and hence the most important thing in life is to fear God.

How does Ecclesiastes relate to the NT? The NT acknowledges that we live in a fallen and frustrating world (see Rom. 8:18–25). The creation is subject to futility, but Jesus Christ has come and inaugurated the kingdom, with the promise that the fullness of the kingdom will arrive. A new creation has dawned and will be consummated. Human beings show their fear of God (see 2 Cor. 5:11–21) by being reconciled to God through Jesus Christ. Through Christ the new creation has arrived (2 Cor. 5:17; Gal. 6:15), and "new heavens and a new earth" are coming "in which righteousness dwells" (2 Pet. 3:13).

18

SONG OF SONGS

Introduction

Interpreting Song of Songs (also known as Song of Solomon) is no easy task. Scholars have read it allegorically, dramatically, cultically, in terms of a wedding or even a funeral, or from a feminist perspective, or as a counter to what we find in the prophets. Space is lacking to adjudicate these different readings here. I think that Garrett persuasively identifies the weaknesses in these other readings and rightly classifies Song of Songs as love poetry,[1] and there seems to be a general consensus today that the book consists of love poems. An older view, that there are three characters (the maiden, a shepherd boy, and Solomon) is also generally rejected, and for good reason, since there is no evidence for more than two characters in the poems. The poems focus on the love between a young maiden and the king, and the king is clearly identified as Solomon.[2] It is the king who brought the young woman "into his chambers" (1:4; cf. 1:12; 7:5). A royal wedding is envisioned by the author, for Solomon comes from the wilderness with all the trappings of a king (3:6–11).[3] Solomon arrives with a retinue of soldiers and with a magnificent carriage, both of which are redolent of royalty. This is presumably Solomon's wedding day, the day on which the one upon whom the crown rests will marry (3:11; cf. 8:11–12). The love poetry of Song of Songs, then, focuses on the love between the king and a young maiden.[4]

---

1. Garrett, *Song of Songs*, 59–91.
2. Rightly Campbell, "Song of David's Son," 21–22; Hamilton, "Messianic Music," 336. Against B. Webb (*Five Festal Garments*, 20), who says that Solomon is not the suitor.
3. See Hamilton, "Messianic Music," 337.
4. On the importance of Solomon for the book, see Childs, *Old Testament as Scripture*, 575.

Bliss of Married Love

Song of Songs celebrates the ecstasies and delights of sexual love in marriage. Hebrew culture was not plagued by asceticism or a negative view of the body, which unfortunately entered into Christian tradition through a wrong understanding of the Scriptures. The bliss of married love is not described crassly or literally. Instead, the author celebrates the joys of love in imagery that is delicate and lyrical. Love is as intoxicating as wine (1:2). The woman is as beautiful as a rose or a lily (2:1–2), and love is as inviting as fragrant perfume that overwhelms the senses (1:12–13), or is as pleasant as eating delightful fruit (2:3–5). The joy of love is comparable to the arrival of spring after a dreary and cold winter (2:10–13). The clouds part, and the sun comes out. The rains end, and flowers and fig trees bloom. The fragrance of the spring summons lovers to the beauty of marital love. The king is dazzled by the beauty of his beloved (4:1–5; 6:5–9; 7:1–6). He is overcome when he looks into her eyes and gazes upon her hair and mouth and cheeks and neck. Her breasts are as lovely as two fawns. He exclaims, "You are altogether beautiful, my love; there is no flaw in you" (4:7). Song of Songs displays the same kind of delight in sexual union that we find in Prov. 5:15–19.[5]

The Maiden's Virginity

King Solomon longs for this maiden to come to him and to be his bride (4:8). Her beauty has captivated and overwhelmed him (4:9–11), but she is a "garden locked" and "a fountain sealed" (4:12). She is a virgin, and the king longs to come into the garden and enjoy its fruit (4:16). He wants the winds of love to blow so that the fragrance of love will be his. Some of the details of the book are difficult to interpret. Garrett probably is correct in saying that Song of Songs describes in highly symbolic language the maiden's fear of losing her virginity (3:1–4).[6] The young girl both fears and longs for a union with her lover. She longs for his embrace and love, for love is intoxicating and frees her from being alone (cf. Gen. 2:18). At the same time, she is reluctant to surrender her virginity, for once she gives herself to a man, there is no turning back.

It seems that 5:1 describes the wedding night, when the bride and the king make love, and lovemaking is signified by the gathering of fragrant spices, by eating from the sweetness of the honeycomb, and by drinking wine and milk.

5. See B. Webb, *Five Festal Garments*, 29.
6. For a helpful summary, see Garrett, *Song of Songs*, 113–14.

The experience fills both with ecstasy, but the woman is haunted by the loss of her virginity. She is both thrilled and repulsed by love. There is no going back now, for she has entered a new world as the wife and lover of the king. The subsequent chapters confirm the king's love for her, granting her assurance that giving herself to Solomon was worth the cost. Her heart now belongs to the king, whose strength and handsomeness stand out among men (5:9–16). Now bride and groom belong to one another. "I am my beloved's and my beloved is mine" (6:3; cf. 7:10). Sexual consummation is as delightful as delicious fruit (7:8) and as satisfying as aged wine (7:9; cf. 7:12–13).

Song of Songs is not an allegory; it describes in poetic terms the love between a maiden and King Solomon. A significant theme is contained in the refrain "Do not stir up or awaken love until it pleases" (2:7; 3:5; 8:4). Marriage and the loss of virginity for the woman are irrevocable, and hence they must not be pursued too quickly. Marriage and sexual union should not be urged upon those who are not prepared to make a wholehearted commitment to one another. One must be ready for such love and commitment and be prepared for the complete surrender of one's life to another, for a new life is commencing that leaves childhood and adolescence behind. Those who are inclined to marry too quickly should be restrained so that they do not rush into sexual experiences and marriage when they are not ready for such (cf. 8:9).

A Foretaste of Paradise

Clearly, Song of Songs communicates the beauty and depth of sexual love. The joys are described in paradisiacal terms with language reminiscent of Eden.[7] There is no hint of death in the book until near the end (8:6). Both bride and groom are young and beautiful and strong. They are not weakened by sickness or besmirched with any physical blemishes.[8] Their love and sexual joys are as verdant as the spring with trees budding and flowers blooming and the sun shining. Marital love between a husband and wife, and the sexual ecstasy that accompanies that love, hearkens back to paradise, to the love that God intended husband and wife to enjoy in the good creation. "These are symbols of paradise, and in this setting love is innocent and ideal, like that of Adam and Eve before the fall."[9] Such love, in light of the entire canon of Scripture, is

7. See Dumbrell, *Faith of Israel*, 282–83; Campbell, "Song of David's Son," 26; Hamilton, "Messianic Music," 340–42.

8. This is not to say that there are not any negative elements in Song of Songs. See B. Webb, *Five Festal Garments*, 30–31.

9. Ibid., 21.

a foretaste of the joy and delights that await the redeemed.[10] Revelation 21–22 teaches that paradise will be regained and more, for the new Eden in which humans will partake of the tree of life will never pass away.

The Nature of Love

Song of Songs contributes to the canon in another way, for it contains a theology of love. Perhaps this is captured best by 8:6–7: "Set me as a seal upon your heart, as a seal upon your arm, for love is strong as death, jealousy is fierce as the grave. Its flashes are flashes of fire, the very flame of the LORD. Many waters cannot quench love, neither can floods drown it. If a man offered for love all the wealth of his house, he would be utterly despised." Love's strength is compared to death, which is inexorable and unconquerable. Nothing can dampen or destroy love, for those who love are willing to surrender their lives for the sake of the beloved. Love clearly has a spiritual character that forges a bond with the beloved. Love fortifies a person to endure suffering for the sake of the beloved.

Garrett rightly argues that Song of Songs is not just about physical love.[11] He maintains that the book instructs us about the transforming character of love. Before marriage we have not committed ourselves to another person entirely. The commitment to another person by which we expose our vulnerability becomes a reality when we marry. And such an experience of love relates to all of life. "When people experience love, joy, freedom, or intimacy on any level, they are experiencing something that redeems human nature. Knowing God is therefore the ultimate experience of redemption; every other redemptive experience is real but limited, like a foreshadow."[12]

But the spiritual side of love must not be stressed to the neglect of the physical. Song of Songs reminds us that a love that is merely platonic between a husband and wife, a love that is only spiritual, does not accord with the biblical witness. Delight and ecstasy in the sexual union are the essence of marital love, and hence those who have exalted spiritual love as supreme, as if it is purer than physical love, clearly have strayed from the canonical witness. Garrett rightly remarks, "In some forms of monotheism, however, there is a dark cellar of guilt and suspicion, and sexuality looks up from the bottom

---

10. "Perhaps more than any other Old Testament book, Song of Solomon needs to be interpreted in light of the whole of the Old Testament canon" (House, *Old Testament Theology*, 464). See also Campbell, "Song of David's Son," 18.

11. Garrett, *Song of Songs*, 115.

12. Ibid., 117.

of that cellar. This mentality detests the physicality of the human body with all its appetites and excretions."[13] Such is clearly not the theology of Song of Songs. "To rejoice in the wife of one's youth, to be satisfied by her breasts and captivated by her love is to walk in the path of wisdom that is grounded in the fear of Yahweh."[14] Love is realized in the bodily union of husband and wife, and Song of Songs depicts such joys as delectable. Passion for one another physically and sexually is celebrated in the book.[15] Paul sees regular sexual union as a counter to sexual infidelity (1 Cor. 7:1–5, 9), and Song of Songs agrees. As Garrett says, "The passion that *demands* fidelity is also a *shield* to fidelity. To try to live without the passions of love is not merely frustratingly hopeless; it is unwise, unbiblical, and an open door to the very lusts it is trying to bar. In the Song, right passion is a protection against wrong passion."[16] Indeed, Song of Songs *"celebrates a woman's loss of virginity."*[17] Hence, the theology of the book differs dramatically from the view of many believers in history who have seen the path of asceticism as the path of holiness.

The Canonical Contribution

Most interpreters today reject an allegorical reading of Song of Songs. I share their resistance to allegorizing the book, for such allegorizing is quite subjective. But I also suggest that it is legitimate to read the book at another level.[18] Song of Songs does not consist merely of love poems between an ordinary man and an ordinary woman. It describes love poems between a young maiden and a king—indeed, between a maiden and King Solomon. We have a hint that the book can be read in light of the covenant made with David, the promise that a future son of David will reign forever (2 Sam. 7; 1 Chron. 17; Pss. 89; 132).[19] Canonically and typologically, David points us forward to the Christ, and the NT emphasizes that Christ has a bride—the church (Eph. 5:22–33).[20] There is "a marriage supper of the Lamb" (Rev. 19:9), and the "bride" is "adorned

13. Ibid., 100. See Garrett's summary of the theology of sexuality in the early church (pp. 100–101).
14. B. Webb, *Five Festal Garments*, 32.
15. Rightly Garrett, *Song of Songs*, 102.
16. Ibid.
17. Ibid., 118 (emphasis in original).
18. Garrett (ibid., 98) seems to reject this, but he restricts his interpretation of Song of Songs to the book itself, whereas I contend that it is warranted also to interpret the book in light of the canon.
19. Waltke (*Old Testament Theology*, 163–64) rejects allegory but also argues that Song of Songs can be interpreted typologically. See also Dempster, *Dominion and Dynasty*, 207.
20. See Campbell, "Song of David's Son," 25–26. Song of Songs itself does not emphasize the offspring of the king and his bride. Campbell ("Song of David's Son," 27–28) goes too far here.

for her husband" (Rev. 21:2). The relationship between the king and his wife, so beautifully described in Song of Songs, points us to something greater, something that outlasts the short bloom of youth. Here is a love that will never die, a covenant that will not be severed by death or by unfaithfulness. The whispers or shouts of Eden in marital love find their consummation in delights that will far exceed marital bliss—in the loving relationship between Christ and the church. "From a New Testament perspective, the love depicted in the Song is not only a taste of what is given in creation, but a sign of what will be consummated in the new creation—a sign of the gospel."[21] Such a reading does not need to find an allegorical connection between Christ and the church and Solomon and his bride. It simply recognizes, in light of the canon of Scripture, that the love described in Song of Songs points beyond itself to a love that endures and to a love that is greater than any human love.[22]

The OT itself prepared us for seeing a typological relationship, as the relationship between Yahweh and Israel often is expressed in terms of marital love (cf. Jer. 2–3; Ezek. 16; 23; Hosea 1–3), though Israel is criticized for whoring after other gods and for its unfaithfulness to Yahweh.[23] Song of Songs points ahead to a day when the people of God, the bride of Christ, will be faithful to her husband and king. The joys of such a union will exceed the ecstasies of sexual consummation, and they will not be restricted to the days of one's youth. The bride of Christ will be "without spot or wrinkle or any such thing" and will "be holy and without blemish" (Eph. 5:27) forever and ever. Her union with her Lord and king will never be severed.

Conclusion

Song of Songs represents love poems between the king (Solomon) and his bride. The maiden is hesitant to lose her virginity, for once she enjoys sexual union with her husband, she has left the days of her youth behind forever. A common refrain of the book is that one must not take upon oneself the responsibilities and joys of marital love rashly or too quickly. The book does not, however, criticize marital love. The physical bliss of sexual love is described in Edenic terms; beautiful images and pictures are pressed into service to describe the thrill of love between a husband and wife. Many scholars leave the book

21. B. Webb, *Five Festal Garments*, 34.
22. Campbell ("Song of David's Son," 23–25) argues that Song of Songs is not allegorical but rather typological. The view of Hamilton ("Messianic Music," 339) that the book is not allegorical or typological but actually was intended to be read messianically seems less likely.
23. See Ortlund, *God's Unfaithful Wife*.

there, ruling out any allegorical or typological meaning. I do not embrace allegory for this book, but I believe that a typological reading in light of the whole canon fits well. Just as Israel was the bride of Yahweh, so the church is the bride of Christ. The paradisiacal echoes of love in Song of Songs point forward to the love between Christ and his church (Eph. 5:22–33). Married love, though beautiful and fulfilling, is evanescent. It points to something greater, to a relationship with someone greater, a relationship that will never end. And the love between Christ and the church fits with the theme of this book as well. The message of the Scriptures is not only that Yahweh is king over his people but also that his people will see the King in his beauty, that they will revel in his promise, and that knowing him will be all-satisfying. The Edenic and paradisiacal love between a man and a woman is the closest analogy on earth to the delights and pleasures of the love that marks Christ's relationship to the church.

INTERLUDE

A Synopsis of
ISRAEL'S SONGS AND WISDOM

The books in this collection are remarkably different, for they do not advance the story line of the OT. Indeed, the attempt to see a central theme in the OT is often dashed on the rocks of Wisdom literature. As I argued at the beginning of the book, however, the notion of God's kingdom is sufficiently broad to account well for the themes that we find in the books under consideration here. The kingdom has three dimensions: (1) God's rule; (2) the response of human beings to his rule; and (3) the place of his rule. Certainly, wisdom does not emphasize the place of his rule. We have seen in the previous OT books that the land of Israel and particularly the temple are prominent. But the land and the temple are not prominent in Wisdom Literature. I contend, however, that the second dimension of God's rule becomes the focus in wisdom writings. What does it mean to live under God's rule? We saw that in Proverbs, Ecclesiastes, and Job the fear of the Lord is emphasized.[1] Those who know Yahweh as king fear him, and this is expressed by keeping his commands and doing his will.

Another way of putting this is to say that the wisdom books are God-centered, for what it means to be wise is to fear the Lord.[2] Proverbs is occasionally understood to be a secular book, but this judgment misses what the book is about. Fearing Yahweh is the beginning of wisdom. Proverbs recognizes that Yahweh reigns in the warp and woof of life, that the fear of the Lord

---

1. See Schultz, "Unity or Diversity?," 294–95.
2. See Bartholomew, "Wisdom Books." See also G. Wilson, "'Words of the Wise,'" 181. For an alternative point of view, see L. Wilson, "Book of Job."

320

is inseparable from how one treats the poor, how hard one works, one's sex life, and what one says with the tongue. Living under God's kingship is not an ethereal concept; it touches every area of life. There is no sacred/secular split in Israel, for everything in life is under Yahweh's sovereignty. Indeed, we saw evidence in Proverbs that wisdom is closely connected with Torah, for the commands of parents are closely related to exhortations to bind the Torah to one's heart. In addition, there are indications in Proverbs of a future reward beyond this life, which suggests that Proverbs is not limited to earthly existence, that a future fulfillment of God's promises is envisioned.

Both Ecclesiastes and Job teach that the fear of the Lord is the beginning of wisdom as well, but these books are quite different from the book of Proverbs. Proverbs generally teaches that those who do good are rewarded, that practicing righteousness pays off, and that indulging in evil has negative consequences in this life. Some have oversimplified Proverbs in making this point, for the book is quite aware that righteousness does not always lead to success.[3] Proverbs are generalizations, not promises. And yet we all recognize that Job and Ecclesiastes emphasize the irrationality and absurdity of life. Life is unpredictable and incalculable. Too often the righteous suffer miserably and the wicked flourish. Babies die, women are raped, and children are abused. No one can figure out life "under the sun." Life on earth is not paradise, for no pleasure or wisdom can bring ultimate satisfaction. Both Job and Ecclesiastes have essentially the same advice relative to suffering and the puzzles of life. God is sovereign. He reigns over all. But he has not disclosed, and will not disclose, his plan to human beings. He does what he wills as the great King of the universe, as he makes quite clear in his speech to Job. The Lord knows how to run the universe and needs no help or advice from Job. Indeed, Job has no clue about how God keeps the world running.

So what should the human response be? Human beings must put their trust in God, fear him, and keep his commandments. A day of judgment is coming, and then God will set everything right. In the meantime, human beings are to live one day at a time, enjoying good days as they come, while also recognizing that many things in life are beyond their understanding. They are called upon to trust God as King, and must not attempt to rule the world for him, nor to tell him how to run it. The Lord has his own good reasons for allowing suffering to enter the world. Ultimately, it brings honor and glory to him as Lord and King, but if human beings try to discern why it brings him honor and glory to structure life as he did, they will become frustrated, for although some things can be said about the matter, God does not disclose

3. Rightly Bartholomew, "Wisdom Books," 121.

321

fully the rationale for suffering. Fearing the Lord means trusting God's wise rule of the world instead of arrogating the pretension of being creator and king of the cosmos. The wisdom books are also christological, for Jesus is the wisdom of God. He always feared the Lord, righteously carrying out his will, trusting God to vindicate him on the last day. As the exalted King, he rules the world with wisdom and justice.

Song of Songs celebrates the beauty and paradisiacal character of married love, of love between King Solomon and his young bride. Ecclesiastes says that we should enjoy the pleasures of life while we can, and Song of Songs expands upon that sentiment. Many connections are drawn in the latter book between sexual love and Eden, showing that the greatest pleasures of life hearken back to a time when human beings enjoyed fellowship with God and one another untainted by sin. Contrary to many, I also suggest that Song of Songs should be read typologically. The love relationship between the king and the young maiden points to the love of Yahweh for Israel, and the love of Christ for his church, for Song of Songs points both backward and forward. Married love, sexual love, captures the greatest joys of this life, but these joys do not last forever. They point to something greater, to a relationship with someone greater. They anticipate the church seeing God face to face in the new Jerusalem, to seeing the King in his beauty.

How can we capture Psalms in a summary? Their breadth and depth defy description. Psalms 1–2 set the stage for the whole book, as noted earlier. It has often been pointed out that Ps. 1 is a wisdom psalm and programmatic for the entire Psalter, and so the psalms cannot be separated from wisdom traditions. Blessing comes to the one who meditates upon and obeys the Torah. The psalms are also messianic, focusing upon the covenant made with David, which promises him an eternal dynasty. This is immediately apparent in Ps. 2. The Davidic king whom Yahweh installed will rule the ends of the earth. All will prostrate themselves before him and kiss the son. The promise to Abraham, that all the ends of the earth will be blessed, will be fulfilled through a Davidic king (Ps. 72). Jesus fulfills both wisdom and kingly themes, demonstrating that wisdom converges with messianism.

I argued above that the very structure of the Psalter into five books testifies that the promise made to David has not been revoked. Yahweh's rule over the world will become a reality through Jesus the Messiah. The forward-looking character of the Psalter justifies reading the book messianically, seeing Jesus as the true and final David. He is the one who will free Israel from exile through a second exodus. And that brings us to another major theme in the Psalter: praise. There are praise and lament psalms, but the final word is praise, just as the final psalms of the final book redound with praise. The psalms are full of praise because the presence of God is satisfying and because he will redeem his people. Again and again we read about the joy of seeing the Lord in his temple, of finding one's hunger and thirst satisfied in his presence. And the story of the Psalter as a whole is that God will fulfill his promises to David and to Israel and to the world. And that provokes praise and thanks and incredible joy. When God's kingdom is realized through his anointed one, Jesus Christ, his people will rejoice because they will see their King, and they will be glad in his presence forever.

Part 4

JUDGMENT
AND SALVATION
IN THE PROPHETS

19

ISAIAH

Introduction

Trying to sum up the theology of Isaiah is like trying to describe a magnificent snow leopard to someone who has never seen one. The breadth and depth and beauty of Isaiah exceed our capacity to grasp and my ability to express. The book is clearly split into two main parts: chapters 1–35, which focus on threat from Assyria, and chapters 40–66, which predict return from Babylonian captivity.[1] Chapters 36–39 bridge the two main parts, with chapters 36–37 recounting Jerusalem's miraculous deliverance from the armies of King Sennacherib of Assyria, and chapters 38–39 forecasting exile in Babylon. The great sigh of relief that is exhaled after the deliverance from Assyria is followed by the ominous news that Judah will be conquered by Babylon. But Isaiah does not end with a gloomy report of Israel's exile. He promises the coming of a new exodus, a new creation, and a final atonement for Israel's sins. In one sense, Isaiah portrays the destruction of the present Jerusalem and the promise of a new Jerusalem in the new creation.[2] It is difficult to know where to begin and where to end when studying Isaiah, but perhaps we should begin where Isaiah does—with judgment.

Judgment of Israel[3]

Judgment is a theme that bridges both main parts of Isaiah. Judah is almost destroyed by Assyria because of its sin (chaps. 1–35) and is exiled to Babylon for

1. Childs (*Old Testament as Scripture*, 325–26) rightly observes that from a canonical perspective chapters 40–66 are presented as a prophecy of return from Babylon.
2. Alexander, *Eden to the New Jerusalem*, 50–55.
3. When I use "Israel" in this section, often it generally designates the Jewish people. I do not consistently use the term to designate the northern kingdom. Context makes it clear where Israel is limited to the northern kingdom.

its transgressions (chaps. 40–66).[4] We immediately see that Isaiah is covenantal, for the punishments visited upon Israel were due to its violation of covenantal stipulations according to Lev. 26 and Deut. 27–28.[5] The book opens with Israel compared to a tottering makeshift booth in a vineyard before the Assyrian superpower (1:8). They go through the motions of religion and ritual while at the same time practicing injustice and unrighteousness (1:11–17, 21–23). The problem with the nation is captured in the words of 29:13: "Because this people draw near with their mouth and honor me with their lips, while their hearts are far from me." Israel has rebelled against God and has forsaken the Lord (1:2–5, 28). Strikingly, Jerusalem and Judah are compared to Sodom (1:9, 10; 3:9), so it is hard to imagine them sinking any lower. The powerful in the land, the elders and princes, are accused of "grinding the face of the poor" (3:15). The needy were deprived of justice, the rights of the poor were ignored, and widows and orphans were mistreated. Wealthy women were entranced by and consumed with their clothes closet but were guilty of arrogance and sexual dalliances (3:16–24).

Although Israel was a vineyard cultivated by and cared for by the Lord, they yielded "wild grapes" (5:4), so that there was oppression and injustice instead of righteousness (5:7).[6] Evil was rife in the land, "for everyone is godless and an evildoer, and every mouth speaks folly" (9:17). What does forsaking the Lord look like? How did it express itself in Israel's everyday life? The rich wanted to expand their holdings; they took more property and built bigger and more houses (5:8). They "are heroes at drinking wine, and valiant men in mixing strong drink" (5:22; cf. 28:1, 3). They spent their days stimulating their senses by drinking wine and listening to music (5:11–12). Both literally and metaphorically, prophets and priests "reel with wine and stagger with strong drink" (28:7) to the point where vomit fills their tables (28:8). Israel reversed moral norms, so that what is evil was praised and what is good was censured (5:20).

Israel's root problem was a failure to trust in the Lord. Yahweh promised King Ahaz of Judah that he would protect him from King Pekah of Israel and King Rezin of Syria, but Ahaz refused to trust in the Lord's promise (chaps. 7–8, esp. 7:9–13). So too, Yahweh pledged that he would rescue his people from Sennacherib, but they wanted something more practical and concrete to cling to. They formed an alliance with Egypt to gain security from the Egyptian threat (chaps. 30–31). Though the alliance made good sense politically, it did not accord with the divine plan, for the people did not ask for God's

4. See Routledge, "Narrative Substructure of Isaiah?" 188–89.
5. See Dumbrell, *Faith of Israel*, 109. On echoes of Deuteronomy in Isaiah, see Dempster, *Dominion and Dynasty*, 172.
6. For a helpful discussion on justice in the OT, see C. Wright, *Old Testament Ethics*, 253–80.

direction (30:1–2). The Lord's evaluation of their political savvy is devastating: "For they are a rebellious people, lying children, children unwilling to hear the instruction of the LORD" (30:9). And we read, "Woe to those who go down to Egypt for help and rely on horses, who trust in chariots because they are many and in horsemen because they are very strong, but do not look to the holy one of Israel or consult the LORD!" (31:1).

In the same way, Judah was exiled to Babylon for its sin (chaps. 40–66). Judah did not suffer defeat before the Babylonians simply because it had an inferior army. The core reason is explained in 42:24: "Who gave up Jacob to the looter, and Israel to the plunderers? Was it not the LORD, against whom we have sinned, in whose ways they would not walk, and whose law they would not obey?" Yahweh was not weaker than the so-called gods of Babylon. He handed Israel over to its enemies because of its iniquities (cf. 43:24, 27). Why did Yahweh divorce Israel and send it into exile? "Behold, for your iniquities you were sold, and for your transgressions your mother was sent away" (50:1). Israel had turned toward idolatry and adultery (57:3–8; 65:7). Israel thought that it was righteous, for it found pleasure in drawing near to the Lord (58:2). Unfortunately, its people were greatly deceived (58:1; 65:3–5). Injustice was rife in the land, for their religious devotion was contradicted by their oppression of workers and their failure to care for the poor and hungry (58:3–7).

The rottenness at the heart of Israel is summed up in 59:1–8. The problem was not Yahweh's inability to save, for Israel is told, "Your iniquities have made a separation between you and your God" (59:2). The nation was a mess. Murder, lying, and evil speech were endemic. The courts were full of cases, but deceit and subterfuge plagued the nation, for "no one enters suit justly; no one goes to law honestly; they rely on empty pleas, they speak lies, they conceive mischief and give birth to iniquity" (59:4). They are acting like the offspring of the serpent instead of the offspring of the woman (59:5). They were slow to repent, but quick to pursue evil ends: "Their feet run to evil, and they are swift to shed innocent blood" (59:7). The end result of their sin was utter disaster: "Desolation and destruction are in their highways. The way of peace they do not know, and there is no justice in their paths; they have made their roads crooked; no one who treads on them knows peace" (59:7–8). Israel's sins were multiplying (59:12), and they were refusing to follow Yahweh.

The judgment of Israel for its sin is featured in the day of the Lord. The day of the Lord is a day of both judgment and salvation (2:5–22; 4:2–6; 7:17–20; 10:20; 11:11–16; 13:6–16; 19:16–25; 22:1–25; 24:21; 27:12–13; 28:5; 34:8). The shocking element for Israel was that the day of the Lord did not guarantee their salvation. If they turned toward wickedness (and they had!), judgment would be their portion, for the day of the Lord is particularly directed against those who are proud: "The haughty looks of man shall be brought low, and the lofty pride of men shall be humbled, and the LORD alone will be exalted in that day" (2:11; cf. 2:17). Human beings are judged for their arrogance, pride, and self-importance, for failing to pay tribute to and praise the Lord, and for exalting themselves. On the day when the Lord judges it will be evident that idols are useless, and people will fling them away in disgust (2:20–21), for they will see the "splendor of [God's] majesty" and run from him in terror (2:21). Isaiah reminds Israel of the day of the Lord so that they would trust in God instead of fearing people (2:22), so that they would fear Yahweh instead of fearing the Assyrians.

Israel experienced the curses of the covenant with the result that they were bereft of necessary food and water (3:1). The country unraveled politically, militarily, and socially (3:2–7, 12). The vineyard of Israel was destroyed (5:5–6); that is, Israel went into exile (5:13–14, 26–30; 6:12–13), and thus the proud in heart were humbled (5:15), and God was exalted in judgment: "The LORD of hosts is exalted in justice, and the Holy God shows himself holy in righteousness" (5:16). Indeed, one of Isaiah's favorite terms for God is "Holy one of Israel," which he uses twenty-five times. Yahweh shows his utter uniqueness in his judgment of the wicked and the salvation of his people. The northern kingdom, Israel, experienced the shattering storm of Yahweh's judgment (28:2, 18). Judgment is Yahweh's "strange" work (28:21; cf. 65:6–7, 12), for he longs to save, and yet he judges as well if human beings turn away from his goodness. Yahweh is the thrice holy one (6:3), who cannot tolerate sin. Both the northern kingdom of Israel and Syria were judged via Assyria (7:7–9, 17–25; 8:5–9, 21–9:1; 9:8–10:5). Yahweh sovereignly used Assyria as the rod of his anger to punish Syria, Israel, and even Judah (10:5–34), but ultimately he judged Assyria as well because it became entranced with its military strength, exalting itself over Yahweh. He judged Assyria "burning with his anger" and "his lips full of fury" (30:27). The "Assyrians will be terror-stricken at the voice of the LORD" (30:31). They will be consumed by his wrath (30:33).

Yahweh's judgment was not limited to Israel, as the oracles against the nations demonstrate (chaps. 13–23). Chapters 13–14 focus on the judgment of Babylon, which sent Judah into exile (cf. chaps. 38–66). The day of the Lord's wrath will topple mighty Babylon. They will be enfeebled (13:7) and as overcome as a woman in labor (13:8). Isaiah uses symbolic language to convey God's judgment: the stars, the sun, and the moon will be darkened (13:10). We have seen regularly that human pride provoked God's punishment. So too here: "I will put an end to the pomp of the arrogant, and lay low the pompous pride of the ruthless" (13:11). The arrogance of Babylon was breathtaking, for it considered itself to be godlike in its wisdom and power (14:11–14). Babylon's conceit is evident in its claim "I will make myself like the Most High" (14:14).[7] Babylon will be like an abandoned wife, even though it once reigned as the queen of the nations (chap. 47). Its destruction will be sudden and unexpected (47:11). The judgment of the nations shows Yahweh's sovereignty; his purpose and will cannot be thwarted (14:24–27). God judges the nations because of their pride (see also 23:9), and the judgment advertises the glory of his name.[8]

Tucked into the judgment of the nations is the promise that Israel will be delivered. God's purpose and plan include both judgment and salvation.[9] Even though Israel also faced judgment, punishment was not the last word. Israel will return from exile to Babylon: "The LORD will have compassion on Jacob and will again choose Israel, and will set them in their own land, and sojourners will join them and will attach themselves to the house of Jacob" (14:1). A Davidic king will bring justice (16:5). A new exodus will bring deliverance to the people again.

The judgment of the nations forecasts the impending judgment on the entire earth (chaps. 24–27). The earth will be devastated and desolated by the judgment of Yahweh (24:1–4), and the old creation will stagger and collapse (24:19–23). Music and joy will vanish (24:7–13) from the city of the enemy (25:2; 26:5). The enemy, Leviathan, who is identified as the "serpent" and "dragon" (27:1), recalling Gen. 3:15, will be slain in the sea.[10] In chapter 34 Edom represents the nations opposed to Yahweh, for "the LORD is enraged against all the nations, and furious against all their host" (34:2; cf. 63:6; 66:15–16, 24). The destruction of the nations is conveyed in apocalyptic language of the heavens being rolled "up like a scroll" (34:4). The Lord will thrust his bloody sword into those who oppose him (34:5–7; cf. 63:3) in his "day of vengeance" when he repays the evil done to Zion (34:8; cf. 63:4; 66:6). Edom's land "shall be turned to pitch" (34:9); "its smoke shall go up forever" (34:10), and the land shall be utterly desolate (34:10–15). The NT picks up this language, finding it to be typological of the final judgment (e.g., Rev. 6:12–17).

Jerusalem's Salvation

One of the prominent themes in chapters 1–37 is the promise that Jerusalem/ Zion will not be overthrown.[11] Significantly, Jerusalem is mentioned as the

7. Incidentally, the judgment of Moab (chaps. 15–16) was also due to its overweening haughtiness (16:6).

8. Routledge, "Narrative Substructure of Isaiah," 94–95.

9. Jensen, "Yahweh's Plan in Isaiah," 446.

10. See Dempster, *Dominion and Dynasty*, 182n22.

11. Dumbrell (*Faith of Israel*, 108) sees Yahweh's concern for Jerusalem as the central theme of the entire book.

subject of Isaiah's prophecy from the first verse in the book (1:1). Nor is Jerusalem spared because it is so righteous (5:3); the city is described as a "whore" (1:21). Jerusalem does experience judgment to some extent, for it is besieged by Assyria (29:3). Assyria comes up to the very neck of Judah, to its capital city, and is dangerously close to taking it (10:28–32). As a consequence, Jerusalem suffered food shortages (3:1; cf. 5:14). The city "stumbled" "because their speech and their deeds [were] against the LORD, defying his glorious presence" (3:8), and their rulers mocked the Lord (28:14).

Despite Jerusalem's sins, the Lord promises to spare it from Assyria. The first thirty-seven chapters of the book climax with the deliverance of Jerusalem. Sennacherib is poised to take Jerusalem, for the city is under siege, and the cities surrounding Jerusalem have been taken. The Rabshakeh has no doubts about the outcome. Israel's God will not be able to deliver it from Assyria, for no other gods have been able to prevail over the Assyrians. Yahweh rebuked Assyria for its pride and arrogance, reminding them that they conquered other kingdoms only because he ordained it (37:26–29). Hence, the Lord promises that not even an arrow will fly in Jerusalem (37:33). "For I will defend this city to save it, for my own sake and for the sake of my servant David" (37:35). Yahweh got glory for himself by striking dead 185,000 Assyrians, and their mighty army returned home without taking Jerusalem, without even taking a shot against the city.

Yahweh's protection of Jerusalem was not limited to protection from Assyria. Pekah of Israel and Rezin of Syria plotted to take the city and to set a rival king, Tabeel, upon the throne (chaps. 7–8). The prospect terrified Ahaz and Judah (7:2). Even though Ahaz did not trust in Yahweh, the Lord gave him a sign that he would protect him, a sign that God was with his people ("Immanuel" [7:14]). He promised that before a child reached the age of understanding, both the northern kingdom of Israel and Syria would be overwhelmed by the mighty waters of Assyria (8:6–7).[12] Assyria would reach the neck of Judah (i.e., Jerusalem) but would not conquer it, for God is with his people ("Immanuel" [8:8]). Whatever they may do, the opponents of Judah will not triumph, "for God is with us" (8:10). Judah should not fear the conspiracy of Israel and Syria (8:12), for political realities are not ultimate. Judah must stop fearing people (cf. 2:22) and center themselves on the Lord: "But the LORD of hosts, him you shall honor as holy. Let him be your fear, and let him be your dread" (8:13). Judah is summoned to trust in the Lord, and not to turn to "mediums" and "necromancers" for security (8:19): "Should not a people inquire of their

---

12. The identity of the child is the subject of controversy. I believe that it is Maher-shalal-hash-baz, the son of Isaiah and the prophetess (Isa. 8:3).

God? Should they inquire of the dead on behalf of the living?" (8:19). Judah should rely on the revelation given by Isaiah through the prophetic word (8:20). Yahweh will judge Israel and Syria via Assyria (9:8–10:4), and then when it looks as if Assyria is about to swallow up Jerusalem, he "will lop the boughs with terrifying power; the great in height will be hewn down, and the lofty will be brought low. He will cut down the thickets of the forest with an axe, and Lebanon will fall by the Majestic One" (10:33–34). Jerusalem will be spared from destruction. The NT picks up the "Immanuel" theme (Matt. 1:23) and sees it fulfilled in Jesus of Nazareth. Jesus will save Israel from its sins (Matt. 1:21) and spare it from eschatological destruction.

The same theme is picked up in chapter 29 of Isaiah. Jerusalem will be besieged by the Assyrians, and things will become so bleak that "your voice shall come from the ground like the voice of a ghost, and from the dust your speech shall whisper" (29:4). And yet Ariel (i.e., Jerusalem) will not be taken. The nations poised against the city may think they are about to enjoy Jerusalem as a tasty meal with all its spoils, but that banquet will be a dream (29:7–8). Yahweh will protect Mount Zion from its adversaries. Therefore, Israel should not turn to Egypt for help but rather must trust Yahweh to protect them (chaps. 30–31), for he promises to strike Assyria "with his rod" (30:31). He will fight for his people and set Assyria ablaze (30:32–33). "The LORD of hosts will come down to fight on Mount Zion and on its hill. Like birds hovering, so the LORD of hosts will protect Jerusalem; he will protect and deliver it; he will spare and rescue it" (31:4–5; cf. 33:20–22). Assyria will be destroyed, but by the sword of the Lord, not the swords of humans (31:8–9).

Jerusalem and the Remnant[13]

Considering Isaiah as a whole, of course, we know that Jerusalem was not spared forever. Yahweh saved the city from Assyria, but Babylon razed the city and temple (586 BC), and so the message of deliverance in the 700s BC did not apply in the same way in the 500s. But that leads us to ask about the theology of Isaiah. Is there any long-term significance in the preservation of Zion in the 700s? Does the Lord deliver on one occasion but fail to do so the next time? Is there any enduring theology of Yahweh's protection of Jerusalem in the book? I maintain that there is a durable theology when we consider what Isaiah says about the remnant and about the eschatological promises for Jerusalem.

13. For the theology of the remnant, see Hasel, *The Remnant*.

The book begins with remnant theology. The sin of Zion warrants complete destruction like the overthrow of Sodom and Gomorrah, but Yahweh preserves "survivors" in the land (1:9) so that Israel will not be wiped out totally. Judgment is coming for Jerusalem (4:2–6) by which the Lord will cleanse Jerusalem of evil (4:4), and a "holy" remnant that is "recorded for life" will be left in Jerusalem (4:3). The great vision of the Lord in chapter 6 captures the same theme. Isaiah sees the glory of the Lord and recognizes that he and the people have unclean lips. Therefore, he will be a messenger of judgment, and the nation will almost disappear. Israel cannot survive because of its sins. And yet a remnant will remain, for "the holy seed is its stump" (6:13). The preservation of the remnant shows that there is hope for the future, that the final word is not judgment, but salvation. The mention of the "stump" probably refers to the Davidic king (11:1), even though a different Hebrew word for "stump" is used here. The remnant survives and is represented by its king.

We have already seen the Lord's promise to preserve Judah from the machinations of Israel and Syria in the days of Ahaz (chaps. 7–8). The remnant theme surfaces here as well. Isaiah comments on his family, "Behold, I and the children whom the LORD has given me are signs and portents in Israel from the LORD of hosts, who dwells on Mount Zion" (8:18). How are they signs? They are portents of the truth that the Lord will save his people, that he will deliver a remnant. And the deliverance of the remnant forecasts a future salvation (9:1–7)—a day when evil will be defeated decisively and forever. This is confirmed by 10:19–22. Assyria will be the tool of God's judgment, but a "remnant will return" (10:21; cf. 37:31–32), guaranteeing a day of future salvation (14:1) where there will be a new exodus (see below, 11:11–16) in which the Lord will save Israel (28:5–6). The promise of the remnant is picked up in the NT. Believers in Jesus are the true remnant from Israel (Rom. 11:1–16). The NT does not restrict the remnant to Jewish believers in Christ, for Gentile believers are also the true Israel (Rom. 2:25–29; Gal. 6:16). If the children of Isaiah represent the remnant in Isaiah's day, they point forward typologically to the brothers and sisters of Jesus and the children of God who are members of the church of Christ (Heb. 2:13), the true children of Abraham (Heb. 2:16).

New David

The promise of a remnant and the prospect of future salvation are inseparable from the promise of a new David. Just as the texts on judgment pick up on the curses of the Mosaic covenant from Leviticus and Deuteronomy, so the promise of a new David applies the covenant with David to a new situation

(2 Sam. 7; 1 Chron. 17; Pss. 89; 132). Most likely, the term "branch" (*ṣemaḥ*) refers to the offspring of David, to the promise of a Davidic king. In Jeremiah the term "branch" clearly refers to the promise of a Davidic king (Jer. 23:5; 33:15). In Isa. 4:2–6 the promise of the branch is interwoven with the promise that a remnant will survive after the judgment of Israel is completed. After the judgment comes glory, and the Lord's presence will reside in Israel symbolized by the cloud and the "flaming fire" (4:5), just as he dwelt with his people during the exodus, so that "now the entire city will have become one Holy of holies."[14] Israel will be spared and shielded by the Lord; there will be "shade by day from the heat" and "a shelter from the storm and rain" (4:6). Artistically and symbolically, we are told that the coming David (the coming anointed one) will bring political security and well-being to Israel.

One of the most famous prophecies of a Davidic king is found in 9:2–7. The context of chapters 7–10 must not be neglected. Judah feared a takeover planned by Syria and Israel. Yahweh promised that he would spare Jerusalem, that Assyria would conquer Syria and Israel, and that he would finally judge Assyria (even though Assyria would come up to the very neck of Judah [i.e., Jerusalem]. In the midst of such promises and threats the prophecy of a new David is tucked in. God's people are promised victory over their enemies, and the victory is clearly a military one (9:2–5). But what will account for this great victory? Isaiah explains that a son is coming; a child is on the horizon who will sit on David's throne (9:6–7). He will reign as the governor and ruler over the land forever. Peace, righteousness, and justice will never cease upon his coming. This king is remarkable, for he is a "Wonderful Counselor, Mighty God, Everlasting Father, Prince of Peace" (9:6). "These epithets seem to explode the expectations of this coming king. He is much more than a descendant of David."[15] Clearly, Isaiah's promise of such a king was not fulfilled in his day.

In 11:1–10 another stunning prophecy of a new David is given, and the context is the same as that in chapter 9. The Davidic origin of the ruler is evident, for he is "a shoot from the stump of Jesse, and a branch from his roots" (11:1), which anticipates the servant of the Lord (53:2).[16] He is equipped by the Spirit to rule over Israel, and so he is a Spirit-anointed Messiah (11:2), but the sevenfold work of the Spirit shows that he surpasses all previous kings.[17] Righteousness and justice and peace will be the fruit of his rule, since he will strike down the wicked (cf. 16:5) and vindicate the poor. The consequence

14. Dempster, *Dominion and Dynasty*, 174.
15. Ibid., 175.
16. Dempster says, "They are both compared to a plant growing in difficult circumstances" (ibid., 179).
17. Ibid., 175.

of his rule will be a new creation (11:6–9) wherein the woes of everyday life are a distant memory, and human beings will enjoy "an Edenic paradise."[18] Infants and young children will even be safe near the den of serpents. "They shall not hurt or destroy in all my holy mountain; for the earth shall be full of the knowledge of the LORD as the waters cover the sea" (11:9). The distinctive element of the new creation surfaces here: it comes when there is universal and genuine knowledge of God. This same root of Jesse will bring salvation to the Gentiles (11:10), and the new exodus will become a reality in his day (11:11–16). In due course I will discuss Gentile salvation, the new exodus, and the new creation. At this point it is simply necessary to point out that these blessings become a reality through the Davidic son, the offspring of Jesse, who will fulfill the promises made to David.

It is probable that the cornerstone in Zion that will not be overturned refers to David's rule as well (28:16).[19] The king in chapters 32–33 is not identified as clearly, but when we consider the witness of Isaiah as a whole, when we compare it to what we have seen in chapter 9 and chapter 11, it is fair to conclude that this king is Davidic. In these chapters Israel is warned not to trust foreign alliances to save them from Assyria (chaps. 30–31). They must not look to Egypt for deliverance. Yahweh will be faithful to his people, pledging that "a king will reign in righteousness" (32:1), presumably a Davidic king. God's people will find protection under this king (32:2), and the blind will see and the deaf will hear (33:3–4). Yes, a judgment is coming from Assyria, but it will not finally succeed. Indeed, just as we saw in chapter 11, the coming king is connected with the pouring out of the Spirit (32:15). And when the Spirit arrives, there will be a new creation: "The wilderness becomes a fruitful field, and the fruitful field is deemed a forest. Then justice will dwell in the wilderness, and righteousness abide in the fruitful field. And the effect of righteousness will be peace, and the result of righteousness, quietness and trust forever" (32:15–17).

A new day of justice and *shalom* is coming. Israel must wait for this promise and trust that it will come to pass (33:5–6, 22). Only the righteous will enjoy the salvation and peace coming after the day of destruction (33:14–15). In that day, "Your eyes will behold the king in his beauty" (33:17), and Jerusalem will be transformed and secure. "Behold Zion, the city of our appointed feasts! Your eyes will see Jerusalem, an untroubled habitation, an immovable tent, whose stakes will never be plucked up, nor will any of its cords be broken" (33:20). All of this will become a reality because Israel will enjoy forgiveness of sins (33:24). We see once again the inseparability of the major themes in

18. Ibid.
19. So Hamilton, *God's Glory in Salvation*, 200.

Isaiah. When the new David arrives, Israel will be forgiven its sins, and there will be a new exodus, a new creation, and a new Jerusalem. The wicked will be judged and removed, and there will be peace forevermore. The covenant, the sure mercies given by the new David, will become a reality (55:3).[20] The obedience of the new David will ensure the fulfillment of the covenant.[21]

New Exodus and New Creation

When we consider the book of Isaiah as a whole, we come across something quite curious. Jerusalem was spared from Assyria but not from Babylon (chaps. 38–39). Hezekiah becomes a parable of the nation. When Israel was delivered from Jerusalem, he did not entrust himself anew and afresh to Yahweh but instead trusted in himself.[22] The deliverance of Jerusalem from Assyria did not spell the coming of the new creation. Indeed, Jerusalem was subsequently taken by the Babylonians in 586 BC. It is significant to find, then, that the themes of the new exodus and the new creation span both parts of Isaiah (chaps. 1–37; 38–66). The deliverance of Jerusalem from Assyria points to a future act of salvation that is greater and more permanent than rescue from the Assyrian siege. Israel would be delivered not just from the Assyrians and Babylonians, but from all their enemies. Significantly, the first promise of a new exodus occurs in a text that promises a future Davidic king, and in which the promise of a new creation (the wolf living peaceably with the lamb) is found (11:1–10). Just as Yahweh liberated Israel from Egypt in the first exodus, so he will bring his people back from Assyria, Egypt, and as far as the coastlands in the second exodus (11:11–16). The northern and southern kingdoms would finally live in harmony with each other. Yahweh would strike rivers so that his people, the remnant of Israel, could cross over, and "there will be a highway from Assyria" (11:16). It seems reasonable to conclude from chapter 11 that the new David, the new exodus, and the new creation will commence at the same time. In response, Israel will sing praises to Yahweh for his salvation (chap. 12) and "proclaim that his name is exalted" (12:4). The new exodus, then, becomes the means by which Yahweh establishes his kingdom.[23]

---

20. We clearly have reference to a new David here (Dempster, *Dominion and Dynasty*, 180–81). For the subjective genitive in the phrase "sure mercies of David" (so KJV), see Gentry, "'Sure Mercies of David'"; Dempster, "Servant of the Lord," 159–60. See also Japhet, *Ideology*, 358n44. "Wine and milk" (55:1) represent the blessings of paradise (so Dumbrell, *Covenant and Creation*, 196).

21. So Gentry and Wellum, *Kingdom through Covenant*, 643–44.

22. So Routledge, "Narrative Substructure of Isaiah," 198.

23. So Dumbrell, *Faith of Israel*, 117.

It was noted previously that seeing the King in his beauty means that the new creation is at hand (chaps. 32–33). The blind will see, and the deaf will hear (32:3). The evil and the frustrations of the old creation will pass away (cf. 29:18–19). The desert will be fruitful (32:15), and "My people will dwell in a peaceful habitation" (32:18). Israel's enemies will be long gone (33:18–20), and there will be no more sickness (33:24). This vision of an idyllic future is picked up in chapter 35. The "desert shall rejoice and blossom like the crocus" (35:1). The new creation will provide a vision of God. "They shall see the glory of the LORD, the majesty of our God" (35:2). The Lord will save his people and destroy his enemies (35:4). The blind, the deaf, the lame, and the mute will be healed (35:5–6). The days of sin and sickness will be over, and there will be "streams in the desert" (35:6). No evil will be in the new creation; only those who are holy will dwell there (35:8). Wild animals that maul and destroy will be a distant memory (35:9). The NT picks up these themes of new creation and sees them as fulfilled in Jesus Christ and his ministry (Matt. 11:2–6). The new creation was realized in a way that surprised and scandalized Jesus' contemporaries.

The promise of a new creation belongs to those who are delivered in the second exodus, for chapter 35 of Isaiah concludes with a reference to the new exodus: "And the ransomed of the LORD shall return and come to Zion with singing; everlasting joy shall be upon their heads; they shall obtain gladness and joy, and sorrow and sighing shall flee away" (35:10; cf. 51:11). It is clear from this text that the new creation and the new exodus occur at the same time. When Israel returns from exile, the sorrows of the present world will pass away.

The theme of a new exodus is especially prominent in chapters 40–66, which is hardly unexpected because chapters 38–39 reveal that Judah and Jerusalem will be exiled to Babylon. The new exodus, God's second act of deliverance, occurs only because Jerusalem is forgiven its sins. "Her iniquity is pardoned" (40:2). There will be a highway in the desert, and God's people will return from Babylon (40:3–5). The return from exile is the gospel, the good news that must be proclaimed in Jerusalem (40:9–11); the Lord will bring his people back like a shepherd carries his lambs. The remainder of chapter 40 emphasizes that Yahweh is able to restore his people, for he is the incomparable God. He is the creator of all, and the nations that oppose his purposes "are as nothing before him" (40:17).[24] Israel must not fear that it is too weak to return, for "the Creator of the ends of the earth" (40:28) is their God, and he will give strength to those who are weary (40:29–31). Since Yahweh is the creator and Lord of all, he will provide water and sustenance in the wilderness, just as he did in the first exodus (41:17–18).

24. See Rendtorff, *Canonical Hebrew Bible*, 424–25.

Yahweh will show compassion and mercy on his people once again: "And I will lead the blind in a way that they do not know, in paths that they have not known I will guide them. I will turn the darkness before them into light, the rough places into level ground. These are the things I do, and I do not forsake them" (42:16). The return from exile is described in terms of Israel's "redemption" (35:9; 43:1; 51:10; cf. 41:14; 43:14; 44:6, 23–24; 47:4; 48:17, 20; 49:7, 26; 52:3, 9; 54:5, 8; 59:20; 60:16; 62:12; 63:16), and this redemption is tied to the forgiveness of Israel's sins (44:22). Yahweh will liberate Israel from the ends of the earth because it is called by his name and was "created for [his] glory" (43:7). Israel will pass through the waters safely (43:2). And so the purpose of the new exodus is to display the superiority, glory, and supremacy of Yahweh over all nations.[25]

Indeed, the second exodus demonstrates that Yahweh is superior to idols, for not only did he announce former things but also predicts what will happen in the future (41:22–23). The proof of Yahweh's lordship is that he "tell[s] us what is to come hereafter" (41:23). Yahweh unveils "new things . . . before they spring forth" (42:9), predicting the rise of Cyrus (41:25–26; 44:28; 45:1–3), and that Cyrus will decree the rebuilding of Jerusalem and the temple (44:28). "In the guise of a fictive dispute with the nations and their idols, God demonstrates his power to declare the future and bring it to pass."[26] Yahweh does a new thing in making a way for Israel in the wilderness (43:19), parting the waters just as he did in the first exodus (43:16), and granting a renewed creation (43:19). Just as he promised liberation from Egypt in the first exodus before it came to pass, so he promises beforehand that Israel will be freed in the second exodus. He will bring Israel from the ends of the earth, from east and west and south and north, for the glory of his name (43:5–7). Yahweh is uniquely and exclusively God (46:9–11), which he demonstrates by declaring "the end from the beginning" (46:10). His purposes and plans cannot and will not be frustrated, and he will demonstrate his deity by calling out Cyrus to accomplish his will (46:10–11). Israel will leave Babylon, and, as in the first exodus (cf. 51:9–10), the Lord will satisfy their thirst in the new exodus, and water will flow from the rock (48:20–21). Israel will not "hunger or thirst" when returning to the land (49:9–10). The Lord will, so to speak, level the mountains for his people (49:11).

The themes of new creation and new exodus are closely tied together, for when Israel returns from Babylon, they will find "springs of water," and the heat will not scorch them (49:10; cf. 41:18; 48:19–20). There will be a highway

---

25. So Routledge, "Narrative Substructure of Isaiah," 195.
26. Childs, *Biblical Theology*, 388.

in the desert, and the valleys will be filled and the mountains leveled (40:3–4). The rough ground will become level (42:16). The desert will become like a new Eden. "I will put in the wilderness the cedar, the acacia, the myrtle, and the olive. I will set in the desert the cypress, the plane and the pine together" (41:19). This is confirmed in 51:3: "He comforts all her waste places and makes her wilderness like Eden, her desert like the garden of the LORD." The Lord will "create new heavens and a new earth" (65:17; cf. 66:22). The new creation means a new Jerusalem, where sorrow is absent and joy is prevalent (65:18–19). The creation of a new Jerusalem also means the creation of a new world, a new cosmos. The two are intertwined.[27] Death will not take the life of anyone early (65:20), and life will be rich and satisfying (65:21–22). The theme of a new creation resounds with the language of paradise: "The wolf and the lamb shall graze together; the lion shall eat straw like the ox, and dust shall be the serpent's food. They shall not hurt or destroy in all my holy mountain" (65:25). The crushing of the serpent (see Gen. 3:15) will be completed.

The major themes in Isaiah are interrelated, and hence the new creation is closely tied to the promise of a new Jerusalem.[28] Isaiah prophesies that Jerusalem will shine with light and with the glory of Yahweh (chap. 60; cf. 54:11–12). The new creation and the new Jerusalem cannot be separated from the second exodus, for nations will be drawn by Jerusalem's light, and sons and daughters of Israel will return as well (60:3–4). As Beale observes, the light streaming from Jerusalem resonates with creation themes from Gen. 1, showing that the new Jerusalem is the new creation, which anticipates, of course, the confluence of these themes in Rev. 21–22.[29] It certainly will be a new day, for "the wealth of the nations shall come to you" (60:5). Jerusalem will be rebuilt by foreigners (60:10), and the nations of the earth will stream to Jerusalem, and Yahweh's sanctuary will be gloriously beautiful (60:13). Those who resist Israel will be destroyed (60:12), and enemies will bow before them (60:14). Majesty, wealth, peace, and joy will characterize Jerusalem (60:15–18). The light of the sun will no longer be needed, for "the LORD will be your everlasting light, and your God will be your glory" (60:19), and Israel will never be removed from the land (60:21).

The promise of salvation for Israel in chapter 62 flies in the same orbit as what we saw in chapter 60. Israel is promised a future righteousness and dazzling glory. It will be "a crown of beauty" and "a royal diadem in the hand of your God" (62:3). Instead of experiencing the forsakenness of exile and

27. See Levenson, *Persistence of Evil*, 89–90; Beale, *Church's Mission*, 141.
28. Rightly Dumbrell, *Faith of Israel*, 108.
29. Beale, *Biblical Theology*, 243–44.

divorce from the Lord, they will experience the Lord's delight and joy (62:4–5). Yahweh promised to restore Jerusalem (62:6–7), and its future salvation is sure (62:11). Israel's destiny is remarkable: "They shall be called The Holy People, The Redeemed of the LORD; and you shall be called Sought Out, A City Not Forsaken" (62:12). We have ample evidence that the new exodus, the new creation, and the new Jerusalem are various ways of describing the same future reality. As Dumbrell says, the final chapters of Isaiah are about "the renewal of creation and its submission to divine rule."[30]

What is notable is that the promises of the new exodus were not fulfilled when Israel returned from exile.[31] Nevertheless, those who received the OT as Scripture did not conclude that Isaiah was mistaken. What we have here is an inaugurated return from exile, and NT writers saw the promises of a new exodus, a new creation, and a new Jerusalem to be fulfilled in Christ. Even in Christ, as we will see, there is an "already but not yet" tension, for although the new exodus and new creation have already arrived in Christ, they have not yet come in all their fullness.

The Servant of the Lord

The promises of the new creation, the new exodus, and the new Jerusalem also relate to the servant of the Lord in Isaiah.[32] In chapters 40–66 the servant of the Lord is a major theme. The identity of the servant has been the subject of intense debate, but there is scarcely space here to consider various interpretations. I will focus on the text and attempt to explain thereby the interpretation favored here. We are introduced to the servant in chapter 41, and here the servant is identified as Israel, elected by the Lord (41:8–9; 45:4). Yahweh summons Israel to overcome fear, for he promises to be with them, help them, and strengthen them so that they overcome their enemies (41:10–16). Even though Israel is chosen by the Lord as his servant, it is not a blameless servant. Israel is blind and deaf (42:19) and has failed to keep the law that Yahweh gave (43:20–25), and as a result Israel has suffered the punishment of exile. And yet exile will not be permanent. Yahweh has forgiven the sins of his servant, Israel (44:21–22), and hence Israel can sing the Lord's praises, since the one who created and formed Israel has also redeemed it (see also 48:20), promising that when Israel returns from exile, Jerusalem will be reestablished and the cities of Judah will be inhabited (44:23–28). The Lord is the one and

30. Dumbrell, *Covenant and Creation*, 198.
31. See Childs, *Old Testament as Scripture*, 327.
32. See esp. Dempster, "Servant of the Lord." See also Dumbrell, *Faith of Israel*, 118, 126.

only God, and the only Savior, and he promises to save Israel as his servant (43:10–21). They will experience the joys of the new exodus, the new creation, and the new Jerusalem. Israel as God's chosen servant will serve as his witnesses (43:10, 12; 44:1–2, 8). They will testify of Yahweh, as he himself says, "I am the first and I am the last; besides me there is no god" (44:6). Yahweh is incomparable because he predicts what will happen before it occurs, pledging that Israel will return from exile (44:7–9).

The servant is identified as Israel, but it is clear as well that the servant transcends Israel, that he cannot be limited to Israel.[33] For instance, Yahweh asks who "obeys the voice of his servant" (50:10). Since Israel is asked the question, the servant cannot be equivalent to Israel, for the question is not merely "O Israel, who obeys the voice of Israel?" Isaiah clearly addresses the nation of Israel as a whole, asking if they obey the servant's voice, and thus it is clear that the servant in this text, though part of Israel, is also distinct from Israel. I will argue shortly that the servant transcends Israel in chapters 52–53, but a look at chapters 42 and 49 indicate the same expanded role. The servant in chapter 42 could be identified as Israel, but there are reasons to think that the servant transcends Israel as well. Yahweh delights in this servant (42:1), which stands in contrast with Israel, upon whom the Lord poured out his anger because of their sin (42:24–25). This servant is endowed with the Spirit and "will bring forth justice to the nations" (42:1; cf. 42:4), but righteousness will not be obtained via war, for he will not break a "bruised reed" or extinguish "a faintly burning wick" (42:3).[34] He will be "a light for the nations, to open the eyes that are blind, to bring out the prisoners from the dungeon, from the prison those who sit in darkness" (42:6–7). The servant will bring salvation to the whole earth, not just to Israel.

In 49:3 Israel is actually identified as the servant, and so it may seem that further discussion is not needed. But as we continue to read on in the text, it is evident that things are not so simple, for the servant will also bring Jacob back to the Lord and "bring back the preserved of Israel" (49:6; cf. 49:5). Isaiah also may serve in this text as the Lord's servant, since he was called from the womb, and the Lord prepared his mouth as one who speaks Yahweh's word (49:1–2). Yet it is difficult to see how what is said about the servant can be exhausted by Isaiah either. Isaiah does not bring Israel back to Yahweh, and so another servant must ultimately be in view. The notion that the servant is not merely Israel or Isaiah is confirmed by the promise that the servant will impact the nations: "I will make you as a light for the nations, that my

---

33. Rightly Childs, *Old Testament as Scripture*, 334–35.
34. See Goldingay, *Israel's Faith*, 224.

salvation may reach to the end of the earth" (49:6). Isaiah clearly did not fulfill this prophecy. So Isaiah must be speaking of another servant who saves both Israel and the nations.

Chapters 52–53 demonstrate conclusively that the servant cannot be identified fully with Israel or Isaiah, for the servant atones for the sin of Israel.[35] He bore the griefs and sorrows of his people (53:4). The wounds and crushing that he experienced are because of the transgressions and iniquities of Israel (53:5). He suffered not because of his own sins but rather to bring healing to his people (53:5). The people of Israel, like sheep, have wandered from the right way, "and the LORD has laid on him the iniquity of us all" (53:6). By bearing the iniquities of Israel he would make them righteous (53:11; cf. 53:12). Obviously, the servant cannot be coextensive with Israel if he bears the sins of Israel. Nor can the servant be Isaiah, for Isaiah also had "unclean lips" (6:5) and needed atonement for his sins (6:6–7).[36] "At once Isaiah realizes . . . his own and Judah's failure to reflect Yahweh's kingship at the center of Israel's covenant life."[37] The servant, however, was punished, but not because of his iniquity. Instead, there was no warrant for the sufferings that he endured (53:9). He was as innocent as a lamb and suffered "for the transgression" of the people, not his own sin (53:7–8). He was rejected by those for whom he suffered, and they concluded that he was being afflicted by God when in fact he was suffering for their sake (53:4). His sufferings became the means of atonement (53:12) for the guilt of Israel and the nations (chaps. 42; 49). As a result of his suffering, he would be exalted (52:13) and ultimately prosper (53:10).[38] His suffering would not be the end, for he would see the light of life (53:10) and be raised from the dead, and thus he would share the victory he accomplished with others (53:12).

The last servant text probably is chapter 61. I say "probably" because the word "servant" is not used here, but what is described here fits with the servant's work elsewhere. The language of 61:1, including liberty for those imprisoned and for those who are bound, echoes 42:7. The work of the Spirit-anointed one in 61:1 matches the work of the servant in chapter 42. In addition, in both texts the one who accomplishes this ministry does so by the endowment of the Spirit (42:1; 61:2). The focus is on the fulfillment of prophecy, for when the Spirit comes, it will be "the year of the LORD's favor" and the day when

---

35. Dumbrell (*Faith of Israel*, 123) notes that chapters 49–55 distinguish Israel more clearly from the servant.

36. What is true of Isaiah is also true of Israel. See Routledge, "Narrative Substructure of Isaiah," 189.

37. Dumbrell, *Faith of Israel*, 110.

38. A royal dimension seems present here for the servant. See ibid., 124.

the wicked are punished (61:2). The ruins of former years will be rebuilt, and cities will be reestablished (61:4). Foreigners will be Israel's servants, and Israel will be Yahweh's priests and enjoy the wealth of the nations (61:5–6). It is striking that this is the same language, as noted above (chaps. 60; 62), for the new creation and the new Jerusalem. The new creation and new exodus and new Jerusalem will come only via the servant of the Lord. The one endowed with the Spirit will instantiate this new reality.

If the new creation and new exodus become a reality only through the servant of the Lord, it follows that Israel will enjoy the new Jerusalem, the new creation, and the second exodus only if it is forgiven its sins. Sin is what led Israel into exile, and we have seen at key junctures in Isaiah that Israel will be restored from exile only if and when its sins are forgiven (40:2; 43:24; 44:22). The "servant of the Lord" texts demonstrate that such forgiveness is achieved through the suffering and death of that servant. The threads of the story fit together in Isaiah, and it is only when we see the pattern in the entirety of the book that we discern how the book fits together. The great promises of salvation are dependent upon the work of the servant of the Lord. The servant who fulfills these great promises is Jesus the Christ. He suffered for the sake of Israel and for the sake of the nations to atone for their sins and to grant them forgiveness. The return from exile and the new creation are realized through the work of the Christ in his cross and resurrection. The kingly role of the servant explains how he represents Israel and yet is distinguished from Israel. If we tie the servant to the Davidic promises earlier in Isaiah, it is clear that the servant is a royal figure.

The Spirit

The Spirit's role in the life of the servant was commented on above. The servant is endowed by the Spirit (42:1; 61:1). Only by virtue of the power of the Spirit does he carry out his ministry, by which he suffers for the sins of Israel. If we put all of Isaiah together, we see that the son of Jesse, the Davidic king, is also anointed by the Spirit (11:2). What is remarkable is that in chapter 11 the Spirit-endowed one brings in the new creation, which, as was argued above, is the same blessing brought by the servant of the Lord in chapters 40–66. It seems fair to conclude from Isaiah's own narrative that the servant of the Lord and the future Davidic king are the same person, for both are Spirit empowered and bring about the new creation.[39] Of course, this fits well with

---

39. Others argue that the servant is a royal figure. See Dumbrell, *Faith of Israel*, 119; Dempster, "Servant of the Lord," 155–60.

the NT witness, as we will see. Jesus is the Spirit-anointed Messiah, the royal son of David, the one who will bring in the kingdom of God. But he is also the servant of the Lord, the one who dies as a ransom to deliver his people from their sin (Matt. 20:28).

The coming of the Spirit in Isaiah signals the fulfillment of Yahweh's promises to Israel. Israel suffers judgment because of its sins (32:10–14), but when the Spirit is poured out, the new creation will dawn (32:15–16). Israel will be secure, at peace, and live righteously in the land (32:17–18). Similarly, the end-time blessing for Israel will come when Yahweh pours his Spirit upon Israel (44:3). When the Spirit is dispensed, Yahweh's covenant with Israel will be fulfilled (59:21). We see another indication that Isaianic themes cannot be sundered from one another. The Spirit is the eschatological Spirit who brings eschatological salvation, and the servant of the Lord is endowed with that Spirit, showing that the new creation cannot arrive apart from the Spirit or apart from the servant of the Lord. In the NT Jesus, as the exalted and resurrected Lord (see Acts 2, esp. 2:33), is the one who pours out the Spirit on his people (cf. John 7:37–39). The Spirit is poured out when Jesus is glorified, and the coming of the Spirit signals the arrival of the last days, the fulfillment of all of God's saving promises.

Salvation to the Ends of the Earth

One of the promises made to Abraham was that all nations would be blessed through his offspring (Gen. 12:3). Isaiah does not limit himself to promising blessing for Israel. He dramatically and regularly forecasts salvation reaching the ends of the earth, the inclusion of Gentiles into the people of God. The folding in of Gentiles into salvation fits with Isaiah's unremitting scorn for idolatry. Yahweh, who is the creator of all, belongs to an entirely different category from idols (40:17–20). After all, he truly exists and has always existed, and he did not need human beings to craft him. As the creator of all, he deserves glory and honor and praise (42:8). Isaiah derides the folly of idolatry (44:9–20). Why would someone worship something made by human hands, especially when part of what is worshiped is used to fuel a fire? Idols are futile because they can neither save nor deliver (45:20; cf. 57:15), but Yahweh is the creator and redeemer. The problem is that people have to carry their idols instead of their idols carrying them (chap. 46). But Yahweh, in contrast to the idols, carries his people, even to old age (46:3–4). Yahweh is incomparable (46:5), showing that he is the true God because he declares from the beginning what will happen in the future (46:9–10). Yahweh also shows that he is the true and only God because his salvation reaches the whole world. The injunction to multiply and fill the earth found in Gen. 1:28 will be fulfilled, for Yahweh will "[enlarge] all the borders of the land" (26:15; cf. 27:6).[40]

The salvation of the Gentiles commences with the beginning of the book (2:1–4). In the last days Jerusalem's temple will be exalted as supreme, and "many peoples" will travel to seek Yahweh, longing to be taught "his ways" so that they "may walk in his paths" (2:3). The Torah of Yahweh will stream out from Jerusalem, and all people will enjoy the new creation (2:3–4). According to the NT, the promise found here is fulfilled in the gospel going out from Jerusalem (Acts 1:8) to the ends of the earth. Dempster rightly says that "Isaiah reverses Babel,"[41] and the book of Acts proclaims that this promise of universal salvation begins to be fulfilled on the day of Pentecost (Acts 2:1–11), which is in its own way a reversal of Babel. Isaiah teaches that war will be a distant memory, and peace will reign. The salvation of Gentiles will occur through Jesse's son, the one endowed with the Spirit (11:1–9), the one who will bring in the new creation. This "root of Jesse" will be "a signal for the peoples," and "the nations" will "inquire" of him (11:10). The restoration from exile (11:11–16), it seems, includes the salvation of the Gentiles (11:12).

The oracles of the nations (chaps. 13–23) stress Yahweh's judgment of the nations, but there are also some windows that forecast future salvation for some. For instance, Isaiah forecasts a day when those from Cush will bring tribute to the Lord (18:7). Indeed, what we read here echoes 2:1–4, where all nations will stream to Zion, the mountain of the Lord. Here Cush brings its tribute to Mount Zion. Chapter 19 is surely one of the most stunning and surprising texts in all of Scripture. The first part of the chapter emphasizes the judgment that will strike Egypt (19:1–17), but suddenly the tone changes. "Five cities" in Egypt will "speak the language of Canaan," and they will "swear allegiance to the LORD of hosts" (19:18). There will be an altar and pillar to Yahweh in the land (19:19), and Yahweh will save them from their enemies (19:20). Isaiah clearly refers here to the salvation of Egypt, for they "will know the LORD" and "worship" him with "sacrifice and offering" (19:21). Yahweh will strike them in judgment but will also heal them so that they return to him (19:22). The salvation envisioned is not limited to Egypt, for Assyria will also be included as a work of the Lord's hands (19:25). "Egypt and Assyria are significant as Israel's first and most recent oppressors, and probably represent

---

40. So Beale, *Biblical Theology*, 752–54.
41. Dempster, *Dominion and Dynasty*, 174.

all her political enemies."[42] If this is the case, then the salvation here encompasses the whole world. In any case, how shocking and delightful it is to read that Assyria and Egypt are placed on the same level as Israel, as "a blessing in the midst of the earth" (19:24). Canonically, NT writers find fulfillment in the spread of the gospel to all nations, which is rehearsed in the book of Acts and in the Pauline Letters.

The salvation of Gentiles finds further expression in chapters 40–66. The Spirit-endowed servant "will bring forth justice to the nations" (42:1). In language reminiscent of 2:3, the coastlands will "wait for his law" (42:4; cf. 51:4). The servant will serve as "a light for the nations" (42:6; 49:6) so that they experience salvation as well.[43] The purpose is that the Lord's praises will resound to "the end of the earth" (42:10), so that glory is given to the Lord (42:12). This salvation will reach even kings and princes (49:7). Remarkably, nations will be sprinkled by the atoning work of the servant, and kings will perceive and grasp what many in Israel fail to understand (52:15).[44] We see another connection between the servant of the Lord and the Davidic king in the promise of salvation to Gentiles in 55:3–5.[45] David, like the servant, does not only save Israel, he also functions as "a witness to the peoples, a leader and commander of the peoples" (55:4). There is another strand of evidence that the servant of the Lord and the Davidic king are the same person in the Isaianic vision.

Isaiah, more than any other OT writer, stresses that there is only one God. Since Yahweh is the one and only God and there are no other gods beside him, there is only one way of salvation (45:21). This truth is expressed concisely in 45:22: "Turn to me and be saved, all the ends of the earth! For I am God, and there is no other." The universal reach of salvation in Isaiah surfaces in chapter 56 as well. Both foreigners and eunuchs ought not to think they are excluded from the Lord's people (56:3).[46] Gentiles who love Yahweh's name and serve him will enjoy his presence in the temple and offer their prayers to him there (56:6–7). Yahweh's glory is expressed in the truth that he will gather others to himself apart from Israel (56:8). The new Jerusalem will not be limited to Jews. Gentiles and kings will be attracted to the light emanating from Israel (60:3; 62:2), and all the good things belonging to Gentiles will stream toward

42. Routledge, "Narrative Substructure of Isaiah," 192n30.
43. So also Dumbrell, *Faith of Israel*, 120.
44. The work of the servant echoes here the Day of Atonement in Lev. 16. So Dempster, *Dominion and Dynasty*, 178.
45. Rightly Dempster, *Dominion and Dynasty*, 179. Contrary to Childs (*Old Testament as Scripture*, 335), who sees no redactional connection between the servant texts and the places that promise a future messianic king.
46. See Gentry and Wellum, *Kingdom through Covenant*, 447–48.

Israel (60:6–7, 10). So, Gentiles too will share in the messianic feast on the last day and will enjoy resurrection from death (25:6–8).[47]

We have seen that Isaiah emphasizes that Yahweh is the holy one of Israel, and he will receive glory and praise for saving Israel and the nations and judging the wicked. Robin Routledge argues that glory and holiness are closely related: "Holiness may be seen as an inward characteristic; it is an essential divine attribute, intimately related to who God is. Glory is the outward manifestation of that holiness: the radiant splendour of the presence of God."[48] Or, as Dumbrell says, the obedience of the nations is "a result of the establishment of the Kingdom of God, where God himself rules from the reconstituted centre of Zion."[49]

Conclusion

We need to step back and consider how Isaiah relates to the story line of the Scriptures as a whole. The Lord promised that the offspring of the woman would triumph over the serpent. The promise of offspring was then narrowed down to Abraham and his offspring. The land of Canaan would be given to Abraham's offspring, and blessing would come to the whole world. As time passed, the Lord clarified that the triumph over the serpent would be realized through David's dynasty, through a son of David. When we come to Isaiah, we see that the promise seems to be in jeopardy. The people through whom the promised offspring is destined to come have turned to other gods. Both Israel and Judah are sent into exile for their sins, facing judgment from Yahweh for their failure to abide by covenant stipulations. The message of Isaiah is that Yahweh has not abandoned his promises. A new David is coming, and there will be a new exodus and a new creation. Yahweh will pour out his Spirit, especially upon his servant, and this servant will bring in the new creation and the new exodus. But he will do so in a most unusual way. He will suffer for the sins of the nation and secure forgiveness of sins through his suffering. We have seen that this suffering servant and the texts on a new David in Isaiah should be melded together. In other words, the suffering servant and the new David are the same person, and the NT witness proclaims that this one is none other than Jesus of Nazareth, the Christ of God. The salvation accomplished by the servant extends to the

47. For a persuasive and subtle defense of resurrection in the OT, see Levenson, *Restoration of Israel*.

48. Routledge, "Narrative Substructure of Isaiah," 194.

49. Dumbrell, *Covenant and Creation*, 198.

entire world. He will bring in a new creation. Indeed, this salvation will reach to the ends of the earth, so that Gentiles will be included. Hence, the kingdom of God will become a reality through this servant, and the promise of worldwide blessing made to Abraham and the promise of triumph over the serpent will become a reality.

20

JEREMIAH

Introduction

If we were to sum up the book of Jeremiah, we could say that it is a book of judgment and restoration, a book that assures the wicked that they will be punished and at the same time promises future salvation for the people of God. The ministry of Jeremiah began during the reign of Josiah. Jeremiah started prophesying about 626 BC, ministering until Judah went into exile (586 BC), and the book closes with the release of Jehoiachin in 562 BC (52:31–34). Jeremiah was taken to Egypt along with other exiles, and we do not hear from him thereafter. Jeremiah's calling as a prophet reflects the major themes of the work. The sovereignty of Yahweh in summoning Jeremiah into ministry is emphasized, for the Lord consecrated and appointed him to be a prophet before he was born (1:5), placing his authoritative words in Jeremiah's mouth (1:6–9). Jeremiah's ministry is summarized in 1:10: "I have set you this day over nations and over kingdoms, to pluck up and to break down, to destroy and to overthrow, to build and to plant." Jeremiah's task reflects the central themes of the book. As a prophet, his words have intrinsic power, for through his words judgment (breaking down and destroying) and salvation (building and planting) will take place. But first comes judgment, and then comes salvation. So my outline of the theology of the book finds its locus in 1:10, for we find there both judgment and salvation.

Judgment

Doubtless the theme of judgment dominates the book. From the outset Jeremiah prophesies that enemies will come from the north and visit destruction on Judah and Jerusalem (1:13–15). That the enemy will arise from the north is a repeated theme (4:6; 6:1, 22–26; 10:22; 13:20; 25:9). Jeremiah predicts that Nebuchadnezzar of Babylon will come to Jerusalem, raze the city and its temple, and send the people into exile (5:14–17; 6:1–9; 21:7; 22:4–5; 25:1–18, 29–31; 27:19–22; 32:28–35). The prophecy was fulfilled in 586 BC, just as the Lord said (chaps. 39; 52), and the exile in Babylon would last seventy years (25:11, 12; 29:10), after which Israel would be restored to the land.[1] We should note also that the judgment is not restricted to Israel. Yahweh is the Lord over the entire earth, and he will judge and punish the nations as well (chaps. 46–51), though some promises of salvation are inserted into the narrative as well (see below). Babylon in particular will suffer judgment for its pride and great evil (chaps. 50–51).

Why did Judah suffer judgment and exile? The reason lies in the covenant, which is one of the most prominent themes in Jeremiah. Repeatedly Jeremiah calls attention to the covenant violations of Israel.[2] Judah did not keep the stipulations of the covenant that were handed down on Mount Sinai. Jeremiah shares this perspective with Isaiah and all the prophets, though it seems to receive particular emphasis in Jeremiah. The covenantal character of the book ties Jeremiah to the earliest books in Israel's canon, particularly to Exodus, Leviticus, and Deuteronomy, which feature Yahweh's covenant with Israel and threaten Israel with judgment if the covenant is violated.

The covenantal and Deuteronomic character of Jeremiah surfaces in chapter 11, where the curses of the covenant come to the forefront.[3] If Israel obeyed the voice of their covenant Lord, they would be his people (11:4). Just as Israel transgressed the Lord's commands in the past, so they were doing in Jeremiah's day, and thus they would face judgment as previous generations did (11:6–8). Yahweh would inflict his wrath upon Israel and Judah for violating his covenant and worshiping other gods (11:10–13). What we see in Jeremiah, then, is that Judah did not submit to Yahweh's lordship; they did not give themselves to their covenant king. Such defection is shocking and astonishing, for Yahweh's lordship was scarcely oppressive. He nurtured and cared for his people, and yet still they despised his rule (chap. 2).

Israel's covenant defection is described from many angles, and one of the words often used to describe their apostasy is "forsake" (*ʿāzab*) (e.g., 1:16; 2:17, 19; 5:7). Israel forsook the Lord, who is "the fountain of living waters,

---

1. I use "Israel" in a broad sense quite often in my discussion of Jeremiah. On the complexity of Jeremiah's usage of "Israel," see McConville, *Judgment and Promise*, 29–33.

2. See McConville, "Jeremiah," 758.

3. On the Deuteronomic character of Jeremiah, see Childs, *Old Testament as Scripture*, 347–48.

and hewed out cisterns for themselves, broken cisterns that hold no water" (2:13; cf. 17:13). Israel's forsaking of the Lord manifested itself in serving and worshiping other gods (5:19; cf. 16:11; 19:4), which, of course, violates the very first command in the Decalogue—the covenant document between Israel and Yahweh (Exod. 20:3). They brought offerings to Baal and Molech with the hope that these gods would provide their needs (7:9; 11:13, 17; 19:5; 32:29, 35; cf. 12:6). The covenantal nature of their defection is clear, for "they have forsaken the covenant of the LORD their God and worshiped other gods and served them" (22:9). What it means to be the people of Yahweh is to fear him rather than idols (chap. 10). Israel has failed to see that Yahweh is incomparable. "There is none like you, O LORD; you are great, and your name is great in might" (10:6), and hence he must be feared (10:7). As 10:10 says, "The LORD is the true God; he is the living God and the everlasting King." Unlike idols, he is the creator of all (10:12–13).

The covenant, of course, cannot be separated from the Torah. Israel, says the Lord, has "forsaken my law" (9:13; cf. 16:11). The Deuteronomic flavor of Jeremiah is obvious, for Jeremiah imitates Deuteronomy's style in using parallel verbs to underscore Israel's unfaithfulness. We read in 9:13 that Israel did not "obey" Yahweh's "voice" or "walk in it." The covenantal character of Jeremiah is evident in 7:23 as well: "But this command I gave them: 'Obey my voice, and I will be your God, and you shall be my people. And walk in all the way that I command you, that it may be well with you'" (cf., e.g., Exod. 19:5–6; Lev. 26:3; Deut. 5:29, 33). Israel, however, traveled in the opposite direction, stubbornly following their own way from the very beginning and refusing to listen to the words of the prophets (7:24–26). Israel adhered to the external trappings of religion, devoting themselves to temple worship (chap. 7) and to the offering of sacrifices (6:21; 7:21–22; 11:15; 14:12). They apparently conceived of the temple as a kind of talisman, as if its presence would shield them from judgment (7:4). Jeremiah reminded them that Shiloh, even though it was the place where the ark rested, was not spared (7:12, 14; 26:6).

Israel's rejection of Yahweh, its forsaking of him, is deeply personal and treacherous (3:8, 11; 5:11). Judah's defection from the Lord is adulterous, showing itself to be a whore (2:20; 3:1–3, 6, 8–9; 13:27).[4] Abandoning the Lord is analogous to a wife being unfaithful to her husband (3:20). Israel's adultery and whoredom are made manifest in Israel's devotion to and worship of other gods (3:1–9; 5:7; 13:27). Violating the covenant must not be construed merely as failing to keep God's commands. Judah rejected its covenant Lord, who had saved them and delivered them from enemies. Both Judah and

4. On this theme in Jeremiah, see Ortlund, *God's Unfaithful Wife*, 83–99.

Israel were to cling to Yahweh like a loincloth clings to the waist (13:1–11). If they trusted and clung to the Lord, he would receive "praise" and "glory" (13:11), but they did not do so. The term "cling" (*dābaq*) is covenantal (e.g., Gen. 2:24; Deut. 4:4; 10:20; 11:22). So Judah, just like Israel (3:1, 8), will be divorced by Yahweh for failing to cling to and trust in the Lord (cf. 17:5). He will send them into exile. Judah, however, was unmoved and untroubled by its whoredom. Its people thought that they had matured, but in fact they had become accustomed to their sins, to the point where they did not even blush at their abominations anymore (6:15; 8:12).

The Deuteronomic and covenantal character of Israel's judgment pervades Jeremiah. Israel was judged because they did not fear Yahweh (3:8; 5:22, 24; 26:19). They were stubborn and rebellious like the wilderness generation (5:23), and their forsaking of the Lord manifested itself in violations of the stipulations of the covenant (5:25). They refused to care for the poor, sojourners, widows, and orphans (5:28; 7:6; 22:3). They were greedy for financial profits and their own interests instead of doing what was honorable before God and what was right before others (6:13; 8:10). They found no delight in God's word, scorning it instead (6:10), and so they pursued evil and were guilty of stealing, murder, adultery, lying, and idolatry (7:9). Adultery and lying and deceit were pandemic in the land (9:2–9; 23:10, 14; 29:23). They poured out the blood of the innocent (7:6; 19:4; 22:3, 17). Shockingly, they even offered their children in sacrifices, which was utterly inconceivable to Yahweh (7:31; 19:5; 32:35; cf. Lev. 18:21; 20:2–5). Their defection from Yahweh showed up concretely in their everyday life, so that they failed to observe the Sabbath (17:21–24, 27). Sin was deeply imprinted in their character, seemingly as unchangeable as the spots on a leopard (13:23). As we read in 17:1, "The sin of Judah is written with a pen of iron; with a point of diamond it is engraved on the tablet of their heart, and on the horns of their altars." The depth of sin exceeds the capacity of human beings to understand it and eradicate it (17:9).

We saw earlier that Israel is threatened with exile, and the book culminates with the judgment of Israel and its leaders (chaps. 39; 52), so that both Jerusalem and its temple are destroyed. The judgment of Israel represents a kind of de-creation (4:23–26). The waste and desolation of the world before creation (cf. Gen. 1:2) returned, so that there was, so to speak, no light, no human beings, no birds, and everything was desolate. The judgment threatened and poured out upon Israel represented the curses of the covenant. Yahweh withheld rain to spur them to repent (3:3; cf. Deut. 28:24). Sword, famine, and pestilence struck Israel because of their refusal to obey the Lord (11:22; 14:12, 15–16, 18; 15:2–3; 16:4; 18:21; 21:7, 9; 24:10; 27:8, 13; 29:17–18; 32:24, 36; 34:17; 38:2; cf. 42:16–17, 22; 44:12–13, 27). Such punishments clearly hearken back to the curses of the Sinai covenant (Lev. 26:16–17, 25–26, 33, 36–37; Deut. 28:21–22, 25) and culminate in Israel's exile (Lev. 26:33; Deut. 28:64).

The stubbornness and sheer blindness and obtuseness of God's people are evident in chapters 40–45. What Jeremiah prophesied has come to pass. Jerusalem and its temple have been taken. Judah is in exile. A new leader, Gedaliah, was appointed, but he and some of his followers were brutally murdered by Ishmael. Johanan defeated Ishmael and became the new leader of Israel, but he feared Babylonian recriminations for the rebellion incited by Ishmael and desired along with others to flee to Egypt. Johanan appealed to Jeremiah, saying that he wanted to seek out and do Yahweh's will. If Yahweh wanted them to stay in Israel, they would do so. But the claim that they were willing to do Yahweh's will was a ruse. When Jeremiah declared that they should stay in Israel, they repudiated his words at once. Indeed, they even maintained that the exile came upon them because they ceased making offerings to false gods. Hence, they dragged Jeremiah off with them to Egypt, where he predicted that they would face judgment. These chapters illustrate Israel's need for true repentance and a new heart. Even after being punished, they were still impervious to the Lord's direction.

Jeremiah and the Leaders of Israel

Much of the conflict in Jeremiah exists between him and the leaders of the land. Kings, priests, prophets, and the wise are indicted for their crucial role in swaying the people from trust in and obedience to the Lord. Judah will be judged because of the evil perpetrated by Manasseh as king (15:4). Zedekiah was warned that judgment would come if he did not surrender to Babylon (21:4–10; 24:8–10; 27:12–13; 37:1–10, 17). The kings in Judah were bringing disaster upon themselves because they exploited resident aliens, the poor, widows, and orphans, enshrining injustice instead of justice (21:12; 22:2–3). If a king devotes himself to living in a splendid palace while at the same time oppressing the poor and even shedding blood (22:13–18), that king will be destroyed. King Jehoiakim could not endure the prophet Uriah's indictment of his reign, and so he had Uriah murdered (26:20–24). Jehoiakim's resistance to the Lord's direction is dramatically set forth in chapter 36. The words of Jeremiah's prophecy, words of impending judgment, were put on a scroll by Baruch and read before the king. Jehoiakim responded by cutting off portions of the scroll as it was read and burning them in the fire. The king did not repent by tearing his garments, nor did he show any fear in rejecting the word of the Lord (36:24), and so his offspring would not sit on the throne, and he would die without dignity, and the punishment predicted for Judah and Jerusalem most certainly would come (36:30–31).

Zedekiah imprisoned Jeremiah because the latter predicted that Jerusalem would be captured by the Babylonians (32:3) and that Zedekiah would be judged by Nebuchadnezzar (32:4; 34:2–3, 21). Zedekiah's mistreatment of Hebrew slaves well represents why he deserved judgment, for he began by doing the right thing and granted them liberty, but then reversed course and enslaved them again (34:8–16). Zedekiah's lack of courage and policy of injustice manifested themselves in his treatment of Jeremiah, for he allowed officials to beat and arrest the prophet (37:12–16). McConville says, "The condemnation of Zedekiah and his associates is not a divine *fiat* which they could not resist, but a consequence of their determined choice."[5] Zedekiah moderated the punishment when Jeremiah pled for relief (37:17–21), but he was like a reed in the wind and permitted Jeremiah to be thrown into a cistern to die at the behest of officials who viewed Jeremiah as a traitor (38:1–6). Only the intervention of an Ethiopian (Ebed-melech) spared Jeremiah's life (38:7–13). Indeed, Zedekiah failed to follow the Lord's instructions because he feared the Judeans (38:19) more than the words of the Lord (38:20–23), and hence he endured the punishment of being blinded, seeing his sons slain before Nebuchadnezzar, and languishing in prison until he died (39:5–7; 52:9–11).

The shepherds—the kings and leaders in Israel—were punished for transgressing God's will (2:8). They did not seek the Lord's will in leading the nation (10:21). As shepherds, it was their responsibility to care for and nurture the sheep—the people of Israel (23:1–4). Instead of caring for the sheep, they exploited and abused them. The priests deserved judgment as well (1:18; 2:26; 4:9; 8:1; 13:13; 23:33–34; 32:32; 34:19; 52:24–26) for their ungodliness (23:11). They did not seek the Lord (2:8; 14:18) but instead followed the lying inclinations of the prophets (5:31; cf. 18:18), presumably to put more money into their own hands (6:13; 8:10). The priest Pashhur beat Jeremiah and imprisoned him (20:1–6). Pashhur seems to have been a prophet also, for he prophesied, though falsely, that Judah would be spared from Babylon. The priests and prophets called for Jeremiah's execution because he predicted that Jerusalem would fall and the temple would be destroyed (chap. 26). The officials and people were more attuned to the Lord than the religious leaders, for they at least recognized that Jeremiah might be speaking the Lord's words, and that they needed to repent of their evil.

Nor was there any help in their so-called wise ones, for they were wise, so to speak, only "in doing evil" (4:22). They claimed to be wise, but they were

---

5. McConville, *Judgment and Promise*, 123.

actually fools because they rejected the Lord's word (8:8–9), and yet they were full of self-confidence and pride, convinced that wisdom would never perish from them (18:18). Those who are truly wise boast not in their wisdom but rather in their knowing the Lord (9:23–24). "Exulting has Yhwh alone as its proper basis."[6] A person's life is not determined by one's autonomy. "I know, O LORD, that the way of man is not in himself, that it is not in man who walks to direct his steps" (10:23).

Jeremiah saves his most substantial criticism for the prophets. Instead of prophesying in accordance with the Lord's word, they "prophesied by Baal" (2:8; 23:13). The prophets were ungodly (23:11); "they commit adultery and walk in lies; they strengthen the hands of evildoers, so that no one turns from his evil" (23:14). They are full of hot air when they proclaim that judgment will be averted (5:9–10), but they pursued falsehood because the people were attracted to such a message (5:31). The prophets filled people with a false comfort since they promised them peace and security in Yahweh's name (14:13–16), but they were not sent by Yahweh (23:21). They supported their prophecies by appealing to supernatural revelation; they claimed to have received God's word in dreams (23:25), but they were "dreaming" and disseminating the "deceit" of their own minds (23:26), even stealing their so-called messages from other false prophets (23:30). They were popular prophets because they said that it would be "well" with those "who despise the word of the LORD" (23:17). And hence the prophets gained a financial reward from proclaiming what the people desired to hear (6:13; 8:10). Their prophecies lacked substance and truth because they did not stand "in the council of the LORD to see and hear his word" (23:18). True prophets turn people back from evil (23:22) and announce the coming "storm of the LORD" (23:19). The words of the false prophets were like straw (23:28), which the fire of the Lord will consume (23:29), for they really have no word at all (23:34–38). God's word is a mighty hammer that dashes in pieces those who oppose him (23:29). Such prophets will be judged (2:26, 30; 4:9; 8:1–2; 13:13; 23:12, 15).

Along the same lines, there was resistance to the prophecies of Jeremiah because he proclaimed upcoming disaster (11:21). As noted previously, Pashhur the priest was a false prophet, and he responded to Jeremiah's prophecies of destruction by beating and imprisoning him (20:1–6; see also chap. 26). Jeremiah's conflict with the prophets is illustrated by his interaction with Hananiah (chap. 28). Hananiah prophesied that the articles of the temple, the exiles, and King Jeconiah would return from Babylon in two years. Jeremiah

6. Goldingay, *Israel's Life*, 57.

did not initially condemn the prophecy but warned the people that a prophet's legitimacy was measured by whether his words came true. Hananiah proceeded to break the yoke on Jeremiah's neck, signifying that Israel would be liberated from bondage. Hananiah's prophecies of liberation were fantasies of his own imagination, and Jeremiah predicted the latter's death, which duly occurred, verifying that Hananiah was a false prophet and that Jeremiah truly stood in the Lord's council (cf. 29:8–9, 21).

Jeremiah's words are the words of the Lord, the words that the Lord placed in his mouth (1:9). In contrast to the false prophets, Jeremiah did not proclaim his own message to the people. He was "full of the wrath of the LORD" (6:11) because the Lord's message against Israel was one of judgment. Jeremiah's words were the fire that would set Israel ablaze (5:14). Even though Jeremiah proclaimed judgment against his people, he found joy in the Lord's word: "Your words were found, and I ate them, and your words became to me a joy and the delight of my heart, for I am called by your name, O LORD, God of hosts" (15:16). Reality is complex. At one level the Lord's words were delightful, but they were also difficult because they promised punishment. Jeremiah, therefore, faced fierce criticism for his prophecies (20:8) and was charged, as was noted above, with being a traitor. Naturally, he became reticent to announce such a dire future. And yet the word of the Lord has an inherent power that cannot be resisted: "If I say, 'I will not mention him, or speak any more in his name,' there is in my heart as it were a burning fire shut up in my bones, and I am weary with holding it in, and I cannot" (20:9).

We must add to the mix Jeremiah's grief and tears over the fate of his people (4:19; 8:18; 9:1; 13:17; 14:17). He was as gentle and harmless as a lamb, and yet the people conspired against him (11:19), though he longed for his people to be spared from what was coming (17:16). He did not enjoy the normal joys of life (15:17), and, per the Lord's instructions, he refrained from marriage (16:1–4) as a testimony to the judgment and exile impending. It is important to see that Jeremiah's words and experiences were his own but also have "a representative function."[7] Indeed, in some instances it is difficult to determine whether the grief is Jeremiah's or the Lord's (see 8:18–9:1), suggesting that Jeremiah's grief reflects the Lord's grief, that Jeremiah in his person and experience represents Yahweh to the people.[8] As McConville says, "Jeremiah in his suffering is conveying something of God's desire for his people."[9] "Jeremiah's proclamation consisted not just of his words, but was represented by his whole

---

7. McConville, "Jeremiah," 760. See also Dumbrell, *Faith of Israel*, 139.
8. McConville, "Jeremiah," 760.
9. Ibid.

life."[10] He also anticipates in his suffering the work of Jesus Christ, showing that the message of the prophet and the life of the messenger are inseparable, and this truth comes to its fullest expression in Jesus Christ.[11]

And yet at the same time Jeremiah prayed for the Lord to pour out vengeance on those who would not repent (11:20; 12:3; 15:15; 17:18). Jeremiah's admonitions were for Israel's good, intending to bring them peace through repentance (18:20). Still, things got so bad that he was instructed not to pray for the people (7:16; 11:14; 14:11; cf. 15:1). Israel responded with vitriolic anger, and therefore Jeremiah prayed that they would not be forgiven and would experience Yahweh's anger (18:21–23). It is tempting to think that both grief for Israel and a desire for vengeance could not be in Jeremiah's heart, but such a response is simplistic. Emotions, as we know, are complex, and it is not surprising that Jeremiah shed tears for his people but also longed for their punishment. Israel's recalcitrance and persistence in evil were maddening and frustrating, leading to the conclusion that judgment was deserved. At the same time, their resistance to the Lord brought grief. It would also be a mistake to conclude that Jeremiah's prayers for vengeance represent a bad attitude. Actually, his tears and his call for judgment both reflect the word of the Lord, for the Lord both grieved for his people and poured judgment out on them in anger.[12] The Lord promises Jeremiah that his plea for vengeance will be answered (11:21–23). He does not reject Jeremiah's prayer as inadequate.

This is not to say that Jeremiah is beyond correction in the book. The people's opposition to him wore him down (15:10). Jeremiah wonders if God will defend and protect him (15:17–18). Will the Lord be like "waters that fail" (15:18)? His only hope for healing and salvation was the Lord, and therefore Yahweh was his praise (17:14). Yahweh promises that he will protect and defend him, as long as Jeremiah speaks his word (15:19–21; cf. 1:8, 18–19). Such protection did not mean that Jeremiah was spared from physical beatings and imprisonment (20:1–6; cf. 37:11–16; 38:4–13). Jeremiah wonders if the Lord deceived him, for his words of judgment had not come to pass, and the people were mistreating and deriding him (20:7–8, 10). And yet Jeremiah is persuaded that those who oppose him will see the Lord's vengeance, and Jeremiah will be vindicated (20:11–12). He praises Yahweh for the promise that his life will be delivered from his enemies (20:13). But at the same time

10. Childs, *Old Testament as Scripture*, 349. "But there is an incarnational aspect in that he embodies the experience of the people and also of Yahweh, without ever ceasing to be an individual personality" (Dumbrell, *Faith of Israel*, 139).

11. McConville, "Jeremiah," 765.

12. For the representative and incarnational role of Jeremiah here, see ibid., 760. For his full discussion of the matter, see McConville, *Judgment and Promise*, 61–78.

he curses the day he was born (20:14–18), for when he sees the judgment coming, he rues his entrance into the world. Jeremiah's despair reflects the experience of Judah, which "raises . . . the possibility of a death of Judah, or perhaps a never having been."[13] But Jeremiah's survival also forecasts hope and preservation for Judah, for judgment is not the last word.[14] Once again the representative ministry of Jeremiah manifests itself.

Repentance and Salvation

Judgment is not permanent in Jeremiah, for ultimately Israel will be saved and restored from exile. Jeremiah often calls upon the people to repent, for repentance would save them from judgment, though he also predicts that they will not repent and, because of their hardness of heart, he is instructed not to pray for them (7:16; 11:14; 14:11). A common word for such repentance is "return" (šûb) (3:1, 7; 4:1; 18:11; 23:14, 22; 25:5; 26:3; 34:15; 35:15; 36:3, 7). Yahweh calls upon his people to return to him with all their hearts (3:10; cf. 3:12, 14). They must admit that they have sinned and violated Yahweh's commands (3:13; cf. 3:22–23, 25). Various metaphors depict repentance: it means breaking up the fallow ground of their hearts and not sowing among thorns (4:3); it means cutting back the foreskin of their hearts (4:4). Judgment did not come upon Israel immediately for their sins, for the Lord is patient, but judgment will come because "they have refused to repent" (5:3; cf. 18:8). Their stubbornness hardens them from returning to the Lord (8:5; cf. 15:7). Genuine repentance would mean that they were genuinely sorry for their sin (4:8; 6:26) so that they cleanse themselves of evil (4:14). The Rechabites stand out as an exemplar for Israel. They followed the rather strange instructions of their father about refraining from wine and living in tents, and yet Israel refused to pay heed to what Yahweh demanded of the people he had rescued from slavery (chap. 35).

Jeremiah's ministry was not only to pluck up and destroy but also to build and to plant (1:10; 18:19; 24:6; 31:28; 32:41; 42:10). Promises of salvation and restoration are sprinkled throughout the work and then burst into full flower in the center of the book (chaps. 30–33). In the midst of exhortations to repent, which Judah did not heed at the time, Jeremiah contemplates what will happen when repentance becomes a reality. Then Israel will have leaders ("shepherds") who will feed them faithfully (3:15). The ark of the Lord will be a thing of the past and will not even be sought (3:16), apparently

13. McConville, *Judgment and Promise*, 75.
14. Ibid., 75–76.

because a newer and greater reality will commence. Jerusalem will be the place where Yahweh reigns, and his reign will not be limited to Israel, for all the nations shall come to Jerusalem and evil shall be a thing of the past (3:17). Judah and Israel will be harmonious and united (3:18). Israel's exile will not last forever; they will return to the land again (12:15), and the nations that swear allegiance to Yahweh's name will share the blessing of belonging to the Lord (12:16).

In the midst of Jeremiah's denunciations he prays for Israel (14:7–9), for the only hope for Israel is the intervention of God himself. The prayer commences with the acknowledgment of Israel's sins; the only basis for confidence is if Yahweh acts for his "name's sake" to save his people (14:7). Israel calls upon the Lord not to be like a traveling stranger or like a warrior who cannot save (14:8–9). Yahweh dwells with his people, and his name is upon them, and so they entreat him not to abandon them. The end of the chapter concludes with a similar prayer (14:19–22). Here Jeremiah asks whether Yahweh hates his people and has rejected them forever (14:19). The fundamental problem with the people is their sin. So Jeremiah begs the Lord to remember his covenant with Israel, to preserve them "for your name's sake" (14:21). Idols cannot bring rain or fruitfulness. Israel's only hope for renewal and restoration is the Lord, for he can do all things (14:22).

We find a similar note of hope in 16:14–21. Exile will not be the final reality for Israel. There will be a new exodus (16:14–15). Yahweh will send fishers and hunters to bring his people back (16:16). Here the role of the apostles as "fishers" is anticipated (cf. Matt. 4:19; Mark 1:17).[15] Even the nations will recognize, in fulfillment of the promise to Abraham (cf. Gen. 12:3), that idols are worthless, that salvation is only in the Lord (16:19–20). Then "they shall know that my name is the LORD" (16:21). The promise of salvation includes even some of the enemies of Israel (48:47; 49:6, 39), though no such hope is offered to Babylon.[16] Yahweh will set his favor on the "good figs" in exile and bring them back to Israel (24:5–6). And he will perform heart surgery on them: "I will give them a heart to know that I am the LORD, and they shall be my people and I will be their God, for they shall return to me with their whole heart" (24:7). The call for repentance would not be heeded during Jeremiah's day, but it would become a reality in the future. The last word for Israel is not exile. There is "a future and a hope" for Israel (29:11), and their "fortunes" will be restored (29:14), which becomes a major theme in chapters 30–33 (30:3, 18; 31:23; 32:44; 33:7, 11, 26; cf. Deut. 30:3).

15. Rightly Gentry and Wellum, *Kingdom through Covenant*, 489–90.
16. See McConville, "Jeremiah," 763.

Chapters 30–33, which are a book of comfort and promise, begin with the assurance that Israel will return from exile after a time of punishment (30:1–11, 17–18). One of the dominant themes, as McConville notes, is that the plans of Yahweh for his people will be fulfilled.[17] Israel will be full of praise and will be safe and secure in the land (30:19–20). A priest-king will come, a ruler, whom God will bring near to himself (30:21–22).[18] God's covenant with his people will be a reality as he cares for them and rules over them as their God (30:22; 31:1). Yahweh could never take his love from Israel, for he "loved them with an everlasting love" (31:3). Music will resound, and vineyards will be planted when Israel is restored (31:4–5, 7). Israel will come from the ends of the earth and will weep at the mercy of the Lord (31:8–10). It will then be clear that Yahweh ransomed and redeemed Israel (31:11). Weeping will be short-lived, for Israel "shall be like a watered garden" (31:12), and the young will dance and the old will rejoice (31:13). The greatest blessing will be the Lord's presence with his people. The Lord says, "My people shall be satisfied with my goodness" (31:14). They will see the King in his beauty! The grief of exile will be temporary (31:15–19), for Ephraim is Yahweh's "dear son," his "darling child" (31:20). Yahweh cannot reject his own, and so Israel will return from exile (31:21). A woman (the people of Israel) will encircle and conquer "a man"—that is, the pagan nations (31:22). Every person will be satisfied and refreshed by the Lord (31:25).

A new covenant is promised, which would be different from the Sinai covenant (31:31–32), for although the Lord was gracious to his people in liberating them from Egypt, Israel did not abide by the stipulations of the covenant. By way of contrast, "it will not be possible to breach the new covenant."[19] The new covenant is of a different character, for now the Lord will write his law on the hearts of his people so that they will obey him (31:33).[20] Israel would experience what it means for Yahweh to be their God and to live as his people. "The new covenant . . . is a way of solving the basic problem identified in earlier parts of the book . . . , namely, the failure of the covenant people to be faithful."[21]

Every member of the covenant people would know the Lord (31:34).[22] Every member of the covenant family would have the law written on their hearts.

17. McConville, *Judgment and Promise*, 92–93.
18. See Gentry and Wellum, *Kingdom through Covenant*, 513–15.
19. Dumbrell, *Faith of Israel*, 145. However, Dumbrell (p. 146) underestimates the newness of the new covenant.
20. See Hafemann, "Covenant Relationship," 51. Although I would identify the covenant as "new" rather than designate it as "renewed."
21. McConville, "Jeremiah," 761.
22. See Hafemann, "Covenant Relationship," 54–55.

The old covenant was "tribal" in that representatives—such as prophets, priests, and kings—mediated the Lord to the people (cf. 31:29–30). But now God's people will relate to him more directly, since the law is planted on each member's heart.[23] The basis of this transformation is the forgiveness of sins (31:34), in which sins will be remembered no more. "The forgiveness of which this verse speaks is so comprehensive that sin has finally been dealt with in the experience of the nation and individual believer."[24] "I will cleanse them from all the guilt of their sin against me, and I will forgive all the guilt of their sin and rebellion against me" (33:8). The old covenant had "faulty mediators," but the new covenant will have a mediator who "is without sin."[25] Canonically, the promise of the new covenant is fulfilled in Jesus Christ, through whom the law has been written on the hearts of his people (Rom. 2:25–29; 2 Cor. 3:4–11), since he has fully and finally forgiven the sins of his people through the sacrifice of himself (Heb. 8–10).[26] How sure is the covenant promised by Jeremiah? As sure as the sun, moon, and stars (31:35–36)! It can no more be revoked than one can measure the heavens or plumb the foundations of the earth (31:37). Jerusalem will again be sacred to the Lord (31:38–40).

Israel's return from exile and future are exemplified in Jeremiah buying a field in Anathoth from his uncle (chap. 32). The old exodus becomes the pattern and hope for a new exodus (32:17–22). Jeremiah, though he knows the creed (32:17), has a difficult time believing that the Lord will restore Israel, and hence the Lord reminds him that nothing is beyond the Lord (32:27). The Lord will gather Israel after their exile, and they will be his people, and he will be their God (32:37–38). The covenant will be fulfilled, and Israel will enjoy Yahweh's presence. The essence of the new covenant is reiterated. The Lord will transform his people through this everlasting new covenant.[27] "I will put the fear of me in their hearts, that they may not turn from me" (32:40). Yahweh will overflow with joy in doing good to his people and planting them in the land (32:41; cf. 32:43; 33:6–7). Israel will luxuriate in the goodness of the Lord, which he will shower upon them (33:9), and will overflow with joy (33:11).

If the promise of a Davidic heir seems to be withdrawn in 22:30, we quickly learn that such a reading is mistaken, for 23:5–6 (cf. 33:17) promises that a future David will sit on the throne.[28] The promises made to David are irrevocable,

23. So Gentry and Wellum, *Kingdom through Covenant*, 646–47.

24. Dumbrell, *Faith of Israel*, 146. See also Williamson, *Sealed with an Oath*, 155–56.

25. Gentry and Wellum, *Kingdom through Covenant*, 510.

26. The promises of the new covenant were not fulfilled fully when Israel returned from exile. See Williamson, *Sealed with an Oath*, 157–58.

27. In support of the notion that the "everlasting covenant" is another way of speaking of the "new covenant," see Gentry and Wellum, *Kingdom through Covenant*, 521.

28. See McConville, "Jeremiah," 765–66; Dumbrell, *Faith of Israel*, 142.

just as the covenant (Noahic) with respect to day and night and the seasons will continue until the end of history (33:20–21). The new covenant promises will become a reality during his reign, so that "justice and righteousness" will be established in the land (23:5), and Israel and Judah will be saved (23:6; 33:16). He will be given the name "The LORD is our righteousness" (23:6). There seems to be a suggestion here that the righteousness that Israel needs from the Lord will be theirs through the future Davidic king. Indeed, the new David is placed on the same level as Yahweh: "They shall serve the LORD their God and David their king" (30:9), suggesting the high stature of this future Davidic ruler. This future king, this "righteous Branch" (33:15), is raised up by the Lord (23:5; 30:9), and his offspring will be as numerous as the sand on the seashore (33:22), suggesting that the promise of countless offspring made to Abraham is fulfilled through a son of David.[29] If the kingship is irrevocable, so too is the priesthood (33:18, 21–22). The Levitical priests will continue to offer sacrifices in perpetuity.

Clearly, the promise of a new David, according to the NT, is fulfilled in Jesus Christ. The Lord raised him up as the Messiah of Israel and the Lord of the world. The righteousness that believers enjoy is theirs via their union with Christ (Rom. 5:15–19; 2 Cor. 5:21). The promise of worldwide blessing through the offspring of Abraham and David becomes a reality through Jesus. If we pay heed to Hebrews, what Jeremiah says about the Levitical priests abiding forever is not literally true. But Jeremiah writes in accord with the language and expectations of his day, and what he says about the priesthood is fulfilled in the permanent and irrevocable Melchizedekian priesthood of Jesus (Heb. 7:1–10:18).[30]

Conclusion

The OT promises that Israel will see the King in his beauty. The promises made to Adam (Gen. 3:15), Abraham (Gen. 12:1–3), and David (2 Sam. 7) will bring blessing to the whole world and undo the devastation introduced by Adam and Eve. Israel, whom Yahweh chose to be his people, would represent Yahweh to the world. But everything went horribly wrong. Instead of worshiping and obeying the Lord, Israel abandoned him and turned to other gods. They violated the stipulations of the covenant repeatedly. Therefore, the Lord threatened the nation with exile and exiled them to Babylon for

---

29. See Dempster, *Dominion and Dynasty*, 167.

30. Alternatively, perhaps what is said about Levitical priests is fulfilled in the priesthood of all believers. See Gentry and Wellum, *Kingdom through Covenant*, 528.

their transgressions. And yet Yahweh's covenant promises were not repealed. Jeremiah teaches that a new covenant is coming, a covenant that is irrevocable, a covenant by which sins will be fully and finally forgiven, and by which a new David will sit on the throne. This king will be Israel's righteousness and will bring about a new Eden.

21

LAMENTATIONS

Introduction

The placement of Lamentations between Jeremiah and Ezekiel fits because both prophets predict the destruction of Jerusalem and see their prophecies come to pass. Lamentations contemplates poetically what happened to the people of the covenant when they were exiled to Babylon in 586 BC. The grief of Israel is set forth within a disciplined poetic framework. The book has five chapters, and the first four chapters are an acrostic, whereby each verse begins with the first letter of the Hebrew alphabet and the chapters conclude with the last letter of the alphabet. Chapter 3 differs, for it consists of sixty-six verses, and each letter of the Hebrew alphabet is used three times. The unique layout of chapter 3 signals that it is the center of the book and the most important chapter. Chapter 5 lacks the acrostic pattern, but there is still a matching structure, for the chapter has twenty-two verses, which conforms to the number of letters in the Hebrew alphabet.

The form of the work reminds us that grief is powerfully communicated through poetry, for poetry captures and conveys emotion in an artistic form that causes the reader to pause and reflect on the experience relayed. Poetry has an ineffable character that makes it ideal for communicating either joy or sorrow. As Barry Webb notes, "The acrostic form of the poems has the effect of giving grief a shape which is itself a kind of resolution. Grief itself, by its very nature, is a rather formless thing. The mind of a person in deep sorrow characteristically moves in circles, returning again and again to the source of grief, unable to leave it and unable to resolve it. What the acrostic form does is to allow the grief to be fully expressed, and yet at the same time set limits to it."[1] Norman Gottwald says that the form brings "about a complete cleansing of conscience through a total confession of sin."[2] As he points out, the sins of Israel through the acrostic are confessed from A to Z.[3] The poetic nature of Lamentations is instructive in another way. As we examine the structure of the poem, we see clearly that the climax of the book comes not in the concluding chapter but rather in the middle of the book (chap. 3). Chapter 3, then, becomes the hermeneutical key for unlocking the theology of the entire book.[4] We should interpret the book not from the perspective of the uncertain statement that concludes chapter 5, but instead from the standpoint of hope found in chapter 3.

If we were to sum up Lamentations at the outset, how does it fit with the theology set forth in the rest of the OT? The first thing to notice is that this book is rooted in the Lord's covenant with Israel. Jerusalem and its temple are destroyed, and the people have gone into exile. Why has all this happened? Because God's people have violated the stipulations of the covenant.[5] They have not submitted to God's lordship, to the will of Yahweh their king. The acknowledgment of sin demonstrates that the book is not only a lament but also a confession of sin.[6] Is the story over? Has everything failed forever? The whole experience with Israel seems to have been a shocking false start, for hundreds of years have passed, and now they are forsaken and devastated. "It is a book that presses us to the brink of the failure of the old covenant through the sinfulness of the people of God."[7] But judgment is not the last word. Hope is. The Lord's covenant promises are not withdrawn from his people. He will have mercy on his people again and be faithful to them. Their enemies will be judged, and the Lord will reign as king over his people.

Agonizing Judgment at Yahweh's Hand

Upon digging a bit deeper into the book, the first thing that strikes a reader is the experience of judgment. Lamentations lingers over the suffering and anguish in Israel. Jerusalem in exile is like a widow among the nations (1:1; 5:2). Tears are her portion (1:2, 16; 2:11, 18; 3:48–49), and she has no one to comfort her in her sorrow (1:2, 17, 21). The festivals and feasts of the Lord are

---

1. B. Webb, *Five Festal Garments*, 61.
2. Gottwald, *Book of Lamentations*, 30.
3. Ibid.
4. See Childs, *Old Testament as Scripture*, 594; B. Webb, *Five Festal Garments*, 60.
5. Dumbrell, *Faith of Israel*, 296.
6. B. Webb, *Five Festal Garments*, 74.
7. Ibid., 79.

all but forgotten (1:4; 2:6), and her enemies rejoice over her destruction (1:5, 7, 21; 2:15–16), showing that they were not her allies (1:19). The precious things in the city and the temple are stolen (1:10). Her princes, who were supposed to lead the nation, are stripped of their power and dignity (1:6; 2:9; 4:7–8; 5:12). Her king, the anointed one, who was charged with leading the nation under Yahweh's lordship, is in exile (2:6, 9; 4:20). No word of the Lord is given to the prophets (2:9), for they did not proclaim Yahweh's word to the nation but instead spoke soothing words when words of reproof were needed (2:14; cf. 4:13). Nor were the priests spared judgment (1:4, 19; 4:16), for they too committed iniquity to further their own interests (4:13).

The entire nation groans under affliction. Elders are dishonored (4:16; 5:12) and are stunned in their sorrow (2:10; cf. 1:19). Women are raped by the enemy (5:11; cf. 2:10), and both young and old are killed (2:21). Strong young men are pressed into forced labor (5:13). Dancing and joy and mirth are a distant memory (5:14–15). Children have gone into captivity (1:5; cf. 1:16), suffer from starvation (2:19; 4:4), and are even eaten by their mothers (2:20; 4:10).

Israel's grief, groaning, and oppression at the hand of its enemies elicit sympathy from readers. It is somewhat astonishing, then, to see the forcefulness with which the author emphasizes that Yahweh is behind Israel's suffering. Israel's exile to Babylon was not the result of fate or chance. "Jerusalem sinned grievously" (1:8; cf. 1:14; 2:14; 4:13, 22; 5:7, 16) and became unclean (1:9) because of its rebellion against Yahweh's lordship (1:20; 3:42).[8] Israel's punishment, then, was not arbitrary or capricious but righteous, expressing Yahweh's justice (1:18).[9] Yahweh "inflicted" "sorrow" upon his people "in the day of his fierce anger" (1:12). "The LORD gave full vent to his wrath; he poured out his hot anger" (4:11). He left Israel "stunned" and "faint all day long" (1:13), and he gave them "into the hands of their enemies" (1:14). "The LORD himself has scattered them" (4:16). He stamped on Judah like it was grapes in a winepress (1:15). In his anger he flung Jerusalem from heaven to earth (2:1) and "broke down the strongholds of the daughter of Judah" (2:2). When Israel needed help, he withdrew support (2:3), so that he "has become like an enemy" (2:4). He is the one who "laid in ruins his meeting place" and "made Zion forget festival and Sabbath" (2:6). It is Yahweh who "determined to lay in ruins the wall of the daughter of Zion" (2:8). Israel abandoned its covenant with Yahweh, and so he did "what he purposed; he has carried out his word" (2:17), so that the enemy rejoiced over Israel's fall.

8. Rightly House, *Lamentations*, 320.
9. So also ibid., 324.

The ferocity of the language for Yahweh's judgment and its relentless character are striking. As Webb remarks, "The language is violent and the emotion intense."[10] The "I" in chapter 3 stands for Israel as God's people.[11] Yahweh shrouded Israel in darkness (3:2). He caused Israel's skin to shrivel up and broke its bones (3:4). "He has besieged and enveloped me with bitterness and tribulation" (3:5). He walled Israel up and put chains on his people (3:7), and he refused to listen to its prayer (3:8). Yahweh is like a ravaging animal intent on destroying Israel, so that he is likened to a bear and a lion (3:10) that "tore me to pieces" (3:11). Yahweh stretched out his bow and sent his arrows flying against Israel (3:12), filling them with bitterness and making their teeth grind (3:15–16). Israel was experiencing judgment from their king. As Claus Westermann says, "God directs not just the history of Israel; God directs the history of all peoples. It is God who effects wars, determining who will be the victors and who the vanquished."[12] Gottwald remarks, "No accident, no demon, no foreign god was responsible for the plight of Israel, but Yahweh alone."[13] Everything that happens, both good and evil, comes from his hand. "Who has spoken and it came to pass, unless the Lord has commanded it? Is it not from the mouth of the Most High that good and bad come?" (3:37–38). The calamity that struck Israel fulfills what the Lord ordained and what he prophesied would happen (see Lev. 26; Deut. 28) if they violated covenant stipulations.

Hope for the Future

At first glance, it might seem to be disastrous news that Israel's punishment was the personal expression of Yahweh's anger. What hope was there for Israel if Yahweh was against them? In fact, however, the rule of Yahweh in this situation was also the basis, indeed the only basis, for hope. Israel's defeat was not merely a result of the way the political winds were blowing, as if it were subject to the military power and prowess of other nations. Israel's enemies could not and would not touch it unless the nation had sinned and Yahweh had handed them over to their adversaries. The author of the book is hopeful that judgment is not permanent.[14] Interjected and

10. B. Webb, *Five Festal Garments*, 67.
11. This is disputed. The majority opinion is that an individual is in view (see Childs, *Old Testament as Scripture*, 592–93). But even if that is the case, the individual still represents the nation. Perhaps Dempster (*Dominion and Dynasty*, 209) is correct in seeing a reference to the king who represents the nation, though that is not clear to me in the text.
12. Westermann, *Lamentations*, 222–23.
13. Gottwald, *Book of Lamentations*, 77.
14. See House, *Lamentations*, 324.

sprinkled throughout the judgments and woes of Israel are short prayers wherein Yahweh is summoned to come to his people's aid.[15] Yahweh is still the God and king of Israel,[16] so the author suddenly interjects, "O LORD, behold my affliction, for the enemy has triumphed!" (1:9). He appeals to Yahweh's mercy, believing that when the Lord sees the suffering of his people, whom he loves, he will intervene on their behalf. We find a similar prayer in 1:11, "Look, O LORD, and see, for I am despised," and in 1:20, "Look, O LORD, for I am in distress." The author is convinced that the same Lord who ravaged his people like a lion or a bear still cares for his people and is able to reverse their fortunes, and so he calls upon his God, "Look, O LORD, and see!" (2:20).

The whole of chapter 5 is a prayer to the Lord. The author calls upon the Lord to remember his people and to "see our disgrace" (5:1). He calls upon the Lord, precisely because the Lord reigns, because he rules over all: "But you, O LORD, reign forever; your throne endures to all generations" (5:19). Hence, the author wonders why the Lord has forgotten and forsaken his people (5:20), calling upon him, "Restore us to yourself, O LORD, that we may be restored! Renew our days as of old" (5:21). The same Lord who destroyed them can also renew them. The book ends not on this positive note but rather with a question. Is the Lord so angry that he will never show mercy again (5:22)? As noted earlier, chapter 5 does not represent the climax of the book, so the last verse should not be given undue weight.[17] The key to the book is found in its center, chapter 3. Still, the author wants to leave the readers pondering the future of Israel. Their sin is grievous so that they don't deserve redemption.

We noted earlier the unrelenting opposition of Yahweh to Israel in chapter 3, but the tone changes in the middle of the chapter. The author remembers the Lord's covenant with his people and is renewed with hope (3:21). The covenant faithfulness of Yahweh is expressed in the most famous lines of the book, picking up the language of Exod. 34:6:[18] "The steadfast love of the LORD never ceases; his mercies never come to an end; they are new every morning; great is your faithfulness" (3:22–23). The judgment had been devastating, but Yahweh is merciful and gracious and "does not willingly afflict or grieve the children of men" (3:33). "Begrudgingly, regretfully, if there is no other way toward his higher purposes, he may unleash the forces of evil, but 'his heart'

---

15. See Gottwald, *Book of Lamentations*, 91–94.

16. For the emphasis on God's rule and sovereignty in Lamentations, see House, *Lamentations*, 329.

17. B. Webb (*Five Festal Garments*, 75) perhaps overemphasizes the role of this verse.

18. Ibid., 69. Also, House (*Lamentations*, 320) notes the contribution of Deut. 30.

is not in it!"[19] Perhaps Dempster is correct in seeing a reference here to the Davidic promise, the pledge that one of David's sons would reign.[20] Those who were under Yahweh's judgment should bear the judgment humbly and hopefully (3:27–29), for "the LORD is good to those who wait for him, to the soul who seeks him" (3:25). The author is confident in the Lord's love: "For the Lord will not cast off forever, but, though he cause grief, he will have compassion according to the abundance of his steadfast love" (3:31–32). The author never presumes on Yahweh's grace and mercy, but he is confident of it, for he knows that Yahweh is Israel's "portion" (3:24). "God's people remain God's people."[21] "The ground of hope is in the unshakable nature of Yahweh's justice and love. His constancy guarantees that the disappointments and defeats are not ultimate inasmuch as sovereign grace stands behind and beyond them (3:36–39)."[22] He calls upon the Lord, therefore, as the king and sovereign one to judge Israel's enemies and to have mercy upon Israel (1:21–22). Indeed, the author is confident (3:59–66) that Yahweh "will repay them" (3:64), and that his "curse will be upon them" (3:65),[23] so that he "will pursue them in anger and destroy them from under your heavens" (3:66). The author is convinced that the cup of God's wrath will be drunk by Edom (4:21–22). The judgment of enemies may seem unrelated to contemporary readers, but such a reversal shows that the punishment of Zion has ended, and that exile is over (4:22).

Conclusion

Lamentations starkly describes the anguish of Jerusalem and Judah. Exile and desolation are its portion because the nation departed from the covenant, transgressing what Yahweh commanded. The punishments were inflicted by pagan nations, but ultimately the Lord himself was Israel's adversary, turning against his people for their faithlessness. But since Yahweh was the one who judged Israel, he was also the one who could save them. Therefore, there was reason for hope. Their king and covenant Lord would not forget his promises of salvation. He would be the portion and joy of Israel again. "The special contribution of Lamentations is to confront us with the terrible reality of the wrath of God, and so bars the way to any resolution less than the one the New

---

19. Gottwald, *Book of Lamentations*, 98. Gottwald (pp. 101–2) goes on to say that there is a recognition of levels of God's will in Lamentations, a "permissive and primary will," when we recognize the emphasis on divine sovereignty and divine mercy.

20. Dempster, *Dominion and Dynasty*, 210.

21. House, *Lamentations*, 324.

22. Gottwald, *Book of Lamentations*, 108.

23. House, *Lamentations*, 327.

Testament finally provides."[24] The agony and desolation of standing under God's wrath, so powerfully communicated in Lamentations, finds its apex in the suffering of Jesus the Christ, who was forsaken by God.[25] The giving oneself up to suffering in Lamentations (3:27–30) anticipates the Isaianic servant of the Lord who willingly bears suffering, though in the latter case he does so for the sins of his people.[26] The sufferings of Israel and of the world, which find their root in human sin, were also experienced by the true Israel, the servant of the Lord. Hence, the forgiveness pleaded for and the hope persisting in Lamentations find their resolution in the sufferings and glories of Jesus Christ, for the hope in Lamentations reaches its goal in the resurrection of the Christ.

---

24. B. Webb, *Five Festal Garments*, 81.
25. See Gottwald, *Book of Lamentations*, 64.
26. So ibid., 105–6.

22

EZEKIEL

Introduction and Ezekiel's Call

We saw that the themes of judgment and salvation are central in Jeremiah, and the same is true of Ezekiel. Ezekiel's ministry started after Jeremiah's (593 BC), being directed especially to the exiles in Babylon and extending until at least 571 BC. Ezekiel's call as a prophet is relayed in chapters 1–3. Upon reading the first chapter of Ezekiel, one might think that the prophet suffered from a nightmare.[1] In the midst of a storm he saw four living creatures with wings and faces. Their faces had four dimensions, such that they looked like human beings, lions, oxen, and eagles. The creatures were "like burning coals of fire" (1:13), and they were darting hither and thither with amazing speed. In addition, he saw wheels that corresponded with each of the four living creatures, and the wheels traveled beside the four living creatures and were full of eyes on their rims. We are told in chapter 10 that these strange living creatures are cherubim (10:15–16, 20). The cherubim are closely associated with God's presence in the OT. They prohibit the way to the tree of life in the garden (Gen. 3:24) and were placed above the mercy seat, where Yahweh met with Israel (Exod. 25:18–22; 1 Sam. 4:4; 2 Sam. 6:2; cf. 1 Kings 6:23–29; 8:6–7; 2 Kings 19:15).

It is not surprising, then, that Ezek. 1 concludes with a vision of Yahweh (1:26–28). The words "likeness" and "appearance" dominate these verses, for the glory of the Lord cannot be fully seen or fully expressed.[2] Yahweh's ap-

---

1. Incidentally, I should add that Ezekiel uses many images from creation in chapter 1 and elsewhere in the book. See Duguid, "Ezekiel," 229.
2. See Goldingay, *Israel's Faith*, 25.

pearance is as brilliant and bright as a raging fire. Ezekiel's vision echoes the vision of the Lord vouchsafed to Moses and the elders (Exod. 24:10). The glory was so stunning that Ezekiel fainted. The vision conveys the transcendent glory, holiness, and sovereignty of God.[3] The vision sets us up for the remainder of the book. How can this glorious and holy God continue to abide with his people when they have turned aside to abominations and defiled themselves by their sin? As Gentry and Wellum say, the motion in the chapter shows that "God is getting ready to move out!"[4] Ezekiel unfolds how Yahweh, as the sovereign Lord of Israel, handed his people over to judgment, removing the glory of his presence from them. At the same time, the book promises that the beauty of the Lord's presence will be restored to Israel. They will once again live under the dominion of their king.

At the same time, the vision of Yahweh is the means by which Ezekiel is called as a prophet (chaps. 2–3). The Spirit entering into Ezekiel signifies that he speaks from God, not from his own wisdom or on the basis of his own inspiration. Ezekiel is identified as "son of man" ninety-three times in the book, and this phrase underscores Ezekiel's mortality and frailty. Hence, he needs the Spirit's "empowerment."[5] His effectiveness, like that of Jeremiah (Jer. 1:5–10) and Isaiah (Isa. 6), does not stem from his own giftedness. Indeed, Ezekiel was called to prophesy to a "rebellious house," a term used fourteen times in Ezekiel, seven of these in chapters 2–3. Israel is "impudent and stubborn" (2:4) and like "briers and thorns" and "scorpions" (2:6). Ezekiel ate the scroll of the Lord's words, which signified that he was willing to hear and obey Yahweh's instructions. The words were "sweet as honey" because they were the words of God (3:3), but at the same time they were hard words, words of "lamentation, mourning, and woe" (2:10). Israel should have listened to Ezekiel's words, for they were the people of God and could understand what he was saying. But they resisted because of their stubbornness (3:7).

Ezekiel was commissioned by God and empowered by the Spirit to speak words of judgment to the exiles, whether they would hear him or not. He was the watchman for Israel, threatening death to those who persisted in sin and promising life to those who would repent (3:18–21; 33:1–9). Indeed, it seems that Ezekiel could speak only words of judgment from the Lord (3:24–27). His muteness means that words of salvation did not apply to his generation.[6] But his muteness ended when it was reported that Jerusalem was taken (33:21–22),

---

3. So Block, *Ezekiel: Chapters 1–24*, 106–7.
4. Gentry and Wellum, *Kingdom through Covenant*, 471.
5. Dempster, *Dominion and Dynasty*, 168.
6. Dumbrell, *Faith of Israel*, 155. For a full discussion, see Block, *Ezekiel: Chapters 1–24*, 154–61.

for now the prophecy Ezekiel uttered about judgment was fulfilled, and he promised future salvation.

Judgment: Yahweh Abandons the Temple

Ezekiel began his ministry proclaiming the removal of the glory of the Lord from Israel, warning the Lord's people of the judgment to come. As a prophet, he illustrated and exemplified the judgment to come with dramatic signs. For instance, in chapter 4 he built miniature siege works with an iron griddle, a brick, and other articles to represent the upcoming siege of Jerusalem. Ezekiel also lay on his left side for 390 days and then on his right side for 40 days to symbolize the punishment to be inflicted on Israel and Judah, respectively.[7] Ezekiel's diet would also forecast the hardship that would ensue with the siege, for he consumed rationed amounts of food and water to signify the difficulty that Jerusalem would face. A similar sign was acted out in chapter 5. Ezekiel shaved his head and beard: one-third of his hair was then burned in the city, one-third was struck with a sword, and one-third was thrown to the wind. Again, the sign spelled the future punishment of Jerusalem because of its wickedness and failure to do Yahweh's will. Yahweh will unleash his judgments, he tells the people, because "you have defiled my sanctuary with all your detestable things and with all your abominations" (5:11). The sign that Ezekiel enacted would become a reality: one-third would die from disease, one-third would die from war, and one-third would be scattered to the winds with violence pursuing them (5:12). Thus, Yahweh's fury and anger would be vented upon his people.

Along the same lines, Ezekiel acted out going into exile (chap. 12). He prepared baggage to carry, put it on his shoulder, dug through a wall, left at dusk, and covered his face so that he would not see the land. So too, Israel and its king would be taken into exile by the Babylonians and be scattered among the nations. In the same vein, Ezekiel ate his food tremulously and drank water while trembling to signify Israel's state during exile (12:19). These signs were given to assure Israel that the judgment would certainly come and that it was imminent (12:22–28). Similarly, chapter 7 heralds the imminence of the end. Yahweh will punish Israel for all their "abominations" (7:3). He will neither "spare" nor "pity" (7:4). He will "pour out" his "wrath" and "spend" his "anger" (7:8). Sword, pestilence, and famine await Israel (7:15; cf. 5:12, 17; 6:11, 12; 12:16; 14:21). When these judgments come, Israel will know that Yahweh

---

7. The days reflect "the number of years Israel was in Exile in Egypt" (cf. Exod. 12:40), showing that the number is symbolic (Dempster, *Dominion and Dynasty*, 168).

is Lord (7:4, 9, 27). We see two of Ezekiel's favorite expressions in these verses. Israel will suffer because of its "abominations," a term used ninety-three times to describe the horror of Israel's sins. Remarkably, the term is absent from the oracles against the nations, so it is reserved to highlight Israel's defection from Yahweh. Another common expression is that Yahweh does what he does so that Israel "will know that I am the LORD." Variants of this phrase occur seventy-two times. Most often, the phrase is found in contexts of judgment so as to emphasize the ultimate reason why the judgment is inflicted upon Israel. The nation will recognize and know that Yahweh is Lord, that he is the sovereign king and the one and only true God. As Childs says, "The dominant feature of the book of Ezekiel is its stark theological understanding which views everything from a radical theocentric perspective."[8]

Furthermore, this recognition is not restricted to Israel. In the oracles against the nations Yahweh's judgments will lead them to acknowledge his lordship as well (25:7, 11, 17; 26:6; 28:22, 23, 24, 26; 29:6, 9, 16; 30:8, 19, 25, 26; 32:25; 35:4, 9, 12, 15; 38:23; 39:6, 7). Yahweh is the king and sovereign over the entire world. There is no place anywhere where his lordship will be disputed or where his great name will be rivaled. The nations face judgment particularly because of their response to Israel. Ammon, for instance, rejoiced over the profanation of the sanctuary (25:3, 6). Moab and Seir cursed Israel (25:8), whereas Edom and the Philistines will face vengeance because they took revenge upon Israel (25:12–17). Tyre anticipated financial profits from Israel's fall (26:2). Though Tyre was the center of trade (chap. 27), it would fall because of its pride (28:1–18), for it claimed to be godlike on account of its wealth while practicing iniquity. Egypt will also face judgment (chaps. 29–32) as the great dragon opposed to Yahweh (29:3; 32:2). It will be judged because it was a basis of false confidence for Israel (29:6–10, 16). Just as Assyria was brought down because of its pride in its majesty, likewise Egypt will be brought low (31:2–18). The judgment of Edom is located at a different place in the book (chap. 35), in the midst of the oracles of restoration for Israel. The oracle is placed here because Edom represents all the nations that resisted Yahweh and hated Israel (35:5, 10, 15).

The sword will be unleashed against Israel for its evil (chap. 21). The horror of the judgment provokes groaning and grief (21:6). Those who think that they are strong will melt before the intense judgment impending (21:7, 15). The siege of Jerusalem will assuage Yahweh's wrath (24:7–8). The city will not be spared, and Yahweh will be unrelenting because of its uncleanness (24:13–14). The death of Ezekiel's wife ("the delight of your eyes" [24:16]) functions as a parable of the anguish about to strike Jerusalem (24:21–24).

8. Childs, *Old Testament as Scripture*, 361.

Ezekiel often stresses that Israel will be judged for being unclean. Yahweh tells them, "You defiled my sanctuary with all your detestable things" (5:11; cf. 23:38), probably a reference to their idolatry (20:7, 18, 31; 22:3, 4; 23:7, 13, 17, 30; 36:18; 37:23). They are also defiled because of "all their transgressions" (14:11; cf. 20:43; 36:17), and they defile their neighbor's wife through adultery (18:6, 11, 15; 33:26; cf. 22:11). Fundamentally, Israel "defiled [Yahweh's] holy name" (43:7–8). The treachery of Israel's sin against Yahweh is depicted in two chapters that describe Israel's sin as whoredom (chaps. 16; 23), where the language used is shocking and X-rated.[9] Jerusalem was an abandoned infant, but Yahweh showed mercy to her so that she lived (16:6). He entered into a covenant with her, betrothed her to himself, and arrayed her with beautiful clothes and jewelry (16:7–14). But instead of being grateful, Jerusalem "trusted in" her "beauty" (16:15) and "played the whore" with other gods (16:16; cf. 16:17) by sacrificing her children to them (16:20–21). And Jerusalem played the whore with not one lover only, but also with the Egyptians (16:26), the Assyrians (16:28), and the Chaldeans (16:29). She became "a brazen prostitute" (16:30), but she was worse than a prostitute because she played the whore for free! Indeed, she paid her lovers instead of vice versa (16:33–34). Therefore, Yahweh would pour out his wrath on his people and judge them for their treachery (16:38–43). The language in chapter 23 is also shockingly crass. Both Samaria and Jerusalem, identified as Oholah and Oholibah, have been whores since their time in Egypt (23:3), and Samaria continued her whoredom with Assyria (23:5–8), and thus suffered exile (23:9–10). Remarkably, Jerusalem did not learn the lesson from seeing what happened to Samaria, but instead she played the whore with both Assyria and Babylon (23:11–18), and therefore she will suffer the punishment of exile as well (23:22–34). Israel's sin did not consist merely in transgression of the law. The covenant with Yahweh was not an impersonal contract. Spurning Yahweh was a rejection of his lordship and love and thus is compared to adultery.

The judgment was impending because of covenant violations, particularly because Israel worshiped other gods, thus violating the first commandment (Exod. 20:3; Deut. 5:7). The glory of God, which resided in the temple, could not dwell among a people whose allegiance was elsewhere. Ezekiel's vision in chapter 8 unveils the cancer within Israel. The temple had been compromised. There was an "image of jealousy" (8:5) near the altar gate, and such flagrant rejection of God's covenant presence will, Yahweh says, "drive me far from my sanctuary" (8:6). At the entrance of the court were "vile abominations" (8:9), and seventy elders were offering incense to "creeping things and loathsome

9. See Ortlund, *God's Unfaithful Wife*, 101–36.

beasts" (8:10). The closer one got to the temple, the worse things got. At the "entrance of the north gate" of the temple (8:14) women were weeping for the Sumerian god Tammuz (8:14). And yet most shocking of all, in the inner court of the temple, at the entrance, twenty-five men were worshiping the sun (8:16). The beauty of God's presence, his glory, must withdraw from a people who spurned Yahweh's majesty (9:3). Hence, in Ezekiel's vision executioners entered the city, striking down in judgment those who sinned, beginning from the temple—Yahweh's sanctuary among the people. Only a remnant was spared, for they had a mark upon them to protect them from the looming wrath.

The fires of judgment descended from the cherubim who guarded the divine presence (10:1–6). Meanwhile, the glory of Yahweh departed to the threshold of the temple. The vision of Yahweh and the cherubim that commenced the book takes center stage here. The cherubim and the divine presence were slowly withdrawing from the temple (10:15–18). Ezekiel attests elsewhere that the elders of Israel were treasuring idols in their hearts (14:3–7). The sword will be unleashed against Israel (11:9–10, 21). The cherubim and the divine glory abandoned the temple and the city (11:22–23). Yahweh's presence among them was a thing of the past. Ezekiel wondered if there would be no remnant, no promise, no future (9:8; 11:13). Judgment would not be the last word, but more on that in due course.

The evil of the land had reached its zenith, and so even if Noah, Daniel, and Job were to intercede for Israel, it would be to no avail (14:13–21). Israel's judgment was not arbitrary. When Yahweh entered into covenant with them, he gave them his statutes and laws, promising them life if they kept them (20:11, 13, 21; cf. Lev. 18:5). But Israel flouted Yahweh's precepts, disregarding the Sabbath, which was the sign of the covenant between Yahweh and Israel. Chapter 20 clarifies that Israel violated Yahweh's will all through history, from the time of the exodus onward. They would live if they kept Yahweh's commands, but they failed to observe his rules. So when Ezekiel says that Yahweh "gave them statutes that were not good and rules by which they could not have life" (20:25), he is not denigrating the content of the law.[10] The rules were defective because they could not bring life, and they could not bring life because Israel could not keep them. Ezekiel, then, really says nothing different from what Paul says about the law in Rom. 7.

Judgment was imminent for the nation, but chapter 18 introduces an important clarification. Sin and judgment are ultimately an individual reality.

---

10. But, against House (*Old Testament Theology*, 337–38), Ezekiel is not speaking of a "false law." Ezekiel uses hyperbole to underscore the truth that Israel cannot keep God's law. For a full discussion of the verse with a different interpretation than is supported here, see Block, *Ezekiel: Chapters 1–24*, 636–41.

Sons do not die for the sins of their fathers, nor are they spared by the righteousness of their fathers. The one who sins will experience judgment and death, and the one who does what is righteous will find life. Hence, one must not blame fate or think it is too late to turn to righteousness. At the same time, one must not rest on past accomplishments, thinking that now a turn toward evil will escape judgment. Yahweh shows mercy to those who forsake evil and pursue righteousness, but he will not grant amnesty to those who renounce what is good, even if they had practiced righteousness for many years previously. Ezekiel emphasizes often the sin of elders and kings, and the impact of leaders is substantial. Nevertheless, individuals still bear responsibility for their own decisions and their own lives. Hence, a mark of protection is placed upon those who forsake evil (9:4); they will be protected when the judgment falls. And yet the matter is not simplistic. Apparently, some of the righteous will suffer because of the sins of the wicked (21:3–4).

Ezekiel 18 (18:9, 13, 17, 19, 21–24, 28; see also 33:1–20) also assists us in understanding what it means to say that one who keeps the law will live (20:11, 13, 21; cf. Lev. 18:5). Those who live are those who keep the covenant stipulations. What does that mean concretely? Ezekiel does not leave us wondering:

> If a man is righteous and does what is just and right—if he does not eat upon the mountains or lift up his eyes to the idols of the house of Israel, does not defile his neighbor's wife or approach a woman in her time of menstrual impurity, does not oppress anyone, but restores to the debtor his pledge, commits no robbery, gives his bread to the hungry and covers the naked with a garment, does not lend at interest or take any profit, withholds his hand from injustice, executes true justice between man and man, walks in my statutes, and keeps my rules by acting faithfully—he is righteous; he shall surely live, declares the Lord GOD. (18:5–9)

Of course, looking at Ezekiel as a whole, we see that this is precisely what Israel failed to do, as we noted in the discussion of chapter 21 above. Hence, judgment would come upon the nation. For they shed blood (22:3, 4, 6, 9, 12, 13, 27; 23:37, 45), violate the Sabbath (22:8), have sex with women who are menstruating (22:10), commit sexual sin (22:11; 33:26), take bribes and interest (22:12), and cheat to gain financial advantage (22:13). Chapter 18 adds another crucial truth that we should attend to: "For I have no pleasure in the death of anyone, declares the Lord GOD; so turn, and live" (18:32; cf. 18:23). Yahweh judged Israel, but he took no delight in such judgment. He longed for Israel to repent and turn to him for life.

As noted, individuals are judged for their sin, and yet leaders shoulder a particular responsibility for the sin of the people (chaps. 17; 19). The princes shed blood in the land (22:6, 27; cf. 11:1; 21:12). The leaders are designated as shepherds in chapter 34. The shepherds were guilty of feeding themselves instead of the sheep (34:2–3). They failed to strengthen the weak, heal the sick, bind up the injured, and seek those who were straying; instead, they exerted their authority brutally and harshly (34:4). Since the leaders failed to care for the sheep, the latter were dispersed (34:5–6), and the former will be judged for their failure (34:10). And, as we will see below, the Lord himself will shepherd the sheep and care for them.

The priests flouted the Torah, failed to observe the Sabbath, and did not distinguish between what was holy and what was unclean (22:26; cf. 44:23; Lev. 10:10). The prophets prophesied falsely, applying whitewash to the sins of the people (13:10; 22:28). They prophesied "from their own hearts" (13:2) instead of in accord with the word of Yahweh (13:6–8), proclaiming "peace" when in fact Jerusalem was destined for defeat (13:10, 16). They neither patched up the gaps in the wall of the city nor strengthened the wall for battle (13:5). On account of their errant words Yahweh judged them (13:9, 11, 14), so that they faced his wrath (13:15). The same judgment applies to the prophetesses (13:17–23). They profaned Yahweh's name with their lies and prophesied to get food. Indeed, says Yahweh, they "have disheartened the righteous falsely, although I have not grieved him, and you have encouraged the wicked, that he should not turn from his evil way to save his life" (13:22). The sin of Israel was pervasive. Prophets, priests, princes, and people—all of them wandered from the right way. There was no one to turn away God's wrath on the nation.

Salvation and Restoration

The claim that the people will know Yahweh as Lord is not restricted to judgment. Israel will come to know that Yahweh is Lord by their return from exile as well, when they come back to the land (20:42, 44; 36:11, 38; 37:6, 13–14; 39:22, 28). Moreover, some texts seem to include Gentiles in prophesying about future salvation (36:23, 36; 37:28). God's purpose, whether in salvation or judgment, is that all peoples everywhere acknowledge his lordship, that they confess him as the almighty king.

Yahweh sent Israel into exile and abandoned the temple because it violated the covenant, because of its abominations and uncleanness. The judgment was not irrevocable, however, for he spared a remnant (14:22). The preservation of a remnant signaled the Lord's intention to bring Israel back from exile, to regather them from the nations where they were scattered (20:39–44). Even though the sanctuary was removed from Jerusalem, Yahweh was "a sanctuary" for those in exile (11:16), and he will restore them to the land of Israel (11:17). The restoration will not be merely physical, for it would do little good to return Israel to the land if they came back unchanged. Yahweh promised to root out their "detestable things" and "abominations" (11:18). He would give them "one heart" and "a new spirit," removing the "heart of stone," and giving them "a heart of flesh" (11:19).[11] As a result of such a divine work, Israel would live in accordance with Yahweh's commands and rules (11:20), and the covenant formula would be reality (cf. 36:28).[12] Israel would truly be Yahweh's people, and he would be their God.

God's gracious work is picked up and reiterated in 36:26–27: "And I will give you a new heart, and a new spirit I will put within you. And I will remove the heart of stone from your flesh and give you a heart of flesh. And I will put my Spirit within you, and cause you to walk in my statutes and be careful to obey my rules." The new feature is the pronounced emphasis on the indwelling Spirit (36:27),[13] who will enable Israel to fulfill the Lord's commands. The promise of restoration is of a piece in chapters 36–37 with Israel's restoration to the land. If Ezekiel earlier prophesied against the mountains (6:2–3), now he prophesies a new day for them (36:1–8), for now the mountains "will yield fruit to my people Israel, for they will soon come home" (36:8). The promise of many offspring will be fulfilled, and the cities will be rebuilt and inhabited (36:10–11). Yahweh "will do more good to you than ever before" (36:11), and they will no longer be bereaved of children (36:14) or experience "the reproach of the nations" (36:15). Yahweh acted because his "holy name" was "profaned" (36:20) and because he had concern for his "holy name" (36:21; cf. 20:44) and would "vindicate the holiness of [his] great name" (36:23; cf. 20:41).[14] Ultimately, he acted not for Israel's sake, "but for the sake of [his] holy name" (36:22). God's ultimate purpose, then, is the fame of his own name.[15] His reputation and honor are preserved by the salvation of his people. Therefore, he sprinkles "clean water" to cleanse Israel from their defilements (36:25). Israel should realize that the new creation that will come (36:29–30) is not for their sake (36:32). They should "loathe" themselves for their "iniquities and abominations" (36:31) and feel shame for their wickedness (36:32; cf. 20:43). A new Eden is coming, and the deserted and desolate places will be inhabited (36:35), and Israel will, in fulfillment of the promise of Abraham, increase like a flock (36:37–38).

11. The new heart and spirit are anthropological here so that they refer to the human heart and spirit, not the Holy Spirit (so Block, *Ezekiel: Chapters 1–24*, 353).

12. So ibid., 354.

13. See Block, *Ezekiel: Chapters 25–48*, 355–56.

14. See Dumbrell, *Faith of Israel*, 161.

15. See Block, *Ezekiel: Chapters 1–24*, 48.

Such promises for Israel were difficult to believe, given the desolate state of the nation. The nation was like dead, sun-bleached bones (chap. 37).[16] They had no life of their own. But Ezekiel was to prophesy to the bones (37:4), for the word of the Lord grants life where there is death (37:5–10).[17] The bones represent Israel in exile, whose hope for the future was extinguished (37:11). But the Spirit will indwell them and give them life, and will raise Israel from the dead (37:12–14).[18] Israel will return from exile to the land (37:21), and the north and the south will be reunited (37:15–22). They will no longer be defiled with sin but will be cleansed from evil and forgiven for their transgressions (37:23). The "covenant of peace" will "be an everlasting covenant" (37:26). And the glory that left the temple will return. Yahweh will "set [his] sanctuary in their midst forevermore" (37:26). The wonder of this covenant is God's presence with his people. They will see the King in his beauty. "My dwelling place shall be with them, and I will be their God, and they shall be my people. Then the nations will know that I am the LORD who sanctifies Israel, when my sanctuary is in their midst forevermore" (37:27–28). The NT writers, of course, see the resurrection as fulfilled in Jesus Christ, whose resurrection signaled the arrival of the new age promised in the OT. Indeed, in Jesus Christ Israel is reunited (see Acts 8:4–25), for the inclusion of the Samaritans in God's saving purposes signals the reuniting of Israel. Indeed, Jesus is the true temple, who dwells in the midst of his people through the Holy Spirit.

Another feature of this future bliss, according to Ezekiel, is the arrival of a new David. The kingdom will be taken from Zedekiah and given to a future Davidic heir (21:26–27). There seems to be an allusion to Gen. 49:10 in 21:27, for Ezekiel looks forward to the day when the kingdom will be restored: "This also shall not be, until he comes, the one to whom judgment belongs, and I will give it to him" (21:27).[19] The coming David is also described as a shepherd: "My servant David shall be king over them, and they shall all have one shepherd" (37:24). Then Israel will walk in the Lord's rules (37:24), and this David's rule will never end: "David my servant shall be their prince forever" (37:25).[20]

Chapter 37 actually picks up the thought of chapter 34 here. As noted earlier, the shepherds of Israel were indicted for caring for themselves rather than for the sheep. Yahweh promises that he will become the shepherd for

16. See the study of this chapter in Levenson, *Restoration of Israel*, 156–65.
17. The coming of life to the bones picks up the imagery and the process of the original creation of human beings (see Gen. 2:5–7; Job 10:8–9, 11). See ibid., 159.
18. Levenson (ibid., 161) remarks that Ezekiel's promise of Israel's revival would carry no weight if his vision of the resurrection was deemed incredible.
19. So Dempster, *Dominion and Dynasty*, 171.
20. On the messianic character of the text, see Block, *Ezekiel: Chapters 25–48*, 423.

Israel, that he will seek out the sheep who have been lost, heal those who are injured, help those who are weak, and bring back those who are scattered (34:11–13, 16). Yahweh will feed them, so that they lie down in good pastures (34:14–15), and will vindicate the righteous and judge the wicked (34:20, 22). The picture gets more complex, for Yahweh will appoint his servant David to be the shepherd of and provider for Israel (34:23). "I, the LORD, will be their God, and my servant David shall be prince among them" (34:24).[21] Then the "covenant of peace" will be a reality, and life in the wilderness will be secure (34:25). The Lord will send "showers of blessing" (34:26), and the trees will be heavy with fruit (34:27). Israel will know Yahweh and will be free from its enemies (34:27–31).

This new David should be linked with the "sprig" that Yahweh "will plant on a high and lofty mountain" (17:22),[22] and the mountain here is Mount Zion.[23] This sprig will branch out and bear fruit and become a mighty cedar, giving rest to "birds of every sort" (17:23).[24] It may be that the prince who plays such a major role in chapters 40–48 is also messianic, that he is a further description of the Davidic shepherd who will reign over Israel,[25] but Block raises serious questions about seeing the prince in chapters 40–48 as messianic.[26] For instance, the prince must offer a sin offering for himself (45:22). Resolving this issue is quite difficult, but perhaps the prince is a messianic figure, and we must interpret the language used here symbolically, as we do the rest of the temple vision, so that the more prosaic or literalistic features of the prince's responsibilities should not be pressed.[27] In any case, Iain Duguid sums up nicely Ezekiel's view of this future ruler: he "is a powerful ruler, but at the same time a gentle shepherd."[28]

The NT writers found Jesus of Nazareth to be the fulfillment of these Davidic prophecies. In John's Gospel, for example, Jesus is the good shepherd

21. This shepherd, though a servant, has a high stature and role. See Duguid, *Leaders of Israel*, 46–49.

22. See Block, *Ezekiel: Chapters 1–24*, 552–54.

23. Levenson, *Program of Restoration*, 7; Duguid, *Leaders of Israel*, 44.

24. See Levenson, *Program of Restoration*, 77–84, but Duguid (*Leaders of Israel*, 45) rightly points out that there is no diminution of the kingship here.

25. So Levenson, *Program of Restoration*, 57–69; Duguid, *Leaders of Israel*, 50–55. Duguid (*Leaders of Israel*, 11–33) provides a careful study of the words "prince" (*nāśî'*) and "king" (*melek*).

26. Block, *Ezekiel: Chapters 1–24*, 59–60, 504–5; Block, *Ezekiel: Chapters 25–48*, 742–46; see also Rendtorff, *Canonical Hebrew Bible*, 257–58.

27. Some scholars see a critique of the monarchy in these chapters; for discussion of the matter, see Stevenson, *Vision of Transformation*, 109–23. Dumbrell (*End of the Beginning*, 58) rightly says that one of the main points is that God rules over Israel.

28. Duguid, *Leaders of Israel*, 55.

who gives his life for the sheep (10:14–15). Ezekiel puts side by side the promise of forgiveness and cleansing with the arrival of the new David (37:23–25), but the NT clarifies that the shepherd, the Davidic king, sacrifices his own life for the good of the sheep, so that they can be cleansed of their sin and enjoy the promise of the new creation. As the good shepherd, Jesus heals those who are sick, seeks those who are lost (Luke 15), and brings back those who are scattered. The covenant of peace has become a reality through him.

In Ezekiel the identity of Gog from the land of Magog (chaps. 38–39) is obscure and disputed.[29] Clearly, though, it represents a nation that will attack Israel in the future. Gog will attack restored and regathered Israel "in the latter years" (38:8).[30] The assault will be frightening, for the enemy will be like a dark "cloud covering the land," like a horde (38:9), "a great host, a mighty army" (38:15). They will come upon Israel while it is dwelling "securely" to take goods for themselves (38:8, 11, 14). Gog's attack will be a stunning failure. Yahweh will "vindicate [his] holiness before their eyes" (38:16). God's "blazing wrath" and jealous anger will be poured out on Gog and his hordes (38:18–19). All creation will war against the enemies of the Lord (38:20). Yahweh will "rain" on Gog "torrential rains and hailstones, fire and sulfur" (38:22), and Yahweh's "greatness" and "holiness" will be evident to all nations, and all will confess that Yahweh is Lord (38:23). The battle is described in exaggerated terms, depicting a holy war.[31]

Chapter 39 reprises the judgment on Gog from another angle. Yahweh is the king of history, for he is the one orchestrating events so that Gog turns against Israel (39:2). Then Yahweh will judge Gog, so that his "holy name" is known in Israel, and the nations will know that Yahweh is Lord, "the Holy One of Israel" (39:7). Then the hordes of Gog will be buried in Israel, showing the massive extent of Yahweh's victory over the enemy,[32] and birds and beasts will feed on the flesh of Israel's enemies (39:9–19). Yahweh's forgiveness of Israel and restoration of the nation come about because Yahweh is "jealous for [his] holy name" (39:25). "Above all else, this complex divine speech expresses Yahweh's divine determination once and for all to reveal to nations his holiness, and to his own people his covenant loyalty."[33] Israel will know that Yahweh is their God when they return from exile, when Yahweh pours out his Spirit on the nation (39:28–29).

29. For a helpful summary, see Block, *Ezekiel: Chapters 25–48*, 432–36.
30. Cf. Dumbrell, *Faith of Israel*, 165.
31. See ibid., 165–66. Hence, we must beware of trying to interpret the prophecy literally (rightly Block, *Ezekiel: Chapters 25–48*, 431).
32. Dumbrell, *Faith of Israel*, 165.
33. Block, *Ezekiel: Chapters 25–48*, 431.

The last chapters of the book (chaps. 40–48) are quite difficult, for here we find a long description of a new temple. It is not my purpose here to linger on the details of these chapters. As Thomas Renz says, "The architectural design of the temple embodies the holiness of God."[34] It probably is the case that these chapters do not envision the building of a literal temple, for sufficient instructions are lacking to complete such a structure.[35] Block says, "The description of the temple is not presented as a blueprint for some future building to be constructed with human hands."[36] It describes "spiritual reality in concrete terms."[37] The new temple does not constitute the rebuilding of the old one.[38] "The details are not a plan for physical rebuilding."[39] No blueprint for building the temple exists here, for vertical dimensions are entirely lacking.[40] The temple represents a new Eden, a cosmic mountain (40:2) where Yahweh dwells with his people.[41] "The sanctity of the new temple is expressed by its measurements."[42] And, "like Moses, Ezekiel sees the pattern of a new sanctuary on the mountain and describes it twice."[43] Israel should be ashamed of their iniquities when they learn that Yahweh will show mercy on them and dwell among them again (43:10–11). The glory of God departed from the old temple because of Israel's sin, but now the glory of God comes from the east to dwell in the new temple (43:1–5). The temple represents God's "throne," where he reigns over Israel (43:7), and Yahweh's presence with his people, where, he says, "I will dwell in the midst of the people of Israel forever" (43:7).[44] That which defiles God's holy name will be a distant memory (43:7), and all that is abominable must be removed from Israel in order for God to dwell among them (43:8–9).[45] Levenson remarks, "Ezekiel's tour of Zion is a foretaste of ultimate redemption."[46]

Human beings must not enter the east gate of the temple because the Lord entered the temple via the east (44:2). Nothing unclean or profane should be admitted into the Lord's sanctuary (44:6–9). The sanctuary will be a holy

34. Renz, "Zion Tradition," 93.
35. Rightly, Beale, *Church's Mission*, 335–64. Against Levenson, *Program of Restoration*, 45–46.
36. Block, *Ezekiel: Chapters 1–24*, 59. See also Block, *Ezekiel: Chapters 25–48*, 505–6, 510–11.
37. Block, *Ezekiel: Chapters 1–24*, 59.
38. Renz, "Zion Tradition," 91.
39. Dumbrell, *Faith of Israel*, 167.
40. See Stevenson, *Vision of Transformation*, 5, 21, 23, 28, 35.
41. See Levenson, *Program of Restoration*, 37; Dumbrell, *Faith of Israel*, 166.
42. Dumbrell, *Faith of Israel*, 167.
43. Ibid.
44. See Levenson, *Program of Restoration*, 17.
45. See Stevenson, *Vision of Transformation*, 42–43.
46. Ibid., 18.

district in the midst of the land (chap. 45). There are gradations of holiness, with the inner sanctum of the temple being the most holy, and as one progressively moves away from the temple, holiness diminishes.[47] Boundaries separate the holy from the unholy, with the holiest area being in the center.[48] Kalinda Stevenson observes that the word for "walls" in these chapters always refers to city walls and never to temple walls, suggesting that the temple represents a city,[49] which nicely anticipates Rev. 21–22, where the new Jerusalem is God's temple. A river will flow from the temple (47:1–12). Clearly, the river is symbolic, for it is a very strange river, beginning as a trickle but growing larger and deeper and faster without tributaries, such that it eventually becomes impassable.[50] And trees, like the tree of life, grow on both sides of the river (47:12).[51] The fruit and leaves never fail, and the leaves provide healing (47:12). Clearly, here we have the picture of a new Eden. The land and Jerusalem will be divided as an inheritance for Israel (47:13–48:23).[52]

Ezekiel ends fittingly with these words: "And the name of the city from that time on shall be, The Lord Is There" (48:35). The Lord departed from the temple and Jerusalem because the city was defiled and unclean, but the departure is not permanent. Ezekiel suggests that there is a new and better Jerusalem coming, one that transcends the earthly Jerusalem, just as the coming temple transcends the existing temple. And that city and temple will be marked by the presence of the Lord.[53] They will see the King in his beauty. Levenson argues, "The society imagined and prescribed by the program of restoration of Ezek. 40–48 is a theocracy, a kingdom of God."[54] He goes on to

47. See Dumbrell, *Faith of Israel*, 168.
48. See Stevenson, *Vision of Transformation*, 43–44.
49. Ibid., 44.
50. "Virtually every detail of the vision is unrealistic and caricatured. Streams do not issue forth from temple thresholds, nor do they increase geometrically in size and volume, from a mere trickle to an unfordable stream in the desert, without benefit of tributaries. Waters do not flow over or through hills. When fresh water contacts putrid water . . . the influence is from foul to fresh, not the reverse. . . . Trees do not break the seasonal patterns and produce fruit every month of the year, nor do the leaves of these trees have medicinal value. All these features suggest an impressionistic literary cartoon with an intentional ideological aim" (Block, *Ezekiel: Chapters 25–48*, 701).
51. See Levenson, *Program of Restoration*, 13.
52. Block (*Ezekiel: Chapters 25–48*, 740) gives six features of Ezekiel's territorial vision. Among other things, he notes that "tribal territories" are given "without respect to—nay, in defiance of—the geographic grain." The "territorial allocations . . . are governed more by ideal than historical reality." The heartland of the city is "a perfect square." Block concludes, "In the light of all these considerations, a literal fulfillment of these conditions is obviously not anticipated."
53. House (*Old Testament Theology*, 327) says that the presence of God is the central theme of Ezekiel.
54. Levenson, *Program of Restoration*, 129.

say, "In other words, the focus of Ezek. 40–48 is on the structures of encounter between God and man, the service man in his ideal condition can and must render to God."[55] The temple described in Ezekiel is fulfilled in the new heaven and new earth that are coming (see Rev. 21–22), where the new creation is described as a temple to signify that the whole earth is indwelt by God, that God's presence fills the entire cosmos.[56]

Conclusion

The glorious presence of Yahweh is the focus of Ezekiel. The Lord withdrew from the temple, where he specially dwelt and reigned over Israel, because of the sin of Israel. The temple was not a magical place that protected Israel regardless of how it behaved. Yahweh could not dwell in the midst of Israel because of its abominable behavior and its uncleanness. Israel was defiled by idolatry and violated the other stipulations of the covenant as well. Hence, the nation was expelled to Babylon. But the Lord's gracious reign over Israel was not over. He would restore and save them for the sake of his great name, because his reputation was irretrievably tied to the fate of Israel. Therefore, the Lord promised to do a great spiritual work among his people, fulfilling his promise to Abraham. He would put his Spirit in them and give them the strength to observe his commands. Israel was like dead, sun-bleached bones, but the Lord, by his Spirit, would give them life so that they would prosper again. The covenant with David would be fulfilled as well. A new David would arise who would shepherd God's flock, and he would truly care for God's people. The Lord himself would dwell among his people. The chapters on the new temple, which should not be interpreted literally, indicate that the glory of Yahweh will return to Israel. They will see the King in his beauty. When the Lord dwells among his people, the covenant of peace will be established, and a new creation will arrive. We have another hint here, which is picked up in Rev. 21–22, that the new creation and the new temple are two different ways of describing the same reality. When God reigns over all, his presence will abide with his people.

---

55. Ibid.

56. For the notion that Rev. 21–22 is intended to be a fulfillment of the temple described in Ezek. 40–48, see Beale, *Church's Mission*, 346–53; see also my discussion of Rev. 21–22 in chapter 34 below.

23

DANIEL

Introduction

The book of Daniel addresses the situation of Israel in exile (605–536 BC), calling upon Israel to recognize that God rules over all and will bring in his kingdom, and therefore they should not compromise with paganism. Even though Israel was in exile, Yahweh still reigned over history. His purposes and program for Israel would not be ultimately frustrated. His saving promises for Israel would be fulfilled despite Israel's sin and violation of the covenant. The Aramaic part of the book (chaps. 2–7) is chiastic.[1]

Yahweh's sovereignty over history	The interpretation of Nebuchadnezzar's statue dream (chap. 2)	The interpretation of Daniel's dream of the beasts and the son of man (chap. 7)
Yahweh's deliverance of his own	The deliverance of Shadrach, Meshach, and Abednego from the fiery furnace (chap. 3)	The deliverance of Daniel from the lions' den (chap. 6)
Yahweh's humbling of the proud	The humbling of Nebuchadnezzar (chap. 4)	The humbling of Belshazzar (chap. 5)

Chapter 1 seems to emphasize the same theme as chapter 3 and chapter 6: the faithfulness of Daniel and his friends under pressure. Chapters 8–12 expand upon chapter 2 and chapter 7, focusing upon Yahweh's sovereignty over history. The three themes that we will investigate in Daniel, then, are (1) the deliverance of the faithful (chaps. 1; 3; 6); (2) the humbling of the proud (chaps. 4–5); and (3) Yahweh's sovereignty over history (chaps. 2; 7;

---

1. See Dumbrell, *Faith of Israel*, 304.

8–12). Of course, the themes do not fit quite so neatly, and so they overlap in the book.

The Deliverance of the Faithful

The book of Daniel begins with Israel being taken into exile in 605 BC. King Jehoiakim was taken to Babylon, as were vessels from the temple, which then were placed in the temple of Nebuchadnezzar's god (1:1–2). The reference to "the land of Shinar" (1:2) recalls Gen. 11:2 and the tower of Babel. Hence, Nebuchadnezzar is viewed "as the humanistic reviver" of what happened at Babel.[2] If we read Daniel in light of the rest of the canon, we see that exile was the result of Israel's violation of covenant stipulations (Lev. 26:33, 39; Deut. 28:64). Daniel and his three friends were intellectually gifted and had opportunities to serve the king. But the young Hebrews were required to eat the king's food (1:5). Daniel, however, resolved not to partake of the king's food and wine, which he considered to be defiling (1:8). We are not told why the king's food and wine were defiling. Perhaps they were unclean or offered to Babylonian idols, or perhaps the Hebrews wanted to distinguish themselves from Babylonian culture.[3] In any case, Daniel boldly asked if he and his three friends could restrict themselves to vegetables and water (1:12), and God so worked that the request was granted (cf. 1:9). Indeed, God gave these young men wisdom and intellectual skill as well so that they distinguished themselves before Nebuchadnezzar (1:17–20). We see here the twin themes of God's sovereignty and the commitment of the four young Hebrews to live in a way that pleased God.

If Israel is to be restored from exile, they must serve Yahweh and resist idolatry. Shadrach, Meshach, and Abednego in chapter 3 function as a model for all Israel. They were threatened with death if they refused to bow down to the ninety-foot-tall image of gold erected by Nebuchadnezzar. "The image in this chapter is clearly a symbol of his worldwide dominion."[4] Nebuchadnezzar wanted others to see and acknowledge his greatness, thereby replicating Babel (cf. Gen. 11:1–9).[5] These three men demonstrated their devotion to Yahweh and their obedience to the Torah by refusing to serve and worship false gods (3:18), and they were rescued by the Lord from the scorching furnace by which

2. Ibid., 305.
3. See Shepherd, *Daniel*, 71–72.
4. Dumbrell, *Faith of Israel*, 306.
5. Shepherd, *Daniel*, 76; Dumbrell, *Faith of Israel*, 306. Dumbrell says, "It requires an allegiance that is akin to worship."

the furious Nebuchadnezzar intended to kill them for their defiance. Such deliverance should not be interpreted as a promise that individual Israelites were guaranteed that they would be spared suffering if they refused to worship idols. Instead, the point of the narrative is that Israel would ultimately be delivered by the Lord if they served him. Israel was in exile because of its sin and would be restored to the land and experience Yahweh's promises if they served the Lord as did Shadrach, Meshach, and Abednego.

The story of Daniel in chapter 6 has a similar function. Daniel, like his friends in chapter 3, faced persecution from Babylonian officials. They conspired against Daniel by banning prayer to anyone but the king for thirty days. Daniel refused to compromise and continued to pray publicly to the Lord. Like his three friends, Daniel faced imminent death for his defiance of the king. He was placed in a lions' den, but Yahweh again intervened, shutting the mouths of the lions so that Daniel was delivered and his enemies were punished. Perhaps Daniel here functions as "a second Adam" to whom the beasts were subject.[6] Daniel's devotion to the Lord should be interpreted along the same lines as the rescue of his three friends. If Israel followed Daniel's example, they would be restored to the land and enjoy the blessing promised. Furthermore, the uniqueness of Yahweh was recognized by unbelievers: "He is the living God, enduring forever; his kingdom shall never be destroyed, and his dominion shall be to the end. He delivers and rescues; he works signs and wonders in heaven and on earth" (6:26–27). Even in Israel's exile Yahweh was the sovereign God, who reigned over all.

The Humbling of the Proud

If Israel repents and serves and worships the Lord, they will be restored from exile, for Yahweh is the sovereign king. In the same way, the rulers of Babylon, even though they rule the world, were not greater than Yahweh and would be humbled if they arrogantly exalted themselves against him. Two examples of such humbling are provided. First, Daniel interprets Nebuchadnezzar's dream of a magnificent tree that holds sway over the earth (chap. 4). The tree, representing Nebuchadnezzar,[7] would be chopped down, and Nebuchadnezzar would be struck with insanity if he remained haughty. The significance of the dream is explained to Nebuchadnezzar in advance so that he would forswear pride and avoid judgment. Daniel specifically counsels the king to practice "righteousness" and to show "mercy to the oppressed" (4:27).

---

6. Dempster, *Dominion and Dynasty*, 214.
7. Dumbrell (*Faith of Israel*, 307) thinks that the reference is to the tree of life—a new Eden.

Instead, Nebuchadnezzar takes credit for the glory of his kingdom and thus is stripped of his kingdom and becomes insane for seven years. Ultimately, Nebuchadnezzar recognizes Yahweh's sovereignty after he humbles himself before the Lord. "I blessed the Most High, and praised and honored him who lives forever, for his dominion is an everlasting dominion, and his kingdom endures from generation to generation; all the inhabitants of the earth are accounted as nothing, and he does according to his will among the host of heaven and among the inhabitants of the earth; and none can stay his hand or say to him, 'What have you done?'" (4:34–35). It became clear to him "that the Most High rules the kingdom of men and gives it to whom he will" (4:25). Nebuchadnezzar confessed his relationship before the one true God, saying "I . . . praise and extol and honor the King of heaven, for all his works are right and his ways are just; and those who walk in pride he is able to humble" (4:37). Nebuchadnezzar understood what it means to be a creature, for the creature acknowledges the sovereign rights and goodness of the creator and walks humbly before him (cf. Mic. 6:8).

King Belshazzar functions as the mirror image of his father, Nebuchadnezzar, in chapter 5. He and his nobles committed the flagrant evil of taking the vessels that had been captured from the Jerusalem temple and drinking from them (5:3–4). Mysterious human fingers suddenly appeared, writing words on the palace wall. One of the typical themes of Daniel surfaces at this point. None of the king's astrologers, enchanters, and advisers could interpret what happened. Only Daniel was able to unlock the significance of the writing on the wall, explaining to the king that the days of his kingdom have come to an end (5:26–30). Most important, Belshazzar did not learn the lesson of humility from his father (5:18–21). Daniel explains to him, "You . . . have not humbled your heart, though you knew all this, but you have lifted up yourself against the Lord of heaven" (5:22), and this was manifested in his drinking from the temple vessels instead of honoring the God of the universe (5:23). How tempting it would have been for the Jews in exile to transfer their affections to the Babylonian superpower and to their gods, but the narratives in chapters 4–5 reminded them that Babylonian kings were also subject to Yahweh, that they reign only at his direction, that the gods of the Babylonians are figments of the imagination, and that Yahweh is supreme and must be honored above all.

Yahweh's Sovereignty over History

Chapter 2 and chapter 7 together sketch out the future until the arrival of the kingdom of God. The chapters interpret each other, for, as we noted above, they are in a chiastic relationship. In chapter 2 Nebuchadnezzar came up with the novel idea of requiring the sorcerers and Chaldeans to tell him not only the interpretation of the dream but also what he dreamed in the first place. Naturally, Nebuchadnezzar's enchanters and magicians were nonplussed, for such a requirement was unheard of. Daniel, however, was able to explain to Nebuchadnezzar not only the interpretation of the dream but also its content. Daniel reminds the reader of Joseph. "Both were captives at the royal court, both succeeded where the professionals failed, both were promoted as a result, and, most important, both operated in an Israel that stood before an exodus."[8] Such ability was not native to Daniel. Yahweh answered prayer in disclosing such mysteries to Daniel (2:17–19), so that Daniel praised God for revealing hidden things to him (2:20–23), and he explained to Nebuchadnezzar that such knowledge was given to him by God (2:27–28, 30; cf. 2:47). The significance of the dream is explained before it was relayed by Daniel: "[God] changes times and seasons; he removes kings and sets up kings; he gives wisdom to the wise and knowledge to those who have understanding" (2:21). The course of history is determined by God; human beings do not ultimately secure the future by their own actions.

In Nebuchadnezzar's dream he saw a massive statue with a head of gold, its chest and arms made of silver, its middle and thighs of bronze, and its legs of iron, with the feet being a mixture of iron and clay (2:31–33). A stone struck the statue on the feet, and the whole statue collapsed, and the stone became like a mountain that filled the earth (2:34–35). Daniel then provides an interpretation of the dream (2:36–45). The statue stands for human governments that represent a subversion of what God intended when he made human beings in his image (cf. Gen. 1:26–27).[9] The head of gold was the Babylonian kingdom ruled by Nebuchadnezzar. Remarkably, the second and third kingdoms are explained in one verse (2:39), probably referring to Media-Persia and Greece, respectively.[10] Attention is fixed on the fourth kingdom (2:40–43), most likely Rome, which crushes all opposition. Human kingdoms are not the last word, for the stone represents the kingdom of God (cf. Isa. 28:16), which will shatter and bring down all human kingdoms (2:44–45).[11] The kingdom of God "shall stand forever" (2:44). It is clear from Daniel's vision that history will last longer than expected, but the people of God should be full of hope, for the kingdoms of the world will not endure. Only the kingdom of God will remain. As Goldingay says, "God's kingdom comes without human

---

8. Ibid., 305.
9. Dempster, *Dominion and Dynasty*, 214.
10. Shepherd (*Daniel*, 74) thinks that the only referent described is Babylon, and that the reader should not seek further information.
11. Shepherd (ibid., 75) sees a messianic reference here.

cooperation. . . . God establishes it. . . . A human response is required, but it is not human action that brings in God's rule."[12] God's kingdom will fill the earth (2:35), fulfilling the mandate originally given to Adam (cf. Gen. 1:26).[13] Furthermore, we will see from Daniel 7 that the rule of God will be established through a "son of man."

Daniel's vision and dream in chapter 7 match chapter 2. Here the four kingdoms are described as four beasts: Babylon as a lion, Media-Persia as a bear, Greece as a leopard, and Rome as an indescribably ferocious beast (7:1–8). The four beasts represent "four kings" and kingdoms that reign over the world (7:17). The kingdoms and kings are described as beasts because they are cruel and rapacious, destroying and devastating those under their rule.[14] Their governance is not congenial to human life and flourishing; rather, it is destructive and dehumanizing. The focus, as in the dream in chapter 2, is on the fourth beast (7:19–26). Its terrible nature is emphasized, with teeth that devour and claws that tear (7:19, 23). A "horn," a human ruler, arises who prevails over the saints by putting them to death (7:21), elevating himself above the Lord (7:25). The reign of three and a half years should be interpreted symbolically, denoting a period of time when the evil horn will rule. The reign of the beasts will not endure forever, as 7:9–14 demonstrates. The Ancient of Days reigns on his throne, his white clothing denoting his holiness, and his white hair his wisdom and eternity. The flames on the throne indicate that the Ancient of Days must not be trifled with; he can easily destroy his enemies. Indeed, when the books of the courtroom are opened, the fourth beast and the horn are destroyed with flaming fire, and the rule of the other beasts is taken away.

The scene in the heavenly courtroom shifts. Suddenly "one like a son of man" comes to the Ancient of Days, and the kingdom is given to him (7:13–14). "All peoples, nations, and languages should serve him; his dominion is an everlasting dominion, which shall not pass away, and his kingdom one that shall not be destroyed" (7:14). The term "serve" (*pĕlaḥ*) and his riding on the clouds point to the son of man having divine stature.[15] The reference to the son of man also shows that the kingdom to come is one that is humane and civilizing (for "son of man" in Aramaic refers to human beings) in contrast to the terrors inflicted by the beastly kingdoms.[16] Unlike the ferocious beasts,

---

12. Goldingay, *Israel's Faith*, 368.

13. So Beale, *Biblical Theology*, 111.

14. See Lucas, "Daniel," 234.

15. So Shepherd (*Daniel*, 90), pointing to Dan. 3:12, 14, 17–18, 28; 6:17, 21 in the MT. Shepherd (p. 91) says that a reference to angels is ruled out if worship of the son of man is in view.

16. "A typically vague apocalyptic designation of what appears to be in this context a human being" (Dumbrell, *Faith of Israel*, 308).

he does not take the kingdom for himself, but God gives the kingdom to him.[17] The son of man is a new Adam fulfilling the role of kingship originally given to Adam.[18] At the same time, riding on the clouds is what God does (cf. Ps. 104:3; Isa. 19:1).[19] Daniel links the son of man with the rock in chapter 2, suggesting an identity between the two.[20]

Daniel saw a vision of a son of man receiving the kingdom, but when he explains the vision, the kingdom is given to the saints: "But the saints of the Most High shall receive the kingdom and possess the kingdom forever, forever and ever" (7:18). Nothing more is said about the son of man in the interpretation of the vision. The horn rules for a while, "until the Ancient of Days came, and judgment was given for the saints of the Most High, and the time came when the saints possessed the kingdom" (7:22). When the court is in session, sovereignty will be removed from the horn and he will be destroyed (7:26). "And the kingdom and the dominion and the greatness of the kingdoms under the whole heaven shall be given to the people of the saints of the Most High; their kingdom shall be an everlasting kingdom, and all dominions shall serve and obey them" (7:27). Some understand the saints to denote angels, but the phrase "the people [ˈam] of the saints" (7:27) almost certainly denotes human beings. This fits with "son of man," for that term also denotes a human being. What Daniel prophesies, then, is that beastly kingdoms will reign over much of history and will introduce much devastation, but finally and ultimately the people of Yahweh will be vindicated and will reign over the world.

One other feature of the parallel should be noted. Just as the beastly kingdoms are represented by kings, so too the saints may be represented by an individual as well.[21] The saints are included corporately in their leader. So there are good grounds for thinking that the interpretation of Dan. 7 found in the Gospels fits with the context of Daniel's vision. Jesus is the Son of Man, the king, the stone, who represents the saints. The saints triumph insofar as they belong to him and are united to him. His victory is their victory. The Son of Man will crush the head of the serpent, the ferocious and beastly kingdoms that oppress human beings and advance evil.

Chapters 8–12 focus in more detail on the span of history sketched in by chapter 2 and chapter 7.[22] Chapter 8 focuses on the conflict between Media-Persia and Greece, the former described as a ram and the latter as a male goat.

17. Dempster, *Dominion and Dynasty*, 217.
18. On this theme, see Beale, *Biblical Theology*, 188–99.
19. Dumbrell, *Faith of Israel*, 308.
20. Dempster, *Dominion and Dynasty*, 217, 221.
21. See Dempster, *Dominion and Dynasty*, 216; Dumbrell, *Faith of Israel*, 308.
22. Dumbrell (*Faith of Israel*, 304) thinks that chapters 8–12 expand upon chapter 7.

Media-Persia corresponds to the chest and arms of silver (2:32, 39) in the vision of the great statue and to the bear (7:5) in the vision of the beasts. Greece corresponds to the middle and thighs of bronze (2:32, 39) in the vision of the statue and to the leopard (7:6) in the vision of the beasts. The male goat shattered the power of the ram (8:5–7, 21), standing for the decisive defeat of Media-Persia by Alexander the Great, which took place in 334–331 BC. The reign of Alexander was short-lived, and his kingdom was divided into four parts (8:8, 22). The vision focuses on the little horn that sprouted from the four kingdoms that survived after Alexander, which is identified as Antiochus Epiphanes (reigned 175–164 BC), one of the Seleucid rulers (8:9–14, 23–25). Antiochus persecuted and killed the saints, throwing some of the stars to the ground and trampling on them (8:10). Furthermore, for 2,300 days, approximately three and a half years (perhaps 167–164 BC),[23] he defiled the temple in Jerusalem by offering his sacrifices on the altar (8:12–14). Finally, however, he would be defeated (8:25). The chapter expands on the theology of chapter 2 and chapter 7. Israel will face defeat before powerful enemies, but ultimately it will triumph.

A further explanation of the course of history is offered in chapter 9. In 539 BC, the first year of the reign of Darius the Mede (9:1), Daniel, upon reading the prophecies of Jeremiah, which said that Israel would suffer captivity for seventy years (Jer. 25:11–12; 29:10), prayed that Yahweh would show mercy and forgive the sins of Israel. Israel experienced the curses of the covenant (Lev. 26:14–44; Deut. 28:15–68), particularly exile (Lev. 26:33, 39; Deut. 28:36–37, 64–65), because it failed to observe the covenantal stipulations (Dan. 9:11–14). Daniel prayed that Yahweh would show mercy to his people and his sanctuary for his great name's sake and return Israel from exile (9:15–19).[24] Gabriel was sent to Daniel to assure him that his prayer was answered (9:20–23). But the prayer was answered in a surprising way. Yes, Israel would return from exile, but the fullness of what God promised would not become a reality when Israel returned from captivity in Babylon.

What Yahweh promised Israel would become a reality only after "seventy weeks" (9:24). That is, the exile would fully end not after seventy years, but after 490 years. "The point of this reinterpretation is not that Jeremiah was mistaken in his prophecy, but that which he correctly envisioned was further clarified by a fresh illumination of Scripture through the spirit."[25] Israel's sins would then be atoned for, and their transgressions would no longer be held against them (9:24). "Everlasting righteousness" would finally be a reality, and

23. See Dempster, *Dominion and Dynasty*, 218.
24. On the centrality of God's concern for his own name, see Shepherd, *Daniel*, 96.
25. Childs, *Old Testament as Scripture*, 617.

all prophecies and visions would be fulfilled (9:24). Daniel 9:26 reveals, rather cryptically, the basis of the forgiveness of sins. The "anointed one" (messiah), after sixty-nine weeks (483 years), would be put to death. The precise dating of what Daniel teaches here is disputed, but the building of Jerusalem probably commences with the work of Nehemiah in rebuilding the wall in 445 BC. Hence, 483 years would bring us to the life, ministry, and death of Jesus of Nazareth in the late 20s and early 30s AD. But even then, the struggle would not be over, for "the prince who is to come" (9:26) would destroy Jerusalem and the temple. This most likely refers to the destruction of the temple by the Romans in AD 70. It is attractive in some ways to see a reference to the Christ when "the prince who is to come" is mentioned,[26] but the destruction of the city by the prince's people more naturally refers to Rome, given the active verbs, than it does to the Jews.[27] Hence, 9:27 also refers to the prince who opposes God's people. He would make a covenant with those who oppose God's people and would oppose divine worship.[28] Abominations are coming, Daniel predicts, and the process will be long, but finally and ultimately the one who brings desolation will find himself desolate. The exile, then, will last much longer than Israel would anticipate, but ultimately God's people will triumph, and their sins, which led them into exile in the first place, will be removed forever. And the most holy place, the new temple, the new cosmos according to Rev. 21–22, will be anointed (9:24), and God will dwell with his people forever. Then they will see the King in his beauty.

Chapters 10–12 close out the book with another vision of what is to come. In chapter 10 Daniel sought the Lord with fasting for three weeks. An angelic figure appeared to Daniel and strengthened him, informing him what was to come. Chapter 11 focuses on the conflict between the Ptolemies and Seleucids, who respectively ruled over Israel (from the third century to the second century BC). The focus is on Antiochus Epiphanes (11:21–35), who opposed "the holy covenant" (11:30). "Forces from him shall appear and profane the temple and fortress, and shall take away the regular burnt offering. And they shall set up the abomination that makes desolate" (11:31); that is, offerings will be made in the temple to a foreign god (cf. 1 Macc. 1:54, 59). Some Jews will compromise, but others will take action (11:32), presumably referring to the Hasmonean revolt (cf. 1 Macc. 2–4). A great conflict would ensue, and some of those who belong to Yahweh would suffer, but they would "receive a little help" (11:34), from the Hasmoneans. Those who suffer would be refined and purified (11:35).

26. For this interpretation, see Gentry, "Daniel's Seventy Weeks," 32–33, 40.
27. For a contrary interpretation, see ibid., 38–39.
28. Conversely, it could refer to the covenant that the Messiah makes with his people (see ibid., 37–38).

The subsequent verses do not match the life of Antiochus Epiphanes and probably denote a future opponent of the people of God (11:36–45) of whom Antiochus functions as a type.[29] He will exalt himself as divine and blaspheme the one true God (11:36). Thousands who belong to the people of God will fall before him (11:41), but he will not ultimately triumph (11:45). Those who belong to Yahweh will be delivered at the time Michael arises (12:1). The righteous dead will rise again in triumph (12:2), and the wise will shine like the stars (12:3).[30] The promises to Abraham will be fulfilled, but Daniel clarifies that they will be realized in an unanticipated way. It will take a resurrection, the commencement of a new era, for the promises of Abraham to come to pass in their fullness.

Conclusion

Daniel emphasizes Yahweh's sovereignty over history. "Above all, the witness of the book is theocentric."[31] He reigns and rules over all. Kings and kingdoms derive their authority and power from him. They are not autonomous and do not determine their own destiny. What Daniel particularly emphasizes is that Israel's victory will not come soon. The restoration from exile (536 BC) is not the end of Israel's suffering, nor is it Israel's final triumph. Many kingdoms will reign before the kingdom of God arrives in power. Those who know their God must, like Daniel, Shadrach, Meshach, and Abednego, refuse to compromise with paganism. Whatever the cost, they must not worship other gods and violate the covenant. That is what got them into exile in the first place. They must, like Daniel (chap. 9), plead to the Lord to forgive them and must turn from evil. Nor does the book of Daniel promise deliverance from suffering for those who obey Yahweh. The latter chapters of the book (chaps. 7–12) make it plain that those who are faithful to the Lord will suffer. Thereby they will be refined and purified so that they are worthy to enter the kingdom. The fullness of God's promises will not be realized until seventy sevens have elapsed. But God's kingdom will come. The saints will triumph. Even those who have died will be raised from the dead and enjoy the kingdom forever. The offspring of the serpent—those brutish and ferocious rulers of human beings—will be crushed. The stone from the mountain will crush them, and this stone is none other than the Son of Man—the one born of woman, Jesus the Christ.

29. See Childs, *Old Testament as Scripture*, 619. For another interpretation, see Parry, "Desolation of the Temple."
30. For discussion of the resurrection in Dan. 12, see Levenson, *Restoration of Israel*, 181–200.
31. Childs, *Old Testament as Scripture*, 621.

<h1 style="text-align:center">24</h1>

THE BOOK OF THE TWELVE

Introduction

The Book of the Twelve, also known as the Minor Prophets, has existed as a collection from very early times.[1] Since these twelve books focus on many of the same themes, they will not be studied individually here (though unique contributions will be noted). The purpose here is to lift out particular themes that recur in the Book of the Twelve, to discuss their role in the theology of the OT, and to discern how they fit into the story line of OT theology. I will insert comments here and there, however, to signify how the Twelve relate to one another. House maintains that sin, judgment, and restoration actually fit the order of the books.[2] It is more convincing to say that these are regular themes in the Twelve as a whole, and it is harder to see a distinct progression.[3]

Covenant

Virtually everything said about the Twelve could be fit under the category of covenant. This is hardly surprising, since the Twelve assume that Israel is the special people of Yahweh, called by him to covenant obedience. Israel must submit to its king and lord. What is striking in the Twelve is how Israel has deviated from its covenantal obligations. We see this immediately in the first

---

1. For recent study on the Twelve, see Nogalski, *Book of the Twelve*; House, *Unity of the Twelve*; Nogalski and Sweeney, *Book of the Twelve*; Redditt and Schart, *Book of the Twelve*; Seitz, *Prophecy and Hermeneutics*.
2. See House, *Unity of the Twelve*.
3. Rightly Dempster, *Dominion and Dynasty*, 182n23.

book of the Twelve, Hosea. The prophet ministered in the eighth century BC (1:1), before Israel was exiled to Assyria (722 BC). Israel was called upon to be faithful to Yahweh as a wife is to be faithful to her husband. Hosea's marriage to a prostitute, Gomer, illustrates Yahweh's relationship to Israel (chaps. 1–3).[4] Readers must have discernment and wisdom to unlock the message of Hosea (14:9). The importance of this wisdom is confirmed by the placement of this admonition at the conclusion of the book.[5] Israel was guilty of "whoredom by forsaking the LORD" (1:2; cf. 2:4–5; 3:3; 4:10–15; 5:3–4; 6:10; 9:1). Israel's worship of and reliance on other gods (especially Baal worship) demonstrates that "sin" is not merely a failure to keep covenantal stipulations. Forsaking and abandoning Yahweh is treachery and betrayal. Israel, the wife of Yahweh, did not understand that he was the one who lavished good gifts on her (2:8), gifts that Israel turned around and used to worship Baal. As Christopher Wright says, Israel was called upon to "acknowledge God's sovereignty in the *economic*, as well as the *religious*, sphere."[6] Israel did not "return" to Yahweh (7:10) but instead they "strayed" from him (7:13). Instead of crying to Yahweh from their hearts, they rebelled against him (7:14) and "forgot [their] Maker" (8:14; cf. 13:6).

Israel, Yahweh says, has transgressed covenantal stipulations as well: "They have transgressed my covenant and rebelled against my law" (8:1). There is a controversy, a lawsuit (4:1), with Israel because of its lack of "faithfulness" and "steadfast love" and because there is "no knowledge of God in the land" (4:1).[7] Deficiency in knowledge is highlighted: "My people are destroyed for lack of knowledge; . . . you have rejected knowledge" (4:6); "The spirit of whoredom is within them, and they know not the LORD" (5:4). They needed "the knowledge of God rather than burnt offerings," for they did not realize that Yahweh desired "steadfast love and not sacrifice" (6:6). Their lack of knowledge of God was evident in their disobedience. They were guilty of "swearing, lying, murder, stealing, and committing adultery; they break all bounds, and bloodshed follows bloodshed" (4:2; cf. 6:9; 7:4). The sins listed here represent violations of the Decalogue, even though the transgressions are not specifically said to violate that code. Clearly, then, Israel transgressed covenant obligations. They had "forgotten the law of [their] God" (4:6), and "like Adam they transgressed the covenant" (6:7). The sin of Israel was pervasive. Priests (4:4, 6, 9; 5:1; 6:9; 10:5), prophets (4:5; 9:7–8), kings (5:1; 7:3, 5,

4. The most likely reading is that Hosea was asked "to marry someone who was sexually promiscuous before marriage" (House, *Old Testament Theology*, 349).
5. Cf. Childs, *Old Testament as Scripture*, 382–83.
6. C. Wright, *Old Testament Ethics*, 97.
7. On this topic, see Huffman, "Covenant Lawsuit."

7; 8:4, 10; 10:7, 15; 13:10–11), and other rulers have transgressed (4:18; 5:10; 7:3, 5, 16; 8:4, 10, 15; 13:10).

Because Israel defected from the covenant, they are threatened in Hosea with the curses of the covenant. Yahweh would refuse to show mercy and forgive Israel (1:6; cf. 4:9–10) and would deprive the nation of physical provisions (2:9): "I will put an end to all her mirth, her feasts, her new moons, her sabbaths, and all her appointed feasts. And I will lay waste her vines and her fig trees, of which she said, 'These are my wages, which my lovers have given me.' I will make them a forest, and the beasts of the field shall devour them" (2:11–12). The punishments here echo the curses of the covenant (cf. Deut. 28:16–18, 22–24, 38–40). Hosea says that Israel will be defeated by its enemies (5:8–9; cf. 8:7) and will be exiled to Assyria (9:3, 7, 17; 10:6–7; 11:5–6; cf. 12:2; 13:7–16; cf. also Deut. 28:47–52, 64–65).

The punishment of the nation in Joel also reflects Israel's failure to abide by the covenant, even though the term "covenant" is not used.[8] Joel describes the judgment as "the day of the LORD." Such a judgment is covenantal (the nature of the judgment will be discussed when the day of the Lord is addressed below). Israel's special status as the covenant people of the Lord is prominent in Amos as well.[9] They are Yahweh's chosen people, but as his elect, they will be punished for their transgressions (3:2). Judah will be punished for rejecting "the law of the LORD" and for violating "his statutes" (2:4). Israel will face punishment particularly for their callous mistreatment and exploitation of the poor (2:6–7), forgetting Yahweh's covenantal love in freeing them from Egypt and in giving them victory over their enemies (2:9–10). Their hearts were drawn to their beautiful ivory houses rather than to the Lord (3:15). They "trample on the poor and . . . exact taxes of grain from him," while building for themselves "houses of hewn stone" (5:11). Rich women are compared to "cows of Bashan," and they are denounced as those "who oppress the poor, who crush the needy" (4:1). They "are at ease in Zion" (6:1), enjoying their ivory beds, sumptuous meals, elegant music, and refined wine (6:4–6). At the same time, they participate gladly in worship, attending the appointed feasts for Israel and offering required sacrifices (5:22–23; cf. 4:4–5). But all of this means nothing to Yahweh. Indeed, it provokes him, for they abandoned justice (5:24) and schemed about ways to extract more money from the poor (8:4–6; cf. 5:12).

8. Determining a date for Joel is notoriously difficult. Since I am using a canonical approach and the text does not specify a date, I simply follow the canonical order here and make no attempt to resolve when the book was written.

9. Amos prophesied during the reign of Uzziah in Judah and Jeroboam in Israel (1:1), which would place him in the eighth century BC.

Amos emphasizes the covenantal judgments that will come upon Israel for its sins. Yahweh's justice is impartial. He judges not only the nations for practicing evil (1:3–2:3)[10] but also his own people when they depart from his ways. When Israel faces battle, it will find itself running from the enemy (2:14–16; cf. Deut. 28:25). The judgments are not the result of chance and cannot be attributed to political circumstances that are outside Yahweh's dominion. The impending disaster comes from the Lord (3:6; cf. 5:16–17) in fulfillment of his prophetic word (3:8). Yahweh inspired Amos to prophesy that Jeroboam would be destroyed and Israel would be taken into exile (7:10–17; cf. 3:11–15; 6:7–14; 7:7–9; 8:1–3; 9:1–4, 8). Israel would be taken to Assyria with "hooks" and "fishhooks" (4:2). Of course, the judgment of exile itself is the climax of the covenant curses (see Lev. 26:33, 39; Deut. 28:49–52).

Yahweh was patient with his people, for he is slow to anger (see Exod. 34:6). Amos's prayers stemmed judgments that Yahweh threatened to send upon his people (7:1–6). The Lord gave Israel many chances to turn to him before exile arrived, calling for them to seek him (5:4, 6; cf. 5:14). Other covenant judgments preceded exile. He sent famine (4:6; Lev. 26:26), withheld rain (4:7–8; Lev. 26:19; Deut. 28:23–24), sent locusts to devour fruit (4:9; Deut. 28:38–40), and unleashed pestilence and war (4:10; Lev. 26:25) so that Israel would return to him, but they refused to do so.

Micah prophesied probably in the latter part of the eighth century BC (1:1), and his book has many intertextual connections with Isaiah.[11] The covenantal nature of Micah's accusations against Israel and Judah is evident. Yahweh functions as a witness against his people from his temple (1:2). He will come and judge his people for their transgressions (1:3–7), particularly their idolatry, which violates the first and fundamental principle of the covenant (see Exod. 20:3). But their sins did not end there. They spurned the tenth commandment by coveting and acted on their coveting by stealing (2:2), thereby taking advantage of the poor (2:8–9). Rulers did not shepherd the people, but instead were like ravaging animals that tore the skin off them so that they could eat their flesh (3:2–3). The prophets declared holy war against those who did not provide them food (3:5; cf. 3:8–11). Micah brought a covenant lawsuit against his people (6:1–3). Yahweh showered his goodness on Israel by freeing them from Egypt and turning the curses that Balak wanted Balaam to impose upon Israel into blessings (6:4–5). What it means for Israel to be in covenant with Yahweh is to "walk humbly" with him and "to do justice and to love kind-

10. The judgment of the nations in Amos picks up this theme from the end of Joel (Seitz, *Prophecy and Hermeneutics*, 120).
11. See Childs, *Old Testament as Scripture*, 435–36.

ness" (6:8). But instead, Israel turned to violence and theft (6:10–12). Because Israel violated the covenant, they were threatened with covenant curses. They would experience famine (6:14; Lev. 26:26) and would not enjoy the harvest of oil and wine (6:15; Deut. 28:39–40). Samaria would be destroyed (1:6), and devastation would come to many cities in Israel (1:10–16). Jerusalem would be ruined as well (3:12), and the people would be exiled to Babylon (4:10).

Habakkuk provides no definite information in regard to the date of his writing, but his book was written probably in the late seventh century BC, since he predicts the Babylonian exile. Judah would face punishment at the hand of the Chaldeans (1:5–11) for its violence (1:2), iniquity (1:3), and failure to observe the Torah (1:4). We have already seen that exile is the result of covenantal defection, of a failure to trust in and obey the Lord.

When we come to the book of Haggai, a new period of Israel's history after the exile is in view. Haggai can be dated very specifically to 520 BC (1:1, 15; 2:1, 10, 20). The nation had experienced the covenant curse of exile but had also been the recipient of the Lord's mercy and so has returned to the land. Still, the issue is whether Israel will be faithful to the Lord of the covenant. Haggai rebuked the people of the nation for lavishing attention on their own houses while neglecting to rebuild the temple (1:9–11; cf. 2:16–19). Since they disregarded the temple, their harvest of food and drink was pitiful (1:6, 9). In other words, they were facing some of the curses of the covenant (cf. Lev. 26:26). The words of Haggai provoked the leaders and the people to work on the temple (1:12–17). Zechariah began his ministry at the same time as Haggai, and, like Haggai, he was concerned with the rebuilding of the temple. Zechariah issues a reminder that the prophetic threats against God's people became a reality, so Israel should repent to avoid judgment (1:2–6), for Yahweh's curse remains on those who practice evil (5:1–4). Israel suffered exile because they hardened their hearts to Yahweh's commands, refusing to practice justice, oppressing the poor and disadvantaged (7:8–14; cf. 8:16–17).

A definite date for Malachi is not available in reading the book, but a post-exilic date is supported by its place in the canon and its contents. Israel was promised great blessing, but Malachi challenges Israel to live in accordance with the covenant. They are summoned to remember the commands of the covenant given to Moses at Horeb (4:4) and warned that they will face a curse if they fail to keep its stipulations (4:6). Yahweh is coming to his temple, and no one who is wicked will be able to stand when he appears (3:1–2). He will judge "sorcerers," "adulterers," and those who oppress the poor and sojourners and engage in lying (3:5). The root problem is that they did not fear and honor Yahweh (3:5). Israel was plagued with cynicism (cf. 2:17) and had qualms about Yahweh's goodness, doubting whether the Lord loved them even though he showed them his love concretely in favoring them and judging Edom (1:2–5). The problem with Israel was not trivial. How would the promises of the covenant ever be fulfilled, since the people dishonored and despised the Lord (1:6)? Priests showed their loathing for the Lord "by offering polluted food upon my altar" (1:7) and by offering blind and defective animals in sacrifice (1:8). The law specifically prohibited the latter from being sacrificed (Lev. 22:22; Deut. 15:21).

If the foundation of the biblical message is the centrality and glory of God, then it follows that Yahweh's name would be great to the ends of the earth (1:5), and Yahweh promises that his name will be honored wherever the sun rises and sets, but Israel profaned his name with their offerings (1:11–12, 14). They dishonor the Lord by rejecting him as boring (1:13). The Lord also summons priests "to give honor to my name" (2:2), and he will curse them if they refuse to do so. Yahweh made a covenant with Levi so that priests would fear him and stand "in awe of my name" (2:5). When priests fear Yahweh, they give "true instruction," live godly lives, and turn "many from iniquity" (2:6). But the priests of Malachi's day "corrupted the covenant of Levi" (2:8), and thus they would face judgment (2:9).

The unrighteousness of Israel was also evident in their marriages. They profaned the covenant by their faithlessness to one another (2:10), particularly by marrying foreign women who did not worship the Lord (2:11). Again, Israel would not know Yahweh's blessing if they abandoned him. Nor is the Lord impressed with tears and lamentations of so-called repentance when Israelites were divorcing and oppressing their wives (2:13–16). Israel would know Yahweh's favor only if they repented (3:7), but they were not giving the tithes that Yahweh commanded and were facing the consequences (3:8–11; cf. Deut. 4:40; 12:28). They were complaining that "it is vain to serve God" (3:14), thinking that the living of a righteous life was futile, even believing that those who pursued evil would be blessed (3:14–15). A day of judgment was coming when the arrogant would be annihilated by fire (4:1). The righteous, upon hearing such exhortations, encouraged one another. They responded rightly because they "feared the LORD and esteemed his name" (3:16). Such fear of the Lord is the right response of the creature before the creator.

The Day of the Lord and God's Rule over the Whole World[12]

The day of the Lord is a theme noted previously (see Isa. 2:11–22; 3:7, 18; 4:1–6; 13:6–13; Ezek. 13:5; 30:3). The term should not be limited to the formal

12. See House, "Day of the Lord."

expression "day of the LORD," for sometimes the same notion is present with just the word "day." Furthermore, the separation expressed by having a section called "Covenant" and one where we focus on the day of the Lord is largely artificial, for in many instances the day of the Lord represents Yahweh's covenant judgment or covenant salvation. In this section I will concentrate on the day of the Lord insofar as it relates to judgment. It should be noted that the day of the Lord is integrally linked to the theme of God's rule and kingdom, for the Lord reasserts his rule over the world on the day when he judges the wicked and saves his people.[13]

The first book in which the day of the Lord dominates as a theme is Joel. The book opens with a description of the devastating and unprecedented effects of locusts that have swarmed over Israel (1:2–4). Vines and figs (1:7) and grain and drink offerings (1:9, 13) are a thing of the past. The wheat and barley harvest was ruined (1:11). "The vine dries up; the fig tree languishes. Pomegranate, palm, and apple, all the trees of the field are dried up, and gladness dries up from the children of man" (1:12). Israel is summoned to "weep and wail" (1:5) and to "lament like a virgin" who has lost her bridegroom (1:8). Priests should "put on sackcloth and lament" (1:13), and Israel should fast and "call a solemn assembly" (1:14), gathering at the temple to beseech the mercy of the Lord. The locust plague was not just a chance happening, according to Joel, an unfortunate conglomeration of circumstances that destroyed Israel's economy. It was instead a manifestation of Yahweh's covenant judgment upon his people, as Deut. 28:38–40 demonstrates.

Indeed, it seems that Joel describes the locust judgment as the day of the Lord (1:15–20),[14] which picks up on the locust and darkness plagues in Exodus.[15] Nevertheless, it is not a day of salvation but rather one of judgment and destruction. Probably the day of the Lord is described as a locust invasion in 2:1–11 as well.[16] The locusts are God's army sweeping through the land, bringing "a day of darkness and gloom, a day of clouds and thick darkness" (2:2).[17] Apocalyptic language is used to describe the day of the Lord, which is presented as a locust invasion: "The earth quakes before them; the heavens tremble. The sun and the moon are darkened, and the stars withdraw their

---

13. See ibid., 181–82.

14. Some scholars identify this as a drought instead of seeing a reference to the locust plague. I contend that the author describes the results of the locust plague in dramatic and symbolic terms.

15. So Sweeney, "Place and Function of Joel," 143–44.

16. So Dumbrell, *Faith of Israel*, 186. Some scholars think a literal army is in view here, but it is more likely that symbolic language describing an army portrays a locust invasion in apocalyptic terms.

17. The relationship between the first two chapters of Joel is debated. Childs (*Old Testament as Scripture*, 390–91) rightly says that the two chapters are more closely related than some suggest.

shining" (2:10). What is remarkable, however, is that the day of the Lord is one of judgment. Israel cannot count on salvation if it is not obeying the Lord. "For the day of the LORD is great and very awesome; who can endure it?" (2:11). Hence, chapter 2 resumes themes from chapter 1. Israel, says the Lord, must "return to me with all your heart" (2:12) and "rend your hearts and not your garments" (2:13). The people should fast and gather together and implore Yahweh to show mercy (2:15–17). Joel appeals to the covenant revelation of Yahweh in Exod. 34:6, giving Israel motivation to return: "For [the LORD] is gracious and merciful, slow to anger, and abounding in steadfast love; and he relents over disaster" (2:13). Because the people turned to Yahweh, he removed the locusts from Israel and restored the grain and new wine (2:19–23), and so an even greater punishment was averted (at least temporarily).[18] Israel will be glad and give praise to Yahweh (2:26), for Yahweh is "in the midst of Israel" (2:27). Christopher Seitz argues that Joel's intervening role between Hosea and Amos is significant, for it teaches that Yahweh will forgive if Israel repents.[19]

The astonishing element in Joel is that the day of the Lord means judgment for the wicked in Israel. We will see in due course that salvation is also promised for Israel in the day of the Lord, but the Twelve also emphasize God's righteous judgment of his people. Amos rebukes those who desire the day of the Lord to come, reminding the wicked that it will be a day "of darkness, and not light" (5:18; cf. 5:19–20). Unless they repent and obey Yahweh, those who comfort themselves with the thought of being delivered on the day of the Lord are deluded.

The other book of the Twelve in which the day of the Lord signals judgment for Israel (and the world) is Zephaniah, written late in the seventh century BC, before the Babylonian exile occurred in 586 BC. The day of the Lord is conceived of as a sacrifice whereby those who do not know and obey Yahweh will be consumed (1:7). The coming judgment is described in cosmic terms, terms that even exceed the judgment under Noah (1:2–3), for the impending devastation includes not only all human beings but also the fish of the sea and the birds of the air. "In the fire of his jealousy, all the earth shall be consumed; for a full and sudden end he will make of all the inhabitants of the earth" (1:18). As D. W. Baker says, "Their punishment could be seen as an 'uncreation,' since the order of destruction in Zephaniah exactly reverses that of creation in Genesis."[20] Judah faces judgment for its violation

---

18. According to Seitz (*Prophecy and Hermeneutics*, 125–26), we see in Joel the repentance called for in Hosea. He writes, "In so doing, we are drawn back into the world of Hosea to learn again what the character of God is really like" (p. 126).

19. Ibid., 209.

20. Baker, "Zephaniah," 255.

of the covenant, for its idolatry especially among the priests (1:4–5). Judah has defected from the Lord so that they do not follow him, "seek" him, or "inquire" of him (1:6). Zephaniah often uses the word "day" to designate the judgment that is coming (1:7, 8, 9, 10, 14, 15, 16, 18; 2:2, 3; 3:8), and in two instances specifically he calls it the "day of the LORD" (1:7, 14), though it is evident that the same event is in view. I will note in the next section that Zephaniah also uses "the day" to refer to God's saving work, showing that the day of the Lord is one of judgment and salvation. It seems that there is continuity in Zephaniah (and the other prophets) between days of the Lord in history (like the judgment of Jerusalem in 586 BC) and the final day of the Lord. In other words, there are days of the Lord before the arrival of the final day of the Lord. Zephaniah warns that the day will be one of punishment for those who reject Yahweh and indulge in sin (1:8–13, 17), and those who dismiss Yahweh from everyday life (1:12).[21] One ought not think that the day will bring only gladness: "A day of wrath is that day, a day of distress and anguish, a day of ruin and devastation, a day of darkness and gloom, a day of clouds and thick darkness" (1:15). Trumpets will blare out warnings, and cities will come crashing down (1:16).

The response that Zephaniah calls for resonates with themes found in Joel. The people of Judah, says Zephaniah, should assemble before the day of Yahweh's wrath comes, and they should "seek the LORD" and "seek righteousness" and "humility," so that "perhaps you may be hidden in the day of the anger of the LORD" (2:3). The coming judgment will affect not only Judah, for, as we have already seen, the day has universal dimensions. Hence, the Philistines, Moab, the Ammonites, the Cushites, and Assyria will also be judged on that day (2:4–15). Indeed, the judgment on these nations is connected with a promise of salvation for Israel (2:7, 9), anticipating again the theme of judgment and salvation relative to the day of the Lord. But Zephaniah returns to Jerusalem in chapter 3, predicting its judgment for its rebellion and oppression of others (3:1). Jerusalem, personified as a woman, has not drawn near to God and has refused to listen to his voice of correction or to trust in him (3:2). Her leaders are fierce animals destroying those whom they serve (3:3). Her prophets and priests distort and twist God's revelation for their own purposes (3:4). When the Lord rises to judge the entire earth (cf. 1:2–3, 18), Jerusalem will not be spared (3:8). In "the fire of [the Lord's] jealousy all the earth shall be consumed" (3:8), and those who are proud will be removed from the nation (3:11).

21. Zephaniah disputes the idea that Yahweh is "as irrelevant to life as the other gods, as though Yahweh were not a serious player in the life of the world" (Brueggemann, *Theology of the Old Testament*, 137).

The day of the Lord also plays a major role in Obadiah. The phrase "day of the LORD" is restricted to verse 15, but the word "day" refers to the day of judgment ten times in verses 11–14.[22] All ten of these examples refer to the judgment that was poured out on Jerusalem and Judah in 586 BC, confirming the prophecies of Zephaniah and others that Judah would be punished for violating the covenant. Obadiah warns Edom, however, that the historical day of judgment upon Jerusalem anticipates a greater and climactic day of the Lord (v. 15), fulfilling the prophecy of Amos (9:12).[23] The judgment meted out on Jerusalem will be returned upon Edom, and hence it must avoid gloating or rejoicing in Jerusalem's misfortune. Edom will be judged for its arrogance and delusive self-confidence, for thinking itself to be impervious to harm (vv. 3–4). The judgment on Edom also represents salvation for Israel (I will comment on this in the next section). Edom will be judged, but those on Mount Zion will escape and possess the land (vv. 17–21). It seems that Edom/Esau in Obadiah is not limited to the nation of Edom. As Childs says, the judgment of the day of the Lord here is "directed to all the nations."[24] "Edom is now understood as a representative entity, namely, the ungodly powerful nations of this world which threaten the people of God."[25] There are other indications in the OT that Edom and Esau are a symbol for unbelieving nations generally (cf. Isa. 34; 63:1–6; Lam. 4:21–22; Ezek. 35; Mal. 1:2–5), so that the judgment of Edom represents the arrival of the kingdom, just as verse 21 in Obadiah attests.

The reference to the day of the Lord in Obadiah and the coming of the kingdom function as a good transition to the next topic, for Yahweh's judgment over the nations shows that he is Lord, that he is the king over all the earth. His lordship over the nations is emphasized in Amos 1:3–2:3, where various nations are judged by Yahweh for their transgressions. "God's ability to judge these lands demonstrates his sovereignty over the whole earth."[26] Yahweh is not merely the Lord over all Israel; he reigns over the entire earth. Indeed, as we will see shortly in discussion of the promises of salvation, the realization of God's saving promises is intertwined with the judgment of the wicked.

We see this same theme in the book of Nahum, which predicts the judgment of Assyria. As Childs says, "The destruction of Nineveh is . . . explicitly

22. There are a number of intertextual connections between Obadiah and Joel. See Sweeney, "Place and Function of Joel," 147.

23. On days of the Lord and the day of the Lord, see Rendtorff, *Canonical Hebrew Bible*, 701–5. On the link between Edom in Amos and Obadiah, see Seitz, *Prophecy and Hermeneutics*, 138–39.

24. Childs, *Old Testament as Scripture*, 414.

25. Ibid., 415. Seitz (*Prophecy and Hermeneutics*, 138–39) rightly says Edom is not just a "metaphor" here, and yet the historical referent goes beyond Edom.

26. House, *Old Testament Theology*, 359.

derived from the nature of God," and 1:1–8 offers "a theological interpretation of how to understand the oracles of judgment which constitute the main portion of the book."[27] Nahum does not call this judgment a "day of the Lord," but conceptually it falls under the same idea. Yahweh's judgment over Assyria represents his day of victory over them, demonstrating his sovereignty over an evil kingdom.[28] Yahweh's character does not consist only of his love: "The LORD is a jealous and avenging God; the LORD is avenging and wrathful; the LORD takes vengeance on his adversaries and keeps wrath for his enemies. The LORD is slow to anger and great in power, and the LORD will by no means clear the guilty. His way is in whirlwind and storm, and the clouds are the dust of his feet" (1:2–3). The whole of creation melts and shakes before the sovereign God, such that no one can stand in his presence, no one can endure his anger (1:5–6). The Lord is good, but his goodness and grace and mercy are reserved for "those who take refuge in him" (1:7).

Heschel reflects on why it is difficult to comprehend God's anger: "Is it not because we are only dimly aware of the full gravity of human failure, of the sufferings inflicted by those who revile God's demand for justice? There is a cruelty which pardons, just as there is a pity which punishes. Severity must tame whom love cannot win."[29] The Lord's adversaries stand no chance (1:8). The gods and kingdom of Assyria will fall, showing that Yahweh is the one and only supreme king (1:14). This represents good news, the gospel, for Israel, for the end of Assyria's reign spells peace for Israel (1:15). Chapters 2–3 depict the judgment and battle against Assyria in vivid terms. Its doom is certain because Yahweh is "against" it (2:13; 3:5). Thereby Yahweh's justice will be revealed in the judgment of the wicked.

Yahweh's sovereignty is also evident in Habakkuk. Yahweh raised up the Babylonians to judge Judah (1:5–11), which provokes Habakkuk to wonder about Yahweh's justice, since the Babylonians are more evil than Judah (1:12–2:1). Yahweh instructs Habakkuk to wait and to trust in him, for the righteous live by faith (2:4). The judgment on Babylon will not come immediately, but come it will (chap. 2). Those who trust in false gods will not be delivered by their idols, for idols lack breath and life (2:18–19). Yahweh reigns from his heavenly temple, and he will assess and judge all those who practice evil (2:20). Babylon will be destroyed and the new creation will dawn: "For the earth will be filled with the knowledge of the glory of the LORD as the waters cover the sea" (2:14). As Childs says, "The prophet learns that both the punishment of

27. Childs, *Old Testament as Scripture*, 443.
28. Hence, the judgment also functions typologically. See ibid., 444–45.
29. Heschel, *The Prophets*, 296. Heschel writes, "Divine justice is not the antithesis of love, but its counterpart, a help to justice as demanded by true love" (p. 297).

disobedient Israel by means of the Babylonians, and the subsequent destruction of that arrogant nation, belong to the one consistent purpose of God."[30]

The book of Jonah takes us in a different direction. Reading the prophecies of judgment upon the wicked could sow in Israel a wrong understanding. So it is significant that Jonah comes after Obadiah, correcting a false conclusion that might be drawn from Obadiah.[31] After all, the promise of Abraham was that the nations would be blessed through him, and we have seen in the prophets many examples of Israel being judged for its own wickedness. There is no inherent delight in the judgment of those who give themselves to wickedness. Jonah, in wanting to see Nineveh destroyed, represents a natural inclination in Israel, but it is an inclination that must be repudiated. As a reading of the entire book demonstrates, Yahweh's reason for calling Jonah to proclaim judgment upon Nineveh was so that Nineveh would repent. This is the very thing that Jonah feared, and therefore he fled to Tarshish (chap. 1) to preclude such an outcome (4:2). Jonah knew that what Exod. 34:6 said about Yahweh's covenant with Israel was not limited to Israel. He well knew, as he said to Yahweh, "You are a gracious God and merciful, slow to anger and abounding in steadfast love, and relenting from disaster" (4:2). What he should have seen, and, as the preservation of the book suggests, eventually did see, is that Yahweh's graciousness to him was no different from his graciousness to Nineveh. As Childs says, "Jonah is thankful for his own deliverance, but resentful of Nineveh's inclusion within the mercy which had always been restricted to Israel."[32]

Jonah deserved to be judged and destroyed because he disobeyed the divine commission to proclaim judgment upon Nineveh, and yet Yahweh had mercy upon him. The large fish that swallowed Jonah became the means of his salvation. He saw that salvation is of the Lord, and that those who call to him in their distress, as he did in the belly of the fish, are saved by the Lord's mercy, and hence the Lord deserves praise and thanksgiving (2:9).[33] Yahweh reigns from his holy temple in heaven (2:4, 7), and those who belong to him will reside with him in his temple, which represents his reign over all the earth. Yahweh made his sovereign reign over all things very plain to Jonah by bringing a storm upon the sea so that he could not escape to Tarshish (1:4–16), by appointing a fish to swallow Jonah (1:17), by commanding the fish to disgorge Jonah (2:10), by appointing a plant to grant Jonah shade (4:6), and by appointing a worm

---

30. Childs, *Old Testament as Scripture*, 453.

31. So Seitz, *Prophecy and Hermeneutics*, 120–21, 146–47, 212.

32. Childs, *Old Testament as Scripture*, 424. At least it was restricted to Israel in Jonah's view.

33. Chapter 2 is not a plea for deliverance but rather is a psalm of thanksgiving for deliverance via the fish (so Childs, *Old Testament as Scripture*, 423).

to destroy the plant (4:7–8). The sovereign Lord is also compassionate, relenting from judgment when people repent (3:5–10; 4:11). We learn from Nahum that Yahweh is a mighty and just king who inflicts righteous judgment upon those who persist in evil,[34] but Jonah reminds readers that Yahweh is good, that he longs to save, and that his salvation extends to the ends of the earth. "The final form of the story does seek to address the issue of God's salvation being extended to the nations as well as to Israel."[35] Jonah and all the people of God should rejoice in such a salvation.

Future Promises of Salvation

Yahweh shows his lordship and manifests his kingly power in judging the wicked and condemning them for their evil. But as we saw with the book of Jonah, Yahweh's kingdom is not restricted to judging the wicked. The saving promise that commenced with Gen. 3:15 and is reiterated in the covenants with Abraham and David is also picked up in the Book of the Twelve. The day of the Lord is not merely a day of judgment; it is also one of salvation. The coming kingdom will bring blessing and joy to the world, so that it becomes even better than Eden.

The promise of salvation begins with the first book of the Twelve, Hosea. Yahweh rejects Israel, saying that they will not receive mercy and are not his people (1:6, 9). The abandonment of Israel, however, is not Yahweh's final word. He will not utterly destroy Israel as he destroyed the cities of the plain during the days of Lot (11:8–9; cf. Gen. 18). Yahweh will roar like a lion, and Israel will return from exile (11:10–11). The promise of Abraham, which pledges that Israel will be as numerous as the sand on the seashore (Gen. 22:17; 32:12; cf. 1 Kings 4:20), will become a reality in the future (1:10). Israel will again live as God's children and receive his mercy (1:10–2:1). The judgment upon Israel represents a severe mercy according to chapter 2. Yahweh will remove from Israel all the joy and fruitfulness derived from false gods. Once in the wilderness, Israel will realize that her only husband is Yahweh and will forsake Baal worship (2:14–17). The language used is very similar to the covenant promises found in Jeremiah, Ezekiel, and Isaiah. Yahweh, as the bridegroom and husband, says to Israel, "I will betroth you to me in faithfulness" (2:20; cf. 2:21). Israel's faithfulness is the result of Yahweh's work in the people's hearts. Therefore, a new creation will dawn, and Israel "will lie down in safety" (2:18).

34. In that sense, Nahum answers the concern found in Jonah (see Seitz, *Prophecy and Hermeneutics*, 147–48, 212).
35. Childs, *Old Testament as Scripture*, 425.

There is the recognition in chapter 3 that Israel's return to the Lord will not happen soon. Israel will pass "many days without king or prince, without sacrifice or pillar, without ephod or household gods" (3:4). But the day will come when they "shall return and seek the Lᴏʀᴅ their God, and David their king, and they shall come in fear to the Lᴏʀᴅ and to his goodness in the latter days" (3:5). Israel's apostasy is self-destructive, for when they return, they will come to the one who provides them with every good thing. Another striking feature of what is predicted here is the promise that they will seek out "David their king" (3:5). This promise is addressed to the northern kingdom, which rejected Davidic kings, and yet in the future they will seek a king from David's line. Clearly, the promise does not envision the literal return of David but rather forecasts a future king from David's line in the last days, and according to the NT, this prophecy is fulfilled when Israel seeks Jesus the Christ.

Israel is summoned to return to Yahweh, knowing that he will heal them and bind up their wounds, that he will raise them up on the third day so that they would have life (6:1–2).[36] Here, life refers to the resurrection (see also 13:14),[37] and the reference to three days, in terms of the NT witness, suggests a reference to Christ's resurrection, for he embodies the destiny of his people. Israel, according to Hosea, should seek to know Yahweh, for his goodness is "sure as the dawn," and he will pour out blessings on his people (6:3). The same language of repentance and return concludes Hosea (chap. 14). Yahweh promises that he will intervene: "I will heal their apostasy; I will love them freely" (14:4). The promise of healing matches the new covenant in Jeremiah and the covenant of peace in Ezekiel. Israel will blossom and thrive under Yahweh's gracious care (14:5–7).

Joel too looks forward to an eschatological work of Yahweh by which he will save Israel. But there are hints that the salvation will extend beyond Israel as well. The Spirit will be dispensed to "all flesh" (2:28), which fulfills what is anticipated in Num. 11:25–29, and is picked up by Peter on the day of Pentecost (Acts 2:16–21). Joel announces that the day of the Lord is coming in which all will be assessed and judged by Yahweh, but those who call upon Yahweh will be rescued from his negative verdict (2:31–32; 3:16). On that day Yahweh will restore his people and judge those who have abused them (3:1–16). Then Yahweh will dwell "in Zion, my holy mountain" (3:17). The whole universe will be a new temple, and there will be a new Jerusalem (3:17), anticipating the vision of John in Rev. 21–22. A new creation will dawn where

---

36. Intertextual connections between Hosea and Isa. 26–27 suggest that the former anticipated the resurrection of the dead (see Levenson, *Restoration of Israel*, 202–4). Cf. Hosea 13:14 with Isa. 26:19; Hosea 13:13 with Isa. 26:17–18; Hosea 13:14; 14:5–6 with Isa. 26:19.

37. See ibid., 205–6.

"mountains shall drip with sweet wine, and the hills shall flow with milk" (3:18). We see a picture very similar to what is found in Ezekiel (chap. 47). "A fountain shall come forth from the house of the LORD and water the valley of Shittim" (3:18). From God's new temple, from the place where he reigns as king, he will pour his goodness out upon his people. Yahweh "dwells in Zion" (3:21) and in Judah and Jerusalem (3:20), but he will avenge the wicked who resist his people (3:19).[38]

Amos focuses on the judgment that Israel deserves and will receive for its sins, but he also envisions a day when Yahweh will save his people. Like Hosea, Amos anticipates the coming of a future Davidic king. The "fallen booth" of David will be repaired, raised up, and reestablished (9:11).[39] When the kingdom is restored, Israel will conquer its enemies, described here as Edom (another indication that "Edom" is used to designate Israel's enemies in general). There is a hint here, however, also picked up in the NT (see Acts 15:16–18), that more than judgment is anticipated for Gentile nations. Yahweh speaks of "all the nations who are called by my name" (9:12), suggesting that they belong to him because of their identification with his name.[40] The coming Davidic king will save not only Israel, but also the Gentiles. The new creation, such a prominent theme in the prophets, is coming. "The mountains shall drip with sweet wine" (9:13). Israel's fortunes will be restored, so that cities will be rebuilt, and God's people will enjoy gardens and vineyards (9:14) and never again will suffer exile (9:15).

We noted earlier that the day of the Lord in Obadiah is one of judgment, but it is also one of salvation. The judgment of Edom, representing all nations opposed to Yahweh, also signals the deliverance and rescue of Israel from its enemies. Joel refers to those who will escape and be rescued on the day of the Lord (2:32; 3:16), and Obadiah picks up the same theme. Some in Mount Zion will escape when the fierce day of the Lord arrives; they will "be holy" and inhabit the land (v. 17). Obadiah emphasizes also that Israel will possess the land of its enemies (vv. 18–20), suggesting that the whole world will be under the dominion of the Lord on that future day.[41] The book ends upon such a note: "Saviors shall go up to Mount Zion to rule Mount Esau, and the

---

38. On the close connection between Zion and kingdom, see Rendtorff, *Canonical Hebrew Bible*, 578–81.

39. Sailhamer (*Old Testament Theology*, 250–51) sees this as a fulfillment of the triumph over Moab prophesied in Num. 24:17–19.

40. "Edom . . . seems to be a paradigm for repentant Gentiles, who will finally share in the covenant promises" (Dumbrell, *Faith of Israel*, 198).

41. Sailhamer (*Old Testament Theology*, 251) argues that Obadiah therefore fulfills the promise of salvation found in Amos 9:11–12 (see the LXX), for when Edomites believe, they are no longer Edomites but rather belong to Israel.

kingdom shall be the LORD's" (v. 21). Childs observes, "The climactic note of the coming of God's kingdom sounds the central theme of the final oracle"; and, "The canonical shape of the oracles of Obadiah has interpreted the prophetic message as the promise of God's coming rule which will overcome the evil intent of the nations, even Edom, and restore a holy remnant to its inheritance within God's kingship."[42] The emphasis upon Mount Zion and the kingdom suggests that Yahweh reigns from his new temple (which in the NT is the entire universe), from a renewed Zion.

The future salvation of Israel receives some prominence also in Micah. Israel would go into exile because of its sins and refusal to keep covenant stipulations. But exile is not the final reality. Yahweh will reassemble his people, his flock, his remnant, and bring them back to the land (2:12–13).[43] And the kingship will be renewed, for the king will lead them back from exile along with the Lord (2:13). As we saw in Hosea (3:5), the relationship between the king and Yahweh is very close, suggesting a very prominent place for the ruler of Israel.

In Mic. 4:1–3 is a prophecy also found in Isa. 2:1–4.[44] Micah looks to the future, to "the latter days," when "the mountain of the house of the LORD" will be exalted, and all peoples, not just Jews, will come to the temple to worship Yahweh (4:1). The law will flow from Zion, and so people will come to his mountain to hear his instruction (4:2). Then peace will dawn worldwide. War will be forsaken, and each person will be "under his vine and under his fig tree" (4:4). Yahweh "will assemble the lame and gather those who have been driven away" (4:6), and they will be gathered as Yahweh's people, as his remnant (4:7). The return from exile seems to be coincident with the coming of the kingdom (4:10): "And the LORD will reign over his people in Mount Zion from this time forth and forevermore" (4:7; cf. 4:8). As we have seen often in the prophets, so too in Micah the salvation of Israel is coterminous with the destruction of the nations (4:11–5:1). Israel's ruler, who will lead them to victory, will come from Bethlehem, from the tribe of Judah (5:2). Micah says that this ruler's "coming forth is from of old, from ancient days" (5:2), which probably means that "his coming was predicted from long ago, thus harking back to the passages in Genesis and Numbers that anticipate such an individual."[45] Canonically, this is the same one who is described in Davidic terms by both Hosea (3:5) and Amos (9:11). As the shepherd and ruler, says

---

42. Childs, *Old Testament as Scripture*, 415.

43. Against Dumbrell (*Faith of Israel*, 208), who sees this as a judgment oracle.

44. The relationship between Isaiah and Micah as well as Micah and Jeremiah is instructive. See Seitz, *Prophecy and Hermeneutics*, 127–28.

45. Dempster, *Dominion and Dynasty*, 185. House (*Old Testament Theology*, 370) thinks that the reference shows that he is a "supernatural figure" and eternal.

Micah, he will lead Israel to victory (5:5–6) and bring them security: "For now he shall be great to the ends of the earth" (5:4), and "he shall be their peace" (5:5). Israel will be a blessing among the nations (5:7–8).

Micah closes by considering the future of Israel. Israel has fallen, but it will rise; it sits in the darkness now, but it will see the light again (7:8–9). The enemies will be destroyed, and Israel's walls will be rebuilt (7:10–11). There will be a new exodus (7:15), and Yahweh will shepherd his people again (7:14). The promise of Gen. 3:15 will be fulfilled, for the enemies of Yahweh "shall lick the dust like a serpent, like the crawling things of the earth; they shall come trembling out of their strongholds; they shall turn in dread to the LORD our God, and they shall be in fear of you" (7:17). The offspring of the serpent will be destroyed, and Yahweh will fulfill the covenant that he made with Abraham, showing "steadfast love," just as he promised (7:20). And he will fulfill that covenant fundamentally by forgiving Israel's sins, "by pardoning iniquity and passing over transgression for the remnant of his inheritance" (7:18). A great day of salvation is coming, for Yahweh "will again have compassion on us; he will tread our iniquities underfoot. You will cast all our sins into the depths of the sea" (7:19).

The book of Habakkuk does not as clearly predict that Yahweh will fulfill his promises for Israel. A careful reading of the book demonstrates, however, that an eschatological promise for Israel remains. Babylon will ultimately be judged for its evil, and "the earth will be filled with the knowledge of the glory of the LORD as the waters cover the sea" (2:14). What will happen to Israel when the earth universally knows the Lord's glory? In chapter 3 Habakkuk appropriates the language of the exodus, praying that the Lord will again work on behalf of his people. The book concludes with Habakkuk waiting for "the day of trouble to come upon people who invade us" (3:16), which almost certainly also involves salvation for Israel. The judgment coming from Babylon is described poetically as fig trees not blossoming, the lack of produce from vineyards and olive trees, and shortage from the herd (3:17). The judgment from Babylon represents not a new creation but rather a de-creation. But judgment is not forever, for Habakkuk will "rejoice in the LORD," and such rejoicing never takes place in a vacuum but rather is rooted in Yahweh's saving work on behalf of his people (cf. Pss. 28:7; 32:11; 35:9; 64:10; 68:4; 97:12; Isa. 41:16; 61:10; Joel 2:23; Zeph. 3:14; Zech. 10:7).[46] Habakkuk specifically mentions that his joy is in "the God of my salvation" (3:18),[47] suggesting that

---

46. Various verbs for "rejoice" are used, but the idea communicated is the same.

47. There is likely an allusion to Gen. 3:15 in Hab. 3:12–13 (so Hamilton, *God's Glory in Salvation*, 253).

Yahweh's saving work for Israel is in view. Ultimate victory will come, for having feet like a deer echoes the words of the Davidic king (see 2 Sam. 22:34; Ps. 18:33) who triumphs over his enemies. For Habakkuk, treading on high places (3:19; see also Amos 4:13; Mic. 1:3; cf. Deut. 32:13; 33:29; 2 Sam. 22:34; Ps. 18:33) signifies victory and triumph over those in opposition, so there are good reasons to think that Habakkuk anticipates salvation and deliverance for Israel ultimately.[48] Hence, the whole of Habakkuk summons one to faith in God's promises (2:4). "The prophet's testimony (3.18–19) witnesses to this faith which rejoices in God's salvation and awaits the end in spite of a human situation which oppresses the people of God."[49]

As we noted previously, Zephaniah emphasizes the day of the Lord when Yahweh will judge the wicked in Israel and in the whole world. In that sense, Zephaniah expands upon the judgment forecast in the preceding book, Habakkuk.[50] As Childs says, Zephaniah contains a "radically theocentric perspective."[51] The day of the Lord is one not only of judgment but also of salvation. Remarkably, this salvation will reach to the Gentiles: "I will change the speech of the peoples to a pure speech, that all of them may call upon the name of the LORD and serve him with one accord" (3:9). Here we have echoes of Babel (Gen. 11:1–9) and the rebellion against God in Genesis, where the people were conspiring to make a name for themselves instead of honoring the Lord. In the future the nations will be united in serving the Lord and will invoke him as their God. Such a change will be the result of Yahweh's sovereign work, for he is the one who grants them such "pure speech." It is a bit difficult to determine in 3:10 whether the worshipers are only Israelites who have been exiled or whether Gentiles are also included, but the word "peoples" in 3:9 suggests that Gentiles are in view as well.[52] In any case, future worship in Yahweh's temple is envisioned. Such worship should not be understood in literal terms, since the NT presents the whole universe as Yahweh's temple. Clearly, Zephaniah draws on the Abrahamic promise of blessing for all nations.

Those who are proud and arrogant will not enjoy the future days of blessing, which are reserved for those who are "humble and lowly," for those "who seek refuge in the name of the LORD" (3:12). Injustice and evil speech will not be found in Israel (3:13), and Israel will rejoice because Yahweh will clear away their enemies (3:13–15). The theme of the kingdom is prominent

---

48. See Goldingay, *Israel's Life*, 791.
49. Childs, *Old Testament as Scripture*, 453.
50. So Seitz, *Prophecy and Hermeneutics*, 213. But, he notes, Zephaniah also predicts the future mercy of the Lord, which is unpacked in Haggai and Zechariah.
51. Childs, *Old Testament as Scripture*, 461.
52. House, *Old Testament Theology*, 382.

here, showing that the salvation of Israel and of the whole world means the coming of the kingdom. "The King of Israel, the LORD, is in your midst; you shall never again fear evil" (3:15). Yahweh will not only reign as king, he also will dwell in Israel's midst. The promises enunciated in Gen. 3:15, which were repeated and expanded to Abraham and David, will become a reality. Zephaniah says that Zion will no longer fear (3:16), for "the LORD your God is in your midst, a mighty one who will save; he will rejoice over you with gladness; he will quiet you by his love; he will exult over you with loud singing" (3:17). Not only will Yahweh be king but also those who belong to him will be secure in his love and experience the intense joy of knowing his love for them. They will see the King in his beauty and will experience the richness of knowing God. The days of reproach and humiliation will be over, and those who belong to Yahweh will be gathered to him (3:18–19). When their fortunes are reversed, the people of God will be praised and renowned in the whole earth (3:19–20).

Haggai focuses on the temple and the need for the people of God to devote themselves to its rebuilding. In the midst of such exhortations Haggai receives an oracle in which Yahweh promises to shake both the heavens and the earth, the sea and the dry land (2:6). The universal nature of the shaking accords with Zephaniah's emphasis on a universal judgment. When the whole world is shaken, says Haggai, then "the treasures of nations" will be brought to Jerusalem and will fill the temple (2:7). Yahweh promises, "The latter glory of this house shall be greater than the former. . . . And in this place I will give peace" (2:9). This prophecy certainly was not fulfilled in the Second Temple period. Some argue that it will be fulfilled with a literal future temple, but it is more likely that this prophecy will be fulfilled in the new universe that is coming, the new cosmic temple in which Yahweh will dwell as king.[53] This accords with the appropriation of this text in Hebrews (12:26–28), for there is no indication of a future temple in Hebrews, and such a temple fits awkwardly with the definitive and final sacrifice of Christ in the book. In Hebrews the realization of this prophecy means the arrival of "a kingdom that cannot be shaken" (12:28). Haggai ends on a similar note. Yahweh pledges again that he will "shake the heavens and the earth" (2:21), which means the ousting of kingdoms opposed to the Lord (2:22). No kingdom that exalts itself against the kingdom of the Lord will prevail. Yahweh's kingdom will be established through Zerubbabel, for he is Yahweh's "signet ring" by whom the Lord's authority is exercised in the world (2:23). Zerubbabel, as a descendant of David, fulfills the promise that a ruler will come from David's line (cf. 2 Sam. 7;

53. See Childs, *Old Testament as Scripture*, 469–70.

1 Chron. 17).[54] The Davidic hope is not surrendered; it is reaffirmed. Obviously, the hopes and dreams associated with David did not come to pass under Zerubbabel. The fulfillment of Yahweh's kingship came later, just as we saw with the temple, in an unexpected way, in Jesus the Christ.

The eschatological character of the book of Zechariah is well known, though it is difficult to interpret. Zechariah, like Haggai, focuses on the temple, and it is not surprising that Jerusalem and the temple figure prominently in his eschatological vision, given the focus of chaps. 1–8.[55] The central theme of the book is the kingdom of God,[56] but the kingdom is realized in God's presence with his people. "For Zechariah, Jerusalem's chief glory was the presence of God in it, powerfully symbolized by the temple."[57] Zechariah encourages Israel, for Yahweh is "exceedingly jealous for Jerusalem and for Zion" (1:14). Jerusalem will be rebuilt and "without walls" since it is so large (2:4), and yet it will be secure, for, as Yahweh declares, "I will be to her a wall of fire all around. . . . I will be the glory in her midst" (2:5). Yahweh will dwell in the midst of his people (2:10), and his salvation will be extended to the nations, so that they will also be the people of the Lord (2:11). Judah will be "his portion," and Jerusalem will be chosen (2:12). Yahweh's jealousy and wrath for Jerusalem (8:2) will lead to its salvation. He will "dwell" in the city, and Jerusalem "shall be called the faithful city, and the mountain of the LORD of hosts, the holy mountain" (8:3). The joy of the city will be great, with people living to an old age and children playing joyfully and safely in the streets (8:4–5). Israel will be gathered to the Lord, and the covenant will be a reality. He will be their God, and they will be his people (8:8), and the new creation will dawn (8:12). In those days salvation will extend beyond the borders of Israel so that the nations are also included, and Gentiles will long to be part of the Jewish people (8:22–23).[58] In the NT this promise of salvation is realized when Gentile believers are identified as true Jews, as truly circumcised, and as the true children of Abraham (Rom. 2:25–29; 4:9–16; Gal. 3:6–9; 6:15; Phil. 3).

For Zechariah, Joshua's role as high priest and the forgiveness of his sins, symbolized in the removal of his dirty garments and his being clothed in pure

54. So House, *Old Testament Theology*, 385–86. Dumbrell (*Faith of Israel*, 228–29) downplays this idea, though he does not deny the messianic connection altogether.

55. There is continuity between chapters 1–8 and chapters 9–14 in seeing Jerusalem's special place and final salvation, the judgment of the nations and their salvation, the coming new creation, the giving of the Spirit, a messianic figure, and the centrality of the covenant. See Childs, *Old Testament as Scripture*, 482–83.

56. See B. Webb, *Message of Zechariah*, 153.

57. Ibid., 34.

58. The return from Babylon takes on eschatological significance in Zechariah (so Childs, *Old Testament as Scripture*, 477–79).

garments (3:1–5), signify that Yahweh will raise up "my servant the Branch" (3:8). The word "branch" has messianic associations (see Isa. 4:2; Jer. 23:5; 33:15; cf. Zech. 6:12).[59] When the branch comes, Yahweh will "remove the iniquity of this land in a single day" (3:9). Read canonically, this almost certainly refers to Jesus' atoning work on the cross, where sins were cleansed once-for-all through his sacrifice. Such forgiveness of sins would lead to the coming of the kingdom, to the fulfillment of all of God's promises, for then "every one of you will invite his neighbor to come under his vine and under his fig tree" (3:10). A crown is placed on Joshua's head as the high priest (6:11), but there is likely expectation of a separate individual, the "Branch," as the one who will build the Lord's temple and will rule (6:12–13).[60] It is possible that the references here are to Joshua the priest instead of a king from David's line. In any case, "6:13 points forward to a time when the kingship and the priesthood are united in a way not seen before, for 'the counsel of peace will be between both of them.' Given the eschatological and apocalyptic character of Zechariah, I think it would have been fairly clear that Joshua and Zerubbabel were not themselves this Branch but they pointed forward to someone greater."[61] The role of the priest and king is resolved in Jesus Christ, for he is conceived of as a priest-king, and the temple he builds is not a literal one but instead consists of the new people of God, the church of Jesus Christ. In chapter 4 the prominent role of Joshua (chap. 3) seems to be matched by that of Zerubbabel. Together they are the two olive trees, "the two anointed ones who stand by the Lord of the whole earth" (4:14).[62]

Chapters 9–14 of Zechariah are apocalyptic and notoriously difficult to interpret. Israel's enemies will be destroyed (9:1–8), and Yahweh will protect his people "at [his] house" (9:8). The daughter of Zion will rejoice because a humble king is coming to bring salvation (9:9), which the NT sees fulfilled in Jesus' entry into Jerusalem the week before his passion (Matt. 21:5; John 12:15). The promise that salvation would reach the ends of the earth, as was promised to Abraham, will be fulfilled, for "he shall speak peace to the nations; his rule shall be from sea to sea, and from the River to the ends of the earth" (9:10). This humble king, who will come from Judah (10:3–4), is likely the same person as "the Branch" in chapter 3 and chapter 6.[63] We would read

59. See Dempster, *Dominion and Dynasty*, 186; House, *Old Testament Theology*, 389–90. For doubts about this, see Rose, *Zemah and Zerubbabel*, 91–141.

60. Dempster, *Dominion and Dynasty*, 186–87. Dumbrell (*Faith of Israel*, 223) sees two crowns here, one for Joshua and one for Zerubbabel. Against Rose (*Zemah and Zerubbabel*, 47–48), who goes on to argue that the crown does not signify coronation (pp. 50–59).

61. This comment is from Joshua Greever.

62. Against this, see Rose, *Zemah and Zerubbabel*, 177–207.

63. So B. Webb, *Message of Zechariah*, 131.

9:1–8 wrongly if we restricted the fate of Gentiles to judgment, for it is clear that some among the nations will enjoy peace. The means of this peace are communicated in 9:11: prisoners will be set free by "the blood of my covenant with you,"[64] which in the NT is understood as a reference to the death of Jesus Christ, by which those imprisoned are set free (cf. Luke 4:18). The salvation and judgment described in chapters 10–11 occur through the humble king who brings salvation (9:9–10). As Barry Webb says, "The arrival of the Messiah . . . will be the time for false shepherds to be judged, for the dispersed flock to be regathered, and for a new Israel to be created."[65] The rejection of the shepherd in chapter 11 is also understood in the NT to be a reference to Jesus (11:12–13; cf. Matt. 26:15; 27:9–10). As Webb remarks, "It is impossible to be in relationship with God unless we are prepared to be ruled by him."[66] And we see in that chapter that those who reject the true shepherd will end up being ruled by evil leaders. Those who belong to the people of God will triumph over their enemies (9:13–10:12), for the Lord "will save them, as the flock of his people; for like jewels of the crown they shall shine in his land" (9:16).

Chapter 12 also looks forward to the day when Yahweh will save his people. Jerusalem and Judah will conquer their enemies, and Jerusalem will be inhabited again (12:1–6). Salvation will be poured out for Judah and Jerusalem (12:7). On that day "the house of David shall be like God" (12:8) in the conflict with enemies (12:9). Yahweh will "pour out . . . a spirit of grace and pleas for mercy" on his people, including the house of David (12:10). Israel will look on the one whom they pierced and mourn sorrowfully in repentance (12:10–14). A fountain will be opened "to cleanse" Israel "from sin and uncleanness" (13:1), and the fountain suggests, as Webb points out, an "overflowing, never-failing, inexhaustible supply."[67] Israel's cleansing means that false prophets will be removed from the land, and there will be pure devotion to the Lord (13:2–6). For the writers of the NT, the one pierced is Jesus Christ (John 19:34, 37; Rev. 1:7), and through the shedding of his blood full cleansing from sin is now available.

Zechariah says that the Lord will extend his sword against his own shepherd and scatter the sheep (13:7; cf. Matt. 26:31), and he will save a purified remnant (13:8–9). It seems that the king of these chapters and the shepherd who is smitten are identical.[68] The nations will attack Jerusalem again (chap. 14), but Yahweh will come down on the Mount of Olives and defeat them

64. See ibid., 133–34.
65. Ibid., 143.
66. Ibid., 154.
67. Ibid., 163.
68. So ibid., 41, 169–70. On the messianic teaching of Zechariah, see Duguid, "Zechariah," 259.

(14:1–4). "Then the Lord my God will come, and all the holy ones with him" (14:5; cf. 1 Thess. 3:13), and the new creation will dawn (14:6–7, 10). "On that day living waters shall flow out from Jerusalem" (14:8), much like the waters that flow from the temple (see Ezek. 47:1–12; cf. Joel 3:18). A plague will strike those who oppose the Lord (14:11–15). So with the salvation of the Lord's people, the destruction of his enemies, and the arrival of the new creation, the fulfillment of God's promises will be realized. The kingdom will then be a reality: "And the Lord will be king over all the earth. On that day the Lord will be one and his name one" (14:9). No other gods will be worshiped and venerated. All will worship Yahweh as king at the feast of Booths (14:16), and those who fail to do so will be punished (14:17–19). Everything everywhere will be holy to Yahweh (14:20). "Every pot" in Jerusalem and Judah will be dedicated to the Lord (14:21), so that the Lord will be worshiped on that day. In the new creation holiness will pervade the whole cosmos. This is another way of portraying the truth that the universe will be a cosmic temple, and the prescriptions in the temple will apply to the whole creation.[69]

Malachi looks forward to the day when Yahweh's name "will be great among the nations" (1:11; cf. 1:5, 14). A messenger will come to prepare the way before Yahweh himself comes to his temple to purify his people (3:1–5). Yahweh will be faithful to his covenant promises to his people, for he does not change (3:6). When the day of judgment arrives, those who fear Yahweh's name will rejoice, and "the sun of righteousness shall rise with healing in its wings. You shall go out leaping like calves from the stall" (4:2). The wicked will be destroyed who repudiate and transgress the Mosaic law (4:3–4), but Elijah will come and restore God's people to a heart of repentance before the day of judgment commences (4:5–6).

---

69. Dumbrell, *End of the Beginning*, 26.

INTERLUDE

A Synopsis of
JUDGMENT AND SALVATION IN THE PROPHETS

The prophets do not advance the story line of the OT, but they do provide insight into Israel's history, helping us to understand it at a deeper level. Most of the prophets are preexilic, warning Israel and Judah about the dangers of forsaking the Lord. A few of the prophets are exilic or postexilic, reflecting on Israel's state after its people have returned to the land. To summarize the prophets: they focus on judgment and salvation. Yahweh reigns over all things for his glory both in judging and saving his people.

The judgment threatened typically is exile. God's people have failed to observe the stipulations of the covenant, and thus they are threatened, as we find in Lev. 26 and Deut. 28, with exile unless they repent and obey their covenant Lord. Another way of putting this is to say that Israel and Judah are warned about the impending day of the Lord. There are "days" of the Lord in history when he judges his people, and there is a final day, which will be a culminating judgment. Both Israel and Judah thought of the day of the Lord as one of salvation, a day when they would be delivered and the Gentile nations judged. Such an interpretation of the day of the Lord is partially right, for God will judge wicked nations and rescue his people. But the prophets warn Israel and Judah that they are living like the pagan nations, and hence the day of the Lord will be one of darkness, not light. They will not rejoice on the day of the Lord; rather, they will be filled with gloom unless they turn from their sin. The prophets repeatedly warn the people of their sin, especially indicting prophets, priests, and kings for failing to shepherd and teach the people well. These leaders promised peace when there is no peace, safety when disaster is coming, assurance when Israel should be scared to death. Most notably, Hosea,

Jeremiah, and Ezekiel describe Israel's sin as whoredom. Israel has not just violated the law; they have committed treachery by abandoning their Lord, who nurtured them, protected them, fed them, and sustained them. They have committed the sin of finding God to be boring, so they found more excitement and security in other gods. Because both Israel and Judah abandoned and forsook the Lord, he sent them into exile.

Exile is not a permanent condition. Yahweh had not abandoned his people. The promise that the offspring of the woman would triumph over the serpent was not withdrawn. The promise made to Abraham of offspring, land, and worldwide blessing would still be fulfilled, as would the promise that a king from David's line would reign. The prophets promise that Israel will return to the land. A new exodus is coming! Yahweh will go before the nation and bring them back to Israel. The Lord does not only promise a new exodus but also a new creation. The mountains will drip with sweet wine, and all of nature will be transformed, for there will be a new heaven and a new earth. The Lord also pledges to make a new covenant with his people. Yahweh would write his law on the hearts of his people. He would pour out his Spirit, and the Spirit would indwell their hearts so that they would do his will. Israel would gladly submit to Yahweh's rule, and the coming new creation would be a new paradise, but it would be a paradise better than the old paradise, for nothing will ever defile it.

Yahweh also promises a new temple. Here an interesting feature of these prophecies should be noted. They were fulfilled in an "already but not yet" fashion. Israel returned from exile, but the promises found in Isaiah, Jeremiah, and Ezekiel were not realized in their fullness. They rebuilt the temple, but it was nothing like the temple that Ezekiel foresaw. Daniel explains that the exile will last longer than Israel might imagine, that other kingdoms would rise and fall before the kingdom of God arrives. Israel should continue to follow the Lord, for his kingdom will come in its fullness.

And that leads us to another feature of the prophets. There will be a new David. It is quite clear that the new creation and the new exodus will become a reality only when the new David arises. He will rule over all creation; the new covenant will be a reality when he arrives. He will shepherd Israel with love and care, unlike the shepherds who preceded him. And we saw reasons in Daniel to connect the son of man with the stone that shatters worldly kingdoms. It is clear from Jeremiah, Ezekiel, and Zechariah that the new David will shepherd and rule God's flock, but this seems to be the same function of the stone in Daniel (cf. Isa. 28:16) and the son of man. So there are reasons to think that the new David and the son of man describe the same person, for the kingdom will be given to the son of man, but Isaiah makes it very plain that the new David will rule (9:2–7), that he is the Spirit-anointed leader of God's people (11:1–9).

What is fascinating is that Isaiah makes it plain that the promises of a new exodus and new creation will come about only via the servant of the Lord. Israel will experience return from exile only if their sins are forgiven, and it is the servant of the Lord who bears the sins of the people. He is the shepherd, as Zechariah says, who is struck for the sake of the people. But we have also seen that the new creation and the new exodus become a reality through the new David, so we have reasons to think that the new David, the son of man, and the servant of the Lord have the same referent. The promises made to Abraham and to David will become a reality through a new David, the servant of the Lord, and the son of man, and the NT proclaims that Jesus is the son of David, the messianic king, the servant of the Lord, and the Son of Man.

The promises of the prophets are not restricted to Israel but have a universal dimension. The salvation brought about by this new David, this son of man, and this servant of the Lord will extend beyond Israel so that Gentiles will be included. Judgment looms for those who refuse to submit to their king, but there is salvation for Gentiles who put their hope in the Lord and the Davidic king. The prophets, from Hosea to Malachi, teach that Gentiles will believe and hope in this Messiah. Yahweh's name will be great among the nations (Mal. 1:11, 14). The Egyptians and Assyrians will worship alongside Israel (Isa. 19). The remnant of Edom will be called by Yahweh's name (Amos 9:12). God will pour his Spirit on all, not just Israel (Joel 2:28), for, as the message of Jonah suggests, Gentiles will be included among the people of God. The servant will be a light for all nations, and his message will go to the ends of the earth (Isa. 42:4, 6; 49:6). Nations will stream to Jerusalem to hear Yahweh's word (Isa. 2:1–4; Mic. 4:1–4). Yahweh will change the speech of Gentiles so that they speak the language of Zion (Zeph. 3:9). All of God's promises to Abraham will be fulfilled, for the blessing will not be limited to Israel but instead will encompass the whole world. Israel and the entire world will sing because the king is in their midst (Zeph. 3:15). The judgments due to their sin will be removed. Everyone will "worship the King, the LORD of hosts" (Zech. 14:16), "and the LORD will be king over all the earth" (Zech. 14:9). The Lord will rule in the new creation, the new Jerusalem, and the new temple, but the most beautiful thing will be his presence. They will see the King in his beauty, for as Ezekiel said about the new temple, "The LORD is there" (Ezek. 48:35).

A BRIEF RETROSPECTIVE
OF THE OLD TESTAMENT STORY

Interludes have been inserted along the way so that the big picture of the OT story line will not be lost. Here I want to summarize that story briefly because we have come to the end of the OT.

God created the universe and Adam and Eve for his glory. Adam and Eve were created to rule the world, more specifically the garden that they inhabited, for God. They were Yahweh's vice-regents and were to rule the garden in submission to him. But instead of relying upon and obeying God, they listened to the voice of the serpent and did not submit themselves to God's lordship. The earth was blighted with the curse, as sin and death entered the world. The Lord promised victory through conflict: the offspring of the woman would triumph over the serpent.

The conflict immediately began, as the offspring of the serpent, Cain, killed the offspring of the woman, Abel. And things got worse. By the time of Noah, the entire world, except for Noah's family, belonged to the serpent. It seemed as if victory was out of reach for the righteous. But the Lord is always the king and sovereign one. He judged the world by sending a flood, destroying those aligned with the serpent, anticipating thereby the final judgment. He then made a covenant with Noah, promising to spare the world until the victory was achieved. The promise of preservation was important, for human beings had not changed since the flood. The tower of Babel illustrated that human beings still lived for their glory instead of living for the sake of God's kingdom. God, in his grace, had not abandoned human beings. He called Abraham to be his own, pledging land, offspring, and universal blessing. The offspring of Abraham would defeat the serpent.

And yet it took years and years before Abraham and Sarah had a single child, and by the end of Genesis, the number of offspring is not as the sand on the seashore, for they top out at about seventy. God was teaching the people that victory over the serpent would not be easy, that the conflict would be arduous and long. At the opening of Exodus, the promise of countless offspring begins to come to pass, though Pharaoh, as the offspring of the serpent, tries to destroy Israel. But Yahweh reigns as king and warrior, freeing his people from Egyptian slavery so that they left Egypt (the exodus) and traveled to the land of promise. The second great promise, that of the land (a new garden of Eden), was about to be fulfilled.

Israel needed to learn, however, what it meant for Yahweh to dwell in their midst. He made a covenant with Israel through Moses, requiring that his people live by the stipulations of the covenant. If they failed to do so, he would evict them from the land. They would be able to stay in their "new Eden" only if they obeyed. Otherwise, like Adam, they would be expelled from their inheritance. The Lord specially dwelt with Israel via the tabernacle, for the glory and wonder of his presence are what made Israel distinct among all peoples. But one cannot come into God's presence on one's own initiative. He is the holy one of Israel, and so access to him is not free and unhindered, for human beings are unclean due to their sin. Sacrifices must be offered so that sins will be atoned for, and only those who are designated by the Lord (the priests) can offer sacrifices and enter the holy place and the holy of holies. Numbers reminds us why Israel needs sacrifices, for instead of trusting the Lord and doing his will, the people refused to enter the land of promise, and as a consequence they perished in the wilderness. Deuteronomy represents the renewal of the covenant for a new generation. Israel would enter the land and flourish in it if they feared, obeyed, and loved the Lord, walking in all his ways and commands.

Arriving at Joshua, we see that the second element of the promise to Abraham is fulfilled. Israel dispossessed the Canaanites and entered the land of promise. It seemed that worldwide blessing could not be far behind. However, Adam was still in Israel. During the time of the judges Israel oscillated between trust and unbelief, between worshiping Yahweh and giving themselves to idols. Hence, the Lord gave them over to their enemies until they called on the Lord and repented. He then sent judges/saviors to deliver his people. The cycle repeated itself over and over. It became apparent that Israel needed a king to deliver them (Judg. 17:6; 21:25). What was intimated earlier in the Pentateuch (Gen. 17:6, 16; 49:8–12; Num. 24:17) now becomes clearer. Victory over the serpent would come to pass through a king, and Ruth forecasts the coming of this king, for she gives birth to one of David's ancestors.

The books of 1–2 Samuel recount the rise of David as king. The day of the judges ends, and Saul is appointed as the first king. Saul, however, replicates the life of Adam and Israel (cf. the episode of the golden calf and the book of Judges). He begins by trusting and obeying the Lord but then turns aside to evil. Hence, the kingdom is removed from him, for he shows himself to be the offspring of the serpent, and David is then anointed as king. Hannah's song is programmatic in 1–2 Samuel. Yahweh exalts the humble and puts down the proud. Saul persecutes and tries to kill David, for Saul is the offspring of the serpent, but Yahweh's plans and purposes cannot be frustrated. Since David trusts in and obeys the Lord, he is granted a permanent dynasty. The offspring of the woman, who will triumph over the offspring of the serpent, will come from the line of David.

Israel seems to be on the cusp of worldwide blessing under David and Solomon. During Solomon's reign the temple was built, and Israel was safely established in the land. But both David and Solomon, after they had reigned for some time, wandered from the Lord. Solomon's defection was so great—he turned to idolatry—that the kingdom over which he reigned was divided after his death. Henceforth, the nation was split into two parts, Israel in the north and Judah in the south. Though some of the kings in the south followed the Lord (none of the kings of the north were faithful), both Judah and Israel violated the covenant, and so both kingdoms were sent into exile, Israel in 722 BC and Judah in 586 BC. Instead of worldwide blessing, things were going backward! Israel was no longer in the land. Like Adam, they were evicted from their "Eden," and the temple, the place of Yahweh's presence, was destroyed. The Lord's gracious reign over the whole world seemed farther away than ever. Nevertheless, the Lord promised that Israel would return from exile, and the people did return, build the temple, and restore the city of Jerusalem. And yet things were at a low ebb in Israel. The new temple scarcely matched the former one, and Jerusalem did not enjoy the freedom and influence that it had in Solomon's day. Still, the promise for Israel was not withdrawn; victory over the serpent was still forthcoming.

The songs of Israel and the wisdom tradition depart from the narrative, but they still fit within the story line. They examine what it looks like to live under Yahweh's reign. Proverbs, Ecclesiastes, and Job are well identified as Wisdom literature. Some scholars claim that Proverbs contradicts what we find in Ecclesiastes and Job. It is better to say that the perspectives in the books are not at variance with one another but rather are complementary. Even in Proverbs we see that the righteous do not always prosper, so we must beware of a simplistic and one-dimensional appropriation of its message. All the wisdom books teach that the fear of the Lord is the heart of wisdom, so the books are not secular, nor do they separate faith from the concrete details of everyday life. Indeed, it is commonly acknowledged that wisdom draws on creation traditions, and there are a number of intertextual links between Proverbs and Deuteronomy. What it means to live under Yahweh's lordship is to fear him and to keep his commands. Ordinarily, those who fear the Lord will experience blessing in this life, but Job and Ecclesiastes indicate that there are many anomalies. Life in this world will not necessarily turn out well for the righteous. Life is mysterious, baffling, and absurd for those under the sun, and human beings lack the capacity to discern a larger plan. Those who fear and love the Lord must not think that they will be spared suffering, or that they will be able to fathom the mysteries of human existence. God reigns over all, but he has not explained to human beings the full rationale of his reign. Human beings are called upon to fear the Lord and to submit to his lordship by obeying him. Ultimately, though, it will go well with those who fear the Lord. Those who trust and obey him will find life. From a canonical perspective, the only truly wise person is Jesus Christ. He is the only one who invariably lived righteously by fearing the Lord and keeping his commands.

Song of Songs celebrates married love, comparing it to the pleasures and innocence of Eden. The love between King Solomon and a maiden anticipates the love between Christ and the church, so that Song of Songs is not limited to the temporary and passing experience of human love but rather points to something deeper and to a permanent reality. Capturing the message of the Psalter is quite difficult, but it does no wrong to the book to say that its theme is that the Lord reigns. A scan of the five books of the Psalter shows that they move from David's reign to exile to a renewal of the promise of a Davidic reign. In other words, the psalms fit with the theme propounded here. God will bring in his kingdom; he will destroy the reign of the serpent through a Davidic king. Hence, the Psalter concludes with a note of praise, for when Yahweh is present with his people, they will praise him.

The OT concludes with the prophets. The prophets warn Israel and interpret for them the significance of the covenant. Why were Israel and Judah sent into exile? Because they violated the stipulations of the Mosaic covenant. They failed to obey their master and king. Hence, the day of the Lord for disobedient Israel and Judah would be a day not of deliverance, but of disaster. We see the fulfillment of these prophecies in 1–2 Kings and 1–2 Chronicles, which recount the story of the demise of Israel and Judah.

And yet the prophets do not stop there. The promise of Gen. 3:15 has not been overturned. The promises to Abraham (land, offspring, and worldwide blessing) have not been withdrawn. So the prophets are full of hope. A new exodus, like the first exodus and even greater, is coming. A new creation will dawn. A new covenant will be established, whereby Yahweh writes his law on the hearts of his people. And a new David will arise. The promise that blessing will come through David is reiterated, not rejected. Indeed, this future deliverer is also described as the son of man and the servant of the Lord. He will restore Israel by suffering for their sake, by absorbing the punishment that they deserve so that their sins are forgiven. And he is the glorious son of man who will receive the kingdom from the Father. The saints who belong to him will reign with him. They will reign because they belong to the new David, who has suffered for them and received the kingdom as their representative and king. Indeed, the prophets make it clear that these blessings are not only for Israel. The universal promises made to Abraham will be fulfilled. Gentiles too will be members of the new covenant, beneficiaries of the new exodus, and recipients of the new creation. Their king will be the new David, who atones for their sins as well. The promise of universal blessing made to Abraham will be fulfilled.

The prophets after the return from exile (Haggai, Zechariah, Malachi) surprise us, for we expect at the return from exile the fulfillment of the promises of a new creation. We anticipate that the curse will be lifted entirely. Instead, Israel returned from exile as expected, but things are at a low ebb. For those who have read the story carefully, this is no surprise. Every stage of the story has been fulfilled much more slowly than we would have ever imagined. The hope is not abandoned, but it is delayed. The victory over the serpent will come. The new creation will dawn, and a new David is still coming. The slowness of the triumph etches on our minds the depth and breadth of human sin, but also the miracle of God's grace. The Bible is the story of the triumph of the kingdom, and the story plays out as it does because thereby it brings glory to God.

PROLOGUE TO THE
NEW TESTAMENT

The OT clearly leaves us with an unfinished story. The serpent was not yet crushed. The promise that Israel would dwell in the land was contradicted by the exile, and even when Israel repossessed the land, they were either under the thumb of foreign powers or barely hanging on to independence. The promises of the new covenant, the new exodus, the new creation, and the new David obviously were not realized. Yahweh ruled as the sovereign king over the entire earth, but his saving promises for Israel and the world remained unfulfilled. The NT witness claims that the promise of a kingdom, anticipated in the OT, is fulfilled in Jesus Christ. The new creation, the new covenant, and the new exodus have arrived in Jesus Christ. This is just another way of saying that the kingdom has come, and NT writers most often describe what has happened in Christ as the coming of the kingdom.

But how should the NT be approached?[1] Should we study each book separately? We could study all the Gospels together, or, since the Synoptics share to a remarkable degree the same content, we could separate the Synoptics from John's Gospel. But then we divide Luke from Acts, two volumes that clearly form one work and were written by the same author. Along the same lines, John's Gospel could be examined together with the Johannine Epistles and even the book of Revelation because all of them belong to Johannine tradition. We face the same kinds of issues in considering Paul. Each letter could be studied separately, or we could combine them together and look for

---

1. I worked out many of these themes in my NT theology, but space is lacking to defend here what was asserted there. For a more detailed explication of NT theology, see Schreiner, *New Testament Theology*.

common themes that permeate all the Pauline Epistles. So too, we could treat the letters of 1–2 Peter as a unit, or we could study each letter individually. A good argument can be made for putting 2 Peter with Jude as well because their content is so similar.

So how should we proceed? I suggest, as I did in my introduction to the OT, that those who insist on "one right way" are mistaken. It is legitimate and fruitful to examine the biblical story line from many different perspectives and angles.[2] Just as it does not matter greatly whether we study OT theology with the canon derived from the Hebrew Bible or one that relies upon the English Bible,[3] so also a variety of approaches will unearth the riches found in the NT. We must beware of thinking that we can exhaust the subject under consideration through a particular method, particularly if we believe in the divine authority and inspiration of the Scriptures. We do not need to agonize over choosing one approach rather than another. Instead, we should recognize that studying biblical theology is like looking through a kaleidoscope. The perspective from which we view the subject will bring some things to the forefront rather than others. This is not to say that biblical theology is arbitrary and without any controls. It is legitimate to dispute whether the perspective advocated truly fits with the text. What should be rejected is the notion that there is only one window into what the text says.

I am dividing the NT into five larger sections: (1) the Synoptic Gospels and Acts; (2) John's Gospel and the Johannine Epistles; (3) the Pauline Epistles; (4) the remainder of the NT Epistles; and (5) Revelation. Under the first category I will examine Matthew and Mark separately and then study Luke-Acts together.[4] Of course, there are advantages to studying all the Synoptics together, but it is also illuminating to put Luke and Acts together, since they were written by the same author. Examining the Gospel of Luke along with Acts assists us in exploring Lukan theology. I also elect to put the Gospel of John with the Johannine Epistles for the same reason. Whatever one's view of authorship, these books belong canonically to Johannine tradition.[5] There are advantages to considering each of the Pauline Epistles separately, for then specific features of his theology are not neglected. But the survey character of this work is amenable to considering all the Pauline Epistles together. I

2. See Poythress, "Kinds of Biblical Theology."
3. See pp. xv–xvi.
4. For a programmatic study, see Tannehill, *Narrative Unity of Luke-Acts*.
5. I am not trying to hide my view of authorship. I believe that the Gospel of John, the Johannine Epistles, and Revelation were written by the apostle John. So too, I think that all thirteen letters ascribed to Paul are authentic, and that the letters of 1–2 Peter are genuinely Petrine. It is not my purpose in this book, however, to answer historical-critical questions or to defend the historical accuracy of the Scriptures.

hope that the main features of his theology will be delineated through this approach. The remainder of the NT Epistles will be examined in the next section. I will examine 2 Peter along with Jude because their content is so similar. The remaining letters will be studied individually. Finally, Revelation will conclude the book. Revelation could be studied along with the rest of Johannine tradition, but it uniquely and fittingly closes the canon, and thus a separate consideration makes good sense.

Part 5

THE KINGDOM IN MATTHEW, MARK, AND LUKE-ACTS

25

THE GOSPEL
ACCORDING TO MATTHEW

Fulfillment and Christology

The OT closes on a note of anticipation, and the NT opens on a note of fulfillment. The kingdom of God has come, and this is evident because Jesus is risen from the dead, and "all authority in heaven and on earth" is his (28:18). The very first verse of Matthew resonates with OT themes and covenants: "The book of the genealogy of Jesus Christ, the son of David, the son of Abraham" (1:1). The words translated "the book of the genealogy" (*biblos geneseōs*) recall the first book of the Bible, which is the only other place where the phrase *biblos geneseōs* occurs (Gen. 2:4; 5:1), suggesting here the inauguration of the new creation in Christ.[1] The references to David and Abraham hearken back to OT covenants. The promise to Abraham included land, offspring, and blessing (Gen. 12:1–3). Matthew does not concentrate on the land promise, but the offspring, as we will see, is Jesus himself. Matthew particularly underscores that the blessing will reach the whole world (both Jews and Gentiles), indicating that the people of God, the new Israel, includes both Jews and Gentiles.[2]

1. Beale, *Church's Mission*, 171; France, *Gospel of Matthew*, 26–28.
2. In identifying the church as the new Israel, I am not arguing that it is continuous with Israel in every respect, for in the new covenant every believer is regenerate, indwelt by the Spirit, and has access to God through Christ. OT believers were regenerate, but they were not indwelt by the Spirit and had access to God through mediators. See Gentry and Wellum, *Kingdom through Covenant*, 685–90.

Matthew also proclaims that Jesus is the Christ, the son of David. The promise of a Davidic dynasty, signaled in the first verse of Matthew, finds its fulfillment in Jesus of Nazareth. The kingdom has come because the king has come. Since Jesus is the true offspring of Abraham and David, his connection to David receives particular emphasis in the genealogy (1:6, 17).[3] Jesus does not often assert that he is the Christ or the son of David in Matthew, probably because such a title had political associations that were liable to be misunderstood. But Matthew, in composing his Gospel, regularly identifies Jesus as the Christ. The title "Christ" is used quite often in the birth narratives (1:1, 16, 17, 18; 2:4), so that the reader knows from the outset that Jesus is Christ the king. The most important text is 16:13–20, where Peter declares that Jesus is the Christ, though subsequent events reveal that Peter did not understand the nature of Jesus' messianic ministry. Peter's declaration functions as one of the climaxes in Matthew's narrative, demonstrating that Jesus' disciples are finally beginning to grasp his identity. The kingship of Jesus is apparent also in texts where he is identified as the son of David. What is striking is the social status of those who identify him as such: blind persons (9:27; 20:30–31), a Canaanite woman (15:22), crowds of common people (21:9), and children (21:15). The religious leaders did not understand how Jesus could be both the son of David and David's lord (22:41–46). They refused to believe Jesus was the Christ and the Son of Man, and they mocked him for claiming to be the Christ (26:63, 68). Those who had the lowest social status recognized that Jesus was the king, and that the kingdom was becoming a reality through him.

Matthew's genealogy also focuses on the exile to Babylon (1:11, 12, 17), suggesting that the exile had ended, that the new exodus had begun with the coming of Jesus Christ. Christology and the fulfillment of God's saving promises are woven together in Matthew. The kingdom is realized as Jesus rescues his people from exile. Jesus is "Immanuel" (1:23), and as Immanuel he will "save his people from their sins" (1:21). We scarcely see at this point in the narrative how Israel will be saved, but the story culminates in the cross and resurrection, indicating that Israel will be saved through Jesus' suffering and death. Such a reading fits with the context of Isa. 7–8, where the prophecy of Immanuel is found. Just as Judah was saved from the Syrian-Ephraimite plot in Isaiah's day, so the people of God will be delivered in a climactic and definitive way through Jesus Christ. The high Christology of Matthew surfaces from the outset of the book and forms the backbone of the entire narrative. Not only is he the Christ, the son of David, but also he is God himself. Indeed,

3. Note how Matthew emphasizes that Joseph is David's son (1:20).

the importance of this theme is evident, for Matthew both opens and closes the book with the theme that God is with his people in Jesus. Jesus says, "And behold, I am with you always, to the end of the age" (28:20).

The reference to Isa. 7:14 in 1:23 is the first of Matthew's fulfillment quotations, and the repeated emphasis on the fulfillment of prophecy ties the first Gospel in the NT canon firmly to the OT witness. Some of the fulfillment citations seem strange to us and are difficult to interpret. Even if we cannot discern why Matthew finds a connection to the OT in some of his prophecies, it remains a stubborn fact that Matthew sees in Jesus Christ the realization of OT promises. The theme of fulfillment is not limited to places where the word "fulfill" occurs. For instance, Jesus' birth in Bethlehem fulfills the promise that the Messiah would be born in Bethlehem (2:5–6; cf. Mic. 5:2). The Davidic character of the promise is evident, for he is the one "born king of the Jews" (2:2). In Mic. 4–5, however, the coming of a ruler means that Israel would be restored from exile, that God would intervene and vindicate his people. In Matthew, then, Christology is tied to the fulfillment of OT promises: the return from exile will take place through the king of the Jews.

We find a similar circle of ideas in the remainder of Matt. 2. At first glance, seeing Jesus as the son called out of Egypt (2:13–15) in fulfillment of Hosea 11:1 is exceedingly strange because that verse is not a predictive prophecy, and the son there is clearly Israel, which was freed from Egypt. A closer look at Hosea 11 indicates that in that very chapter Hosea draws a typological lesson from Israel's exodus from Egypt. Just as Yahweh delivered Israel from Egypt, so too he would free them from Assyrian rule and fulfill his promises to Israel. Matthew picks up this typological stream. Just as Israel survived Pharaoh's wrath in Moses' day, so also Jesus was shielded from Herod, the offspring of the serpent of his day. Matthew also begins to develop the theme here that Jesus is the true Israel. Just as Yahweh delivered Israel at the exodus, he also delivers Jesus, the true Israelite, from his enemies.

The last fulfillment formula in chapter 2 is perhaps the strangest one, for Matthew sees a fulfillment in Jesus being called "a Nazarene" (2:23), but where in the OT do we find a prophecy about a Nazarene? Probably two OT texts are in view, indicating the richness and depth of the fulfillment theme in Matthew. First, the instructions about a Nazirite (Num. 6:1–21) point to Jesus as the one who is supremely and totally dedicated to the Lord. Second, in Isa. 11:1 the branch from Jesse is called a *neṣer*. Jesus is the promised descendant from Jesse, the true Davidic king, and if we read on in Isa. 11, we see that he is the one who is the Spirit-anointed Messiah, the one who will bring in the new creation, where the knowledge of the Lord will extend throughout the whole world (Isa. 11:2–9).

Matthew's fulfillment theme continues in chapter 3. The Baptist has come to proclaim the kingdom of heaven, which is another way of saying that he announces the coming new creation and new exodus. It is clear that the kingdom of heaven represents the arrival of the new exodus and new creation, for Matthew cites Isa. 40:3 (Matt. 3:3), a text that promises Israel's return from Babylon. Matthew adds that John's clothing and food were similar to what Elijah wore (cf. 2 Kings 1:8). The allusion to Elijah confirms that the day of fulfillment has arrived, for Elijah is the messenger who will arrive and prepare the way before the Lord comes to his temple (see Mal. 3:1; cf. 4:5). Jesus plainly identifies the Baptist as Elijah (17:10–13), verifying that John is the eschatological forerunner of the Messiah. There is still another connection with Matthew's message. We have already seen Jesus is Immanuel ("God with us"), and so Jesus' cleansing of the temple (21:12–13) represents the Lord coming to his temple, where he judges those who are impure (see Mal. 3:1–5).

The fulfillment theme continues apace in Matthew. John consents to baptize Jesus "to fulfill all righteousness" (3:15). According to Matthew, Jesus has no need of baptism for confession of sin, and thus we see Jesus as the true Israel representing the people. But how does Jesus represent his people? His baptism in the waters of the Jordan represents a new exodus (he, so to speak, crosses the Jordan into the land), and the descent of the dove signifies the onset of the new creation (cf. Gen. 1:2; 8:8–12,[4] which fits with Isa. 32:15; 44:3, linking the Spirit to the new creation work of God). It is here that the story line of the Gospel as a whole comes in, for Jesus fulfills all righteousness by his ministry, death, and resurrection.[5] As 1:21 says, "He will save his people from their sins." Jesus emphasizes that he must die to fulfill the Scriptures (26:54, 56), and so he represents his people in his death as the servant of the Lord.

Such claims are not imposed upon the narrative; they emerge in the account of Jesus' baptism. As Jesus is baptized, the heavens open (3:16), signifying a transcendent and otherworldly revelation of God (cf. Ezek. 1:1). A voice from heaven speaks: Jesus is God's "beloved Son" (3:17). Israel was God's son and his firstborn (Exod. 4:22), and the Davidic king is also God's son (2 Sam. 7:14; Ps. 2:7, 12). There may also be an allusion to Isaac as the only son of Abraham (Gen. 22:2, 12).[6] The OT allusions clarify that Jesus is the Son of God, and hence he is the true Israel and the true king. He embodies Israel in his person.

4. For support of this notion, see Beale, *Biblical Theology*, 412–13.
5. For an elegant and persuasive study on the resurrection, see N. T. Wright, *Resurrection of the Son*. The resurrection plays a central role, for Jesus' resurrection indicates that he reigns as Lord and king, and that the new creation has come (so Beale, *Biblical Theology*, 247–48).
6. Beale (ibid., 414–15) makes a good case for an allusion to Isa. 63:11–15; 64:1, where God's people traverse the water, and the Spirit leads them through the wilderness into the land.

The words "with whom I am well pleased [*eudokēsa*]" at Jesus' baptism allude to Isa. 42:1, where Yahweh expresses his delight in the servant of the Lord. An allusion to Isa. 42 fits with what we find elsewhere in Matthew, for later in his Gospel Matthew cites Isa. 42:1–4 (12:18–21). There is another connection with the Matthean baptismal scene, as Yahweh gives his Spirit in Isa. 42:1 to the servant, and Jesus at his baptism is endowed with the Spirit. Furthermore, the "servant" text points to Isa. 53, where the servant surrenders his life so that Israel can be forgiven. It seems, then, that Jesus represents his people and fulfills all righteousness by atoning for Israel's sins. Jesus' role as the servant of the Lord is also suggested by 20:28: "The Son of Man came not to be served but to serve, and to give his life as a ransom for many."[7] The word "many" perhaps alludes to Isa. 53:12, which speaks of the servant bearing the sins "of many." The notion of a suffering Son of Man finds its roots in Daniel's vision of the son of man (7:9–14).[8] The ransom saying accords with Jesus' intention to fulfill all righteousness, for he came to be a servant, to give his life in place of others so that they might be liberated from the guilt of their sin.

The importance of Jesus' death is not only communicated by the story line itself, where Jesus' death and resurrection function as the climax of the story, it also matches the plot of the story as a whole, for the story culminates and climaxes in Jesus' death and resurrection. Matthew also points to the programmatic importance of Jesus' death by punctuating the latter half of his Gospel with predictions of Jesus' passion and resurrection (16:21; 17:22–23; 20:17–19).

What Matthew emphasizes, then, is that the kingdom of God arrives through Jesus' death and resurrection. The significance of Jesus' death is explicated also at his last meal with his disciples. He declared, "For this is my blood of the covenant, which is poured out for many for the forgiveness of sins" (26:28). The word "covenant" takes us back to the OT. Moses sprinkled blood on the people when the Sinai covenant was established with Israel (Exod. 24:8). Furthermore, the phrase "blood of the covenant" occurs in Zech. 9:11 (*en haimati diathēkēs*), providing the basis for release of prisoners.[9] Final and definitive forgiveness of sins, therefore, is secured through the new covenant (see Jer. 31:31–34).[10] Jesus' death fulfills God's covenant promise to cleanse his people of their sins, atoning for their transgressions by shedding his blood on their behalf.

7. For a rigorous and persuasive study on preexistence in the Synoptics, see Gathercole, *The Preexistent Son*.
8. Beale, *Biblical Theology*, 193–99.
9. This text was pointed out to me by Joshua Greever.
10. On the new covenant in the NT, see Dumbrell, *End of the Beginning*, 79–118.

Jesus' death and resurrection provide the context and backdrop for his declaration that the sins of the paralytic are forgiven (9:2). When questioned by the scribes, Jesus did not qualify his words by saying that it was actually God who forgave the sins of the paralytic. Instead, he emphasized his own authority to forgive sins by healing the paralytic (9:2–8). Jesus demonstrated that he had the same authority as God. Psalm 103:3 speaks of God as the one "who forgives all your iniquity, who heals all your diseases," and Jesus showed that he has the same status as God by forgiving the paralytic's sins and by healing his disease.

Indeed, Jesus is the Danielic "son of man" to whom authority was given (Dan. 7:13–14), which was expressed in the forgiveness of the paralytic's sins (9:6). The reference to the Son of Man in 9:6 is important, for in Daniel (7:18, 22, 27) the "son of man" is exalted to God's right hand and receives the kingdom for the saints.[11] Hence, as the Son of Man, Jesus fulfills the role that Adam was intended to carry out inasmuch as human beings were called upon to rule the world for God's glory (see Ps. 8). Another way of putting it is that Jesus is the corporate Son of Man representing the saints, the people of God. His exaltation as the Son of Man and the Son of God at the resurrection indicates that forgiveness of sins is offered on the basis of his cross and resurrection.

Jesus is identified thirty times as the Son of Man in Matthew. I have already argued that the term hearkens back to Dan. 7:13–14 in Matthew's Gospel. As the Son of Man, Jesus is the true Adam, who exercises the rule that Adam was supposed to carry out. As a human being, Jesus' authority was hidden and veiled, for he had nowhere to lay his head (8:20), and he ate and drank as all other human beings (11:19), and hence human beings were unsure about his identity (16:13; cf. 12:32). His authority and majesty were particularly veiled and obscured by his suffering. Matthew's Gospel is punctuated by predictions that the Son of Man would suffer and die (12:40; 17:9, 12, 22; 20:18, 28; 26:2, 24–45). His suffering concealed his authority and glory, an authority that belonged to him even on earth, for he forgave sins as the Son of Man (9:6) and was Lord of the Sabbath (12:8). Many of the Son of Man sayings that promise suffering also emphasize Jesus' resurrection, conveying his sovereignty over death and the arrival of the new creation. Though the glory and authority of the Son of Man are obscured, they will become evident to all, for he will come in glory, judge the wicked, vindicate the righteous, consummate the kingdom of God, and bring to completion all of God's promises (10:23; 13:41; 16:27,

---

11. The literature on the Son of Man is immense. For studies that are particularly helpful, see S. Kim, "Son of Man"; Caragounis, Son of Man; Gentry, "Son of Man." For some useful histories of interpretation, see Burkett, Son of Man Debate; Müller, The Expression "Son of Man." In support of Jesus as the corporate son of man of Dan. 7, see Beale, Biblical Theology, 393–401.

28; 19:28; 24:27, 30, 37, 39, 44; 26:64).[12] As the Son of Man, he will judge the world at the final judgment (25:31–32). Then the new creation and the new exodus and the new covenant will be fulfilled in their entirety. Then all will see the King in his beauty.

We have been looking at the fulfillment theme in Matthew, focusing on its christological and soteriological dimensions. We have seen that the new creation and the new exodus became a reality through the one who fulfills the promises to Abraham, Israel, and David, through the one who is the servant of the Lord and the Son of Man and the king of all. The portrait of Jesus is difficult to sketch because of its depth and complexity. Jesus' uniqueness also shines through in the temptation by the devil (4:1–11). In these temptations Jesus is identified as the Son of God. Just as Israel as God's son was tempted forty years in the wilderness, so Jesus was tempted forty days by the devil. Jesus, however, proves himself to be the true Son of God, the true Israel, by his trust in God and obedience to him.[13]

Jesus' sonship goes beyond his being the true Israel. We have already seen at Jesus' baptism that he is identified as God's "beloved Son" (3:17), and this designation is repeated at the transfiguration (17:5).[14] Jesus is specially and uniquely related to God. Demons recognize his special relationship with God and identify him as the Son of God (8:29). Indeed, since he is the Son of God (11:27), he alone truly knows the Father, and only the Father truly knows him. Indeed, no one can come to know the Father unless the Son chooses to reveal the Father to him.

The disciples also confessed that Jesus was the Son of God (14:33; 16:16; cf. 26:63). Perhaps the disciples were only thinking of Jesus as the son of David in calling him the "Son of God," for in the OT the Davidic king is identified as God's son (e.g., 2 Sam. 7:14; Ps. 2:7, 12; Isa. 9:6), or perhaps they had a flash of insight in which they recognized that Jesus was uniquely related to God. In Matthew's eyes, however, such statements clearly designate Jesus as the Son of God in the fullest sense, given the story line of the Gospel as a whole (see also 21:37–38; 22:2). Jesus is the virgin-born Son of God and the one acclaimed as the Son at both his baptism and his transfiguration.

---

12. On the kingdom of God in Jesus' teaching, see Beasley-Murray, *Jesus and the Kingdom.*

13. Beale (*Biblical Theology*, 401–29) rightly argues that "Son of God" is not radically different from "Son of Man," and the latter designates Jesus as the true human being, the one who fulfills the commission given to Adam. "Son of God" also includes the notion of Jesus' deity. See also S. Kim, "*Son of Man.*"

14. "Jesus' transfiguration served as the confirmation for their confession, for they saw the heavenly glory upon him. Likewise, it guaranteed them the promise Jesus had given them in anticipation of his end. . . . At the same time, the event revealed the greatness of renunciation Jesus took upon himself through the way to the cross" (Schlatter, *History of the Christ*, 296).

Indeed, even though Jesus' opponents mock him for not being the Son of God because he does not come down from the cross (27:40, 43), a centurion recognizes that Jesus is the Son of God, not in spite of his suffering on the cross, but because of it (27:54). Finally, Matthew concludes with the baptismal formula in 28:19, demonstrating the majesty of the Son, for he is clearly equal to the Father.

The authority and the rule of Jesus are not limited to his titles. His unique status and position are evident throughout Matthew's Gospel. He takes the initiative to call others to be his disciples (4:18–22; 9:9), whereas in standard Jewish practice a person would ask a rabbi for permission to become a disciple, and it was understood that one would not be a disciple forever. Being Jesus' disciple, however, never ends.[15] Interestingly, the disciples are called to be fishers of people (4:19), recalling the prophecy of Jer. 16:14–16, where fishers will assist in returning Israel from exile. Those who are disciples of Jesus must follow him without reservation and whatever the cost (8:18–22). Jesus clearly is no ordinary person. Anyone who loves a family member more than Jesus is "not worthy" of him (10:37). One must be willing to take up one's cross and to die for Jesus' sake (10:38; cf. 16:24–25). Indeed, one will find life only if one loses it for Jesus' sake (10:39). Jesus tells a rich young man that he will enjoy eternal life (19:16) only if he gives up all his possessions and follows Jesus as a disciple (19:21).

Jesus' stature is evident, for he says that those who come to him will find rest, insisting that human beings should take his yoke, his teaching, upon themselves (11:28–30). The rest anticipated at the first creation (see Gen. 2:1–3) is now being offered by Jesus.[16] He is the bridegroom, introducing the new wine, designating the fulfillment of God's saving promises (Joel 3:18; Amos 9:14), which become a reality through him (9:14–17). When a storm batters the Sea of Galilee, he issues the word, and the storm abates (8:23–27). Such sovereignty belongs to God, for as Ps. 107:29 says of the Lord, "He made the storm be still, and the waves of the sea were hushed." Similarly, Jesus walked on the water (*epi tēs thalassēs peripatounta* [Matt. 14:26]), which is the prerogative solely of Yahweh, who "trampled the waves of the sea" (*peripatōn hōs ep' edaphous epi thalassēs* [Job 9:8]).

The majesty of Jesus indicates that he is the king who brings in the kingdom, for he is the Son of Man, the Son of God, the servant of the Lord, the son of Abraham, and the true descendant of David. He is the Christ whom

15. See Meier, *Mentor, Message and Miracles*, 52–55. For an explication of the high Christology in the call to discipleship, see Hengel, *Charismatic Leader*, 3–15.
16. See Beale, *Church's Mission*, 178.

Israel longed for, the true son, the true Israel, who always did the will of the Lord. At the same time, he is the preexistent one, the one who has come from another realm, Immanuel, the one who has authority in heaven and earth, who will abide with his disciples until the end of history.

Kingdom of Heaven[17]

The lordship of God is expressed in the emphasis on the kingdom in the Gospels and Jesus' teaching. Adolf Schlatter remarks that Jesus did not rely on technique, nor did he try to manipulate his hearers to bring in the kingdom, for he believed that God's kingdom was God's work, and that it would be advanced through the proclamation of God's word.[18] The expression "kingdom of God" occurs four times in Matthew, which might make us think, at first glance, that the kingdom is not very important in Matthew. But Matthew, in contrast to both Mark and Luke, uses the expression "kingdom of heaven" thirty-two times.[19] Older dispensational thought distinguished between the "kingdom of God" and the "kingdom of heaven," but today very few argue for a dispensational understanding of the distinction. The usual scholarly explanation today is that the Gospel of Matthew was addressed to Jews, and the Jews often reverentially avoided using God's name.[20] The term "heaven," it is argued, was a reverential substitute for "God." If this is the case, then the expressions "kingdom of God" and "kingdom of heaven" refer to the same reality and should not be distinguished.

Recent work by Jonathan Pennington on the term "heaven" in Matthew, however, has demonstrated the inadequacy of the scholarly consensus in Matthew.[21] It is quite unlikely that Matthew used the term "heaven" to avoid referring to God out of reverence, for he refers to God more than fifty times elsewhere in the Gospel and actually uses "kingdom of God" on four

17. The next four paragraphs on the kingdom of heaven are taken, with minor changes, from Schreiner, *New Testament Theology*, 45–47.

18. Schlatter, *History of the Christ*, 113.

19. Pennington remarks, "'Kingdom of heaven' is found nowhere else in the OT, NT, or any preceding Second Temple literature. Similar phrases appear occasionally in the Apocrypha, but kingdom of heaven is found only in literature which postdates Matthew. Even these occurrences are quite infrequent (e.g., twice in the Mishnah and three times in the Gospel of Thomas)" (*Heaven and Earth*, 2–3).

20. See Dodd, *Parables of the Kingdom*, 34; Meier, *Mentor, Message and Miracles*, 239.

21. Pennington (*Heaven and Earth*, 67–76) summarizes his thesis on heaven in Matthew with four points: (1) we see a preference for the plural form *ouranoi*; (2) we find an emphasis on the word pair "heaven and earth"; (3) Matthew regularly refers to the Father in heaven; (4) the phrase "the kingdom of heaven" is prominent in Matthew.

occasions.[22] Moreover, Jewish evidence that the term "heaven" was used to avoid the name of God out of reverence is lacking. Hence, it is more persuasive to argue that Matthew uses the term "heaven" for a particular purpose in the narrative.

The substance of Pennington's case is as follows. When "heaven" (*ouranos*) is used in the singular without the term "earth" or its equivalent nearby, it usually refers to the sky (16:1–3; cf. 6:26; 8:20; 13:32; 14:19; 26:64).[23] The plural "heavens" (*ouranoi*), however, typically refers to the invisible divine realm (e.g., 3:16–17; 5:12, 16; 18:10; 19:21). When the pair "heaven and earth" is used, it may denote the entirety of the universe created by God (5:18; 11:25; 24:35; cf. Gen. 1:1). But even more common in Matthew is the use of "heaven" and "earth" to contrast life according to God's will and ways with life lived according to human standards. In 6:1–21 Jesus' instructions on righteousness point to a heaven-versus-earth contrast, whether the issue is almsgiving, prayer, or fasting. The contrast between heaven and earth is illustrated in 6:19–20: "Do not lay up for yourselves treasures on earth, where moth and rust destroy and where thieves break in and steal, but lay up for yourselves treasures in heaven, where neither moth nor rust destroys and where thieves do not break in and steal" (cf. 5:34–35; 6:10; 11:23;[24] 21:25;[25] 28:18).

Matthew uses the plural "heavens" to speak of the Father in heaven on thirteen occasions, and "kingdom of heaven" thirty-two times to contrast the heavenly and earthly realm. The usage here confirms that the plural "heavens" refers to God, while the singular "heaven" refers to the sky.[26] In other words, Matthew intentionally uses "heaven" and "earth" to contrast God's ways with those of human beings. The disjunction between God's ways and ours is also evident in (1) the "heaven and earth" pairs; (2) the emphasis that the Father is in heaven (separated and exalted above human beings); and (3) the contrast between the heavenly kingdom and the kingdoms that are earthly and wicked. Hence, the expression "kingdom of heaven" focuses on the truth that God's kingdom is from above. His kingdom is not an earthly one but rather represents his sovereignty and rule over all other kingdoms and all other so-called

22. Pamment ("Kingdom of Heaven") suggests a less convincing distinction. She claims that "kingdom of heaven" refers to an imminent but future coming of the kingdom, whereas "kingdom of God" refers to the kingdom already actualized in the present.

23. Matthew 23:22 seems to be an exception where the singular "heaven" appears to refer to God's realm; "the powers of the heavens" in Matt. 24:29 also seems to be an exception (see also Matt. 24:31).

24. The contrast here is between heaven and Hades.

25. Here Matthew contrasts what is from heaven with what is from human beings.

26. The singular is also used in "heaven and earth" pairs, following the pattern of the LXX, regardless of the referent.

gods. In particular, Matthew emphasizes the inbreaking of God's heavenly kingdom in Jesus.[27] The earthly and inhumane kingdoms described in Dan. 7 are giving way to the kingdom from above with the coming of Jesus Christ.

Both the Baptist and Jesus and Jesus' disciples proclaimed that the kingdom was imminent (3:2; 4:17; 10:7). The promises found in the OT were above and beyond the reach of human beings. They would be realized only through a transcendent and supernatural work of God himself. The kingdom does not become a reality through the effort and work of human beings. Human beings may pray for the kingdom, but they cannot bring it to earth. The imminence of the kingdom manifested itself in a way that baffled and surprised both the religious leaders and Jesus' disciples, for Jesus taught that the kingdom of heaven was already present in his ministry but was not yet consummated.

The arrival of the kingdom of heaven meant that God's enemies would be destroyed, and that the godly would enjoy a new world where peace reigned. But Jesus said that those who were poor in spirit enjoyed the blessings of the kingdom during the present evil age (5:3). Everyone believed that those who were persecuted were waiting for the coming kingdom so that they would be relieved of their suffering, but Jesus also taught that the persecuted enjoyed the kingdom now, in the midst of their sufferings (5:10).

Matthew emphasizes the mysteries of the kingdom in parables (13:11). Perhaps the most surprising feature is that the kingdom arrives without an immediate final judgment. In the OT the coming of the kingdom means the consummation of God's purposes. But Jesus clearly teaches that the kingdom is inaugurated without being consummated. Hence, there is a messy and unexpected segment of time in which the kingdom of heaven coexists on earth with the kingdom of darkness. In the parable of the sower (13:1–9, 18–23), for instance, the "word of the kingdom" (13:19) does not reign supreme over all; it is effective only in some hearts, for many reject the message. They remain fixated upon earthly reality and fail to see the implications of their rejection of the message, and hence they pursue the joys of this present age or become consumed in its stresses and strains. The parable of the weeds and wheat is somewhat similar (13:24–30, 36–43). The kingdom does not come with apocalyptic power and transform the world immediately. Those who are evil continue to dwell with "the sons of the kingdom" (13:38). We expect from the OT that the coming of the kingdom would mean the instantaneous eradication of evil. But the parable of the wheat and weeds clarifies that evil will persist until the day of judgment, and then the good will be segregated from the evil (cf. 13:47–50). The kingdom has come, and yet the wicked are not removed

27. For a survey on the kingdom of heaven in Matthew, see Kingsbury, *Matthew*, 128–60.

from the earth immediately. The kingdom of heaven is at work during the present evil age, and at its conclusion the wicked will be cast "into the fiery furnace," where "there will be weeping and gnashing of teeth" (13:42). At the same time, the promise of Daniel that the righteous "shall shine like the brightness of the sky above" (Dan. 12:3) will be fulfilled, for "the righteous will shine like the sun in the kingdom of their Father" (Matt. 13:43).

The mysterious nature of the kingdom is unpacked in the parables of the mustard seed and leaven (13:31–33). Most expected the kingdom to come with unrivaled power so that opponents would be swept away and the righteous would live in peace and joy. The parable of the mustard seed points to a far different state of affairs. The kingdom's arrival would be small and virtually unnoticeable. Evil would not be trounced immediately. Instead, there would be no apparent change in the world at all. Life would go on as usual, even though the kingdom had arrived in Jesus' person. Since the kingdom is small, its presence is evident only for those with eyes to see. Evil persists until the day of judgment, and only then will it be removed from the world. The parable of the leaven communicates the same truth. The inauguration of the kingdom was hidden, like leaven is hidden in flour. Hence, the coming of the kingdom in Jesus Christ was obscured from the world's vision. The fullness of the kingdom would arrive when the whole was leavened, when Jesus Christ came again, vindicating the righteous and judging his enemies. We can see, then, why many did not believe that Jesus was the Christ, for he proclaimed a kingdom that did not match their expectations. They believed that the kingdom involved the dethronement of their enemies and the exaltation of the righteous. Jesus proclaimed that the kingdom had indeed come, but its presence was hidden and small, and that the great day of judgment was still future. This "already but not yet" character of the kingdom constitutes the mystery of the kingdom.

The hiddenness of the kingdom is picked up in the parable of the treasure in the field (13:44). The value of the kingdom is not apparent to those in the world, especially since it did not arrive on the scene with apocalyptic power. But those with eyes to see perceive that nothing compares to the joy of possessing the treasure of the kingdom, and therefore they give up all they have to enter the kingdom. The kingdom is of inestimable value, like a pearl (13:45–46), so that one surrenders everything else to acquire it. Those who enter the kingdom understand that nothing can be compared to being invited to the wedding banquet (22:1–13), and hence the kingdom is the center of their existence. The incomparable treasure of the kingdom is part of the mystery of the kingdom as well because its value is not apparent to many.

Nothing compares to the riches of the kingdom, and hence all people everywhere must strive to enter it. The kingdom belongs to both Jews and Gentiles who put their faith in Jesus, as the centurion in Capernaum did (8:1–13). The kingdom is gracious, available to those who have spurned the Lord all their lives if they turn and repent (20:1–16). Those who are poor in spirit enjoy the kingdom (5:3), and therefore the kingdom is given not to those who are morally virtuous but instead to those who recognize their moral poverty. Those who admit their inadequacy, however, are strengthened by the power of the kingdom. Therefore, their "righteousness exceeds that of the scribes and Pharisees" (5:20), and they obey Jesus' teachings (7:21). We see the same pattern later in Matthew's Gospel. Only those who humble themselves like children and admit their need for righteousness by turning and repenting will enter the kingdom (18:3–4; cf. 19:14). The kingdom is for those who acknowledge their evil, just as children look to adults for sustenance and strength. Humility never leaves one unchanged, for it produces the willingness to forgive those who have injured us (18:23–35). Those who have experienced the power of the kingdom live in a new way, like the wise virgins rather than the foolish ones (25:1–13).

I began the discussion of Matthew by emphasizing the fulfillment of God's promises in Jesus Christ, noting especially that the promise of the coming kingdom was realized in Jesus Christ. If we examine Isaiah, we see clearly that the new creation, new exodus, the gospel, and the coming kingdom are different ways of describing the same reality. The "good news" in Isa. 40:9 is that Israel will return from Babylon, but the good news will come to pass because of Yahweh's rule (Isa. 40:10), because of his sovereign power. We find the same truth in Isa. 52:7. The good news of salvation and return from exile can be described in the words "Your God reigns."

The coming of the kingdom in Jesus indicates that the new exodus has been inaugurated, that God is reigning in a saving way over his people. As noted above, God's reign in Isaiah is also described in terms of the new creation. We see the new creation dimension of the kingdom in Jesus' miracles, healings, and exorcisms. The summary statements in Matthew show that the kingdom has come in Jesus' works.[28] He proclaimed "the gospel of the kingdom and heal[ed] every disease and every affliction among the people" (4:23). "And Jesus went throughout all the cities and villages, teaching in their synagogues and proclaiming the gospel of the kingdom and healing every disease and every affliction" (9:35). We see the same connection in the ministry of the Twelve, whom Jesus instructs, "And proclaim as you go, saying, 'The kingdom of heaven is at hand.' Heal the sick, raise the dead, cleanse lepers, cast out demons" (10:7–8).

---

28. On the connection between Jesus' healings and the coming of the kingdom, see Twelftree, *Jesus the Miracle Worker*.

The healing of Peter's mother-in-law signifies restoration to the creation ideal (8:14–15). Her healing is immediately followed up by a summary statement of Jesus' healings and exorcisms (8:16). Jesus' healings and exorcisms are tied to one of Matthew's fulfillment formulas: "This was to fulfill what was spoken by the prophet Isaiah: 'He took our illnesses and bore our diseases'" (8:17). Matthew cites Isa. 53:4 here. Jesus as the servant of the Lord frees Israel from sickness and demonic powers. If we consider the context of Isa. 53, we note that the servant of the Lord atones for the sin of his people, that he suffers in their place, so that they are forgiven through the work of the servant.[29] What this means is that Jesus' healings and exorcisms are tied to his atoning work, to his giving his life as a ransom for many. Another way of putting it is that all sickness and demonic oppression are due to sin. This is not to say that someone's sickness necessarily is the result of personal sin, as if sickness is visited upon someone for a particular transgression. It is to say, however, that there will be no sickness or demonization in paradise, that a new world is coming that is free from disease. Jesus' healings and exorcisms, then, point to the new creation, to a world in which sin and demonic oppression do not exist. Triumph over healing and demons, however, comes only through the cross. Final victory over demons and illness comes only because Jesus crushed the serpent at the cross.

That creation is out of whack is also suggested by the storm that assails the sea (8:24–27). Jesus rebuked the winds and waves (8:26), just as he rebuked demons (17:18). Jesus also showed his authority over disease by healing a woman who suffered from hemorrhages for twelve years and by raising Jairus's daughter from the dead (9:18–26). Jesus exercised his kingly authority over demons, disease, and death. Triumph over these foes clearly indicates the arrival of the kingdom. This is confirmed by Jesus' response to the Baptist's doubts about him (11:2–3): "Go and tell John what you hear and see: the blind receive their sight and the lame walk, lepers are cleansed and the deaf hear, and the dead are raised up, and the poor have good news preached to them" (11:4–5). Jesus appeals here to OT prophecies, seeing a fulfillment of Isa. 29:18 and Isa. 35:5–6. What is remarkable, however, is that both of these prophecies envision the arrival of God's kingdom and the new creation. When the blind see and the deaf hear, "Lebanon shall be turned into a fruitful field" (Isa. 29:17). Similarly, the healing work of Jesus is associated with the new creation and the kingdom in Isa. 35: "The wilderness and the dry land shall be glad; the desert shall rejoice and blossom like the crocus; it shall blossom

---

29. The servant of the Lord has been examined in depth by many. For one of the most illuminating discussions theologically, see Dempster, "Servant of the Lord."

abundantly and rejoice with joy and singing. The glory of Lebanon shall be given to it, the majesty of Carmel and Sharon" (Isa. 35:1–2). We should note also that Matthew specifically links Jesus' healing ministry with the proclamation of the good news. Furthermore, in Isa. 35 the new creation is linked with the return from exile (Isa. 35:10). We have further evidence that the gospel, return from exile, the new creation, and the kingdom are different ways of describing the same reality.

In Matthew's Gospel the inseparability of the kingdom and Jesus' power over demons is confirmed.[30] After Jesus cast out a demon and was criticized by opponents as being in league with Beelzebul, he affirms, "But if it is by the Spirit of God that I cast out demons, then the kingdom of God has come upon you" (12:28). The expulsion of demons signals the inauguration of the kingdom of God.

The kingdom is inaugurated in the ministry and person of the king, Jesus the Messiah. His healings, exorcisms, teaching, and parables indicate that the kingdom of heaven has arrived. The transcendent rule of God has come to earth in Jesus the Christ, fulfilling the promises of a new creation and a new exodus.

Life in the Kingdom

The Father inaugurated his saving reign, his kingdom, in Jesus. But who will enjoy his saving rule? And what does it mean to live under this rule? Both of these topics are closely related in Matthew. First and foundationally, those who enter the kingdom are saved from their sins by Jesus (1:21). They are ransomed from death by Jesus' death (20:28). He poured out his blood so that they would enjoy forgiveness of sins (26:28). Those who benefit from Jesus' death put their trust in him (cf. 8:10, 13; 9:2, 22, 28–29; 15:28; 17:20).

For Matthew, faith is empty without a corresponding change of life, and thus he emphasizes the radical change in disciples.[31] The Beatitudes indicate who will enjoy the blessings of the kingdom (5:3–12). Those who are "poor in spirit" (5:3) and free of pride (cf. 2 Sam. 22:28) are contrasted with the wicked and proud, who trust in themselves (cf. Pss. 10:7–9; 14:3–4).[32] End-time satisfaction (cf. Pss. 17:14–15; 107:9) will be granted to those who recognize that they lack righteousness (5:6) and hence seek for it ardently. Eschatological

---

30. On the coming of the kingdom in the casting out of demons, see Kallas, *Synoptic Miracles*.
31. For a helpful summary of the meaning of righteousness in Matthew, see Matera, *New Testament Theology*, 30–36.
32. All these OT texts contrast the "poor" with the wicked, who are arrogant.

comfort will be given to those who mourn (5:4). Matthew probably draws on Isa. 61:2, where comfort is promised to mourners. Isaiah in the same context envisions return from exile for Israel (61:2, 4), predicting the work of the Spirit-anointed one who will "bring good news to the poor" (61:1). According to Matthew, possession of the new earth, the coming new creation, will be granted to those who are meek (5:5). The saying stems from Ps. 37:11, "But the meek shall inherit the land." Those who inherit the land are described in this psalm as those who "trust in the Lord" (37:3), who "wait for the Lord" (37:9, 34), "those blessed by the Lord" (37:22), those who are "righteous" (37:29). These different descriptions give a thickness and a depth to meekness, showing that the meek are those who trust in the Lord and wait for him. In the same way, Matthew underlines that those who show mercy and grace to others will themselves receive mercy (5:7). The "pure in heart" will see the King in his beauty (5:8). In the OT it is the pure in heart who can ascend the Lord's holy hill (Ps. 24:3–4), and it is recognized that only the Lord can create a pure heart (Ps. 51:10). Matthew offers assurance that the kingdom belongs even now to those who are persecuted and despised as Jesus' disciples (5:10–12).

The Beatitudes, as observed above, are infused with OT allusions and echoes,[33] which fits with Matthew's emphasis on fulfillment. The fulfillment theme is picked up in 5:17–48. Jesus came to fulfill the law, not to abolish it (5:17–20). The focus here is on obedience, on a righteousness greater than that of the religious teachers. The rest of Matt. 5 (5:21–48) works out what this greater righteousness looks like, describing the life of those who are members of the kingdom. The command against murder is not limited to the outward act; it also includes anger (5:21–26). Similarly, the prohibition of adultery must be interpreted in terms of the tenth commandment, which condemns coveting, so that lust and divorce are also adulterous (5:27–32). The demand to speak the truth cannot be circumvented with casuistic oaths (5:33–37; 23:16–22). Nor does one properly interpret the OT if one resorts to personal vengeance (5:38–42). The commands regarding an eye for an eye and a tooth for a tooth are found in civil contexts in the OT (Exod. 21:22–25; Lev. 24:19–20; Deut. 19:21), and the principle enunciated is that the punishment must be proportional to the crime. The standard for civil justice, however, must not be applied to personal relationships. There is never any defense for personal vengeance. So too, Matthew shows, the OT is wrongly interpreted as teaching that one can hate one's enemies (5:43–47; cf. Exod. 23:4–5; Job 31:29–30). Instead, rightly understood, it calls upon disciples to love their enemies. The standard demanded is perfection (5:48), just as the Father is perfect. Naturally, there is

33. I am using the terms "allusions" and "echoes" nontechnically here.

forgiveness for those who sin (6:12), and yet Matthew makes it clear that only those who live transformed lives will enter the kingdom.

The narrow gate does not designate putting one's trust in Jesus as Savior (although Matthew certainly thinks that salvation is only through Jesus); but in context Matthew refers to a righteousness that exceeds the scribes and Pharisees (7:13–14). False prophets are discerned by their fruits (7:15–20); this warning focuses on the kind of life that purported prophets lead. Spiritual activity must not be confused with genuine life, for some so-called disciples of Jesus who invoke him as Lord may not actually be his followers (7:21–23). Some may prophesy in Jesus' name and even perform exorcisms and miracles without being his disciples. The real test is obedience. Those who practice unrighteousness demonstrate that Jesus never knew them, that they only seemed to belong to the people of God (7:23). One is either foolish or wise. Either one builds on a solid foundation by hearing and doing Jesus' words, or one hears what Jesus commands and fails to obey him (7:24–27). Only those who hear and keep Jesus' words will be protected when the stormy winds of judgment arrive. "Each person" will be repaid "according to what he has done" (16:27). Those who are faithful in serving God as their master will be rewarded accordingly (25:14–30; cf. 24:42–51). There will be a final judgment whereby the sheep are separated from the goats (25:31–46), and the sheep will be rewarded with eternal life (25:46) for the good that they have done—that is, their care for poor and imprisoned brothers and sisters in the faith (25:40).

What it means to be Jesus' disciple is to seek his kingdom and his righteousness above all else (6:33). It means that he is the treasure and joy of one's heart (6:20–21). Those who seek his kingdom will not be plagued with worry about riches and provisions for everyday life (6:25–34). They will not serve money rather than God (6:24), for they will recognize that they have a Father who loves them and attends to them, caring for every need they have (6:26, 30, 32). If fellowship with God is the joy of one's heart, then one will not practice righteousness in order to be praised by people (6:1–18). Fasting, prayer, and charitable giving will be motivated by a desire to please and honor God. Prayer will not be offered in a panic or from a spirit of superstition, for believers realize that they have a Father who knows and cares about their needs (6:7–8; cf. 7:7–11).[34] The center of life for believers should be God himself, and therefore they pray that his name will be honored and valued above all else (6:9).[35] And

---

34. On the significance of the Father in Jesus' teaching, see Jeremias, *Prayers of Jesus*, 11–67; idem, *New Testament Theology*, 61–68; M. Thompson, *Promise of the Father*, 35–55, 133–54; Lee, *From Messiah to Preexistent Son*, 122–36.

35. Schlatter comments, "The first longing Jesus awakened in the disciple was directed toward the honoring of the divine name, rule, and will" (*History of the Christ*, 160). He goes on to

they pray for the coming of his kingdom (6:10), for the arrival of his rule where God's will is carried out everywhere.

The People of God

In the OT Israel is God's son and the chosen people of the Lord. Abraham and the patriarchs were promised universal blessing for the nations (Gen. 12:3; 18:18; 22:18; 26:4; 28:14), and the prophets and the psalms also look forward to the day when salvation will be extended to all peoples. Matthew underscores that such promises are fulfilled in Jesus Christ. We saw earlier that Jesus is the true Son of God and the Son of Man, who corporately represents his people. Jesus is the true Israel, and thus those who belong to Jesus Christ, whether Jews or Gentiles, are members of the true Israel. This should not be interpreted to say that Matthew is opposed to or negative toward the Jewish people. Matthew's Gospel shows a concern for the salvation of both the Jews, as the chosen people of the Lord, and the Gentiles.

Matthew displays a tension and balance between the promise being for the Jews and the good news being extended to the Gentiles. The Jewish character of Matthew's Gospel is immediately evident, for he begins with a genealogy, tracing Jesus to David and Abraham. He emphasizes that Jesus fulfills OT prophecies and the OT law. When Joseph heard the angel declare that Jesus would "save his people from their sins" (1:21), surely he understood "his people" here to refer to the Jews. Similarly, the book of Micah prophesies that the coming king "will shepherd my people Israel" (2:6). Quite striking are the statements lacking in the other Gospels. In Matthew, Jesus instructs the Twelve on their mission, "Go nowhere among the Gentiles and enter no town of the Samaritans, but go rather to the lost sheep of the house of Israel" (10:5–6). Jesus speaks in a similar way to a Canaanite woman when she solicits help for her daughter: "I was sent only to the lost sheep of the house of Israel" (15:24). The disciples will not finish evangelizing Israel before the Son of Man comes (10:23).

The restriction to Israel should not be read as a permanent program for the disciples. They restricted themselves to Israel for a limited period of salvation history, during the time in which Jesus conducted his earthly ministry, just as Jesus mainly confined himself to Israel during his ministry, for the promises were first given to the Jews.

When we read Matthew's Gospel as a whole, however, it is clear that Jesus' disciples, after his death and resurrection, were called upon to proclaim the

---

say, "All human needs were subsumed under the one aim: that God would receive what was due him, the honor due his name, the revelation of his power to all, and the doing of his will by all."

good news to all nations in fulfillment of the promise made to Abraham that all nations would be blessed through him. Actually, there are anticipations of the inclusion of the Gentiles all through the Gospel, so that this theme is actually more prominent than one might expect from the statements that restrict the disciples' mission to Israel during Jesus' earthly ministry. For example, we see in Jesus' genealogy the inclusion of Gentiles, for all the women named in the genealogy are Gentiles: Tamar, Rahab, and Ruth (1:3, 5). Interestingly, Bathsheba as a Jewish woman remains unnamed, while her Gentile husband, Uriah, is specifically mentioned (1:6). Hence, these names forecast the Gentile mission. I noted earlier that 1:21 speaks of Jesus saving "his people from their sins," which certainly would refer to Israel in Joseph's mind, but in light of the entire Gospel of Matthew the definition of "his people" almost certainly expands to include Gentiles. We see the same sort of thing in 2:1–12. Jesus is the "king of the Jews" (2:2), but magi from the east, who were Gentiles, were the ones who came to worship him (cf. Ps. 72:10–11; Isa. 60:6), while those in Jerusalem were "troubled" (2:3). And even though the disciples were initially restricted to Israel (10:5–6), Jesus anticipates that their witness will ultimately include the Gentiles (10:18). Similarly, Jesus originally rejects the plea of the Canaanite woman because he was sent to Israel (15:21–28), but nevertheless he heals her daughter, implying that salvation will extend outside of Israel. Nor is physical descent from Abraham necessarily an advantage, for God can produce Abraham's sons from stones (3:9), and if he can do that with stones, certainly he can do the same with Gentiles. With the coming of Jesus the great light prophesied for the Gentiles has become a reality (4:14–16; cf. Isa. 9:1–2).

The faith of the centurion in Capernaum stands as a paradigm of what is to come, for his faith is unmatched in Israel (8:10). Jesus predicted that many Gentiles would enjoy the messianic feast in the last day, while at the same time the chosen people, "the sons of the kingdom," would be on the outside, "weeping and gnashing their teeth" (8:12). That the end-time banquet was intended for more than Israel was anticipated in Isa. 25:6, which prophesies "for all peoples a feast of rich food." The story of the centurion is replicated by the repentance of the people of Nineveh and the faith of the queen of the South, both of whom heeded God's call to repent in contrast to the Israel of Jesus' day (12:41–42), so that the Israel of Jesus' day looks much like the Israel that failed to believe when the prophets preached. Perhaps Gentiles are included as the eleventh-hour workers in the parable of the vineyard (20:1–16; cf. 22:9–10), so that they are the last who are now first. It is also likely that the four thousand who are fed are Gentiles (15:32–39). And perhaps the Gentiles are in view as well in the statement "The kingdom of God will be taken away from you and given to a people producing its fruits" (21:43).

We must beware of an opposite extreme here, for some have taken Matthew to renounce any future mission to Israel, but this sits awkwardly with the Jewish character of Matthew's Gospel as a whole, and with the emphasis on Jesus fulfilling the OT law. The church consists of "repentant and restored Israel composed of Gentiles as well as Jews."[36] Furthermore, Jewish evangelism is included in Jesus' final commission to his disciples (28:18–20), where he exercises his authority as the Danielic son of man.[37] Jesus' disciples are instructed to make disciples of all nations, both Jews and Gentiles.

If there are any doubts about the inclusion of the Gentiles in the people of God, Matthew removes them in 24:14: "And this gospel of the kingdom will be proclaimed throughout the whole world as a testimony to all nations" (see also 28:18–20). We have seen in this chapter that the kingdom and the gospel are closely related hearkening back to Isaiah. Now it is confirmed that the good news of the kingdom includes the Gentiles, which fits with what Isaiah, who proclaims the good news of the kingdom (40:9–10; 52:7), also teaches (2:1–4; 11:10; 12:4–5; 18:7; 19:16–25; 24:13–16; 25:6–8; 42:1–7; 45:20–25; 49:7–8; 52:15; 55:4–5; 56:3–7; 66:19–20). The announcement of the Lord's salvation is not restricted to Israel; it belongs to all peoples everywhere. Jesus commands his followers, "Go therefore and make disciples of all nations" (28:19). The worldwide blessing pledged to Abraham would become a reality through the gospel proclaimed by the disciples. We can say, then, that Matthew sees Jesus as the true Israel, the true Son of God, and the true Son of Man. He embodies Israel in his person, and hence all those who belong to him, both Jew and Gentile, are part of restored Israel.

Matthew, uniquely among the Gospels, includes sayings of Jesus about the church. The selection of the Twelve (10:1–4) indicates that they are the nucleus of a new Israel, that the Twelve now represent the twelve tribes of Israel. Only those who align themselves with the Twelve and the kingdom message that they proclaim (which centers on Jesus [see 10:5–11:1]) belong to the true Israel. Those who do the Father's will belong to this family (12:46–50), for God can make children of Abraham from stones (3:9).[38] Those who are Jesus' "sons" live like the Father (5:9, 44–48), for they are sons because they are identified with Jesus as the Son of Man.[39]

Jesus promises to build his new assembly, his church, which is an amazing statement of authority because the *qāhāl* ("assembly" [*ekklēsia* in the LXX]) in the OT was Yahweh's. Jesus guarantees that the "gates of hell" will not

36. Matera, *New Testament Theology*, 44.
37. Beale, *Biblical Theology*, 390–91.
38. See Beale, *Biblical Theology*, 424–25.
39. Ibid., 425–27.

triumph over the church (16:18; cf. Job 38:17), and thus death will not conquer the people of God. Jesus will build his church on the rock, which is identified as Peter. It is likely that both Peter and his confession are the foundation upon which the church is established. Peter also stands for the apostolic circle as the first among equals. The foundation of the church will be the apostolic witness, where the gospel of Christ is proclaimed. To say that the church is given the keys (16:19) means that the church is granted authority to proclaim the gospel, to certify who belongs to the people of God, to build up fellow believers, and to exclude those who are not genuinely believers.[40] The authority of the church is picked up again in 18:15–20. The church is to be a community of love and accountability. Those who sin must be reproved and led to repent so that the holiness of the community and its devotion to goodness are not compromised. Those who stubbornly persist in evil are to be excluded from the church. The church gathers in the name of Jesus, and when it truly acts in his name, his will is carried out on earth.

Conclusion

Matthew is the Gospel of fulfillment. The promises made to Abraham and David, the blessings for Israel and the whole world, are realized in Jesus of Nazareth. Jesus is the true Israel, the Messiah, the Son of Man, the Son of God, the servant of the Lord, and Immanuel. He shows his authority and uniqueness by forgiving sins, calling people to be his disciples, walking on water, and stilling storms. Jesus saved his people from their sins by giving his life as a ransom as the servant of the Lord. This Gospel concludes with the cross and resurrection, climaxing the narrative with these great events. Hence, the promised kingdom is obtained only by those who receive forgiveness of sins through Jesus' death and resurrection. The kingdom —the transcendent kingdom of heaven—has arrived in Jesus' ministry. His works of power, exorcisms, healings, and raising of the dead signaled the arrival of the new creation and the new exodus. They point to life in the world to come. Remarkably, the kingdom has an "already but not yet" dimension in Jesus' ministry. The kingdom, which has penetrated the present age in Jesus' ministry, is hidden, small, and obscure. But the victory over the serpent has been won in the cross and resurrection of the Christ. Those who belong to the Christ receive forgiveness of sins through him and put their trust in him. Matthew also emphasizes that those who are disciples live transformed lives. Only those who obey the Christ

---

40. See Leeman, *Surprising Offence of God's Love.*

will receive eternal life.[41] Finally, the kingdom is for both Jews and Gentiles who are part of the restored Israel. Disciples are mandated to proclaim the gospel to the ends of the earth, to all peoples without exception. Jesus has called out a new community, the church of the Christ. This community is the new and true Israel, and it is to be marked by obedience to the apostolic gospel. Those who live contrary to that gospel are to be removed from the church, for the final separation between good and evil, which will be carried out at the final judgment when Jesus returns, is anticipated now by the community of the disciples, which stands in contrast to the world.

---

41. As Schlatter says, "To obtain life and to obtain God's rule is one and the same thing" (*History of the Christ*, 120).

26

THE GOSPEL
ACCORDING TO MARK

Introduction

Mark's Gospel overlaps significantly with Matthew's, though certainly it has
distinctive features. Mark, like Matthew, sees a fulfillment of OT revelation
in Jesus Christ. In unpacking Mark's Gospel, I will concentrate on three main
themes: kingdom, Christology, and discipleship. The focus on the kingdom fits
well with the major theme of this work, for Mark teaches that God's kingdom
has arrived in Jesus. I will argue as well, however, that both Christology and
discipleship are closely related to the kingdom.

Kingdom

The kingdom of God has broken into the world with the coming of Jesus
Christ.[1] In another sense, of course, God has always reigned as king over all
(Ps. 103:19). He always has been and always will be the sovereign king over all
that happens. But when Mark declares that the kingdom of God has arrived
in Jesus Christ, he is not merely saying that God rules over all things everywhere. The kingdom of God in Mark refers especially to God's saving rule, to
the fulfillment of his saving promises. The coming of the kingdom, in other
words, means that the promise of victory over the serpent (see Gen. 3:15);

---

1. See Marshall, *New Testament Theology*, 60–62, 64–65, 78–81. As Matera says, "Everything Jesus says or does is in some way related to the proclamation of the kingdom" (*New
Testament Theology*, 12).

the promise of worldwide blessing made to Abraham, Isaac, and Jacob; the promise of a kingdom that would never end made to David; and the promise of a new covenant, a new exodus, and a new creation are now fulfilled in Jesus. The righteous will finally be vindicated, and the wicked will be punished.

The kingdom's arrival is a supernatural work of God. Human beings cannot bring in the kingdom.[2] The parable of the unstoppable seed in Mark's Gospel illustrates the nature of the kingdom (4:26–29). The seed represents the message of the kingdom. This message of the kingdom, as 1:14–15 clarifies, is nothing other than the gospel, the good news that Isaiah heralded about return from exile, about God's saving reign over his people (Isa. 40:9–10; 52:7). Mark 4:26–29 shows that the kingdom breaks into the world and advances through the word of God. Human beings gaze at its progress in amazement, because they cannot comprehend how the seed, the message proclaimed, bears fruit. But grow it does until the day of harvest arrives.

The message of the kingdom, after many years in which the Jews languished under foreign rule (much like the time of the exodus!), suddenly appeared with the coming of John the Baptist.[3] The Baptist strode into history as an Elijah-like figure (1:6; cf. 2 Kings 1:8), proclaiming the need for Israel, as did the prophets of old, to confess their sins. The Baptist preached in the wilderness and baptized in the Jordan (1:4–5), for Israel was, so to speak, still wandering in the wilderness like the generation that left Egypt under Moses. They needed to cross the Jordan again, cleansed and purified so that they could enjoy God's saving rule.[4] For the kingdom of God which signifies God's saving rule also spells judgment for those who are not right with God. Mark introduces the Baptist with a mixed citation, quoting from both Malachi and Isaiah, though Mark says only that he is quoting Isaiah (1:2–3). It is not as if

---

2. What Ladd says about the kingdom in general applies to Mark as well: "The Kingdom can draw near to men (Matt. 3:2; 4:17; Mark 1:15; etc.); it can come (Matt. 6:10; Luke 17:20; etc.), arrive (Matt. 12:28), appear (Luke 19:11), be active (Matt. 11:12). God can give the Kingdom to men (Matt. 21:43; Luke 12:32), but men do not give the Kingdom to one another. Further, God can take the Kingdom away from men (Matt. 21:43), but men do not take it away from one another, although they can prevent others from entering it. Men can enter the Kingdom (Matt. 5:20; 7:21; Mark 9:47; 10:23; etc.), but they are never said to erect it or to build it. Men can receive the Kingdom (Mark 10:15; Luke 18:17), inherit it (Matt. 25:34), and possess it (Matt. 5:4), but they are never said to establish it. Men can reject the Kingdom, i.e., refuse to receive it (Luke 10:11) or enter it (Matt. 23:13), but they cannot destroy it. They can look for it (Luke 23:51), pray for its coming (Matt. 6:10), and seek it (Matt. 6:33; Luke 12:31), but they cannot bring it. Men may be in the Kingdom (Matt. 5:19; 8:11; Luke 13:29; etc.), but we are not told that the Kingdom grows. Men can do things for the sake of the Kingdom (Matt. 19:12; Luke 18:29), but they are not said to act upon the Kingdom itself. Men can preach the Kingdom (Matt. 10:7; Luke 10:9), but only God can give it to men (Luke 12:32)" (*Presence of the Future*, 193).

3. For a study of the Baptist, see R. Webb, *John the Baptizer*.

4. See Meier, *Mentor, Message and Miracles*, 46.

Mark is ignorant of the OT context. He signals to his readers that Malachi must be interpreted through the lens of Isaiah, which means that Malachi must be understood in terms of return from exile, for the Isaiah citation (Isa. 40:3) has to do with Israel's return from captivity. In other words, if Mal. 3:1 is interpreted correctly (in light of Isa. 40), it will be understood that the Lord's messenger who will prepare his way will appear in a most unlikely place: the desert. The Lord is coming to his temple as Malachi prophesied, but the people must be ready and must turn from their sins. John announced that a great deluge of the Spirit was coming (1:8), for the prophets promised a coming day of the Spirit (Isa. 32:15; 44:3; Ezek. 36:26–27; Joel 2:28). When the Spirit is given, the exile will be over, the new exodus will begin, or as Mark puts it, the kingdom will come.[5] The Baptist was the Elijah who would come before the day of the Lord commenced (cf. Mal. 4:5–6), which, as we saw in the OT, is a day of salvation and judgment.

The kingdom, John predicted, would arrive in Jesus. What did the kingdom look like when Jesus came? Jesus, like the Baptist, proclaimed that the kingdom had arrived, that the good news of Yahweh's salvation for Israel was at hand, summoning the people to repent and to believe the good news (1:14–15). He called on the Twelve to travel with him and to preach the kingdom (3:13–19; cf. 6:7, 13). They were to be the fishers of people (1:16–20), the fishers prophesied by Jeremiah to return Israel from their captivity (Jer. 16:14–16). But the focus of the kingdom was Jesus himself, for the kingdom arrived in his person (see the next section) and his ministry. Fresh winds were blowing in Israel, the winds of grace and mercy and peace, for Jesus had power over demons, disease, and death. Such power was nothing less than the power of the kingdom. People were stunned at Jesus' authoritative teaching, for unclean spirits were cast out at his word (1:21–28; cf. 3:11).

The story of the Gerasene demoniac (5:1–20), which Mark lingers over longer than does any other Gospel, illustrates the point. No one could help this man. He was at the mercy of a legion of demons. He had superhuman strength but lived in cemeteries, isolated from society. The man was suicidal and self-destructive, cutting himself with rocks. Modern readers may be disturbed by what happened to the pigs, but the fate of the pigs demonstrated to the onlookers the extent to which the man was demonized. When the kingdom comes, human beings are restored to their rightful condition. They become sane and sensible (5:15). No demon anywhere is a match for Jesus. The hardest

---

5. On the theme of a new exodus in Mark, see Watts, *Isaiah's New Exodus*. On the link between the new exodus and Christology, though in Luke's Gospel, see Strauss, *Davidic Messiah*, 261–336.

cases melt at the power of his word, so that a boy who has had a demon all his life, whom no one else can help, is delivered, not by some long process of exorcism, but by the simple word of Jesus (9:14–29). Jesus' authority over the demons indicates the coming of the kingdom, the arrival of the new creation. When the kingdom comes, the power of demons is stripped away, and human beings are freed from everything that dehumanizes them.

Another sign of the old creation was the presence of disease and death. Jesus reigned over these as well (1:29–34; 3:11; 5:21–23, 35–43). The paralyzed man was healed at Jesus' word (2:1–12). A tenacious hemorrhage that a woman suffered from for twelve years, which no doctor could heal, ceased when she touched Jesus (5:24–34). Jesus should have become unclean when the woman touched him, but the situation was reversed. Jesus' cleanness, the power of his holiness, eradicated the uncleanness in the woman. Her healing is framed by the story of Jairus's daughter (5:21–23, 35–43). In the old creation death reigns, but in the kingdom proclaimed by Jesus life triumphs over death, so that his touch again produces life, raising the young girl from the dead. Isaiah promised that when the new exodus and new creation arrived, "the eyes of the blind shall be opened, and the ears of the deaf unstopped" (Isa. 35:5). And Mark shows that Jesus made the deaf to hear (7:31–37) and the blind to see (10:46–52). Of course, the new world had not yet arrived in its fullness, for death, demons, blindness, and deafness were not eliminated completely. There was an "already but not yet" dimension to Jesus' ministry.[6] The kingdom had come in his person and ministry, but it was not yet consummated. The kingdom had not arrived in all its fullness.

If the kingdom wasn't fully realized, there were stunning signs that it had been inaugurated in Jesus. Lack of food was no obstacle. The mountains seemed to be dripping with sweet wine (cf. Joel 3:18; Amos 9:14). Mark reports that Jesus fed five thousand and then four thousand in the wilderness (6:30–44; 8:1–10). Clearly, he was a new and better Moses.[7] The creation itself is disordered because of the sin of human beings, so that earthquakes, hurricanes, tornadoes, and floods wreak untold damage. But Jesus has authority over storms and calms them at his word (4:35–41), with the same authority that he exercised over demons. Here is a foretaste of the new world that is coming, when the words "Peace! Be still!" (4:39) will be true throughout the cosmos.

The coming of the kingdom introduces a newness not present in the old covenant. The new wine of the kingdom has arrived, and disciples should

---

6. The "already but not yet" tension in Jesus' teaching has long been recognized. See Jeremias, *New Testament Theology*, 96–108; Kümmel, *Promise and Fulfillment*; idem, *Theology of the New Testament*, 33–39; Ladd, *Theology of the New Testament*, 54–102; Goppelt, *Ministry of Jesus*, 43–76.

7. On this theme in Matthew, see Allison, *New Moses*.

no longer drink the old wine of the former covenant (2:21–22). Jesus is now the sovereign interpreter of the law (7:1–23). The purity laws are no longer binding for those who are Jesus' disciples (7:19). The day in which the temple will continue to exist is coming to an end (chap. 13). A new era has arrived in which forgiveness is secured through Jesus' death instead of through sacrifices in the temple.

The kingdom's arrival anticipates a new and transformed universe, but such a kingdom is tied up with and inseparable from the forgiveness of sins. Jesus' table fellowship with sinners (e.g., 2:13–17) points toward the messianic banquet on the last day (see Isa. 25:6–8), showing that sinners may experience now the mercy of the kingdom through Jesus the Christ. The new wine (see Joel 3:18; Amos 9:14) was now available in Jesus (2:18–22), for he is the bridegroom of the wedding feast that has even now begun. The forgiveness given to the paralytic (2:1–12) shows that healing of the body cannot be separated from cleansing from sin, and that it is in fact ultimately rooted in such forgiveness (cf. Ps. 103:3). Jesus' lordship and healings on the Sabbath (2:23–3:5) point to the final Sabbath rest (cf. Gen. 2:1–3), the consummation of God's creation purposes.

As in Matthew, in Mark the parables are crucial for understanding the kingdom. The parable of the sower indicates that when the kingdom comes, only some will receive its saving word (4:1–9, 13–20). Many will reject the kingdom because they fail to understand its message or because they find pleasure in the present evil age or become consumed with the worries of this life or refuse to endure persecution. The arrival of the kingdom will not be evident to all. Indeed, God must give understanding for one to understand and to embrace the kingdom (4:10–12, 33–34). Those who are turning against Jesus (3:6, 21–35) will be hardened and turned over to further darkness so that they fail to perceive the truth. The kingdom cannot be discerned or evaluated or tested by human intelligence or by empirical sciences; it is a testimony given by the Son of what the Father revealed to him, and it is to be received by faith. The parable of the mustard seed illustrates the mystery of the kingdom (4:31–32), for the kingdom is present but invisible to human perception. Only those granted sight will be able to see that the kingdom has truly come.

The Person of the King

The kingdom was present because the king had come. When Jesus announces that the time is fulfilled and the kingdom is at hand (1:14–15), he makes this announcement because he is present. Mark forges a connection between the gospel, which the Jews are to believe in (1:15), and the "gospel of Jesus Christ, the Son of God" (1:1). The first verse of the book sets the agenda for Mark. The good news of return from exile and the new creation, the good news of the kingdom, centers on Jesus the Messiah, who is also the Son of God.

The first verse of Mark leads us to think that this Gospel will often feature that Jesus is the Christ. Surprisingly, the theme is absent to a remarkable degree, provoking in scholarship discussion of the so-called messianic secret. For instance, Jesus commands those whom he heals not to make known the healing (1:44; 5:43; 7:36). He forbids the disciples who saw the transfiguration to make it known (9:9), and he charges demons not to spread the news that he is the Son of God (3:12). Presumably, he prohibited the man whom he healed of blindness from going to his village for the same reason (8:26). And when Peter declares that Jesus is the Messiah, Jesus enjoined the disciples not to tell anyone else (8:30). Jesus' reticence to use the title "Christ" ("Messiah") almost certainly was due to the political explosiveness generated by the appellation (cf. *Pss. Sol.* 17–18). Jesus did not want to foment a political revolution in which he was hailed as a messianic leader who would remove the Romans from power.[8]

The first time Jesus embraces the title "Messiah" is when Peter confesses him as the Christ at Caesarea Philippi (8:29). Jesus does not solicit the crowds to identify him as the son of David or as the Christ. Instead, he asks Peter about his identity when he is alone with the disciples and far from Jerusalem. Indeed, one of the prominent story lines in Mark is the blindness of the religious leaders, the crowds, and even the disciples. Human beings are unable to comprehend Jesus' identity apart from the gracious work of God. So it is quite fitting that a blind man perceives who Jesus is and identifies him as the son of David (10:47–48). The man who is blind truly sees who Jesus is, and even more significant, he understands Jesus' identity as the Christ as Jesus is traveling to Jerusalem to die on a Roman cross.

The religious leaders were unable to grasp Jesus' identity, for they did not see how he could be both David's son and David's lord (12:35–37). They believed that if Jesus claimed to be the Christ, then he was guilty of blasphemy (14:61–64). Remarkably, the title "Christ" and the designation of Jesus as the king of the Jews become prominent only near the end of Mark's Gospel, particularly in chapter 15. One only understands Jesus as Messiah if one sees that he is the crucified Messiah. Pilate asks Jesus if he is "the King of the Jews," and Jesus retorts that Pilate and all those accusing him have identified him as such (15:2; cf. 15:9, 12), since they are putting him to death as a king. Irony pervades Jesus' passion. The inscription on the cross identifies Jesus as "the

---

8. For an important study in this area, see Hengel, *Victory over Violence*.

King of the Jews" (15:26), and what Pilate wrote is the truth, even though he did not realize it. When the soldiers hailed Jesus as "the King of the Jews" (15:18), they were truly hailing the one who was king of the Jews and of the whole world. The religious leaders mocked Jesus, saying that he would be Christ the king only if he came down from the cross (15:32), failing to realize that he was proving himself to be the Messiah by his crucifixion.

Jesus' authority pervades Mark's Gospel. He calls disciples to follow him (1:16–20), casts out demons with a word, declares that the paralytic is forgiven of his sins (2:1–12), identifies himself as the end-time bridegroom (2:19–20), claims to be the Lord of the Sabbath (2:23–28), says that those who do God's will are part of his family (3:31–35), stills a storm with his words (4:35–41), sends others out to preach the kingdom (6:7–13), feeds crowds of five thousand and four thousand (6:30–44; 8:1–10), functions as the interpreter of the law (7:1–23), demands that people follow him (1:17; 2:14; 8:34; 10:21), warns that those who are ashamed of him and his words will be punished (8:38), teaches that children should be received in his name (9:37), cleanses the temple (11:15–17), identifies himself as the last and the most important of God's messengers (12:1–12), triumphs in controversy with religious leaders (11:27–12:44), predicts the destruction of the temple (13:1–37), calls on his disciples to bear witness to him before governmental authorities (13:9), claims to be the Son of God (14:61–62), and, most important of all, is raised from the dead (16:1–8).

Mark's portrait of Jesus as the Son of God is featured from the first verse of the book.[9] Some manuscripts lack the appellation "Son of God" in 1:1, but the reference to the Son of God there almost certainly is original. Since the title appears in the first verse of this Gospel, the recognition that Jesus is God's Son is a central theme of the work. Indeed, the title appears as an inclusio, for the book concludes with a centurion declaring that Jesus is the Son of God when he dies upon the cross (15:39). Mark signifies that no one truly understands Jesus as God's Son unless they identify him as the crucified Son of God. The kingdom that Jesus proclaims becomes a reality through his death and resurrection.

The declaration that Jesus is God's Son appears at crucial events in Mark's Gospel. At Jesus' baptism, where he is anointed for ministry by the Holy Spirit, the divine voice from heaven identifies Jesus as his Son (1:11). As we saw in Matthew, Jesus is identified here not only as the Son but also as the servant of God, with whom God is "well pleased" (cf. Isa. 42:1). Again, Jesus' sonship is tied to the cross, to his suffering for the sake of his people. Jesus is again identified by the divine voice from heaven as the Son of God at the transfiguration

---

9. For insightful discussion, see Thielman, *Theology of the New Testament*, 61–64.

(9:7), demonstrating that he is the new and better Moses, superior to the law and the prophets. Moses and Elijah appeared with him, but the divine voice declared that they must listen to Jesus (9:7), which is a clear allusion to Deut. 18:15, which promises the coming of a prophet like Moses (cf. Deut. 18:19). Jesus is both the Son of God and the final prophet. Jesus' transfiguration reveals his glory as the Son of God, but the cross is also in view, for Jesus spoke of rising from the dead (9:9–10), indicating that he is the crucified and risen Son of God. The story of the transfiguration unveils the true significance of Jesus' person, anticipating the power and glory of the kingdom when Jesus is revealed in his glory. The parable of the wicked tenants confirms the close relationship between Jesus' suffering and death and his sonship (12:1–12). The parable suggests that the tenants will slay the son, but the son who is slain will become the cornerstone of a new temple (12:10). He will be raised from the dead, and the new age will commence with his resurrection. God will triumph over his enemies; he will conquer the serpent, through the death and resurrection of the Son of God.

Jesus is also the glorious Son of Man, who receives the kingdom from the Father (cf. Dan. 7:13–14).[10] He has authority to forgive sins, just as he forgave the sins of the paralytic (2:10). As the Son of Man, he is also "lord even of the Sabbath" (2:28). Jesus' lordship, however, is inseparable from his going to the cross. Mark emphasizes repeatedly that the Son of Man would be betrayed (14:21, 41) and suffer (8:31; 9:12–13; 10:33) just as it was predicted in the Scriptures. The Son of Man would come again in glory (8:38; 13:26; 14:62) after he was raised from the dead (8:31; 9:9; 10:34). The kingdom has arrived in the person of the Son of Man, but first comes suffering and then glory. The kingdom clearly has an "already but not yet" dimension, for the fullness of glory is not yet a reality. Even more important the glory is realized for human beings only through the death of the Son of Man. As the servant of the Lord (cf. Isa. 52:13–53:12), he came "to give his life as a ransom for many" (10:45). Those who were enslaved by their sin are freed by the Son of Man taking their punishment upon himself. Here Mark picks up Dan. 7, where the son of man represents the saints who will receive the kingdom after suffering. Mark (and all the Gospel writers) indicates that Jesus is the son of man of Dan. 7. The saints receive the kingdom by belonging to him. Since they belong to Jesus, who is the Son of Man, they share his death and resurrection and thus belong to the era of the kingdom inaugurated by Jesus.

Mark clearly teaches that the kingdom comes only through the cross, for Jesus' work and ministry is all of a piece. One segment of his life cannot be

10. See ibid., 68–71.

separated from another. His healings and exorcisms cannot be sheared off from the cross and resurrection, as if the former were ultimately possible without the latter. At the Last Supper Jesus' blood and body signify, akin to the prophetic signs in the OT, Jesus' impending death (14:22–25). The shedding of his blood is covenantal (cf. Exod. 24:8), which is "poured out for many" (14:24). The pouring out of Jesus' blood signifies the giving of his life (cf. Lev. 17:11), indicating that atonement for sins is secured through Jesus' sacrifice, so that those who put their faith in him are saved on the basis of his death on their behalf.

Other hints suggest that Jesus' death provided atonement, that his death spared disciples from God's wrath.[11] The story of Barabbas is not merely one with historical interest (15:6–15). Jesus died in place of Barabbas, and because Jesus died, Barabbas lived. The story of Barabbas is paradigmatic, and readers should see in Barabbas their own story. They too deserve to die because of their sins, but Jesus died in their place so that they could enjoy life. In the same way, Jesus is "delivered into the hands of men" (9:31). In the OT Israel was "delivered into the hand of the enemy" (Lev. 26:25), cast into exile when it sinned (cf. 2 Kings 17:39–40). Conversely, those whom God favors are saved from the hand of the enemy (e.g., Exod. 3:8; 2 Sam. 22:1; Ezra 8:31). When Jesus was delivered into the hands of his enemies, therefore, he faced the judgment of God, taking upon himself the punishment that Israel deserved. Along the same lines, when Jesus was dying, his enemies mocked him, "wagging their heads" (*kinountes tas kephalas autōn* [Mark 15:29]). The same verb and object are used in Jer. 18:16 (see also Lam. 2:15) to describe the response to the defeat that Israel will face at the hand of its enemies. Those who see the judgment inflicted upon Israel "shall shake their head" (*kinēsousin tēn kephalēn autōn*). Similarly, the passersby realized that Jesus was facing God's judgment. What they did not perceive was the deeper truth in their words "He saved others; he cannot save himself" (15:31). If he saved himself, there was no hope for others, but by suffering for the sake of others, he died in their place. The darkness in the land (15:33) also signified that judgment was falling upon Jesus (cf. Exod. 10:21–22; 1 Sam. 2:9; Ps. 107:10). He took the darkness of God's anger upon himself so that his people would enjoy the light of salvation.

Discipleship

The first half of Mark's Gospel (1:1–8:30) focuses on Jesus' identity. The issue before the readers is whether Jesus' disciples will recognize that he is

11. On this topic, an important work is Bolt, *The Cross from a Distance*.

the Messiah. As noted above, Jesus did not openly proclaim or teach that he was the Messiah, and hence recognizing him as such was a matter of spiritual perception. In the story line of the Gospel the religious leaders are blind, even saying that Jesus cast out demons by their ruler, Beelzebul (3:6, 22). His family failed to see who Jesus was, concluding that he was mentally unstable (3:21, 31–35). Demons truly know who Jesus is (3:11), but they hate and despise him. Controversy swirled over Jesus' identity, and he was thought to be John the Baptist, Elijah, or another one of the prophets (6:15–16).

Even Jesus' disciples struggled to grasp his identity. Jesus privately explained parables to them (4:33–34) so that they could comprehend the mystery of the kingdom (4:11). But this should not be interpreted to mean that they immediately grasped who Jesus was. When he stilled a storm, his disciples were filled with astonishment, wondering about his identity, but, according to the narrative, they come to no clear conclusion (4:35–41). Jesus also walked on the Sea of Galilee, approaching the disciples' boat after feeding the five thousand (6:45–52). The disciples thought that Jesus was a ghost, but he identified himself, saying, "It is I. Do not be afraid" (6:50). The "It is I" statement probably hearkens back to Exod. 3:14 and the "I am" declarations of Yahweh in Isaiah (e.g., Isa. 41:4; 43:10, 25; 45:18, 22). This certainly would fit with walking on water, for such an act is possible only for the Lord (cf. Job 9:8). But the disciples were dulled in their comprehension. They were amazed, but they "did not understand about the loaves, but their hearts were hardened" (6:52). Clearly, they understood that Jesus provided enough food to feed more than five thousand people. What they did not grasp from this event and his walking on the water was who he really was. They were not blind in the same way as the religious leaders and Jesus' family. Nor were they opposed to him as the demons were. And yet their hearts were impervious and resistant to the Lord. They did not truly see who Jesus was, and no one can be a disciple of Jesus and fundamentally misunderstand his identity.

Still, the disciples were not in the same place as the religious leaders or the crowds who misunderstood Jesus. The disciples loved Jesus and believed in him, at least to some extent. And yet they did not fully realize who Jesus was, and so their vision was obscured from seeing him with full clarity. When Jesus warned the disciples, "Beware of the leaven of the Pharisees and the leaven of Herod" (8:15), they took him literally and started discussing with one another their failure to bring bread for the journey (8:16). The obtuseness of the disciples amazed Jesus (8:17–21). He wondered how they could fail to perceive and understand what was right in front of them. Jesus asked them if their hearts were hardened so that they were prevented from comprehension. Did they fail to see with their eyes and hear with their ears? Did they fail to reflect on the significance of Jesus feeding the five thousand and the four thousand? So Jesus repeated, "Do you not yet understand?" (8:21). Apparently, the disciples lacked perception regarding Jesus' identity.

The miracle story in 8:22–26 signifies the problem with the disciples. This is one of the strangest stories in the Gospels. Jesus laid his hands on the blind man and spit on his eyes, asking him what he saw. The man observed people walking, but they looked like trees. In other words, he did not see clearly and distinctly. So Jesus laid his hands on the man again, and this time his sight was completely "restored, and he saw everything clearly" (8:25). What is the point of this story? It makes no sense to say that Jesus could not heal the person entirely at the first touch, as if he needed to work in two stages to cure the man of blindness. It was a genuine healing, but it is a story with a point, with a lesson for readers. The story symbolizes the spiritual perception and vision of Jesus' disciples. They were like this blind man, unable to perceive who Jesus was. They needed a touch from Jesus in order to truly understand him. It is no accident, then, that the story that immediately follows is of Jesus asking his disciples at Caesarea Philippi about his identity (8:27–30). The people's answers were flawed, seeing him as John the Baptist, Elijah, or one of the prophets (8:27–28). But Peter and the disciples had received a touch from Jesus. The blindness had been lifted from their eyes, and so Peter rightly confessed that Jesus is the Christ (8:29).

The two-stage healing of the man, however, still applies to the disciples. They understand that Jesus is the Messiah, but they had no conception about the nature of his messiahship. They had no categories for a suffering Messiah. Hence, they needed a second touch from Jesus to perceive clearly what it meant for him to be the Messiah. At the end of the day, they did not truly understand Jesus as Messiah if they did not grasp that he had come to suffer. Furthermore, the nature of Jesus' messianic calling as a suffering Messiah is wedded inseparably to what it means to be a disciple. Jesus' mission and the disciples' calling shed light on each other. We see this directly in the account that follows Peter's declaration that Jesus is the Christ (8:31–9:1). Jesus began to explain frankly to the disciples that he would be rejected by the religious leaders, suffer, die, and then be raised. Peter was shocked by such an announcement, rebuking Jesus, presumably because such a destiny did not accord with his understanding of a triumphant Messiah. Jesus struck back at Peter, staggering him by saying, "Get behind me, Satan!" (8:33). These words were not intended for Peter's ears only, for Jesus looked at all the disciples in saying them, indicating that Peter's words reflected the sentiments of all the disciples. It was not enough for the disciples to have just one healing touch from Jesus and to understand that he was the Messiah.

Such a view was satanic if it also denied that his destiny as the Messiah was suffering and death.

It was imperative that the disciples understand Jesus' destiny as Messiah, that he was called to suffer and die. Indeed, Jesus' destiny functions as the pattern for disciples.[12] If they want to follow Jesus as disciples, they must deny themselves and take up their own crosses and follow Jesus (8:34). In other words, they must give their lives entirely to Jesus. They must be willing to die for his sake, for unless they lose their life for Jesus' sake, they will suffer eternal loss (8:35–37). Only those who are willing to face shame for belonging to Jesus and for heeding his teaching will enter the kingdom. The suffering of disciples is a corollary to Jesus' suffering. This is clarified when we recognize that the three passion predictions in Mark (8:31–33; 9:30–32; 10:32–34) are immediately followed by texts that unfold the nature of discipleship (8:34–9:1; 9:33–50; 10:35–45). We have already examined the first passion prediction (8:31–33) and Jesus' teaching on discipleship. In the second passion prediction Jesus clearly predicts his death and resurrection (9:30–32). The cluelessness of the disciples is evident, for they were discussing at the same time which one of them was the greatest (9:33–34). Such a desire to be great showed resistance to God's rule in their lives.[13] They failed to see the inseparable connection between Jesus' destiny and theirs. Jesus was giving up his life for the sake of others, but the disciples were consumed with their own status and reputations. The true disciple lives as a servant of others, receiving children in Jesus' name (9:36–37) instead of engaging in self-promotion. Disciples are fixated on their own glory if they suspiciously cast aside any fellow disciple who is not exactly like them (9:38–41). No true disciple causes others to stumble in their faith (9:42), for a true disciple seeks to build up the faith of others, not tear it down. Furthermore, the true disciple shows no mercy to sin in his or her own life (9:45–50). Sin is dealt with severely and completely so that it does not gain a foothold in one's life.

The last passion prediction of Jesus is the starkest and most specific (10:32–34). The utter rejection that Jesus was facing was incomprehensible to the disciples, particularly since their eyes were fixed on the glory that they anticipated for themselves in the coming kingdom. James and John obviously were not attuned to what Jesus was saying, for while he was speaking of the cross, they were thinking of their crowns, soliciting Jesus for the privilege of sitting at his right and left hand in glory (10:35–37). They needed a radical reorientation of their thinking, for they would confront a baptismal deluge

12. See Best, "Discipleship in Mark."
13. So Schlatter, *History of the Christ*, 298.

of suffering just as Jesus would (10:38–39). If they were not prepared to suffer, they would be liable to fall prey to false Christs (13:4–13, 21). The fate of the master and the fate of the servant could not be wrenched apart. The path to glory for one would be the path to glory for the others. The rest of the disciples were not free from the same ambitions that fired the hearts of James and John, for they were angry upon hearing about their request (10:41). Jesus instructed them that they must liberate themselves from selfish ambition, for ruling over others is what animated authorities in the secular sphere (10:42). Instead, they were to be free from the slavery of self-ambition so that they could be liberated to be the slave and servant of others (10:43–44). Here Jesus is their supreme exemplar, for he surrendered his life so that the guilt of sin would be expunged from those who put their trust in him (10:45). Those who are disciples keep the Great Commandment, for they love the Lord with all of their being and love their neighbor as well (12:28–34). They must be ever vigilant and alert, for evil is perpetually near and cannot be conquered by those who fall into lethargy (13:33–37; cf. Peter's denials in 14:66–72).

We have seen that the three passion predictions are linked with three texts on discipleship. Here a few other threads on discipleship must be picked up. Those who are disciples recognize Jesus' identity as Messiah and Son of God and follow him as disciples. They also receive the kingdom like children (10:15). Only those who are humble and teachable enter the kingdom, those who recognize their need for the power of the kingdom to be saved. The story of the rich man that immediately follows illustrates the point (10:17–31). He wanted to know what he must do to obtain eternal life and enter the kingdom. Apparently, he thought that his observance of the commandments qualified him for entrance, but Jesus pierced through his defenses, spying out his violation of the first and tenth commandments. The rich man had another god that possessed his heart, and thus Jesus insisted that the man must give up the treasures of earth and follow Jesus in order to enjoy the treasures of heaven. But he was not humble like a child, clinging to his riches instead. Jesus emphasizes that only God can change the human heart, that entering the kingdom can be explained only by his grace (10:28–31). Bartimaeus illustrates the life of a true disciple, one who would enter the kingdom of God. When he was healed of blindness, he followed Jesus as a disciple on the road to Golgotha (10:46–52). He was a genuine disciple of Jesus, for he was willing to follow Jesus even to the point of death.

Mark emphasizes, then, that the sons and daughters of the kingdom are those who are disciples of Jesus. Membership in the kingdom is attained not by Jewish descent but rather by repenting and believing the gospel of the kingdom proclaimed and instantiated by Jesus of Nazareth.

Conclusion

Mark, like Matthew, emphasizes that God's kingdom has come in Jesus of Nazareth. The kingdom has arrived supremely in his person. No one description suffices to capture who Jesus is. He is the final prophet, the Messiah, the Son of Man, the Son of God, and his authority manifests itself in many other ways. The kingdom has come in its saving power through Jesus, and it is evident in his healings, exorcisms, table fellowship, and preaching. Jesus' healings and exorcisms anticipate the new creation.[14] The new exodus has arrived in his preaching. Those who belong to Jesus have, so to speak, crossed the Jordan and now live in the land of promise. The kingdom is present now, but it is not yet consummated. The final judgment is delayed for the future. In fact, the kingdom is present only for those who have eyes to see, since those who reject its rule are not immediately judged. The kingdom has come like a mustard seed, such that the world cannot perceive it. The kingdom has come in the king, but the king, astonishingly, brings members into the kingdom through suffering, by becoming a ransom for many and by pouring out his blood of the covenant. The king's suffering is part of the mustard-seed character of the kingdom. Those who enter into the kingdom do so by receiving it like children. Those who try to enter as kings cannot enter. Indeed, the disciples of Jesus are called to be like their master, to serve one another in love and to forsake trying to be great. The glory of the kingdom will finally belong to those who give up trying to be glorious and are willing to suffer and to live as Jesus' disciples.

14. They also point to who Jesus is. See Marshall, *New Testament Theology*, 85.

27

THE GOSPEL
ACCORDING TO LUKE
AND THE ACTS OF THE APOSTLES

Introduction

As noted in the two preceding chapters, the kingdom is quite prominent in
Matthew and Mark, and the same is true in Luke-Acts. In this chapter I will
combine Luke and Acts because they are by one author, and Acts continues
the narrative from Luke's Gospel (Acts 1:1). Luke-Acts accounts for more
than 25 percent of the NT, thus playing a major role in the NT canon. The
overarching theme from which I will explore Luke-Acts is the kingdom. The
following topics will be explored in considering Luke-Acts: the kingdom and
salvation history, the kingdom and the Spirit, the kingdom and the king, the
kingdom and prayer, the kingdom and salvation, the kingdom and missions.

The Kingdom and Salvation History

The Gospel of Luke, not surprisingly, has much in common with both Matthew
and Mark. The word "kingdom" occurs forty-six times in Luke. Most of these
instances relate to the kingdom of God, showing how prominent the theme is
in this Gospel. We see the importance of the kingdom in summary statements
about Jesus' ministry: "I must preach the good news of the kingdom of God
to the other towns as well; for I was sent for this purpose" (4:43; cf. 16:16).[1]

---

1. On God's plan or purpose in Luke-Acts, see Squires, *Plan of God*; Reasoner, "Theme of
Acts"; Peterson, "Motif of Fulfillment."

Clearly, the purpose of Jesus' ministry was to proclaim the kingdom of God. We read later in the narrative, "Soon afterward he went on through cities and villages, proclaiming and bringing the good news of the kingdom of God" (8:1). Once again the kingdom is the burden of Jesus' ministry. Furthermore, when he commissions the Twelve, "he sent them out to proclaim the kingdom of God" (9:2; cf. 9:11). In the same way, he appointed seventy-two others to preach the kingdom (10:9, 11). And when disciples pray, they are to pray for the coming of the kingdom (11:2), and they should seek the kingdom above all else (12:31).

Even though the word "kingdom" appears relatively infrequently in Acts (8x), the theme is of central importance in the book.[2] In the forty days between Jesus' resurrection and ascension he spoke to the disciples about the kingdom of God (1:3). Indeed, Acts begins and ends with a reference to the kingdom, for when Luke sums up Paul's ministry in Rome in the last verse of the book, he says he was "proclaiming the kingdom of God and teaching about the Lord Jesus Christ with all boldness and without hindrance" (28:31). The theme of the kingdom, then, functions as a framing device in Acts, indicating that the message of the entire book focuses on the kingdom. Paul proclaimed the kingdom when Jews from Rome visited him in prison (28:23). The Christ-centeredness of the kingdom is evident in 28:23, 31. Indeed, 28:23 says that Paul was "testifying to the kingdom of God and trying to convince them about Jesus both from the Law of Moses and from the Prophets." Luke makes it clear that the message of the kingdom fulfills the OT Scripture and that it centers on Jesus Christ. Those who proclaim Jesus Christ and his suffering and his glory proclaim the message of the kingdom (cf. Luke 24:25, 27, 44–46). We see the same connection in 8:12. When Philip visited Samaria, "he preached good news about the kingdom of God and the name of Jesus Christ" (8:12). It seems that preaching about Christ and the gospel also constitutes a proclamation of the kingdom. Paul ministered for three months in the synagogue in Ephesus, "reasoning and persuading them about the kingdom of God" (19:8). And when he summarizes his three-year ministry in Ephesus, he describes it as "proclaiming the kingdom" (20:25). It is quite clear, then, that the kingdom is central in Acts, even though the term itself is used infrequently. Indeed, we see that proclaiming Jesus as the Christ in his death and resurrection constitutes the preaching of the kingdom in Acts.

Luke particularly features history in his presentation, emphasizing in the prologue of his Gospel that he relied on eyewitness testimony and carefully

2. See esp. A. Thompson, *Acts of the Risen Jesus.*

researched other writings to convey the truth of what happened (1:1–4). Luke carefully identifies the year John the Baptist began his ministry, tying it to the fifteenth year of the emperor Tiberius and to the rule of Pilate, Herod Antipas, Philip, and Lysanias, and to the high priestly ministry of Annas and Caiaphas (3:1–2). Often in Acts he names or identifies local leaders in the various places the apostles ministered. For Luke, the fulfillment of the kingdom in salvation history is grounded in real history.

The theme of fulfillment emerges in the very first verse of Luke's Gospel. He writes "a narrative of the things that have been accomplished among us" (1:1), but the word translated as "accomplished" (*peplērophorēmenōn*) is better translated as "fulfilled" (cf. 1:20, 45).[3] The fulfillment of the covenant stands out as a major theme in chapter 1. Mary's song (1:46–55) is replete with echoes of Hannah's song (1 Sam. 2:1–10), and we see that fulfillment of God's covenant promises is inseparably intertwined with the kingdom.[4] Mary anticipates the realization of the covenant promises made to Abraham (1:54–55), longing for the coming of the kingdom, where the rich, the proud, and the mighty are routed, and the poor, the humble, and the weak who belong to the Lord are exalted (1:51–53). The priest Zechariah is more specific. The Lord has acted to fulfill the covenants made with both David and Abraham (1:68–75). The redemption anticipated in the first exodus is now fulfilled in the second exodus through the Christ, the son of David (1:68–69). The promise made to Abraham is near. Israel will be saved from its enemies so that it can serve the Lord.[5] The kingdom is at hand!

The Spirit and the Kingdom in the Gospel of Luke

Starting a new topic here is somewhat artificial because what was said about the kingdom above could fit here as well. A new topic is introduced here, however, because Luke particularly ties together the Spirit and the kingdom.[6] Hence, I will focus on that theme here. The role of the Spirit comes to center stage in the ministry of the Baptist. He is "filled with the Holy Spirit" while in the womb of Elizabeth (1:15), and he is like a Nazirite (cf. Num. 6:1–21),

---

3. Though two different Greek words are used to designate such fulfillment.

4. Hahn (*Kinship by Covenant*, 234–37) persuasively argues that in Luke-Acts covenant is integral to the kingdom.

5. Matera (*New Testament Theology*, 74) rightly notes how Luke emphasizes that "today" salvation history is being fulfilled (2:11; 4:21; 19:9; 23:43).

6. For excellent surveys of scholarship relative to the Holy Spirit with a focus on Luke-Acts, see Menzies, *Empowered for Witness*, 17–45; Turner, *Power from on High*, 20–79.

totally dedicated to the Lord (1:15). He is a Spirit-filled prophet like Elijah (1:16–17, 76–77; 7:26–27) who is called to bring Israel back to the Lord (cf. Mal. 4:5–6), for the new exodus is at hand (3:4–6), summoning Israel to repent or to face the wrath of the Lord (3:3, 7–9).

Jesus was conceived by the power of the Holy Spirit apart from a human father (1:34–35) and was anointed by the Spirit for ministry at his baptism (3:21–22), and thus was full of the Spirit after his baptism (4:1). The Spirit "led" him into the desert, where he was tempted by the devil (4:1–13). Jesus faced forty days of testing in the wilderness and did not capitulate to sin, whereas Israel was punished forty years in the wilderness for its transgressions. After Jesus triumphed over the devil, he returned from the wilderness "in the power of the Spirit" (4:14). The passage that perhaps contains the "genetic code" for all of Luke-Acts is 4:16–30. Jesus read from the Isaiah scroll (see Isa. 58:6; 61:1–2), claiming that the Spirit of the Lord was upon him. He was "anointed" (4:18) at his baptism to carry out his ministry, which included proclaiming good news to the poor, freedom for those imprisoned, sight for the blind, and liberty for those crushed. It is the year of the Lord's favor (cf. Isa. 61:2), which most likely means that Jesus was anointed to return Israel from exile, to restore them to living under the Lord's blessing. The return from exile represents the dawning of God's kingdom, so we can conclude that Jesus was empowered by the Spirit to bring in the kingdom.

We need not linger over Jesus' healings and exorcisms in Luke because we saw that they were part and parcel of the kingdom in both Matthew and Mark. What is clear is that such acts of power were manifestations of the kingdom (4:31–44), for Luke ties Jesus' healings and power over demons to his proclamation of the good news of the kingdom (4:43). There is also a close connection to the programmatic speech at Nazareth (4:16–30), for in healing those blighted by disease (5:12–26; 14:1–6) and those terrorized by demons (8:27–39; 9:37–42; 11:14; 13:10–17), Jesus was freeing the oppressed (4:18). The interpretation offered here is confirmed by 7:21–22. The Baptist wondered if Jesus was truly the Christ. His doubts are not surprising, since he languished in prison. But Jesus points him to the fulfillment of prophecy: "The lame walk, lepers are cleansed, and the deaf hear, the dead are raised up, the poor have good news preached to them" (7:22). The list here is strikingly similar to what we read in 4:18–19, but in this instance Luke also draws on Isa. 29:18 and 35:5–6. Isaiah 35 is a remarkably clear passage on the return from exile (35:8–10) and the dawning of the new creation (35:1–2, 6–7). But this is another way of speaking of the coming of the kingdom. And the link between Luke 4:18 and 7:21–22 shows that the kingdom arrives because Jesus is empowered by the Spirit. The kingdom has arrived for those who have eyes to see, even if it is not consummated.[7]

Elsewhere Luke says that Jesus' expulsion of demons represents the finger of God and the arrival of the kingdom (11:20). It is a bit surprising that Luke does not refer to the Spirit here, given his interest in the Spirit and also the reference to the Spirit in the Synoptic parallel (Matt. 12:28). But the meaning is not remarkably different. The kingdom has come by the power of God. The emphasis on the Spirit does not lead to the conclusion that the kingdom has been consummated. It is like a mustard seed and leaven (13:18–21). To the world, the kingdom is insignificant and hidden, for the wicked have not yet faced judgment. Nevertheless, God's ruling power, his saving power, is at work in the world.

The "not yet" character of the kingdom is also evident, for Jesus predicts an interval before the consummation of the kingdom. Scholars too often have overemphasized the immediacy of Jesus' teaching on the end. But Jesus also warned that the time before the consummation of the kingdom would seem long to human beings. The stresses would be so great that they would be tempted to give up altogether and surrender their faith (18:1–8). Jesus corrects the notion that the kingdom will necessarily arrive imminently, crafting a parable designed for those who supposed "that the kingdom of God was to appear immediately" (19:11). The man in the parable travels to "a far country to receive . . . a kingdom and then return" (19:12). The words "far country" suggest that the delay may be significant.

Jesus also admonished his disciples regarding the coming of the kingdom (17:22–37). Many will claim that the end is at hand, asserting even that they had seen the Christ. The disciples should not anticipate a sudden release from their suffering; they will face opposition during their generation. The end will come suddenly and unexpectedly, just as the flood arrived in Noah's day and as fire from heaven destroyed Sodom in Lot's day. Similarly, the destruction of Jerusalem and end of history will not occur immediately (21:5–36). Wars, earthquakes, famines, and unrest do not necessarily denote the end of history. Such things characterize human life throughout the present evil age. The Son of Man will come, and although the time is not calculable, there will be an interval. To sum up, it is evident that there is an "already but not yet" character to the kingdom in Luke. The kingdom has come, God's saving promises are being fulfilled, as is evidenced by the work of the Holy Spirit in Jesus, and

7. In the same way, Jesus' table fellowship with sinners forecasts the coming messianic banquet (cf. Isa. 25:6–8), including the feeding of the five thousand (9:10–17), the Last Supper (22:7–38), and the meal at Emmaus (24:13–35). See Hahn, *Kinship by Covenant*, 222–23.

yet the kingdom has not come in its fullness. The wicked have not yet been judged, and the righteous still face trials and suffering until Jesus returns.

The Kingdom and the King

Jesus Is the Messianic King

What Luke, along with Matthew and Mark, emphasizes is that the kingdom has arrived in the person of the king. Jesus declares to the Pharisees that "the kingdom of God is in the midst of you" (17:21). The words translated "in the midst of you" (*entos hymōn*) are aptly rendered by the ESV here. Jesus is not saying to the Pharisees, who opposed and doubted him, that the kingdom was inside them. He was claiming that the kingdom was among them, that it was present in his person. It was hidden from them like leaven in flour. The kingdom comes through the Christ, the son of David. The promise of world-wide blessing made to Abraham and the promise that kings would come from him (Gen. 17:6; 35:11) would be fulfilled through a Davidic king, in accord with the covenant made with David (2 Sam. 7). The Lukan birth narratives, therefore, emphasize that Jesus is the son of David.[8] Mary's husband, Joseph, is from "the house of David" (1:27; cf. 2:4), and Jesus' genealogy stretches back to David (3:23–38; cf. 3:31). Mary is informed in no uncertain terms that Jesus is the Messiah: "The Lord God will give to him the throne of his father David, and he will reign over the house of Jacob forever, and of his kingdom there will be no end" (1:32–33). Jesus' identity as the Messiah and the reign of God's kingdom are closely linked here, showing that the realization of God's kingdom promises will come about through him. Zechariah recognizes that Jesus is from David's house (1:69), and the angels declare to the shepherds, "For unto you is born this day in the city of David a Savior, who is Christ the Lord" (2:11). In the same way, Simeon too recognizes that Jesus is the Christ (2:26).

Hahn nicely summarizes eight ways in which the Lukan Jesus fulfills the covenant with David and restores the kingdom:[9] (1) Jesus' kingdom is based on God's covenant with David (1:32–33; 22:20, 29; cf. 2 Sam. 7:9, 12, 14, 16); (2) like David, Jesus is the Son of God (1:35); (3) Jesus is the Christ (2:26; cf. 2 Sam. 23:1); (4) "Jesus' royal mission is bound up with Jerusalem";[10] (5) Jesus' mission centers on the temple; (6) Jesus restores the twelve tribes of Israel and

---

8. On the Christology of Luke's Gospel, see Buckwalter, *Luke's Christology*.
9. Hahn, *Kinship by Covenant*, 218–19.
10. Ibid., 218 (italics removed).

David's kingdom, for he ministers in Judea, Samaria, and Galilee;[11] (7) Jesus' rule is over all peoples and nations; and (8) Jesus rules forever.

Even though Luke emphasizes that Jesus is the Messiah and it is a central part of his theology, Jesus, as we saw in Matthew and Mark, is reticent to identify himself during his ministry as the son of David or as the Christ. Jesus compares himself to David with respect to his actions on the Sabbath (6:3), but he makes no direct statement about being the Davidic heir. The demons know that Jesus is the Christ, but he forbids them from speaking for that very reason (4:41). Peter confesses that Jesus is the Christ, and Jesus does not reject the title but forbids him from spreading such news (9:20–21). A blind man recognizes that Jesus is the son of David (18:38–39) and follows him toward Golgotha (18:43), and the crowds acclaim him as king on the Sunday before his death (19:38), but these events occur at the end of Jesus' ministry, and hence a political misappropriation of Jesus' messiahship is precluded. Jesus suggests that the Messiah is both David's lord and David's son (20:41–44), but even here he makes no direct statements. Jesus identifies himself as the Christ at his trial (22:67–71; cf. 23:2), but for this he is condemned, not praised. On the cross Jesus was mocked for being the Christ and the king of the Jews (23:35–39), though Luke wants readers to see that he was the Christ precisely because he suffered, for it was ordained that the Christ would suffer and then enter into glory (24:26–27; 46).

The pattern in Luke's Gospel is fascinating, for the two frames of the book (the birth narrative and the Passion Narrative) emphasize that Jesus is the Christ, while the body of the book does not. Why is this? It is because Jesus' messiahship can be understood only in the light of the cross, and the Jews would have latched onto the political dimensions of Jesus being the son of David if he emphasized such during his ministry. Even the disciples had difficulty in grasping why Jesus as the Christ had to suffer. This reading of the evidence is confirmed by the book of Acts. There, Jesus is freely acknowledged to be the Christ (2:38; 3:6, 20; 5:42; 8:5, 12; 9:22, 34; 10:36, 48; 11:17; 13:22–23, 34; 15:16, 26; 16:18; 18:5, 28; 24:24; 28:31),[12] for after the cross and resurrection there was no danger of Jesus being called upon to serve as an earthly king. Those proclaiming the gospel in Acts prove from the Scriptures that the Christ was called upon to suffer before entering into glory (3:18; 17:3; 26:23), and Jesus' resurrection proves that he is truly the Christ, so that now he is the exalted Messiah (2:31, 36; 4:10).

11. Ibid., 220–21. Jesus fulfills the prophecy of Ezek. 37 in reuniting true Israel during his mission.

12. I am assuming that the verses which tie Jesus to David also indicate that he is the Christ.

Jesus Is the Lord of All

We see a similar phenomenon regarding Jesus' lordship.[13] To say that Jesus is Lord is to acknowledge that he reigns and rules, that he is the king of all. In Luke's Gospel Elizabeth recognizes that Jesus is Lord while he is still in Mary's womb (1:43),[14] and Zechariah predicts his son, John, will prepare the Lord's (i.e., Jesus') way (1:76). The angels declare to the shepherds that Christ is the Lord (2:11). Peter, distressed at his own sinfulness, invokes Jesus as Lord (5:8; cf. 9:54; 10:17; 12:41; 19:31, 34; 22:33, 38, 49; 24:34), in a scene reminiscent of the theophany to Isaiah (Isa. 6). In some texts those who call Jesus "Lord" may simply mean "sir" (cf. 5:12; 7:6; 9:59; 11:1; 13:23, 25; 17:37; 18:41; 19:8), but even in these cases Luke wants readers to see a deeper meaning.[15] Certainly Jesus saw himself as Lord, for he identifies himself as such in teaching his disciples (6:46; 20:42, 44). Luke also regularly identifies Jesus as "Lord" when there is no necessity in the narrative to do so (7:13, 19; 10:1, 41; 11:39; 12:42; 13:15; 17:5, 6; 18:6; 22:61; 24:3). Such a narrative device reveals that Jesus' lordship is central to Luke's purpose, for he reminds the reader of Jesus' lordship regularly.

Elizabeth acknowledged Jesus as Lord while he was in the womb (1:43), indicating that Jesus was Lord from his conception. The lordship of Jesus gains even more prominence in Acts, expanding upon what is already present in Luke's Gospel. Alan Thompson says that Luke's second volume should be designated "The Acts of the Risen Jesus" (cf. 1:1), which is just another way of saying "The Acts of the Risen Lord."[16] The term "Lord" is used ninety-nine times in Acts, and about half of them refer to Jesus. Jesus, as the result of his resurrection, is now the exalted Lord, sitting at the right hand of the Father (2:34–36; 5:31). Indeed, he shares the same status as God, for "he is Lord of all" (10:36). The divine status of Jesus is also attested by Stephen invoking Jesus as Lord in prayer (7:59–60), and it is suggested by Jesus' appearance to Paul (9:5, 17, 27; 22:8, 10; 26:15) and his speaking in a vision to Ananias (9:10–15) and to Paul (22:17–21). Furthermore, disciples were baptized "in the name of the Lord Jesus" (8:16; 19:5)[17] and believed in Jesus as Lord (9:42; 11:17; 14:23; 16:31; 18:8; 20:21; cf. 11:21). In Luke's Gospel Jesus' glory and lordship were veiled by his humanity and suffering. But at his resurrection,

---

13. Matera (*New Testament Theology*, 67) says that "Lord" and "Messiah" are the two most prominent titles for Jesus in Luke-Acts.

14. For a profound and persuasive study of Jesus as Lord in Luke's Gospel, see Rowe, *Early Narrative Christology*.

15. See ibid.

16. A. Thompson, *Acts of the Risen Jesus*, 49.

17. On the importance of name Christology, see Hartman, *Name of the Lord Jesus*.

Jesus is exalted as Lord, and Acts often points to his lordship. How does this relate to the kingdom? The kingdom was inaugurated in Jesus' ministry, but it reached a new stage with his death and resurrection, for now Jesus sits at the right hand of God as Lord and Christ. Of course, there is still a future consummation. As Acts makes clear, the restoration of all things has not yet occurred (3:20–21). Still, Jesus reigns now, though the universe awaits the day when everything will be put under his feet (2:32–36; cf. Luke 20:42–43).

Jesus' Authority

The authority of Jesus pervades Luke-Acts, revealing his kingship and lordship. In Luke's Gospel demons recognize him as "the Holy One of God" (4:34; cf. Acts 16:18). He summons people to be his disciples and to follow him (5:27; 9:23, 59; 18:22). He claims to be "lord of the Sabbath" (6:5) and the bridegroom (5:34). He stills a storm, which only God can do (8:23–25), and forgives and heals the paralytic (5:17–26). He shares the same name as God himself and, therefore, the same status and dignity as God. Children are to be received in his name (9:48), and demons were subject to the disciples in Jesus' name (10:17). The disciples must proclaim from east to west and north to south that forgiveness of sins may be obtained through his name (24:47; cf. Acts 2:38; 8:12; 9:15, 21; 10:43; 22:16).

In Acts "name" theology is even more prominent. Joel 2:32 proclaims that everyone who calls on Yahweh's name will be saved, but Acts applies this OT promise to Jesus (2:21; cf. 9:14), showing that he is equal to Yahweh. Indeed, Jesus' name is the only name by which salvation comes (4:12)! Baptism, initiation into the people of God, must take place in Jesus' name (2:38; 8:16; 10:48; 19:5), and apostles heal in his name (3:6, 16; 4:7, 10, 30). The apostles suffered for the sake of Jesus' name (5:41; cf. 9:16; 21:13), and Jesus' name was honored (19:17). Contemporary readers may neglect the significance of name Christology. God's name in the OT reflects his uniqueness, reminding us that he alone is God and Lord. Luke highlights Jesus' stature and dignity by teaching that Jesus shares the same divine name as Yahweh.

Son of Man and Son of God

The titles "Son of Man" and "Son of God" are quite common in the Gospel of Luke. Interestingly, both titles are far more common in Luke's Gospel than in Acts, for in Acts both "Son of Man" and "Son of God" occur only once. However, the title "Son of God" appears six times in Luke. Jesus, as the virgin-conceived child, is the holy one, the Son of God (1:35). The devil

(4:3, 9) and demons (4:41) know that he is the Son of God, but they do not gladly embrace him as such. Jesus' genealogy stems from Joseph to Adam to God, so that he is the Son of God (3:23–38). Jesus never declares himself as the Son of God until just before his death, when he is questioned by the chief priests and scribes (22:66–71). The only place the title "Son of God" occurs in Acts is after Paul's conversion, when he proclaims Jesus as the Son of God (9:20). The title "Son of God" conveys Jesus' unique relationship to God and, as we saw in Matthew and Mark, identifies Jesus as the true Israel and the true Davidic king.

The title "Son of Man" functions in Luke's Gospel in much the same way as it does in Matthew and Mark. As the Son of Man (cf. Dan. 7:13–14), Jesus has the authority to forgive sins (5:24), and he is "lord of the Sabbath" (6:5). Since Jesus is the Son of Man, his glory is obscured from the eyes of human beings, and hence they may revile him (7:34; 9:26; 11:30; 12:10) or his disciples (6:22). He does not enjoy a royal welcome on earth (9:58). The Son of Man has been commissioned to suffer and to die and then to rise from the dead (9:22, 44; 18:31–33; 22:22, 48; 24:7). He dies as the Son of Man for the salvation of lost human beings (19:10). Ultimately, life will be given only to those who confess and acknowledge the Son of Man (12:8; 21:36), for he is coming again in glory and will judge all (12:40; 17:22, 24, 26, 30; 18:8; 21:27; 22:69).

In Acts the Son of Man only appears in 7:56, where he stands at God's right hand when the heavens are opened during Stephen's defense. This likely means that the Son of Man supports Stephen's case by vindicating him before God. The Son of Man fits well with the kingdom theme in Luke-Acts. Just as the kingdom is already present but not yet consummated, so too the Son of Man in Luke-Acts brings in the kingdom through his suffering and his glory. And yet the glory of the Son of Man, just like the glory of the kingdom, is hidden from the world. The kingdom will come in its fullness, and the Son of Man will come in glory.

Jesus' Resurrection

Luke particularly emphasizes the resurrection of Jesus, and the resurrection is not just a bizarre event in history. It attests that Jesus reigns at God's right hand as Lord and Christ (Acts 2:36), and that the new age has dawned.[18] According to Luke's Gospel, Jesus predicted during his ministry that he would be raised after his death (9:22; 18:33; cf. 11:29–30). The truth of the resurrection

18. On the importance of the resurrection in Acts, see A. Thompson, *Acts of the Risen Jesus*, 76–83.

in history is important to Luke. Jesus demonstrated concretely to his disciples that he had conquered death (24:13–48), convincing them that they were not dreaming or hallucinating. Acts confirms that the resurrection of Jesus is no fable; it did not happen "in a corner" (26:26). Many convincing proofs attested to the reality of the resurrection (1:3). The apostles witnessed firsthand that Jesus was risen (3:15; 10:40–41; 13:31), and the resurrection is also verified by the OT Scriptures (2:24–36; 13:32–37).

The disciples in Acts were persecuted, especially by the Sadducees, because of the hope of the resurrection (4:1–3; cf. 5:17). Paul's claim to believe in the resurrection precipitated dissension between the Pharisees and Sadducees at his trial (23:6–10), and Paul was convinced that he was on trial because of his belief in the resurrection (24:15, 21; 26:6–8; 28:20). We have an interesting paradox here. On the one hand, Christ's resurrection indicates that the new age has arrived (cf. Isa. 26:19; Ezek. 37:1–14; Dan. 12:1–3) and that God's saving promises (his kingdom) are being fulfilled. On the other hand, those who belong to Christ are still being persecuted (4:1–22; 5:17–32; 6:8–8:4; 12:1–24; 13:45, 50; 14:1–6, 19; 16:19–24; 17:5–9, 13–14; 18:12–17; 19:23–41; 20:3). The age to come had arrived in Christ, and yet there was an interval before the kingdom was consummated. There was an "already but not yet." Still, Jesus, as the risen and exalted Lord, pours out the Spirit on his disciples (2:33), granting forgiveness and repentance to Israel (5:30–31). The lordship of Jesus is inseparable from his resurrection, for the resurrection functions as the proof and emblem of his lordship, showing that Jesus now reigns over all. He now reigns as Lord and Christ (2:36).

Salvation in Luke-Acts

Jesus' Death

The centrality of salvation in Lukan thought is well recognized.[19] It has often been said that Luke minimizes the atonement, emphasizing instead Jesus' exaltation as Lord.[20] Luke omits the ransom statement found in Mark 10:45, and even in Acts there is no explicit statement connecting Jesus' death with the forgiveness of sins.[21] Certainly, we do not find in Luke the kind of detailed atonement theology that is present in Paul's writings. Nevertheless, scholars have underestimated Luke's theology of the atonement, and I will argue here that it plays a larger role than many have admitted. The Last Supper saying in

19. See Marshall, *Luke*; Green, "'Salvation to the End of the Earth.'"
20. On the significance of atonement in Luke-Acts and for a thorough discussion of the whole matter, see Kimbell, "Atonement in Lukan Theology."
21. On Lukan anthropology, see Stenschke, *Luke's Portrait of Gentiles*.

Luke 22:19–20, almost certainly part of the original text,[22] shows that Jesus' death was atoning: "'This is my body, which is given for you. Do this in remembrance of me.' And likewise the cup after they had eaten, saying, 'This cup that is poured out for you is the new covenant in my blood.'" The Last Supper is a Passover meal,[23] and in the Passover the blood of the lamb was spilled in place of the firstborn in each Israelite house. So too, Jesus gave his body, surrendered his life, to give life to his people. The new covenant resonates with OT themes, including the sacrificial covenant blood that inaugurated the Mosaic covenant (Exod. 24:8), and the new covenant that secures forgiveness of sins (Jer. 31:31–34). Luke here indicates that the pouring out of Jesus' blood provides atonement for the sins of the people. Acts 20:28 also emphasizes the blood of Jesus, for he acquired the church "with his own blood." The shedding of his blood is the means by which the church becomes his possession, and the sacrificial language used here indicates that his blood has an atoning function.

Luke teaches that Jesus is the Isaianic suffering servant who bears the sins of Israel (see Isa. 53). Luke does not cite the clearest verses about the servant's atoning death, and yet the several allusions to Jesus as the servant indicate that he saw Jesus as the servant of the Lord who suffers for the sake of others.[24] In Luke's Gospel when Jesus is baptized, God identifies him as his Son, with whom he is well pleased (3:22), which is a clear allusion to Isa. 42:1, where the ministry of the servant of the Lord is described. And we read in 22:37 that Jesus "was numbered with transgressors," a citation of Isa. 53:12, which also states that the servant "bore the sin of many," thus emphasizing here that Jesus died to secure forgiveness for others. Acts 8:32–35 also quotes Isa. 53:7–8, and Philip interprets the text for the Ethiopian eunuch by pointing him to Jesus. Even though Isa. 53:7–8 does not specifically refer to the atonement, it is legitimate to conclude that the whole of Isa. 53 applies to Jesus. Jesus is identified as God's servant (*pais*) in several texts in Acts (3:13, 26; 4:27, 30). It is quite likely that there is an allusion to the Isaianic servant, for we see in these verses a reference to Jesus' suffering (3:13; 4:27) and his resurrection and glorification (3:13, 26; cf. Isa. 52:13; 53:11–12). In light of what Luke teaches about the servant of the Lord, it is plausible to conclude that Jesus' death as the servant is the basis for forgiveness of sins.

Other strands in Luke-Acts support the atoning nature of Jesus' death. In Luke's Gospel, for instance, Jesus endured the cup that God gave him (22:42). In the OT the "cup" most often refers to the wrath God pours out upon those who have sinned against him (e.g., Pss. 11:6; 75:7–8; Isa. 51:17, 22; Jer. 25:15,

22. J. Petzer, "Luke 22:19b–20"; K. Petzer, "Institution of the Lord's Supper."
23. Köstenberger, "Last Supper."
24. On the servant of the Lord in Luke-Acts, see Strauss, *Davidic Messiah*, 317–33.

17, 28; 49:12; Hab. 2:16–17). Hence, Jesus took upon himself the wrath that sinners deserved so that they would be freed of their sins. The account of Barabbas makes the same theological point. Luke emphasizes, through the words of Pilate, the decision of Herod, and the words of one of those crucified, that Jesus was innocent (23:4, 14, 15, 22). He had "done nothing wrong" (23:41). And yet Barabbas, who was truly guilty, was released, and Jesus died in his place (23:16–25). The point of the story is not that Barabbas believed that Jesus was the Christ. Luke makes a narratival point: the guilty one was counted as innocent because Jesus, the innocent one, took upon himself the death that Barabbas deserved. The repentant thief on the cross probably conveys the same message (23:39–43). He acknowledged that he suffered justly for his sins but asked Jesus to remember him. Jesus' promise that he would be in paradise is most likely based on his suffering on the cross for the thief's sake.

The breaking of the bread in Luke-Acts (Luke 22:19; 24:30, 35; Acts 2:42, 46; 20:7, 11) probably alludes (but cf. Acts 27:35) to Jesus' act of self-sacrifice, where his life was given (broken) for the forgiveness of his people. Luke also emphasizes that Jesus was "hung on a tree" (Acts 5:30; 10:39; 13:29). The term "tree" (*xylon*) is used only five times, whereas the term "cross" (*stauros*) occurs twenty-seven times. Hanging on a tree alludes to Deut. 21:23, where one hung on a tree is cursed by God, and so Luke is suggesting that Jesus absorbed the curse that sinners deserved. Finally, the gospel proclaimed in Acts (see the next section below) links forgiveness of sins with Jesus' death, and though precision is lacking, Luke, given the OT context of wrath and punishment for sin, likely sees Jesus' death and resurrection as the means by which sins are forgiven.

I am not suggesting that Luke's theology of atonement is as clearly explicated as Paul's, but the evidence sketched in above suggests he had a theology of atonement.

The Kerygma

The gospel proclaimed in Acts fits with what we have seen in the Gospels. We see this gospel in Acts particularly in Peter's speeches (2:14–39; 3:12–26; 4:8–12; 5:29–32; 10:37–43) and in Paul's speech in Antioch (13:16–41). The kerygma can be seen as an expansion of Mark 1:14–15: "The time is fulfilled. The kingdom of God is at hand; repent and believe in the gospel."[25] First, the age of fulfillment has dawned. We read in 2:16, "This is what was uttered through the prophet Joel." Or as 3:18 says, "But what God foretold by the mouth of all the prophets . . . he thus fulfilled." Peter goes on to say, "All the prophets who have spoken,

25. See Dodd, "Framework of the Gospel Narrative."

from Samuel and those who came after him, also proclaimed these days" (3:24; cf. 3:25; 13:27–29). Second, the age of fulfillment has been realized in the ministry, death, and resurrection of Jesus in accord with the Scriptures. Jesus is the son of David and the promised Messiah (2:30–31; 13:23). His life and ministry glorified God, for he was "attested to you by God with mighty works and wonders and signs" (2:22). Peter, in speaking to Cornelius and his friends, notes "how God anointed Jesus of Nazareth with the Holy Spirit and with power. He went about doing good and healing all those who were oppressed by the devil, for God was with him" (10:38). Jesus' death was part of God's preordained plan, though those who killed him are held responsible for their evil deed (2:23; 3:13–15; 4:10; 5:30; 10:39; 13:26–29). God vindicated Jesus after he was crucified by raising him from the dead (2:24–32; 3:15; 4:10; 5:30; 10:40; 13:30–37). The resurrection of Jesus is a major theme in Acts, as we have seen, and it is argued that his resurrection fulfills OT prophecies, particularly Ps. 16:9–11.

Third, by virtue of his resurrection Jesus has been exalted to the right hand of God (2:32–36). Jesus is now the exalted "Lord and Christ" (2:36). He is glorified at the right hand of the Father (3:13) and is now the "head of the corner" (4:11). "God exalted him at his right hand as Leader and Savior" (5:31). The kingdom has come, since Jesus reigns as king. Fourth, now that Jesus is exalted as Lord and king, the Spirit is poured out on his disciples (2:17–21, 33; 5:32).

Fifth, the messianic age will reach its consummation in the return of Christ. The first four themes here feature what God has already accomplished in Christ, but believers still await the finale. God's enemies will not be vanquished until God makes Christ's "enemies [his] footstool" (2:35). The "times of refreshing" are still future and will arrive when Jesus comes to restore everything in accordance with prophecy (3:20–21). The new creation will come in its fullness, and final and definitive victory over the serpent and his offspring will be a reality. A day of judgment is coming when Jesus, as "the one appointed by God," will be the "judge of the living and the dead" (10:42; cf. 17:31).

Finally, there is an appeal for repentance, an offer of forgiveness, and a promise that the Holy Spirit will be given to those who receive the promise of salvation by baptism (2:38–39; 3:19, 26; 4:12; 5:31–32; 10:43; 13:38–39).

Repent and Believe

It is appropriate here to say a bit more about faith and repentance because they play a significant role in Luke-Acts and are necessary for salvation.[26] For

---

26. On the close relationship between faith, repentance, baptism, and so forth, see Stein, "Baptism in Luke-Acts"; see also idem, "Baptism and Becoming a Christian."

Luke, they are two sides of the same coin. Paul summarizes his ministry in terms of "testifying both to Jews and to Greeks of repentance toward God and of faith in our Lord Jesus Christ" (Acts 20:21). Luke can describe priests who were saved as those who "became obedient to the faith" (Acts 6:7). And we read in Acts 11:21 that those "who believed turned to the Lord," with the word "turned" here being synonymous with "repented." True belief always leads to repentance, and there is never true repentance that can be separated from belief.

All people everywhere are called upon to repent (Acts 17:30; cf. 14:15; 15:19), indicating that salvation is available for those who have sinned and failed to please God (see also Luke 5:32; 15:7–10). Clearly, repentance is not optional, for it is regularly associated with forgiveness of sins, and hence it follows that those who fail to repent will be judged. The Baptist proclaimed "a baptism of repentance for the forgiveness of sins" (Luke 3:3; cf. Acts 13:24; 19:4). And the apostolic witness after Jesus' resurrection also sees repentance as a condition for forgiveness: "Repent therefore, and turn again, that your sins may be blotted out" (Acts 3:19; cf. Luke 24:47; Acts 2:38; 5:31; 8:22; 26:18). Those who fail to repent are heading for judgment and will perish (Luke 10:13; 13:3, 5; 16:30), but conversely those who repent will find life (Acts 11:18). Repentance is not limited to a mental frame of mind; it embraces the whole person. Believers must "bear fruit in keeping with repentance" (Luke 3:8). Those who repent must perform "deeds in keeping with their repentance" (Acts 26:20). Repentance is proved by the new life that follows repentance (cf. Acts 11:23; 13:43; 14:22). The call to repent fits with Jesus being Lord, for since Jesus is the risen Lord, all people everywhere must repent and put their faith in him in order to be saved.

The necessity of faith is communicated in the Gospel of Luke. Jesus declares to a sinful woman, whose tears dripped on his feet and who wiped his feet with her hair and anointed them with perfume, that her sins were forgiven (7:36–50). The story concludes with Jesus saying to her, "Your faith has saved you; go in peace" (7:50). The woman was saved and forgiven of her sins, not because of her virtuous life, but because she trusted in Jesus and God.[27] "Your faith has saved you" is a repeated refrain in Luke's Gospel, being declared to the woman saved from her hemorrhage (8:48), to the Samaritan who returned to give thanks for being cleansed from leprosy (17:19), and to the blind man who followed Jesus as he traveled to Jerusalem to die (18:42). Some have understood Jesus in literal terms, as if he were only speaking of physical healing.

27. Lack of space precludes further comment here, but I think that there is evidence that her trust was not only in God but also in Jesus.

The ESV follows this interpretation by rendering the phrase as "your faith has made you well." It is far more likely, however, that the saying is polyvalent, referring both to physical healing and spiritual salvation, and the former is the emblem of the latter. Luke has prepared us for this, for the paralytic's healing signifies that he has been forgiven of his sins (5:17–26; cf. Ps. 103:3). And the first use of the phrase "your faith has saved you" (7:50) clearly refers to the salvation that saves from sin, suggesting that the subsequent references have to do with more (though not less) than physical healing. And there are hints that the phrase designates more than physical healing in two of the other instances as well. All ten lepers were cleansed, but only the Samaritan returned to thank and glorify God, showing that he was distinct from the rest, that a spiritual work occurred in him that was lacking in the other nine who were healed physically (17:11–19). Similarly, when the blind man's sight was restored, he followed Jesus and gave glory to God (18:43). Clearly, he was not only saved from physical blindness, spiritual sight was also granted to him so that he followed Jesus.

The inseparable connection between faith and salvation is evident in the parable of the four soils. Those who do not believe in the word proclaimed are not saved (8:12). Indeed, only persevering faith truly saves. Those who "believe for a while" and then "fall away" when difficult times come are not saved (8:13). Temporary faith is not saving faith; only a faith that endures through the difficulties of life is genuinely saving. Jesus' words to Jairus when he feared for his daughter's life sum up well Luke's message to his readers: "Do not fear; only believe" (8:50). Even though the story of the tax collector and the Pharisee does not use the words "faith" or "believe," the emphasis on God's grace given to the undeserving is clear in the story (18:9–14). The justified one is the one who confesses that he is unworthy, who does not brag about what he has done for God but instead implores God for mercy. Faith looks to God for help and salvation, recognizing that Jesus is a physician who came to heal those who are sick with sin (5:31). The parables in chapter 15 also make the same point, especially the parable of the prodigal son (15:11–32). He is "found" and "alive" again (15:32) because he trusted in the mercy of his father. He did not come to the father arrogantly, claiming to have fulfilled what the father commanded. He came humbly and with brokenness, asking the father for mercy. The older brother in the prodigal son parable was outside the circle of the family, just like the Pharisee in 18:9–14, because he claimed to be good, because he was filled with self-righteous haughtiness.

The book of Acts repeatedly teaches that one must believe to be saved. Paul said to the Philippian jailer, "Believe in the Lord Jesus, and you will be saved, you and your household" (16:31). Christians often are designated as "believers" or as those who have "believed" (e.g., 2:44; 4:4, 32; 5:14; 8:12; 9:42; 10:45; 14:1, 23; 15:5; 16:1; 17:12, 34; 18:8; 19:18; 21:20, 25; 22:19). The hearts of unbelievers are "cleansed . . . by faith" (15:9). Paul exhorted Felix and Drusilla to put their "faith in Christ Jesus" (24:24; cf. 26:18) for salvation. Those who believe receive forgiveness of sins (10:43). It is recognized that justification cannot come via the law (13:38), for no one can keep the law and gain salvation thereby (15:10), and hence salvation is by grace (15:11).

The emphasis on persevering in faith that is present in Luke's Gospel we also see in Acts. Just as repentance is borne out by fruit that accompanies it, so genuine faith is not temporary. It perseveres through the stresses and difficulties of life, for the kingdom is only entered through many troubles (14:22). Ultimately, faith is a gift of God. God "opened a door of faith to the Gentiles" (14:27). Those whom he "appointed to eternal life believed" (13:48). First comes God's appointment and ordination, and as a consequence or result belief follows. This fits with the observation that people believed "through grace" (18:27). Those who know the Son are blessed beyond description, for the Son has chosen to reveal the Father to them (Luke 10:22–23).

Discipleship

Here I am using a separate category for discipleship, but this should not be misconstrued, for all those who repent and believe are also disciples. In other words, if one does not become and remain a disciple of Jesus, then one will not be saved. However, a separate category is warranted because Luke says much about discipleship, and so obviously it is important in his thinking. Those who are disciples live under Jesus' lordship and submit to his rule in their lives.

One of the central themes of Luke-Acts is captured in Luke 19:10: "For the Son of Man came to seek and to save the lost." This declaration concludes the story of Zacchaeus (19:1–9), who, as a tax collector, was a collaborator with the Romans and also skimmed money off the top for himself. Zacchaeus was one of the lost whom Jesus came to save, and he was rescued from sin, not because of the good he had done, but because of the mercy of God. But that is not the whole story. Zacchaeus also followed Jesus in discipleship. He repented of his sins, demonstrating his repentance by repaying those whom he cheated and by giving half his money to the poor.

Those who follow Jesus must be utterly and totally committed to him. They leave the comfort of hearth and home for his sake (9:57–58). Family must no longer be first in their lives; the kingdom of God must be their foremost passion (9:59–62). Jesus' call is shocking: "If anyone comes to me and does not hate his own father and mother and wife and children and brothers and sisters, yes, and even his own life, he cannot be my disciple. Whoever does not bear his own cross and come after me cannot be my disciple" (14:26–27). He demands supremacy in the lives of those who claim to be his followers. They must count the cost realistically before deciding to follow him (14:28–32).[28] They must renounce everything in order to be his disciples (14:33). The rich ruler functions as an example (18:18–30). He thought of himself as a man who kept the commandments, but Jesus directed him to sell all his possessions in order to obtain eternal life. A careful reading of the story reveals that eternal life (18:18), treasure in heaven (18:22), entering the kingdom (18:25), and being saved (18:26) refer to the same reality. The rich ruler disclosed that he worshiped another god, that he coveted his riches, for he could not part with his wealth and follow Jesus.[29] Since he was unwilling to be a disciple, he was unsaved. He needed the "impossible" work, which is possible only with God, to become a disciple of Jesus (18:27). Apparently, this "impossible" work had taken place in Peter and the other disciples, for they left everything for the sake of the kingdom (18:28–30).

In the ancient world women were considered second-class citizens and often were scorned, but Jesus saw them as persons with dignity and worth. It has often been noted that Luke has a particular interest in women, and many women function as examples of disciples. For instance, Mary the mother of Jesus submitted herself as the Lord's servant to God's word (1:38). Elizabeth, along with her husband, Zechariah, was blameless (not sinless) in her obedience (1:6). Anna devoted herself to the Lord from a young age (2:36–38). Mary the sister of Martha and Lazarus demonstrated that she was a disciple by listening intently to the Lord's teaching (10:38–42). Luke mentions a number of women who traveled with Jesus and supported his ministry financially (8:1–3). Other examples are Philip's daughters, who functioned as prophets (Acts 21:9), and Priscilla, who, along with her husband, instructed Apollos (Acts 18:26).

Jesus' passion predictions function much like they do in Mark's Gospel. In Luke's Gospel Jesus predicts his passion (9:21–22) and follows this with instruction on discipleship (9:23–26). Disciples must deny themselves and follow Jesus and lose their lives for his sake. If they give up their lives, they will gain them in the new world that is coming. When Jesus announces a second time that he will be handed over to others, the disciples remain baffled (9:44–45). And they certainly do not understand what it means to be a disciple of Jesus, for they dispute which one of them is the greatest and exclude those

---

28. See Schlatter, *History of the Christ*, 106.

29. Schlatter remarks, "What Jesus had against the rich . . . was that they slid into complete dependence on their wealth" (ibid., 166).

who are colaborers with them (9:46–50), and they want to call fire down on their enemies (9:51–56).

Disciples must beware of hypocrisy (11:37–52) and must fear God more than what other people think of them (12:1–12), for everyone who denies the Son of Man because of fear of others will be denied by him on the last day. Disciples must be faithful servants, obediently doing the will of the master, lest they suffer punishment instead of reward when he returns (12:35–48; cf. 19:11–27). The judgment will come as in the days of Noah and in the days of Lot, and so disciples must be ready (17:20–37) and be willing to lose their lives in order to keep them on the last day (17:33). When the stresses and strains of life seem unbearable, disciples must not confess a false Christ (21:7–11); rather, they must be ready to suffer and die for the sake of the Christ (21:12–19). Hence, they must always be on the alert (21:34–36). The long period of time before Jesus returns, at least from a human perspective, may cause them to deny the faith (18:1–8). They must faithfully persevere in faith and prayer, confident of final vindication. They must "strive to enter through the narrow door" (13:24), for this is the only pathway to enter the kingdom (13:22–30). Many will be in anguish because they failed to respond to the summons when it came. People say that they want to be part of the end-time kingdom feast, but actually other things interest them much more, and so they decline to come (14:15–24).

Jesus came to proclaim the gospel to the poor (4:18), which refers to those who are materially and spiritually poor. True disciples, according to Luke, do not set their affections on the riches of this world. The kingdom will come in its fullness, so that those who are poor in the present age will be rich on the last day, and vice versa (1:53; 6:20–26). How foolish it is to grasp after riches in the present age and forget the age to come. The parable of the rich man and Lazarus illustrates this truth (16:19–31). The rich man, during his earthly life, lavishly enjoyed the good things of this world, paying no heed to Lazarus, who suffered in his poverty. But at the end things will be reversed. Lazarus finds blessing, joy, and comfort in Abraham's presence, and the rich man is tortured for his evil. Those who seek the kingdom show concrete and practical concern for the poor (14:12–14). The rich may forget about the kingdom, building bigger barns and calculating their investments, thinking that they will enjoy a long retirement, where they can relax and enjoy the good things of life (12:15–21). Unfortunately, they have forgotten about the kingdom and are "not rich toward God" (12:21). Actually, they are fools, for they live as if this world is the final reality, when in fact death is at hand (12:20).

How dangerous riches are because they can choke out the word of the kingdom (8:14). Human beings can become consumed with the necessities of everyday life so that they worry and fret instead of trusting in their Father, who knows what they need (12:22–30). Disciples will be freed from anxiety over things when they believe that their Father loves them, and that it is his "good pleasure to give them the kingdom" (12:32). They must seek the kingdom above all else (12:31), surrender any claim to their possessions (12:33), and make God their treasure and joy instead of the things of this world (12:34). The rich ruler was excluded from the kingdom (18:18–30) because his wealth had become his god and his treasure. He could not surrender it and follow Jesus, for he found his security, significance, and joy in what he owned. One of the reasons the Pharisees rejected the message of Jesus is that they loved money (16:14–15). Even the temple had become a place of financial impropriety (19:45–46).

Peter and the other disciples demonstrated that the kingdom was their treasure because they left everything to follow Jesus (18:28–30), just as the poor widow gave up everything she owned for God's sake (21:1–4). Luke is not formulaic. He does not teach that everyone must sell all possessions in order to be disciples. According to the Baptist, the work of the kingdom is evident in those who share an extra garment with others (3:11). Tax collectors demonstrate their new life by being just and honest instead of cheating their payers (3:12–13), and soldiers must desist from taking the wages of others (3:14). When salvation reached Zacchaeus, he did not give up everything he owned; instead, he gave half of his wealth to the poor and repaid those he cheated (19:1–10). In Acts John Mark's mother apparently had a large enough house for the church to meet in (12:12). She did not sell her house, but rather she used her wealth for the sake of the kingdom. Ananias and Sapphira were struck dead by God not because they were required to sell everything that they owned but because of their hypocrisy and dishonesty (5:1–11). Peter specifically says that their possessions were their own, and they were free to do with them whatever they wished (5:4). Those who live for the kingdom, however, are remarkably generous, like Barnabas, who sold a field and gave the money to help fellow believers (4:36–37). Early believers did not practice an enforced communism, but neither did they consider their money to be their own, and so they freely gave of what they owned to assist others, so that no one was lacking the necessities of life (2:44–45; 4:32–35). Hence, when there was a famine in Jerusalem, believers in Antioch rushed in to assist (11:28–30), and when the Hellenistic widows were not being cared for with provisions of food, the apostles saw to it that the problem was remedied (6:1–6). Those who were godly gave alms (10:2). True disciples know and experience that, as Jesus said, "it is more blessed to give than to receive" (20:35).

Conclusion

Salvation in Luke-Acts is obtained through Jesus' death and resurrection and is a gift of his grace. Those who believe and repent are saved. They are members of the kingdom of God. But Luke stresses that those who are truly part of the kingdom are Jesus' disciples. They live a new life under his lordship. They give their lives over to their Lord and serve him instead of following their own desires. Their riches and all that they have belong to their master.

The Spirit and the Kingdom and Acts

In Luke's Gospel Jesus is the one anointed with the Spirit. The kingdom has come with Jesus and in his person because he is specially endowed with the Spirit. What we see in Acts is the pouring out of the Spirit through Jesus (2:33). The one who was the bearer of the Spirit in Luke's Gospel now becomes the one through whom the Spirit is poured out in Acts. In other words, the kingdom now expands; it reaches the ends of the earth through the work of the Spirit.

In the book of Acts the role of the Holy Spirit in mission is particularly highlighted. The theme of Acts is set forth in 1:8: "But you will receive power when the Holy Spirit has come upon you, and you will be my witnesses in Jerusalem and in all Judea and Samaria, and to the end of the earth." The Holy Spirit will empower the disciples to testify to the gospel of Christ throughout the world, and hence their witness is the means by which the kingdom will reach the entire world, fulfilling the promise to Abraham and the prophecies in the prophetic books and the psalms.[30]

In Acts we see the outward thrust of the gospel and the Holy Spirit's impetus in Philip's encounter with the Ethiopian eunuch, for the Spirit prompted Philip to approach the chariot of the Ethiopian and to speak to him (8:29). Similarly, the Spirit carried Philip away to Azotus so that he could preach the gospel in the area around Caesarea (8:39–40). Peter first brought the gospel to the Gentiles when he preached to Cornelius and his friends. It was the Spirit who spoke to Peter, confirming that he should go to Cornelius and proclaim the gospel to him and his cohorts (10:19; 11:12).

We have seen a pattern whereby the Spirit propels people to proclaim the gospel to those outside the circle of the Jewish community, beginning with the Ethiopian eunuch and then on to the Gentiles. But an even more significant development commenced in Acts 13. Paul and Barnabas launched an intentional mission to bring the gospel to Gentiles. It was the Holy Spirit who

30. See Hahn, *Kinship by Covenant*, 231.

spoke to them while they were worshiping the Lord, instructing the church to "set apart" Paul and Barnabas for the mission to the Gentiles (13:2). The first designed mission to the Gentiles had its impetus from the Spirit, so that Luke can say that they were "sent out by the Holy Spirit" (13:4). The Spirit confirmed that Gentiles could belong to the people of God without being circumcised (15:28–29), testifying that the spread of the gospel apart from the law was God's will. Sometimes the Spirit guided messengers not to go to a certain area (16:6–7), showing again that the Spirit was steering the church in its mission.

I noted above that the kingdom of God functions as an inclusio in Acts because it is the subject of both Jesus' teaching (1:3) and Paul's preaching (28:31). We also saw in the Gospel of Luke that the Spirit is linked with the spread of the kingdom. So there are good reasons in Acts to conclude that the spread of the kingdom, the expansion of the gospel, is due to the work of the Spirit. In Acts Luke particularly emphasizes that those who are filled with the Spirit speak the word of the Lord (2:4; 4:8, 31; 9:17; 13:9). Jesus' disciples, through the power of the Holy Spirit, proclaim the gospel; that is, they proclaim, as Paul says in 28:31, the kingdom of God in teaching about Jesus Christ. Hence, the conversion of three thousand people in chapter 2 represents the restoration of Israel under Jesus as the exalted and reigning Davidic Messiah, fulfilling OT promises that the people of God would be united under a Davidic king.[31] The gathering in chapter 2 of Jews "from every nation under heaven" (2:5) signifies that the restoration prophesied in Ezek. 37 was becoming a reality.[32]

The Spirit also provides indisputable evidence that one belongs to the people of God. Luke focuses on four main events in Acts with reference to the Holy Spirit: Pentecost (2:1–41), the ministry to the Samaritans (8:4–25), the gospel going to Cornelius (10:1–11:18), and Paul's ministry to the Ephesian twelve (19:1–7). Various terms are used for the granting of the Spirit for these four events: (1) "receiving" (*lambanō*) the Spirit (Pentecost [1:8; 2:33, 38]; Samaria [8:15, 17, 19]; Cornelius [10:47]; Ephesian twelve [19:2]); (2) "pouring out" (*ekcheō, ekchynnō*) of the Spirit (Pentecost [2:17, 18, 33]; Cornelius [10:45]); (3) "giving" (*didōmi*) of the Spirit (Samaria [8:18]; Cornelius [11:17; 15:8]); (4) the Spirit "coming," "coming upon" (*erchomai, eperchomai*) (Pentecost [1:8]; Ephesian twelve [19:6]); (5) the Spirit "falling upon" (*epipiptō*) (Cornelius [10:44; 11:15]); (6) being "baptized" (*baptizō*) with the Spirit (Pentecost [1:5]; Cornelius [11:16]); and (7) being "filled" (*pimplēmi*) with the Spirit

31. So ibid., 232–33.
32. So A. Thompson, *Acts of the Risen Jesus*, 109–12.

(Pentecost [2:4]). The main point in every instance is the role of the Spirit in the extension of the kingdom. The day of Pentecost represents a reversal of the tower of Babel (see Gen. 11:1–9),[33] but it also signals an advance in redemptive history. Jesus is now exalted as Lord and Christ (2:36) and thus pours out the Spirit in fulfillment of the eschatological promises (cf. Isa. 32:15; 44:3; Ezek. 36:26–27; 37:14; Joel 2:28). In Exod. 23:16 Pentecost is the feast of "firstfruits," while Tabernacles is the feast of "ingathering." Hence, the gift of Pentecost signifies that the new age has begun (it is the firstfruits), though it is not yet consummated. The consummation will come on the day of ingathering (the return of Jesus). Pentecost reveals that Jesus was not only the bearer of the Spirit but also the one who pours out the Spirit.

The giving of the Spirit in Samaria signals the unification of the people of God. Perhaps Luke sees here a fulfillment of Ezek. 37:15–22, where Judah and Israel are reunified because God has granted his Spirit (Ezek. 37:14).[34] Ezekiel foresees a day when the new David arrives (37:24), and Israel is restored from exile (37:21). All of these promises are fulfilled in Christ, for he is the new David, he pours out his Spirit, the return from exile has arrived in forgiveness of sins, and Israel is now restored as a people under the lordship of Jesus.

The coming of the Spirit upon Cornelius and his friends is the first clear example of the inclusion of Gentiles into the people of God. The reception of the Spirit signals that the Gentiles truly belonged to the Lord, that they were equal members in the people of God. The inclusion of the Gentiles fulfills OT expectations (cf. Gen. 12:3; 18:18; 22:18; 26:4; Pss. 22:27; 47:1, 9; 67:1–7; 72:17; 96:1–3; Isa. 2:1–4; 19:16–25; 45:22–25; 49:6–7; 52:15; 55:3–5; 66:18–19; Amos 9:11–12; Zeph. 3:9–10). The age of promise had arrived, for the good news was extending to the farthest reaches of the world in fulfillment of the promise to the patriarchs. The Spirit also was given to the Ephesian twelve, who previously were disciples of John the Baptist. The eschatological kingdom focus of the gift is evident once again. The Baptist, despite his many gifts, lived in the age before the fulfillment of the promise. Hence, Paul asks if the twelve have received the Spirit (19:2). Paul wanted to know whether they lived in the age of fulfillment or the age of promise. The granting of the Spirit through Jesus' name shows Jesus' superiority over the Baptist. The Baptist lived in the era of hope and anticipation, but the giving of the Spirit demonstrates that kingdom promises were available through Jesus the Christ. The theme of Jesus' superiority over the Baptist picks up themes from Luke 1, where Jesus' conception (by a virgin) was better than John's (to an old, barren couple), and

---

33. See Beale, *Church's Mission*, 202–3.
34. See A. Thompson, *Acts of the Risen Jesus*, 112–16.

Jesus' birth accompanied by angels shone brighter than John's (accompanied by the restoration of Zechariah's ability to speak).

To sum up, the Spirit is the gift of the risen Christ to the church, showing that God's kingdom had arrived, and that the end-time promises were being realized. The gift of the Spirit represents the fulfillment of God's promises to Israel. Indeed, the gift of the Spirit to the Samaritans represents the fulfillment of the promise of the restoration of Israel in Ezek. 37. But the new era involved more than the restoration of Israel. The message of the kingdom via the power of the Spirit was reaching to the ends of the earth, and Gentiles were included in this saving message. The promises of universal blessing given to Abraham and confirmed in the prophets and the psalms were becoming a reality through the power of the Holy Spirit.

Prayer and the Kingdom

Prayer in Luke-Acts is not merely an act of private piety; it is forged with the coming of the kingdom, the fulfillment of God's saving promises. In Luke's Gospel this is evident in the prayers of both Zechariah and Anna (1:13; 2:37). Anna's prayers focused on "waiting for the redemption of Jerusalem" (2:38). Along the same lines, Jesus was baptized while praying (3:21), when he was anointed by the Spirit for ministry. Indeed, Jesus departed from crowds to pray, for he knew his ministry depended on God's power (5:16). The disciples were called by Jesus to proclaim the kingdom of God, and so they were vital to his mission. Hence, it is not surprising that Jesus spent a whole night praying before selecting them (6:12). In all these examples prayer is an engine for ministry, for the advance of the kingdom, and is not confined to private piety.

No one perceives the nature of the kingdom without understanding Jesus' identity, nor can anyone understand who Jesus is on the basis of his or her own wisdom; hence, Jesus is praying when he asks the disciples who he is (9:18). Similarly, he is praying when he is transfigured (9:28), presumably so that the disciples would understand that they were catching a glimpse of the kingdom of God in his person (9:27). Disciples are to pray for the coming of the kingdom (11:2) and for strength and faith to persist until the end (11:4; 18:1–8; 21:36; 22:40, 46), for the Father is eager to answer the prayers of those who seek him (11:5–13).

In Acts the disciples pray for the coming of the kingdom, for the coming of the Spirit with power (1:12–14). Such prayers were geared, then, to the spread of the gospel to the ends of the earth, so that the worldwide blessing promised in the OT would be realized. The disciples also pray that they will select the right person (the twelfth apostle) for the ministry of the kingdom (1:24–25) and pray boldly for courage to proclaim the word in the midst of opposition (4:23–31). There was a keen recognition that their courage would last and the word would spread only if God strengthened them, and hence the members of the early church devoted themselves to prayer (2:42).

Prayer recognizes complete dependence upon God, and thus the apostles, as the leaders of the church, were to devote themselves particularly to prayer (6:4; cf. 6:6; 9:40). Peter and John prayed that the Samaritans might receive the Spirit (8:15), which would advance the kingdom. Saul was praying when Ananias entered and healed him, so that he would be set free for ministry (9:11). And prayer was offered before Cornelius and his friends received the Spirit (10:2, 4, 30–31). In the case of Cornelius we see the first example of Gentiles being folded into the people of God. Paul and Barnabas were called to the first intentional mission to Gentiles when they were fasting and praying (13:2–4). And churches were established and secured through prayer (14:23). Clearly, in Luke-Acts there is a close connection between the advance of the kingdom and prayer. The kingdom does not arrive through human invention or contrivance; it is a stunning and miraculous work of God, and the prayer of the early church signaled absolute dependence upon him. Furthermore, prayer played a significant role in key turning points (e.g., Pentecost, the inclusion of the Samaritans and Gentiles) in the mission of the church.

Mission and the Kingdom

The missional character of Luke-Acts has been evident throughout the previous discussion, but here I will comment briefly on this matter because the spread of the gospel to the ends of the earth is central to Luke-Acts. More specifically, the inclusion of Gentiles in Luke-Acts will be featured, for in this way the promise of worldwide blessing made to Abraham is fulfilled. Acts, of course, features prominently the mission to Gentiles and their being folded into the people of God. But the Gospel of Luke also anticipates the inclusion of Gentiles, for in the birth narrative the angel promises that the good news through Christ "will be for all the people" (2:10). When we consider Luke-Acts as a whole, with its emphasis on the folding in of the Gentiles, we are right to conclude that Gentiles are also in view here. This fits with the words of Simeon in Luke's Gospel when he speaks of salvation "prepared in the presence of all peoples" (2:31). Jesus is "a light of revelation to the Gentiles" (2:32), which alludes to Isa. 42:6; 49:6, where it predicted that the servant of the Lord will be a light for the nations.

The blessing will come to the Gentiles only through Jesus' suffering as the servant on the cross, which is another indication that the different strands of Lukan thought cannot ultimately be separated from one another. Luke's Gospel cites Isa. 40:3–5, seeing in the Baptist's ministry preparation for the Messiah's entrance into Israel (3:4–6). Included here is the statement that "all flesh shall see the salvation of God" (3:6). Given the universal dimensions of Lukan thought, "all flesh" cannot be restricted to Israel. If Gentiles are in Luke's purview here, we see another indication that the various Lukan themes are stitched tightly together, for on this reading Gentiles are within the circle of those restored from exile. And restoration from exile is another way of talking about the coming of the kingdom.

It is often acknowledged that Luke 4:16–30 is programmatic for all of Luke-Acts, foreshadowing many of the central themes in both volumes. Here Jesus emphasizes that Elijah ministered to a woman of Zarephath in Sidon, and Elisha healed Naaman the Syrian of leprosy (4:26–27). What is remarkable is that both of these persons were Gentiles, forecasting the Gentile mission that is so prominent in Acts. The book of Acts is anticipated in another way, for the Jews become angry with Jesus for emphasizing the inclusion of the Gentiles while they themselves are excluded (4:28–29). This pattern is replicated in Acts a number of times where the Jews are angry about the inclusion of the Gentiles (13:45–51; 14:1–5, 19; 17:5–9, 13–14; 18:4–8, 12–17; 19:8–9; 20:3; 22:17–24; 23:12–31; 25:2–3; 28:17–28).[35] In Luke's Gospel the faith of the centurion also forecasts what we see in Acts, for his faith is more remarkable than anything Jesus saw in Israel (7:1–10). Perhaps Gentiles are also in view in the parable of the tenants in the reference to giving the vineyard to others (20:16), though it is difficult to be sure. The Gospel of Luke ends much like Acts begins, for Jesus says that "repentance and forgiveness of sins should be proclaimed in his name to all nations, beginning from Jerusalem" (24:47). Luke picks up from Isaiah and Micah that the word of the Lord would go out from all nations to Jerusalem (Isa. 2:2–4; Mic. 4:1–2). Acts 1:8 resumes this same theme, for the disciples are to be Jesus' witnesses beginning in Jerusalem to the very ends of the earth. The notion that salvation reaches the ends of the earth stands as a fulfillment of Isa. 49:6, which predicts the Gentile mission.

The proclamation of the gospel to the ends of the earth is doubtless one of the central themes of Acts. The pouring out of the Spirit "on all flesh" (2:17) includes Gentiles along with Jews, particularly since the remainder of Acts

35. In NT scholarship the anger of the Jews and the inclusion of the Gentiles are occasionally put forth as evidence of Luke's anti-Semitism. It is not my purpose to engage in apologetics here, but I maintain that such claims are unconvincing.

indicates that the Spirit is given not only to believing Jews but also to Gentiles who believed that Jesus is the Christ. Peter emphasizes in his speech in chapter 3 the special role of the Jews in salvation history: they are the children of the covenant, and God sent the message of salvation to them first (3:24–26). The prophecies made in the OT are being fulfilled. But these prophecies included the Gentiles. Peter cites the promise made to Abraham, "And in your offspring shall all the families of the earth be blessed" (3:25; cf. Gen. 12:3). From the very beginning the promise made to Abraham was not restricted to Israel; it was intended to bring blessing to the whole world.

In Acts the first significant movement toward the Gentile mission (the encounter with Stephen [6:8–8:4]) demonstrates the sovereignty of the Lord in the extension of the gospel throughout the world. Luke does not criticize the apostles or the church for failing to bring the gospel to the Gentiles. On the contrary, he emphasizes the Lord's sovereignty in using circumstances and opening doors for the Gentile mission. Stephen was charged for sitting loose to the law and the temple. He defended himself by appealing to the progress of redemptive history, for it is evident that the Lord often worked outside the temple and the land of Israel. Furthermore, Stephen saw a pattern of rebellion in Israel's history, such that they invariably failed to discern God's messengers from Joseph to Moses to Jesus. Stephen's words precipitated such rage in his opponents that they stoned him to death. As a result, persecution broke out and scattered the church, but such persecution led to the spreading of the gospel outside Jerusalem (8:4), so that Philip preached the gospel in both Samaria (8:4–25) and to the Ethiopian eunuch (8:26–40). In both instances the gospel transcended Jewish boundaries.

The cultural breach between Jews and Samaritans rendered them suspect in Jewish eyes, and eunuchs were considered unfit for the Lord's assembly (see Deut. 23:1), though their inclusion in Acts fulfills Isa. 56:3–7.[36] The conversion of Paul is rehearsed three times in Acts (chaps. 9; 22; 26). It is not my purpose here to explore the differences between the accounts. The crucial, unifying theme is that Paul was called as an apostle particularly to bring the gospel to the Gentiles (9:15; 22:17–21; 26:17–18). The reason why Paul occupies so much space in Acts is not primarily because Luke had a biographical interest in his story, but because he played a significant role in the gospel going forth to the Gentiles.

The Cornelius event plays a pivotal role in the Acts narrative (10:1–11:18). Here is the first clear example of the gospel extending to the Gentiles. The narrative underscores the role of divine sovereignty. Peter had no thought or

36. See esp. A. Thompson, *Acts of the Risen Jesus*, 116–18.

inclination of going to Caesarea to proclaim the good news to Gentiles. Events transpired that virtually compelled him to visit Cornelius and his friends. An angel appeared to Cornelius in Caesarea, telling him to summon Peter, who was in Joppa. As messengers from Cornelius were approaching, Peter had a vision in which he was commanded by God to eat unclean animals (contrary to Lev. 11; Deut. 14). While Peter was reflecting on the import of the vision, messengers from Cornelius arrived at the house of Simon the tanner, where Peter was staying. The Spirit instructed Peter to go with them. Upon arriving, Peter proclaimed the gospel of Christ, but he did not invite the hearers to repent and believe. Nevertheless, the Holy Spirit fell upon the Gentiles present, and they spoke in tongues. Peter and his friends were astonished, concluding that God had given to the Gentiles the same gift they themselves had received at Pentecost, and so the Gentiles were baptized as converts to Christ. Peter rightly emphasizes that God gave the Gentiles eternal life, and those hearing the news in Jerusalem "glorified God, saying, 'Then to the Gentiles also God has granted repentance that leads to life'" (11:18).

Another notable feature of the Cornelius story is the evident salvation-historical shift with reference to the OT law. Clearly, the purity and food requirements of the OT were no longer required for disciples of Jesus Christ. The laws separating Jews from Gentiles were falling aside. Now there is one people of God, centered on Jesus Christ instead of being built around the Torah. The decisive issue was whether one believed in Jesus Christ and repented of one's sins.

The rest of Acts is devoted to the Pauline mission. We see the first conscious mission to the Gentiles in chapters 13–14 as Paul and Barnabas traveled to Cyprus, Pisidian Antioch, Iconium, Lystra, and Derbe. In the midst of significant opposition many believed, particularly among the Gentiles. Paul never abandoned his mission to the Jews, but he turned again and again to the Gentiles, especially when the Jews rejected the gospel. Luke again attributed salvation to the sovereign work of God (13:48). When Luke sums up the trip, he says that God "opened a door of faith to the Gentiles" (14:27).

The success of the Gentile mission provoked what was perhaps the most significant controversy in the NT era. Some Jewish Christians insisted that Gentiles must be circumcised in order to belong to the people of God (15:1, 5). If circumcision were required, the church of Jesus Christ would be fundamentally Jewish in that it would be required to observe the OT law. The people of God would be centered on Torah instead of Christ. Paul had already taught that justification and forgiveness did not come via obedience to the law (13:38–39), and Peter sided with Paul and Barnabas, arguing that the Cornelius event demonstrated that the Holy Spirit is given by faith apart from the law

(15:7–9). No one is able to keep the OT law sufficiently to obtain salvation, and hence salvation is by grace (15:10–11). James concurred with Peter, and the church as a whole also agreed that circumcision would not be required for salvation (15:13–29). The church and the apostles formally ratified what was anticipated in the salvation of Cornelius and his friends. The OT law was not required for salvation. With the fulfillment of God's promises and the coming of the kingdom, the era of the Mosaic covenant was no longer in force. It was now the time of the new creation and the new covenant, and so the regulations of the Sinai covenant were no longer the charter for the people of God. The church has not replaced Israel, but "it is that portion of Israel that has repented and believed in Jesus as the Messiah."[37] The Davidic kingdom has been restored, and believing Gentiles are included in the people of God.[38]

The remainder of Acts relates the story of Paul as he brought the gospel to various locales, particularly to what is now called "Europe." Paul's travels and trials brought him before governors, kings, and perhaps even the emperor (in fulfillment of 9:15–16). Ultimately, Paul landed in Rome and proclaimed the gospel there (chap. 28). Rome scarcely represents the ends of the earth. Luke is not suggesting that the mission is completed. He was well aware of geographic locales to which the gospel had not yet reached. The gospel going to Rome signified, however, the remarkable progress of the gospel, showing that the promise of 1:8 was on the way to being fulfilled. After all, the gospel had reached the Roman capital through an apostle. Acts appropriately concludes by emphasizing Paul's bold proclamation of the kingdom (28:31).

Conclusion

The coming of the kingdom surely is central in Luke-Acts. Luke shares many themes with Matthew and Mark, emphasizing that the kingdom has come with the arrival of the king. Jesus, according to Luke, is the Messiah, the Son of Man, the Son of God, the final prophet, and the Lord of all. The kingdom has arrived in and through him, in his miracles, healings, and exorcisms. The resurrection of Jesus shows that the kingdom has dawned, that the new age has begun in fulfillment of Isa. 26; Ezek. 37; Dan. 12. Jesus now reigns as the resurrected Lord in heaven, seated at the right hand of God.

37. Matera, *New Testament Theology*, 75. Matera rejects the idea that the church is the new Israel (p. 81), but identifying the church as the new Israel is acceptable if it is understood not as a replacement of Israel but rather as a restored Israel composed of both Jews and Gentiles. Furthermore, the new Israel is the "new man" (Eph. 2:15) in Christ (see Gentry and Wellum, *Kingdom through Covenant*, 689–90).

38. See Hahn, *Kinship by Covenant*, 234.

Although some think that Luke has no theology of atonement, a careful reading shows that the atonement is foundational to his thinking. Only those who repent and believe enter the kingdom, for believers put their trust in Jesus the Christ, who atoned for their sins in his cross and resurrection. Luke fills out what it means to believe, for true believers are disciples of Christ. Their riches and every part of their lives are given to Jesus Christ. Luke does not teach that disciples are perfect, but he certainly teaches that they are transformed, and that they submit to the lordship, to the kingship, of Jesus.

Luke also particularly emphasizes the resurrection and the gift of the Spirit. Jesus is the one anointed and empowered by the Spirit in his ministry. The kingdom advances through his Spirit-endowed ministry while he is on earth. As the resurrected and exalted Lord, he pours out his Spirit upon his followers. Both the resurrection and the granting of the Spirit indicate that the new age has arrived. In Christ the new covenant, the new exodus, and the new creation have come, but this is just another way of saying that the kingdom has come. There is no idea here of the kingdom being consummated. The day of judgment and final salvation has not yet arrived. The kingdom is already present but not yet completed.

The Spirit is poured out on the disciples especially for the sake of mission. The church is strengthened by the Holy Spirit to bring the message of Jesus, the kerygma, to the ends of the earth. Both the Spirit and prayer in Luke-Acts are intimately tied to the advance of the kingdom, to the proclamation of the gospel to the ends of the earth, fulfilling the promises made to Abraham and the prophets of worldwide blessing. Of course, the promises found in David and the prophets are fulfilled as well, for they both emphasize that universal peace will be attained through a Davidic heir, through a Davidic king.

INTERLUDE

A Synopsis of
THE KINGDOM IN MATTHEW, MARK, AND LUKE-ACTS

The Synoptic Gospels and the book of Acts, despite all their diversity, have
something in common. All of them proclaim that the king has come, that
Jesus of Nazareth is the Son of Man, the Son of God, the Messiah, the final
prophet, the true Israel, and the Lord of all. Jesus fulfills the promise made to
David that his dynasty would never end, that a king would always sit on the
Davidic throne. By virtue of his resurrection and exaltation he is now seated
at God's right hand and reigns from heaven.

The kingdom prophesied in the OT has come, for the king has come. The
day of fulfillment has arrived in Jesus' ministry, death, and resurrection. The
age to come has invaded history, for Jesus is risen from the dead. By virtue of
Jesus' death forgiveness of sins (cf. Jer. 31:34) is available for those who belong to him. The presence of the kingdom manifested itself in Jesus' healings,
exorcisms, and nature miracles. These miracles anticipate the new creation
that is coming, the day when all that is wrong with the world will be made
right. Amnesty is offered to all those who have defied the king's lordship, but
the day of forgiveness will last for a limited time, for the king will return to
the earth and finish what he has started. Then the devil and his cohorts will
be destroyed forever, though the crushing blow (cf. Gen. 3:15) already was
delivered at Jesus' death and resurrection.

Luke particularly emphasizes, though the theme is not absent from Matthew and Mark, that the kingdom advances through the power of the Holy
Spirit. The gospel of the kingdom will be heralded to the ends of the world,

and Acts testifies that such a mission is carried out through the work of the Holy Spirit, animating and strengthening disciples to testify to the gospel of Jesus Christ. The people of God consists of all those who belong to Jesus Christ. The twelve apostles represent the new and restored Israel—the new twelve tribes, so to speak. All those who accept the apostolic testimony about the Christ are members of God's kingdom. The restored and new Israel is not limited to the Jewish people. Gentiles who repent of their sins and put their faith in Jesus Christ and are baptized in his name also belong to the new people of God. Luke particularly emphasizes in Acts the expansion of the people of God. The promise that Israel and Judah would be reunified is fulfilled when the Samaritans believe (Acts 8; cf. Ezek. 37). The folding in of the Gentiles fulfills the universal blessing pledged to Abraham and the other patriarchs.

Those who are members of the kingdom repent of their sins and put their faith in Jesus Christ. They submit to Jesus' lordship and his reign as disciples. True disciples are obedient to God and do what Jesus commands them to do. They live a new life as members of the kingdom, bearing fruit that is pleasing to God.

Part 6

ETERNAL LIFE
IN THE GOSPEL
AND EPISTLES OF JOHN

28

THE GOSPEL
ACCORDING TO JOHN
AND THE JOHANNINE EPISTLES

Introduction

The Johannine portrait of Jesus, as all acknowledge, differs remarkably from
the one in the Synoptic Gospels, though there are striking points of contact as
well.[1] Both elegant simplicity and profound depth characterize John's writings.
Here I treat the Gospel and the three letters together, for most acknowledge
that they stem from the same writer. One might insist that Revelation be
included here as well because its author is John (Rev. 1:9), and certainly it
would be legitimate and even illuminating to do so. I have suggested in this
book that there are many different ways to write a biblical theology, and we
should reject the path of taking one approach to the exclusion of others. The
subject matter of NT theology cannot be mastered by adopting a particular
method or approaching the subject in "the right way." Doing NT theology
is somewhat like shaking a kaleidoscope. Different angles of looking at the
material yield complementary and beneficial insights into the theology of the
Scriptures. I have chosen here to separate Revelation because it plays a definitive and climactic role as the concluding book of the canon, and thus it also
makes good sense to detach it from other Johannine literature.

1. I will use "John" and "Johannine" here, but I am not making any particular claim about
authorship, though I believe that it is most credible to attribute the Gospel, the three epistles,
and even Revelation to the apostle. For a theology of John's Gospel and the Johannine Epistles,
see Köstenberger, *John's Gospel and Letters*.

Another daunting issue is how to investigate the themes in John. The central Johannine themes are textured in such a way that they overlap significantly, and unraveling one strand and separating it from others seems to produce distortions. Unfortunately, any explanation of John cannot reproduce the beauty or power of his work. I want to begin, therefore, with a more modest question. How do the Johannine writings contribute to the theme of this work? One of the key verses in John's Gospel is 14:9, where Jesus says to Philip, "Whoever has seen me has seen the Father." This means that we see the King in his beauty only when we see Jesus, when we acknowledge that Jesus shares the identity of the one God.[2] John clearly identifies Jesus as the king of the Jews, as we will see in more detail in due course. What is surprising, however, is how rarely he refers to the kingdom. The "kingdom" (*basileia*) belonging to Jesus and God is mentioned only five times in John's Gospel (3:3, 5; 18:36 [3x]). But Jesus as the Christ, as the messianic king, is a major theme in John's Gospel and the Johannine Epistles. In fact, the stated purpose of this Gospel is that people believe that Jesus is the Christ and God's Son (20:30–31), and this plays a central role in the Johannine Epistles as well (1 John 2:22–23; 3:23; 4:2, 14–15; 5:1, 5, 6, 9–13; 2 John 7, 9). Hence, the purpose of the Gospel and the Epistles is seeing and believing that Jesus is the true king and God's Son, and when one sees who he truly is, then one will believe in him.

Has John abandoned the eschatological framework of the Synoptic Gospels and Acts? Is it a reflective and ontological work lacking the dynamism of the other Gospels? Such a perspective would misjudge John's writings. John is more reflective and discursive than the Synoptics, but an eschatological framework and emphasis are not abandoned. Indeed, Johannine eschatology also reveals itself in his emphasis upon eternal life.[3] The life of the age to come has penetrated history. So it is not as though John has abandoned the eschatological vision of the Synoptics; rather, he looks at the same theme from a fresh angle.

For heuristic purposes, John 14:6 will function as the basis for the outline of Johannine theology. There Jesus identifies himself as "the way and the truth and the life." I am not claiming that the outline accords with the specific intention of 14:6, but that dividing Johannine theology in accord with this verse proves illuminating. First, Jesus is the life. Here the focus will be on eternal life and Christology, showing that the former is inseparable from the latter. Second, Jesus is the truth. Here the fulfillment of the OT will be especially featured, so that Jesus' role as the true temple, the true manna, the true shepherd, and

---

2. See Bauckham, *God Crucified*.
3. See Dodd, *Interpretation of the Fourth Gospel*, 144–50; Ladd, *Theology of the New Testament*, 290–305; Thielman, *Theology of the New Testament*, 161–69.

so forth will be discussed. Finally, the third section will consider Jesus as the way to God, where the centrality of the cross, the need for belief, the work of the Spirit, the place of assurance, and the emphasis on divine sovereignty will be consulted. These discrete categories are somewhat artificial. They clearly bleed into one another, but I hope that the proposed outline will shed some light on John's theology.

Jesus as the Life

Life

It has often been recognized that whereas the Synoptic Gospels focus on the kingdom, the Gospel of John emphasizes life, particularly eternal life. John uses the word "life" (*zōē*) thirty-two times and the term "eternal life" seventeen times. The term "eternal life" refers to the life of the age to come, reflecting the common Jewish distinction between this age and the age to come. "Eternal life," then, refers to life in the new creation, to the hope of the coming age, when death would be defeated.[4] In that sense, it reflects an idea that is quite similar to the notion of the kingdom. Indeed, in the Synoptic story of the rich ruler, eternal life and inheriting the kingdom mutually explicate each other (Matt. 19:16, 23, 24 pars.). John's Gospel overlaps with the Synoptics, for in the story of Nicodemus, entering the kingdom (3:3, 5) and believing to receive eternal life (3:15) are closely linked. John, of course, particularly emphasizes that one must believe to have life (e.g., 3:15–16, 36; 5:24; 6:35, 40, 47; 11:25; 20:31), and later I will explore the centrality of belief.

The issue here, however, relates to the nature of eternal life, and what must be emphasized is its eschatological and Jewish character. The eschatological character of life is confirmed by its close association with resurrection. It is those who are raised from the dead who enjoy life (5:21). The resurrection in 5:21 refers to life before death, but in 5:29 "the resurrection of life" clearly has to do with life after death (cf. 6:40). Jesus' words in 11:24–26 are also instructive, for resurrection life is granted before death, but they also guarantee physical resurrection after death. The resurrection, according to the OT (Isa. 26:19; Ezek. 37; Dan. 12:2), is indisputably eschatological, signifying the end of history and the fulfillment of God's promises. The close tie between eternal life and resurrection in John demonstrates the OT character of John's thought.

---

4. The polarity between life and death is part of John's well-noted dualism. See Köstenberger, *John's Gospel and Letters*, 277–92.

John's conception of life does not only draw upon the OT. He offers his own unique contribution, for he emphasizes repeatedly that eternal life belongs to those who believe in Jesus (3:15, 16, 36; 5:24; 6:35, 40, 47; 11:25; 20:31), obey him (3:36), come to him (5:40), and follow him (8:12). Given the Jesus-centered character of this Gospel, it is scarcely surprising that John connects life so closely to Jesus. Life finds its origin in Jesus (1:4; 5:26). He came to grant life to human beings (10:10), and he grants it to whom he wishes (5:21, 28–29; 6:27, 33; 10:28; 17:2). Jesus speaks the words of life (6:63, 68). The life that Jesus gives is tied particularly to the cross, to his giving of himself as the bread of life (6:35, 40–41, 47–48, 50–51, 53–54, 58), to his laying down his life for the sheep (10:11, 15, 17, 28; cf. 15:13). Furthermore, eternal life is qualitative; it means one knows the Father and Jesus the Christ (17:3). The Gospel also stresses that the life of the age to come is realized for believers.[5] Even before death believers have "passed from death to life" (5:24).[6] They enjoy "eternal life" now (10:28), so that one has life before physical death (11:25–26), although, as noted above, a future physical resurrection is also strongly emphasized, contrary to the view of some scholars who think that John has no interest in a future physical resurrection.

The purpose of John's Gospel (20:30–31) underscores that believers partake of life now. John's Gospel draws from the OT by connecting the life of the age to come to the resurrection. What is distinctive, however, is the focus on Jesus as the Messiah and the Son of God. Life comes from him and is gained only by believing in him, and he secures it for his own by his death on the cross. John's realized eschatology, his emphasis that life is available now, also flows from his Christology. Believers have life now because Jesus has conquered death by virtue of his resurrection. Through Jesus' death and resurrection the life of the resurrection—the life of the age to come—is now available to believers. For us, the link between eternal life and Christology is a commonplace, but John's emphasis on such a connection is nothing short of astonishing, and it represents a startling new emphasis.

The letter of 1 John is remarkably similar. In his Gospel John desires his readers to know that they have eternal life (20:30–31), and the purpose in 1 John is the same (5:12–13). Life centers on Jesus and has entered into history in the person of Jesus, who was touched, seen, and heard (1:1–2). The "antichrists" denied that Jesus came in the flesh, but those who propound such teaching do not belong to the Father (2:18–23). Eternal life is given to those who believe

---

5. This is a common observation in Johannine scholarship. See Köstenberger, *John's Gospel and Letters*, 297.

6. The coming of the hour signifies, as Beale (*Biblical Theology*, 131–33) says, a "staggered" fulfillment of Dan. 12:1. See Dan. 12:1 in the LXX and John 5:24.

in and have the Son (5:11–13, 20). As in John's Gospel, so too in 1 John those who believe in Jesus enjoy life now. Life in the person of Jesus has reached into history, so that even now believers have left death behind and have been ushered into the realm of life (3:14–15). The life of the age to come has arrived, and such life is available because Jesus, as the Christ and the Son of God, has died for the sake of his people, so that they currently enjoy the forgiveness of sins. There is still a "not yet" in Johannine eschatology, for "the darkness is passing away and the true light is already shining" (2:8), but the darkness has not yet been eclipsed. It still exists. So too, "the world is passing away," but the day has not yet arrived when those who do God's will abide forever (2:17). Believers still wait for the day of Jesus' appearing (2:28; 3:2), and only on that day will they be perfected and be like him entirely.

John's teaching on eternal life, though it uses different terminology than the Synoptics, indicates that the age to come has arrived with the coming of Jesus the Christ. The life of the age to come belongs now to those who put their trust in Jesus as the Messiah and the Son of God. Eternal life has arrived in the present era since Jesus is risen from the dead. His triumph over death demonstrates that life has now conquered death. John emphasizes realized eschatology, but there is still a "not yet" in his eschatology. The resurrection and final judgment are still future, and the world and evil have not yet been eliminated. Jesus has not yet returned and brought disciples to himself (John 14:1–3). What John accents, however, is that the life of the age to come belongs to believers now, and hence they can be assured of life in the future.

Jesus as Messiah and King

John's Gospel was written to help people believe that Jesus is the Christ and God's Son and thereby obtain life (20:30–31). Clearly, then, John ties Christology, specifically Jesus' status as the Messiah, to the reception of eternal life. It is somewhat remarkable that John does not argue more specifically in his Gospel that Jesus is the Messiah. But the purpose statement clarifies that Jesus' signs (sēmeia) were given so that people would embrace Jesus as the Messiah, and thus Jesus' signs are designed to lead to the conclusion that he is the Christ and the Son of God.

One of the interesting features in John's Gospel is the robust discussion over the identity of the Messiah/Christ. The Baptist repeatedly insists that he is not the Messiah (1:20, 25; 3:28), which shows, incidentally, the high esteem that John garnered during his ministry. Jesus' disciples almost immediately recognized and confessed him to be the Messiah (1:41–49), but the encounter with Nathaniel demonstrated that the faith of the disciples, though genuine, was superficial.

Intense discussion about Jesus' identity marks chapter 7. The people were confused because the authorities criticized Jesus but did not arrest him, provoking them to wonder if the religious leaders truly believed that he was the Messiah (7:26). The people also had reservations about whether Jesus was the Messiah, for they were convinced that they knew where he was from, and he did not fit the qualifications for being the Messiah (7:27, 41–42). John does not answer the question at the literal level by proving apologetically that Jesus was a son of David and hailed from Bethlehem. He answered the objections at an entirely different level, contending that he was sent by God into the world (7:28–29, 33). Those who are open to doing what God desires will know whether Jesus is truly from God (7:17). Assurance about Jesus' identity is not ultimately an intellectual matter, nor can it be proved empirically beyond dispute, for recognition of Jesus as the Christ depends upon the state of one's heart, on whether one is truly willing to do God's will. Those who do not submit to his lordship will not see the Christ embodied in Jesus' signs.

Debate continued to simmer over whether Jesus was the Messiah. Some believed Jesus was the Christ because of the signs he performed (7:31). On another occasion doubts arose about Jesus because he predicted his death, but they believed that the Christ would never perish (12:34). Even though the Johannine style differs remarkably from the Synoptics, we see a theme that was also prominent in the Synoptics. Many rejected the idea that Jesus could be the Christ because they found the notion that he would die, especially via the cross, intolerable. The religious leaders protested that they truly wanted to know whether Jesus is the Christ (10:24); however, Jesus does not answer them directly but instead appeals to his works to validate his self-claims (10:25), indicating that their protestations were hollow. The hostility of the Jewish leaders toward Jesus expressed itself when they persecuted those who confessed Jesus as the Christ by expelling them from the synagogue (9:22; 12:42).

John often calls attention to Jesus' signs, for they provoked intense discussion about Jesus' identity (e.g., 3:2; 4:48; 7:31; 9:16; 11:47; 12:18), but often they were misread (2:23–25). Sometimes the misinterpretation was extraordinarily close to being correct. When Jesus fed the crowd of five thousand, the people concluded rightly from the sign that Jesus was the prophet and king (6:14–15). But apparently, they only wanted a king who would feed them when they were physically hungry (6:26). They did not want a king who would die, whose flesh they would have to eat and whose blood they would have to drink in order to gain life (6:51–58). Since the Jews were prone to misunderstand Jesus, he did not directly proclaim that he was the Messiah. Indeed, he announces himself as the Messiah only to a Samaritan woman (4:25–26), for there was no potential in Samaria for a political movement that would crown Jesus as the Messiah. Apart from the disciples in chapter 1, and Peter's confession that Jesus is "the Holy One of God" (6:69), the only person who recognized Jesus as the Christ was Martha, the sister of Mary. Indeed, her words anticipate the purpose of John's Gospel, for she declares, "You are the Christ, the Son of God, who is coming into the world" (11:27). Spiritual perception belongs not to the elite, to the religious leaders but to humble believers such as Martha.

The signs that Jesus did indicated that the promise of the new creation found in the OT Scriptures was realized in Jesus. In the OT the coming of the new David was inseparable from the arrival of the new creation. For instance, we read in Amos 9:11–15 that the rebuilding of David's house is coincident with the mountains dripping with wine. It is highly significant, therefore, that in John's Gospel Jesus' first miracle took place at a wedding (2:1–11), which anticipates the eschatological banquet where "well-aged wine" and "aged wine well refined" is enjoyed, and death is wiped out forever (Isa. 25:6–8). Furthermore, at the wedding Jesus turned water into wine. Those with ears to hear and eyes to see would perceive that the miracle hearkened back to Amos's promise that the mountains would drip with wine when the Messiah arrived (cf. Joel 3:18).

Jesus' other signs also point to the new creation. The healing of the royal servant's son (4:46–54) points to the day when sickness will be eradicated (cf. Isa. 35), the restoration of the sight to the blind man (chap. 9) to the fulfillment of OT promises (cf. Isa. 29:18; 35:5), and the raising of Lazarus (chap. 11) to the future resurrection (cf. Isa. 25:7–8; Ezek. 37; Dan. 12:2). The appropriate response to Jesus' signs is to believe in him (cf. 2:11; 4:53; 9:36–38). It was hard to conceive of anyone doing more signs than Jesus did, and hence many believed (7:31; 10:40–41; 11:47–48), and yet others failed to believe that Jesus was the Messiah, despite the signs (12:37). According to John, the signs functioned as compelling evidence for belief in Jesus as the Messiah, and the failure of some to believe demonstrated their love for the glory that comes from human beings instead of the glory that comes from God (5:42–44; 9:22; 12:43–44).

Identifying Jesus as "king" is another way of designating him as the Messiah. When Nathaniel declares that Jesus is the "Son of God" and "the King of Israel" (1:49), he is confessing that Jesus is the Messiah. Nathaniel's confession functions as a framing device (cf. 20:30–31), showing that Jesus' royal status functions as a major theme in the book. Such a judgment is borne out by a careful assessment of other evidence.

We find, for instance, that the word "king" appears mainly in the Passion Narrative or in texts associated with the Passion Narrative, where it is found fourteen times. The central theme is that Jesus is a humble king who suffers for the sake of his people. He does not conquer his enemies through violence but triumphs over his adversaries through suffering. Therefore, Jesus entered Jerusalem humbly on a donkey instead of on a conquering warhorse (12:13–15). The passion account is filled with irony. Pilate sarcastically asked Jesus whether he was a king, and Jesus replied that Pilate did consider him to be a king (18:37), for he was on trial and eventually put to death for political reasons. Indeed, what finally convinced Pilate to crucify Jesus was the accusation that Jesus was a rival king to Caesar (19:12). The irony is thick here, for Jesus was scarcely a rival to Caesar in terms of military power, but by putting Jesus to death, Pilate unleashed forces by which Caesar and all political rulers would be overthrown.

Another irony is that the Jews, who had longed and prayed for the Messiah for centuries, failed to recognize him when he came (1:11). Instead, they preferred Caesar's rule over them, confessing that they "had no king but Caesar" (19:15). Pilate correctly, though ironically, proclaimed Jesus as "the King of the Jews" (18:39) and said to the Jews, "Behold your King," when he was about to crucify him (19:14). What neither Pilate nor the Jews apprehended was that Jesus' crucifixion qualified him to be king. The soldiers rightly clothed Jesus with a purple robe and cried out, "Hail, King of the Jews" (19:3), even though they were mocking Jesus with their actions and statements. In the same way, Pilate was guided by God in affixing to the cross the statement "Jesus of Nazareth, King of the Jews" (19:19). The Jews tried to dissuade Pilate, asking him to rewrite the statement so that it read only that Jesus claimed to be the king of the Jews, but Pilate stood firm and refused to countenance their request (19:21–22). Unwittingly, Pilate posted the truth before all, identifying Jesus as the king of the Jews. John makes it abundantly clear that Jesus was a suffering and crucified Messiah. His suffering did not disqualify him from being the Messiah but rather was constitutive of his messiahship, for the true Messiah, the true king, would suffer for the sake of his people.

The Christology of 1–2 John calls attention to the same theme. Jesus is a human and suffering Messiah. Those who are from the antichrist rebuff the claim that the human Jesus is the Christ (1 John 2:22). The "Word became flesh" in Jesus (John 1:14). According to John, such a teaching is not inconsequential, for those who reject the incarnation deny the Son and therefore do not belong to the Father (1 John 2:23; cf. John 5:22–23). As John says later, "Every spirit that confesses that Jesus Christ has come in the flesh is from God, and every spirit that does not confess Jesus is not from God. This is the spirit of the antichrist" (1 John 4:2–3). To detach the human Jesus from the Messiah is tantamount to saying there is no Messiah, and hence such teaching is that of the antichrist.

According to 2 John, the problem persists, for "deceivers . . . do not confess the coming of Jesus Christ in the flesh. Such a one is a deceiver and the antichrist" (v. 7). The antichrists likely acknowledged the coming of the Christ, but they rejected the notion that Jesus was human, probably because they believed that the divine could not be identified with corrupt humanity. Such "progressive" teaching, according to John, lands one outside the circle of the saved, for anyone who makes such claims "does not have God" (v. 9). Only those who continue in the teaching about the Christ, only those who persevere in the faith belong to the Father and Son (v. 9). In 1 John the writer explains why the humanity of Jesus as the Christ is a nonnegotiable. Jesus came both by the water of baptism and by the blood of the cross (5:6–8). If one denies the humanity of Jesus, then the atoning work of the cross is surrendered. And if there is no atonement, then there is no forgiveness of sins, and thus the goal of granting readers assurance, of giving them confidence that their sins are forgiven, vanishes (2:12–14; 5:13, 20). All those and only those who are born of God believe that Jesus is the Christ (5:1).

Those who have eternal life acknowledge that Jesus is the Messiah and the king. Jesus' signs attest to his kingship, but he did not often proclaim himself as the "Christ," for that term was laden with political associations and prone to be misunderstood. John particularly uses the term "king" of Jesus in the Passion Narrative, underscoring that Jesus was the crucified and risen Messiah. Those who truly understand Jesus' kingship grasp that he was a suffering king, that he gave his life so that those who trust in him would live.

Jesus as the Son of God

We can be briefer in thinking about Jesus as the "Son of God," for that term is closely tied to "Messiah," as we have already seen. Indeed, in both John's Gospel and 1 John belief in Jesus as the Son of God is necessary to have assurance of eternal life (John 20:30–31; 1 John 5:12–13; cf. John 3:16; 6:40). We saw earlier that in John's Gospel both Nathaniel (1:49) and Martha (11:27) confessed Jesus as the Christ and the Son of God, fulfilling the purpose of this Gospel. The Baptist fulfilled his unique role as a witness, as the friend of the bridegroom, in proclaiming the sonship of Jesus (1:34). The title "Son of God," however, is not completely synonymous with "Messiah." One must believe "in the name of the only Son of God" (3:18) and obey him (3:36) in order to live. "Name" theology is associated only with God, and hence the title "Son of God" also points to deity. The divine character of the Son of God is verified by his ability to raise the dead, both spiritually (5:25) and physically (11:4, 27), for only God can grant life to those who have died.

The Son's divinity is also apparent because he sets free those who are in sin (8:36), but no human being possesses such power. We are not surprised to learn, therefore, that some charge Jesus with blasphemy for claiming to be God's Son (10:36; 19:7).

John affirms six times that the Father sent the Son (John 3:17; 5:23; 10:36; 1 John 4:9, 10, 14), and the sending of the Son, especially in John's Gospel, with its clear teaching on preexistence and its high Christology, implies the Son's deity. Indeed, Jesus is the "only [*monogenēs*] Son" (John 3:16, 18; 1 John 4:9; cf. John 1:14, 18), demonstrating his uniqueness as God's Son. In John's Gospel it is noted that the Father receives glory particularly through the Son (11:4; 14:13; 17:1). Indeed, the Father has a special love for the Son (3:35; 5:20), and the Son demonstrates his love for the Father by carrying out his will (5:19), and the Father shows his love for the Son by granting him authority to judge all on the last day (5:22, 27). The deity of the Son is without dispute, for all must honor the Son in the same way they do the Father (5:23). If they fail to grant honor to the Son, they do not honor the Father. John tolerates no attempt to diminish the glory and worship that must be given to the Son.

In 1 John the title "Son of God" is closely tied to John's emphasis on assurance. Jesus, as God's Son, came "to destroy the works of the devil" (3:8). Here John probably has the cross in mind (cf. 3:5; John 1:29). John features elsewhere the centrality of Jesus' atoning work in speaking of his sonship: "the blood of Jesus his Son cleanses us from all sin" (1 John 1:7). The Father sent the Son so that human beings would enjoy life, and life is obtained through the Son, who was commissioned to offer himself as "the propitiation for our sins" (1 John 4:9–10). Fellowship with God is conditioned upon fellowship with both the Father and the Son (1 John 1:3), so that only those who confess the Son as coming in the flesh belong to the Father (1 John 4:2–4; 2 John 7–9). The sending of the Son, which points to his deity, is reiterated in 1 John. Jesus was sent as "the Savior of the world" (4:14), so that human beings may enjoy life (4:9–10). As we saw in John's Gospel, so too in 1 John "name" is collocated with "Son," and again "name" theology points to deity (3:23; 5:13), and it is linked again with the assurance that believers have life (5:13). Only those who have the Son have life, John insists (1 John 4:15; 5:5, 11–12; 2 John 8–9), and believers can be confident of the truth, for God has borne witness about his Son (5:9–10).

The title "Son of God" indicates that Jesus is king and divine. Those who trust in him are assured of eternal life, for they are trusting in the name, in the very character, of God. Even though Jesus is God's Son, John's Gospel and especially 1 John emphasize Jesus' atoning work on the cross as the Son of God, for his suffering on the cross is the means by which believers are cleansed of their sins.

Son of Man

John uses the title "Son of Man" thirteen times, all of them in the Gospel. When we consider John's usage of the title, we are immediately struck by its authority. The term "Son of Man" is associated with ascending, descending, being lifted up, being glorified, and the granting of life. Such authority fits with Dan. 7:13–14, where the son of man receives from the Ancient of Days authority to rule. John's portrait of the Son of Man finds its roots, then, in the OT and resonates with the OT promises of the coming of the kingdom. Just as angels ascended and descended upon Jacob's ladder, so that Bethel became the house of God for Jacob (see Gen. 28:12–17), Jesus is the ladder, the pathway between earth and heaven (1:51). No one will reach God's house unless Jesus prepares a room for him or her (14:2–3).[7] The Son of Man has "descended from heaven" and brings life to those who believe in him by being lifted up on the cross (3:14–15). The lifting up refers to the cross, and thereby John emphasizes that the cross is the pathway to Jesus' exaltation and authority (8:28; 12:34). In the same way, he speaks of Jesus' death as the Son of Man being in his glorification (12:23; 13:31). Jesus' death is the hour of his triumph, not the occasion of his shame and dishonor. Here John picks up Isaiah's language about the servant of the Lord: "Behold, my servant shall act wisely; he shall be high and lifted up, and shall be exalted" (Isa. 52:13). For John, the cross is the pathway by which the Son of Man ascends "to where he was before" (6:62). The Son of Man will receive the promised Danielic kingdom through suffering. That the cross is the means by which Jesus is lifted up on high and glorified is counterintuitive and contrary to Jewish expectations. Despite the distinctiveness of John's Gospel, the message is the same as that of the Synoptics. Suffering is the pathway to glory for Jesus, and thus the only way to obtain life is to eat Jesus' flesh and drink his blood (6:53). Those who do not believe will find that Jesus as the Son of Man is their judge (5:27).

Conclusion

Jesus is the Messiah, the Son of God, and the Son of Man. Remarkably, all of these titles point to the cross and are linked to eternal life, for the only way one can enjoy eternal life is by believing that Jesus is the Messiah, the Son of God, and the Son of Man. But John says something more radical. One can have life only by believing in Jesus as the crucified and risen Messiah, Son of

7. Beale says that Jesus views himself as "the temple stairway" (*Church's Mission*, 195), and that Jesus does what Adam should have done in linking "heaven to earth" (p. 196).

God, and Son of Man. Since Jesus is risen from the dead, the age to come, eternal life, is available now for those who put their faith in Jesus.

Jesus as the Truth

The artificiality of the distinctions drawn for the major sections in this study of Johannine theology is apparent, for we cannot neatly divide Jesus as the life from Jesus as the truth. In this section I focus on Jesus' fulfillment of the OT. This is not to say, of course, that what was examined above (Jesus as Messiah, Son of Man, Son of God, and the realization of eternal life in him) does not richly fulfill the OT. All of the topics investigated above fit with the notion of promise and fulfillment. For instance, the OT predicts a coming messiah, and Jesus is that Messiah. A son of man will arrive on the scene (Dan. 7:9–14), and Jesus is that Son of Man. The OT promises that a day of resurrection is coming, and Jesus is the life promised in the OT Scriptures.

Perhaps it will be helpful to say that the topics explored under Jesus as the truth center on the deeper meaning disclosed in Jesus than was apparent upon the first reading of the OT. For instance, the word of God in the OT represents divine oracles and utterances. But John tells us that the word in the OT points to *the* Word, to a divine speech that bursts the boundaries of OT revelation even if it stands in continuity with it. In the same way, there is more complexity in the "I am" statements than most reading the OT could imagine. God's identity is "thicker" than is apparent in reading the OT, for Jesus shares the identity of God as "I am." We see as well that Jesus is the true temple, true manna, and the true vine. Special days such as the Sabbath and feasts such as Tabernacles, Passover, and Dedication find their true meaning and fulfillment in him.[8]

Jesus as the Word

John's high Christology manifests itself from the outset of his Gospel, where Jesus is identified as the Word (1:1, 14). The primary background is the OT, for the opening of this Gospel ("in the beginning" [1:1]) echoes the "in the beginning" of Gen. 1:1. The Word is the agent of creation in John (1:3), and in Gen. 1 God created by means of his word ("God said" [1:3, 6, 9, 11, 14, 20, 24, 26]). The effectiveness of God's word permeates the OT. "By the word of the LORD the heavens were made" (Ps. 33:6). God's word is personified as the

---

8. See Hoskins, *Jesus as the Fulfillment*; Köstenberger, *John's Gospel and Letters*, 413–35; Matera, *New Testament Theology*, 268–69.

agent of deliverance: "He sent out his word and healed them" (Ps. 107:20). God's word functions as his agent by which he accomplishes his will upon earth: "He sends out his command to the earth; his word runs swiftly" (Ps. 147:15). Nothing can hinder or prevent his word from being realized. God says of his word, "It shall not return to me empty, but it shall accomplish that which I purpose, and shall succeed in the thing for which I sent it" (Isa. 55:11). We see the same theme in the Second Temple writing Wisdom of Solomon: "Your all-powerful word leaped from heaven, from the royal throne, into the midst of the land that was doomed, a stern warrior carrying the sharp sword of your authentic command, and stood and filled all things with death, and touched heaven while standing on the earth" (Wis. 18:15–16 NRSV). Word and wisdom are closely allied in biblical thought, for wisdom also becomes the agent by which God created the world (Prov. 8:22–31), and in Second Temple literature wisdom is equated with Torah (Sir. 15:1; 19:20; 24:23) and is the means by which God created the world (Wis. 7:26; 9:1–3).[9]

John's notion of the Word, though it echoes the OT and Second Temple Jewish literature, also transcends them. In previous traditions God's word is personified, but it is not considered to be a separate hypostasis. John 1:1–2 both distinguishes the Word from God ("the Word was with God," "he was in the beginning with God") and identifies the Word as God ("the Word was God"). John thereby introduces complexity into the identity of God. There is one God, and yet the Father is God, and the Word is God. The Word has explicated God to human beings (1:18). Thomas confesses that Jesus is "my Lord and my God" (20:28), so that the theme that Jesus is fully divine bookends this Gospel. The mystery grows even deeper however. The Word is not only God but also "became flesh" (1:14), which clarifies how he could explain who God is to human beings. The creator of the world also entered into the world (1:3, 10). Anyone who has truly seen Jesus has also seen the Father (14:9). Jesus as the Word is the revelation of the Father, explicating God to us. Nor is this knowledge abstract. Jesus came and revealed that he is "the way, and the truth, and the life," that he is the only way to God (14:6), that one becomes a child of God through Jesus (1:12–13).

The "word" in the opening verses of 1 John confirms the practical dimensions of John's thought (1:1–2). Here the "word" refers to both the message of the gospel and the messenger (Jesus Christ). Certainly, John refers to Jesus, for he emphasizes that he heard, saw, and touched him (1:1), pointing to the revelation of the Word in history, to the incarnation of the Word. God manifested

---

9. On the importance of wisdom, see Witherington, *Jesus the Sage*; Schnabel, *Law and Wisdom*.

himself to the world through the Word, and the Word is the means by which human beings may enjoy "eternal life" (1:2) and have "fellowship" with both the Father and the Son (1:3). We can say, then, that Jesus as the Word is God's final and definitive message to human beings. The words of the OT point toward and climax in Jesus as the Word, as the incarnate one of the Father. As the Word, he reveals and discloses the Father to human beings, making known to us what God is like.

"I Am" Sayings

The close connection between Christology and soteriology is evident in the "I am" sayings in John's Gospel.[10] These "I am" sayings are rooted in the OT. In one of the most famous texts in the OT God reveals himself to Moses as "I AM WHO I AM" (Exod. 3:14). The "I am" language is featured particularly in Isaiah (41:4; 43:10, 25; 45:22; 46:9). Isaiah emphasizes Yahweh's sole sovereignty over history. He is the one and only "I am." Yahweh is the incomparable God; no one like him exists. For Jesus to appropriate "I am" statements and apply them to himself, therefore, is nothing short of astonishing. He is clearly identifying himself as God, indicating that the identity of the one God has a fuller dimension than was clear from the OT. The "I am" declarations are never presented abstractly by John; they are vitally connected with soteriology, showing that Jesus is the only way of salvation.

Perhaps the best way to proceed is to observe Jesus' "I am" statements in the order in which they appear in John's Gospel. An "I am" statement, of course, may simply be a way of self-identification, as was the case with the blind man (9:9). But when Jesus takes "I am" on his lips, he is clearly doing more than identifying himself. The context of the texts where the phrase is used and the OT background demonstrate that Jesus is identifying himself as divine. We have already noted 4:26, where Jesus identifies himself as the Messiah by saying, "I am" (*egō eimi*). Possibly Jesus is simply claiming to be the Messiah here, and we should not read anything more into the "I am" statement. But given the significance of the phrase elsewhere in this Gospel, there is likely a deeper meaning. Jesus also uses "I am" (*egō eimi*) in revealing himself to the disciples when he walks upon the water (6:20), and only God can walk on the sea (Job 9:8), and therefore he discloses himself as the sovereign one, the one who rules over nature.

The "I am" statement in 6:20 seems particularly pregnant, for it is tied to the feeding of the five thousand (6:1–15) and to Jesus' claim "I am the bread of

---

10. For helpful studies, see Ball, *"I Am" in John's Gospel*; C. Williams, *I Am He*.

life" (6:35, 48; cf. 6:41, 51). Jesus directly contrasts his claim to be the bread of life to the manna that was given to Israel in the wilderness (6:31). The manna that Israel received in the wilderness did not produce life, for all those who ate of the manna died (6:49). Manna was a gift of God for Israel, and yet manna anticipates and directs believers to something greater than physical sustenance. Jesus, therefore, is the true manna, the true bread of God, for as the living bread, he grants eternal life to those who eat his flesh and drink his blood (6:54). The OT account of the Lord providing his people with manna points to something (to someone!) deeper and more profound than provision for physical needs. True life comes from feeding on Jesus spiritually. The realistic language of eating Jesus' flesh and drinking his blood (6:51–58) conveys the truth that Jesus is true food for those who put their trust in his atoning death. Those who feast on him by faith and look to his death in their place as the means of life will never die (by way of contrast, all those who ate manna died).

The soteriological slant of the "I am" declarations is evident when Jesus says, "I am the light of the world" (8:12; 9:5). Here Jesus fulfills the lighting ritual practiced during the feast of Tabernacles (*m. Sukkah* 4:1, 9–10; 5:2–4), for he is the true light for human beings, as is often noted in John's Gospel (cf. 1:4, 5, 8, 9; 3:19–21; 11:9, 10; 12:35, 36, 46). The ritual lighting was not merely functional, nor did it just point to the past work of Yahweh in the exodus; it anticipated a future work of God, an illumination that would far exceed what Israel had experienced thus far. Indeed, Jesus demonstrates that he is the world's light by granting sight to a blind man (chap. 9), and not merely physical sight. The man sees who Jesus truly is (9:35–38), while the Pharisees remain blinded by their sin (9:39–41). The narrative in chapters 8–9 is thick with "I am" statements. The obtuseness of those who refuse to believe is a matter of great consequence, for unless people trust that Jesus is "I am," they will "die in [their] sins" (8:24). The only way for sins to be forgiven is if Jesus is lifted up on the cross, and when he is lifted up, he says, people will "know that I am [*egō eimi*]" (8:28). The most stunning and revealing "I am" declaration appears in chapter 8 as well. In the midst of a vigorous and heated dispute with so-called believers, Jesus claims, "Before Abraham was, I am" (8:58). Jesus certainly draws here on the texts cited from Exodus and Isaiah at the beginning of this discussion. To claim that he existed before Abraham was alive can only be understood as a claim to deity. Apparently, the Jews understood it in such a way, for they picked up stones to execute Jesus (8:59). Nor is the soteriological thrust absent, for the self-revelation of Jesus appears in a discussion on how one can be free from the bondage of sin (8:32–36).

Jesus also declares, "I am the door of the sheep" (10:7) and "I am the good shepherd" (10:11, 14), showing that Jesus is the true shepherd. The text is rich with associations from Ezek. 34. There, Yahweh says that he will seek out and gather his sheep and bring them back from exile (34:11–13). He promises to nourish and feed his flock, to care for the sick and weak and protect them from predators (34:14–22). Remarkably, David also plays a role as the shepherd of the sheep (34:23–24). Like Yahweh, he will feed the flock, and the covenant of peace and the new creation will dawn under this Davidic ruler (34:24–31). Clearly, Jesus fulfills what we find in Ezekiel, though there is a surprising feature in John's Gospel that was not apparent in Ezekiel in that both the divine and Davidic dimensions of the shepherd find their fulfillment in Jesus. As the good shepherd, Jesus will save his flock, and thus we see again that the "I am" declarations are tied to soteriology, for one can be part of God's fold only through Jesus. Jesus as the good shepherd gave his life on the cross for the sake of the sheep (10:15), demonstrating that he prized the welfare of his flock over his own life.

Jesus' statement "I am the resurrection and the life" (11:25) is linked with his raising of Lazarus from the grave. The resurrection, as Martha clearly understands, is an eschatological event (11:24). Martha's understanding accords with the OT, for Daniel locates the resurrection (12:2) at "the time of the end" (12:9). In the same way, Isaiah prophesies that the resurrection will come (26:19) on the day when God punishes the wicked and vindicates his people (chaps. 24–27). The promise of the resurrection in Ezek. 37 is found in a discourse that is emphatically eschatological, for Judah and Israel will be unified, God's people will be cleansed of their sins, a new David will reign as king, an everlasting covenant of peace will commence, and God will dwell with his people. In John's Gospel we see that the resurrection of the age to come has arrived in the person of Jesus, for he is "the resurrection and the life." Those who believe in Jesus will "never die" (11:26), for resurrection life is already theirs. They will die physically (11:25), but their physical death is not permanent, for they will be raised to new life (11:26). The discourse and the event, as we see in other "I am" statements, are intertwined.

In 13:18–19 Jesus announces the future before it occurs, so that his disciples will know of him, "I am" (egō eimi). Here John echoes Isaiah, where Yahweh is known as the true God because he declares what is to come before it occurs (41:22–23; 42:9; 44:7; 45:11). We see again the Johannine conviction that the God of Israel is revealed in the person of Jesus, that Jesus as the Word has explained the Father (1:18), that the one who has seen Jesus has seen the Father (14:9), and that the Father is in Jesus and Jesus is in the Father (10:38; 14:10–11). The ontological and soteriological converge in Jesus' famous words "I am the way, and the truth, and the life. No one comes to the Father except through me" (14:6).

Jesus also declares, "I am the true vine" (15:1; cf. 15:5). In a famous text Isaiah identifies Israel as Yahweh's vineyard (5:1–7), and other OT texts likewise designate Israel as God's vine (Ps. 80:8, 14; Jer. 2:21; 8:13; 12:10; Ezek. 17:6–8; Hosea 10:1; cf. Ezek. 19:10, 12). Israel, as Isa. 5:1–7 explains, did not fulfill its role as the people of God. It was not the obedient son of God. John explains, however, that the true vine of God, the true Israel, is Jesus himself, for he was truly God's obedient Son. Only those who abide in him and keep his commands are part of the people of God (15:4–10). The true Israel cannot be equated with the ethnic people of God; mere ethnic descent without obedience means nothing. All those who belong to Jesus are members of the true Israel; they are part of his flock (10:16), members of the true Israel because they abide in Jesus. Israel, as we saw in the Synoptic Gospels, is redefined in terms of Jesus himself.

Jesus also said three times to those arresting him, "I am" (*egō eimi* [18:5, 6, 8]). His pursuers fell back, as do those who experience a theophany, but Jesus handed himself over to them. Jesus is "I am," and yet he is also the one who came to suffer on the cross and to die for his flock.

Jesus' "I am" declarations in the Gospel of John hearken back to the OT, showing that Jesus shares the same identity as the God of Israel (8:58). The "I am" statements are not abstract statements; they are connected with John's soteriology. Jesus is the way and the truth and the life (14:6). He is the light of the world (8:12), granting illumination to those who are physically and spiritually blind. He is the true shepherd, the true Davidic king, for God's flock, and the only door into the sheepfold (chap. 10). He is the resurrection and the life (11:26), so that the life of the age to come is given only to those who abide in Jesus as the true vine (15:1).

Jesus as the True Temple

The prominence and the importance of the temple in Judaism are well known, for the temple was the place where sacrifices were offered to secure atonement. The significance of the temple is evident from Stephen's conflict with Hellenistic Jews recorded in Acts 6–7. One of the primary reasons Stephen was accused and killed was his criticism of the temple, and, of course, such criticisms also were directed against Jesus at his trial (Matt. 26:60–61). The cleansing of the temple in John's Gospel (2:13–22) represents Jesus' judgment on the house where Israel met with God. John clearly indicates that greed had subverted the true purpose of the temple. Jesus alludes to Jer. 7:11 here, and in chapter 7 Jeremiah reminded the people that Shiloh was not spared, nor will the Solomonic temple in Jerusalem be spared if the people do not repent. Similarly, Jesus forecasts the fate of the Jerusalem temple in John. Remarkably,

John does not include Jesus' prophecy from the Synoptics that the temple would be destroyed (Matt. 24:2 pars.), but the incident of the temple cleansing in John subtly suggests the temple's destruction.

Intriguingly, the temple is identified as Jesus' body (2:21), though the Jews believed that he was speaking of the structure in Jerusalem. Jesus used an imperative verb, instructing the Jews to "destroy" the temple (2:19). The command may have an implicit condition, such that Jesus is not mandating the destruction of the temple but rather is saying that if they destroy the temple, he will restore it in three days. In any case, by murdering Jesus, the Jewish opponents destroyed the true temple, Jesus' body. And John probably also implies that the physical structure was also destroyed by the Jews. Interestingly, Jesus' words about the temple answer the charge recorded in the Synoptics that Jesus said he would destroy the temple (Matt. 26:61 par.). The facts of the case are exactly the opposite. The Jews destroyed their own temple because of their wickedness, whereas Jesus was full of godly zeal for God's house (John 2:17; cf. Ps. 69:9). Indeed, the Jews destroyed the true temple Jesus at the cross, but Jesus raised up the new temple (his body) after three days (see John 2:19–21).[11] We noted in the OT, particularly in the psalms, that Israelites journeyed to the temple to see the Lord and to dwell in his presence. But Jesus is the true temple. John declares that Jesus "tabernacled [*eskēnōsen*] among us" (1:14), so that those who see Jesus gaze upon the Lord, and those who see him see the King in his beauty.

The Samaritan woman in John 4 raised a dispute about the temple (4:20). Samaritans believed that worship should be conducted in the temple built on Mount Gerizim, while Jews were persuaded that the temple should be in Jerusalem. The Hasmonean leader John Hyrcanus destroyed the Samaritan temple on Mount Gerizim in 128 BC. Jesus clearly sided with the Jews on this matter, affirming that worship in Jerusalem was divinely ordained (4:22). But with the coming of Jesus, the old question of where to worship is no longer relevant (4:21). Human beings must worship "in spirit and truth" (4:23). If we put this text together with the discussion about the temple in John 2, we see that worship in the Jerusalem temple is irrelevant, for now Jesus is the true temple. Those who belong to Jesus will find a place in the Father's house (14:1–3), and they will be part of God's true temple (cf. 15:1) if they belong to Jesus.

Jesus as the True Rest

John devotes relatively little attention to the Sabbath in his Gospel. On the Sabbath Jesus, by his words, healed a man who was unable to walk and

11. On the theme of the new temple, see Dumbrell, *End of the Beginning*, 37–76.

instructed him to carry his bed (5:8). Jesus did not have to heal the man on the Sabbath, nor was the man required to pick up his bed. Surely Jesus could have explained that he should return to fetch it the next day. When Jesus was challenged about the healing, he did not respond with a halakic ruling to defend the lawfulness of his actions (but cf. 7:22–23). Instead, he boldly claimed to be working on the Sabbath, defending such work by saying that he was engaging in activity just like the Father (5:16–17). Here we have the suggestion that true rest comes from Jesus instead of from the institution of the Sabbath. The grace of Jesus has replaced the grace of the law (1:17). Jesus truly makes people whole (7:23), and thus the Sabbath rest is fulfilled in him. We see a similarly provocative scene played out in chapter 9 in the restoration of the blind man's sight. Here again Jesus healed on the Sabbath, though in this case he did not merely speak to the man but instead applied mud to his eyes and instructed him to wash in the pool of Siloam (9:6–7, 11, 14–15). The Pharisees were scandalized that Jesus healed on the Sabbath (9:16). Since Jesus could have healed the man simply by speaking (cf. 5:8–9), it seems that he deliberately acted to aggravate the religious leaders. Apparently, Jesus wanted to show that wholeness comes from him, that the true rest promised in the Sabbath is found in the Son of Man, who is the light of the world (9:5).

Conclusion

Much more could be said as to how the OT finds its fulfillment in Jesus. The words of the OT anticipate Jesus as the Word, who reveals the Father. The "I am" statements pick up on OT realities, indicating that all of them find their climax and consummation in Jesus. He is the good shepherd, the true vine, the light of the world, the bread of life, and the resurrection and the life. The temple and the Sabbath are temporary realities, indicating that God's presence is now localized in Jesus, and that true rest is found in him. Other feasts—such as Tabernacles, Dedication, and Passover (see below), also find their fulfillment in Jesus. John teaches that God's salvation, promised and pledged in the OT, has become a reality in and through Jesus. He is the true revelation of God.

Jesus as the Way

I have already indicated that the categories used in this discussion of John are somewhat artificial and do not fit perfectly. Still, I hope that they are of some help in considering John's theology. In this last section I will consider

Jesus as the way (14:6). He is the way to God, and thus John's theology of the cross will be unpacked here. At the same time, human beings would never come to God apart from the work of the Spirit, and so John's theology of the Spirit will be sketched in as well. The way to God is accessible only to those who believe and obey. John's theology of belief is multifaceted and must be explored in more detail, and it is tied to his view of assurance. Finally, why do human beings believe and obey? John's theology of gift reveals that salvation and even belief are granted by God and are a consequence of his grace.

Theology of the Cross

Jesus came to die. John impresses that fact on readers from the beginning of his Gospel.[12] The summons to believe in him as the Messiah and the Son of God is a summons to believe in the crucified one. Jesus' coming and his death are a revelation of the love of God for the world (John 3:16–18; 13:34–35; 1 John 3:16; 4:9–10). According to John, Jesus' death fulfilled God's plan. He was slain just as OT prophecy predicted he would be. Several themes converge when thinking of Jesus' death. John presents Jesus as the lamb of God and the Passover sacrifice so that OT sacrifices are picked up and interpreted to point to Jesus. In his death Jesus is lifted up and glorified. Jesus' death was appointed for him by God; he died at the destined hour and in fulfillment of prophecy. John often teaches that Jesus gave his life for others so that his death provided atonement for sin.

In John's Gospel the Baptist proclaimed Jesus as "the Lamb of God, who takes away the sin of the world" (1:29; cf. 1:36). It is difficult to know whether the reference is to sacrificial lambs in general, to the lamb of Isa. 53:7, or to the Passover lamb. Given the prominence of the Passover theme in John, it seems likely that the Passover sacrifice is particularly in view. Precise chronology is difficult in John, but in any case the Passover is closely associated with Jesus' death (11:55; 12:1; 13:1; 18:28, 39; 19:14). Jesus' washing of his disciples' feet, which occurs "before the Feast of the Passover" (13:1), symbolizes the cleansing of the disciples from sin (13:10; 15:3). Indeed, those who are not washed have no "share" (*meros*) with Jesus (13:8); that is, they do not belong to him. Jesus' death is presented as a Passover sacrifice (18:28, 39; 19:14), so that his death becomes the means by which those who belong to Jesus are liberated from their sins, just as the blood of Passover lambs spared the firstborn of Israel when they were freed from Pharaoh's subjugation. True freedom, then, does not come by being freed from Egyptian bondage. The

12. On the theology of the cross in John, see Köstenberger, *John's Gospel and Letters*, 525–38.

political liberation of a nation is not the essence of freedom. True freedom comes when human beings are freed from their sin, and such freedom is rooted in Jesus' sacrifice as the lamb of God, the one who takes the wrath upon himself that Israel deserved.

Instructively, Jesus' death is described as his "lifting up" (*hypsoō*) and his glorification, stressing that Jesus triumphed in his death. Jesus' lifting up is compared to the lifting up of the serpent in the wilderness (3:14). In the OT, Num. 21:5–9 describes how serpents caused the deaths of many Israelites in the wilderness. Nevertheless, God was gracious calling upon Moses to make a bronze serpent, providing life to those who had been bitten if they looked at the raised serpent. Perhaps the point of comparison is that trusting in the crucified Jesus seemed to be the pathway to death, not life. Like gazing upon the uplifted bronze serpent, maintaining faith in the one lifted up on the cross seems counterintuitive. John stresses with the expression "lift up" that Jesus' death on the cross is the means of his exaltation to the right hand of God. Via the cross, the one who descended also ascends to God (3:13) and enters his presence as the triumphant one. The cross is the pathway to the crown. Human beings will know Jesus as "I am" and truly grasp his identity when he is lifted up on the cross and exalted to God's right hand (8:28), and Jesus will effectively draw both Jews and Gentiles to himself (12:32; cf. 12:20–24) when he is lifted up on the cross.

Along the same lines, the cross of Jesus is portrayed as his glorification (12:16, 23; 13:31–32; 17:1, 4–5). Human beings consider the cross as Jesus' degradation and shame, but in God's eyes it is his "finest hour," for the cross reveals the character of God, displaying his sacrificial and suffering love for human beings. The language of glorification also points to Jesus' exaltation, for the cross is the means by which Jesus was honored and exalted. John draws here on Isa. 52:13, which predicts the exaltation of the servant. The whole of Isa. 52:13–53:12 clarifies that the glorification of the servant will come not despite his suffering, but through it. Jesus is glorified precisely because he was crucified.

Since Jesus' death is described as both a lifting up and glorification, we are not surprised that he often speaks of himself as "going" to God. The two verbs for "going" (*hypagō* and *poreuomai*) are basically synonymous and represent a common Johannine pattern of varying his style (*hypagō*: 7:33; 8:14, 21, 22; 13:3, 33, 36; 14:4, 5, 28; 16:5, 10, 17; *poreuomai*: 7:35; 14:2, 3, 12, 28; 16:7, 28; 20:17). What was not apparent to the Jews or to Jesus' disciples was that he was going or returning to God via the cross, and it is only because he goes to the cross that he is able to send the Spirit (16:7) and to bring the disciples to himself in the future (14:1–3). John does not, then, refer to "going" to God in a general way. The journey back to God is exclusively through the cross, and those who want to live in God's presence likewise will do so only via the cross.

John regularly uses the term "hour" (*hōra*) to designate the time of Jesus' death (2:4; 4:23; 5:25; 7:30; 8:20; 12:23, 27; 13:1; 16:32; 17:1; cf. 19:14). We could describe it as Jesus' "finest hour," for Jesus' death was no accident, and he could not and would not die before the appointed time set by the Father. His death fulfilled the prophecy of Caiaphas, who spoke better than he knew as high priest (11:49–52); that is, Jesus died for the sake of and instead of the nation so that the Jews would not perish, though John is quick to add that Jesus' death was not restricted to Jews but also included Gentiles. Jesus laid down his life for his sheep, and his flock extends beyond the Jews to include Gentiles (10:11, 15–18). Like a grain of wheat, he must die to bear fruit (12:24) and draw Gentiles into the circle of the people of God (12:21, 32). The death of Jesus is so vital because he dies as the shepherd to spare his flock from death and destruction. Although many scholars dispute and doubt it, John apparently views Jesus' death as sacrificial and substitutionary.

Since Jesus' death fulfills God's plan, John especially emphasizes divine sovereignty during the Passion Narrative. What happened to Jesus cannot be ascribed to the cruelty of fate or to events spinning out of control. Instead, God supervised and superintended every detail. Hence, when Jesus knew death was about to befall him, he did not flee in fear and even offered himself to his captors (18:4–7; cf. 13:3), knowing that God was ruling even in such a dark hour. Jesus' captors fell to the ground in fear before Jesus, as one falls on the ground during a theophany, and hence Jesus virtually had to hand himself over to his captors. When Peter tried to rescue Jesus by slashing off the ear of the high priest's servant Malchus, Jesus informed Peter that he had come to drink "the cup" given him by the Father (18:10–11). The OT associations suggest that the cup designates God's wrath (see Pss. 11:6; 75:7–8; Isa. 51:17, 22; Jer. 25:15, 17, 28; 49:12; Hab. 2:16–17). Jesus willingly and gladly accepted what the Father destined for him. When Pilate questioned Jesus, the roles seemed reversed, such that Jesus interrogated Pilate as if the latter were the defendant and Jesus the plaintiff (18:33–38). Similarly, when Pilate asserted his authority over Jesus, Jesus struck back, claiming that the authority that Pilate exercised was derived from God, and therefore Pilate did not enjoy independent authority (19:8–12). Jesus' death represents his conquest over evil, so that he surrenders his life by exclaiming triumphantly, "It is finished" (19:30).

John also emphasizes the fulfillment of prophecy in Jesus' death. Not one of those given to Jesus was lost (18:8–9), and death by crucifixion was in accord with what was destined (18:31–32). Soldiers cast lots for Jesus' clothing (19:24), just as Ps. 22:18 predicted. In the same way, Jesus thirsted on the cross

(19:28) in accord with Ps. 69:21. Jesus was spared from having any of his bones broken, and John sees this as a fulfillment of prophecy (19:33–36). It is difficult to know for certain whether John is reflecting on the Passover (Exod. 12:46; Num. 9:12) or sees a fulfillment of Ps. 34:20. Perhaps the emphasis on the Passover in John makes the former more likely. Finally, the piercing of Jesus (19:34) fulfills Zech. 12:10 (19:37). It is striking that John calls attention to the fulfillment of prophecy in detail in the death of Jesus. Even seemingly minor events take place according to divine prediction, showing that Jesus' death was not accidental. Instead, what God had always intended became a reality.

The death of Jesus was no accident; it accorded with God's plan from the beginning. The details of his death fulfilled Scripture, and all that happened in his passion was determined by God. His death took place at the hour destined by God and not before. The terms "glorify" and "lift up" describe Jesus' death, for even though he was dishonored by human beings, his death was the means by which he was exalted to God's right hand. The death of Jesus took place to provide salvation for those who put their faith and trust in him (20:30–31). Jesus was God's Passover lamb who gave his life for the sake of his people. He died for others so that they would not perish (11:51–52), giving his life for the sake of his sheep (10:15). According to 1 John, Jesus' death was the supreme revelation of God's love (4:9–10). His blood was the means by which believers are cleansed of their sins (1:7), for he died as an advocate—the righteous one giving his life for the unrighteous (1:9; 2:1–2). Jesus' death functioned as a propitiation (2:2; 4:10), taking the punishment upon himself that sinners deserved. It is Jesus' blood that takes away sin (1:7; 5:6), which explains further why Jesus' humanity was so important to John, for apart from the spilling of his blood there is no salvation. Hence, as Jesus says in John's Gospel, people must eat his flesh and drink his blood for eternal life (6:52–58), for he gives his crucified flesh (6:51) for the life of the world.

The Spirit of Truth, Life, and Assurance

John's theology of the Spirit shares some themes with the Synoptic Gospels but also characteristically moves in fresh directions.[13] I will sketch in John's portrait of the Spirit under the themes of truth, life, and assurance.

First, the Spirit is the Spirit of truth. The Gospel begins with the Baptist bearing witness to Jesus (1:6–8), and the role of "witness" is a rather prominent theme in this Gospel in its own right (1:26–36; 3:26–30; 5:31–39; 8:13–19;

13. For a helpful study, see Burge, *Anointed Community*.

10:25; cf. 19:35; 21:24).[14] Interspersed in the Baptist's witness we find a reference to the Spirit's role as a witness. The Baptist observed that the Spirit like a dove descended and remained on Jesus (1:32–33), equipping him for ministry. The Spirit's descent on Jesus also functions as a witness to Jesus as the truth, demonstrating that Jesus is the Messiah (cf. Isa. 11:1–5). Jesus speaks the words of God, communicating truth received from above. Jesus utters truth because God has given the Spirit to him "without measure" (3:34). It seems, then, that the Spirit inspired Jesus to proclaim God's speech, that the Spirit was the agent by which Jesus revealed the truth.

John identifies the Spirit as the Paraclete (*paraklētos*) four times (14:16, 26; 15:26; 16:7), though it should be noted that Jesus is also identified as a Paraclete in 1 John 2:1, suggesting that the Spirit takes up Jesus' role after the latter's exaltation. The meaning of the term has been intensely debated in scholarship, but no consensus has been reached as to its definition. Probably the best approach is to discern the meaning in context, though the word itself must play a role in determining its definition. In some instances *paraklētos* likely has a legal dimension, and so often it is rendered as "advocate." For instance, in 14:16–17 the Spirit is the legal advocate for the truth, and the truth ultimately is Jesus (14:6). The Spirit's role as a witness to the truth is evident in the second case where *paraklētos* is used, for the Paraclete will teach the disciples and bring to their mind everything Jesus taught them (14:26). Or, as Jesus says later, the Paraclete, "the Spirit of truth," "will bear witness about me" (15:26), just as Jesus bore witness to the Father (3:32). The Paraclete's role as a prosecuting attorney seems evident in 16:7–11. "He will convict the world concerning sin and righteousness and judgment" (16:8). He will convict and reprove the world because it fails to see the truth in Jesus. The world does not realize that disbelief in Jesus represents the fundamental sin of humanity (16:9). The world also lives under the illusion of its righteousness, for it does not perceive and behold Jesus or realize that he resides with God (16:10). Nor does the world grasp that its judgment is certain because the ruler of the world, Satan himself, was judged at the cross (16:11). John has in mind here an "effective" conviction of the Spirit. Obviously, he does not mean that everyone will believe. His point is that some in the world will put their trust in Jesus because the Spirit will convince them that Jesus is the way, the truth, and the life.

The Spirit does not function as an independent or autonomous witness. The Father "gives" the Paraclete (14:16), sending him by his own authority (14:26). At the same time, the Paraclete is also sent by the Son (16:7), for Jesus says,

14. See Boice, *Witness and Revelation*.

"I will send [him] to you from the Father" (15:26). The close relationship and equality of the Father and Son are also reflected, for "the Father will send" the Paraclete "in my [Jesus'] name" (14:26). The Father does not work apart from the Son in sending the Spirit. Indeed, the Spirit is given only after Jesus is glorified (7:39). The Spirit "proceeds from the Father" (15:26), deriving his authority from Jesus, so that the Spirit speaks only what he hears from the Son (16:13). The Spirit does not work apart from Jesus; he always witnesses to the truth in Jesus. The Spirit does not have an independent ministry; he came to bring glory to Jesus (16:14) and was sent by the Father in Jesus' name so that Jesus would be honored. Jesus "baptizes with the Holy Spirit" (1:33). The Spirit does not come on his own initiative or to bring attention to himself; he witnesses to and about Jesus (15:26), and he does not draw on his own resources in speaking truth but rather declares what has been given to him by Jesus.

The Spirit's dependence on the Father and the Christ and also his role in bringing glory to Jesus fit with the function of Jesus' farewell discourse in John (chaps. 13–17). Since Jesus was leaving and returning to the Father, the Spirit will come and dwell with and in the disciples (14:17). The Spirit's presence with them will compensate for Jesus' departure. In Jesus' absence the Spirit will be his stand-in, reminding them what Jesus taught them and instructing them in the future (16:13). The indwelling Spirit instantiates Jesus' presence, just as Jesus explained (1:18) and revealed (14:9) the Father. The disciples will know when the Spirit comes that Jesus is in them (14:20). The Spirit's devotion to Jesus and his role of calling attention to Jesus explain why he is not given until Jesus is glorified, for otherwise he would rivet attention on himself.

In 1 John the Spirit's role in witnessing to Jesus continues. "Spirits" must be tested, "for many false prophets have gone out into the world" (4:1). The Spirit testifies that the historical Jesus is the Christ (4:2). Those who do not confess Jesus as the human Messiah imbibe the spirit of the antichrist (4:3). Similarly, John reminds his readers of the anointing that they received (2:18–27). The context is quite similar to 4:1–6, where John warns against a defective Christology. So too here, those who deny Jesus as the historical and human Christ are liars and antichrists. Believers, however, stand in a different place, for they know the truth and have received the anointing. The anointing likely represents the work of the Spirit, which teaches believers the truth about Jesus the Christ. The anointing work of the Spirit in 1 John is remarkably similar to the Spirit's ministry of testifying to Jesus in the Gospel of John.

In 1 John we have a final text that impresses upon readers that the Spirit witnesses to the historical Christ (5:6–8). Jesus was empowered by the Spirit for ministry at his baptism, but the Spirit did not depart from him at the cross. The Spirit continued to testify that Jesus is the Christ at his death, where he spilled his blood for the salvation of human beings. The Spirit does not bear witness in a vacuum, nor does he work directly upon the minds of believers apart from history. The Spirit's work of teaching and testifying is tied to historical events, to Jesus' baptism and crucifixion. John emphasizes the eyewitness character of revelation both in his Gospel (e.g., 21:24) and in 1 John (e.g., 1:1–4). A mystical, intuitive, or immediate witness of the Spirit is denied by John, for the Spirit always witnesses to Jesus. Worshiping God "in spirit and truth" (John 4:23–24) becomes a reality only through the Holy Spirit. True worship is not realized through human reflection or intelligence. Given the Holy Spirit's role in calling attention to Jesus Christ, the Spirit inspires true worship by directing people to Jesus Christ. Human beings truly worship when they believe Jesus is the Christ, and that he is glorified and exalted via the cross.

The Spirit is not only the Spirit of truth; he is also the Spirit of life. New life cannot be produced by human beings, for it is the miraculous work of the Holy Spirit. John's Gospel records how Nicodemus was impressed with Jesus and acknowledged that he was from God, given the signs that he did (3:2). Jesus brushed aside Nicodemus's commendation, maintaining that one must be born again in order to see God's kingdom (3:3). New life cannot be generated by human beings (3:6). Indeed, Jesus emphasizes that new life is incalculable, for the Spirit sovereignly blows wherever he wishes (3:8), granting new life at his discretion.

Jesus says something quite similar in 6:63: "It is the Spirit who gives life; the flesh is no help at all. The words that I have spoken to you are spirit and life." Human beings are unable to produce life because of their weakness, whereas the Spirit is a spirit of power who can beget life where there is none. The life given by the Spirit, however, is tied to the words of Jesus, and in chapter 6 in particular to Jesus being the bread of life, to eating Jesus' flesh and drinking his blood. Hence, the Spirit gives life as he attests to Jesus' giving his flesh for the life of the world (6:51). The Spirit grants life, then, based on the atoning death of Jesus Christ. The Spirit confirms that Jesus ascends to the Father (6:62) through the cross, so that the cross is the way to life.

John's Gospel also closely associates the Spirit with water. The meaning of the reference to water in 3:5 is contested. Possibly it refers to Christian baptism, and John probably wants readers to see an allusion to baptism, where the sins of believers are cleansed. But the key for interpreting the verse is discerning the OT background. The OT context is Ezek. 36:25–27, where the Spirit replaces the heart of stone, granting a soft and compliant heart of flesh instead. The Lord promises, "I will sprinkle clean water on you" (Ezek.

36:25), and the water that cleanses, given the parallelism in Ezek. 36:25–27 and John's appropriation of the Ezekiel text, probably refers to the Holy Spirit. The Spirit gives life, for those who are beneficiaries of the Spirit's work keep the rules and regulations given by Yahweh (Ezek. 36:27).

Two other texts in John's Gospel forge a link between the Spirit and water. At the feast of Tabernacles Jesus invited the thirsty to come to him and drink (7:37–39). Jesus promises, in accord with Scripture, that "rivers of living water" will flow from those who believe in him. John clarifies that the living waters refer to the Spirit, who will be granted to the disciples after Jesus is glorified. Here it is difficult to discern which Scripture texts are being drawn from. Perhaps one text is Isa. 12:3: "With joy you will draw water from the wells of salvation." John may also be alluding to Ezek. 47, where the water flowing from the temple begins as a trickle and becomes a mighty flood. The water makes stale water fresh (47:8–9) and is the source of life and healing (47:12).[15] Hence, John shows that the water of the Spirit grants salvation and refreshes by dispensing life. Human beings are dead and desiccated without the Spirit, but the Spirit revivifies, just as water invigorates a thirsty traveler.

We also find a reference to water in John 4. A direct reference to the Spirit is lacking, but the link between water and the Spirit in other Johannine texts, especially 7:37–39, suggests that the Holy Spirit is in view here as well. Isaiah 44:3 also forges a connection between water and the Spirit, and this verse may have informed John's usage: "For I will pour water on the thirsty land, and streams on the dry ground; I will pour my Spirit upon your offspring, and my blessing on your descendants." Jesus informed the Samaritan woman that if she knew who he was, she would have asked him for "living water" (4:10). This living water would quench the thirst of her soul forever (4:13–14), for it would become a spring within, "welling up to eternal life" (4:14). This water of life within most likely is an indication of the Holy Spirit. The reference to eternal life strengthens this suggestion, for we have already seen that the Spirit is the Spirit of life. Those who are parched and dead are granted life by the Spirit.

The Spirit of life is given to believers after Jesus' death, when he is glorified. Perhaps 19:30 should be understood along these lines. When Jesus died, "he handed over the Spirit." Contrary to the ESV ("his spirit"), there is no pronoun "his" in the original text. It is possible, then, that John communicates symbolically that the Spirit is given at Jesus' death, for Jesus' death in John's Gospel constitutes his glorification, and the Spirit is granted when Jesus is glorified (7:39).

---

15. Beale also sees allusions to Joel 3:18 and Zech. 14:8, showing that Jesus himself is "the new 'holy of holies'" (*Church's Mission*, 197).

The meaning of 20:22 is controversial. Jesus breathed on the disciples, saying, "Receive the Holy Spirit." When was this speech-act fulfilled? Was it immediately when Jesus spoke, or was it later, on the day of Pentecost? I tend to think that Jesus speaks symbolically here, and the words uttered on this occasion were fulfilled on Pentecost, which was well known to John's readers. But we can skip over the debate about when Jesus' words were fulfilled and focus instead on the meaning of his words. In any case, Jesus grants the Spirit of life to his disciples after his glorification. The eschatological gift of the Spirit is granted to Jesus' disciples, and therefore they enjoy life.

John also emphasizes that the Spirit grants assurance. This theme is especially prominent in 1 John, but it is not completely absent in the Gospel, where it is present by implication. John's Gospel was written so that people would know that they have eternal life if they believe that Jesus is the Christ and the Son of God (20:30–31). The Spirit becomes a means of assurance, for those who enjoy the Spirit as living water find that the Spirit springs up to eternal life (4:14). The Spirit grants life that is imperishable, life that cannot be quenched by death. Similarly, the Paraclete will abide with the disciples "forever" (14:16). His residence in believers is not temporary but permanent, and such permanence suggests life that is inviolable, which in turn grants assurance. The convicting work of the Spirit (16:7–11) also fortifies assurance and confidence, for he will convince believers that Jesus is truly the Christ. The language of "convicting" (*elenchō*) suggests persuasion (cf. John 8:46; 1 Cor. 14:24), and those who are persuaded by the Spirit have a deeply rooted confidence that Jesus is indeed the Son of God and the Messiah.

The theme of assurance relative to the Spirit comes to the forefront more directly in 1 John. John penned the epistle so that readers would be convinced that they have eternal life (5:13). Those who did not belong to God had left the church (2:19), but believers enjoy an "anointing" (*chrisma*) from God so that they know the truth (2:20). The anointing, as noted above, almost certainly refers to the Spirit. The truth that the Spirit confirms is that the historical Jesus is the Christ, the one sent by God to accomplish salvation through the cross (2:22–23). John says twice that believers can have confidence that God abides in them because God has given them his Spirit (3:24; 4:13). Such assurance cannot be separated from keeping God's commands and believing that Jesus is the Christ (3:23–24). The Spirit is present in those who love one another (4:12), and such love is grounded in God's love manifested in Jesus Christ (4:7–11).[16] For anyone who claims assurance from the Spirit but fails to

---

16. Schlatter says that the disciples "tolerated no hatred among themselves except hatred of sin" (*Theology of the Apostles*, 41).

love fellow believers, violates God's commands, or disbelieves that Jesus is the Christ, such assurance is illusory. The assurance derived from the Spirit cannot be detached from other grounds of confidence taught by John. However, even though the Spirit and the other grounds of assurance are inseparable, this is not to say that they are indistinguishable. Assurance from the Spirit is not the same thing as keeping the commandments, believing Jesus is the Christ, and loving one another. The Spirit personally and persuasively convinces believers that they truly belong to God and Christ so that they know that they enjoy eternal life.

In Johannine thought the Spirit glorifies and calls attention to Jesus Christ. His ministry is never isolated or separated from Jesus Christ. The Spirit is the Spirit of truth, but invariably he witnesses and attests to the truth in Jesus. Similarly, the Spirit grants life, but he grants life only because Jesus is now lifted up and glorified. The Spirit sovereignly gives life because Jesus is the crucified and glorified one, and so he honors Jesus in granting life. The Spirit is also the Spirit of assurance, but again the assurance is tied to the historical work of Jesus as the Christ. He assures those who believe that Jesus is the Christ and who keep his commands that they truly belong to God. The Spirit is an advocate of Christ, teaching and convicting human beings about the truth in Jesus.

Believing and Obeying

The verb "believe" (*pisteuō*) occurs ninety-eight times in the Gospel of John, and nine times in 1 John. The noun "faith" (*pistis*) occurs only once in the Johannine Gospel and Epistles, in 1 John 5:4. In this one instance the noun carries the same meaning as the verb. Not every use of "believe," of course, refers to trusting in Jesus or God, but the vast majority do, so it is evident that believing is a major theme in John. Furthermore, the centrality of believing is evident from the purpose statement in the Gospel and 1 John. John wrote his Gospel so that his readers would believe that Jesus is both the Christ and the Son of God (20:31; cf. 11:27). Indeed, the importance of belief is particularly underscored, for John uses *pisteuō* twice in 20:31, a crucial verse, emphasizing that life is obtained by believing in Jesus. Similarly, 1 John was written so that the readers would be assured of eternal life, which is given only to those "who believe in the name of the Son of God" (5:13). The purpose of the Baptist's ministry as described in John's Gospel can be summarized compactly. He bore witness to Jesus as the light so "that all might believe through him" (1:7). And 5:30–47 emphasizes that the Father, the Baptist's ministry, Jesus' works (cf. 10:25, 37; 12:37), and the Scriptures function as witnesses so that people would "believe the one whom he has sent" (5:38). Those who believe in Jesus are spared judgment, while those who disbelieve already experience judgment before the age to come arrives (3:18). Those who do not believe in Jesus will "die in [their] sins" (8:24). Conversely, those who believe in Jesus "shall never die" (11:26). Those who have new life believe that Jesus is in the Father and the Father is in him (14:10–11), for the fundamental sin is the refusal to believe in Jesus (16:9). Human beings are inclined to dream about the great things that they can accomplish for God's sake, but the work that God requires is believing not doing, so that human beings "believe in him who he has sent" (6:29). Eternal life is obtained not by working for God but rather by trusting in the Christ.

John communicates the vitality of faith in a variety of ways, using different verbs and images to convey the breadth and depth of what it means to believe, so that the notion that faith is mere intellectual assent is avoided. Faith is described as "receiving" (*lambanō*). Those who trust in Jesus welcome him as the Messiah and Son of God (1:12; 5:43; 13:20; cf. 1 John 5:9). They receive his testimony and pay heed to his words (3:11, 32, 33; 12:48; 17:8). Faith both welcomes and cherishes the words of Jesus and the testimony of witnesses that points to Jesus.

Faith obeys Jesus. The parallelism in 3:36 is most interesting, for "disobeying" (*apeitheō*) is contrasted with "believing" in him, indicating that disobedience is an expression of unbelief. John cannot conceive of those who believe in Jesus but fail to obey him. Those who trust in Jesus "keep" (*tēreō*) his word and his commandments (8:51, 52; 14:15, 23, 24; 15:10), for those who refuse to keep Jesus' commands do not truly love him. Jesus identifies his disciples as those who keep his word (17:6). Similarly, Jesus' disciples "follow" (*akoloutheō*) him (1:37–38, 40, 43; 8:12; 12:26; 21:19, 22), just as sheep follow only their shepherd (10:4–5, 27). Those who refuse to follow Jesus do not truly believe in him and are not truly his disciples. We see the same theme in 1 John. Those who truly know Jesus keep his commands (2:3–6; cf. 3:22; 5:3). They are not sinless (1:7–2:2), but they do not persist in a life of sin (3:4–10; 5:18). Sin does not dominate their lives, and they do not give themselves over to evil.

Another way of putting this is that those who believe in Jesus "abide" or "remain" (*menō*) in Jesus (15:4–5). Those who do not continue in Jesus will be cast aside and perish forever (15:6). True disciples continue in Jesus' words (8:31; 15:7); they remain in Jesus' love by keeping his commands (15:9–10). The same truth is taught again in 1 John. Those who remain in Jesus live as he lived (2:6; cf. 3:24) and do not give themselves over to a life of sin (3:6). They continue in the light by loving brothers and sisters (2:10), by caring for the needy and indigent (3:17). Those who do not truly belong to the people of God demonstrate their inauthenticity by leaving the church, by failing to abide (2:19), whereas those who truly belong to God remain within the circle of apostolic teaching (2:24, 27). As 2 John 9 says, faithful believers do not "progress" beyond apostolic teaching about the Christ; they continue to uphold an orthodox Christology.

In the OT and in John "hearing" (akouō) occasionally denotes obedience, in the sense that those who truly hear obey. Such a meaning for "hearing" derives from the OT, where hearing often has the idea of obeying. We see this meaning in John's Gospel when Jesus says to adversaries, "You cannot bear to hear my word" (8:43). Conversely, the one who is of God "hears the words of God" (8:47). The sheep hear the voice of the shepherd (10:3, 16, 27) but refuse to listen to false shepherds (10:8). Along the same lines, we find in 1 John that those who belong to God listen to and therefore obey the apostolic message (4:6). A genuine hearing of Jesus' words provokes one to action, such that the hearing has a practical effect in everyday life.

The richness of the Johannine conception of faith is confirmed by the many terms that express the nature of faith. One of the most prominent, of course, is "love" (agapaō), which is the antithesis of "hate" (miseō). John's Gospel observes that unbelievers are drawn toward the darkness and "love" it (3:19), while they "hate" the light because it exposes their evil (3:20), for they love the approval of human beings more than the glory of God (12:43). Those who truly belong to the Father love Jesus (8:42), demonstrating their love for Jesus by keeping his commands (14:15, 21, 23, 24; cf. 1 John 5:2).

The vigor and the dynamism of faith are expressed with words of motion. I have already noted that John's Gospel uses the word "follow" to denote the vitality of faith. Other verbs of motion are used as well: "come," "enter," and "go." For instance, those who shrink from evil do not "come" (erchomai) to the light, for they flinch at the appearance of the light (3:20). Conversely, believers, whose works have a divine origin, come to the light (3:21). People must come to Jesus to obtain life (5:40; cf. 6:35, 37, 44–45, 65; 7:37; 14:6). Similarly, faith is portrayed as "going": Peter says to Jesus, "Lord, to whom shall we go? You have the words of eternal life" (6:68). Faith is also described as "entering." Jesus uses the image of the door of the sheepfold, saying that he is the door, and so, "If anyone enters by me, he will be saved and will go in and out and find pasture" (10:9). John would not recognize as faith what many today identify as faith, for faith is never separated from activity.

The vivacity of faith is also conveyed by sensory metaphors. Faith "beholds" (theaomai) the Son, seeing and perceiving him for who he really is (6:40; cf. 12:45). The necessity of "seeing" Jesus is communicated particularly in the healing of the blind man (chap. 9; cf. 11:9). His physical healing represents the granting of spiritual sight as well, for the story concludes with his believing that Jesus is the Son of Man and worshiping him. Conversely, the Pharisees who claim to see are blind because they refuse to see Christ for who he truly is. Indeed, those who give themselves to sin have not really seen Jesus (1 John 3:6). In John's Gospel some Greeks want to see Jesus (12:21), but they cannot truly perceive him apart from his death (12:24), his being lifted up on the cross (12:32). Only if one sees that Jesus is the Messiah and Son of God on the cross does one truly grasp who he is.

Two other sensory metaphors for faith are "drinking" and "eating," both of which convey the notion that faith is absorbed and takes residence in a person. Those who believe in Jesus drink of the water that he gives them, and he slakes their thirst forever (4:14; 7:37). So too, those who eat Jesus' flesh and drink his blood obtain eternal life (6:50–56). Only those who put their faith in Jesus' bloody death have life. Believing in Jesus is not a passive activity. Those who come to him and believe in him eat and drink of him, so that they ingest his life in themselves.

The vitality of faith is confirmed by 1 John, where John writes to grant assurance to those who stayed in the church rather than departing with the secessionists (2:19). The emphasis on assurance pervades the letter. John writes so that his readers will know they have eternal life (5:13). Fathers, the young, and children are assured that they truly know the Father, and that their sins are forgiven (2:12–14). I noted above that the Spirit was given (3:24; 4:13) and believers received the anointing (2:20, 27) to give them confidence that they belonged to God. The readers are exhorted to remain in Christ so that they will have boldness before God (2:28), and then John immediately emphasizes that they are truly God's children and have the certain hope of being like Christ (3:1–3). They can be sure of the message that John proclaimed because he received it as an eyewitness (1:1–4), and hence they should test the spirits and reject those that do not accord with the apostolic witness (4:1–6). Since the readers have received God's love, they are free from all fear of punishment (4:17–18). Their hearts can be full of assurance even when they feel condemned, for God is greater than their hearts (3:19–21).

This message of assurance is tied to the authenticity and reality of their faith, and John emphasizes in 1 John that faith expresses itself in the confession of sin (1:6–10), in keeping commands (2:3–6), in living a life of righteousness (3:4–10), in loving brothers and sisters (2:7–11; 3:11–22; 4:7–21), and in confessing Jesus as the Christ (2:18–23; 4:2–3; 5:6–7; cf. 2 John 7–9). Faith rests on Christ's atoning work, where God's love is manifested in history, but it is always connected to life. Faith is not an abstract or ethereal reality separated from ordinary life; rather, it reveals itself in orthodox Christology and in love and righteousness.

For John, believing is a dynamic and vital reality. Believing that Jesus is the Christ and God's Son is necessary in order to enjoy eternal life. John uses many different terms and expressions to convey the nature of faith. Faith obeys, keeps, abides, follows, comes, enters, goes, eats, drinks, loves, hears, and sees. All that God requires for life is belief in the Son, but faith is no cipher for John. Faith "is the victory that has overcome the world" (1 John 5:4).

The Divine Gift of Life

The last theme I will consider in John is the theology of divine gift.[17] Faith, according to John, is not ultimately a human work but rather is given to human beings by God. In his Gospel John observes that those who believe are born of God (1:13). Those who are born again and born anew (an example of John's regular use of double meanings) are regenerated because of the sovereign work of the Spirit (3:1–8). We see a remarkable example of the same theology in 1 John, where he uses the same construction to say that those who practice righteousness (2:29), who triumph over sin (3:9), who love (4:7), and who believe (5:1) have been born of God. In every case the verb for "born" (gennaō) is in the perfect tense, showing clearly that new birth precedes practicing righteousness, avoiding sin, loving, or believing Jesus is the Christ. Certainly, John does not intend to say that a person first practices righteousness and as a result of that righteousness is born of God, or first triumphs over sin and subsequent to such victory is born of God, or first loves and as a consequence of that love is born of God. Instead, being born of God comes first, and the result is righteousness, triumph over sin, love, and belief. Those who are born of God overcome the world (5:4). It is evident, then, that righteous living, love, and faith in Jesus as the Christ are gifts of God, fruits of God's sovereign and saving work in the lives of human beings.

The theology of gift accords with the emphasis on God's love in 1 John, which is supremely manifested in the cross of Christ. The love of human beings is an answering and responding love, for love for God is a consequence of first being loved by him (4:19), since Jesus as the Christ and the Son of God surrendered his life for believers (3:16). Out of love God sent his Son as an atoning sacrifice so that believers could enjoy life and be spared from the ravages of eternal death (4:9–10). God's gift of love expresses itself in the inclusion of believers into his family so that they are his children (3:1–2).

The obedience of believers is also a gift. It is, as John's Gospel says, "carried out in God" (3:21). True life is not grasped autonomously. Instead, the Son grants life to those to whom he wishes (5:21). Human beings are prone

---

17. On the relationship between divine sovereignty and human responsibility in John, see Carson, *Divine Sovereignty*.

to think that they are capable of believing and coming to Jesus. After all, believing in him and coming to him satisfy the thirst and hunger of one's soul (6:35). Jesus clarifies, however, that only those given by the Father to the Son come to him (6:37). Indeed, those who are not given by the Father to the Son are unable to come and believe (6:44; cf. 14:6). In other words, the desire to believe is granted by God, and if that desire is not fanned into existence by God, it will never appear. The gift of life, once granted, is irrevocable, for those given by the Father to the Son will never be lost and will experience the resurrection of life (6:39–40). Only some, in fulfillment of the covenant promise of Isa. 54:13, are truly taught by God (6:45), for those who have the Father as their teacher are those who are "drawn" by God (6:44). Those who do not believe were not "granted" by the Father to the Son (6:65). Hence, Peter cannot boast about perceiving that Jesus is "the Holy One of God" (6:69), for he made such a statement because he was chosen (6:70).

Jesus shepherds his own as the good shepherd, but how does one become part of his flock? John impresses upon readers the necessity to believe, and yet belief cannot be generated by human beings on their own. Only those who belong to Jesus' flock believe (10:26). Only those who belong to God hear his word (8:47). The circle of faith is beyond human ability because of human selfishness and blindness, but Jesus tells his disciples that he brings others into his fold (10:16). Jesus grants eternal life to those granted to him by the Father, and that life is indefectible (10:28–29). No one can remove them from his or the Father's protection. Those whom the Father gave to Jesus kept his word (17:6), and Jesus prays that they will be preserved until the end (17:9–12), and his prayer certainly will be answered.

INTERLUDE

A Synopsis of
ETERNAL LIFE IN THE GOSPEL AND EPISTLES OF JOHN

Given that John scarcely uses the word "kingdom," how does his theology fit with what is being argued for in this book? Certainly we must beware of suppressing the distinctive contribution of each of the writers of Scripture and of mashing them together so that the diversity of Scripture is squashed. We must let John be John, so that we hear his voice. God has given four Gospels with all their diversity and distinctiveness, for we need four Gospels to communicate the richness and depth and breadth of Jesus Christ.

Yet the differences between John and the Synoptic Gospels and Acts could be exaggerated. The purpose statement in John's Gospel emphasizes the importance of believing that Jesus is the Christ, and Christology, as we saw above, has to do with kingship. In order to be saved and to have life, one must believe that Jesus is the king and the Son of God. The emphasis on belief and Jesus' kingship puts us in the same circle as the Synoptics and Acts, where it is shown that one must repent and believe that Jesus is Lord in order to be saved. We saw in the Synoptics that repentance and belief cannot be separated from a life of discipleship, and this accords with what John teaches. We saw in John's writings that those who believe in Jesus are transformed. They obey, keep, abide, love, follow, enter, go, come, hear, eat, drink, love, see, and so on. This is John's distinctive way of saying that those who believe that Jesus is the Messiah live under his lordship and rule. The manner of expression differs from the Synoptics, but the substance of what is said is remarkably similar.

John, of course, stands out as distinctive. He emphasizes the life that is granted to believers instead of emphasizing the kingdom. Jesus, according

537

to John, has been raised from the dead, and so eternal life, the life of the age to come, has invaded the present age. John emphasizes realized eschatology: those who believe in Jesus already enjoy the life of the age to come. But again we must beware of overstating our point. We saw above that there is a future eschatology in John. He recognizes that there is an already and a not yet. Furthermore, we saw in the Synoptics that "life" and the "kingdom" are two different ways of expressing the same reality. Those who live are in the kingdom, and those who are in the kingdom enjoy life. John points to the same reality, for in chapter 3 of his Gospel, where John speaks of the kingdom, Nicodemus is told that he must be born again to enter the kingdom, clearly showing that life is given to those in the kingdom. The Synoptics argue along the same lines, for the rich ruler will enter the kingdom, will have eternal life, only if he becomes a disciple of Jesus (Matt. 19:16–30 pars.).

Another very significant point of contact exists between the Synoptics and Acts and the Johannine writings. Just as the kingdom is an "already but not yet" reality in the Synoptics and Acts, so too eternal life fits with the "already but not yet" schema in John. John, along with Matthew, Mark, and Luke, believes that the age to come has arrived but is not consummated. John emphasizes life to describe the nature of what God grants to believers. He gives them life in Christ.

John provides an angle different from that of the Synoptics. All of the Gospels have high Christology, but in John's Gospel Christology reaches its zenith. Those who have eternal life know God and Jesus Christ (17:3). Jesus is the Word of God (1:1), and as the Word, he is fully divine. He explains the Father to human beings (1:18), and anyone who has seen Jesus has seen the Father (14:9). We could say that John differs from the Synoptics and Acts in that he focuses on seeing Jesus. The goal of the kingdom comes into sharper focus in John, for the kingdom is delightful, not merely because of God's rule, but because we will see the King in his beauty. The kingdom brings joy because believers will enjoy God's presence forever. They will "see" Jesus "as he is" (1 John 3:2), and they already see him now as the Word "made flesh" (John 1:14).

Christology plays a central role in John. Who is this Christ, this king, who explicates the one true God to human beings? John, in both his Gospel and his epistles, emphasizes that Jesus is the incarnate one, that he was truly a human being. He is, as John emphasizes over and over, the Christ, which means that he is the son of David. At the same time, he was truly God (John 1:1; 20:28) and the Lord of all. Just as we saw in Matthew, Mark, and Luke, Jesus is the Son of God and the Son of Man. He is the unique Son of God and fulfills what is promised about the Son of Man in Dan. 7:9–14. Christology in John is tied to soteriology, and hence Jesus as the Son of God and Son of

Man brings salvation to his people. Most of the "Son of Man" statements are linked to the cross, where Jesus is lifted up and glorified. Jesus as the lamb of God gives his life for the world. The indissoluble link between Christology and soteriology is also evident in the "I am" sayings. Jesus is the bread of life, the light of the world, the good shepherd, the door of the sheep, the resurrection and the life, the way and the truth and the life, and the true vine. Ontology feeds into and supports soteriology. Jesus saves because of who he is. John's style and expression differ from the Synoptics and Acts, but the content is the same in this respect: life is obtained through Jesus' suffering and resurrection. Jesus came so that human beings would not be condemned, so that they would enjoy life.

John especially overlaps with Luke in emphasizing that life comes from the Holy Spirit. The life of the age to come is a miracle, John teaches, a gift of God's sovereign and unpredictable grace. John does not say that God is king when he describes God's sovereignty, but again the concept of God's rule is surely present in the emphasis on his sovereignty in salvation and the events of Jesus' passion. John also stresses that the Spirit bears witness to Jesus, that he glorifies and honors Jesus, and shines the light on Jesus so that human beings will believe in him. The Spirit grants assurance to believers that Jesus is really the Christ, and that they belong to the people of God.

John does not emphasize the people of God in his Gospel. It has often been perceived as an individualistic Gospel. This observation perhaps is overstated, for John, in both his Gospel and his epistles, emphasizes love for brothers and sisters (John 13:34–35; 15:12–17; 21:15–17; 1 John 3:10–18, 23; 4:7–21; 5:2; 2 John 1, 5; 3 John 1, 6). John's Gospel teaches that those who follow Jesus are part of his flock (chap. 10; cf. Ezek. 34), but the flock is not limited to Israel, for Gentiles too will be folded into the flock and be united with the Jews so that there is one flock (10:16). The people of God from all over the world will be gathered together as one (11:51–52), and Jesus, by becoming a grain of wheat, will draw both Jews and Gentiles to himself (12:20–32). Jesus' conversation with the Samaritan woman and ministry among the Samaritans (4:4–42) suggest the unification of the people of God in Jesus. All those who follow the shepherd are part of the one flock (10:16). Jesus is the true Israel as the true vine (15:1), and thus all those who are joined to him and abide in him are part of the restored and new Israel in Jesus. Jesus prays that this flock, which comes to faith via the witness of the Twelve, will be one (17:20–26), that they will be united in love and harmony, for they are united with the Father and the Son. John, then, is not radically different from what we see in the other three Gospels and in Acts. Jesus is the true Israel, and those who belong to Jesus belong to this restored and new Israel.

Part 7

THE END
OF THE AGES HAS COME
ACCORDING TO
THE APOSTLE PAUL

29

THE THEOLOGY OF PAUL

Quite obviously, Paul's theology plays a major role in NT theology, for he wrote thirteen letters, and thus nearly half of the NT canon in terms of books comes from Paul.[1] There is virtue in reading each letter individually and constructing the theology of each epistle separately.[2] However, this book uses more of a wide angle and synthetic lens, and thus I will examine all of the letters together in unfolding Paul's theology.[3]

Unlike the Synoptics, Paul does not typically use the word "kingdom" to describe the fulfillment that has come in Christ. The term is not entirely absent, as we will see, but Paul's theology must be understood against the larger canvas of fulfillment in Christ. The eschatological promises of the OT are now fulfilled in Christ. As we examine Paul's theology, however, it becomes evident that there is an "already but not yet" dimension to the fulfillment. God's promises have been realized in Jesus Christ, and yet they have not reached their consummation. God's saving promises have been inaugurated but not yet consummated. Such a theme runs like a thread through all of Paul's theology. Whether we think of Christology, the new creation work accomplished by Christ, the new life that Christians live, the new people of God, or the new heaven and new earth, eschatological tension characterizes Paul's thought.

---

1. Pauline authorship of the Pastoral Epistles, Ephesians, Colossians, and 2 Thessalonians is disputed. I think that all of them are authentic, but it is not the purpose of this work to defend such a notion. I am writing a canonical biblical theology, which accepts what the canon says about authorship without trying to defend it historically.

2. On Pauline theology, see Dunn, *Theology of Paul*; Schreiner, *Paul*; Schnelle, *Apostle Paul*. For helpful and lucid surveys of Paul's letters theologically, see Marshall, *New Testament Theology*, 209–469; Thielman, *Theology of the New Testament*, 219–479; Matera, *New Testament Theology*, 105–258.

3. On the core of Paul's theology, see Plevnik, "Center of Pauline Theology."

The New David

Jesus is identified as the Christ about 375 times in Paul's writings. Often the title has been regarded as insignificant for Pauline theology, but this is almost certainly wrong. Paul was raised and nurtured in the OT Scriptures, which promised a coming David. The OT texts that promise an eternal dynasty and the coming of a new David were not rejected by Paul. Paul sees a fulfillment of the messianic prophecies in the OT and thus states frequently that Jesus is the Christ.[4] He does not elaborate on the theme, presumably because the majority of his letters were written to churches that he planted, where Jesus' messianic status was demonstrated from the OT when the churches were evangelized (see Acts 13:13–41). But he hardly understood "Christ" to be Jesus' last name. Interestingly, in Romans, written to a church that Paul neither established nor had visited when he wrote the letter, the Davidic and messianic role of Jesus is defended in the introduction of the letter (1:3). The presence of this theme in the introduction is significant, for Paul introduces his gospel here (1:1), and thus Jesus' Davidic heritage constitutes a central theme in the Pauline gospel. In 2 Timothy Paul reaffirms that Jesus is the offspring of David (2 Tim. 2:8), and again emphasizes that this accords with his gospel.

The connection between Jesus as the fulfillment of the Davidic promise and the gospel is quite interesting, for we have seen that the gospel promises return from exile (see Isa. 40:9; 52:7). Isaiah and the other prophets believed that the return from exile would become a reality with the arrival of a new David (Isa. 9:7; 11:1, 10; Jer. 23:5; 30:9; 33:17, 21–22, 26; Ezek. 34:23–24; 37:24–25; Hosea 3:5; Amos 9:11). Another piece of evidence points to Jesus' messianic identity, for Paul speaks of his reign (1 Cor. 15:25; 2 Tim. 2:12), and almost certainly the reign refers to his reign as the Messiah, as the son of David. Indeed, the text in 1 Cor. 15:24–28 contributes significantly to the "already but not yet" theme in Paul's writings. Jesus as the Davidic Messiah now reigns from heaven. He is the exalted Christ, and yet his enemies are not yet completely routed. The final destruction of demons and death is still to come, so that believers await the fulfillment of the prophecy of Ps. 110:1, when everything will be placed under Jesus' feet. This same theme appears in Eph. 1:20–22. Jesus was enthroned at his resurrection as Lord over all, so that all demonic beings are even now subservient to his authority (cf. Col. 2:10), and Jesus also reigns as Lord over the church. Even now Jesus is Lord over the universe. The notion that Jesus is the Christ fits with the theme of this work. Jesus is the messianic king, the sovereign one sitting at God's right hand, ruling even now from heaven.

4. See N. T. Wright, *Climax of the Covenant*, 41–55.

Our entrance point into Pauline Christology is that Jesus reigns as the Christ, as the new and better David. Such a theme is connected to Jesus as the new and better Adam, for just as Israel and David were, at one level, new Adams, Jesus is superior to both Adam and David, succeeding where they failed. We have an implicit connection here to Gen. 3:15, for a promise was given that an offspring of the woman would triumph over the serpent, which suggests that there would be a second Adam, who would succeed where the first Adam failed. The first Adam brought death into the world, but the last Adam—Christ (1 Cor. 15:45)—brought life by virtue of his resurrection from the dead (1 Cor. 15:21–22). The resurrection of the Christ signals the dawning of the new creation, for Christ at his resurrection triumphed over both sin and death (Rom. 6:8–10). The first Adam was responsible for the old evil age of death and sin (Rom. 5:12–19), but Jesus, as the second Adam, the last Adam, conquered the twin towers, the evil powers, of sin and death (Rom. 5:12–19). He cleaned up the mess that Adam spawned and more, for human beings do not only return to the Adamic state; they now enjoy the righteousness and life given to them by the last Adam. The first Adam tried to become like God and to be independent of God by transgressing his command in the garden (Gen. 3:1–6). But the last Adam was the obedient one (Rom. 5:19; Phil. 2:8), surrendering his life on the cross for the sake of his people. Surely, Phil. 2:6–11 cannot be limited to Adam Christology, but Adam should not be washed out of the text either.[5] Adam subverted his role as a creature to reach deity; Jesus, by contrast, did not exploit his deity but instead surrendered his life for the sake of human beings and their salvation (Phil. 2:6–8).

Jesus is not only the last Adam and the new David, he is also the offspring of Abraham. Indeed, Paul argues that he is the only true offspring of Abraham. Abraham, like Israel and David, was a new Adam of a sort,[6] but the promises could never be fulfilled in him, since he did not invariably trust in and obey God. The promises of land, offspring, and blessing given to Abraham are fulfilled in Christ. Hence, the only way to belong to Abraham is if one is united with Christ (Gal. 3:29). Here we see Paul's missionary theology. It is extraordinarily easy, especially for academicians, to forget that Paul was a missionary who had a passion to spread the gospel to the entire world. The promise to bless the whole world, both Jews and Gentiles, would become a reality through Jesus Christ, who was the true son of Abraham. Ethnic descent did not guarantee participation in the blessing of Abraham. Gentiles who belonged to Jesus Christ and were circumcised in heart were true Jews and

5. See Martin, *Hymn of Christ*; N. T. Wright, *Climax of the Covenant*, 56–98.
6. I say "of a sort" since Abraham, unlike Adam before the fall, was not free from sin.

truly circumcised (Rom. 2:26–29; Phil. 3:3; Col. 2:11). In Christ the eschaton had dawned, for the worldwide blessings promised to Abraham were now becoming a reality.

Paul uses the expression "Son of God" or "Son" seventeen times in reference to Jesus. He picks up the language here of Israel being God's son (e.g., Exod. 4:22–23; Jer. 31:20). The Davidic king is also identified as God's son (e.g., 2 Sam. 7:14; Ps. 2:7, 12; cf. Isa. 9:6). Jesus is the true Son of God, who invariably obeyed his Father. Paul often describes Jesus as God's Son when considering his death on the cross (Rom. 5:10; 8:3, 32; Gal. 2:20; 4:4). Here the obedience of the Son is featured, for he fulfilled the Father's will by dying for sinners. Jesus is now the exalted and reigning Son of God, fulfilling the purpose of the covenant with David (Rom. 1:4), and as David's son he will subject himself to the Father on the last day (1 Cor. 15:28). In the meantime, believers await the coming of the Son (1 Thess. 1:10). Believers now belong to the Son's kingdom (Col. 1:13) and enjoy fellowship with the Son (1 Cor. 1:9; cf. Eph. 4:13). Jesus is the unique and distinctive Son of God (Rom. 1:3), who preexisted as God's Son. Clearly, as the Son of God, Jesus enjoys a special relationship with God. Israel and David were called upon to reign as new Adams and as sons/son of God. But both Israel and David ultimately failed to do God's will. Only Jesus was the true Adam and the true Son of God, and hence the rule belonging to Adam was given to him, and this is attested by his resurrection from the dead.

The fulfillment of redemptive history is emphasized with Jesus being the exalted Lord. Here the promises of a new Adam, a new Israel, and a new David are again featured, though the lordship of Jesus cannot be limited to his humanity, for Paul picks up OT texts where Yahweh is Lord and applies them to Jesus. The hymn in Phil. 2 represents a striking example of this. Jesus is crowned as Lord because he did not take advantage (see 2:6 in NRSV, HCSB) of being equal to God. He did not exploit his being in the form of God. Rather, he took on humanity and humbled himself by suffering death on a cross (2:7–8). Therefore, God granted him the name above all names and exalted him as Lord, so that every knee would bend before Jesus and every tongue would acclaim him as Lord (2:9–11). Paul certainly alludes here to Isa. 45:23, with its proclamation that every knee will bow before Yahweh and every tongue profess allegiance to him. Paul makes a similar move in Rom. 10:13, where he asserts that "everyone who calls on the name of the Lord will be saved." The Lord here clearly is Jesus (cf. Rom. 10:9, where one must confess Jesus as Lord and believe in him to be saved). Paul cites Joel 2:32, where the Lord upon whom one must call certainly is Yahweh, and so there is no doubt that Jesus shares the same status as God (cf. 2 Cor. 4:5).

Those who are illuminated and energized by the Holy Spirit proclaim Jesus as Lord (1 Cor. 12:3). As Lord and creator, he enjoys the same stature as Yahweh (1 Cor. 8:5–6).[7] The day of the Lord in the OT is the day of Yahweh, but for Paul, the day of the Lord also belongs to Christ (1 Cor. 1:8; 5:5; 2 Cor. 1:14; 1 Thess. 5:2; cf. Rom. 2:16; Phil. 2:16; 2 Thess. 1:10).[8] Indeed, Paul links "name" with Christ's lordship, and "name" theology reaches back to the OT, stressing the deity of Christ (1 Cor. 1:2, 10; 5:4; 6:11; Eph. 5:20; Phil. 2:9–10; Col. 3:17; 2 Thess. 1:12; 3:6; cf. Eph. 1:20–23; Col. 3:23). The glory of Christ is supported by baptism being in his name (cf. 1 Cor. 1:13–16). The transcendence of the Lord is evident in many other texts as well. He is the "Lord of glory" (1 Cor. 2:8), the one who grants grace (2 Cor. 1:2; 13:14; Gal. 1:3; Phil. 1:2; 1 Thess. 1:1), peace (2 Cor. 1:2; Phil. 1:2; 1 Thess. 1:1; 2 Thess. 3:16), mercy (2 Tim. 1:16, 18), understanding (2 Tim. 2:7); delivers from afflictions (2 Tim. 3:11); grants strength to resist temptation (2 Thess. 3:3); repays the righteous and wicked (Eph. 6:8; Col. 3:24; 2 Tim. 4:8, 14); strengthens human beings (2 Tim. 4:17); is sovereign over what happens to each person (1 Cor. 16:7); and apportions each person's lot in life (1 Cor. 7:17). He is coming again in transcendent power and glory and will judge the righteous and wicked (1 Cor. 1:7; 4:5; Phil. 3:20; 4:5; 1 Thess. 3:13; 4:15–16; 5:23; 2 Thess. 1:7, 9; 2:1, 8; 1 Tim. 6:14–15). Prayer is directed to him (2 Cor. 12:8; 1 Thess. 3:11, 12; 2 Thess. 2:16; 3:5), songs are sung to him (Eph. 5:19), and he is to be trusted (Eph. 1:15; Phil. 1:14; cf. 2 Cor. 3:16) and rejoiced in (Phil. 3:1; cf. 1 Cor. 1:31; 2 Cor. 10:17) and loved (1 Cor. 16:22; Eph. 6:24; cf. 1 Cor. 1:9). Believers celebrate a meal in which Jesus is honored as Lord (1 Cor. 10:16–17, 21; 11:23–26).

I have suggested in this book that one of the fundamental themes in the Scriptures is that Yahweh is Lord. Paul augments and refines what we find in the OT by emphasizing the lordship of Jesus. Those who submit to God as Lord (i.e., to the Father as Lord) also submit to the Son, to the Christ, as Lord. Indeed, if one does not submit to the Son's lordship, one does not submit to the Father. The Lord of the universe is the second and last Adam, the offspring of Abraham, the new and final David. He is also "in the form of God" (Phil. 2:6) and "the image of the invisible God" (Col. 1:15). Everything was created by him and for his sake (1 Cor. 8:6; Col. 1:16). He is preeminent over all (Col. 1:17–18) because he is seated at God's right hand and rules over all (Eph. 1:20–22; Col. 2:10). Indeed, there are good reasons to conclude that Jesus is

---

7. On the lordship of Jesus, see Capes, *Old Testament Yahweh Texts*.

8. In a few of these texts it is disputed whether the referent is Christ, but I will not linger over this here.

specifically identified as God in two texts (Rom. 9:5; Titus 2:13). Jesus is the king of all, and all the promises of the kingdom find their fulfillment in him.

New Creation and Old Creation

In Gen. 3:15 we see the promise of victory over the serpent.[9] The triumph over evil pledged at the beginning is elaborated upon in the covenants with Abraham—and David and in the new covenant. When the kingdom comes, when God reestablishes his lordship over the world, there will be a new David, a new exodus, a new covenant, and a new creation.[10] Above we examined the promise of a new David and other dimensions of Pauline Christology, for as creator and redeemer and Lord, Jesus will fulfill the promise to restore God's lordship over the world. The world is blighted by death, demons, and sin. Jesus as Lord has triumphed over them all through his death and resurrection. Indeed, he has fulfilled the promise of a new exodus, a new creation, and a new covenant, though in an inaugurated but not consummated manner. It is fitting to describe what Christ has accomplished as the new David in terms of the new creation. The old creation, the fallen creation, came into the world through Adam's sin (Gen. 3). The new creation has arrived in Jesus Christ.

New Creation and Resurrection

How do we know that the new creation is present? In the OT the new creation arrives on the day of resurrection. The resurrection is the day when Israel will be delivered (Dan. 12:1–2), and it will occur at the time of the end (Dan. 12:9). Isaiah 24–27 teaches that the resurrection will mean the demise of the city of man and the exaltation of the city of God.[11] The Lord will reign on Mount Zion (24:23) on that day, and hence the day of resurrection is the day of God's redemptive rule over the world. On the Lord's mountain there will be an eschatological feast, and death will be swallowed up forever (25:6–8), and the righteous will be raised from the dead (26:19). Leviathan will be defeated (27:1), and Israel's sin will be atoned for (27:9) when they

9. See esp. M. Hubbard, *New Creation*, emphasizing the anthropological nature of the new creation; Beale, *Church's Mission*, seeing the new creation as both cosmological and anthropological. See also, more recently, Jackson, *New Creation*.

10. On the notion that Paul's thought is fundamentally eschatological, see Ridderbos, *Paul*. Beker (*Paul the Apostle*) emphasizes the apocalyptic character of Pauline theology. See also Pate, *End of the Age*.

11. In using the terms "city of man" and "city of God" here, I am reaching back to the work of Augustine.

return from exile (27:12–13). According to Ezek. 37, Israel will be unified on the day of resurrection, for the Spirit will breathe on them and give them life. In that day a new David will rule over them (37:24–25), their sins will be cleansed (37:23), Yahweh will be their sanctuary forever (37:27–28), and they will enjoy a covenant of peace in their land (37:25–26).

Paul was convinced that the new creation and the time of the end had arrived in Christ, for Jesus was risen from the dead. The OT texts cited above demonstrate that the day of resurrection is inseparable from the coming of the new David, the cleansing of sins at the cross, the defeat of Satan (Leviathan), the outpouring of the Spirit, and the unification of the people of God in Christ. Hence, the kingdom of God has dawned with the coming of Jesus and his resurrection (cf. Rom. 1:4). Now that Jesus has conquered death, death has been defeated forever (Rom. 6:9). The age to come has invaded history in Jesus' resurrection (1 Cor. 15:1–28), though there is an "already and not yet" dimension to the resurrection. Jesus has been raised from the dead, but the resurrection of believers is a future event. Jesus' resurrection demonstrates, however, that the age to come has arrived, that the new creation is here.

Old Creation and Sin

The old creation was subjected to frustration and futility because of human sin (Rom. 8:18–25). Corruption and death characterize the old creation. Through Adam sin and death entered the world (Rom. 5:12–19), so that in Adam "all die" (1 Cor. 15:22). As the sons and daughters of Adam, human beings are "by nature children of wrath" (Eph. 2:3). Because of Adam's one sin all people enter the world condemned, spiritually dead, and as sinners (Rom. 5:15–19). Death and sin reign as the twin towers, as cosmic powers over the world. The old creation has both cosmic and anthropological dimensions. In Pauline thought spiritual death (separation from God) cannot be sundered from physical death and final judgment. Hence, the final triumph of sin is death, for in death sin exacts its wages (Rom. 6:23). Human beings are not only subject to sin; in the old creation they are subservient to Satan, who is "the prince of the power of the air" (Eph. 2:2).

Sin, going back to Gen. 3, is inseparably intertwined with the old creation. Thorns and thistles and pain in childbirth are the consequences of sin. The fundamental sin, the root sin, consists in the refusal to give praise and thanks and glory to God (Rom. 1:21).[12] Human beings worship the creature rather than the creator, turning to idols instead of giving thankful praise to the living

---

12. For an insightful study on thanksgiving, see Pao, *Thanksgiving*.

God (Rom. 1:22–25). The myriad of sins that human beings commit are a result and consequence of idolatry (Rom. 1:24–32). God hands human beings over to sin because they chose independence over dependence, because they wanted to get glory for themselves instead of giving it to God. Despite the reservations of some scholars, Rom. 14:23 is a general statement: "Whatever does not proceed from faith is sin." If human beings are not trusting in God and relying upon his strength, they are sinning. Faith gives all glory to God, believing that he will carry out what he promised (Rom. 4:20–21). Sin gives all glory to self, refusing to believe in God's Word and promises so that one trusts in one's own wisdom and intellect (Rom. 1:21–22; Eph. 4:18). But such a mind distorts reality, for nothing is more false than the denial of God and the exaltation of the self. Human beings live in accord with the purpose of their existence if they glorify God in everything, even in eating and drinking (1 Cor. 10:31). And God is supremely glorified in Christ when human beings "do everything in the name of the Lord Jesus, giving thanks to God the Father through him" (Col. 3:17). Those who are truly God-centered and God-glorifying are Christ-centered and Christ-glorifying. It was God, after all, who exalted Jesus as Lord, so that the universal lordship of Jesus brings glory to God (Phil. 2:11). Those who honor God, then, put their faith in Jesus Christ, trusting in him rather than in themselves for salvation (Rom. 3:22, 26; 10:11; Gal. 2:16, 20; 3:22; Eph. 1:13, 15; 3:12; Phil. 1:29; 3:9; Col. 1:4; 2:5).[13]

Since sin refuses to trust in God or Christ, boasting or pride is the mark of idolatry. Human beings especially take pride in their observance of the law (Rom. 3:27) and try to establish their own righteousness (Rom. 10:3), and so they place their confidence in the flesh rather than the Spirit (Phil. 3:2–3). Human beings want to secure "a righteousness of [their] own that comes from the law" (Phil. 3:9), but the only true righteousness is that which comes from God, a righteousness obtained "through faith in Christ" (Phil. 3:9). Many today vigorously question such a reading because of the work of the new perspective on Paul, whereby the issue is seen to be boundary markers and ethnic identity rather than self-righteousness. Certainly, boundary markers were disputed in Paul's day, and the unity of Jews and Gentiles in the people of God was very important to Paul. Nevertheless, a contrast between self-righteousness and the righteousness from God, between boasting and trust in God, cannot be washed out of these texts. The old perspective

---

13. Most of these examples of faith in Christ stem from texts that are greatly disputed today, for many scholars believe that we have a subjective genitive in these texts, so that the reference is to the "faithfulness of Christ" instead of "faith in Christ." For a recent work that chronicles the debate, see Bird and Sprinkle, *Faith of Jesus Christ*. For a defense of the objective genitive reading, "faith in Christ," see Schreiner, *Galatians*, 163–66.

reading is fundamentally right in this regard. "Works of law" (Rom. 3:20, 28; Gal. 2:16; 3:2, 5, 10) refers not just to boundary markers but rather to all the law commands (note Gal. 3:10). A wider frame for "works of law" is evident in Galatians, for the Galatians desired to be under the law as a whole (Gal. 4:21), and Paul's polemic is not limited to boundary markers, but includes the entirety of the law. In the same way, the Jewish problem with the law is not limited to boundary markers in Romans. In fact, when sins are listed, the moral norms of the law are mentioned (Rom. 2:21–24). Nothing is said about excluding Gentiles from the promise. Human beings want to secure a right standing before God on the basis of their obedience.

We have another indication of a fundamental opposition between "works of law" and faith. Paul shifts from speaking of "works of law" (Rom. 3:20, 28) to "works" (*erga*) in general (Rom. 4:2, 6; cf. 4:4). Here "works" clearly refers to the actions or deeds that human beings do to commend them to God, for Abraham did not live under the law. Paul does not criticize works per se. If Abraham did the required works, he could legitimately boast in God's presence (Rom. 4:1–5). Boasting is excluded because Abraham was ungodly, because he failed to do what God demanded. The case is quite similar with David (Rom. 4:6–8), for he was justified apart from works. It is clear that Paul reflects on David's adultery with Bathsheba and murder of Uriah, since he quotes Ps. 32, where David confesses his sins. Hence, the focus is scarcely on boundary markers here. The old perspective has it right at this point. Boasting is excluded because of human disobedience (Eph. 2:8–9; Titus 3:5). Hence, the grace of God, instead of human performance, is featured as the ground of salvation (Rom. 11:5–6; 2 Tim. 1:9).

The irrationality of human beings comes to the forefront when we think of human works. Paul emphasizes the universality of human disobedience (Rom. 1:18–3:20; Gal. 3:10; 5:3). No one does what God requires. "All have sinned and fall short of the glory of God" (Rom. 3:23). And yet human beings still live under the illusion that they can be justified before God, even though they fall far short of what God requires. Both human disobedience and human boasting rob glory from God.

In the new creation the promised circumcision of the heart (see Deut. 30:6) becomes a reality. Since the law is abolished, God has now created "one new man" in Christ (Eph. 2:15). The old age reflected division between Jews and Gentiles, where the Jews were God's theocratic people who observed the law of Moses given by their king and Lord. But the wall that separates Jews and Gentiles has been torn down through the death of Christ (Eph. 2:14). Jesus took the curse of the law upon himself (Gal. 3:13) and freed all those who were subject to the law's curse (Gal. 4:4–5).

We will see shortly that one of the marks of the new creation is the gift of the Spirit, and one of the most common Pauline contrasts is the opposition between the flesh and the Spirit. In the polarized opposition between the flesh and the Spirit we see Paul's apocalyptic theology, the antagonism between this age and the age to come. Those who are in the flesh are sons and daughters of the first Adam. Those who are in the flesh are unregenerate (Rom. 7:5), for by definition those who are in the flesh are not indwelt by the Holy Spirit (Rom. 8:9; cf. Col. 2:13). Therefore, they have no inclination to do God's will, and indeed they have no ability to practice what God commands (Rom. 8:5–8). When those who are in the flesh carry out their desires, they do what displeases God (Eph. 2:3).[14] The works of the flesh exclude people from God's eschatological kingdom (Gal. 5:16–17, 19–21; cf. 5:22–23; 6:8), for those who do what the flesh desires reveal that they never lived under God's rule.

The New Creation and Its Relationship to Law and Righteousness

An eschatological contrast in Pauline theology exists between this age and the age to come (Eph. 1:21), between the law and the Spirit. This age represents the old creation, whereas the age to come represents the new creation. Believers must not let their thoughts and actions be shaped by the old age (Rom. 12:2; Eph. 2:2; 1 Tim. 6:17; 2 Tim. 4:10; Titus 2:12). The values and intellectual judgments of this age are flawed, for they led the rulers of this age to crucify Christ (1 Cor. 1:20; 2:6, 8; cf. 3:18). Believers have been delivered by the cross of Jesus Christ from "the present evil age" (Gal. 1:4).

The new creation in Christ Jesus means the end of the old creation. No longer will demons, disease, disobedience, the devil, and death rule. Christ's death and resurrection constitute the decisive victory over sin and death (see Rom. 6:1–11). The promised new creation in Isa. 43:18–19; 65:17; 66:22 has come in Jesus Christ. Hence, all those who belong to Christ are a new creation (2 Cor. 5:17).[15] The new has come in the midst of the old. Because the new creation has come, Christians are no longer under the old covenant and the Sinai law. The law given to Moses was intended to be in force as long as this age lasted. But with the onset of the new creation and the fulfillment of God's promises, the age of the law covenant has been concluded (cf. Rom. 6:14–15; 7:4–6; 2 Cor. 3:4–18; Gal. 3:15–4:7; Eph. 2:15). The arrival of the new creation

14. Schlatter says about the flesh, "The constitution of our body results in the fact that we bear within ourselves an infinite number of passions, constantly having needs, constantly nurturing cravings, so that our lives and aspirations consist in the fulfillment of our desires" (*Theology of the Apostles*, 206).
15. For the OT background, see Beale, *Biblical Theology*, 299–302.

explains why circumcision is no longer necessary (Gal. 6:15), for circumcision was part of the old order, being required for members of the covenant with Moses (Eph. 2:11–22; cf. Lev. 12:3). In Galatians Paul argues repeatedly that the readers cannot return to Torah now that the Christ has been crucified. To do so would be to return to the "present evil age" (Gal. 1:4). It would say that Christ died for nothing (Gal. 2:21), as if the sacrifices of the law could remove the curse instead of Christ (Gal. 3:13). Sonship and redemption came not through the law but rather through the cross (Gal. 4:4–5). If one relies on circumcision and the old creation for salvation, then one is severed from Christ (Gal. 5:2–4) and removes the scandal of the cross (Gal. 5:11). It is as if a spell has been cast upon those who turn to the law for salvation, for they have forgotten the saving message of the cross (Gal. 3:1). Boasting only in the cross and not in circumcision is characteristic of those who belong to the new creation (Gal. 6:14–15).

Those who trust in their circumcision and the law for salvation show that they are still members of the old creation, for they actually trust in the flesh and their own righteousness instead of relying on the righteousness of God in Jesus Christ (Phil. 3:2–9). Jesus' resurrection functioned as his vindication, showing that he was crucified not because of wickedness on his part (1 Tim. 3:16).[16] Believers are righteous, therefore, because they are incorporated into Jesus as the crucified and risen Lord.[17] They are "in Christ" instead of "in Adam" (e.g., Rom. 6:1–11; Eph. 1:3–14).[18]

The close connection between Christ's resurrection and righteousness assists us in seeing that righteousness belongs to believers because they are part of the new creation. The righteousness of God is a gift given to believers from God (Rom. 1:17; 3:21–22; 10:3; 2 Cor. 5:21; Phil. 3:9). It is God's own righteousness given to believers who put their trust in Christ Jesus. Their righteousness is not in themselves, therefore, but rather belongs to them because they are united to Christ. The righteousness of God is given to them because Christ became sin for them, absorbing the punishment that they deserved (Rom. 3:25–26; 2 Cor. 5:21).[19] He took upon himself the curse that believers deserved for failing to do God's will (Gal. 3:13). Christ absorbed the sin of believers, and believers received the righteousness of God in Christ by way of exchange. This reading of what took place in the cross is sometimes said

16. See esp. Beale, *Biblical Theology*, 493–94.
17. Bird, "Incorporated Righteousness."
18. For a useful study of the "in Christ" formula in Paul's writings, see Seifrid, "In Christ"; see also Moule, *Origin of Christology*, 54–63; Campbell, *Paul and Union with Christ*.
19. For the notion that Paul's atonement theology was influenced by martyr traditions, see J. Williams, *Maccabean Martyr Traditions*.

to be a modern innovation, but it is an old interpretation, going back to the *Epistle of Diognetus*:

> But when our wickedness had reached its height, and it had been clearly shown that its reward, punishment and death, was impending over us; and when the time had come which God had before appointed for manifesting His own kindness and power, how the one love of God, through exceeding regard for men, did not regard us with hatred, nor thrust us away, nor remember our iniquity against us, but showed great long-suffering, and bore with us, He Himself took on Him the burden of our iniquities, He gave His own Son as a ransom for us, the holy One for transgressors, the blameless One for the wicked, the righteous One for the unrighteous, the incorruptible One for the corruptible, the immortal One for them that are mortal. For what other thing was capable of covering our sins than His righteousness? By what other one was it possible that we, the wicked and ungodly, could be justified, than by the only Son of God? O sweet exchange! O unsearchable operation! O benefits surpassing all expectation! that the wickedness of many should be hid in a single righteous One, and that the righteousness of One should justify many transgressors! (9:2–5).

God's righteousness represents God's character, an attribute of God, if you will. And the righteousness of God has been granted to believers as a gift, so that they stand in the right before God by faith.[20] They share the same status as the resurrected Christ, for they are united to Christ in both his death and resurrection. Hence, God's righteousness is also a gift of the new age.[21] The verb "justify" (*dikaioō*) supports such an interpretation. The verb is clearly forensic, indicating God's verdict or law court declaration regarding human beings (e.g., Rom. 2:13; 3:20, 24, 26, 28; 4:2, 5; 8:30, 33; 1 Cor. 4:4; Gal. 2:16; 3:8, 11, 24; 5:4; 1 Tim. 3:16; Titus 3:7). These texts emphasize that the verdict of righteousness is obtained by faith rather than by works. It is given to those who believe, not to those who work for God (Rom. 4:5), since no one's obedience is sufficient to obtain a favorable verdict. It is not surprising, then, that justification is closely aligned with grace (Rom. 3:24; 5:2; Gal. 2:21; 5:4; cf. Eph. 2:8), since human beings deserve not vindication but rather condemnation.[22] Justification is a stunning gift that awakens thankfulness and joy in those who receive it. Such a verdict of righteousness is also eschatological (Gal. 5:5). The

---

20. For helpful entries into the discussion, see Brauch, "Appendix: Perspectives on 'God's Righteousness'"; Reumann, *Righteousness in the New Testament*.

21. On the eschatological character of justification, see Gaffin, *"By Faith, Not by Sight."*

22. For a defense of the cruciality of justification, see Seifrid, *Christ, Our Righteousness*; Fung, "Status of Justification by Faith." Schlatter observes that opponents attacked Paul's view of justification because it was "the centerpiece of his preaching which set it apart from other forms of Christianity" (*Theology of the Apostles*, 239).

end-time pronouncement by the judge of the universe has been announced in advance. The future has broken into the present, so that believers in Christ Jesus are now declared to be in the right before him. Believers grasp this verdict by faith, for it is hidden from the world and cannot be proved or demonstrated. The final heralding of the verdict will be on the last day. Therefore, believers are already righteous in Christ, but that verdict has not yet been promulgated throughout the world. They are righteous because they belong to the Christ, who has been declared to be righteous at his resurrection.

New Creation and the Gospel

The onset of the new creation means that the new exodus prophesied in the OT prophets, especially Isaiah, has become a reality. Paul does not use the language of exodus specifically. However, he often speaks of his "gospel" (noun *euangelion* [59x], verb *euangelizō* [21x]). The background most likely lies in Isa. 40:9; 52:7, where the good news is the return from exile. The importance of the gospel for Paul is evident, for he was commissioned and called to preach it (Rom. 1:1; 1 Cor. 1:17; 9:16), and it is of first importance, centering on Christ's death and resurrection (1 Cor. 15:1–11) and unveiling "the glory of Christ, who is the image of God" (2 Cor. 4:4). Here Paul picks up the whole message of Isa. 40–66, particularly Isa. 53, for the new exodus becomes a reality only through the forgiveness of sins. The truth of the gospel is nonnegotiable (Gal. 2:5, 14), and thus those who proclaim a different gospel will be cursed eschatologically (Gal. 1:8–9; cf. 2 Thess. 1:8). The gospel was revealed to Paul by the risen Christ on the road to Damascus (Gal. 1:11–17; cf. Eph. 3:7; 1 Thess. 2:4). As a missionary, Paul was driven to preach the gospel in virgin regions where Christ was not named previously (Rom. 15:20–24; 2 Cor. 10:13–16; cf. Rom. 1:15–16; 15:16; Gal. 1:16; Eph. 2:17; 3:8), for the gospel was always intended for all nations (Gal. 3:8). Actually, the bringing of the gospel to the ends of the earth fulfills a new creation promise as well, for Isa. 66:18–21 predicts the nations will come and see Yahweh's glory, envisioning some coming from the farthest reaches of the earth to worship Yahweh. Such an extension of the gospel certainly fits with Paul's conception of his mission.

New Creation and Redemption

The language of redemption resonates with themes of the new exodus. The first exodus anticipates and foreshadows (Exod. 6:6; 15:13; Deut. 7:8; 9:26; 13:5; 15:15; 21:8; 24:18; Ps. 106:10), as we already saw in the prophets, a new exodus, a return from exile (Isa. 35:9; 41:14; 43:1, 14; 44:22–24; 52:3; Jer.

31:11; Mic. 4:10; Zech. 10:8). Paul sees that new exodus fulfilled in an "already but not yet" fashion in the redemption accomplished by Christ. According to Paul, human beings need liberation from sin, and so redemption consists of forgiveness of sins (Rom. 3:24; Eph. 1:7; Col. 1:14). Such redemption has been accomplished in the cross of Christ, where he took the curse that sinners deserved (Gal. 3:13) and freed those who were under the law (Gal. 4:5; cf. Titus 2:14). Redemption in Rom. 3 is closely linked with Jesus functioning as the mercy seat (3:25), the place where God's wrath is appeased. God thereby vindicates his righteousness, for he has judged sin in the death of Christ. Sin has not been passed over without punishment. The punishment that sinners warranted by virtue of their sins has been absorbed by Jesus Christ. Even though believers are now liberated from sin through the cross work of Christ, they still await final redemption (Eph. 4:30). The redemption of the body will take place on the day of resurrection (Rom. 8:23).

New Creation and the Holy Spirit

We saw in the OT that the new creation is inseparable from the gift of the Spirit (e.g., Isa. 32:15; 44:3; Ezek. 36:26–27; Joel 2:28).[23] The outpouring of the Spirit signifies that the last days have arrived. If the last days and new creation are present, then observing a rite from the old creation, such as circumcision, is passé. The Galatians, for instance, know that they are members of the new people of God because they received the Holy Spirit by faith, not by observing the Mosaic law (Gal. 3:2, 5). In Pauline theology the Spirit is the mark of conversion, the indisputable sign that one belongs to the people of God (Rom. 5:5; 8:9). Thus, true Jews are marked not by ethnicity or physical circumcision but rather by circumcision of the heart, which is the result of the Holy Spirit's work (Rom. 2:28–29). "Regeneration" and "renewal" are the result of the Spirit's supernatural work (Titus 3:5), and these terms themselves designate the fulfillment of God's promises, the arrival of the new creation through the Holy Spirit.

In Paul's soteriology the Holy Spirit plays an indispensable role. The Spirit, for instance, plays a role in justification, sanctification, and baptism (1 Cor. 6:11; 12:13). In 1 Cor. 6:11 sanctification is definitive (i.e., positional) and refers not to ongoing growth in the Christian life but rather to the work of the Spirit in setting a person apart at conversion (see also 2 Thess. 2:13). Paul also teaches that no one confesses Jesus as Lord apart from the Holy Spirit (1 Cor. 12:3). Conviction that the gospel is the truth comes from the Holy Spirit

23. On the Spirit in Paul's theology, see Fee, *God's Empowering Presence*.

(1 Thess. 1:5), and believers are "born according to the Spirit" (Gal. 4:29) and receive the Spirit when they are saved (Rom. 8:16; 1 Cor. 2:12; Gal. 3:14; 4:6). The Spirit indwells the individual Christian (1 Cor. 6:19) but also dwells in the church corporately (1 Cor. 3:16; Eph. 2:22). The Spirit certifies that one is a child of God (Rom. 8:16) and guarantees as the firstfruits of God's work (Rom. 8:23) eschatological salvation (2 Cor. 1:22; 5:5; Eph. 1:13–14; 4:30; cf. Gal. 5:5), so that those who have the Spirit now will experience the final resurrection (Rom. 8:11). The Spirit is the gift of the new age, functioning as a pledge and promise that God will bring to completion what he has begun.

The coming of the Spirit represents the arrival of the power of the age to come during the present evil age. There is a close connection between the Spirit and power (Rom. 15:13, 19; 1 Cor. 2:4). Believers are empowered to live in a way that pleases God if they walk by the Spirit (Gal. 5:16; cf. Eph. 3:16), are led by the Spirit (Rom. 8:14; Gal. 5:18), march in step with the Spirit (Gal. 5:25), and sow to the Spirit (Gal. 6:8). Eschatological tension is evident, for the Spirit battles with the flesh (Gal. 5:17; cf. Rom. 8:10), but the accent in Paul's theology is on the power of the Spirit to overcome sin, though sin persists until the day of redemption. There is a progressive change "from one degree of glory to another" from the Spirit (2 Cor. 3:18). Those who are indwelt by the Spirit produce "the fruit of the Spirit" (Gal. 5:22–23; cf. Rom. 8:5–6). Elsewhere Paul says that joy comes from the Holy Spirit (1 Thess. 1:6; cf. Rom. 14:17), and that love is a work of the Spirit (Rom. 15:30; Col. 1:8). Believers are liberated from the power of sin and death through the Holy Spirit (Rom. 8:2), so that those who have the Spirit fulfill "the requirement of the law" (Rom. 8:4). They serve in a new way by virtue of the Holy Spirit (Rom. 7:6), for "the letter kills, but the Spirit gives life" (2 Cor. 3:6), and as a result those who are indwelt by the Spirit are given the freedom to obey (2 Cor. 3:17). They slay by the Spirit "the deeds of the body" (Rom. 8:13). Believers do what pleases God as they are filled with the Spirit (Eph. 5:18), and the filling probably denotes both the Spirit as the means by which believers obey and the content with which believers are filled. The Spirit also enlightens believers so that they are able to grasp spiritual realities (1 Cor. 2:10–16).

New Creation: Reconciliation and Triumph over Evil Powers

Paul also argues that believers are reconciled to God in Christ.[24] Reconciliation means that friendship with God has been restored, so that the fellowship

---

24. Beale ("Reconciliation in 2 Corinthians 5–7") argues that the reconciliation stems from the promise of a new creation in Isaiah.

Adam enjoyed with God in the garden has been renewed and amplified. Reconciliation in Pauline theology is invariably dependent upon the cross of Christ (Rom. 5:10; 2 Cor. 5:18–21; Eph. 2:16; Col. 1:20). Paul emphasizes, therefore, the hostility of human beings toward God, so that the breach in their relationship with God must be repaired. Reconciliation is not only with God but also with one another. Jews and Gentiles are now united with one another through the cross of Christ (Eph. 2:11–22). Through Jesus' atonement the promise given to Abraham that all peoples would be blessed comes to realization. The cosmic scope of reconciliation is quite astonishing, for all things have been reconciled in Christ, even things in heaven (Col. 1:20). Here the new creation dimensions of reconciliation are quite evident. The reconciliation of all things does not mean that salvation reaches all, but rather that the entire universe is pacified and submitted to the Son. When all is said and done, the entire universe will bring glory to God and be under his dominion. The aim of reconciliation is the joy and exultation in God that will well up in the heart of those reconciled, for those who are reconciled in God rejoice in him (Rom. 5:11), as there is nothing more satisfying and fulfilling than knowing and seeing God.

The triumph over evil powers fits nicely after reconciliation. The drama of Scripture is the conflict between the offspring of the woman and the offspring of the serpent. Human beings enter into the world subject to the "prince of the power of the air" (Eph. 2:2). Satan is "the god of this world," blinding human beings from the beauty of the gospel (2 Cor. 4:4). Human beings wage war not merely against visible enemies, but against spiritual forces in the heavens (Eph. 6:12). Satan and demonic forces, however, were dealt a mortal blow at the cross (Col. 2:10–15), so that Jesus as the exalted Lord rules over all demonic powers (Eph. 1:20–22). At the cross Jesus stripped them of their authority and power, and hence the cosmic battle has been won once for all. In response, believers must put their trust in Christ and clothe themselves with the grace and the power that are theirs in Christ (Eph. 6:10–12). No heavenly powers or spiritual rulers can separate believers from Christ's love (Rom. 8:38) now that he has rescued them and won the victory at the cross. Indeed, heavenly beings see the church of Jesus Christ and God's redeeming plan and marvel at his wisdom (Eph. 3:10).

New Creation: The Kingdom, Salvation, and Inheritance

The eschatological character of Paul's thought and its rootedness in the OT are apparent in the foregoing discussion. We see these same themes in his use of the terms "kingdom" and "kingdom of God." After reading the

Synoptic Gospels, we are struck by how rarely Paul speaks of the kingdom of God. However, scholars perhaps have underestimated the significance of this terminology in Paul's thought, for the word "kingdom" and the phrase "kingdom of God" occur fourteen times in Paul's writings. The expression reaches back to the OT, where the notion of God's reign and rule over his people and over the whole world is prominent, but it also is quite possible that Paul draws here upon the teaching of Jesus about the kingdom. Paul often uses "kingdom" terminology to refer to the future kingdom that is coming, to God's reign over the universe. Indeed, the arrival of the kingdom means the destruction of demonic powers and of death (1 Cor. 15:26). Jesus will hand over the kingdom to the Father on the last day, and demonic powers will be nullified (1 Cor. 15:24). When the kingdom comes, God will be "all in all" (1 Cor. 15:28). God's power and beauty will be featured when the kingdom is consummated.

The promise of universal blessing given to the patriarchs and confirmed in the prophets and the psalms will be fulfilled in the coming kingdom of God. Abraham's children and heirs would only enjoy the promise if they kept "the way of the LORD by doing righteousness and justice" (Gen. 18:19). So too, Paul warns his readers that only the righteous will inherit the kingdom of God. Those who give themselves over to evil will be excluded (1 Cor. 6:9–10). Paul reminds the Galatians that those who practice the works of the flesh "will not inherit the kingdom of God" (Gal. 5:21). Ephesians has an interesting twist, for the kingdom belongs not only to God but also to Christ. Still, the same emphasis on obedience for entrance into the kingdom is underscored: "For you may be sure of this, that everyone who is sexually immoral or impure, or who is covetous (that is, an idolater), has no inheritance in the kingdom of Christ and God" (Eph. 5:5). Human beings are inclined to hope for and think the best, and so Paul admonishes them not to be deceived (1 Cor. 6:9; Eph. 5:6), for those who give themselves over to evil will face God's wrath and be excluded from the kingdom. Believers are made worthy of the kingdom by their righteous conduct and perseverance in faith (1 Thess. 2:12; 2 Thess. 1:5). The day of judgment will arrive, when Jesus appears and the kingdom is consummated (2 Tim. 4:1). Those who "fought the good fight" and "kept the faith" and who loved Jesus' appearing (2 Tim. 4:7–8) will be rescued from evil and inducted into the heavenly kingdom (2 Tim. 4:18).

For Paul, as we saw above, the kingdom often is future. At the same time, the kingdom is an eschatological reality that has broken into the present. Believers have been "transferred" "to the kingdom of his beloved Son" and freed from Satan's dark realm (Col. 1:13). The power of the kingdom is now unleashed, and it is manifested in "righteousness and peace and joy in the Holy Spirit"

(Rom. 14:17). The collocation between the kingdom and the Spirit reminds us of Luke, who forges a close connection between the two. Where the Spirit is working to transform human beings, the kingdom is active. The power of the kingdom is also presently unveiled (cf. 1 Cor. 4:20) in the gospel that Paul proclaims (see 1 Cor. 1:18–4:21), for the gospel is God's power for salvation (Rom. 1:16; cf. 1 Cor. 1:18). The Spirit, the gospel, and the kingdom are three different ways of communicating God's saving work in the present evil age. There is a present dimension to the kingdom, for believers are now called to the kingdom that they will inherit eschatologically (1 Thess. 2:12), and believers presently work for the kingdom of God (Col. 4:11).

The eschatological character of Paul's thought is evident in his understanding of salvation. Salvation is fundamentally an end-time reality. Those who are justified and reconciled through Christ's death can be confident that they will be saved on the day of judgment (Rom. 5:9–10). These two verses also capture the fundamental meaning of salvation; it means that one will be rescued and delivered. Believers enjoy the certain "hope of salvation" (1 Thess. 5:8), for God has appointed them to escape wrath and "to obtain salvation through our Lord Jesus Christ" (1 Thess. 5:9). The final separation between the wicked and righteous is a regular theme for Paul, and he often speaks of the deliverance that the righteous will receive as salvation. For opponents of the gospel there will be "destruction," while those who belong to God will experience "salvation" (Phil. 1:28). Since salvation is an eschatological reality, it "is nearer to us now than when we first believed" (Rom. 13:11).

As is typical in other arenas of Pauline thought, salvation has an "already but not yet" character. The eschaton has broken into the present, and thus believers are already saved (Eph. 2:5, 8; 2 Tim. 1:9; Titus 3:5; cf. 1 Cor. 1:18; 15:2; 2 Cor. 2:15). The end-time gift belongs now to those who believe in Jesus Christ. Paul particularly stresses that those who believe enjoy salvation. Those who are justified will be saved (Rom. 5:9), but justification is by faith, and hence those who believe will be saved on the day of redemption. Paul prays for the salvation of the Jews (Rom. 10:1), and salvation will be given to those who believe that Jesus is Lord and that God raised him from the dead (Rom. 10:9; cf. 10:10), so that those who call on the Lord's name in faith will be saved (Rom. 10:13). God saves "those who believe" in the message of Jesus as the crucified and risen Lord (1 Cor. 1:21; 15:1–11). They enjoy forgiveness of sins. One of the classic statements of this reality is found in Eph. 2:8, where Paul asserts that believers are saved by grace through faith, not by works. Indeed, it is characteristic of Paul to say salvation cannot be obtained through works (2 Tim. 1:9; Titus 3:5). That fits nicely, of course, with the Pauline emphasis that justification is by faith, not by works.

The language of heirs and inheritance in Paul's writings is eschatological, looking to the final reward. Abraham and those who share in the Abrahamic promise are heirs "of the world" (Rom. 4:13; see also 4:14). Paul does not often refer to the land promise of the OT, but the promise of land given to Abraham finds its fulfillment here. According to Paul, the entire world is now the object of the promise, indicating that the whole earth will gladly serve the Lord as the sovereign king. This reading of inheritance is justified, for elsewhere Paul speaks of those who will inherit the kingdom of God (1 Cor. 6:9–10; 15:50; Gal. 5:21; Eph. 5:5). The entire world, then, will be God's kingdom, his inheritance. In other texts the inheritance focuses upon the eschatological reward for believers (Rom. 8:17; Gal. 3:18, 29; 4:1, 30; Eph. 1:11, 14; Col. 1:12; 3:24; Titus 3:7). The nature of the reward in some texts is vague, but it seems from Col. 3:24 that Paul refers to the eschatological reward that believers will receive—their final salvation.

The New Creation as a Gift of God's Electing Grace

The salvation that believers enjoy is ultimately a gift. In other words, God gets the glory for salvation because he chose and elected believers to be saved. He chose both Jewish and Gentile believers in Christ before the world began (Eph. 1:4) for "the praise of his glorious grace" (Eph. 1:6). Paul certainly has salvation in mind in referring to election, for election is closely linked to predestination, which in turn is connected to adoption (Eph. 1:5), to being a son or daughter of God.[25] He chose the foolish and despised "so that no human being might boast in the presence of God" (1 Cor. 1:27–29), and hence the one "who boasts" should "boast in the Lord" (1 Cor. 1:31). Modern readers, even scholars, typically raise "justice" questions relative to election, but for Paul, being chosen is a matter of mercy and grace, not desert, so the choosing of any brings astonishment and wonderment and joy. This is especially apparent in Rom. 9–11, where words for "mercy" occur nine times and "grace" four times. The selection of Isaac rather than Ishmael and of Jacob rather than Esau is attributed to the mercy of God.[26] Paul emphasizes that God will fulfill his covenant promises to the Jews because the fulfillment of the promises depends upon divine election. God does not elect based upon foreseeing the good that human beings will perform (9:11), and thus the promise will be secured because it depends upon God's choice. Election and a theology of

25. On election, predestination, and calling in Pauline theology, see Schnelle, *Apostle Paul*, 400–403.
26. "God's hatred of Esau does involve ultimately that holy revulsion that is directed against the accursed Satan, his demonic hosts, and his human seed" (Kline, *Kingdom Prologue*, 187).

grace are closely linked in Paul's thought. As Paul says, "So too at the present time there is a remnant, chosen by grace. But if it is by grace, it is no longer on the basis of works; otherwise grace would no longer be grace" (11:5–6).[27] If election is repudiated, a theology of works reasserts itself, such that salvation is no longer entirely of grace. Paul did not promulgate a theology of election for speculative reasons but rather to preserve the grace and mercy and freedom and sovereignty of God in salvation.

A common objection is that Rom. 9 refers to the historical destiny of nations instead of to salvation. Some limit what Paul says to the political history of peoples and nations because he refers to Isaac and Ishmael, to Jacob and Esau, and to Pharaoh. Such a reading, though it has a certain plausibility initially, goes astray because it fails to read the text in context. The issue that troubles Paul is Israel's exclusion from salvation (not its political fate). He is so troubled by Israel's separation from Christ that he is even willing to be cursed forever so that Israel would be saved (9:1–5). Indeed, the issue throughout all of Rom. 9–11 is salvation. Hence, Paul prays for Israel to be saved (10:1) and promises a future end-time salvation for Israel (11:26). There are no grounds for thinking that Paul addresses a different topic in chapter 9. The soteriological character of chapter 9 is apparent, for the phrases "children of God" and "children of promise" (9:8) obviously relate to salvation, not merely to the historical destiny of nations. Furthermore, the contrast between "calling" and "works" demonstrates that soteriology is the subject of concern (9:11). The contrast between "destruction" and "glory" points in the same direction (9:22–23), for the former word is regularly used by Paul to indicate the final judgment that unbelievers will face. It is acceptable to speak of "historical destiny," as long as it includes and indeed features the notion of salvation, but those who use the term often limit its meaning to the political fate of peoples.

Others want to say that Paul speaks of corporate rather than individual election here. The Greek singulars used in 9:15–21, however, demonstrate that such a conclusion is faulty. Indeed, separating the individual from the corporate is a false dichotomy that should be laid to rest permanently. Certainly Paul is concerned about Israel's corporate destiny, but that in no way precludes the role of the individual. I have already mentioned that chapters 9–11 should be read as a unit. When Paul speaks in chapter 10 of the need to believe in order to be saved, he is not speaking only corporately; individuals must believe in order to be saved.

In any case, divine election is pervasive in Pauline theology. The faith, hope, and love of the Thessalonians are grounded ultimately and finally in God's

---

27. See Schnelle, *Apostle Paul*, 71–72.

election (1 Thess. 1:4–5). In 2 Thess. 2:9–12 Paul reflects on unbelievers who are deceived and refuse to love the truth. The condition of unbelievers leads him to consider the place of believers (2 Thess. 2:13). They are not in the circle of the saved because they are nobler or wiser or more inclined to godliness than unbelievers. Whether Paul speaks of "firstfruits" or "from the beginning" in 2 Thess. 2:13, his point is that believers are saved because they are chosen by God. They cannot take any credit for seeing the light. All unbelievers are duped and blinded by Satan (2 Cor. 4:4). The salvation of believers is analogous to the first day of creation (2 Cor. 4:6). Just as God said, "Let there be light," so too he has shone in the hearts of believers so that they see the beauty and glory of God in Christ. They see the King in his beauty because of the wondrous grace and election of God. They are humbled and grateful because belonging to the people of God is undeserved.

When Paul speaks of God foreknowing those whom he predestined (Rom. 8:29), the word "foreknow" (cf. Gen. 18:19; Jer. 1:5; Amos 3:2) refers to those upon whom God set his covenant affection, those who are chosen to be his people. The "golden chain" of salvation cannot be severed, for all those foreknown and predestined are also glorified (Rom. 8:29–30), and therefore salvation is God's work from first to last, from beginning to end. Part of this golden chain is "calling" (*kaleō*): "Those whom he called he also justified" (Rom. 8:30). It is evident from this verse alone that this calling is effectual, that it is a supernatural work. After all, only those who believe are justified. But Paul says that all those who are called are justified. It must follow, then, that calling does not merely mean "invited to believe"; rather, calling creates faith, so that all those and only those who are called are justified.[28] The same notion is evident in other texts as well. The gospel is "preached" (*kēryssō*) to all, both Jews and Gentiles (1 Cor. 1:21), but the "called," and only the called and all the called, see that Christ is the "power" and "wisdom" of God (1 Cor. 1:24). The gospel is proclaimed to all, but only those who are called embrace the gospel. It is hardly surprising, then, that Paul immediately explains "calling" (1 Cor. 1:26) in terms of God "choosing" (*eklegomai*) some rather than others (1 Cor. 1:27–28; cf. Rom. 9:11–12, 24–26). God's calling is his supernatural power by which he summons things into existence that did not exist formerly (Rom. 4:17). Indeed, calling relates to the central theme of the present book, for God "calls you into his own kingdom and glory" (1 Thess. 2:12). Human beings are full of praise for being inducted into the kingdom, for those so transferred know that they deserved to reside in the kingdom of

28. Schnelle comments, "Faith does not rest on human decision but is a gift of God's grace" (ibid., 521).

darkness (Col. 1:13). They know they were called not on account of their works (Rom. 9:12; 2 Tim. 1:9). God has granted life to those who were dead in their transgressions and sins (Eph. 2:1–6).

Conclusion

The "new creation," a term that really is another way to refer to God's kingdom, has come. It has come because Jesus is risen from the dead, and so the promises of a new exodus (the gospel) have arrived. Believers in Jesus Christ are the chosen of the Lord. They are God's people, the new Israel of the Lord. The age to come now overlaps with this present evil age, according to Paul. The end-time gift of righteousness is given to believers, showing that the last days have come. In the OT the Holy Spirit was promised in the last days, and one of the main themes of Pauline theology is that the Spirit has been poured out on God's people. Pauline theology is richly textured, so that he speaks of reconciliation, redemption, righteousness, salvation, triumph over evil powers, and so forth. In every instance there is an "already but not yet" dynamic. Salvation is inaugurated but not yet consummated. The kingdom has penetrated this present evil age, but the kingdom has not come in all its fullness. Believers still await the day of their own resurrection (1 Cor. 15:20–28). There is a temporal interval between their resurrection and the resurrection of Jesus Christ. The future inheritance for believers is sure. They will, like Abraham, be heirs of the world (Rom. 4:13).

New Life and New Covenant

We should not expect the categories used here to fit perfectly, for Paul's theology defies a packaged analysis that explains every dimension of his thought. Above, I discussed the Spirit under the topic of new creation, but the Spirit is also the agent by which believers live a life that is pleasing to God, empowering them to do what God commands. The new life, which is a gift given to believers at conversion, is to be lived out in the concrete and particular circumstances of everyday life. Believers live under the lordship of Jesus by means of the power of the Spirit. Believers are to glorify God in everything (1 Cor. 10:31) and do everything in Jesus' name (Col. 3:17). They are to live "worthy of God" (1 Thess. 2:12), "worthy of the Lord" (Col. 1:10), "worthy of the calling" (Eph. 4:1; cf. 2 Thess. 1:11), "worthy of the gospel of Christ" (Phil. 1:27), and "worthy of the kingdom" (2 Thess. 1:5). They must "discern what is pleasing to the Lord" (Eph. 5:10) because he is their master.

Christians are to manifest "the fruit of the Spirit" (Gal. 5:22–23) and to bear "fruit in every good work" (Col. 1:10).[29] They have died with Christ so that they "would bear fruit for God" (Rom. 7:4) and be "filled with the fruit of righteousness" (Phil. 1:11). Christians are to live not for themselves but rather for the sake of their Lord (Rom. 14:7–9). They have a new master and king, and their bodies are no longer to be used to carry out their own will, and hence they should "glorify God" in their bodies (1 Cor. 6:19–20). Believers "no longer live for themselves, but for him who died and rose on their behalf" (2 Cor. 5:15). The law no longer exercises authority over them, and thus they now "live to God" (Gal. 2:19). Their goal is to magnify Christ in their remaining time on earth (Phil. 1:20), for living to them is Christ (Phil. 1:21). Christ is their life (Col. 3:4).

Paul's exhortations may be explained in terms of the indicative and imperative, which is another way of reflecting on Pauline eschatology.[30] The indicative represents what believers already are in Christ, while the imperative means that they are to appropriate the grace granted to them. Christ is already the Lord, but believers are to live out his lordship in everyday life. The indicative/imperative tension in Paul's thought is expressed well in 1 Cor. 5:7: "Cleanse out the old leaven that you may be a new lump, as you really are unleavened. For Christ, our Passover lamb, has been sacrificed." The imperative is to remove the old leaven (i.e., to cast the person committing incest out of the church). The evil must be removed from the church so that the lump will be pure. Clearly, the purity of the church is dependent upon heeding the imperative. But suddenly the indicative intervenes, lurching us in a new direction. Paul states that believers are already a new lump. They are unleavened in Christ. Since Christ has been sacrificed as the Passover lamb, all leaven has been removed from their lives (cf. Exod. 12–13). The indicative does not cancel out the imperative but rather is its foundation. Believers should cleanse themselves from evil because they are already cleansed. They should become what they are; they should be what they are becoming. They do not attain purity by removing sin from their midst, for they are already pure and holy in Christ. And yet they are to realize experientially and existentially what they are eschatologically.

29. For a helpful work on the moral life of believers, see J. W. Thompson, *Moral Formation according to Paul*.

30. For two important essays on the indicative and imperative in Pauline theology, see Bultmann, "Ethics in Paul"; Parsons, "Being Precedes Act." Schnelle (*Apostle Paul*, 546–51) disputes the notion that the indicative and imperative are basic for Pauline ethics. However, his objections do not stand, for the substance of his critique questions how the indicative and imperative make sense. But this is precisely the point. The tension between the indicative and imperative, though not fundamentally irrational, cannot be fully explicated. It is analogous to explaining how the soul and the body interact. Often the most fundamental truths in life are beyond our understanding.

Another famous example is found in Phil. 2:12–13: "Therefore, my beloved, as you have always obeyed, so now, not only as in my presence but much more in my absence, work out your own salvation with fear and trembling, for it is God who works in you, both to will and to work for his good pleasure." Believers are summoned to obey. Another way of putting it is that they are to work and accomplish their salvation. Surely, this is one of the most astonishing things Paul ever wrote, one that would be rejected by many readers of Paul as contrary to his thinking were it not found here. The imperative stands out in all its starkness: accomplish your salvation! Nevertheless, the imperative ultimately cannot be segregated from the indicative. The "for" grounding 2:12 is crucial in interpreting these verses, showing that 2:12 cannot be interpreted apart from 2:13. Paul's call to accomplish salvation should not be interpreted as a call to autonomy. In fact, any work believers do is a consequence of, a result of, God's work. Ultimately, what is done is God's work, and human beings cannot take any credit for obedience. The call to obey is not canceled or nullified but is set in its proper context and given a full explanation. Even desires for what is good and true and right come from God. The imperative can become a reality only because of the indicative. Grace precedes and undergirds demand.

Another illustration of the indicative and imperative occurs in Rom. 6. Believers have died to sin in baptism, for they have died with Christ and will be raised with him. Because they are united with Christ, they share his victory over sin and death. The "old person" (*ho palaios anthrōpos* [Rom. 6:6]), the old Adam, has been crucified with Christ, who is the new person (Eph. 2:15). Sin's tyranny and dominion have been dethroned. Believers have a new Lord and a new king, and sin is no longer the master, since they are united with Christ. The indicative is that believers have died to sin, and the power of the resurrection is now theirs. The death of the old person in Adam matches what Paul teaches in Colossians. Believers "have put off the old self [*ton palaion anthrōpon*] with its practices" (Col. 3:9), and they have put on the new person (Col. 3:10).

And yet Paul commands believers "to put off your old self" (*ton palaion anthrōpon* [Eph. 4:22]) and "to put on the new self" (*ton kainon anthrōpon* [Eph. 4:24]). The old person has been crucified with Christ, and yet the old self must still be put off. Thus, believers are "to put on the Lord Jesus Christ" (Rom. 13:14). Perhaps we see a hint in Colossians of the tension between the old and new person, for even though believers have put on the new person, there is a process of renewal in the image of the creator (Col. 3:10). As we saw in Rom. 6:1–10, believers have died to sin, but they must count themselves as "dead to sin and alive to God in Christ Jesus" (Rom. 6:11). They must not let sin "reign" in their bodies or "obey its passions" (Rom. 6:12). They must give their members to God (Rom. 6:13). If they present their members to sin, they will face eternal death (Rom. 6:16, 23). The threat in the imperative is quite remarkable. Obedience is not optional. Those who give themselves over to sin will not enjoy eternal life. Once again, the imperative stands forth in all its starkness, showing that the new life of believers is no abstraction. And yet the imperative is grounded in and even secured by the indicative. After the stirring commands in Rom. 6:11–13, we read in 6:14, "For sin will have no dominion over you, since you are not under law but under grace." This is not a command; it is a promise. On the one hand, believers are exhorted to pursue obedience lest they die; on the other hand, they are promised that they will not surrender to evil, for the grace that has captured them will triumph.

We see the same theme in Rom. 6:17. "But thanks be to God, that you who were once slaves of sin have become obedient from the heart to the standard of teaching to which you were committed." If believers pursue evil, they face the certain prospect of eternal death. They must take this warning seriously and avoid such a consequence. At the same time, Paul is confident that they will not succumb to evil, for they have had a heart transplant. God has handed believers over as slaves to righteousness (Rom. 6:18, 22). The indicative guarantees that the imperative will be kept without canceling out the authenticity of the imperative.

The eschatological character of Paul's thought surfaces in his theology of the law, his explanation of the Mosaic covenant. We can look at the matter from this angle. The kingdom that the Lord promised would not be secured through the Torah. The Jews believed that the law was the pathway to life (*m. 'Abot* 2:7), but Paul, who was nurtured in the law and almost certainly propounded as a Pharisee the notion that the law produces life, came to a shockingly different view. He came to believe that the law multiplied transgression instead of diminishing it (Rom. 5:20). The "I" in Rom. 7 discovers that the law exacerbated and stimulated sin. The command against coveting provoked all kinds of coveting (7:7–8). The law was intended to bring life, but the end result, because of human disobedience, was death (7:10–11). The problem is not with the content of the law, for the law represents God's holy and perfect will (7:12; cf. 7:16). The culprit is sin, which takes the law into its orbit so that sin uses the law as a platform for its advance (7:8, 11). The law has no power to rescue or transform those "sold under sin" (7:14)—that is, those who are "captive" to sin (7:23).

The weakness of the law (Rom. 8:3) is not isolated to Romans. Paul's statement about the law in 1 Cor. 15:56 is enormously interesting: "The sting of death is sin, and the power of sin is the law." It is difficult to overestimate the significance of what we find here. Suddenly the law surfaces in a chapter devoted to the truth of the resurrection. It is quite clear from 1 Corinthians that the law was not a subject of controversy in the church, for the church struggled with antinomianism. Despite the emphasis on obedience and keeping God's commands in 1 Corinthians, Paul makes a statement that matches what we find in Romans, confirming that what was said about the law in Rom. 7 was fundamental to Paul's theology. When Paul writes that "the power of sin is the law," it is clear that sin uses the law for its own purposes, and thus the law does not suppress sin but increases it instead.

It is likely that the same perspective is reflected in Galatians, when Paul comments that the law "was added because of transgressions" (*tōn parabaseōn charin* [Gal. 3:19]). Despite the view of some commentators, it is scarcely likely that the point is that the law restrains transgressions. Such a view would play into the hands of the Judaizers, who insisted that the Galatians get circumcised and observe the Mosaic law. Nor is there any clear contextual warrant for thinking that "defining sin" is intended. Instead, Paul emphasizes in Galatians that those who attempt to be righteous by law are "under a curse" (Gal. 3:10).

The "under" phrases in Paul's writings underscore that those who are under law are in the old age of redemptive history, that they live under the sway of sin's power. Scripture locked all "under sin" (Gal. 3:22), and all were "captive under the law" (Gal. 3:23). The Son of God was "born under the law" in order to free those "under the law" (Gal. 4:4–5). Before faith, human beings "were enslaved under the elements of the world" (Gal. 4:3 [my translation]). Those who are "led by the Spirit" are not "under the law" (Gal. 5:18). Now that Christ has come, believers are no longer "under a pedagogue" (Gal. 3:25 [my translation]). The "under" phrases show that to be "under law" is equivalent to being "under sin" (see also Rom. 6:14–15; 1 Cor. 9:20). Furthermore, "under law" should be interpreted in a redemptive-historical sense, so that it refers to this present evil age instead of the age to come. Both sin and the law are elements in the old creation. This is not to say that the law is itself sinful. Far from it. Indeed, it is spiritual (Rom. 7:14). Still, the law is limited to the old age in redemptive history. It follows, therefore, that believers are no longer under the law (Rom. 6:14; 1 Cor. 9:20; Gal. 3:25). The era of the pedagogue has ended, for it was intended by God to rule over human beings for a limited period of time. The history of Israel confirms that those who were under the law were under the authority of sin. Both Israel (722 BC) and Judah (586 BC) were sent into exile because of their failure to observe the law. Freedom to keep God's law would commence with the coming of the kingdom, with the arrival of the new covenant, by which the law is written on the heart.

The contrast between the old age and the new, between the old creation and the new, is clearly evident in the claim that the law is no longer in force. The Sinai covenant was an interim covenant given 430 years after the promise given to Abraham (Gal. 3:15–18), and it was never intended to be in force forever. God designed the law to function as an authority only until the promised offspring should arrive (Gal. 3:19). Now that the Christ has come, the new creation is present (Gal. 6:15) and the present evil age (Gal. 1:4) has concluded. The age of the pedagogue (*paidagōgos*), where the law functioned as a babysitter, has ended (Gal. 3:24–25). The era of the law is coterminous with the rule of the elements of the world (Gal. 4:3), but Christ has now liberated human beings from the law and the elements (Gal. 4:4–5). Believers are now God's children (Gal. 3:26; 4:6–7) and no longer live in the old era of redemptive history. The opponents in Galatia required circumcision for salvation as the initiation rite to life under Torah (Gal. 2:3–5; 4:21; 5:2–4; 6:12–13). Imposing circumcision fails to recognize that the new age has arrived in the death and resurrection of Christ. Circumcision is part of the old creation, but now the new creation has dawned. We find the same perspective elsewhere. The purity and food laws of the Mosaic covenant and its feast days and Sabbaths (Rom. 14:5–6, 14, 20; Col. 2:16–17) point to Christ and have now passed away. Believers have died with Christ and now belong to the one who has risen from the dead, to the one who has inaugurated the new creation, and hence they have died to the rule of the law (Rom. 7:4–6). The covenant with Moses is "old" (2 Cor. 3:14) and has come to an end (2 Cor. 3:11). Christ is the goal to which the law always pointed, and he is also the end of the law (Rom. 10:4), for when the goal of the law is reached (i.e., Christ), it also comes to an end.

The setting aside of the Mosaic covenant does not mean that believers live immoral lives. They fulfill the law of Christ (Gal. 6:2; cf. 1 Cor. 9:21), which is exemplified most profoundly in Jesus' own life and death, in the giving of his life for the sake of others. The law of Christ is summed up in the command to love one's neighbor as oneself (Rom. 13:8; Gal. 5:14; cf. Lev. 19:18), in the call to live for the benefit and edification of others instead of living for oneself. The law of Christ includes some of the commands of the Sinai law (e.g., Rom. 13:9; Eph. 6:2).[31] Such commands are authoritative not because they are part of the Mosaic law, for the law has come to an end. They still function as God's word and command because they summarize what is loving, because they reflect the character of God. They are authoritative because they are God's will, not because they are part of the Mosaic covenant.

---

31. Schnelle (*Apostle Paul*, 551–58) underestimates the role that the OT continues to play in Pauline ethics.

Since Christians live between the times, between the inauguration and consummation of God's purposes, they still need commands. When the new creation arrives in its fullness, commands will no longer be needed. In the meantime, Paul's letters are full of exhortations. Even those who are spiritual (Gal. 6:1), those who are empowered by the Holy Spirit, profit from moral instruction. Believers need to be reminded to walk in the Spirit, be led by the Spirit, to march in step with the Spirit, and to sow to the Spirit (Rom. 8:14; Gal. 5:16, 18, 25; 6:8). They need imperatives to live out the indicative reality of life in Christ. Christians who are doing well still need imperatives (1 Thess. 4:1–2, 9–10), for there is always room for growth so that believers are conformed even more to Christ. Believers have not yet arrived at perfection (Phil. 3:12–16), and so they must follow the Lord until the day of redemption.

The moral exhortations given to Christians do not merely consist of generalities. Paul does not only say that they should yield to the Spirit and follow the course of love. Love has specific contours and features that are clearly identified, so that Christians must abstain from sexual sin (1 Cor. 6:12–20; 1 Thess. 4:3–8), from homosexual relations (Rom. 1:26–27), from divorce (1 Cor. 7:10–16), from incest (1 Cor. 5:1–2), and so forth. Paul regularly traces out for readers what is pleasing to God in vice and virtue lists (Rom. 1:29–31; 12:9–21; 13:13; 1 Cor. 6:9–10; 2 Cor. 12:20–21; Gal. 5:19–23; Eph. 5:3–5; Phil. 4:8; Col. 3:5, 8–9, 12–13; 1 Tim. 6:4–5; 2 Tim. 2:22; 3:2–4). Paul recognizes that there is not an ethical rule for every situation (Eph. 5:10). Believers must pray and seek the Lord to discern his will (Phil. 1:9–11; Col. 1:9–11). They need spiritual wisdom because the circumstances of life are too complex to be formulated with rules that apply to every situation. The priority of love and the need for wisdom, however, do not preclude the need for specific ethical exhortation, as the vice and virtue lists clearly demonstrate. Husbands, wives, children, and slaves are given particular commands (Eph. 5:22–6:9; Col. 3:18–4:1).[32] Paul does not merely tell them to act in a loving manner; he provides instructions relative to their station in life. Paul does not have a casuistic ethic that attempts to address every conceivable situation. At the same time, he does not fall prey to vague generalities and merely say that believers should follow the Spirit. Some specifics are given to delineate the pathway of love. Love cannot be captured exhaustively by particular directives. Love goes beyond commands, but it never contravenes such commands.

---

32. Paul's teaching on women and slavery has been the subject of particular interest in our day. For more detailed discussion, see Schreiner, *New Testament Theology*, 772–76, 794–800. Suffice it to say here that Paul never endorses or commends slavery as a system but rather regulates an existing evil institution.

The kingdom has come, and believers must live under the rule of their king. Paul teaches that the Holy Spirit empowers and transforms Christians so that they are enabled to please God. Paul does not teach perfectionism. The "already but not yet" persists. There is a tension between the indicative and the imperative. The indicative reflects what God has accomplished for believers in Christ; the imperative calls upon believers to live upon the basis of the indicative. They are to be what they are. They are to be now what they will be on the last day. The last days have arrived. Believers are no longer under the Torah, for the Mosaic law was temporary and never was intended to be permanent. The new covenant, now present on the basis of the cross and the resurrection of Jesus Christ, is marked by the gift of the Holy Spirit. Believers are to follow the law of Christ and are to love as Christ did. Obeying moral norms that reflect God's character should mark their lives, as they live in dependence upon the Holy Spirit.

The New People of God

The eschatological character of Paul's thought manifests itself in his theology of the church. Paul conceives of the church as God's new temple and as the body of Christ and as the new Israel. We will look at the last of these three ideas first. In the OT Israel was the people of the Lord. Often the word *synagōgē* is used in the Greek translation of the OT (the LXX) to designate the congregation of Israel (e.g., Exod. 12:3, 6; 16:1; 17:1; Lev. 4:13; 8:3; 10:6). Paul does not use the word *synagōgē*; rather, he employs the closely related word *ekklēsia* ("gathering" or "church"), which is also used for the gathering of Israel in the LXX. In the LXX there is one instance where both the noun and the verb form of the word *ekklēsia* occur together, particularly emphasizing the gathering of Israel (Deut. 4:10). In two instances the verb "gather" (*ekklēsiazō*) is used with *synagōgē* as the object (Lev. 8:3; Num. 20:8), featuring again the assembling of Israel together. The noun "gathering" (*ekklēsia*) is also used regularly for the gathering of Israel (e.g., Deut. 4:10; 18:16). Israel is "the assembly of the Lord" (*ekklēsia kyriou* [Deut. 23:1, 2, 3, 8 [LXX 23:2, 3, 4, 9]; 1 Chron. 28:8; 29:20; Mic. 2:5) or the "assembly of God" (*ekklēsia theou* [Neh. 13:1]). In other texts we find the phrase "assembly of Israel" (*ekklēsia Israēl* [Deut. 31:30; 1 Kings 8:14, 22, 55; 1 Chron. 13:2; 2 Chron. 6:3, 12, 13; 10:3]).[33]

---

33. We also see "the assembly of the sons of Israel" (Josh. 8:35 [LXX 9:2–3]), "the assembly of the people of God" (Judg. 20:2), "the assembly of the people" (Ps. 107:32 [LXX 106:32]), and "the assembly of all the tribes of Israel" (Judg. 21:5).

Paul uses the term *ekklēsia* ("assembly" or "church") sixty-two times. We see "all the churches of Christ" (Rom. 16:16), "the church of God" (1 Cor. 1:2; 10:32; 11:22; 15:9; 2 Cor. 1:1; Gal. 1:13; 1 Tim. 3:5, 15), "the churches of God" (1 Cor. 11:16; 1 Thess. 2:14; 2 Thess. 1:4), "the church of the saints" (1 Cor. 14:33). The assemblies are also delineated in accord with geography: "the church at Cenchreae" (Rom. 16:1); "the church of God that is in Corinth" (1 Cor. 1:2); "the churches of Galatia" (1 Cor. 16:1); "churches of Asia" (1 Cor. 16:19); "the church of God that is at Corinth" (2 Cor. 1:1); "the churches of Macedonia" (2 Cor. 8:1); "the churches of Galatia" (Gal. 1:2); "the churches of Judea that are in Christ" (Gal. 1:22); "the church of the Thessalonians in God the Father and the Lord Jesus Christ" (1 Thess. 1:1); "the churches of God in Christ Jesus that are in Judea" (1 Thess. 2:14); "the church of the Thessalonians in God our Father and the Lord Jesus Christ" (2 Thess. 1:1). It is also apparent that some of the churches assembled in homes (Rom. 16:5; 1 Cor. 16:19; Col. 4:15; Philem. 2). As Udo Schnelle says, "For Paul, the local congregation represents the whole church in a particular location."[34]

What was the assembly of Israel in the OT—that is, the Lord's assembly or God's assembly—is now made up of both Jews and Gentiles who believe in Jesus Christ. The "churches of the Gentiles" (Rom. 16:4) are now the assemblies of the Lord. Just as Israel was beloved (Deut. 32:15 LXX; 33:12; Isa. 44:2; Jer. 11:15; cf. Hosea 2:23), so the church is God's beloved (Rom. 9:24–25; 1 Thess. 1:4).[35] Just as Israel was the elect people of God, so now the church is God's elect people (Rom. 9–11).[36] Hence, the church's identity with Israel is revealed when Gentiles are told that Israelite ancestors are "our fathers" (1 Cor. 10:1), and that Christ is "our Passover lamb" (1 Cor. 5:7).[37] The church of Jesus Christ, then, is the true and new Israel. Prophecies originally given to Israel are fulfilled as well in Gentile believers because they are integrated into Israel and are Abraham's children through Christ (Gal. 3:16).[38] Believers in Christ are true Jews and the true circumcision (Rom. 2:28–29; Phil. 3:3; cf. Col. 2:13–14). They are the children of Abraham (Rom. 4:9–25; Gal. 3:6–9) and the children of God (Rom. 8:14–17; Gal. 3:26; 4:6; cf. Gal. 4:28, 31).

Since the Torah has been abolished (Eph. 2:15), Jews and Gentiles are now unified in Christ (Eph. 2:11–22). They have been reconciled (whether far from

34. Schnelle, *Apostle Paul*, 560–61. He goes on to say, "The whole church is present in the local congregation, and the local congregation is a part of the whole church" (p. 561).
35. Beale, *Biblical Theology*, 669–70; cf. Schnelle, *Apostle Paul*, 561.
36. On election, see the section "The New Creation as a Gift of God's Electing Grace" above.
37. So Schnelle, *Apostle Paul*, 564.
38. Beale, *Biblical Theology*, 671. See all of Beale's chapters 21–22.

God or near him) to Christ and to one another through the cross. Hence, Gentiles are fellow citizens with Jews in the people of God. The mystery hidden in the OT is now revealed. Jews and Gentiles are coheirs and members of the same body through the gospel (Eph. 3:5–6). Gentiles are now part of the true Israel because they are united to Christ, who is the true Israel of God,[39] in contrast to "Israel according to the flesh" (1 Cor. 10:18), which is separated from God. The Christ dwells in Gentile believers (Col. 1:27), just as he indwells Jewish believers. Gentiles have been grafted onto the olive tree of God's people (Rom. 11:17–24). Identifying believers in Christ as the true and new Israel does not preclude a future for ethnic Israel. Indeed, in Rom. 9–11 Paul promises a future salvation for Israel. Ethnic Jews who trust in Christ will be grafted back onto the olive tree (11:23–24). "All Israel will be saved" (11:26).[40] They will become part of the church of the Lord, part of God's assembly when they are converted, so that they are united with Gentile believers in Christ.

The newness of the people of God is signified through the church being described as Christ's body (1 Cor. 12:27; Eph. 1:23; 4:12; 5:23; Col. 1:24; cf. 1 Cor. 12:12; Eph. 5:30). Believers "are one body in Christ" (Rom. 12:5). Paul often uses the image of the body without designating it specifically as the body of Christ (e.g., Rom. 12:4; 1 Cor. 12:13–17; Eph. 3:6; 4:4, 16; Col. 2:19; 3:15), though in context the relation to Christ is implicit or obvious. The newness of the people of God is evident in the phrase "body of Christ." Scholars often try to locate the origin of the metaphor, though no certain conclusion has been established. What is clear is that the church as Christ's body, as those who are incorporated into Christ, represents Christ to the world. The church is clearly an eschatological reality, for it arrives on the scene with the coming of the Christ in the fullness of time. Indeed, Eph. 1:22–23 clarifies that Christ rules over the world even now, as the one exalted over all powers and authorities. The church represents his fullness in the present evil age.

The unity of the church is one of the central Pauline themes. Believers are one in Christ (Rom. 12:5; 1 Cor. 12:12, 20; Eph. 2:16; 4:4; Col. 3:5; cf. Eph. 3:6). All believers are "baptized into one body" (1 Cor. 12:13). Because the body is united in Christ, no member of the body is inferior or superior (1 Cor. 12:14–26). Disputations over food, which particularly divided Jews and Gentiles, become occasions in which Paul exhorts the church to love one another, to desist from judging or condemning one another, and to understand the perspective of those with whom they disagree (Rom. 14–15; 1 Cor. 8–10). The

39. Rightly ibid., 653–54.
40. Rightly Schnelle, *Apostle Paul*, 566, 591.

importance of unity is highlighted in the Letter to the Philippians, the entirety of which can be understood as a call to unity (1:27–2:5; 4:2–3).[41]

We also see the end-time character of Pauline thought relative to the church being God's temple.[42] In the OT, God dwelt in the tabernacle and the temple. We saw in Psalms that the psalmist often longed to make a pilgrimage to the temple to gaze upon and drink in the beauty of the Lord. In the NT John emphasizes that Jesus is the new temple, that the temple has been replaced by Jesus himself. According to Paul, the OT teaching on the temple anticipates and points to Jesus' dwelling in the church. The indwelling Spirit signifies that the church is God's temple (1 Cor. 3:16). As the temple, the church is holy (1 Cor. 3:17), and thus those who destroy it will be destroyed themselves (cf. Lev. 10:1–3). The distinction between the church and the world is evident in 2 Cor. 6:16. The OT promises of the Lord dwelling with his people (Exod. 29:45; Lev. 26:12) through the tabernacle are now realized in the church as God's temple. The church of the living God must not tolerate partnership with idols, for the true and living God dwells in the church, as he did in the temple under the old covenant. The temple theme confirms that the Lord did not merely come to save individuals. He desired to reflect his glory through a corporate people, through the church of Jesus Christ, as the church enjoys the beauty and joy of God's presence, as they see and know the King in his beauty. Clearly, the temple connotes the holiness of the people of God. Believers must refrain from what is unclean and refuse to imitate the evil practiced by unbelievers (2 Cor. 6:17), cleansing themselves "from every defilement of body and spirit, bringing holiness to completion in the fear of God" (2 Cor. 7:1).

The church is also conceived of as a household (Eph. 2:19), which in the context of Eph. 2 most likely refers to the temple, though notions of a house as a home may be in view as well. This household is inclusive, so that both Jews and Gentiles are citizens. The cornerstone of the house is Christ, from whom the entire house takes its shape (Eph. 2:20), and the teaching of the apostles and the NT prophets functions as the foundation of the house. The church corporately is a "holy temple" (Eph. 2:21), the place where God specially resides with his people.

The church celebrates baptism and the Lord's Supper. Baptism is the initiation rite into the eschatological people of God. Baptism is Christ-centered, for those who are baptized are clothed with Christ (Gal. 3:27), and those who are baptized have died with Christ and have risen with him (Rom. 6:1–5; Col.

---

41. See Peterlin, *Disunity in the Church*. In my view, however, Peterlin takes his thesis too far.
42. Beale (*Church's Mission*, 246) overreaches, however, in saying that Paul was also thinking of the temple as a garden "at some level" in 1 Cor. 3. See his discussion on pp. 246–50.

2:11–13). Baptism signifies the washing away of sins (Eph. 5:26) and is closely associated with receiving the gift of the Holy Spirit (Titus 3:5). Baptism signifies the unity of the people of God (1 Cor. 12:13), for there is "one baptism" (Eph. 4:5). Those who are baptized are justified and sanctified (1 Cor. 6:11); they belong to Christ now instead of to the world.

Paul mentions the Lord's Supper only twice (1 Cor. 10:16–17; 11:17–34), but this should not be interpreted to say that it was insignificant in Paul's thought. The reference to the practice in 1 Corinthians indicates that it was a regular feature in his churches. The Lord's Supper reminds believers of their unity, for they all feed on one loaf (1 Cor. 10:16–17), which means they all share in the benefits of what Christ accomplished for them. When sharing in this meal, believers recognize their fellowship with one another, for they all derive their life from Jesus Christ. The bread and cup symbolize the life that Jesus Christ gave for them. His sacrificial blood is the basis of their life together. Hence, it is intolerable that the rich should mistreat the poor during the supper (1 Cor. 11:17–34). Callous disregard for indigent Christians means that participants are partaking of the body and blood of the Lord in an unworthy way. Remembering the Lord and the new covenant inaugurated in his blood means that believers care for and love one another. Those who participated sinfully were judged by the Lord. Anyone who treats fellow believers unmercifully is hardly remembering the forgiveness of sins that is dramatically symbolized in the supper.

Each member of the church plays a crucial role in Paul's theology, for they are endowed with spiritual gifts (Rom. 12:3–8; 1 Cor. 12–14; Eph. 4:7–16). The gifts are not to be used to advertise or show off one's own spirituality. They are intended for the edification of others (1 Cor. 12:7; 14:1–19; Eph. 4:12–16), to strengthen fellow believers in the faith. The participation of every member does not mean that there was no place for leaders or for official ministries in the Pauline churches. Some are called to be elders or overseers or pastors[43] (Eph. 4:11; Phil. 1:1; 1 Tim. 3:1–7; 5:17–22; Titus 1:5–9) and deacons (Phil. 1:1; 1 Tim. 3:8–13; cf. Rom. 16:1–2). Some have mistakenly thought that structure and offices did not coexist with the work of the Spirit and charismatic gifts. However, the two are not contradictory but complementary. Anyone who is familiar with charismatic churches today knows that often leaders in such churches are quite strong.

The most important requirement for teachers was their godliness (1 Tim. 3:1–13; Titus 1:5–9). The focus was not on their skills but rather on their conformity to Christ. This is not to say that skills were ignored altogether. Elders

---

43. In my judgment, these three terms designate the same office.

had a particular responsibility to teach and lead the congregation (1 Tim. 3:2, 4–5; 5:17; Titus 1:9; cf. 1 Tim. 2:12). The Pastoral Epistles emphasize repeatedly the importance of teaching being in accord with the gospel, warning the readers about the dangers of heresy (1 Tim. 1:3–20; 4:1–16; 6:3–21; 2 Tim. 1:3–14; 2:1–4:5; Titus 1:10–2:15). If the church departs from the truth of the gospel, its witness to the love of Christ will be lost. Nor is such a concern limited to the Pastoral Epistles. Paul warns against a false gospel in the strongest terms in Galatians, pronouncing an irrevocable curse on those who proclaim a deviant message (1:8–9). The truth of the gospel is the burden of the whole of Romans (see esp. 6:17). The teaching of the gospel is of first importance (1 Cor. 15:1–11). Paul is concerned to remind his readers that he and the other apostles proclaimed the same message (1 Cor. 15:11; Gal. 2:1–10). Indeed, in virtually all of his letters Paul contends against false teaching in one form or another. According to Paul, the church of Jesus Christ would retain its vitality only if it faithfully passed on and retained the truth of the gospel.

The OT promise from the beginning was that blessing would reach the whole world and include all peoples. This promise is fulfilled in Jesus Christ. The blessings promised to Israel now belong to the new Israel, composed of Jews and Gentiles, in Christ. Hence, the church is now God's assembly, his gathered people. The divisions between Jews and Gentiles have been erased through Christ's death, so that now Gentiles are fellow members with Jews in God's temple—that is, the church. The church is Christ's body and God's temple, and hence it communicates God's presence to the world. The unity of the church is a major Pauline theme, for love is the signature of the people of God and the evidence that the Spirit resides in the church. The people of the church celebrate its new life together in baptism and the Lord's Supper, and the Lord grants gifts to the church for the building up of one another in love. Leaders in particular are called upon to guard the gospel and to teach it faithfully, for love in the church will be squelched if error becomes predominant.

The New World Coming

The OT often emphasizes the place, the land, where Yahweh dwells with his people and where his promises will be fulfilled. What is quite surprising when we read Paul is how little he refers to the land promise. Paul emphasizes, as was noted above, the salvation that awaits God's people, their future and final redemption, and their final sanctification. The physical dimension of salvation certainly is not abandoned, for the resurrection of the body is a major theme in Paul's writings (Rom. 6:5, 8–9; 8:11; 1 Cor. 15:1–58; 2 Cor. 4:14;

Phil. 3:10; 1 Thess. 4:13–18). Those who claim that the bodily resurrection is already a reality deny the faith (2 Tim. 2:18; cf. 1 Cor. 15:20–28). Paul does not abandon the OT hope and advocate an ethereal, transphysical future. When Jesus returns, believers will be raised from the dead and glorified. The return of Jesus signals the consummation of God's promises and the realization of all that has been pledged to them. Paul does not emphasize, however, the location, the place where believers will reside. It is not that he abandons such a promise. We saw previously that believers will inherit the kingdom, and the kingdom includes the notion of a realm, a place where believers will rule, even though the kingdom is "heavenly" (2 Tim. 4:18), transcending contemporary experiences of the world.

Similarly, the language of inheritance suggests a physical dimension to what is promised in the future. Still, a survey of inheritance language reveals an interesting fact. Paul says very little about the nature or character of the inheritance. In the OT the inheritance, as is especially evident in Joshua, is tied to the promise of the land. The geographical and earthly nature of the inheritance is communicated in detail, for Joshua painstakingly and lovingly relates the allotment of land for each tribe. Clearly, Paul promises a future reward and inheritance, and yet he does not tie it closely or specifically to the land. A reference to the physicality of the promise is not entirely absent, for Abraham is said to be "heir of the world" (Rom. 4:13), and believers as the children of Abraham will obtain the same inheritance. Furthermore, in Rom. 8:18–25 the transformation of creation is featured. The old creation was subjected to sin and frustration because of the sin of Adam and Eve in the garden. The bondage and the corruption of the present creation are temporary. A new day is coming when creation will be liberated from its present subjection. A new creation is coming, free from disease and death and sin.

So why does Paul not call attention to the land, even if the land promise is not jettisoned? We have no certain answer to that question, but it seems that Paul focuses on the wonder and beauty of future fellowship with Christ. The promises of the land are not limited to Israel but are now focused on Christ, on the redemption and salvation that he has accomplished.[44] Dying is gain because then one is "with Christ," which "is far better" (Phil. 1:21, 23). When Paul contemplates the future resurrection and its importance, he concludes the entire discussion by relaying why the resurrection matters to believers, saying, "And so we will always be with the Lord" (1 Thess. 4:17). The focus is not on the resurrection, as important as that is, but rather on the experience of enjoying the Lord forever. The blessings of salvation and the inheritance are

---

44. See Walker, "The Land in the Apostles' Writings," 87–88.

to be prized, but what makes them worth it is the exultation in God through Jesus Christ (Rom. 5:11). It is those who love the Lord who will escape the curse (1 Cor. 16:22; Eph. 6:24). Another way of saying this is that believers will praise and glorify God forever. Perhaps Paul emphasizes the joy and the praise that well up in believers' hearts because a place without a person, a place without praise would not be attractive. Hence, when Jesus returns, believers will marvel and be astonished in his presence (2 Thess. 1:10).

In the same way, those who refuse to believe in Jesus as God's Son will be judged when he returns (Rom. 2:2, 12; 3:6; 14:10; 1 Cor. 5:13; 2 Cor. 5:10; 2 Thess. 1:5; 1 Tim. 5:24; 2 Tim. 4:1, 8). The secrets hidden, particularly secret sins, will be disclosed, and the motives of the heart unveiled (Rom. 2:16; 1 Cor. 4:5). The wrath of God will be poured out on unbelievers (Rom. 2:5, 8; 3:5; 5:9; 9:22; 12:19; Eph. 2:3; 5:6; Col. 3:6; cf. 1 Thess. 1:10; 5:9), on those who do not know God and disobey the gospel (2 Thess. 1:8). Another metaphor that designates the destiny of the disobedient is "destruction" (verb *apollymi* [Rom. 2:12; 1 Cor. 1:18, 19; 10:9, 10; 15:18; 2 Cor. 2:15; 4:3; 2 Thess. 2:10]). Destruction is the converse of salvation, signifying the dissolution of all that brings life and joy and peace. Those who repudiate the good news of Christ will face God's righteous punishment (Rom. 2:5; 2 Thess. 1:5, 8). Paul uses another word for "destruction" (noun *olethros* [1 Cor. 5:5; 1 Thess. 5:3; 1 Tim. 6:9]) to describe their "eternal destruction, away from the presence of the Lord and from the glory of his might" (2 Thess. 1:9). What is striking here is that the final punishment means being shut out from God's presence.

When Paul thinks of the final inheritance, he focuses on a person instead of a place, on fellowship with God and Christ instead of the new universe that is coming. But this comment should not be taken too far. A creation free from groaning and futility is envisioned (Rom. 8:18–25). Christians will be heirs of the entire world (Rom. 4:13). A new Jerusalem is coming (Gal. 4:26), and believers even now are members of the heavenly Jerusalem. Believers will be raised from the dead and inhabit the new world that is coming. All will confess that Jesus is Lord (Phil. 2:11), and every enemy in the universe will be pacified (Col. 1:20). God will be "all in all" (1 Cor. 15:28), and those who do not know God or who disobeyed the gospel will be excluded from God's presence forever (2 Thess. 1:6–10). The long-promised kingdom will be at hand, and believers will enjoy God in Christ forever in the transformed world that God has created.

INTERLUDE

A Synopsis of
THE END OF THE AGES HAS COME
ACCORDING TO THE APOSTLE PAUL

Paul does not use the term "kingdom" often, but it is not the thesis of this book that kingdom terminology is predominant in every biblical writer. The thesis is that conceptually and theologically Paul fits with the remainder of the NT. He often uses the word "Christ" to designate Jesus, indicating that Jesus is the new David promised in the OT Scriptures. Jesus is the Son of God and the Lord of all in Pauline theology. As Lord, he is enthroned on high. By virtue of his cross and resurrection, he has triumphed over his enemies and atoned for sins, winning the victory over the serpent and his offspring per Gen. 3:15.

The resurrection of Jesus, as noted, signifies his victory, his rule over all. And those who belong to Jesus Christ are the beneficiaries of the salvation that he has accomplished. Whether Paul speaks of salvation, redemption, justification, reconciliation, adoption, triumph over evil powers, or other such things, he operates with an "already but not yet" understanding of these great saving realities. Christ has redeemed his people. By virtue of his cross and resurrection, the great act of salvation has been accomplished. As the Synoptic Gospels and the book of Acts proclaim, the kingdom has come! And Paul too can speak of the kingdom in "already but not yet" terms. God has saved his people, and yet God is not finished destroying his enemies. Death is not yet abolished, even though it has been defeated. Demonic beings have been stripped of their power, but their final demise, though certain, is yet to occur. Paul's theology of salvation runs along the same arteries that we have seen in all the Gospels and in Acts. The new David has arrived, and so have the new exodus and the new covenant and the new creation. At the same time, there is an eschatological reservation. The final curtain has not fallen, but the decisive turning point in the play has already taken place.

Jesus as Lord rules over his people, over restored Israel, over new Israel. The church of Jesus Christ is now the Lord's assembly. They are the children of Abraham and the true circumcision. They are the Israel of God. They are Christ's body and temple in the world, manifesting and radiating God's presence to the world. Both the love of the body and the new life that Christians live by the power of the Spirit demonstrate to the world and to angels that the church is the people of God. They are the locus of God's presence in the world. But the church exists in a "not yet" state as well. God's promise of salvation to ethnic Israel will be fulfilled, and those Israelites will become members of the church. Paul does not focus on the land promises, but he does promise that a new world is coming, a transformed creation free from the futility and the devastation that mark the present creation. All believers, along with Abraham, will inherit the promises made to him. They will inherit the world. And those who disbelieve will be excluded from God's presence forever. For Paul, God's presence with his people is the greatest joy of all. He emphasizes the joy of being with Christ and God, of marveling over God's beauty (2 Thess. 1:10). Such will be the occupation of the saints in the world to come.

Part 8

LIVING IN THE LAST DAYS ACCORDING TO THE GENERAL EPISTLES

It should be noted that I have already discussed the Johannine Epistles, which are included in the General Epistles. So, all the General Epistles except the Johannine Epistles are discussed here.

30

THE EPISTLE TO THE HEBREWS

Introduction

The Epistle to the Hebrews fits with what we have found elsewhere in the NT. The kingdom has come in Jesus Christ, but it is not consummated. We see in Hebrews both a linear and a vertical worldview. It is linear and salvation-historical in that the promises of the OT have become a reality in Jesus Christ. It is vertical in that heaven has, so to speak, come to earth. Access to God is now secured through the sacrifice of Jesus Christ.[1] Jesus is God's priest and king and son.[2] Adam, as the son of God and as a priest-king, was to extend God's rule throughout the world. Hebrews shows how Jesus succeeded where Adam failed as God's son and as his priest-king.

The eschatological character of Hebrews shines through the introduction.[3] The prophets spoke the word of God to Israel's ancestors in a variety of ways, but these words, though true and authoritative, are "old" (*palai* [1:1]). Now God has spoken "in these last days by his Son" (1:2). The final and definitive word has been proclaimed in the Son, so that the promises of the prophets are fulfilled in the Son. We see a fundamental contrast between the era of the law and the new covenant inaugurated by the Son. A survey of the letter demonstrates the disjunction between the old age of the law and the new age of the Son. Jesus' superiority to angels is introduced (chaps. 1–2) because the angels were mediators of the law (2:2). So too, both Moses (3:1–6) and Joshua (4:8) are associated with the law and the wilderness generation, and Jesus, as

---

1. On the theology of Hebrews, see Lindars, *Letter to the Hebrews*.
2. Hahn (*Kinship by Covenant*, 278–79, 282) explicates how these three roles are really one and the same role.
3. The classic study on eschatology in Hebrews is Barrett, "Epistle to the Hebrews."

583

God's Son, surpasses them both. Along the same lines, the Melchizedekian priesthood of Jesus is better than the Aaronic and Levitical priesthood (5:1–10; 7:1–10:18). The contrast is between the law and the promise, the old covenant and the new, the former age and the age to come.

Nor should Hebrews be understood as an abstract discussion of salvation history. The author fears that the readers are relapsing to the old covenant, turning back to what was inferior when that which is excellent has arrived. Hence, the entire letter is a sermon (13:22), a homily written to urge the readers not to commit apostasy. They must heed the author's admonitions and warnings in order to obtain eternal life. The theological framework of the letter functions as the foundation for the exhortations and warnings that permeate the letter (2:1–4; 3:12–4:13; 5:11–6:12; 10:26–31; 12:25–29).[4] The main purpose of the letter, then, is hortatory. If the readers turn back to the law for forgiveness and for the cleansing of their consciences, they relapse into the former age instead of living in the new covenant inaugurated through Christ.

Jesus Superior to Angels

The themes introduced above must be probed more deeply. We see in chapters 1–2 that Jesus is superior to angels because of his name, for he is the Son and they are servants. As noted above, the author mentions angels not for the purpose of engaging in an abstract discussion comparing Jesus to angels. Angels are introduced because they were mediators of the law (2:2), and thus Jesus' preeminence over angels demonstrates that the era of the law has passed away, that the readers should not return to the law to find forgiveness of sins. More particularly, the author argues that Jesus is better than the angels because he is the Son. The argument regarding Jesus' superiority has two dimensions. First, Jesus takes precedence over the angels because he is divine. The strikingly high Christology of Hebrews surfaces here. Jesus, like wisdom in the OT (see Prov. 3:19–20; 8:22–31), is the agent through whom God created the world (1:2).[5] Remarkably, the author cites Ps. 102:25–27, which speaks of Yahweh creating the world, and applies it to Jesus (1:10–12), seeing Jesus as the unchanging creator. Jesus is not only the creator of the world but also the one who sustains the created order (1:3). Clearly, he is superior to angels because he is the creator, whereas angels are creatures (1:7). Furthermore, as the eternal Son,

4. Scholars differ about the exact parameters of the warning passages, but it is not crucial for my purposes to resolve that issue.
5. Wisdom points to Jesus. It is the shadow, and Jesus is the substance. There is no conception of an independent hypostasis for wisdom in the OT.

Jesus radiates God's glory and represents his exact nature (1:3). Certainly such statements point to Jesus' deity, for the angels will worship him (1:6), and Jesus is identified as God with the citation of Ps. 45:6–7 (1:8–9). What is quite remarkable about the use of Ps. 45 is that the psalm is about the Davidic king, and so in the same psalm, according to the author of Hebrews, Jesus is the promised Messiah and fully divine.

The author of Hebrews does not indulge in an exercise in Christology for intellectual reasons. Christology functions as the basis of soteriology. The author emphasizes not only Jesus' divinity but also his humanity. As the priest-king, Jesus is "the heir of all things" (1:2). The climax of the beautiful and exalted christological confession in 1:1–4 actually comes in 1:3, where the author says of Jesus, "After making purification for sins, he sat down at the right hand of the Majesty on high." The theology of the entire letter is summed up here. Through Jesus' atoning sacrifice the conscience has been cleansed and forgiveness has been secured. His sacrificial work has been completed, for he now sits at God's right hand. Psalm 110 clearly plays a formative role for the author. There is an allusion to Ps. 110:1 in 1:3, and the same verse is quoted specifically in 1:13. In contrast to angels, who are servants and ministers, Jesus reigns as Son and Lord and as high priest.[6] The author's point is that it is quite incomprehensible that the readers would return to the law and its sacrifices for cleansing after experiencing full and final forgiveness through the Son.

Chapter 2 advances the same theme. It was always God's intention that the world be ruled by human beings. Here the author hearkens back to the original creation, where Adam and Eve were to rule the world for God. Such a privilege never belonged to angels (2:5). The author introduces Ps. 8 (2:6–8), a creation psalm celebrating the dominion over the world given to human beings. The author's reflection upon and interpretation of Ps. 8 is quite fascinating, for he observes that the rule over the world promised to human beings is not a reality (2:8). However, even though the world is not where it should be and where it will be, the rule over the world under human beings has begun in Jesus Christ (2:9). He is now crowned as king (in fulfillment of Ps. 110:1), and yet the pathway to his kingship is quite astonishing, for he was exalted to lordship through his suffering. Jesus' suffering was not for himself alone; it was also intended for his brothers and sisters, for human beings who would be freed from death through his suffering (2:10–18). The penalty that humans deserved for sin was absorbed by Jesus, so that human beings could rule together with the one who is crowned as Lord (2:17). Jesus suffered not for angels (2:16) but rather for human beings, so that the rule exercised by

---

6. See Beale, *Biblical Theology*, 317–19.

Adam and Eve is restored for human beings. Such rule is secured through Jesus' sacrifice as the priest-king, for human beings can rule only when they are cleansed from sin and purged from the selfish will that controls them. It is quite incomprehensible, then, that humans would turn back to the law and Aaronic sacrifices, which neither liberated them from the fear of death nor cleansed them from sins.

Jesus Superior to Moses and Joshua

One of the central themes of Hebrews is that the kingdom has come in Jesus because he reigns as the priest-king (cf. 12:28). The readers were tempted to return to the law, thinking perhaps that true forgiveness was secured through Levitical sacrifices. The author proceeds to argue that Jesus is superior to Moses and Joshua. Moses was esteemed as the servant of the Lord, for the Lord spoke to him "mouth to mouth" (Num. 12:8), and the law and Sinai covenant were mediated by him. Many doubtless thought there was no prophet greater than Moses, for "the LORD knew" him "face to face" (Deut. 34:10). According to Hebrews, "Moses was faithful in all God's house as a servant" (3:5), but Jesus is greater than Moses, for he is the builder of God's house and the Son instead of a servant (3:3, 6). Furthermore, Jesus is "the apostle and high priest of our confession" (3:1), and he secured an atonement that Moses never could win (7:1–10:18).

Along the same lines, Jesus is better than Joshua, for Joshua did not give Israel a lasting and permanent rest (4:8). The rest that his generation experienced pointed to a greater rest, as Ps. 95:11 testifies (4:5). Psalm 95 would not promise a future rest if the rest under Joshua had been ultimate. Under Jesus, who is a greater Joshua (the Hebrew name "Joshua" is transliterated into the Greek name "Jesus") (4:8), the final rest, a Sabbath rest, will be the portion of God's people (4:9). The author reminds the readers that it would be senseless to go "backward" in salvation history. They should be striving to obtain the rest that lies before them instead of returning to an era where no lasting rest was attained. The rest that is envisioned is not merely an earthly rest but a heavenly one. Israel's history from the time of Joshua until the writer's day demonstrates that any earthly rest is temporary. The possession of the land by one generation may be lost in the next. The only rest that is permanent, the only rest that will endure, is a heavenly rest. Christ promises such rest to those who trust in him and obey him.

It seems that the readers were particularly inclined to revert to the sacrifices of the old covenant, to find forgiveness in the offerings and sacrifices of the

Levitical priesthood (7:1–10:18). The old age of the law was looking more attractive than the new age inaugurated by the Son. Their sufferings and persecutions were taking a toll (10:32–34; 12:1–11; 13:3, 12–13), such that they were becoming sluggish and dull in their faith (5:11; 6:12). Apparently, they would not feel socially isolated if they returned to the old covenant, and they may have believed that such sacrifices would expunge guilt from their consciences. The author reminds them of the "already but not yet" character of God's promise. Suffering precedes glory. Jesus "endured the cross" because of the future joy that was promised to him (12:2). Currently, believers must endure the same reproach as Jesus did (13:13), recognizing that "we have no lasting city, but we seek the city that is to come" (13:14). Eating from the altar of the old covenant will not profit the readers, for only grace, which comes from Jesus' sacrifice, will strengthen believers (13:9–12). Foods prescribed by the old covenant are not the pathway to blessing.

The Melchizedekian Priesthood Superior to the Levitical Priesthood

The superiority of Jesus' sacrifice is explicated in 7:1–10:18. The Melchizedekian priesthood of Jesus surpasses the Aaronic priesthood, which was tied to the Mosaic covenant and law. The preeminence of the Melchizedekian priesthood is explained from a curious and mysterious event in Abraham's life. After rescuing his nephew Lot, Abraham returned and was blessed by the priest-king Melchizedek, to whom he paid a tithe (Gen. 14:18–20). The author of Hebrews descries significance in the story, for if Abraham gave a tithe to Melchizedek, then the latter is more important than the former (7:1–10). Indeed, there is a sense in which Levi, since he was a descendant of Abraham, gave a tithe to Melchizedek. Hence, the Melchizedekian priesthood takes precedence over the Levitical.

Melchizedek could easily be overlooked in a reading of the OT, for he appears briefly in Gen. 14 and does not appear again until Ps. 110. This is the same psalm that emphasizes that David's son would also be his Lord, the psalm that the author of Hebrews (see the section "Jesus Superior to Angels" above) used in chapter 1 to establish that Jesus now reigns at God's right hand. Suddenly, without warning and with no foreshadowing of what is to come, Melchizedek bursts upon the scene again after hundreds of years: "The LORD has sworn and will not change his mind, 'You are a priest forever after the order of Melchizedek'" (Ps. 110:4). The author of Hebrews discerns special significance in this verse (7:17, 21). The promise of a Melchizedekian priesthood indicates the eventual obsolescence of the Levitical priesthood. If the Levitical priesthood had truly brought perfection, there would be no need for a Melchizedekian priesthood (7:11). A change of priesthood logically involves a change of law (7:12), and therefore a new priesthood means that the old era of the law has been left behind. Clearly, Jesus is a new kind of priest, a Melchizedekian priest, since he comes from the tribe of Judah instead of the tribe of Levi (7:13–14). What really sets Jesus' priesthood apart is its perpetuity. As Ps. 110:4 says he maintains his priesthood "forever" by virtue of his "indestructible life" (7:16)—that is, because of his resurrection. The law did not bring perfection, but the hope secured by Jesus' priesthood is "better" because through it people "draw near to God" (7:19). The purpose of sacrifices is to have fellowship with God, to enjoy his presence and his love. Levitical sacrifices and the Levitical priesthood did not lead to the desired result, but Jesus' Melchizedekian priesthood is of a different character, for as a result of his priestly work human beings know God.

What sets apart Jesus' priesthood by way of contrast with the Levitical priesthood is the presence of an oath (7:20–22). The Lord swore to the perpetuity of his priesthood, demonstrating that he is the "guarantor of a better covenant" (7:22). The author again highlights and features the permanence of Jesus' priesthood (7:23–25). Levitical priests die, but Jesus, as the resurrected one, continues as a priest forever. The consequences are momentous. As the ever-living one who intercedes for believers, Jesus is able to utterly save "those who draw near to God through him" (7:25). If the readers are concerned about forgiveness and final salvation, they must not forsake the one who truly saves and who introduces them into God's gracious presence. The greatness of Jesus' priesthood is confirmed by another truth (7:26–28). Unlike the Levitical priests, Jesus is perfect. He had no need to offer sacrifice to atone for his own sins. His once-for-all sacrifice secured forgiveness of sins forever. Why, the author wonders, would the readers turn back to a priesthood that is temporary, that does not bring one into God's presence, and that is offered by imperfect priests? For in Jesus they have a priesthood that never ends, and that actually secured forgiveness of sins and granted fellowship with God.

In chapter 8 the author introduces specifically the new covenant, contrasting it with the old.[7] He begins, though, by reasserting his main point: "Now the point in what we are saying is this: we have such a high priest, one who is seated at the right hand of the throne of the Majesty in heaven, a minister in the holy places, in the true tent that the Lord set up, not man"

7. See Lehne, *New Covenant in Hebrews*.

(8:1–2). The letter begins with an allusion to Ps. 110:1 and with the truth that sins have been cleansed by Christ's sacrifice. The author returns to both of these themes here. Jesus fulfills Ps. 110:1. He is seated at God's right and as high priest has offered an atoning sacrifice for sins. What was the purpose and function of the tabernacle/temple and priests if they are no longer necessary? The author argues that the priests and tabernacle were intended as earthly copies of heavenly realities (8:3–6), finding justification for this thought from Exod. 25:40. The argument is not only a vertical one, where the earthly reflects the heavenly; it is also temporal, for what is heavenly has now arrived on the scene. The earthly anticipated the heavenly; the old covenant prepared the way for the new, clearly indicating that the old covenant would cease (8:13). The OT itself prophesied that a new covenant would arrive (8:8–12; cf. Jer. 31:31–34), and that full and final forgiveness of sins would become a reality.

The inadequacy of the tabernacle/temple ritual becomes evident when one reflects on the Day of Atonement (see Lev. 16). The author of Hebrews notes that entrance into God's presence, fellowship with the living God, was limited under the old covenant (9:8). Access to the holy of holies was limited to the high priest, and even so, such access was reserved for only one day a year, and he had to bring in blood in order to avert God's wrath (9:7). The regulations and washings dealt with external and bodily matters, but they are not ultimate; they point to a better time, to "the time of reformation" that has now arrived in Christ (9:9–10). Jesus offered his blood not in an earthly sanctuary but rather in a "heavenly tent," in God's very presence (9:11–14). His sacrifice is clearly better than the sacrifices of animals, for it secured "eternal redemption" (9:12) and truly purifies the conscience (9:14). The readers may have desired to return to old covenant sacrifices because these offered a concrete and practical reminder of the cleansing of sins. The author of Hebrews argues, on the contrary, that true purification is realized only in Christ's atonement.

The sacrifices of the old covenant indicate that the "eternal inheritance" (9:15) will be obtained only through death, through the spilling of blood. Thus, earthly sacrifices function as "copies" (9:23–24) of the sacrifice of Christ, for the latter brings one into the very presence of God. The author of Hebrews does not repudiate OT sacrifices. He does not say that the conception of God's holiness in the OT is primitive and outmoded. He does not reject such sacrifices as too bloody, nor does he opt for a more "spiritual" and less "messy" access to God. OT sacrifices were commanded by God and were fitting for a previous era of redemptive history. They point to another bloody sacrifice. They are typological in nature, anticipating a better sacrifice to come. They show that God's holiness is appeased or satisfied not with the blood of animals but rather with the blood of Christ. God's holiness does not change from the OT to the NT. The severe penalties of the OT are not withdrawn, nor does the author say that God can forgive apart from sacrifices. Instead, he argues for a better and more effective sacrifice, one that brings people into God's very presence. The effectiveness of Christ's sacrifice is evident from its once-for-all character (9:25–28). Unlike OT sacrifices, it did not need to be repeated, for Christ's one sacrifice secured forgiveness of sins forever.

The author pounds home the difference between Christ's sacrifice and the sacrifices of the old covenant. The latter are "shadows," but Christ's sacrifice is the substance, "the true form" to which OT sacrifices pointed (10:1). If OT sacrifices were truly effective, they would not need to be constantly repeated (10:2–4). If sins were truly washed away, and if the conscience were really cleansed, then the sacrifices would have ceased. The inadequacy of such sacrifices is indicated by Ps. 40:6–8 (10:5–10), for the Christ has come not to offer animals but rather to give up his own body to God, demonstrating that as sacrifices the former are obsolete. Clearly, the offering of animals cannot take away sin, for they are unwilling victims that are not conscious of giving their lives for the sake of others. The sacrifice of Jesus is of a different order, for he consciously and willingly gave himself for the sins of others. How can the readers find forgiveness in old covenant sacrifices, the author teaches, when they are so clearly inferior to the sacrifice of Jesus Christ?

More than anything else, the author wants the readers to be assured of the forgiveness of their sins. The OT sacrifices are offered repeatedly, but Jesus by one sacrifice atoned for sins forever (10:11–12). OT priests stand, signifying that their work is never done, but Jesus sits at God's right hand, demonstrating that his work is finished, and that he has fulfilled Ps. 110:1 (10:13). The fullness of what Jesus accomplished is summed up in 10:14: "For by a single offering he has perfected for all time those who are being sanctified." The new covenant promise of forgiveness of sins has become a reality in Jesus Christ (10:16–17), and now that forgiveness has been secured, there is no need for further sacrifices (10:18). The author wants the readers to be full of "confidence," since they can enter God's presence because of Jesus' blood and sacrifice (10:19–20). He is a "great priest" by whose sacrifice they can "draw near with a true heart in full assurance of faith, with our hearts sprinkled clean from an evil conscience and our bodies washed with pure water" (10:22). The entire discussion of OT sacrifices is not an academic exercise or a sterile discussion of the OT cult. The author longs for the readers to have assurance that their sins are forgiven and to rejoice that they can enter God's presence through Jesus' blood. Turning back to the OT cult will not bring forgiveness or assurance.

Admonitions against Apostasy

The "already but not yet" permeates Hebrews. The new age has come in Christ, and believers have now received a kingdom (12:28). The old covenant has been replaced by the new, and yet the author is concerned that the readers might relapse back in to the old covenant. Even though the fulfillment has come, the readers are admonished and warned against apostasy. We must recognize up front that the warning texts must be read synthetically. In other words, all the warnings have the same point: do not commit apostasy. The admonitions drive home this single point by using different language. The variety of terminology does not lead to the conclusion that the warning texts should be isolated from one another. On the contrary, they mutually interpret one another, with each text shedding light upon the others. Hence, in considering the warnings, I will interpret them together instead of looking at each one seriatim. Three questions will be asked of the warnings: (1) To whom are the warnings addressed? (2) What are the readers warned about? (3) What will happen if the readers fail to heed the warnings?

First, to whom are the warnings addressed? Clearly, they are addressed to the readers, to the church or churches to which the letter is sent. They are called "brothers" (3:12), and the author often addresses them as "you" (3:7, 12, 15; 4:1, 7; 5:11, 12; 6:11, 12; 10:36; 12:3, 5, 25), which makes the admonition pointed and specific. But the author often includes himself in the warning as well, using the first-person plural pronoun "we" or "us" (2:1, 3; 3:6, 14; 4:1, 2, 3, 11, 13, 14; 6:1; 10:22, 23, 26; 12:1, 9, 25, 28). The pronouns "we" and "us" support the notion that the warnings are addressed to believers, for surely the author considered himself to be a believer. The author describes the readers in 6:4–5, and the description lends weight to the view that the readers are believers. They are "enlightened" (*phōtisthentas* [6:4]), and the same term is used to describe the generous response of the readers to suffering "after you were enlightened" (10:32). It seems that the enlightenment describes conversion in terms of understanding and revelation. The readers also "tasted the heavenly gift" (6:4). Identifying the "heavenly gift" is not simple, but perhaps it refers to salvation. The author should not be understood to say that they simply "sipped" salvation. Earlier he describes Jesus as one who "taste[d] death for everyone" (2:9). The same verb for "taste" (*geuomai*) is used in both instances, and Jesus did not just sip death but fully experienced it, so the same should be said relative to salvation. The same issue arises in 6:5, where the readers are said to "have tasted the goodness of the word of God and the powers of the age to come." The same verb "taste" (*geuomai*) is used, and once again it denotes a full experience of the power of the coming age and of the word of God.

The most important description of the readers, however, is the statement that they "have shared in the Holy Spirit" (6:4). The word "shared" (*metochos*) is used of "sharing" a heavenly calling (3:1), of "sharing" in Christ (3:14), and "sharing" in discipline (12:8). There is no suggestion that such "sharing" is partial or inadequate in any way. Furthermore, the term comes from the same root as the word used for "partaking [*metechōn*] milk" (5:13) and "shar[ing] [*meteschen*] in flesh and blood" (2:14). Certainly, Jesus was fully and completely made of flesh and blood, and the ingestion of milk was more than a sip. Hence, there is no hint in the words used that the sharing of the Holy Spirit was anything other than the reception of the Holy Spirit. Such an expression makes it quite clear that the author speaks of Christians, for the gift of the Spirit is *the* mark in the NT that certifies that one is a believer (cf. Acts 2:38; 10:47; 15:8–9; 19:2, 6; Rom. 8:9, 16; 2 Cor. 5:5; Gal. 3:2, 5; 4:6; Eph. 1:13–14; 1 John 3:24; 4:13). To sum up, it is quite clear that the author addresses believers in the warnings, those who have received the Holy Spirit.

Second, what are the readers warned about? Again, it is imperative that the admonitions be read synoptically, so that they shed light on one another. The readers must beware of drifting away (2:1), of neglecting such a great salvation (2:3). The peril is that they will harden their hearts (3:8, 13, 15), and that their hearts will go astray (3:10). A hard heart is an unbelieving one, one that falls away from the living God (3:12, 19), so that the word of the gospel is not heeded by faith (4:2). Unbelief is inseparable from and always leads to disobedience and sin (3:17–18; 4:2, 11). Positively, the readers must hold on to their assurance until the end (3:14), and they must strive to enter God's rest (4:11).

The readers have become sluggish and dull (5:11; 6:12). The readers must press on to maturity (6:1) and show diligence until the end (6:11) so that they will obtain the promise and take hold of the hope that lies before them (6:15, 18). They must beware of "falling away" (*parapesontas* [6:6]). Here the other warning texts assist us, for some interpreters interpret the participle *parapesontas* as if the readers had already fallen away. Such an interpretation fails to read the genre and function of the warning correctly. The author consistently warns and admonishes and does not make declarations about the readers. Harold Attridge remarks, "Our author does not accuse his addressees of being in this condition. . . . It is a warning that should remind them of the seriousness of their situation and the importance of renewing their commitment."[8] He worries that the readers by their apostasy will, so to speak, crucify God's Son again and bring public shame on him (6:6).

8. Attridge, *Epistle to the Hebrews*, 171.

The readers must draw near (10:22) and hold on to the faith that they confessed (10:23). Believers must urge one another to do good works, for if they neglect to assemble together with other believers, they will depart from the faith (10:24–25). They must beware of sinning deliberately (10:26), which is equivalent to sinning "with a high hand" in the OT (see Num. 15:30). In other words, they must beware of falling away (6:6), of hardening their hearts (3:8), and of failing to enter God's rest (4:11). Deliberate sin constitutes a willful and permanent rejection of Jesus' sacrifice. It involves trampling Jesus under one's feet, rejecting the blood of his sacrifice as unclean, and insulting the Spirit of grace (10:29). The readers must not jettison the confidence that they exercised when they were first believers (10:35); rather, they must do God's will and endure instead of shrinking back out of fear (10:36, 38–39). Positively, they must exercise faith (10:39). Thus, chapter 11 (widely known as the "faith chapter") fits seamlessly into the letter. It is not an aside or a digression. Those who endure put their trust in God, and they are assured that he will care for them in the future. In chapter 11 the author particularly emphasizes the future reward that belongs to those who believe. For example, Abraham and his descendants looked to the promise that they did not receive in their lifetime (11:8–22). Similarly, Moses renounced the joys of Egypt when he considered the future reward (11:23–28). The author wants his readers to follow the example of the ancestors. They too must put their trust in the God who will finally reward them. The supreme exemplar of faith is Jesus, "who for the joy set before him endured the cross, despising the shame, and is seated at the right hand of the throne of God" (12:2). Thus, the readers must persevere in faith and trust, knowing that those who continue to trust in God will be vindicated and rewarded.[9] And so they must not refuse the word that God is speaking to them (12:25).

Third and finally, what will happen to the readers if they fail to heed the warnings? It seems clear that the consequence is final and irrevocable judgment. If the readers drift from the gospel, if they "neglect such a great salvation," they will not "escape" (2:3). By speaking about not escaping, the author refers to final judgment, for the next warning passage says that those who fall away will not enter God's rest (3:11, 18, 19; 4:1, 3, 5–6, 9–11). The readers wanted to be assured of forgiveness, but as Barnabas Lindars aptly remarks, "Paradoxically they are turning away from the means of reconciliation in the endeavor to find it."[10] In the OT not entering God's rest meant earthly judgment, but Hebrews regularly conceives of OT realities typologically so that they forecast

9. On faith in Hebrews, see Marshall, *New Testament Theology*, 615–17.
10. Lindars, *Letter to the Hebrews*, 69.

what is to come. Furthermore, the earthly points toward the heavenly. Hence, the sacrifices that were offered in the earthly tabernacle anticipated Christ's sacrifice, which secured access to God in his heavenly tabernacle. So too here, the earthly rest points toward the heavenly rest, the heavenly city (11:13–16; 13:14), which awaits the people of God. To speak about the heavenly rest, therefore, is another way of describing the eschatological reward for believers. Those who do not enter the heavenly rest will experience destruction, just as the wilderness generation did.

The immutability of the judgment is confirmed in chapter 6. Those who fall away cannot be restored again to repentance (6:4). The terms "cursed" and "burned" with reference to the "land" in 6:8 belong in the same category. What is burned and cursed is not merely the fruit but the land itself, and the land designates the person under consideration, showing that end-time judgment will fall on those who forsake the Lord. Nor does the phrase "near to being cursed" (6:8) suggest that those who apostatize come close to being cursed but barely escape it. The word "near" here is temporal, indicating that the curse is imminent for those who depart from the gospel. The dire consequences explain the urgency of the warnings. Still, the author is confident that his readers will heed the warnings and escape judgment, for he thinks that they will respond well and enjoy "salvation" (6:9) and "inherit the promises" (6:12). The warnings are the means by which the promises will be secured.

I must emphasize yet again that all the warning texts should be read together. "There no longer remains a sacrifice for sins" for those who turn away from "the knowledge of the truth" (10:26). To say that there is no sacrifice is to say that there is no forgiveness. In other words, the only prospect that awaits those who reject the gospel is "a fearful expectation of judgment and a fury of fire" (10:27). Certainly, this is typical language in the NT for the last judgment. Again the author contrasts the old covenant with the new, so that those who sin under the new covenant face an eternal punishment, not just an earthly one (10:28–29). God's vengeance will be their portion (10:30). The Lord has no pleasure in those who fall away (10:38). Indeed, those who "shrink back" will experience "destruction," whereas those who persevere in faith will "preserve their souls" (10:39). The word used here for "destruction" (*apōleia*) is commonly used for the final judgment (see Matt. 7:13; John 17:12; Acts 8:20; Rom. 9:22; Phil. 1:28; 3:19; 2 Thess. 2:3; 1 Tim. 6:9; 2 Pet. 2:1, 3; 3:7, 16; Rev. 17:8, 11). Along the same lines, those who are not holy will not "see the Lord" (12:14). Like Esau, they will not obtain the inheritance (12:14–17). The author concludes the warnings with the verb "escape" (12:25), forming an inclusio with the first warning passage (2:3) and underlining the severe consequences that will be faced by those who turn away from Christ.

Conclusion

According to Hebrews, the kingdom has come (12:28). Jesus, as the priest-king, is seated at the right hand of God in heaven, after securing complete and final forgiveness of sins. To say that the kingdom has come fits well with the message of Hebrews, for the author argues that the new covenant is a reality and the old covenant has passed away. The OT is not rejected as an inferior revelation. It is read salvation-historically and typologically. OT events, institutions, and persons point forward to Christ as the priest and king, as the one who gives final rest to the people of God. The kingdom and the rule for human beings prophesied in the OT have become a reality through Jesus Christ, for by his death and resurrection he has won the victory over Satan (2:14–15), securing the triumph over the serpent promised in Gen. 3:15. Now the rule over the world given to human beings at creation (see Gen. 1:26–27) is exercised by Jesus Christ and will reach its consummation when he returns (9:28). All human beings who belong to Christ, all who are his brothers and sisters and are part of his family, will rule with him (2:10–18). We see again that the people of God are defined christologically. One must belong to Jesus Christ in order to be part of the offspring of Abraham (2:16). As the priest-king, as the one who is fully human and divine, as the Melchizedekian priest and Davidic king, he is superior to angels, to Moses, Joshua, and Levitical priests. By virtue of his sacrifice and his indestructible life he has won complete salvation for those who are his, so that they enjoy perfection through him.

The last days have arrived. God has spoken finally and definitively in his Son. And yet believers still await the fullness of what God promised. The admonitions and warnings in Hebrews fit with the eschatological tension that marks the letter. The last days have arrived, and the readers have put their trust in Jesus, and yet they are warned against falling away. They must not abandon the gospel that they have received by giving way to unbelief and disobedience as the wilderness generation did. If they fall away, there is no hope for repentance, and they will face final and irrevocable judgment. Those who persevere in faith until the end will receive the final reward. The author of Hebrews understands the land promises of the OT typologically. The rest in the land granted to Israel under Joshua points to a greater rest, a heavenly rest, a Sabbath rest, which will be enjoyed by the people of God. Believers, like the patriarchs, are exiles on earth (11:13–16). They are looking forward to a homeland in the future, a better country, and a heavenly city. They look forward to the city that is coming, the city that endures forever (13:14). The world is not yet subjected to Jesus and to human beings (2:5–8). The land promise will be fulfilled, but it will be fulfilled in a new world, a world where rest is unending and where God resides in the city. Believers even now are members of "the city of the living God" and part of "the heavenly Jerusalem" (12:22), and yet they are exiles on the earth at the same time, awaiting the fullness of what God promised. The greatest blessing is not the land but rather fellowship with God through the sacrifice of Jesus. Jesus, as "the great shepherd of the sheep," has accomplished eternal salvation "by the blood of the covenant" (13:20). Now believers can "enter the holy places through the blood of Jesus" (10:19). Now they can "draw near with a true heart in full assurance of faith" (10:22; cf. 7:19). Believers now have access to God's presence through Jesus, and when they reach the heavenly rest, they will enjoy the radiance and beauty of his presence in an undiminished way forever.

31

THE EPISTLE OF JAMES

It is not far off the target to view the Epistle of James as the Proverbs of the NT, though of course the two books are different as well. Certainly, James bears the marks of OT wisdom material, indicating that James sketches in what it means to live under God's lordship.[1] One of the striking features of James is the infrequency with which the author refers to Jesus Christ. Because of this, some have even wondered if the book is Christian. Clearly, James does not present anything close to a full-orbed Christology, and he does not even mention the cross. We should not make the mistake of thinking that the letter was intended to set forth the whole of James's theology, as if he denied elements of Christian teaching found elsewhere in the NT. In addition, the Christology of James is more advanced than is often recognized.[2] For instance, James identifies himself as a slave of "God and the Lord Jesus Christ" (1:1). James assigns the same status to Jesus as he does to God. The significance of such a statement can scarcely be underestimated, for James, consistent with his Jewish heritage, continues to believe in one God (2:19). And yet Jesus has the same stature as God and is designated as "Lord." Nor should we fail to see that James also refers to Jesus as the Christ (1:1; 2:1). With James's Jewish background, the term "Christ" is almost certainly a title.

The significance of the term "Lord" should also be recognized. In some instances it is difficult in James to know whether the Father or Jesus Christ is called "Lord." Even if we take the most conservative reading and see a reference to the Father as "Lord" unless the text specifically identifies Jesus as Lord (1:7; 3:9; 4:10, 15; 5:4, 10, 11, 14, 15), there are still five clear examples where

1. For a most insightful study on James, see Bauckham, *James*.
2. So also Matera, *New Testament Theology*, 365.

lordship is ascribed to Jesus (1:1; 2:1 [2x]; 5:7, 8). Since Jesus has the same title as God, he clearly shares the same divine identity. Translating the phrase at the end of 2:1 is difficult, but it likely should be rendered "our glorious Lord." Such language hearkens back to the OT, where glory and lordship are ascribed to Yahweh (Exod. 16:7; 24:17; Lev. 9:6; see also Ps. 24:8, 10). James does not dwell on Christ's identity, but it would be a serious mistake to conclude that he had a low Christology, for Jesus as the Christ shares in the glory of God. The sovereignty and lordship of Jesus are also confirmed by his future coming (5:7–8). Jesus now reigns with God and will return again as the conquering king. In the same way, 2:1 refers to "faith in our Lord Jesus Christ." Faith must be directed to God alone, and therefore we see here a remarkably high Christology in that Christians are those who put their trust in Jesus Christ as Lord.[3]

Since the time of Martin Luther it has been doubted whether James's teaching accords with the Pauline gospel. Obviously, Paul's emphases differ from those of James, but many interpreters exaggerate those differences. For instance, James teaches that salvation is a gift of God. God "chose the poor to be rich in faith and heirs of the kingdom" (2:5). Faith here is the consequence of election, and hence it follows that faith is a gift and cannot be construed as a contribution generated by the autonomous will of human beings. The new life of believers is a result of God's will (1:18). He chose to give birth to believers via the "word of truth" (1:18), which is the gospel. Regeneration is a "good" and "perfect" "gift" that streams from above (1:17).

Nor is James a perfectionist who demands flawless obedience for salvation. He recognizes that all believers sin regularly and in a variety of ways (3:2). Such sins do not preclude salvation, and hence those who sin may obtain forgiveness. Those who have compromised with the world and become spiritual prostitutes (4:4) are not bereft of hope. If they repent and turn away from sin and cleanse their hands and mourn over their evil, God will exalt them (4:8–10). This certainly means that they may be forgiven for the evil that they carried out. Indeed, James specifically says that those who have sinned will obtain forgiveness and healing if they confess their wrongs (5:15–16). Similarly, those who have strayed from the truth of the gospel can be brought back (5:19–20). They may be rescued from death, which is the final judgment. Even though they have committed a "multitude of sins," those sins may be covered and forgiven (5:20). The importance of forgiveness in James's theology plays a more central role than is often acknowledged in scholarship. James does not explain how believers receive forgiveness, but he clearly teaches that it

3. Compare 2:7, where "the honorable name" blasphemed is almost certainly Christ's. Hence, Christ can be blasphemed. This is analogous to the OT, where God's name must be honored.

is available, even for those who have sinned egregiously and have wandered from the truth. It has often been pointed out that James reflects the teaching of Jesus, and perhaps here we recognize Jesus' teaching that he came to call sinners, not the righteous (cf. Mark 2:13–17).

James's concern for righteous living is acknowledged by all, but the centrality of faith in his theology must not be neglected, for there are reasons to think that faith is the root from which goodness flows. The difficulties of life test the authenticity of believers' faith (1:3), revealing the object of their trust. James shows dependence upon the teaching of Jesus (Matt. 17:20) in emphasizing the need to ask in faith (1:6), so that it is only prayers of faith that save (5:15). The centrality of faith is particularly emphasized in 2:14–26, where the noun "faith" (*pistis*) occurs eleven times, and the verb "believe" (*pisteuō*) three times. James does not deny the primacy of faith here, nor does he teach that works are the basis of salvation. James's concern is with false faith (2:19), an intellectual faith that registers assent with certain doctrines but remains unaffected in daily life by the creed that is confessed. Such "faith" for James is not saving faith. There is, however, a kind of faith that brings "profit" (2:14, 16), a faith that truly saves and justifies. Such faith results in and leads to works. If works are not produced, then the faith exercised is not saving faith, for true faith manifests itself in works. James does not deny, then, that faith saves. He distinguishes between two different kinds of faith. He counters the idea that faith bereft of works saves or justifies. True faith is transforming and energizing, leading one to a life pleasing to God. There is no contradiction with Paul's teaching on justification here, for Paul also teaches that one must do good works to inherit the kingdom (1 Cor. 6:9–11; Gal. 5:21; cf. also Rom. 2:7; Titus 3:8). Paul's point is that works are not the fundamental basis for one's relationship with God, so that justification is not based on works. James does not differ on this matter, for the works that justify and save are the result of faith, and therefore they are not the basis or foundation of one's salvation.

We see something rather similar with regard to the "word" (*logos*). Regeneration was accomplished "by the word of truth" (1:18), which is to be identified with the gospel (cf. Eph. 1:13; 2 Tim. 2:15). The "word" is the means by which life was generated. In a fascinating phrase James refers to "the implanted word, which is able to save your souls" (1:21). The "implanted word" probably alludes to the new covenant of Jer. 31:31–34, where Yahweh writes his law on human hearts. Salvation cannot be attributed to the autonomous effort of human beings but instead finds its roots in the word that God implants in human beings, for it is the supernatural word of God that delivers on the day of judgment. James, of course, emphasizes that human beings must "do" the word (1:22–25). Hearing the word without doing it makes the word an abstraction, and God's word is never abstract but always concrete, for it is an effective word. Still, the doing of the word is a result of the word being implanted so that the priority of God's work is preserved.

Another way of putting this is that only those who do the will of God will be "heirs of the kingdom" (2:5). Those who flout the dictates of the king will not be allowed to enter his realm. James also speaks of the "law" of God as "royal" (2:8). In other words, it is the law of the sovereign one, the Lord of all, and those who neglect to keep it do so at their peril. James particularly stresses the necessity of doing what the law says (1:25; 2:8–12; 4:11). Believers must keep the law and decrees stipulated by their king. At the same time, James calls it "the law of liberty" (1:25). The context of this expression suggests a close relationship between the law of liberty and "the word" (1:18, 21–23). Just as the "implanted word" resonates with the promise of the new covenant, so too the phrase "law of liberty" evokes the same theme. Believers are not only enjoined to observe and keep the law; there is also the notion that the law frees and liberates, and hence the power to keep the law stems from God's gracious work. Grace precedes and undergirds demand.

James's association with or dependence upon wisdom traditions is reflected in his concern for wisdom (1:5; 3:13–18). We saw in the book of Proverbs that those who live wisely fear the Lord; they live under God's lordship. The same theme is apparent in James. Wisdom is not the same thing as intellectual brilliance or philosophical acumen. Wisdom is a gift of God granted to those who ask God for it (1:5). Those who put their trust in God receive it, but it is withheld from those who are unstable and cannot decide if they want to follow God (1:6–8). The behavioral character of wisdom is obvious in 3:13–18. Wisdom is revealed by one's works, by humility, gentleness, mercy, reasonableness, and righteousness. Foolishness is apparent where there is "jealousy and selfish ambition" (3:14–16). The latter are "demonic" qualities (3:15). It has often been observed that the fruit of wisdom for James is matched by the fruit of the Spirit for Paul (Gal. 5:22–23). There is also a close relationship between the Spirit and wisdom in the Scriptures (cf. Isa. 11:2; Dan. 5:11, 14; Acts 6:3, 10; 1 Cor. 12:8; Eph. 1:17). In light of these connections, it seems that James considers wisdom to be a gift of God (cf. Exod. 31:3; 1 Kings 4:29; Job 32:8; Prov. 2:6; Dan. 1:17), just as the Spirit is given by him.

James emphasizes that the heirs of the kingdom live a new life. Quarreling and fighting cannot mark their relationships with others (4:1–3), and their speech must be healing and refreshing instead of being characterized by bitterness, resentment, and hatred (3:1–12). The stresses and difficulties of life prepare believers for eschatological reward (1:2–4, 12), perfecting their character so that they are mature and godly. James, in dependence upon the teaching of Jesus, emphasizes the danger of riches. Hence, believers must not show partiality to the rich and influential (2:1–13). They must beware of becoming adulterous, falling in love with this world so that they long for its approval and splendor (4:4–6). It is the rich who regularly persecute and defame Christ's name (2:6–7). They are headed for eschatological destruction (1:9–11; 5:1–3), for they oppress and mistreat their workers (5:4–6). They are prone to trust in their own ingenuity and business skills instead of relying on God's will (4:13–17).

James features the arrival of the kingdom by teaching that Jesus is the Lord, demonstrating that he now reigns with God. At the same time, his reign is not consummated, for believers suffer trials and economic deprivation and persecution at the hands of the rich. They must be patient and await the day when Jesus will return and exercise his lordship over all (5:7). God has granted believers faith and new life by the word of the gospel. James calls on his readers to live under the law and rule of their king. The reality of their faith is discerned by their works; the authenticity of their wisdom is manifested by their character. James has no patience with those who say that Jesus is Lord while repudiating his lordship in the way they live their lives. Clearly, his message on this score is derived from Jesus himself (Matt. 7:21–23).

32

THE EPISTLE OF 1 PETER

Perhaps the theology of 1 Peter can be captured with the words "the end of all things is at hand" (4:7). These words illustrate the tension that marks Peter's thought. On the one hand, the decisive work of salvation has been accomplished in Jesus Christ. What the OT promised has been fulfilled in him. On the other hand, the fulfillment has not yet been completed. The end is near, but it has not yet arrived.

It is fitting to begin with the emphasis on fulfillment in 1 Peter. The readers live in a different era from the OT prophets (1:10–12). The prophets longed to see the fulfillment of their prophecies and to experience the salvation and grace they proclaimed. But this privilege was not to be theirs. It belongs instead to those who live on the other side of the death and resurrection of Jesus, to Christians (4:16). Those who believe in Jesus Christ have been born again (1:3). By means of the word of God (1:23–25)—that is, the gospel—they have been regenerated.[1] Believers have been chosen and elected by the Father (1:1–2), set apart by the Spirit (1:2), and forgiven by the sprinkled blood of the Son (1:2). The sprinkling of blood in Israel's covenant with the Lord (see Exod. 24:8) pointed to a more effective and final sprinkling in the death of Christ. The sacrifice of spotless lambs anticipated the sacrifice of the true lamb of God, the sacrifice of Christ as the sinless one (1:18–19). Israel was liberated from Egypt through Yahweh's grace, but Israel's exodus and redemption corresponded to and pointed to a greater ransom: the liberation from a life of futility and sin through the death of Jesus Christ. Peter, more than any other NT writer, emphasizes that Jesus fulfilled Isa. 53, that he was the servant of the Lord who

---

1. As Beale (*Biblical Theology*, 324–26) notes, "born again" indicates the arrival of the new creation.

suffered for the sake of his people (2:21–25). The full forgiveness promised in Isa. 53 is now realized in Jesus Christ. He suffered as the innocent victim, and yet he desisted from rage and threats of revenge. He suffered not because of his sin, for he had none (2:22), but rather as the innocent one he entrusted himself to God and to the promise of the resurrection. His death functions as an example for Christians in their suffering (2:21), but at the same time his death was unique and unrepeatable, for he "bore our sins in his body on the tree" (2:24). His death paid the penalty for sin that could not be paid by human beings. Through his death as the servant of the Lord he secured the definitive and final forgiveness prophesied in the OT.

The substitutionary character of his death is clear, for he suffered "once for sins, the righteous for the unrighteous" (3:18). He suffered in such a way to "bring us to God" (3:18). Peter does not use the same language as Hebrews, but the idea is the same. Through Jesus' death, through the forgiveness of sins achieved by his sacrifice, a new relationship with God has been established. Believers now have access to God and enjoy an unhindered relationship with him since Christ suffered in their place and their sins have been atoned for. Jesus' suffering on the cross opened the doors of access to God's presence but also spelled the defeat of demonic powers (3:19–22). The cross also signals victory over the forces opposed to God's love and his saving work in the world. Jesus was raised by the Holy Spirit after his suffering, and as the victorious Lord and sovereign one, he proclaimed triumph over demons. By virtue of his death and resurrection, a new age in the history of salvation dawned, for Jesus is crowned as victor over demons, and they are subjected to him. Even though Peter does not use the term "kingdom" specifically, the notion is quite similar to what we find in the Synoptic Gospels. The kingdom has been inaugurated in Jesus' triumph over demons at the cross and resurrection.

According to the OT, Israel was God's chosen and elect people (Exod. 19:6), and yet Peter says to his readers, "But you are a chosen race, a royal priesthood, a holy nation, a people for his own possession" (2:9). The church of Jesus Christ is now the true and new Israel. It does not displace ethnic Israel but rather fulfills it, so that Jewish Christians are also members of the true Israel. The new identity of believers is reflected in the language used for unbelievers: "Gentiles" (2:12; 4:3). Most of the believers in 1 Peter probably were Gentiles, but now the language of "Israel" is applied to them, for they belong to the restored and new Israel. On the other hand, those who are unbelievers are labeled as "Gentiles." It seems quite clear, then, that Peter conceives of the church of Jesus Christ as the new and true Israel.

Believers are God's "household," which probably refers to the church as God's temple because there are clear allusions to Ezek. 9 and Mal. 3:1–5 in

1 Pet. 4:17–19. As God's "spiritual house," believers "offer spiritual sacrifices" (2:5). They are the "living stones" (2:5) that constitute the building blocks of the people of God. The distinctiveness of the NT witness shines forth here, for virtually all religions had temples. Peter, however, sees the temple as the people of God. Jesus is the "living stone" of the temple, and believers are "living stones" (2:4–5). The Jerusalem temple has been displaced and fulfilled by a new temple, a new dwelling place of God. Jesus is "the cornerstone" of the temple (2:7). The people of God find their life and basis in Christ as the risen and triumphant and reigning Lord. Jesus is the new temple and believers are part of the new temple as well since they belong to Jesus. The Christ-centeredness of the NT continues in 1 Peter, for the people of God find their life and identity in Jesus the Christ.

The eschatology of 1 Peter is fascinating, for believers live in the days of the fulfillment promised in the OT (1:10–12). And yet the fullness of what God promised has not yet been realized. Believers in Jesus Christ are exiles and sojourners on earth (1:1, 17; 2:11). The point is not that they were literal exiles.[2] It is quite improbable that Peter's readers were actually political exiles, for such a conclusion would mean that those converted were not from the regions addressed in the letter. What Peter emphasizes is their alienation from life in this world. Believers do not fit in with the values and priorities that characterize their society and culture. They have a different destination and long for their future home, which is heavenly (1:4).

A heavenly home should not be understood to be an ethereal and non-physical existence, so that the future inheritance has a Platonic character. The inheritance is heavenly because it transcends life on earth and derives from God himself. Since believers are exiles and sojourners and their inheritance is heavenly, it is not surprising that they are now suffering. The suffering of believers is one of the central themes of 1 Peter.[3] Believers are tested in a variety of ways during this life (1:6–7; 5:10). They were criticized and slandered by unbelievers as those who practice evil (2:12; 3:13–17; 4:12–19). Actually, what unbelievers find off-putting is that Christians no longer join together with them in licentious activities (4:3–4). Peter does not mention physical suffering specifically; nothing is said about believers being put to death. The suffering described does not indicate empire-wide persecution representing the

---

2. Against Elliott (*Home for the Homeless*, 37–49, 129–32; *1 Peter*, 100–102), who understands the term literally and metaphorically, whereas a metaphorical reading is more likely (so Chin, "Heavenly Home"; Feldmeier, *Die Christen als Fremde*, 203–10; Bechtler, *Following in His Steps*, 78–81). For a helpful discussion, see Dryden, *Theology and Ethics*, 126–32. Dryden sees a social component to living as exiles but does not understand the term literally, as Elliott does.

3. See Bechtler, *Following in His Steps*.

official policy of the Roman imperium. Apparently, what was occurring was sporadic persecution, the kind of rejection that was to be expected because believers lived contrary to the social norms of their culture. Therefore, slaves were abused and mistreated by their masters (2:18–21), and wives suffered indignity from unbelieving husbands (3:1).

Since believers live between the times and suffer as exiles, Peter reminds them of their future salvation and end-time inheritance (1:4–9). They are urged to persevere and to continue believing and trusting, for their time of vindication is coming (5:9–10).[4] God rules even during their suffering (5:11), and his lordship will not be overturned, nor should they interpret their difficulties as an indication that the Lord does not reign over all. They are to entrust themselves to God's will in their suffering, knowing that he rules over all that they are experiencing (4:19). The devil, like "a roaring lion," wants to terrify them in their suffering so that they will abandon the faith (5:8). But God has designed suffering for believers' good, to refine and purify them so that the validity of their faith will be evident, which will bring glory when Christ is revealed (1:6–7). The pattern of Jesus is the pattern for disciples as well: first comes suffering, then comes glory (1:11).

Believers are summoned to live a life that is pleasing to God. Such godly conduct will bring glory to God (2:12). The importance of righteous behavior is underscored by the frequent use of the word "conduct" (*anastrophē* [1:15, 18; 2:12; 3:1, 2, 16]). Believers must live holy lives that are distinct from the world and remarkable for their devotion to God (1:14–15). Drawing on the teaching of Jesus (see Matt. 5:16), Peter emphasizes that the good deeds of believers will provoke unbelievers to give glory to God (2:12). As believers refrain from evil desires (2:11), they demonstrate the new life that they enjoy in Christ. The passions that rule unbelievers must be absent from the lives of believers (4:2–4). The sexual sin, wild drinking parties, and idolatry that are typical of Gentiles should not characterize the lives of those who are no longer "Gentiles" (2:12; 4:3) but rather are members of the true Israel. Now they live for "the will of God" instead of "human passions" (4:2). Those who give themselves over to evil will not be spared in the final judgment, while believers who pursue goodness will enjoy eschatological blessing (3:10–12). As those who have been born again, they will love fellow believers with a reality that cannot be contradicted (1:22), and hence malice, jealousy, deception, and envy will not characterize their lives (2:1). The realization that the end is near should stimulate believers to love, prayer, and the use of gifts for the good of others (4:7–11). Peter is

---

4. Dryden (*Theology and Ethics*) rightly underscores the connection between eschatology and ethics in 1 Peter.

particularly concerned that if believers suffer, it is not because they are practicing evil (3:13–17; 4:15–16), for wicked actions will bring disrepute on Christ's name because Christians are known as "Christ followers."

Peter particularly calls attention to the future hope Christians enjoy. Believers are to set their hope not on the comforts of this world but instead on the grace and joy that will be theirs when Jesus Christ is revealed (1:13). Because of Christ's resurrection they have "a living hope" (1:3). Wives are not to put their confidence for happiness in their husbands; they are to hope in God as their ancestors did (3:5). Unbelievers will perceive by the way believers live, by the quality of their lives, that they have put their hope in God (3:15). Believers should be model citizens and obey the government and honor political leaders (2:13–17), but their obedience should never be obsequious or fawning or stem from a sense of awe of those in authority. Peter emphasizes throughout the letter that only God should be feared (2:17; cf. 1:17; 2:18; 3:2, 6, 14, 16). Hence, slaves fear God rather than their masters (2:18), and wives fear God rather than their husbands (3:2, 6). The obedience that believers render to the government, then, is free, representing the freedom of one who obeys in God's presence and for the sake of his name. So too, slaves obey because of their consciousness of God (2:19).

Leaders should shepherd the flock and oversee those under their authority before God (5:1–4). They must not be autocratic, greedy, or lazy. Along the same lines, younger believers must resist their tendency to be critical and rebellious; if they live in God's presence, they will be humble and teachable (5:5). Believers live the kind of lives they do because Jesus Christ is their Lord (3:15), because they have tasted the kindness and goodness of the Lord (2:3). Their goal in life is to "proclaim the excellencies of him who called you out of darkness into his marvelous light" (2:9), for they have experienced the tender mercy of God (2:10). Peter closes his letter with a call to stand fast in God's grace (5:12). The beauty and power of God's grace and mercy must not leave their hearts and minds, and they must plant their feet in the soil of God's love until the day Christ is revealed.

The eschatology of 1 Peter is consonant with that found in the rest of the NT. Peter emphasizes that OT prophecies are fulfilled in Jesus Christ: he is the slain lamb and the suffering servant, and the new exodus (redemption) has become a reality through him. Jesus is Lord and king, for he triumphed over demonic powers at the cross. They are now subject to Jesus as the victorious and ascended Lord. Because of God's work in Christ, believers live between the times. They are born again, redeemed by the blood of Christ, and freed from guilt because the suffering servant died in their place. All of this took place to bring them to God (3:18), so that they could rejoice in his presence forever.

Believers are incredibly blessed and should praise God with all their hearts, for the blessings of Israel are theirs. They are the new temple of the Lord, the place where he dwells. They are his chosen people and his royal priesthood mediating God's message to the world. God's promises to Israel are fulfilled in a restored Israel, a new Israel, an Israel composed of both Jews and Gentiles.

One of the prominent themes of 1 Peter is hope. Believers are to hope in God, for their present circumstances called into question whether Jesus is Lord. They faced persecution and discrimination from unbelievers. The government did not support Christians but instead held them in suspicion. Slaves were mistreated and abused by masters. Wives lived with unbelieving husbands who did not share their faith and were often hostile to it. Believers are to hope in God, for suffering comes first, but then glory. The believers follow the same pattern as their Lord. They will reign one day, but their rule will come after a period of suffering. Believers were exiles and resident aliens in the world and did not fit in with the present regime. They were to show that they had a different master and Lord by their godly conduct while suffering. Christians were called upon to suffer as Christians, with the result that their lives were filled with love, gentleness, kindness, and righteousness. They must live not like the Gentiles but rather like the new Israel of God. Christians could not persist under duress without hope, but Peter reminds them that a new world is coming. Their inheritance and future salvation are sure, and if they continue in faith, they will surely receive the final reward.

33

THE EPISTLES
OF 2 PETER AND JUDE

The epistles of 2 Peter and Jude are rightly studied together because most of what we find in Jude is also found in 2 Peter, particularly 2 Pet. 2. The most plausible explanation is that Peter adapted for his own situation what he found in the Epistle of Jude. Both of these letters unpack part of what it means to live under the lordship of Christ. False teachers have entered the churches, upsetting believers with their teaching and behavior. Both Jude and 2 Peter recall believers to the truth. Jude appeals to "the faith that was once for all delivered to the saints" (v. 3). The opponents in 2 Peter denied the second coming of Jesus Christ (3:4), and so Peter emphasizes the eyewitness character of his testimony, refuting the notion that the second coming is mythical (1:16). The transfiguration, where Peter heard God's voice affirming Jesus as his beloved Son, functions as an anticipation of Jesus' glorious second coming (1:17–18), signifying his rule over all. Eyewitness revelation and written revelation complement each other, and the former assists in interpreting the latter (1:19–21). The word inspired by the Holy Spirit has been accurately interpreted by Peter and the apostolic circle, definitely pointing to Jesus' return. Believers must remember the apostolic word, which represents the instruction of their Lord and Savior (3:1–3; cf. 1:12–15). They predicted that scoffers doubting the Lord's return would arrive on the scene.

The false teachers (2:1) were uniformitarians, asserting that life was stable on earth with no disruptions since the creation of the world (3:4). Peter strenuously disagrees. Creation itself took place at a certain point of time (3:5), indicating that the created world is not eternal, and thus the stuff of this world will not persist forever. Nor is it correct to say that there are no disruptions in the created world, for the flood represented a virtual destruction of the present world, forecasting the final judgment to come (3:6). Just as the ancient world was enveloped in water, so the future world will be consumed by fire (3:7). The day of the Lord will arrive in a surprising manner, the way a thief steals into a house, and the present heavens "will pass away with a roar" and "the heavenly bodies will be burned up and dissolved" (3:10; cf. 3:12). Believers are waiting for "new heavens and a new earth in which righteousness dwells" (3:13). The present world will be transformed, and a new creation will descend (cf. Rev. 21:1–8).

The denial of the return of Christ by the false teachers and their disciples was accompanied by and perhaps even motivated by a libertine lifestyle.[1] If Jesus did not return, then there would be no future judgment of the ungodly. People could live as they pleased without any prospect of judgment or final destruction. The opponents in 2 Peter also drew on Pauline teaching about grace and God's kindness (3:15–16), misinterpreting what Paul wrote in support of their libertinism. The false teachers in Jude practiced the same kind of licentiousness.

Another way of putting this is that the false teachers refused to submit to the lordship of Jesus Christ. The lordship of Christ plays a prominent role in both 2 Peter and Jude. Four times in 2 Peter Jesus is identified as "Lord and Savior" (1:11; 2:20; 3:2, 18), and the emphasis on holiness suggests that Jesus' lordship must be lived out in everyday life, and the word "Savior" indicates that he rescues his people from the dominion of sin. As the Lord, he has "an eternal kingdom" (1:11), and he issues commands as the sovereign one (3:2). Salvation is defined as knowing Jesus Christ as Lord (1:2, 8), but it is a knowledge that must grow and increase (3:18). Those who claim to know him as Lord but depart from following him will not be spared on the day of judgment (2:20).

The lordship of Jesus plays an important role in Jude as well (vv. 4, 14, 17, 21, 25). "Glory, majesty, dominion, and authority" belong to Jesus Christ (v. 25). A person will be saved only if he or she receives mercy from Jesus as Lord and king (v. 21). The false teachers, however, denied Jesus Christ as "Master and Lord" (v. 4). They denied him in their behavior, by rejecting his rule over their lives. We also have a hint that the opponents in Jude rejected the second coming (vv. 14–15). Perhaps that explains why Jude, to defend the second coming of Christ, appeals to 1 Enoch, which asserts that the Lord will come to judge and destroy the ungodly. Contrary to the view of some scholars, it is not completely accurate to say that there is not a theological dimension to

1. As Matera (New Testament Theology, 390) notes, the denial of the second coming is not merely an abstract issue but is intertwined with one's lifestyle.

rejection of Jesus' lordship, for the disavowal of the second coming indicates that they rejected a key theological datum shared by early Christians.

The libertine lifestyle of the false teachers is sketched in quickly by both Peter and Jude. According to 2 Peter, they prize sexual freedom (2:2, 10, 14), material comfort (2:2, 13–14), and are full of boldness and pride (2:10). Far from being embarrassed by their evil, they paraded it in public gatherings of the church (2:13). They promised refreshment and replenishment but actually left their hearers desiccated (2:17). They offered freedom but were enslaved by their own desires and habits (2:19). We see the same constellation of errant behaviors outlined by Jude. The false teachers were sexually loose, rejected authority because of their pride, and criticized persons and things that were far nobler than they (vv. 8, 10–11). They posed great danger in the congregation because they were like "hidden reefs" in the sea, threatening to shipwreck the church (v. 12). Like the false teachers in 2 Peter, they promised much but did not deliver on what they promised, showing that they cared only for themselves (v. 12). They were complainers, grumblers, and scoffers (vv. 16, 18).

Christ is Lord over evil, and hence those who reject his lordship by giving themselves over to evil will be judged. Both Peter and Jude emphasize Christ's second coming, for at the second coming the wicked will be judged for their evil behavior. The final judgment plays a central role in both books. Hence, 2 Peter reminds the readers of the judgment of the angels who sinned and the destruction of Sodom and Gomorrah (2:4, 6). In both instances Peter emphasizes the future judgment to come, seeing the judgment of angels and the cities as prelude and anticipation of a greater judgment to come (see also 2:9). This fits with the typology of the NT whereby OT events are escalated in the NT; earthly judgments function as a prelude of the climactic judgment of the future.

Jude likewise adduces the judgment of the angels and Sodom and Gomorrah, but he adds the judgment of Israel in the wilderness (vv. 5–7). Sodom and Gomorrah's judgment functions as "an example" of those who will perish "in eternal fire" (v. 7). The judgment fell on Israel because they failed to believe (v. 5), and hence their disobedience stemmed from lack of faith. Cain, Balaam, and Korah function as paradigms for the false teachers (v. 11), and the teachers will meet the same fate as these men. On the one hand, Jude clearly identifies the false teachers as unbelievers, describing them as those "devoid of the Spirit" and "worldly" (v. 19). Peter, on the other hand, uses language that emphasizes the fellowship that the false teachers enjoyed with other believers. They lived "among you" and were "bought" by Jesus Christ (2:1). They knew Jesus Christ but have now turned away from the holy commandment by relapsing to their former condition (2:20–21). Like dogs returning to their vomit, and pigs returning to their mud hole (2:22), their return to the "defilements of the world" (2:20) shows that they are not believers in Jesus Christ.

Neither 2 Peter nor Jude restricts itself to judgment and denunciation. Both writers also highlight and celebrate the grace of God. Believers are saved by faith, and this faith stems from the saving righteousness of God (2 Pet. 1:1). Peter uses the word "righteousness" in accord with the OT, where it denotes God's saving activity on behalf of his people. Given the situation of the letter, Peter's emphasis on godly living and his denunciation of evil are unsurprising. Still, Peter does not teach that believers have the wherewithal to produce godliness. It is only by "divine power" that they are enabled to live in a way that pleases God (1:3). God has supernaturally called believers to lives of moral excellence, so that the emphasis lies on the grace of God (1:3). They are partakers of the "divine nature" by virtue of God's gift, not because they have autonomously attained moral virtue (1:4).[2] Jude features the grace of God as well. Though threatened by false teachers, he reminds his readers that God called them to himself, and that Jesus Christ will keep them (v. 1). Indeed, they can be confident of receiving the final reward, for God will keep them from apostasy, and they can be assured that they will be presented "blameless" before God on the last day (v. 24).

The exhortations in both letters, therefore, are rooted in God's grace and power. The readers must resist the blandishments of the false teachers, but they are not called upon to do so in their own strength. Indeed, 2 Peter reminds them that God rescued both Noah and Lot when they were a minority in a sea of evil (2:5, 7, 9), and hence they can enjoy the same confidence in the situations that they face. Faith is the root of moral virtue (1:5–7), but believers must live out and appropriate the grace that is theirs in Jesus Christ. Only those who practice such qualities will enter the kingdom and will be assured now of their calling and election (1:8–11). The love that marks the lives of believers certifies that they are truly believers. Salvation is by God's power and his grace, but the salvation given to believers changes them such that their lives are characterized by holiness. The judgment of the Lord does not strike immediately, for he grants human beings time to repent (3:9, 15). But the end surely is coming, and hence believers must live holy and godly lives (3:11). They must be diligent until the end so that they pass muster when the books of the final court are opened (3:10, 14). They must not be swayed by the false teachers; instead, they must "grow in the grace and knowledge of our Lord and Savior Jesus Christ" (3:18).

Jude shares the same concerns as Peter, worrying that the readers might distort God's grace, using it as an excuse to fall into sin (v. 4). Most of Jude's

---

2. See Starr, *Sharers in Divine Nature*.

exhortations to his readers are indirect, for he warns them about the fate of the false teachers. If the readers capitulate under the spell of the false teachers, they will experience the same fate. God keeps believers from falling (vv. 1, 24), but at the same time believers must keep themselves in the love of God (v. 21) by being strengthened in their faith (v. 20; cf. v. 3), by praying in the Spirit (v. 20), and by waiting for Jesus to return (v. 21). Believers show that they live under God's lordship by submitting to Jesus as Lord in their everyday life.

Both 2 Peter and Jude proclaim that Jesus is Lord. His lordship will be dramatically evident when he returns and judges the ungodly. The rejection of Jesus' return is not an abstract theological mistake. If Jesus is not returning, then people are free to pursue selfish desires. Those who disavowed the second coming of Christ refused his lordship in their daily lives and gave themselves over to evil. Both 2 Peter and Jude teach that those who are disciples show by their godly lives that they are under the lordship of Christ. Believers cannot take any credit for their godliness, for it is a gift of God's grace and calling. Still, believers must do what the Lord commands if they want to confirm their call and election. They show that they are waiting for the return of the Lord by their godly character and by refusing to tolerate the false teachers who were promulgating libertinism. In 2 Peter the author emphasizes that a new world is coming (3:10–13). The present heavens and earth will be purified through fire, and a new heaven and earth will dawn. There the righteousness intended for creation at the beginning, the righteousness that Adam should have lived out, will become a reality. Peter's words on the new heavens and new earth match what we find in Rev. 21–22 and also fit with the promise of a heavenly country and a heavenly city in Hebrews.

INTERLUDE

A Synopsis of
LIVING IN THE LAST DAYS
ACCORDING TO THE GENERAL EPISTLES

Hebrews, James, 1–2 Peter, and Jude were not collected and disseminated together in the earliest period. They have various themes and emphases and were not originally intended to be a separate collection treating the same themes. The main theme that they have in common is this: the lordship of Jesus must be lived out in everyday life. Some of these letters are quite brief or do not have a detailed Christology, but in each of them the lordship of Jesus is emphasized. As Lord and Christ, he rules the world at God's right hand. The author of Hebrews, in particular, emphasizes that Jesus is prophet, priest, and king. He is the final prophet, for the last word has been spoken in him (1:2). He is the Melchizedekian priest through whom the final and effective sacrifice of sins has been offered. And he is the king of the universe, who has sat down at God's right hand. He fulfills the role of Adam and David in subduing all things under his lordship (2:5–18), but he also shares in the divine nature. He rules as the God-man.

Every one of these letters stresses with its own terminology that faith without works is dead, that believers should confirm their call and election, that they must not surrender to a life of licentiousness, and that godly conduct must characterize believers even when they are persecuted. Believers must not abandon Christ to escape persecution and are summoned to persevere in the faith until the end.

The emphasis on godliness does not contradict the Pauline emphasis on faith, nor does it contradict the gospel expressed in the remainder of the

NT. We saw in Paul's letters that true faith expresses itself in love. Hebrews emphasizes that those who follow Christ do so because of their faith. And James teaches that genuine faith, faith that is vital, always expresses itself in works. Both 1–2 Peter and Jude attribute the change in the lives of believers to God's grace, for he chose believers to be his own, called them to himself by his power, equipped them to live righteous lives, and promised to keep them until the end. No "works righteousness" is present here. What we find is that the gospel is a transforming reality that does not leave people in their sin.

The church, made up of both Jews and Gentiles, is the true people of God. It is clearly taught in 1 Peter that the church is the new Israel and the restored Israel. Promises and declarations in the OT related to Israel are applied to the church, showing that the prophecies relative to Israel are fulfilled in the church.[1] The church is God's temple, the place of his presence and glory. Hebrews emphasizes that Jesus is the brother of those who belong to God. If one desires to be part of Abraham's offspring (see 2:16), Jesus must be one's brother. The new people of God are defined by one's relationship to Jesus Christ. It is those who belong to Christ who are part of the family of God.

All of these letters also emphasize the future judgment, which can also be called the "day of the Lord." Jesus is returning (Heb. 9:28; 10:37; James 5:7–9; 1 Pet. 1:13; 2:12; 4:13; 5:4; 2 Pet. 1:16–21; 3:1–18; Jude 14–15). He will judge the wicked and vindicate the righteous. The things of this present world will be shaken (Heb. 12:26–29), and only the unshakable kingdom will remain. The new heavens and the new earth will dawn, and the world will be full of righteousness and peace (2 Pet. 3:10–13). The subduing of the earth, which was Adam's commission, will be fulfilled through Jesus, who conquered the devil and sin by virtue of his death and resurrection. Then the "great joy" promised in Jude (v. 24; cf. 1 Pet. 4:14; 5:4) and the blessing in James (5:11) will be the portion of believers. Then believers will see the good days described in 1 Peter (3:10) and will experience the exaltation pledged in James (1:9). They will be delivered from death and the fear that it brings (Heb. 2:14–15), and they will enjoy the heavenly rest (Heb. 3:12–4:13), that is, the city to come, the heavenly Jerusalem forever (Heb. 11:13–16; 13:14). Then God will be all in all, and believers will be in God's presence because of Christ's taking the penalty that sinners deserved on the cross (1 Pet. 2:24–25; 3:18–22). The final and definitive sacrifice for sins has been offered by Jesus Christ, and therefore believers have boldness to enter God's presence (Heb. 7:1–10:25). As a consequence, believers will stand joyously and gladly in God's presence forever. They will see the King in his beauty.

---

1. I am not arguing here that there are no promises for ethnic Israel. For discussion of Israel in Paul's thought, see chapter 29, esp. the section "The New People of God."

Part 9

THE KINGDOM
WILL COME

34

THE BOOK OF REVELATION

Introduction

The story line of the Bible concludes with Revelation, and not surprisingly the book climaxes with God's reign over all, with the righteous vindicated and the wicked punished, with the righteous rejoicing and the wicked grieving, and with God being glorified and human beings satisfied. But before the end arrives a great conflict between good and evil must be played out. The kingdom will belong to the Lord, and all nations will be blessed, as was promised to Abraham. The new heavens and new earth fulfill the land promise given to the patriarchs, but now the promise encompasses the entire universe. The knowledge of the Lord will cover the earth as the waters cover the sea. John summons his readers, however, to endure a great conflict before the end arrives. The serpent and his offspring are waging total war against the offspring of the woman, and believers were tempted to deny their faith to avoid discrimination, mistreatment, and even death.

Opposition and Persecution

The persecution of the church plays a significant role in Revelation. Rome is figuratively described as Babylon (17:18; see all of chaps. 17–19), and this appellation reverberates with OT themes, for Babylon is the city of man opposed to the city of God in the OT (cf. Gen. 11:9; Isa. 13–14; 47; Jer. 50–51).[1] In Revelation this city, portrayed as a harlot, drinks the blood of the saints

---

1. In using the terms "city of man" and "city of God" here, I am reaching back to the work of Augustine.

(17:6; 18:24; 19:2; cf. 16:6) and functions as the center of an anti-God culture, living luxuriously and sensually but in fierce opposition to God. Babylon is characterized as a harlot not primarily for its sexual vices but rather for its idolatry, for often in the OT harlotry designates those who worship and give their allegiance to other gods. The nations of the world have gladly joined her in prostitution (18:3), devoting themselves to wealth and riches, thereby revealing their allegiance to the dragon rather than the lamb. Richard Bauckham strikingly captures John's vision: "At first glance, she [Babylon] might seem to be the goddess Roma, in all her glory, a stunning personification of the civilization of Rome, as she was worshiped in many a temple in the cities of Asia. But as John sees her, she is a Roman prostitute, a seductive whore and a scheming witch, and her wealth and splendour represent the profits of her disreputable trade."[2]

Opposition to God was not limited to Rome. John describes the entire Roman Empire as a beast that has arisen in antagonism to God. Revelation is infused with the OT, and describing the Roman Empire as a beast (13:1) and more specifically as a leopard, bear, and lion echoes Dan. 7:1–8, 19–21, 23–25, which portrays the empires that opposed the people of God in the OT era. John merges the beasts of Dan. 7 into one terrible creature to show that the beast in Rev. 13 represents the climactic evil empire. The use of the word "beast" indicates that the Roman Empire was not humane; it was not a kingdom that cared for its citizens and existed for their benefit. Instead, it was like a carnivorous animal, rapacious and cruel, ripping open and consuming those who opposed it.

John makes it clear that behind the beast lies the dragon, the devil himself (12:17). The dragon gave his authority to the beast so that people would worship the beast and the dragon (13:4). The beast found an ally in its desire for worldwide dominion in its sidekick, the second beast (13:11–17). The second beast probably represents the religious establishment in Rome. The dragon and the two beasts represent an unholy trinity, aping the things of God so that the second beast looks like a lamb (13:11), and the first beast enjoys a kind of resurrection (13:3, 14). Furthermore, signs and wonders were performed by the second beast (13:13–15), apparently validating its claim to truth.

The true nature of the two beasts manifests itself in their treatment of the people of God. The first beast conquered (i.e., put to death) those who worshiped the true God (11:7; 13:7). Economic discrimination is practiced against those who refuse to worship the beast (13:16–17). Even though Babylon and the beast eventually part ways, they conspire in murdering the saints (17:6;

2. Bauckham, *Book of Revelation*, 17–18.

18:6, 24; 19:2). Ultimately, the slaying of the saints is the work of Satan (cf. 2:13; 20:4), for his wrath reaches its zenith because his time is short (12:12). The devil is none other than the serpent of Gen. 3, who deceived the woman and now deceives the entire world (12:9). His rage against the church is such that he does whatever he can to destroy it (12:14–15), throwing some into prison (2:10) and killing others. Even the Jewish religion takes on a satanic character in its opposition to the true people of God (2:9; 3:9). The battle against the serpent and the offspring of the woman clearly reaches a climax in the book of Revelation.

The short time (12:12) in which the devil attacks the church is the time period between Christ's resurrection and his return. Numbers in apocalyptic literature often are symbolic, and this time period, which extends three and one-half years, designates the time between Christ's resurrection and his return. This time period is described as "1,260 days" (11:3; 12:6), "a time, times, and half a time" (12:14), and "forty-two months" (11:2; 13:5). Clearly, John picks up on the half week in Dan. 9:27. It is clear in Revelation that this time period represents the hour of evil. If "seven" is the perfect number, "three and one-half" represents a deformation of what is perfect. It symbolizes the reign of terror perpetuated by Satan and his minions. During these days the beast will "exercise authority" (13:5) as he attempts to stamp out the people of God.

Another woman, this one representing the church of Jesus Christ, will flee from Satan into the wilderness as she experiences persecution (12:6). The devil will try to destroy the woman, but God will preserve and protect her from satanic attacks (12:14–16). The two witnesses, who also represent symbolically the church of Jesus Christ, will proclaim God's judgment and salvation during this period of time as well (11:3). They are lampstands that proclaim the good news to the world (11:4). They witness to salvation and judgment in Jesus Christ. In the same way, the "holy city" also represents God's people. The city of God will be trampled down by unbelievers (11:2), and the beast will try to wipe out the church through martyrdom (11:7). But God's true temple will not be destroyed (11:1). Satan and the beast may kill them (11:2),[3] but God will keep them from apostasy. The church will not finally be destroyed; it will be vindicated via the resurrection (11:11–12).[4]

One of the fundamental themes of Revelation, therefore, is that believers must endure persecution in order to receive the final reward of the kingdom. If they capitulate and worship the beast, they will face the same judgment as

3. In support of this interpretation, see Beale, *Church's Mission*, 314. See his entire discussion on pp. 313–28.
4. See Beale, *Biblical Theology*, 351–52.

the beast, the false prophet, and Satan, and suffer torment forever (14:9–11). Churches are commended for their endurance and persistence (2:2, 3, 19; 3:10; cf. 1:9), and John summons them to endure to the end and to keep Jesus' commands (13:10; 14:12). Jesus functions as an example for believers because he was "the faithful witness" in his suffering (1:5), and believers, like Jesus, must be faithful even in the midst of opposition and in the face of death.

God's Sovereignty and Christ's Supremacy

Revelation particularly emphasizes God's sovereignty and Jesus' victory over death. The sovereignty of God is underscored in the truth that God is the creator of all (chap. 4). As the sovereign creator, he is worthy of worship and praise and thanks (4:9–11). He is the thrice-holy one, who is utterly unique (4:8; cf. Isa. 6:3). A storm rages before him (4:5) as he reigns as the indescribably beautiful one (4:3). John emphasizes God's sovereignty through the use of the word "throne," which occurs forty-seven times in the book.[5] The authority of Satan and the beast does not rival God's authority. The judgments unleashed on the world through the seals, trumpets, and bowls demonstrate God's sovereignty over all and his awesome holiness. Those who practice evil and refuse to repent will not survive in his presence. Even the reign and authority of the beast ultimately come from God. Four times in chapter 13 we read that the power given to the two beasts was granted to them (*edothē*) by God (13:5, 7, 14, 15). Twenty-one times in Revelation we read the words "it was given" (*edothē*), and in every instance God is the one who does the giving. God is unblemished by evil, and his motivations and actions are not evil, as opposed to those of the dragon and the two beasts. And yet the dragon and the beasts are not outside the realm of God's sovereignty. The powers of evil do not exercise ultimate authority. Knowing about God's rule is not intended to raise questions about God's goodness. Rather, believers are comforted, knowing that their suffering is not due to fate or chance. They are in the hands of God in the midst of the titanic battle that they are facing.

We have a remarkable window into God's sovereign purposes in chapter 17. There we find that the beast and ten kings will turn against the harlot, which is the city of Rome (17:16). They will come to hate her and will act to destroy her. Part of what we see here is the insanity of evil whereby those who are evil cannibalize one another so that evil implodes upon itself. The suicidal character of evil, however, cannot be attributed merely to cause and effect, as if it were a mechanical law of nature. John uncovers why the beast and kings

5. In most cases the throne in view is God's.

attack the harlot in 17:17: "God has put it into their hearts to carry out his purpose by being of one mind and handing over their royal power to the beast, until the words of God are fulfilled." In destroying one another, those who are evil fulfill God's purposes. It may appear that evil will triumph, but God has planned that the dynasty of evil will unravel so that the saints will reign.

Revelation features both the sovereignty of God and the supremacy of Christ. The kingdom that will persist forever is the kingdom of Christ (11:15). One of the remarkable features of Revelation is its extraordinary high Christology, which fits nicely with what we find in the Gospels and Epistles. The high stature of Christ accords with his sovereignty and rule over all. The suffering church is assured that Jesus is "the ruler of the kings on earth" (1:5). The rule of Jesus is due not only to his deity but also to his humanity. The promises made to Adam (Gen. 3:15) and Abraham and David find their fulfillment in him. Jesus has conquered death by his resurrection (1:5). He is "the living one" (1:18), so that he proclaims, "I died, and behold I am alive forevermore, and I have the keys of Death and Hades" (1:18). Death and Hades do not finally rule; Jesus reigns over them.

The apocalyptic vision of the Son of Man also features his glory and sovereignty (1:12–16), his humanity and deity. As the "son of man" of Dan. 7, he is a human being, the one who represents the saints of Israel, to whom the kingdom will be given (Dan. 7:18, 21–22, 25, 27). But he also shares the same identity as God. Like God, his hair is "white wool, like snow" (1:14; cf. Dan. 7:9), showing that he is the eternal one. In the book of Daniel fire streamed from God's throne and the wheels of his throne burned hotly (7:9–10), symbolizing his awesome holiness. So too in Revelation, Jesus' eyes "were like a flame of fire" (1:14; cf. 2:18; 19:12), detecting and destroying evil. The close relationship between Jesus' humanity and divinity is reflected in the contexts in which the phrase "eyes like flaming fire" is found. On the one hand, he has eyes like fire as the Son of Man (1:13–14), but on the other hand, he has eyes like fire as the Son of God (2:18). Jesus is the Son of Man and the Son of God.

Indeed, Jesus is "the first and the last" (1:17). He says, "I am the Alpha and the Omega, the first and the last, the beginning and the end" (22:13). Elsewhere the phrase "Alpha and Omega" describes God (1:8; 21:6), and Yahweh, as the first and the last, is distinguished from false gods in Isaiah (41:4; 44:6; 48:12). A church afflicted by suffering is reminded that both God and his Christ rule over history. Life is not spinning outside of their control, and evil will not have the last word. As the Son of Man and the Son of God, Jesus rules over history and death, and thus believers are strengthened to endure persecution and discrimination.

Below, I will further discuss the significance of Jesus as the lamb, but at this juncture we should notice the equality of the lamb with God. Just as God is worthy of worship as creator of all (chap. 4), so the lamb is praised as the redeemer (chap. 5). The word "worthy" (*axios*) plays a prominent role in chapter 5 (5:2, 4, 9, 12), culminating with the ringing affirmation that the lamb is worthy to be praised (5:12), giving the lamb the same stature as God. Indeed, "blessing and honor and glory" are ascribed to God on his throne and to the lamb (5:13). Salvation is given not only by God seated on his throne but also by the lamb (7:9–10). Human beings are the "firstfruits," not just of God but also of the lamb (14:4). Indeed, the lamb "is Lord of lords and King of kings" (17:14). No temple is needed in the Jerusalem descending from heaven, for the Lord and the lamb are the temple, and they are the light and lamp in the new heaven and new earth as well (21:22–23; 22:3). The water that refreshes and enlivens streams from God's throne and the lamb (22:1). Similarly, those who reign during the thousand years are "priests of God and of Christ" (20:6). John makes it abundantly clear, then, that God and Christ, God and the lamb, share the same authority and sovereignty. Bauckham concludes that Jesus is not designated as "a second god" but rather is included "in the eternal being of the one God of Israel who is the only source and goal of all things."[6] He further observes, "It seems . . . that the worship of Jesus must be understood as indicating the inclusion of Jesus in the being of the one God defined by monotheistic worship."[7]

The Judgment of God

The sovereignty of God and of Christ ensure that the world will be judged for its evil. The seven seal judgments indicate that God is lord over history (6:1–8:5). Whether it is war, famine, or plagues, he is ultimately the one unleashing judgment on the world. He has not forgotten those being martyred. It is not a question *if* the righteous will be vindicated and the wicked will be punished, but *when* (6:9–11). The final day will come when the world as we know it will unravel, and human beings will shrink in fear from "the one seated on the throne and from the wrath of the Lamb" (6:16). The trumpet judgments convey the same reality, though they are an intensification of the seals (8:6–9:21; 11:15–19). What is striking is that human beings refuse to repent even though others are being felled by the judgment of God (9:20–21). The ferocity and intensity of the bowl judgments, which clearly escalate the

---

6. Bauckham, *Book of Revelation*, 58.
7. Ibid., 60.

trumpet judgments, suggest that these judgments occur near or at the end of history (15:1–16:21). The judgments disclose the holiness of God, revealing to all creation that God must be feared (15:4). God's glory is displayed in his wrath and power, which are poured out upon the world (15:7–8).

The kingdom of God and his Christ will come, and it will come through judgment. Nor are the judgments arbitrary and capricious, stemming from a vengeful and bloodthirsty deity. John emphasizes that God's judgments are "just" (16:5, 7), that unbelievers are getting what they "deserve" because they spilled the blood of saints (16:6). So too, Babylon is paid back for her sins (18:5–6). Unbelievers are called upon to repent to receive forgiveness, but the final judgment is a reason for rejoicing (18:20). We think of the rejoicing in modern history when the Nazi regime in Germany fell in 1945 and when several Communist regimes in Eastern Europe collapsed decades later. So too, when Babylon falls, those in heaven will exclaim, "Hallelujah!" (19:1, 3). They will confess that God's judgments are "true and just" (19:2). The triumph of God and Christ in history is no abstraction; it becomes a reality when God's mighty judgments bring down the harlot, the beast, and finally the devil himself. The beast and the false prophet and their armies will be defeated when Jesus returns as Lord on a white horse, judging and making war righteously (19:11–21). The fury of God's wrath will be unleashed on those who are evil, and Jesus will reign as "King of kings and Lord of lords" (19:16). Satan will be cast into the lake of fire at the end of the thousand years (20:10), and all will be judged for what they have done (20:11–15). Those who have practiced evil will be cast into the lake of fire (20:15).

Redemption and the Cross

One of the fundamental questions raised in Revelation is posed in 6:17, where John speaks of the wrath of God and the wrath of the lamb: "The great day of their wrath has come, and who can stand?" Clearly, those who do evil (20:11–15) and fail to repent will not endure the judgment and wrath that will be poured out. Still, are there some who will stand on the day of wrath? Chapter 7 answers the question raised at the conclusion of chapter 6. Those who are sealed and protected by God will be spared from wrath (7:1–8). The 144,000 from the twelve tribes of Israel belong to the Lord. The 144,000 does not refer literally to Israelites; it symbolically describes the entire people of God (both Jews and Gentiles), for several reasons. First, the number 144,000, in accord with apocalyptic literature, is laden with symbolism. The number 12 bears symbolic significance in Scripture, and here we have 12 × 12, then multiplied by 1,000. Thus, the 144,000 represent the full number of the people of God, denoting a countless multitude (7:9). Second, in chapter 14 the 144,000 are those on Mount Zion, which stands for heaven, who have the name of the Father and the lamb inscribed on their foreheads (14:1), showing that they belong to God. The 144,000 are not limited to a remnant of believers. They stand for all of those who will reign with the lamb on Mount Zion. This is confirmed when we read that the 144,000 are described as those "redeemed from the earth" (14:3; cf. 14:4), demonstrating that the 144,000 are all those who have been freed from their sins. To say that they are "firstfruits" does not contradict this notion, as if there are other believers besides themselves, for they are the firstfruits of the new creation, the new world that is coming. Third, we recognize the highly figural and symbolic language employed, for they are described as those "who have not defiled themselves with women, for they are virgins" (14:4). Virginity is not prized as the ideal in the NT, nor is sex viewed as defiling (cf. 1 Tim. 4:1–5). John clearly speaks symbolically, in dependence upon OT revelation, where devotion to Yahweh is expressed in terms of a wife's faithfulness to her husband (see Hosea 1–3; Jer. 2). So here, it means that the 144,000—all those who know the song of redemption (14:2–3)—refuse to commit spiritual adultery. Finally, early in the book Jewish synagogues are identified as synagogues of Satan (2:9; 3:9), suggesting that it is natural for John to symbolically describe the church of Jesus Christ as the new people of God.[8]

To return to the main point: the 144,000, the church of Jesus Christ, is protected from God's wrath because it is redeemed by God. Indeed, the immediately succeeding paragraph in chapter 7 emphasizes this very point (7:9–17). Here the people of God are represented as an innumerable multitude "from every nation, from all tribes and peoples and languages, standing before the throne and before the Lamb, clothed in white robes, with palm branches in their hands" (7:9). This vast multitude is another way of describing the 144,000 from a different angle, but here, instead of being protected from God's wrath, they are rejoicing at God's throne because of their salvation (7:10). They have come out of the suffering and tribulation of the last days and are now receiving their final reward (7:15–17).[9] What accounts for their being in the presence of God? The answer is given in 7:14: "They have washed their robes

8. John is not encouraging or contributing to the hatred of the Jewish people here. John himself was Jewish and did not reject his heritage. We must remember that the Jews were persecuting Christians, and that is why John says they were aligned with Satan, but he would be horrified to discover that Christians used this text to justify discrimination or violence against Jews.

9. The tribulation here fulfills what Daniel prophesied in 12:1, so that the great tribulation actually began in Jesus' ministry and continues to the final day (so Beale, *Biblical Theology*, 210–12).

and made them white in the blood of the Lamb." No one is able to enter the new heaven and earth, since all have sinned. But forgiveness is available for those who repent and believe. Through the lamb's blood they are cleansed.

The cross of Christ, although not specifically mentioned in Revelation (though see 11:8), plays a central role in the book. Believers are part of God's kingdom and his priests (1:6; cf. Exod. 19:6). They are part of a new community, a new polity and rule. They enjoy God's saving rule because they have "been freed from [their] sins by his blood" (1:5). Believers are not intrinsically worthy to be priests and members of the kingdom, but Christ has liberated them by giving his life for their sake. In the same way, chapter 5 plays a central role in the narrative. No human being or angel is worthy to unloose the sealed book, which provokes John to tears because there is no hope for human beings if the book remains sealed (5:4). But then "the Lion of the tribe of Judah, the Root of David" appears as the conquering one (5:5), fulfilling the promise of the Davidic covenant. John is told about the lion, but when he looks, he sees a lamb standing that was slain (5:6). It is abundantly clear that the lion triumphs as the lamb, that victory comes not through destroying one's enemies but rather through suffering for their sake and for their salvation. Judgment will come, but there is a reprieve for those who believe and repent because the lamb has suffered for their sake. Some have been "ransomed" from every tribe and people group by Christ's blood (5:9).

Christ's death is not mentioned often in Revelation, but it is central to the narrative, for it appears at key junctures. For instance, in the introduction of the book we find that Christ's death frees human beings from sin by his blood (1:5). Chapter 5 is the key to the remainder of the book, for unloosing the seals leads to the unfolding of the remainder of the narrative. And the seals are opened only because the lamb was slain and has purchased some from every people group for God (5:6, 9). The centrality of Christ's death is also featured in chapter 12. Chapters 12–14 portray the cosmic conflict between God and the dragon, pulling the curtain of history back and unveiling for us the heavenly battle between Satan and Michael. The crucial war is not on earth but rather in heaven, in the heavenly conflict with Satan and his angels. Fortunately, Michael and his allies triumph over the dragon so that the serpent is evicted from heaven (12:7–9). What must be understood, however, is the reason for Michael's victory, for the basis of his victory is the cross of Christ. This is very similar to what we find in John's Gospel, where the "ruler of this world" is "cast out" through Jesus' death (12:31). The devil has been stripped of his power through the suffering of the lamb. We see earlier in Rev. 12 that the devil tried to destroy the Christ, but Jesus was exalted to God's throne (12:4–5). As we saw in John's Gospel, the "lifting up" or "glorification" of

Jesus signifies that Jesus' death is the means by which he was exalted. So too here. The devil was defeated via the cross. He can no longer accuse believers of their sins, for now they are cleansed "by the blood of the Lamb" (12:11). The decisive victory, the fulcrum of history, has turned with Christ's death, and thus the devil's time is limited before he meets his final demise (12:12). Christ's victory over the serpent belongs only to those who wash their robes in Christ's blood. They may eat of the tree of life and enter the city (22:14).

Endurance and the New Creation

The hinge of history is the cross of Christ. As noted above, however, only those who endure to the end will receive the final reward. The letters to the churches (2:1–3:22) emphasize that believers must conquer and overcome if they want to avoid the last judgment and receive the reward of eternal life (2:7, 11, 17; 3:5, 12, 21; see also 12:11; 21:7). Only those who persevere to the end will receive an inheritance and be a "son" of God (21:7). One must be faithful to death in order to receive the crown of life (2:10; cf. 12:11). Any believer who gives allegiance to the beast will face eternal torment (14:9–11). The new creation is coming, and it will arrive when Jesus returns. Both the beginning and the end of the book emphasize that the time of Jesus' arrival is near (1:1, 3; 22:10). Everyone must be ready, for he comes with the clouds as the glorious Son of Man (1:7; cf. Dan. 7:13). He will come soon (3:11; 22:7, 12, 20) and like a thief (16:15), and he will "repay everyone for what he has done" (22:12).

The new creation will fulfill and exceed what was promised to Adam in the beginning, and what was confirmed and elaborated in the covenants with Abraham and with David and in the new covenant. Just as Adam was a king and priest in the garden, so human beings will be kings and priests in the new creation (1:6; 5:10; 20:6). Just as Adam served in a garden temple, so the whole universe will now be God's temple (7:15–17; 21:1–22:5).[10] Chapters 21–22 are dotted with many allusions to Ezek. 40–48, where Ezekiel detailed the building of the new temple. This confirms what was argued for in Ezekiel, where I defended the notion that Ezekiel did not intend the rebuilding of a literal temple. The many allusions to Ezek. 40–48 in chapters 21–22 yield the same conclusion, for John clearly teaches that there is not a literal temple in the new heaven and new earth. The Lord and the lamb are the temple in the new creation (21:22). The glory of the temple always pointed to a greater glory, the glory of God and the lamp of the lamb (21:23; 22:5). The greatest benefit of the new creation and the new temple will be the presence of God.

10. So Beale, *Church's Mission*, 366–73.

The lamb will shepherd his people forever and will feed his flock living water (7:17). Before God's throne and in his temple there will be no hunger or thirst or tears (7:15–16; 21:4). God will tabernacle with his people and will fully and finally fulfill the covenant promise to be their God (21:3). Just as in the OT the greatest joy of the temple was God's presence, so in the new creation what refreshes human beings is seeing God's face (22:4). The glory of the new creation is seeing the glory of God.

Various pictures are employed to describe the wonder and joy of the new creation. Beale observes, "John's portrayal of the entire new creation as a city, a temple, and a garden is exactly what the OT in various places anticipated."[11] As Beale says, "God's intent all along was to make the entire creation his holy of holies and his dwelling place."[12] Naturally, the language is highly symbolic. It is the marriage of the lamb to his bride, the church of Jesus Christ (19:7–9; 21:9). Just as Israel was God's bride in the OT and as Song of Songs describes the love relationship between a man and a woman, now the consummation and fulfillment of all that preceded has been realized, signifying the intimacy and love and delight that will characterize believers' relationship with God in the new creation. John speaks specifically of "a new heaven and a new earth" (21:1), evoking the promise of Isaiah (65:17; 66:22; see also 2 Pet. 3:10–13). In Revelation the old creation gives way to the new creation (6:12–14; 16:20; 20:11; 21:1). The new Jerusalem descends from God like a "bride adorned for her husband" (21:2; cf. 21:10; Gal. 4:26; Heb. 11:13–16; 12:22–24; 13:14).[13] When it is said that there is no sea (21:1) in the new creation, this should not be taken literally, for the sea is the place of chaos, the place from which the beast came (13:1).

The new Jerusalem is inexpressibly beautiful because it reflects "the glory of God" (21:11). The city is a perfect cube (21:16), just as the holy of holies in Solomon's temple was a perfect cube (see 1 Kings 6:20; Ezek. 41:4). John thereby communicates that God dwells in the city, just as he resided in the holy of holies. The goal of Genesis has now been reached. The whole world is full of the "glory of the LORD as the waters cover the sea" (Hab. 2:14; cf. Isa. 11:9). Now the entire universe is God's temple, and Jesus, succeeding where Adam failed, brings peace through the blood of his cross, reconciling all things in earth and heaven (Col. 1:20). Now "the kingdom of the world has become the kingdom of our Lord and of his Christ, and he shall reign forever and ever" (Rev. 11:15). Now all acknowledge that Jesus is Lord to the glory of God

11. Beale, *Biblical Theology*, 759.
12. Ibid.
13. On the new Jerusalem, see Dumbrell, *End of the Beginning*, 1–34.

the Father (Phil. 2:11); some acknowledge it gladly and with joy, while others who rebelled against him do so grudgingly from their place in the lake of fire. Everyone is safe in the new city because it has a high, impregnable wall that no foe can scale (21:12). John's language is colored by symbolism, as the wall is said to measure 144 stadia (21:17), which is 12 × 12. The symbolic character of what he says is evident, for John tells us that the measurement of an angel was used (21:17). Readers are not supposed to try to figure out what measurements angels use.[14] How could we possibly know? He is clueing in the reader to the figural meaning of what he writes, signifying the unbreachable security in the city.[15] We also know that John writes symbolically in saying of the city, "On no day will its gates ever be shut" (21:25 NIV). It makes no sense to have a high and impregnable wall and then leave the gates open! What John teaches is that no enemy can threaten the new Jerusalem, and furthermore, there will be no enemies who will even try. The darkness of evil will be erased forever.

The names of the twelve tribes of Israel are on the gates, and the names of the twelve apostles are on the foundation of the wall (21:12–14), signifying that the residents of the city are members of the true Israel, and that they belong to the church of Jesus Christ. The true Israel is comprised of those who receive the apostolic testimony about Jesus Christ, and both Israel and the church are one unified people of God. It is significant that they are described as God's "peoples" (*laoi* [21:3]), showing that ethnic groups from all over the world will belong to the people of God. The nations will bring into the city only what is beautiful and lovely (21:26–27). Everything of value and worth from the old creation will be in the new creation. No one will feel loss moving from the old to the new, but all that is desirable in this world will be in the new world. But that is not the half of it, for everything in the new creation will be more delightful than what we enjoy now.

The rivers of Eden (Gen. 2:10–14) and of the Ezekielian temple (Ezek. 47:1–12) point to a greater river in Revelation (22:1). The river from God's throne brings life, and this life is free for the taking for all who are thirsty (22:17). The tree of life in Eden (Gen. 2:9; 3:17, 22, 24; cf. Prov. 3:18; 11:30; 13:12; 15:4) points to the ultimate tree of life in Revelation (22:2, 14, 19). Only those who partake of the tree of life will enter the city of God and experience the healing balm that comes from its leaves and fruit. Then human beings will see God's face and worship him forever and ever (22:3–4).[16]

14. The text could be understood to say that the measure used by human beings and angels is the same. I would suggest, however, that such an observation in a chapter laden with symbolism is prosaic. Rather, John signals to readers in mentioning angels that the measurement is symbolic.
15. See ibid., 4.
16. What makes the city distinctive is God's presence (see ibid., 2).

Conclusion

Revelation is a fitting conclusion to the canon of Scripture. God's kingdom is established in and through Jesus Christ. Jesus, as the lion and the lamb, won the victory over the dragon, the ancient serpent (see Gen. 3:15) by virtue of his cross and resurrection. As the slain lamb, he opens the seals that unfold all of history and bring it to its culmination. The seals, trumpets, and bowls show that God and his Christ are sovereign over all. Those who side with the devil and the two beasts will be judged and destroyed. Babylon, the city of man, will not triumph over the city of God that is coming. Even though saints are now suffering and even dying for Jesus' sake, they will ultimately be vindicated and rewarded. Believers are called upon to endure and to persist until the end. They must not compromise and become part of the evil empire, for if they turn away from Jesus, they will experience the judgments destined for the wicked.

Revelation portrays the church as the new Israel. They are symbolically described as the 144,000 from the twelve tribes of Israel. By way of contrast, Jews are described as a "synagogue of Satan" (2:9; 3:9). Those who truly belong to the twelve tribes of Israel (21:12) confess the message proclaimed by "the twelve apostles of the Lamb" (21:14). The message of Revelation does not differ from mainstream Christian teaching. One becomes part of the new and restored Israel by being freed from one's sins through Christ's blood (1:5). Their garments have been whitened by the lamb's blood (7:14), and they "conquered . . . by the blood of the Lamb" (12:11).

God is the sovereign king over all, according to Revelation. Even when evil seems to reign, God rules over the events of history. Believers may entrust their lives to him, for judgment is surely coming for those who resist his will. The future kingdom that is promised to the patriarchs and the prophets and to the psalmists will surely come. The prayer for God's kingdom to come and for his will to be done will be answered. The new heaven and new earth are coming. The land promise of the OT is dialed up to include the whole universe, and the whole universe is portrayed as God's temple. What makes the new universe so dazzling is not gold or jewels but rather the presence of God. The whole world is his holy of holies. The task given to Adam, to rule the world for God, has been successfully completed by Jesus Christ. The goal of all of redemptive history will be obtained: "They will see his face" (22:4). They will see the King in his beauty.

EPILOGUE

The grand narrative has ended. It began with the sovereign creator, the Lord of all, who created the world and the universe for his glory. As the king, he made human beings, Adam and Eve, to rule the world for him. Adam and Eve enjoyed fellowship with God in Eden, in their garden temple, and they were to extend God's rule from paradise until it encompassed the entire earth. Human beings could function as God's vice-regents only if they ruled the world under God's lordship. They were to trust and obey their sovereign king. But Adam and Eve repudiated God as their king, opting for independence instead of dependence on God.

Human history could have ended there, with the death of Adam and Eve. But the Lord in his grace promised that the offspring of the woman would triumph over the serpent and his offspring (Gen. 3:15). God's reign over the world would be reestablished, but the world would be reclaimed through conflict; a titanic struggle between good and evil would ensue. The outcome, though, is guaranteed from the outset. The offspring of the woman would crush the head of the serpent. Finally and ultimately, the serpent's hostility to and hatred of the Lord would prove to be futile, an insane attempt to topple God's rule.

The story continues with the battle between the offspring, and it immediately looks as if evil will prevail. Cain sides with the serpent and slays righteous Abel. As the narrative unfolds, it becomes evident that victory over the serpent will involve a colossal struggle, for by the time of Noah the entire world, apart from Noah's family, has given itself over to evil. The narrator indicates that the evil that has invaded the human heart and human society is pervasive and intractable (Gen. 6:5). Noah stands apart as righteous, and such righteousness is lonely in a world gone wrong. Still, the Lord reigns over all, and the triumphs of evil are ephemeral. All those living, except for Noah's family, which resided in the ark, are deluged in the judgment of God. God makes a covenant with Noah, promising to sustain the world until the victory over the serpent becomes a reality. The world will not be destroyed again, as it was in the flood, until the final judgment.

The fundamental problem with human beings was not solved by the flood (Gen. 8:21). The tower of Babel illustrates that the human heart had not changed. Human beings continued to flout God's lordship, prizing their own reputation over God's honor (Gen. 11:4). It is clear from Gen. 1–11 that human beings do not have the moral resources for righteousness. Left to itself, as Gen. 1–11 shows, the human community would be marked by savagery and evil. The only hope for redemption, then, is from God himself. Indeed, God chose one man, Abraham, as the one through whom the promise of Gen. 3:15 would become a reality. So in a sense Abraham is a new Adam.[1] The Lord establishes a covenant with Abraham, promising him offspring, land, and worldwide blessing. The narrative in the OT, and indeed in the remainder of the Scriptures, fleshes out these promises. What is remarkable is that Abraham, Isaac, and Jacob did not see worldwide blessing, nor did they live in the land. As the NT states, they lived in tents as sojourners in Canaan during their lives (Heb. 11:9). In fact, it was a massive struggle for Abraham to have even a single child! In the case of both Isaac and Jacob the promises advance slowly and even laboriously. At the conclusion of Genesis Israel's population numbers about seventy. Hardly as many as the stars in the sky or the sand of the sea! In addition, they are in the wrong place. They are in Egypt. The triumph over the serpent, it appears, will be protracted and grueling.

And yet when Exodus opens, Israel's population is exploding. They may be in the wrong place (Egypt), but the promise of countless offspring is becoming a reality. The Lord is also about to fulfill the second covenant promise and bring Israel to the land of Canaan. This means that first they must be liberated from Egyptian slavery, and the Lord frees them with signs and wonders and plagues that devastate Egypt. As the redeemed people of the Lord, Israel must live under Yahweh's lordship and follow covenant stipulations. Just as Adam was a priest and king in the garden, so Israel was to be a priestly and kingly people, mediating blessing to the world. Deuteronomy in particular unpacks what it means for Israel to be loyal to its covenant Lord. They must keep his laws and regulations, love the Lord, fear him, and cling to him. If they obey, covenant blessings will follow. But if they turn away from the Lord, covenant curses will descend upon them.

1. Abraham cannot be completely identified with Adam, for Adam at one time was without sin, and Abraham needed God's forgiveness from the beginning in order to be rightly related to God.

Israel has not only been freed from slavery, they are also the Lord's covenant people. He reigns over them and dwells in them. The Lord specially dwells with his people via the tabernacle, but access to him is not a casual matter. He is the holy one of Israel. Those who do not follow the prescribed ritual will be destroyed in the flames of judgment (Lev. 10:1–2). Yahweh is always and ever the holy one, and thus Israel must offer sacrifices for the forgiveness of sins and must live as a holy people before him.

Israel is the covenant people of the Lord, but the narrative is broken up by egregious sin in Israel. Right after the covenant was ratified, Israel violated the covenant by making and worshiping a golden calf (Exod. 32–34). The covenant was broken, so to speak, before the ink was even dry on the contract. Moses interceded and Israel was forgiven, but Israel's idolatry raised the question of how Yahweh was going to dwell with a recalcitrant people. The people were physically delivered from Egypt, but were they really changed? The answer comes when it is time to enter the land. Even after seeing Yahweh's signs and wonders, they failed to trust him and refused to enter the land of promise, believing that the nations in Canaan were too strong for them.

Yahweh, however, was faithful to his covenant with Israel. He did not withdraw his promise to the patriarchs that they would possess the land of Canaan. In addition, the new generation under Joshua believed God's promises and boldly followed Joshua into Canaan. The conquest clearly was the supernatural work of Yahweh, for Israel won victories over their enemies in unconventional ways (such as marching around a city seven times, blowing on trumpets, and shouting!) to illustrate that it was holy war, that the battle was the Lord's. The second great promise made to Abraham was being fulfilled. Israel had many children and land, and now the world was poised for worldwide blessing. The land of Israel, Canaan, was to be the place where Yahweh ruled over his people. In the time of the judges, however, Israel reverted to rebellion. Instead of influencing the nations around them, Israel was molded and shaped by pagans and worshiped the Baals. Under the judges or saviors, Israel went through a cycle of sin, judgment, repentance, and deliverance. In one sense, Israel was not advancing or regressing but instead was replaying the same loop over and over. The author of Judges remarks that Israel's waywardness revealed that they needed a king (17:6; 18:1; 19:1; 21:25).

Remarkably, when we come to 1–2 Samuel, we see that Israel believed that they needed a king as well. But their longing for a king did not stem from dependence upon the Lord as their king. Israel begged Samuel for a king because they wanted to be like the other nations, and hence their motive for wanting a king was fundamentally secular. However, we already saw in Judges that Israel needed a king. The reality here is complex. Israel needed a king, and Yahweh wanted them to have a king, but they wanted a king for the wrong reasons. Indeed, there are hints in the Pentateuch that the blessing of Abraham would come through a king (Gen. 17:6, 16; 35:11). The scepter would come from Judah, and the people would obey a ruler from Judah (Gen. 49:10). Balaam predicts that a ruler will come from Jacob and crush Moab's forehead (Num. 24:17–19). In other words, this ruler will crush the head of the offspring of the serpent. The book of Ruth likewise clarifies that this ruler will be in the line of David, which is picked up in 1–2 Samuel.

The promise to Abraham, the promise of worldwide blessing, would come, then, through a king. Saul, as the first king, seemed poised to be the fulfillment of the promise. But Saul replicated Adam's sin. Instead of being a vice-regent of God and carrying out his will, he followed his own wisdom and inclinations and rebelled against Yahweh's lordship. Because of Saul's treachery, he was punished with death, and there was no Saulide dynasty. In the meantime, David was anointed as king. David's reliance upon and obedience to the Lord revealed that he was a man after God's own heart. Suffering at the hand of Saul and on the run from various enemies, he consistently trusted in the Lord for help. In his battles against foreign powers he called upon Yahweh to deliver him. As a result, Yahweh promised him an eternal dynasty that would not be revoked (2 Sam. 7). The covenant with David, as the Psalter and a number of prophetic books also attest, is irrevocable. Individual kings may be disciplined for their sin and suffer the wrath of the Lord for their recalcitrance, but ultimately and finally the promise of worldwide blessing will be fulfilled through a Davidic king. The narrative also clarifies, however, that David himself is not the king through whom ultimate blessing will come. He too was flawed, as is evident in his adultery with Bathsheba and murder of Uriah.

Will worldwide blessing, then, be realized with his son Solomon? He was a man of peace who built the temple of the Lord. Israel was happy and satisfied and as numerous as the sand on the seashore. Solomon ruled with wisdom and righteousness. The land of Canaan seemed to be on the verge of paradise. Was the final triumph over evil at hand? Solomon, like Adam in the garden, veered toward evil. He started well but failed to submit to Yahweh's lordship and embraced idolatry. As a consequence, the nation split into two, with a northern and a southern kingdom. Every king in the north was evil, for they repudiated Yahweh's lordship and worshiped idols. The kings in the south were a mixed lot. Some of them truly feared and loved the Lord, but the overall trajectory in the southern kingdom was off-center. The story communicates that Judah and Israel were fundamentally shaped by their kings. As their king fared, so fared the nation. The narrative indicates that the people of God desperately needed a righteous king, a king who would reign over them forever.

The exile that Yahweh threatened against his people was looming. Both in the north and the south the stipulations of the Mosaic covenant were regularly violated. The prophets warned Israel and Judah repeatedly that they would be judged if they continued to flout the Lord's instructions. The day of the Lord would come, and it would be a day of judgment instead of a day of salvation for a disobedient people. The prophets brought covenant lawsuits against Israel, declaring that Israel was guilty before the Lord. Here and there the nation repented and turned toward the light. There were flashes of light in the gloomy darkness. But overall both the northern and southern kingdoms were plunging deeper into evil. Ample time was given for repentance, but finally the judgment threatened became a reality. Both the northern and the southern kingdoms were sent into exile—the north by Assyria in 722 BC, the south by the Babylonians in 586 BC. The promises of Abraham were going backward instead of forward! Now the second element of the promise was no longer true. Israel was not even in the land, and blessing for the whole world seemed farther away than ever.

But the promise had not been withdrawn. The Lord promised in the prophets that his people would return again from exile. He would have mercy on them again. There would be a new exodus, a new liberation from those who held them captive. The Lord would make a new covenant with his people and write his law on their hearts so that they would not stray from him. He would grant them the blessing of the Holy Spirit so that they would be enabled to keep his law and his requirements. There would be a new temple, and the Lord would dwell with his people again. And a new David would arise, a new leader who would shepherd the flock and lead them in righteousness. The new David would not only bring joy and blessing to Israel; the nations of the world would submit to the new David who was coming, and they would be his people. Those who resisted the Lord would be judged and destroyed. The promised universal blessing would become a reality through this son of David, and Israel would find rest under his rule. The new exodus, the new covenant, and the new David are linked with the promise of a new creation. The world would be transformed. The desert would bloom and stream with water. A new temple would be built, and the final day of the Lord was coming, in which he would judge his enemies and free his people. Those who belonged to the Lord would be raised from the dead, and the old creation would pass away. Israel and the nations would live under Yahweh's rule and enjoy the beauty and wonder of his presence.

If we ask how the book of Psalms fits with the story, the answer is variegated. We saw that there was a structure and a story in the psalms from book 1 through book 5. The psalms often reflect on the promise of a Davidic king, looking forward to the day when he would exercise his rule. When we get to book 3 it appears as if the promise to David will not be realized, but the promise to David is reaffirmed in book 4 and in book 5 there is great praise because God will fulfill his promises to David and to the world. Wisdom psalms portray the life of those who live under Yahweh's lordship. The psalms are filled with praises and laments, both individual and communal. The laments in the Psalter are not the last word, for mourning ultimately will turn to praise. The psalms reflect on life in the Lord's presence. Those who dwell in his presence and know his salvation are full of praise and joy. They give thanks because Yahweh is the faithful covenant God, who has rescued them from their enemies. Often in the psalms there is a longing to be in Yahweh's temple, to worship him where he specially dwells with his people. The psalms make it very clear that the kingship of Yahweh is not austere and distant. There is nothing more satisfying and thrilling and exalting than praising him. The psalmist longs to reside in the temple with the Lord in order to find rest in his presence and to praise him for his beauty. Actually, we can also put the canonical message of Song of Songs here as well. For if Song of Songs is not only about human marriage but also the relationship of the people of God to the Lord, then the book conveys the wonder and joy of a relationship with the Lord. Furthermore, what Song of Songs says about the king and his marriage to the young woman points to and anticipates Christ's relationship to the church. So the kingship theme is not absent from the book.

How does the Wisdom literature fit into the story of Yahweh's lordship and kingship? Scholars often say that a theme such as lordship does not fit with Wisdom literature. We must beware of forcing wisdom into categories that are foreign to its spirit and message. Certainly the wisdom books do not unfold a historical narrative, and they have a different function and role than other books in the OT. A different function, however, does not necessarily mean the wisdom tradition cannot be integrated into the theme of God's lordship over his people. Wisdom unpacks what life is like under God's rule. What does it mean to obey the Lord in the warp and woof of everyday life? Wisdom supplies the fine mesh, the details, which are relatively absent in larger historical narratives. Life is made up of individual decisions: living with neighbors, conversing with friends and enemies, doing business in the market, and so on. Wisdom pierces down to particulars, to the daily choices that confront people as they make their way in the world. Living under God's rule is not an abstraction, it is not a pious truth separated from real life; rather, it plays itself out in the concrete circumstances of life.

The OT also ties together wisdom with the king, particularly Solomon. What it means to be a king is to rule wisely. Indeed, Isaiah picks up wisdom themes in prophesying a future king from David's line (Isa. 11:1–9). Jesus is the one who is greater than Solomon, for he is the wisdom of God (Matt. 12:42; Luke 2:52; Col. 2:2–3). There is even a hint of Jesus as the king in Ecclesiastes, for wisdom comes from the "one Shepherd" (Eccles. 12:11), but Jesus, the NT clarifies, is the shepherd-king, the good shepherd who cares for his flock.

The theme that ties together Proverbs, Ecclesiastes, and Job is the "fear of the LORD." The phrase appears at key junctures in each of the books. The connection with Deuteronomy is evident, for in Deuteronomy those who live in covenant with the Lord fear and obey him. In the same way, wisdom teaches that those who know Yahweh fear him. It has often been pointed out that wisdom teaching has many points of contact with creation traditions in Israel. Creation points to Yahweh's rule, to his sovereignty over all. Those who are wise stand in awe of the Lord and feel a holy, though not paralyzing, terror before him. They live wisely because they fear the Lord. What is striking is that wisdom resonates with both creation and covenant traditions in Israel. The rewards that come with obedience emphasized in Proverbs remind us of Deuteronomic themes. We saw a number of intertextual links between wisdom and Torah in Proverbs. Covenant and wisdom are more closely linked than is often acknowledged, suggesting that wisdom is integrated with the remainder of the OT message.

The message of Proverbs is at risk for being oversimplified (actually, Proverbs itself gives plenty of exceptions) and pressed in illegitimate directions. God's rule over the world does not mean that life always makes sense. Ecclesiastes and Job look at life from another angle. Wisdom also recognizes that life under the sun is fleeting and enigmatic and beyond our understanding. The world is twisted and distorted by sin. Human beings must not think that the righteous are invariably blessed and the wicked are punished under the sun. Often the roles are reversed, with the wicked prospering and the righteous suffering. Job and Ecclesiastes teach that what happens in life often seems random and purposeless. Neither Job nor Ecclesiastes denies the sovereignty of God over all that occurs. What they emphasize is that human beings are incapable of discerning a pattern in what occurs. Human beings must trust the Lord as history unfolds, even though they cannot detect where history is going. Still, they are to fear the Lord and do his commands, knowing and trusting that a day of judgment is coming in which all will be made right.

The OT history concludes (Ezra-Nehemiah) with Israel returning from exile. But the return from exile did not bring the expected blessings. A new David ruling over Israel did not appear, and the new creation did not arrive. So the OT concludes on a note of expectation. The great promises for Israel and the world were still not realized. When the NT dawned, Israel was in the land, but the Romans ruled over them. Their king was Herod, who was an Idumean, not a Judean. He certainly was not a new David. It is evident from a book such as *Psalms of Solomon* (chaps. 17–18) that Israel was waiting for a Davidic king who would rule over the Gentiles and bless the righteous. The pious in Israel still believed that the covenant promises would be fulfilled, and they were filled with expectation as the curtain opens on the NT.

In the Synoptic Gospels and Acts we find a focus on the kingdom of God. The NT opens with John the Baptist and Jesus saying that the kingdom of God is near. The kingdom of God is not defined or explained. A definition is not offered because the meaning of the kingdom of God is clear from the OT. The kingdom in Jesus' proclamation refers to the saving promises of God for Israel and to judgment for those who resist his rule over their lives. The coming of the kingdom, then, is just another way of speaking of the new exodus, the new covenant, and the new creation, for it is evident in the OT (e.g., Isa. 40–66) that the new exodus is tied together with the inauguration of the new creation. In the same way, Israel's return from exile is coincident with the realization of the new covenant when the Lord writes his law on the heart. The new exodus and new covenant and new creation fulfill the covenant promises to Abraham, which promised universal blessing. In other words, the arrival of the kingdom means also that the blessing pledged for the whole world is at hand, that the crushing of the serpent's head is accomplished.

The kingdom was present in Jesus' ministry, particularly in his signs and wonders and miracles. For instance, the nature miracles were a prelude to and an anticipation of the new creation, for they represent a coming world in which nature is in harmony with human beings, a world that has no thorns and thistles. In the same way, Jesus' healings were a foretaste of the world to come, in which there would be no disease or death. Demons disfigured and distorted human beings, but Jesus' exorcisms restored human beings to their full humanity so that they function as intended, pointing again to the destiny of all those who enjoy the saving promises of the kingdom. Jesus' miracles and healings and exorcisms demonstrated that the kingdom had arrived in his ministry (Matt. 11:2–6; 12:28), but the presence of the kingdom should not be interpreted to say that the kingdom was also consummated.

Here we find the distinctiveness in Jesus' teaching on the kingdom. The kingdom was inaugurated, but it was not consummated. It was already present but not yet complete. Jesus characterizes this reality as the mystery of the kingdom, which means that something previously hidden has now been revealed. It was not apparent from the OT that the kingdom would come in stages. The Jews expected the kingdom to come with apocalyptic power and to sweep away their enemies. They never envisioned an interval in which the power of the kingdom was at work and yet evil continued to hold sway in the world. Jesus taught that the kingdom was like a mustard seed and leaven. It was like a mustard seed: present in the world but small enough so that many would fail to see it. It was like leaven: hidden and observable only to those with eyes to see.

The kingdom's presence in Jesus meant the inauguration of the new exodus, the new covenant, and the new creation, but it also meant that the new David had arrived. One of the central themes in the Synoptic Gospels and Acts is that Jesus is the new David, the Messiah and king of Israel. In other words, the kingdom was present because the king had arrived. All the covenant promises of the OT were fulfilled in him. He was the true Adam (the true human being), the true Israel, the Son of Man, the Son of God, and the servant of the Lord. He was the obedient son who always did the will of the Father. He was the king of Israel who never deviated from the Lord's ways. The Gospels and Acts make it clear, however, that Jesus was not only the true Israel and the Messiah. God himself had come to rescue his people in Jesus. He was Immanuel, the one who was with his people all their days. In Jesus Christ God himself had come to his temple to cleanse it of evil (Mal. 3:1).

How could Israel enter into the kingdom? Only those who are obedient and forgiven of their sins may be members of the kingdom. Both the Synoptic Gospels and Acts teach that Jesus is the servant of the Lord (cf. Isa. 53). He came to save his people from their sins (Matt. 1:21). He is the Son of Man, who came to give his life as a ransom for many (Mark 10:45). In the Lord's Supper texts Jesus explains that he poured out his blood for the forgiveness of sins to establish the new covenant with his people (see also Acts 20:28). Israel's sin was the reason for their exile, and it was the reason they were unable to enter the kingdom. But Jesus shed his blood for the forgiveness of sins, so that human beings could enter the new creation. The coming of the kingdom is inextricably intertwined with the cross and resurrection of Jesus. The Gospels have been defined by some as Passion Narratives with extended introductions for good reason, even if such a description is a bit of an exaggeration. The kingdom is secured only through the cross and resurrection. The resurrection is not an afterthought but rather is integral to the kingdom, for the resurrection of Jesus demonstrates that the age to come has arrived. Death and sin have been defeated. The new creation dawned with the resurrection of Jesus Christ (cf. Isa. 26; Ezek. 37; Dan. 12). The book of Acts, in particular, features the resurrection, highlighting Jesus' vindication and triumph over death. As the resurrected Lord, Jesus is exalted to God's right hand and reigns now as Lord. He is the reigning king, sitting at the right hand of God, ruling over the world until that day when all his enemies are subjected to him.

Still, forgiveness is not automatic. Repentance and faith are required of those who would be members of the kingdom of God. Those who enter the kingdom turn from their sins and put their faith in Jesus Christ as the Son of God and as Lord of all. Furthermore, they live as subjects of the king. They are his disciples and follow him wherever he leads. True repentance and faith can never be separated from obedience. The obedience of disciples is not perfect, but there is a transformation in their lives. Their obedience is substantial, significant, and observable. They do the will of their Father in heaven and enter through the narrow gate. They put Jesus above father and mother and even their own lives, not counting the cost of following Jesus and submitting to his lordship.

The kingdom, of course, is not only for the Jews. The inclusion of the Gentiles is evident in each of the Synoptic Gospels, but it is especially clear in the "great commission" texts in Matthew (28:18–20) and Luke-Acts (Luke 24:47–49; Acts 1:8). Indeed, the book of Acts records the story of the gospel extending to the entire world. The reunification of Israel prophesied in Ezek. 37 becomes a reality when the Samaritans are folded into the church of Jesus Christ (Acts 8). The belief of the Gentiles fulfills the predictions of the prophets that salvation would extend beyond Israel. Gentiles too are saved through faith in Jesus Christ. The promise of Abraham, which guaranteed that the entire world would be blessed, is becoming a reality through Jesus Christ. Jesus Christ is the true offspring of Abraham, and all those who belong to him constitute the true and new Israel. Jesus' crushing of the serpent's head forms the basis for the gospel's proclamation to the ends of the earth. This does not mean that the kingdom has come in its fullness. The final judgment of those who oppose God and his gospel has not yet been realized. Believers in the present evil age are members of the kingdom, and yet they are persecuted and put to death for their allegiance to Jesus. Still, the promise of the age to come has been poured out. The eschatological gift of the Spirit promised in the prophets has now been given to both Jews and Gentiles who trust in Jesus, repent of their sins, and are baptized. The gift of the Spirit signals that the kingdom has come, that the last days have arrived.

John's Gospel and the Johannine Epistles reflect on the fulfillment in Jesus Christ in distinct, though complementary, ways. John rarely refers to the kingdom of God; instead, he focuses on eternal life. The life of the age to come has arrived in Jesus Christ. This is another way of saying that the new creation has come, for the new creation is characterized by life in all its fullness. John focuses on realized eschatology, emphasizing that eternal life is available now to those who trust and believe in Jesus the Christ. Those who believe have passed from death to life during the present evil age (John 5:24). Eternal life is irrevocable; those who enjoy it will never perish (John 10:28–30). Since Jesus is the resurrection and the life, they possess life by virtue of belonging to Jesus. Indeed, the purpose of both John's Gospel (20:30–31) and 1 John (5:13) is to assure believers that they have eternal life. They have triumphed over death before they die, and nothing can rob them of such life.

The life of the coming age is centered on Jesus Christ. John puts the spotlight on Jesus himself. He is the Messiah, the Son of Man, the Son of God, and the Lord. Indeed, he is the eternal Word of God, the one who has revealed and explained the Father to human beings. Those who have seen Jesus have seen the Father. God encounters human beings through Jesus Christ, for he is the Word made flesh. After Jesus' resurrection Thomas rightly confesses that Jesus is both Lord and God. The "I am" statements in John's Gospel communicate the majesty of his person, hearkening back to the "I am" statements in Exodus and Isaiah. Jesus is the bread of life, the light of the world, the door of the sheep, the good shepherd, the resurrection and the life, and the true vine. He shares the identity of God and existed for all eternity (John 8:58). Eternal life, then, centers on knowing him (John 17:3). For John, eternal life does not merely designate the life of the age to come; it also has a qualitative dimension, for it belongs to those who know and love the Father and Jesus Christ.

The centrality of Jesus shines forth in the Johannine portrait. He is the true vine—that is, the true Israel. He is the true bread, which in contrast to manna, bestows eternal life. The feast of Tabernacles points to Jesus, for he is the light of the world, granting life and light to those in darkness. Passover is fulfilled in Jesus, for he delivers his people from destruction as the true lamb of God who takes away the world's sin. True Sabbath rest is found only in Jesus. The law given through Moses has now been fulfilled and replaced by the grace and truth in Jesus Christ.

Jesus' suffering on the cross, the shedding of his blood, is the basis for the forgiveness of sins. He satisfied the Father's wrath through his suffering (1 John 2:2; 4:10). The cross was the pathway to his exaltation and victory. He has been lifted up and glorified through the cross. Suffering has become the pathway to glory. He is the shepherd of the new people of God, for he has brought into his flock both Jews and Gentiles who trust in him. As the good shepherd, he laid down his life for the sheep. Jesus died, as Caiaphas prophesied (albeit unknowingly), to spare the whole nation from perishing.

The centrality of Jesus and the arrival of the end are also confirmed by the gift of the Spirit. The Spirit is an eschatological gift and is given only when Jesus is exalted, for the Spirit does not operate independently. The Spirit came to glorify and exalt Jesus, convincing people to believe in Jesus and teaching disciples about him. The Spirit is the Paraclete, representing Jesus while Jesus is absent.

The life of the age to come is given to those who believe, to those who trust in Jesus Christ. For John, believing is a vital and dynamic reality, for those who believe come to Jesus, love him, follow him, obey him, drink and eat of him, abide in him, enter God's people through him, keep his commands, and so on. Trusting in Jesus is not an abstract reality. Faith permeates a person's whole being so that one's entire life is changed.

John does not focus on the kingdom explicitly, but his theology runs along the same arteries as the Synoptic Gospels and Acts. John emphasizes that Jesus is the Messiah and the Christ. In other words, he is the son of David, the king of all. What John emphasizes, however, is the nature of life in the kingdom. The story of Adam and Eve and Israel shows that exclusion from the kingdom brings death. But those who believe in Jesus enjoy life in all its abundance. What it means to be in the kingdom is to see who Jesus is, to love him, abide in him, obey him, and know him. The kingdom means the dawning of the new creation, but John reminds his readers that it is about seeing Jesus. It is about seeing and relishing the king, the Messiah and Son of God, in his beauty.

Paul too does not make frequent use of the phrase "kingdom of God," though the phrase is more significant in his theology than is often acknowledged. In any case, the "already but not yet" is woven into the fabric of Paul's theology, showing his belief that the fulfillment of OT promises was secured through the coming of Jesus Christ. The tension between inaugurated and consummated eschatology permeates the Pauline Epistles. The end-time verdict has already been pronounced for believers in Jesus Christ, so that they are now justified. And yet they await the eschatological day when that verdict will be declared to the entire world. Believers are now sanctified in Christ Jesus, but final and complete sanctification will be realized when Jesus Christ returns. Believers are redeemed now through the blood of Christ, but they await the final redemption, the redemption of the body. Christians are the adopted sons and daughters of God, and yet the fullness of adoption will be theirs on the day of resurrection. They are saved through faith in Jesus Christ, but they will also be saved on the last day from the wrath of God.

How is it that the eschatological promises, the promises of the kingdom, are now available for believers? Paul anchors these promises in the death and resurrection of Jesus Christ. Justification, redemption, sanctification, reconciliation, propitiation, and defeat of the principalities and powers have been secured through the death and resurrection of Jesus. In other words, no one can enter the kingdom apart from the forgiveness of sins. Atonement must be accomplished, God's wrath must be satisfied, in order for human beings to be rightly related to him. According to Paul, the death of Jesus provides forgiveness and appeases the wrath of God. Jesus' death does not save apart from his resurrection. Jesus' resurrection demonstrates that God vindicated him as Lord and Messiah, as the righteous one. The resurrection signals the arrival of the new creation, and hence with Jesus' resurrection the blessings of the new creation, listed above, become a reality.

The coming of Jesus Christ means that the old covenant, the Sinai covenant, has passed away, and the new covenant has become a reality. The promises of Abraham are being fulfilled in the gospel of Jesus Christ. Now inclusion in the people of God is not restricted to Israel but is open to both Jews and Gentiles who believe in Jesus. Those who trust in him are truly children of Abraham. Those who belong to Jesus Christ and who have received the gift of the Spirit are truly circumcised. Those who are members of the new creation are the new and true Israel of God. In the church of Jesus Christ the worldwide promises given to Abraham are becoming a reality, for Jews and Gentiles are one body in Christ, equally members of the people of God together.

The fulfillment of God's eschatological promises, the arrival of the new exodus and new creation, is attested by the gift of the Holy Spirit. Paul follows the same line of thought that we saw in the Synoptic Gospels, Acts, and the Johannine literature. The Spirit is the gift of the new age. For Paul, the Spirit guarantees the eschatological inheritance for believers, the final resurrection and the redemption of the body. The Spirit empowers believers now to live in a way that pleases God as they walk in the Spirit, are led by the Spirit, march in step with the Spirit, sow to the Spirit, and are filled with the Spirit. Those who have the down payment of the Spirit look forward to the new creation that is coming, when the old creation, with its sighing and sorrow, its frustrations and futility, passes away, and a new creation dawns in all its glory and beauty.

The kingdom theme is more prominent than one might think in Paul's theology, for a fundamental tenet of his theology is that Jesus is both Lord and Christ. He is the exalted Lord, reigning at the right hand of God the Father. Since he is the exalted Lord, angels and demons are subjected to him. And as the exalted Lord, Jesus is also the head and sovereign over the church. The kingdom of God, God's saving promises, are secured through Jesus Christ. This is scarcely surprising, for Paul's theology is radically Christ-centered. The centrality of Christ does not diminish the glory of God the creator. Paul explicitly teaches that God is glorified when Jesus is acknowledged as Lord (Phil. 2:11). Those who are Christ-centered are God-centered, for it was God's will to subject everything to Jesus Christ, and Jesus Christ always pointed human beings to the Father. Every spiritual blessing in Christ brings glory to God (Eph. 1:6, 12, 14). Everything is to be done in Christ's name and for his sake. Living is Christ and dying is gain, and once one sees the beauty and glory of Christ, then one is willing to give up everything for his sake.

The General Epistles (excluding here the Johannine Epistles) mainly focus on what it means to live under God's lordship. One cannot be a member of God's kingdom or a disciple of Jesus Christ if one does not live righteously. Faith without works, as James insists, is dead. True wisdom is measured not by one's intellect but rather by one's godliness. Peter, in his first epistle, reminds believers that righteous conduct will reveal the reality of their faith, especially in the crucible of persecution. In his second epistle Peter emphasizes the future coming of Jesus Christ, which is the day when his reign will be complete, the day when all God's enemies will be destroyed. In the meantime, false teachers promote libertinism, as if the dawn of grace in Jesus Christ has no bearing on the conduct of believers. The opponents in both Jude and 2 Peter advocate a kind of overly realized eschatology, a distortion of the Pauline theology of grace, which promotes licentiousness instead of righteousness. Both Jude and Peter teach that those who live unrighteously will not enter the heavenly kingdom, for love and obedience confirm one's call and election.

The call for obedience and a life that pleases God finds its roots in Christology. One of the central themes of all the General Epistles is that Jesus Christ is the glorious Lord (James 1:1; 2:1). He reigns on high over demonic powers as a result of his death and resurrection (1 Pet. 3:18–22). He is Lord and Savior, as 2 Peter regularly reminds its readers. Hebrews emphasizes particularly that Jesus is Lord, and that he has sat down at God's right hand. There is not only a change of location here. He sat down because he had offered the final and definitive sacrifice for sins. He has cleansed the consciences of those who have put their faith in him. As the true human being, the Davidic king, and as one who shares in the identity of God as God's Son, he has offered himself on the cross for the forgiveness of sins.

Indeed, Hebrews makes it clear that Jesus is the prophet, priest, and king. What the OT says about these three offices finds fulfillment in Jesus Christ. He is God's final word, the one who has perfected worshipers forever by his sacrifice. Likewise, 1 Peter traces the pathway from the cross to the crown. The blood of covenant animal sacrifices points forward to the blood of Jesus Christ (1 Pet. 1:2). He is God's lamb, redeeming people from their sins (1 Pet. 1:18–19). He is the suffering servant of Isa. 53, taking the penalty that sinners deserved.

Jesus is the true temple, the living stone, forming the cornerstone of God's true and new temple (1 Pet. 2:4–10). The church of Jesus Christ is the new and true Israel, bringing glory to God by declaring his praises and witnessing to their great salvation. By his own death, Jesus has defeated death and its potentate, the devil (Heb. 2:14–15). He has freed human beings who were enslaved to and fearful of death since the days of Adam. Now all those who trust in and obey Jesus are his brothers and sisters. They are the true offspring of Abraham (Heb. 2:16). Jesus is both their brother and their king.

The old age, with its sacrifices and rituals, has ended. The "last days" have arrived (Heb. 1:2). The "faith once for all handed over to the saints" has been given (Jude 3). The new covenant has come, and the law has been written on the heart (James 1:21). The new priesthood has displaced the Levitical priesthood. The Son is superior to the angels, who mediated the law from heaven, and superior to Moses, who mediated it on earth. He is greater than Joshua because he does not merely give earthly rest, but heavenly rest. Believers are promised that they will belong to the heavenly city to come, the new Jerusalem. Peter describes it as a new heavens and a new earth. The earthly promises of Canaan now include the whole world, the entire universe, so that believers enjoy the new creation. Jesus' sacrifice is greater than the Levitical sacrifice, for by his one sacrifice he has accomplished forever complete forgiveness of sins. Believers now enter boldly into God's presence. They enjoy his fellowship without fear because of what Jesus Christ has done for them.

All these letters stress that believers must persevere in faith in order to be saved. James and Hebrews, for instance, forge a close connection between faith and obedience. There is nothing new here. The Gospels, Acts, and Paul also teach that faith without a changed life is an illusion. Faith is an active and living reality. Hebrews stresses that those who have faith venture out, trusting God to take care of them in a world where God's people are under attack. James indicts faith without works, arguing that such faith is not true faith, for genuine faith always expresses itself in works. Hebrews calls on readers to stay true to Jesus until the end. If they fall away from the faith, if they abandon Jesus, they will face eschatological destruction. The heavenly city is reserved for those who do not abandon Jesus, for those who do not harden their hearts in unbelief and disobedience.

Revelation wraps up the entire story. God is glorified and praised in the way history turns out, in both judgment and salvation. God reigns not only in salvation but also in judgment. Those who have opposed God and the gospel of Jesus Christ will face a final reckoning. They will be cast into the lake of fire. Revelation does not introduce a new theme here. All of the NT writers regularly promise a final judgment for those who give themselves over to evil. The kingdom that is coming has no room for the unclean, for the rebellious, for those who have compromised with the earthly city of humankind. God is Lord of history, and evil will not have the last word.

Revelation reminds us that history is not yet complete. Jesus is coming soon, and he will complete all that has been started. Then all of God's promises will be yes and amen. The new creation promised in the OT will finally be a reality. The heavenly city anticipated in the earthly Jerusalem will come down to the present creation, and the latter will be transformed and purified (cf. 2 Pet. 3:10–13). The loveliness of the new Jerusalem is indescribable. The stunning beauty of jewelry and the purest gold give us some intimation of the splendor and magnificence of the coming new world.

Revelation does not offer a different message from the remainder of the NT. Those who make it to the heavenly city do so because of the cross of Jesus Christ. Their robes have been made white by the blood of the lamb. They have been freed from their guilt by his blood. His death was the key to history. The sealed book was only opened because he was the slain lamb, and the ancient serpent was crushed and thrown out of heaven solely because of Jesus' death. The victory over the serpent occurs through the one who is the Christ. Indeed, the Christology of Revelation is quite exalted. The lamb, John instructs us again and again, has the same stature as God himself. God is worshiped as creator (chap. 4), and Christ is worshiped as redeemer (chap. 5). Nor is there any notion here of two Gods. John is well aware of the OT teaching that there is only one God, and he affirms that one must worship God alone (19:10; 22:9). Clearly, Jesus shares the identity of God, showing that there is complexity in the identity of God.

Salvation comes through the work of God—more specifically, the cross and resurrection of Jesus Christ. But John, in accord with what we have seen elsewhere, also calls his readers to obedience. Those who throw in their lot with the beast and false prophet will not enter the heavenly city. Believers must persevere in the faith and be willing to face death for the sake of the gospel. Nor must they ever think that the world is spinning out of control. God the creator rules over the entire world. He has allowed the beast to rule over the world for a short time. Even the slaying of saints is within the realm of God's will. Jesus rules over the kings of the earth, and he has gone before his people, for he too faced death but now is the living one. Believers are not given a philosophical resolution to the problem of evil. They are instructed to trust God and to look to Jesus, who went before them. They are promised a final reward whereby they will eat from the tree of life forever.

The world will be a new temple and a new garden where God dwells. All that belonged to Adam at the beginning will be theirs and more. Those in the new creation know what it is like to be separated from fellowship with God.

They know what it is to be redeemed from the horrific evil that dwelt in their own hearts. They know and exult in the love of God demonstrated in the cross of Jesus Christ. They are safe in the heavenly city, with its impregnable walls. The gates of the city can be left open, for there is no enemy within or without who can conquer God's people now. They will see God's face in the person of Jesus Christ. They will see the King in his beauty, and they will be glad forever.

BIBLIOGRAPHY

Ackroyd, Peter R. *The Chronicler in His Age*. JSOTSup 101; Sheffield: JSOT Press, 1991.

Alexander, T. Desmond. *From Eden to the New Jerusalem: An Introduction to Biblical Theology*. Grand Rapids: Kregel, 2008.

———. *From Paradise to the Promised Land: An Introduction to the Main Themes of the Pentateuch*. Grand Rapids: Baker, 1998.

———. *The Servant King: The Bible's Portrait of the Messiah*. Vancouver: Regent College Publishing, 1998.

Allison, Dale C., Jr. *The New Moses: A Matthean Typology*. Minneapolis: Fortress, 1993.

Armerding, C. E. "Judges." In *New Dictionary of Biblical Theology*, edited by T. Desmond Alexander and Brian S. Rosner, 171–76. Downers Grove, IL: InterVarsity, 2000.

Attridge, Harold W. *The Epistle to the Hebrews*. Hermeneia. Philadelphia: Fortress, 1989.

Baker, D. W. "Zephaniah." In *New Dictionary of Biblical Theology*, edited by T. Desmond Alexander and Brian S. Rosner, 254–55. Downers Grove, IL: InterVarsity, 2000.

Baldwin, Joyce G. *Esther: An Introduction and Commentary*. TOTC. Downers Grove, IL: InterVarsity, 1984.

Ball, David Mark. *"I Am" in John's Gospel: Literary Function, Background and Theological Implications*. JSNTSup 124. Sheffield: Sheffield Academic Press, 1996.

Barrett, C. K. "The Eschatology of the Epistle to the Hebrews." In *The Background to the New Testament and Its Eschatology*, edited by W. D. Davies and D. Daube, 363–93. Cambridge: Cambridge University Press, 1954.

Bartholomew, C. G. "Wisdom Books." In *New Dictionary of Biblical Theology*, edited by T. Desmond Alexander and Brian S. Rosner, 120–22. Downers Grove, IL: InterVarsity, 2000.

Bauckham, Richard. *God Crucified: Monotheism and Christology in the New Testament*. Grand Rapids: Eerdmans, 1999.

———. *James: Wisdom of James, Disciple of Jesus the Sage*. New York: Routledge, 1999.

———. *The Theology of the Book of Revelation*. NTT. Cambridge: Cambridge University Press, 1993.

Beale, G. K. "An Exegetical and Theological Consideration of the Hardening of Pharaoh's Heart in Exodus 4–14 and Romans 9." *TJ* 5 (1984): 129–54.

———. *A New Testament Biblical Theology: The Unfolding of the Old Testament in the New*. Grand Rapids: Baker Academic, 2011.

———. "The Old Testament Background of Reconciliation in 2 Corinthians 5–7 and Its Bearing on the Literary Problem of 2 Corinthians 6:14–7:1." *NTS* 35 (1989): 550–81.

———. *The Temple and the Church's Mission: A Biblical Theology of the Dwelling Place of God*. Downers Grove, IL: InterVarsity, 2004.

Beasley-Murray, G. R. *Jesus and the Kingdom of God*. Grand Rapids: Eerdmans, 1986.

Bechtler, S. R. *Following in His Steps: Suffering, Community, and Christology in 1 Peter*. SBLDS 162. Atlanta: Scholars Press, 1998.

Beker, J. Christiaan. *Paul the Apostle: The Triumph of God in Life and Thought*. Philadelphia: Fortress, 1980.

Berg, Christopher. "'Seeking Yahweh' and Seeking the Purpose of Chronicles." *LS* 9 (1982): 128–41.

Berg, Sandra Beth. *The Book of Esther: Motifs, Themes and Structure*. SBLDS 44. Missoula, MT: Scholars Press, 1979.

Bergen, Robert D. *1, 2 Samuel*. NAC. Nashville: Broadman & Holman, 1996.

Best, Ernest. "Discipleship in Mark: Mark 8:22–10:52." *SJT* 23 (1970): 323–37.

Bird, Michael F. "Incorporated Righteousness: A Response to Recent Evangelical Discussion Concerning the Imputation of Christ's Righteousness in Justification." *JETS* 47 (2004): 253–75.

Bird, Michael F., and Preston M. Sprinkle. *The Faith of Jesus Christ: Exegetical, Biblical, and Theological Studies*. Peabody, MA: Hendrickson, 2009.

Block, Daniel I. *The Book of Ezekiel: Chapters 1–24*. NICOT. Grand Rapids: Eerdmans, 1997.

———. *The Book of Ezekiel: Chapters 25–48*. NICOT. Grand Rapids: Eerdmans, 1998.

———. *Judges, Ruth*. NAC. Nashville: Broadman & Holman, 1999.

Boice, James Montgomery. *Witness and Revelation in the Gospel of John*. CEP. Grand Rapids: Zondervan, 1970.

Bolt, Peter G. *The Cross from a Distance: Atonement in Mark's Gospel*. Downers Grove, IL: InterVarsity, 2004.

Brauch, M. T. "Appendix: Perspectives on 'God's Righteousness' in Recent German Discussion." In *Paul and Palestinian Judaism: A Comparison of Patterns of Religion*, by E. P. Sanders, 523–42. Philadelphia: Fortress, 1977.

Brueggemann, Walter. *Theology of the Old Testament: Testimony, Dispute, Advocacy*. Minneapolis: Fortress, 1997.

Buckwalter, Douglas H. *The Character and Purpose of Luke's Christology*. SNTSMS 89. Cambridge: Cambridge University Press, 1996.

Bultmann, Rudolf K. "The Problem of Ethics in Paul." In *Understanding Paul's Ethics: Twentieth Century Approaches*, edited by Brian S. Rosner, 195–216. Grand Rapids: Eerdmans, 1995.

Burge, Gary M. *The Anointed Community: The Holy Spirit in the Johannine Tradition*. Grand Rapids: Eerdmans, 1987.

Burkett, Delbert. *The Son of Man Debate: A History and Evaluation*. SNTSMS 107. Cambridge: Cambridge University Press, 1999.

Campbell, Constantine R. *Paul and Union with Christ: An Exegetical and Theological Study*. Grand Rapids: Zondervan, 2012.

Campbell, Iain D. "The Song of David's Son: Interpreting the Song of Solomon in the Light of the Davidic Covenant." *WTJ* 62 (2000): 17–32.

Caneday, A. B. "'Everything Is Vapor': Grasping for Meaning under the Sun." *SBJT* 15 (2001): 26–40.

Capes, David B. *Old Testament Yahweh Texts in Paul's Christology*. WUNT 2/47. Tübingen: Mohr Siebeck, 1992.

Caragounis, Chrys C. *The Son of Man: Vision and Interpretation*. WUNT 38. Tübingen: Mohr Siebeck, 1986.

Carson, D. A. *Divine Sovereignty and Human Responsibility: Biblical Perspectives in Tension*. Atlanta: John Knox, 1981.

Cassuto, Umberto. *From Adam to Noah: A Commentary on Genesis I–VI 8*. Vol. 1 of *A Commentary on the Book of Genesis*. Translated by Israel Abrahams. Jerusalem: Magnes, 1961.

Childs, Brevard S. *Biblical Theology of the Old and New Testaments: Theological Reflection on the Christian Bible*. Minneapolis: Fortress, 1992.

———. *The Book of Exodus: A Critical, Theological Commentary*. OTL. Philadelphia: Westminster, 1974.

———. *Introduction to the Old Testament as Scripture*. Philadelphia: Fortress, 1979.

Chin, M. "A Heavenly Home for the Homeless: Aliens and Strangers in 1 Peter." *TynBul* 42 (1991): 96–112.

Clark, W. Malcolm. "A Legal Background to the Yahwist's Use of 'Good and Evil' in Genesis 2–3." *JBL* 88 (1969): 266–78.

Clements, Ronald E. *Old Testament Theology: A Fresh Approach*. Atlanta: John Knox, 1978.

Clines, David J. A. *The Theme of the Pentateuch*. 2nd ed. JSOTSup 10. Sheffield: Sheffield Academic Press, 1997.

Collins, C. John. *Genesis 1–4: A Linguistic, Literary, and Theological Commentary*. Phillipsburg, NJ: P&R, 2006.

Craigie, Peter C. *The Book of Deuteronomy*. NICOT. Grand Rapids: Eerdmans, 1976.

Crenshaw, James L. *Old Testament Wisdom: An Introduction*. 3rd ed. Louisville: Westminster John Knox, 2010.

Davies, John A. "'Discerning between Good and Evil': Solomon as a New Adam in 1 Kings." *WTJ* 73 (2011): 39–57.

De Jong, Stephan. "God in the Book of Qohelet: A Reappraisal of Qohelet's Place in Old Testament Theology." *VT* 47 (1997): 154–67.

Dempster, Stephen G. *Dominion and Dynasty: A Theology of the Hebrew Bible*. NSBT 15. Downers Grove, IL: InterVarsity, 2003.

———. "Magnum Opus and Magna Carta: *The Meaning of the Pentateuch*." *Themelios* 36 (2011): 42–47.

———. "The Servant of the Lord." In *Central Themes in Biblical Theology: Mapping Unity in Diversity*, edited by Scott J. Hafemann and Paul R. House, 128–78. Nottingham: Apollos, 2007.

DeRouchie, Jason S. "Shepherding Wind and One Wise Shepherd: Grasping for Breath in Ecclesiastes." *SBJT* 15 (2011): 4–25.

Dodd, C. H. "The Framework of the Gospel Narrative." *ExpTim* 43 (1932): 396–400.

———. *The Interpretation of the Fourth Gospel*. Cambridge: Cambridge University Press, 1953.

———. *The Parables of the Kingdom*. London: Nisbet, 1936.

Douglas, Mary. *Purity and Danger: An Analysis of the Concepts of Pollution and Taboo*. New York: Routledge & Kegan Paul, 1966.

Dryden, J. de Waal. *Theology and Ethics in 1 Peter: Paraenetic Strategies for Christian Character Formation*. WUNT 2/209. Tübingen: Mohr Siebeck, 2006.

Duguid, Iain M. "Ezekiel." In *New Dictionary of Biblical Theology*, edited by T. Desmond Alexander and Brian S. Rosner, 229–32. Downers Grove, IL: InterVarsity, 2000.

———. *Ezekiel and the Leaders of Israel*. VTSup 56. Leiden: Brill, 1994.

———. "Zechariah." In *New Dictionary of Biblical Theology*, edited by T. Desmond Alexander and Brian S. Rosner, 257–60. Downers Grove, IL: InterVarsity, 2000.

Dumbrell, William J. *Covenant and Creation: A Theology of the Old Testament Covenants*. Carlisle: Paternoster, 1984.

———. *The End of the Beginning: Revelation 21–22 and the Old Testament*. Homebush West: Lancer Books, 1985.

———. *The Faith of Israel: A Theological Survey of the Old Testament*. 2nd ed. Grand Rapids: Baker Academic, 2002.

———. "'In Those Days There Was No King in Israel: Every Man Did What Was Right In His Own Eyes'; The Purpose of the Book of Judges Reconsidered." *JSOT* 25 (1983): 23–33.

Dunn, James D. G. *The Theology of Paul the Apostle*. Grand Rapids: Eerdmans, 1998.

Elliott, J. H. *Home for the Homeless: A Sociological Exegesis of 1 Peter, Its Situation and Strategy*. Philadelphia: Fortress, 1981.

———. *1 Peter*. AB 37B. New York: Doubleday, 2000.

Enns, P. E. "Exodus." In *New Dictionary of Biblical Theology*, edited by T. Desmond Alexander and Brian S. Rosner, 146–52. Downers Grove, IL: InterVarsity, 2000.

Farmer, Kathleen A. *Who Knows What Is Good? A Commentary on the Books of Proverbs and Ecclesiastes*. ITC. Grand Rapids: Eerdmans, 1991.

Fee, Gordon D. *God's Empowering Presence: The Holy Spirit in the Letters of Paul*. Peabody, MA: Hendrickson, 1994.

Feldmeier, R. *Die Christen als Fremde: Die Metapher der Fremde in der antiken Welt, im Urchristentum und im 1. Petrusbrief*. WUNT 64. Tübingen: Mohr Siebeck, 1992.

Fiddes, Paul S. *Past Event and Present Salvation: The Christian Idea of Atonement*. Louisville: Westminster John Knox, 1989.

Fox, Michael V. *Qohelet and His Contradictions*. JSOTSup 71. Sheffield: Almond, 1989.

Frame, John M. *The Doctrine of God: A Theology of Lordship*. Phillipsburg, NJ: P&R, 2002.

———. *The Doctrine of the Knowledge of God*. Phillipsburg, NJ: P&R, 1989.

———. *The Doctrine of the Word of God*. Phillipsburg, NJ: P&R, 2010.

France, R. T. *The Gospel of Matthew*. NICNT. Grand Rapids: Eerdmans, 2007.

Fredericks, Daniel C. *Coping with Transience: Ecclesiastes on Brevity in Life*. BibSem 18. Sheffield: JSOT Press, 1993.

Freedman, David Noel. "The Chronicler's Purpose." *CBQ* 23 (1961): 436–42.

———. *The Unity of the Hebrew Bible*. Ann Arbor: University of Michigan Press, 1991.

Fuller, Daniel P. *The Unity of the Bible: Unfolding God's Plan for Humanity.* Grand Rapids: Zondervan, 1992.

Fung, Ronald Y. K. "The Status of Justification by Faith in Paul's Thought: A Brief Survey of a Modern Debate." *Themelios* 6 (1981): 4–11.

Fyall, Robert S. *Now My Eyes Have Seen You: Images of Creation and Evil in the Book of Job.* NSBT 12. Downers Grove, IL: InterVarsity, 2002.

Gaffin, Richard B., Jr. *"By Faith, Not by Sight": Paul and the Order of Salvation.* Waynesboro, GA: Paternoster, 2006.

Gammie, John G. *Holiness in Israel.* Minneapolis: Fortress, 1989.

Garrett, Duane A. *Job.* Shepherd's Notes. Nashville: Broadman & Holman, 1998.

———. *Proverbs, Ecclesiastes, Song of Songs.* NAC. Nashville: Broadman, 1993.

———. *Song of Songs.* WBC 23B. Nashville: Thomas Nelson, 2004.

Gathercole, Simon J. *The Preexistent Son: Recovering the Christologies of Matthew, Mark, and Luke.* Grand Rapids: Eerdmans, 2006.

Gentry, Peter J. "Daniel's Seventy Weeks and the New Exodus." *SBJT* 14 (2010): 26–44.

———. "Kingdom through Covenant: Humanity as the Divine Image." *SBJT* 12 (2008): 16–42.

———. "Rethinking the 'Sure Mercies of David' in Isaiah 55:3." *WTJ* 69 (2007): 279–304.

———. "The Son of Man in Daniel 7: Individual or Corporate?" In *Acorns to Oaks: The Primacy and Practice of Biblical Theology; A Festschrift for Dr. Geoff Adams*, edited by Michael A. G. Haykin, 59–75. Dundas, ON: Joshua Press, 2003.

Gentry, Peter J., and Stephen J. Wellum. *Kingdom through Covenant: A Biblical-Theological Understanding of the Covenants.* Wheaton: Crossway, 2012.

Goldingay, John. *Israel's Faith.* Vol. 2 of *Old Testament Theology.* Downers Grove, IL: InterVarsity, 2006.

———. *Israel's Gospel.* Vol. 1 of *Old Testament Theology.* Downers Grove, IL: InterVarsity, 2003.

———. *Israel's Life.* Vol. 3 of *Old Testament Theology.* Downers Grove, IL: InterVarsity, 2009.

Goppelt, Leonhard. *The Ministry of Jesus in Its Theological Significance.* Vol. 1 of *Theology of the New Testament.* Translated by John E. Alsup. Edited by Jürgen Roloff. Grand Rapids: Eerdmans, 1981.

Gottwald, Norman K. *Studies in the Book of Lamentations.* SBT. Chicago: Allenson, 1954.

Gow, M. D. "Ruth." In *New Dictionary of Biblical Theology*, edited by T. Desmond Alexander and Brian S. Rosner, 176–78. Downers Grove, IL: InterVarsity, 2000.

Grant, Jamie A. *The King as Exemplar: The Function of Deuteronomy's Kingship Law in the Shaping of the Book of Psalms.* SBLAB 17. Atlanta: Society of Biblical Literature, 2004.

Green, Joel B. "'Salvation to the End of the Earth' (Acts 13:47): God as the Saviour in the Acts of the Apostles." In *Witness to the Gospel: The Theology of Acts*, edited by I. H. Marshall and D. Peterson, 83–106. Grand Rapids: Eerdmans, 1998.

Groves, J. Alan. "Atonement in Isaiah 53: 'For He Bore the Sins of Many.'" In *The Glory of the Atonement: Biblical, Historical and Practical Perspectives: Essays in Honor of Roger Nicole*, edited by Charles E. Hill and Frank A. James III, 61–89. Downers Grove, IL: InterVarsity, 2004.

Hafemann, Scott J. "The Covenant Relationship." In *Central Themes in Biblical Theology: Mapping Unity in Diversity*, edited by Scott J. Hafemann and Paul R. House, 20–65. Nottingham: Apollos, 2007.

Hahn, Scott W. *Kinship by Covenant: A Canonical Approach to the Fulfillment of God's Saving Promises*. New Haven: Yale University Press, 2009.

Hals, Ronald M. *The Theology of the Book of Ruth*. FBBS 23. Philadelphia: Fortress, 1969.

Hamilton, James M., Jr. *God's Glory in Salvation through Judgment: A Biblical Theology*. Wheaton: Crossway, 2010.

———. "John Sailhamer's *The Meaning of the Pentateuch*: A Review Essay." *SBJT* 14 (2010): 62–76.

———. "The Messianic Music of the Song of Songs: A Non-Allegorical Interpretation." *WTJ* 68 (2006): 331–45.

———. "The Seed of the Woman and the Blessing of Abraham." *TynBul* 58 (2007): 253–73.

———. "The Skull Crushing Seed of the Woman: Inner-Biblical Interpretation of Genesis 3:15." *SBJT* 10 (2006): 30–54.

Hartley, John E. *Leviticus*. WBC 4. Dallas: Word, 1992.

Hartman, Lars. *"Into the Name of the Lord Jesus": Baptism in the Early Church*. SNTW. Edinburgh: T&T Clark, 1997.

Hasel, Gerhard F. *The Remnant: The History and Theology of the Remnant Idea from Genesis to Isaiah*. AUMSR 5. Berrien Springs, MI: Andrews University Press, 1972.

Hays, Richard B. *Echoes of Scripture in the Letters of Paul*. New Haven: Yale University Press, 1989.

Hengel, Martin. *The Charismatic Leader and His Followers*. Translated by J. C. G. Greig. Edited by John Riches. SNTW. Edinburgh: T&T Clark, 1996.

———. *Victory over Violence and Was Jesus a Revolutionist?* Eugene, OR: Wipf & Stock, 2003.

Heschel, Abraham J. *The Prophets*. New York: Harper & Row, 1962.

Hess, R. S. "Joshua." In *New Dictionary of Biblical Theology*, edited by T. Desmond Alexander and Brian S. Rosner, 165–71. Downers Grove, IL: InterVarsity, 2000.

Hillers, Delbert R. *Treaty-Curses and the Old Testament Prophets*. BibOr 16. Rome: Pontifical Biblical Institute, 1964.

Hoskins, Paul M. *Jesus as the Fulfillment of the Temple in the Gospel of John*. PBM. Waynesboro, GA: Paternoster, 2006.

House, Paul R. "The Day of the Lord." In *Central Themes in Biblical Theology: Mapping Unity in Diversity*, edited by Scott J. Hafemann and Paul R. House, 179–224. Nottingham: Apollos, 2007.

———. *Lamentations*. WBC 23B. Nashville: Thomas Nelson, 2004.

———. *Old Testament Theology*. Downers Grove, IL: InterVarsity, 1998.

———. *The Unity of the Twelve*. JSOTSup 97. Sheffield: Almond, 1990.

Houston, Walter. *Purity and Monotheism: Clean and Unclean Animals in Biblical Law*. JSOTSup 140. Sheffield: JSOT Press, 1993.

Howard, David M., Jr. *Joshua*. NAC. Nashville: Broadman & Holman, 1998.

———. *The Structure of Psalms 93–100*. BibJudS 5. Winona Lake, IN: Eisenbrauns, 1997.

Hubbard, Moyer V. *New Creation in Paul's Letters and Thought*. SNTSMS 119. Cambridge: Cambridge University Press, 2002.

Hubbard, Robert L., Jr. *The Book of Ruth*. NICOT. Grand Rapids: Eerdmans, 1988.

Huffman, H. B. "The Covenant Lawsuit in the Prophets." *JBL* 78 (1959): 285–95.

Jackson, T. Ryan. *New Creation in Paul's Letters: A Study of the Historical and Social Setting of a Pauline Concept*. WUNT 2/272. Tübingen: Mohr Siebeck, 2010.

Japhet, Sara. *The Ideology of the Book of Chronicles and Its Place in Biblical Thought*. Translated by Anna Barber. Winona Lake, IN: Eisenbrauns, 2009.

Jensen, Joseph. "Yahweh's Plan in Isaiah and in the Rest of the Old Testament." *CBQ* 48 (1986): 443–55.

Jenson, Philip Peter. *Graded Holiness: A Key to the Priestly Conception of the World*. JSOTSup 106. Sheffield: Sheffield Academic Press, 1992.

Jeremias, Joachim. *New Testament Theology: The Proclamation of Jesus*. Translated by John Bowden. New York: Scribner, 1971.

———. *The Prayers of Jesus*. SBT 2/6; London: SCM Press, 1967.

Kallas, James. *The Significance of the Synoptic Miracles*. London: SPCK, 1961.

Kelly, Brian E. "Ezra-Nehemiah." In *New Dictionary of Biblical Theology*, edited by T. Desmond Alexander and Brian S. Rosner, 195–98. Downers Grove, IL: InterVarsity, 2000.

———. *Retribution and Eschatology in Chronicles*. JSOTSup 211. Sheffield: Sheffield Academic Press, 1996.

Keys, G. "Esther." In *New Dictionary of Biblical Theology*, edited by T. Desmond Alexander and Brian S. Rosner, 198–200. Downers Grove, IL: InterVarsity, 2000.

Kidner, Derek. *Ezra and Nehemiah: An Introduction and Commentary*. TOTC. Leicester: Inter-Varsity, 1979.

———. *The Proverbs: An Introduction and Commentary*. TOTC. Leicester: Inter-Varsity, 1964.

———. *Psalms 1–72: An Introduction and Commentary on Books I and II of the Psalms*. TOTC. Leicester: Inter-Varsity, 1973.

Kim, Jinkyu. "The Strategic Arrangement of Royal Psalms in Books IV–V." *WTJ* 70 (2008): 143–57.

Kim, Seyoon. *The "Son of Man" as the Son of God*. Grand Rapids: Eerdmans, 1983.

Kimbell, John. "The Atonement in Lukan Theology." PhD diss., Southern Baptist Theological Seminary, 2009.

Kingsbury, Jack Dean. *Matthew: Structure, Christology, Kingdom*. Philadelphia: Fortress, 1975.

Kiuchi, N. *The Purification Offering in the Priestly Literature: Its Meaning and Function*. JSOTSup 56. Sheffield: JSOT Press, 1987.

Kline, Meredith G. *Kingdom Prologue*. South Hamilton, MA: Gordon-Conwell Theological Seminary, 1993.

———. *Treaty of the Great King: The Covenant Structure of Deuteronomy; Studies and Commentary*. Grand Rapids: Eerdmans, 1963.

Köstenberger, Andreas J. *A Theology of John's Gospel and Letters*. BTNT. Grand Rapids: Zondervan, 2009.

————. "Was the Last Supper a Passover Meal?" In *The Lord's Supper: Remembering and Proclaiming Christ until He Comes*, edited by Thomas R. Schreiner and Matthew R. Crawford, 6–30. Nashville: Broadman & Holman, 2010.

Kraus, Hans Joachim. *The Theology of the Psalms*. Translated by Keith Crim. Minneapolis: Augsburg, 1986.

Kruger, Michael J. *Canon Revisited: Establishing the Origins and Authority of the New Testament Books*. Wheaton: Crossway, 2012.

Kümmel, Werner G. *Promise and Fulfillment: The Eschatological Message of Jesus*. Translated by Dorothea M. Barton. SBT 23. London: SCM Press, 1957.

————. *The Theology of the New Testament according to Its Major Witnesses: Jesus—Paul—John*. Translated by John E. Steely. Nashville: Abingdon, 1973.

Ladd, George Eldon. *The Presence of the Future*. Rev. ed. Grand Rapids: Eerdmans, 1996.

————. *A Theology of the New Testament*. Edited by Donald A. Hagner. Rev. ed. Grand Rapids: Eerdmans, 1993.

Lee, Aquila H. *From Messiah to Preexistent Son: Jesus' Self-Consciousness and Early Christian Exegesis of Messianic Psalms*. WUNT 2/192. Tübingen: Mohr Siebeck, 2005.

Leeman, Jonathan. *The Church and the Surprising Offence of God's Love: Reintroducing the Doctrines of Church Membership and Discipline*. Wheaton: Crossway, 2010.

Lehne, Susan. *The New Covenant in Hebrews*. JSNTSup 44. Sheffield: JSOT Press, 1990.

Leithart, Peter J. *A Son to Me: An Exposition of 1 & 2 Samuel*. Moscow, ID: Canon, 2003.

Levenson, Jon D. *Creation and the Persistence of Evil: The Jewish Drama of Divine Omnipotence*. 2nd ed. Princeton, NJ: Princeton University Press, 1994.

————. *Resurrection and the Restoration of Israel: The Ultimate Victory of God in Life*. New Haven: Yale University Press, 2006.

————. *Sinai and Zion: An Entry into the Jewish Bible*. NVBS. Minneapolis: Winston, 1985.

————. *Theology of the Program of Restoration of Ezekiel 40–48*. HSM 10. Missoula, MT: Scholars Press, 1976.

Levine, Baruch A. *Leviticus*. JPSTC. Philadelphia: Jewish Publication Society, 1989.

Lindars, Barnabas. *The Theology of the Letter to the Hebrews*. NTT. Cambridge: Cambridge University Press, 1991.

Longman, Tremper, III. *The Book of Ecclesiastes*. NICOT. Grand Rapids: Eerdmans, 1998.

Longman, Tremper, III, and Daniel G. Reid. *God Is a Warrior*. Grand Rapids: Zondervan, 1995.

Lucas, E. C. "Covenant, Treaty, and Prophecy." *Themelios* 8 (1982): 19–23.

————. "Daniel." In *New Dictionary of Biblical Theology*, edited by T. Desmond Alexander and Brian S. Rosner, 232–36. Downers Grove, IL: InterVarsity, 2000.

Marshall, I. Howard. *Luke: Historian and Theologian*. Grand Rapids: Zondervan, 1970.

————. *New Testament Theology: Many Witnesses, One Gospel*. Downers Grove, IL: InterVarsity, 2004.

Martens, Elmer A. *God's Design: A Focus on Old Testament Theology*. 2nd ed. Grand Rapids: Baker, 1994.

————. "The People of God." In *Central Themes in Biblical Theology: Mapping Unity in Diversity*, edited by Scott J. Hafemann and Paul R. House, 225–53. Nottingham: Apollos, 2007.

Martin, Ralph P. *A Hymn of Christ: Philippians 2:5–11 in Recent Interpretation and the Setting of Early Christian Worship*. Rev. ed. Downers Grove, IL: InterVarsity, 1997.

Matera, Frank J. *New Testament Theology: Exploring Diversity and Unity*. Louisville: Westminster John Knox, 2007.

Mathews, K. A. "Genesis." In *New Dictionary of Biblical Theology*, edited by T. Desmond Alexander and Brian S. Rosner, 140–46. Downers Grove, IL: InterVarsity, 2000.

———. *Genesis 1:1–11:26*. NAC. Nashville: Broadman & Holman, 1996.

Mays, James Luther. "The Place of the Torah-Psalms in the Psalter." *JBL* 106 (1987): 3–12.

———. *Psalms*. IBC. Louisville: John Knox, 1994.

———. "The Question of Context in Psalm Interpretation." In *The Shape and Shaping of the Psalter*, edited by J. Clinton McCann Jr., 14–20. JSOTSup 159. Sheffield: JSOT Press, 1993.

McCann, J. Clinton, Jr., "Books I–III and the Editorial Purpose of the Hebrew Psalter." In *The Shape and Shaping of the Psalter*, edited by J. Clinton McCann Jr., 93–107. JSOTSup 159. Sheffield: JSOT Press, 1993.

———. "The Psalms as Instruction." *Int* 46 (1992): 117–28.

McCarthy, Dennis J. *Old Testament Covenant: A Survey of Current Opinions*. Richmond: John Knox, 1972.

McConville, J. Gordon. *Grace in the End: A Study in Deuteronomic Theology*. Grand Rapids: Zondervan, 1993.

———. "Jeremiah: Theology of." In *New International Dictionary of Old Testament Theology and Exegesis*, edited by Willem A. VanGemeren, 4:755–67. 5 vols. Grand Rapids: Zondervan, 1997.

———. *Judgment and Promise: An Interpretation of the Book of Jeremiah*. Winona Lake, IN: Eisenbrauns, 1993.

———. *Law and Theology in Deuteronomy*. JSOTSup 33. Sheffield: JSOT Press, 1984.

McConville, J. G., and J. G. Millar. *Time and Place in Deuteronomy*. JSOTSup 179. Sheffield: Sheffield Academic Press, 1994.

Meier, John P. *Mentor, Message and Miracles*. Vol. 2 of *A Marginal Jew: Rethinking the Historical Jesus*. New York: Doubleday, 1994.

Mendenhall, George E. *Law and Covenant in Israel and the Ancient Near East*. Pittsburgh: Biblical Colloquium, 1955.

Menzies, Robert P. *Empowered for Witness: The Spirit in Luke-Acts*. JPTSup 6. Sheffield: Sheffield Academic Press, 1994.

Meyer, Jason. *The End of the Law: Mosaic Covenant in Pauline Theology*. Nashville: Broadman & Holman, 2009.

Milgrom, Jacob. *Leviticus: A Book of Ritual and Ethics*. CC. Minneapolis: Fortress, 2004.

———. *Leviticus 1–16: A New Translation with Introduction and Commentary*. AB 3. New York: Doubleday, 1991.

Millar, J. Gary. *Now Choose Life: Theology and Ethics in Deuteronomy*. NSBT 6. Grand Rapids: Eerdmans, 1998.

Miller, Patrick D., Jr. "The Beginning of the Psalter." In *The Shape and Shaping of the Psalter*, edited by J. Clinton McCann Jr., 83–92. JSOTSup 159. Sheffield: JSOT Press, 1993.

———. *Deuteronomy*. IBC. Louisville: John Knox, 1990.

————. *The Divine Warrior in Early Israel*. HSM 5. Cambridge, MA: Harvard University Press, 1973.

————. "Kingship, Torah, Obedience, and Prayer: The Theology of Psalms 15–24." In *Neue Wege der Psalmenforschung*, edited by Klaus Seybold and Erich Zenger, 127–42. HBSt 1. Freiburg: Herder, 1994.

Mitchell, David C. *The Message of the Psalter: An Eschatological Programme in the Book of Psalms*. JSOTSup 252. Sheffield: Sheffield Academic Press, 1997.

Morris, Leon. *The Apostolic Preaching of the Cross*. 3rd ed. Grand Rapids: Eerdmans, 1965.

Moule, C. F. D. *The Origin of Christology*. Cambridge: Cambridge University Press, 1977.

Müller, Mogens. *The Expression "Son of Man" and the Development of Christology: A History of Interpretation*. London: Equinox, 2008.

Murphy, Roland A. *Ecclesiastes*. WBC 23A. Waco: Word, 1992.

————. "Qoheleth and Theology?" *BTB* 21 (1991): 30–33.

Nicole, Emile. "Atonement in the Pentateuch: 'It is the Blood That Makes Atonement for One's Life.'" In *The Glory of the Atonement: Biblical, Historical and Practical Perspectives: Essays in Honor of Roger Nicole*, edited by Charles E. Hill and Frank A. James III, 35–50. Downers Grove, IL: InterVarsity, 2004.

Niehaus, Jeffrey J. *Ancient Near Eastern Themes in Biblical Theology*. Grand Rapids: Kregel, 2008.

————. "The Central Sanctuary: Where and When?" *TynBul* 43 (1992): 3–30.

Nogalski, James D. *Literary Precursors to the Book of the Twelve*. BZAW 217. New York: de Gruyter, 1993.

Nogalski, James D., and Marvin A. Sweeney, eds. *Reading and Hearing the Book of the Twelve*. SBLSymS 15. Atlanta: Society of Biblical Literature, 2000.

North, Robert. "Theology of the Chronicler." *JBL* 82 (1963): 369–81.

Ollenburger, Ben C. *Zion, the City of the Great King: A Theological Symbol of the Jerusalem Cult*. JSOTSup 41. Sheffield: JSOT Press, 1987.

Olson, Dennis T. *Deuteronomy and the Death of Moses: A Theological Reading*. OBT. Minneapolis: Fortress, 1993.

Ortlund, Raymond C., Jr. *God's Unfaithful Wife: A Biblical Theology of Spiritual Adultery*. NSBT 2. Downers Grove, IL: InterVarsity, 1996.

Pamment, Margaret. "The Kingdom of Heaven according to the First Gospel." *NTS* 27 (1981): 211–32.

Pao, David. *Thanksgiving: An Investigation of a Pauline Theme*. Downers Grove, IL: InterVarsity, 2002.

Parry, Jason Thomas. "Desolation of the Temple and Messianic Enthronement in Daniel 11:36–12:3." *JETS* 54 (2011): 485–526.

Parsons, Michael. "Being Precedes Act: Indicative and Imperative in Paul's Writing." In *Understanding Paul's Ethics: Twentieth Century Approaches*, edited by Brian S. Rosner, 217–47. Grand Rapids: Eerdmans, 1995.

Pate, C. Marvin. *The End of the Age Has Come: The Theology of Paul*. Grand Rapids: Zondervan, 1995.

Pennington, Jonathan. *Heaven and Earth in the Gospel of Matthew*. NovTSup 126. Leiden: Brill, 2007.

Perdue, Leo G. *Wisdom and Creation: The Theology of Wisdom Literature*. Nashville: Abingdon, 1994.

Perrin, Nicholas. "Messianism in the Narrative Frame of Ecclesiastes?" *RB* 108 (2001): 37–60.

Peterlin, Davorin. *Paul's Letter to the Philippians in Light of Disunity in the Church*. NovTSup 79. Leiden: Brill, 1995.

Peterson, David. "Atonement in the Old Testament." In *Where Wrath and Mercy Meet: Proclaiming the Atonement Today*, edited by David Peterson, 1–15. Carlisle: Paternoster, 2001.

———. "The Motif of Fulfillment and the Purpose of Luke-Acts." In *The Book of Acts in Its Ancient Literary Setting*. Vol. 1 of *The Book of Acts in Its First Century Setting*, edited by Bruce W. Winter, 83–104. Grand Rapids: Eerdmans, 1993.

Petzer, J. H. "Luke 22:19b–20 and the Structure of the Passage." *NovT* 26 (1984): 249–52.

Petzer, Kobus. "Style and Text in the Lucan Narrative of the Institution of the Lord's Supper (Luke 22:19b-20)." *NTS* 37 (1991): 113–29.

Piper, John. *The Justification of God: An Exegetical and Theological Study of Romans 9:1–23*. 2nd ed. Grand Rapids: Baker, 1993.

Pitkänen, Pekka. *Central Sanctuary and Centralization of Worship in Ancient Israel: From the Settlement to the Building of Solomon's Temple*. GDNES 5. Piscataway, NJ: Gorgias, 2004.

Plevnik, Joseph. "The Center of Pauline Theology." *CBQ* 51 (1989): 461–78.

Poythress, Vern S. *God-Centered Biblical Interpretation*. Phillipsburg, NJ: P&R, 1999.

———. "Kinds of Biblical Theology." *WTJ* 70 (2008): 129–42.

———. *The Shadow of Christ in the Law of Moses*. Brentwood, TN: Wolgemuth & Hyatt, 1991.

Provan, I. W. "Kings." In *New Dictionary of Biblical Theology*, edited by T. Desmond Alexander and Brian S. Rosner, 183–88. Downers Grove, IL: InterVarsity, 2000.

Reasoner, Mark. "The Theme of Acts: Institutional History or Divine Necessity in History?" *JBL* 118 (1990): 635–59.

Redditt, Paul L., and Aaron Schart, eds. *Thematic Threads in the Book of the Twelve*. BZAW 325. Berlin: de Gruyter, 2003.

Rendtorff, Rolf. *The Canonical Hebrew Bible: A Theology of the Old Testament*. Translated by David E. Orton. Leiden: Deo, 2005.

Renz, Thomas. "The Use of Zion Tradition in the Book of Ezekiel." In *Zion, City of Our God*, edited by Richard S. Hess and Gordon J. Wenham, 77–103. Grand Rapids: Eerdmans, 1999.

Reumann, John H. P. *Righteousness in the New Testament: Justification in the United States Lutheran-Roman Catholic Dialogue, with Responses by Joseph A. Fitzmyer and Jerome D. Quinn*. Philadelphia: Fortress, 1982.

Ridderbos, Herman. *Paul: An Outline of His Theology*. Translated by John Richard de Witt. Grand Rapids: Eerdmans, 1975.

Rodriguez, Angel Manuel. "Substitution in the Hebrew Cultus and in Cultic-Related Texts." PhD diss., Andrews University Seventh-day Adventist Theological Seminary, 1979.

Rose, Wolter H. *Zemah and Zerubbabel: Messianic Expectations in the Early Postexilic Period*. JSOTSup 304. Sheffield: Sheffield Academic Press, 2000.

Routledge, Robin. "Is There a Narrative Substructure Underlying the Book of Isaiah?" *TynBul* 55 (2004): 183–204.

Rowe, C. Kavin. *Early Narrative Christology: The Lord in the Gospel of Luke*. Grand Rapids: Baker Academic, 2009.

Sailhamer, John H. *Introduction to Old Testament Theology: A Canonical Approach*. Grand Rapids: Zondervan, 1995.

———. *The Meaning of the Pentateuch: Revelation, Composition, and Interpretation*. Downers Grove, IL: InterVarsity, 2009.

———. *The Pentateuch as Narrative: A Biblical-Theological Commentary*. Grand Rapids: Zondervan, 1992.

Sanders, E. P. *Paul and Palestinian Judaism: A Comparison of Patterns of Religion*. Philadelphia: Fortress, 1977.

Satterthwaite, Philip. "'No King in Israel': Narrative Criticism and Judges 17–21." *TynBul* 44 (1993): 75–88.

———. "Samuel." In *New Dictionary of Biblical Theology*, edited by T. Desmond Alexander and Brian S. Rosner, 178–83. Downers Grove, IL: InterVarsity, 2000.

———. "Zion in the Songs of Ascents." In *Zion, City of Our God*, edited by Richard S. Hess and Gordon J. Wenham, 105–28. Grand Rapids: Eerdmans, 1999.

Schlatter, Adolf. *The History of the Christ: The Foundation for New Testament Theology*. Translated by Andreas J. Köstenberger. Grand Rapids: Baker, 1997.

———. *The Theology of the Apostles: The Development of New Testament Theology*. Translated by Andreas J. Köstenberger. Grand Rapids: Baker, 1998.

Schnabel, Eckhard J. *Law and Wisdom from Ben Sira to Paul: A Tradition Historical Enquiry into the Relation of Law, Wisdom, and Ethics*. WUNT 2/16. Tübingen: Mohr Siebeck, 1985.

Schnelle, Udo. *Apostle Paul: His Life and Theology*. Translated by M. Eugene Boring. Grand Rapids: Baker Academic, 2005.

Schreiner, Thomas R. *Galatians*. ZECNT. Grand Rapids: Zondervan, 2010.

———. *New Testament Theology: Magnifying God in Christ*. Grand Rapids: Baker Academic, 2008.

———. *Paul, Apostle of God's Glory in Christ: A Pauline Theology*. Downers Grove, IL: InterVarsity, 2001.

Schultz, Richard L. "Ecclesiastes." In *New Dictionary of Biblical Theology*, edited by T. Desmond Alexander and Brian S. Rosner, 211–15. Downers Grove, IL: InterVarsity, 2000.

———. "Unity or Diversity in Wisdom Theology? A Canonical and Covenantal Perspective." *TynBul* 48 (1997): 271–306.

Scobie, Charles H. H. *The Ways of Our God: An Approach to Biblical Theology*. Grand Rapids: Eerdmans, 2003.

Seifrid, Mark A. *Christ, Our Righteousness: Paul's Theology of Justification*. Downers Grove, IL: InterVarsity, 2000.

———. "In Christ." In *Dictionary of Paul and His Letters*, edited by Gerald F. Hawthorne and Ralph P. Martin, 433–36. Downers Grove, IL: InterVarsity, 1993.

———. "Righteousness Language in the Hebrew Scriptures and Early Judaism." In *The Complexities of Second Temple Judaism*, edited by D. A. Carson, Peter T. O'Brien, and Mark A. Seifrid, 415–42. Vol. 1 of *Justification and Variegated Nomism: A Fresh Appraisal of Paul and Second Temple Judaism*. Grand Rapids: Baker Academic, 2001.

Seitz, Christopher R. *The Goodly Fellowship of the Prophets: The Achievement of Association in Canon Formation*. Grand Rapids: Baker Academic, 2009.

———. *Prophecy and Hermeneutics: Toward a New Introduction to the Prophets*. Grand Rapids: Baker Academic, 2007.

Selman, M. J. "Chronicles." In *New Dictionary of Biblical Theology*, edited by T. Desmond Alexander and Brian S. Rosner, 188–95. Downers Grove, IL: InterVarsity, 2000.

Shepherd, Michael B. *Daniel in the Context of the Hebrew Bible*. SBL 123. New York: Peter Lang, 2009.

Sheppard, Gerald T. "Theology and the Book of Psalms." *Int* 46 (1992): 143–55.

Smith, Gary V. "Structure and Purpose in Genesis 1–11." *JETS* 20 (1977): 307–19.

Smith, Mark S. "The Psalms as a Book for Pilgrims." *Int* 46 (1992): 156–66.

Sprinkle, Joe M. "The Rationale of the Laws of Clean and Unclean in the Old Testament." *JETS* 43 (2000): 637–57.

Squires, John T. *The Plan of God in Luke-Acts*. SNTSMS 76. Cambridge: Cambridge University Press, 1993.

Starr, J. M. *Sharers in Divine Nature: 2 Peter 1:4 in Its Hellenistic Context*. ConBNT 33. Stockholm: Almqvist & Wiksell, 2000.

Stein, Robert H. "Baptism and Becoming a Christian in the New Testament." *SBJT* 2 (1998): 6–17.

———. "Baptism in Luke-Acts." In *Believer's Baptism: Sign of the New Covenant in Christ*, edited by Thomas R. Schreiner and Shawn D. Wright, 35–66. Nashville: B&H Academic, 2006.

Stenschke, Christoph. *Luke's Portrait of Gentiles Prior to Their Coming to Faith*. WUNT 2/108. Tübingen: Mohr Siebeck, 1999.

Stevenson, Kalinda Rose. *The Vision of Transformation: The Territorial Rhetoric of Ezekiel 40–48*. SBLDS 154. Atlanta: Scholars Press, 1996.

Strauss, Mark L. *The Davidic Messiah in Luke-Acts: The Promise and Its Fulfillment in Lukan Christology*. JSNTSup 110. Sheffield: Sheffield Academic Press, 1995.

Strom, Mark. *The Symphony of Scripture: Making Sense of the Bible's Many Themes*. Phillipsburg, NJ: P&R, 1990.

Sweeney, Marvin A. "The Place and Function of Joel in the Book of the Twelve." In *Thematic Threads in the Book of the Twelve*, edited by Paul L. Redditt and Aaron Schart, 133–54. BZAW 325. Berlin: de Gruyter, 2003.

Tannehill, Robert C. *The Narrative Unity of Luke-Acts: A Literary Interpretation*. Vol. 1 of *The Gospel according to Luke*. FFNT. Philadelphia: Fortress, 1986.

Terrien, Samuel. *The Elusive Presence: The Heart of Biblical Theology*. San Francisco: Harper & Row, 1978.

Thielman, Frank. *Theology of the New Testament: A Canonical and Synthetic Approach*. Grand Rapids: Zondervan, 2005.

Thompson, Alan J. *The Acts of the Risen Jesus: Luke's Account of God's Unfolding Plan*. NSBT 27. Downers Grove, IL: InterVarsity, 2011.

Thompson, J. A. "The Near Eastern Suzerain-Vassal Concept in the Religion of Israel." *JRH* 3 (1964): 1–19.

Thompson, James W. *Moral Formation according to Paul: The Context and Coherence of Paul's Ethics*. Grand Rapids: Baker Academic, 2011.

Thompson, Marianne Meye. *The Promise of the Father: Jesus and God in the New Testament*. Louisville: Westminster John Knox, 2000.

Turner, Max M. B. *Power from on High: The Spirit in Israel's Restoration and Witness in Luke-Acts*. JPTSup 9. Sheffield: Sheffield Academic Press, 1996.

Twelftree, Graham. *Jesus the Miracle Worker: A Historical and Theological Study*. Downers Grove, IL: InterVarsity, 1999.

VanGemeren, Willem. *The Progress of Redemption: The Story of Salvation from Creation to the New Jerusalem*. Grand Rapids: Baker, 1988.

Van Leeuwen, Raymond C. "Wealth and Poverty: System and Contradiction in Proverbs." *HS* 33 (1992): 25–36.

Viberg, Å. "Job." In *New Dictionary of Biblical Theology*, edited by T. Desmond Alexander and Brian S. Rosner, 200–203. Downers Grove, IL: InterVarsity, 2000.

Vogt, Peter T. *Deuteronomic Theology and the Significance of Torah: A Reappraisal*. Winona Lake, IN: Eisenbrauns, 2006.

Von Rad, Gerhard. *Genesis: A Commentary*. Rev. ed. OTL. Philadelphia: Westminster, 1972.

———. *Holy War in Ancient Israel*. Translated and edited by Marva J. Dawn. Grand Rapids: Eerdmans, 1991.

———. *The Theology of Israel's Historical Traditions*. Vol. 1 of *Old Testament Theology*. Translated by D. M. G. Stalker. New York: Harper & Row, 1962.

———. *Wisdom in Israel*. Translated by James D. Martin. Nashville: Abingdon, 1972.

Vos, Geerhardus. *Biblical Theology: Old and New Testaments*. Grand Rapids: Eerdmans, 1977.

Walker, Peter W. L. "The Land in the Apostles' Writings." In *The Land of Promise: Biblical, Theological and Contemporary Perspectives*, edited by Philip Johnston and Peter Walker, 81–99. Downers Grove, IL: InterVarsity, 2000.

Waltke, Bruce K. *The Book of Proverbs: Chapters 1–15*. NICOT. Grand Rapids: Eerdmans, 2004.

———. *Genesis: A Commentary*. Grand Rapids: Zondervan, 2001.

———. *An Old Testament Theology: An Exegetical, Canonical, and Thematic Approach*. Grand Rapids: Zondervan, 2007.

———. "The Phenomenon of Conditionality within Unconditional Covenants." In *Israel's Apostasy and Restoration: Essays in Honor of Roland K. Harrison*, edited by Avraham Gileadi, 123–39. Grand Rapids: Baker, 1988.

Walton, John H. "Deuteronomy: An Exposition of the Spirit of the Law." *GTJ* 8 (1987): 213–25.

———. "Psalms: A Cantata about the Davidic Covenant." *JETS* 34 (1991): 21–31.

Watts, Rikki E. *Isaiah's New Exodus in Mark*. Grand Rapids: Baker Academic, 2000.

Webb, Barry G. *The Book of Judges: An Integrated Reading*. JSOTSup 46. Sheffield: JSOT Press, 1987.

———. *Five Festal Garments: Christian Reflections on the Song of Songs, Ruth, Lamentations, Ecclesiastes, and Esther*. NSBT 10. Downers Grove, IL: InterVarsity, 2000.

———. *The Message of Zechariah: Your Kingdom Come*. BST. Downers Grove, IL: InterVarsity, 2003.

Webb, Robert L. *John the Baptizer and Prophet: A Socio-Historical Study*. JSNTSup 62. Sheffield: JSOT Press, 1991.

Weinfeld, Moshe. *Deuteronomy and the Deuteronomic School*. Oxford: Clarendon, 1972.

Wenham, Gordon J. *The Book of Leviticus*. NICOT. Grand Rapids: Eerdmans, 1979.

———. "Deuteronomy and the Central Sanctuary." *TynBul* 22 (1971): 103–18.

———. *Genesis 1–15*. WBC 1. Waco: Word, 1987.

———. "The Theology of Old Testament Sacrifice." In *Sacrifice in the Bible*, edited by Roger T. Beckwith and Martin J. Selman, 75–87. Grand Rapids: Baker, 1995.

Westermann, Claus. *Lamentations: Issues and Interpretation*. Translated by Charles Muenchow. Minneapolis: Fortress, 1994.

Whybray, R. N. "Qoheleth, Preacher of Joy." *JSOT* 23 (1982): 87–98.

Williams, Catrin. *I Am He: The Interpretation of "Anî Hû" in Jewish and Early Christian Literature*. WUNT 2/113. Tübingen: Mohr Siebeck, 2000.

Williams, Garry. "The Cross and the Punishment of Sin." In *Where Wrath and Mercy Meet: Proclaiming the Atonement Today*, edited by David Peterson, 68–99. Carlisle: Paternoster, 2001.

Williams, Jarvis J. *Maccabean Martyr Traditions in Paul's Theology of Atonement: Did Martyr Theology Shape Paul's Conception of Jesus's Death?* Eugene, OR: Wipf & Stock, 2010.

Williamson, Paul R. "'Because He Loved Your Forefathers': Election, Atonement, and Intercession in the Pentateuch." In *From Heaven He Came and Sought Her: Definite Atonement in Historical, Biblical, Theological, and Pastoral Perspective*, edited by David Gibson and Jonathan Gibson. Wheaton: Crossway, forthcoming.

———. "Promise and Fulfillment: The Territorial Inheritance." In *The Land of Promise: Biblical, Theological and Contemporary Perspectives*, edited by Philip Johnston and Peter Walker, 15–34. Downers Grove, IL: InterVarsity, 2000.

———. *Sealed with an Oath: Covenant in God's Unfolding Purpose*. NSBT 23. Downers Grove, IL: InterVarsity, 2007.

Wilson, Gerald H. *The Editing of the Hebrew Psalter*. SBLDS 76. Chico, CA: Scholars Press, 1985.

———. *Psalms: Volume 1*. NIVAC. Grand Rapids: Zondervan, 2002.

———. "The Shape of the Book of Psalms." *Int* 46 (1992): 129–42.

———. "Shaping the Psalter: A Consideration of Editorial Linkage in the Book of Psalms." In *The Shape and Shaping of the Psalter*, edited by J. Clinton McCann Jr., 72–82. JSOTSup 159. Sheffield: JSOT Press, 1993.

———. "Understanding the Purposeful Arrangement of Psalms in the Psalter: Pitfalls and Promise." In *The Shape and Shaping of the Psalter*, edited by J. Clinton McCann Jr., 42–51. JSOTSup 159. Sheffield: JSOT Press, 1993.

———. "The Use of Royal Psalms at the 'Seams' of the Hebrew Psalter." *JSOT* 35 (1986): 85–94.

———. "'The Words of the Wise': The Intent and Significance of Qohelet 12:9–14." *JBL* 103 (1984): 175–92.

Wilson, Lindsay. "The Book of Job and the Fear of God." *TynBul* 46 (1995): 59–79.

Witherington, Ben, III. *Jesus the Sage: The Pilgrimage of Wisdom*. Minneapolis: Fortress, 1994.

Wong, Gregory T. K. *Compositional Strategy of the Book of Judges: An Inductive, Rhetorical Study*. VTSup 111. Leiden: Brill, 2006.

Wright, Addison G. "Additional Numerical Patterns in Qoheleth." *CBQ* 45 (1983): 32–43.

———. "The Riddle of the Sphinx: The Structure of the Book of Qoheleth." *CBQ* 30 (1968): 313–34.

———. "The Riddle of the Sphinx Revisited: Numerical Patterns in the Book of Qoheleth." *CBQ* 42 (1980): 38–51.

Wright, Christopher J. H. *Old Testament Ethics for the People of God*. Downers Grove, IL: InterVarsity, 2004.

Wright, N. T. *The Climax of the Covenant: Christ and the Law in Pauline Theology*. Minneapolis: Fortress, 1992.

———. *The Resurrection of the Son of God*. Vol. 3 of *Christian Origins and the Question of God*. Minneapolis: Fortress, 2003.

Zenger, Erich. "The Composition and Theology of the Fifth Book of Psalms, Psalms 107–145." *JSOT* 80 (1998): 77–102.

Author Index

SCRIPTURE INDEX

Subject Index